War and the World

War and the World

*Military Power and the Fate of Continents
1450–2000*

Jeremy Black

Yale University Press
New Haven and London

Set in Adobe Garamond
Printed in Italy

Library of Congress Cataloging-in-Publication Data

Black, Jeremy.
   War and the world: military power and the fate of continents, 1450–2000/Jeremy Black.
   Includes bibliographical references and index.
   ISBN 0–300–07202–3
   1. Military history, Modern.   2. War and society—History.
   3. History, Modern.   4. Europe—History.   I. Title.
   D214.B58   1997
   335′.009—dc21   97–28169
                                                      CIP

A catalogue record for this book is available from the British Library.

10 9 8 7 6 5 4 3 2 1

For Geoffrey Parker

Contents

Illustration Credits

Preface

Appointment to a new post and my decision to offer a course on war 1400–2000 have prompted me to write this book. It reflects many years of teaching military history and is designed as a development from my previous works, especially *European Warfare 1660–1815* (London and New Haven, 1994). As the Introduction makes clear, I seek to adopt new approaches in a number of important respects. Obviously, with a subject of this scale and a work of this size, this book must be regarded as only a contribution; the subject is vast and developing and, as ever with history, it is mistaken to pretend to be definitive, particularly in writing a single-volume world military history that adopts a global perspective. The text seeks to provide essential information as well as to analyse trends. In places there is a plethora of information, especially dates, but they are necessary in order to structure and integrate events of which too few Western readers are aware. The book seeks to provide as comprehensive an account as is possible in the space available. The notes have been kept to a strict minimum, in order to make more space for text and because they are not intended to advertise the scholarship on which this book is based but rather to be useful to a wider readership. They are restricted to direct quotations and, as far as possible, to accessible secondary literature.

Acknowledgements

I am most grateful for the opportunities to develop some of the following arguments provided by invitations to deliver lectures at the Universities of Aberdeen, Bristol, British Columbia, Cambridge, Denver, Dundee, Edinburgh, Illinois (Urbana), Indianapolis, Maine, Manchester, Marburg, Missouri (St Louis), New Hampshire, Northumbria, Odense, Oxford, Plymouth, Southeastern Louisiana, Victoria, Virginia and Yale, and at West Point, at the Royal Military College of Canada, at Brown, Lamar, Lethbridge, McMaster, Pennsylvania State, Rice, St Andrews, Simon Fraser, Stirling, Temple, Texas Christian, Washington (St Louis), Wesleyan (Normal), Western Ontario and Wilfrid Laurier Universities, at Austin College, at Corpus Christi College and Peterhouse College, Cambridge, at the Institute of Historical Research, the German Historical Institute in London, the University of Virginia Alumni Summer School in Oxford and the Open University Summer School in York, at naval history conferences at Dartington and Huddersfield, at the City of London School and at St Swithun's School. I would like to thank Tom Arnold, Chris Bartlett, Ian Beckett, Volker Berghahn, George Boyce, Ahron Bregman, Martin van Creveld, Brian Davies, Kelly DeVries, Jan Glete, Jeffrey Grey, John Hattendorf, Nicholas Henshall, Stewart Lone, Peter Lorge, Piers Mackesy, John Pocock, George Raudzens, Dennis Showalter, Gene Smith, Lawrence Sondhaus, Edward Spiers, Armstrong Starkey, David Stevenson, John Thornton, Spencer Tucker, Bruce Vandervort, Arthur Waldron, Geoffrey Wawro, Scott Wheeler, Russell Weigley and Peter Wilson for their helpful comments on an earlier draft. I am most grateful to Wendy Duery for her secretarial support. It has only been possible to write this book thanks to Sarah's love and attention.

I finished work on this book soon after visiting the U.S.S. *Texas* at San Jacinto Battleground State Historical Park. The occasion, like the trip itself which took me to the Gulf at Galveston, the Mississippi at Baton Rouge and over the causeway across Lake Pontchartrain, brought together two of my great fondnesses, first that of visiting the United States and enjoying its vitality, variety and the company and friendship of Americans, and, second, that of light and water – the spangling of sunlight on the shifting sea, the search for peace in the golden light.

1   *Introduction*

It cannot happen again. That was the optimistic conclusion of Edward Gibbon, writing in the 1770s, as he considered whether contemporary Europe could once more succumb to those whom he termed barbarians. Gibbon's answer was couched in terms of military progress: 'Cannon and fortifications now form an impregnable barrier against the Tartar horse'.[1] This book seeks to use Gibbon's analysis as a point of departure for looking at a series of crucial and related topics that centre on the question of the relationship between the rise of European military power on the global scale and the relative military development and success of non-European peoples. It seeks to demonstrate the adaptability of a broad spectrum of social and political systems to the ultimate challenge of war, and to provide a balance between operational material and the broader contexts subsumed under the heading of 'new military history'.

At the outset, it is necessary to make two points. First, there is no suggestion that the rise of European power should be regarded as good, no question of a triumphalist approach. This is true not only of the consequences of warfare in terms of changes in territorial control, but also of the nature and means of conflict. To kill people more 'effectively' or ruthlessly, is not regarded as a desirable aspect of civilisation or a facet of progress. This point has to be emphasised because such assumptions are latent in much, although by no means all, of the literature on war.

Secondly, this subject is not a *tabula rasa*, although, given its importance, it is surprising that more attention has not been devoted to it. In part, this reflects the relative neglect of military history, especially pre-1900 military history, in academic circles over the last forty years. In part, it is the case that most military history, whether operational or the so-called 'new military history' that adopts a wider social dimension, concentrates on Western history and is very much Euro-centred even when it considers developments elsewhere in the world.

This, in turn, is due to a number of factors. Source availability and linguistic capability are clearly crucial but so also are attitudinal factors that are harder to gauge. First, and linked to issues of data and language, is the heavily positivist nature of most military history, arguably a consequence of the approaches that have been developed to tackle both operational and 'new' military history, the bureaucratic nature of modern European military forces, the types of people that become military historians and the 'culture' of the subject.

In addition, there is the reluctance to grasp the wider global context, or the tendency to approach it as a simple function of a given explanatory model, classically that of the triumph of the West through technology. Intellectually and visually, this is a matter of the 'Rorke's Drift' approach to military history: through technology and a sense of mission, small numbers of Europeans were able to defeat, indeed destroy, the military 'other', that is large numbers of alien non-Europeans. The military culture of the latter was and is largely neglected, not simply because of problems in studying the subject – the objective 'scholarly' aspect; but also because non-Europeans appeared then and now anachronistic and bound to fail.

Indeed, non-Europeans were and are generally seen as of military interest only in relation to the Europeans and, more specifically, if they adopted European weaponry and methods. The former leads to the 'Plassey approach': an emphasis on battles, such as Plassey (1757), that involved Europeans, especially those in which they were successful, rather than on other, often larger, struggles that did not; for example, in the case of India and Plassey, the major battle of Panipat fought four years later between the Afghan invaders and the Marathas, and decisively won by the former, or the Persian invasion of India in 1739 which led to Persian victory at Karnal, to the sack of Delhi, and to the cession to Nadir Shah of Persia of Sind and the Mughal territories west of the Indus River. The Eurocentric Plassey approach has had even greater impact because the American experience can be accommodated by treating the struggle between European and native Americans as an aspect of the wider 'rise of the West'. Thus military history becomes a misleading question of the West versus the Rest.

It would be mistaken to argue that no historians have tackled global military history and military technology. Indeed, three scholars, in particular, have made major contributions. William H. McNeill, a skilled practitioner of global history, in his *The Pursuit of Power. Technology, Armed Force, and Society since AD 1000* (Oxford, 1983),[2] and the innovative military historian Martin van Creveld in his *Technology and War. From 2000 BC to the Present* (New York, 1989), both illuminated the role of the technology of war, although they were less concerned with operational military history, and may be criticised for placing too great an emphasis on technology. Geoffrey Parker in his *The Military Revolution. Military Innovation and the Rise of the West, 1500–1800* (Cambridge, 1988, 2nd edn, 1996) projected European military developments in the sixteenth century on to a global scale.

The current study is an attempt to build on these contributions, not to make points at their expense. In particular, it seeks to build on two of Parker's achievements: first his putting of naval and land warfare in the same frame and, secondly, his bringing together of European and extra-European warfare. Has the subject then been already done and is this book redundant? No; first because Parker, despite the dates of his book, very much concentrated on the period prior to 1650. Secondly, the notion of a European 'military revolution' in the sixteenth century, that Parker took from Michael Roberts, is not without problems.[3] As Parker noted, European success in the New World and in the Indian Ocean in the sixteenth century contrasted with less effective military capability on land elsewhere until the nineteenth century. Thirdly, the subject is a wide one and capable of a number of interpretations.

It is a particular pleasure to me that Geoffrey has accepted the dedication of this volume. His work has always been an inspiration. He is a scholar of great ability, wisdom and fortitude.

2 _Gibbonian Strategies_

It is particularly appropriate to begin by considering the views of Edward Gibbon (1737–94). Aside from his being arguably the greatest historian of the last half-millennium, Gibbon is of particular importance for two reasons. First, he sought not to be Eurocentric, and, within the constraints of the intellectual constructs and scholarship of his period, achieved his goal. This was seen most famously and controversially in Gibbon's treatment of religion: he admired the vigour of Islam and found much to criticise in Christianity. More generally, Gibbon was not a Euro-triumphalist. Secondly, Gibbon was fascinated with the issue of the rise and fall of empires. The generally held notion that he wrote only about the fall of the Roman empire is misleading. In fact, Gibbon covered over a millennium of history. He dealt with the successor states to the Western and Eastern Roman empires, but also ranged more widely, discussing for example Persia (Iran) and, though much more briefly, China.

Gibbon's writing about empire took place against a background of a long European discourse on the subject. This was a discourse that served moralistic and polemical ends and was essentially expressed in moralistic terms. Christian concepts framed the discussion about international relations and, not least for that reason, traditional consideration of such relations made little sense of aggressive actions.

Cultural relativism, rather than Christian conviction, was an important aspect of Gibbon's Enlightenment ideology. He was an intellectual who proclaimed that he was 'a citizen of the world' and did not favour conflict: 'I must rejoice in every agreement that diminishes the separation between neighbouring countries, which softens their prejudices, unites their interests and industry, and renders their future hostilities less frequent and less implacable'.[1] Furthermore, Gibbon sought to fulfil this aspiration not simply in terms of adopting pan-European sentiments, but also by looking at non-European cultures with greater sympathy than his counterparts.

Military developments were crucial in Gibbon's analysis, both in explaining European history and in accounting for Europe's position in the wider world context. In Europe, Gibbon claimed, an absence of gaps in military capability was the underpinning and consequence of the particular nature of political society and international relations. Gibbon argued that a network of states operating in a competitive network of civilised polities was necessary to progress. In his 'General Observations on the Fall of the Roman Empire in the West', an essay written in about 1772, set within his _Decline and Fall of the Roman Empire_ (London, 1776–88), and published in 1782, Gibbon contrasted the centralised government of Imperial Rome, and what he felt was its susceptibility to autocratic abuse, with the multiple statehood of the eighteenth century:

Europe is now divided into twelve powerful, though unequal kingdoms, three respectable commonwealths, and a variety of smaller, though independent, states; the chances of royal and ministerial talents are multiplied, at least with the number of its rulers . . . The abuses of tyranny are restrained by the mutual influence of fear and shame; republics have acquired order and stability; monarchies have imbibed the principles of freedom, or, at least, of moderation; and some sense of honour and justice is introduced into the most defective constitutions by the general manners of the times. In peace, the progress of knowledge and industry is accelerated by the emulation of so many active rivals; in war, the European forces are exercised by temperate and indecisive contests.[2]

For Gibbon, this 'happy mixture of union and independence' had been prefigured in ancient Greece and in Italy during the period of the early Roman republic, and, by the fifteenth century, was well developed in Europe. In contrast, other powers lacked the stimulus of competition and emulation: of situation and process. For example, according to a hostile Gibbon, Byzantium, isolated by language and arrogance, 'was not disturbed by the comparison of foreign merit; and it is no wonder if they fainted in the race, since they had neither competitors to urge their speed, nor judges to crown their victory'. This situation was not challenged until, from the late eleventh century, Western European power was projected eastwards with the Crusades, when 'the nations of Europe and Asia were mingled . . . and it is under the Comnenian dynasty that a faint emulation of knowledge and military virtue was rekindled in the Byzantine empire' (*Decline and Fall* VI. 108–9; VII. 116).

A similar argument has been recently used to explain the failure of Asian powers, such as China, to maintain their early progress in gunpowder weaponry. William McNeill argued that 'once a decisive advantage accrued to central authorities through the use and monopolisation of heavy guns, further spontaneous improvements in gunpowder weapons ceased . . . There was little incentive to experiment with new devices.' He also suggested that there was little incentive to experiment with novel modes of military organisation, an obvious contrast with the developments in European infantry and naval organisation in the sixteenth, seventeenth and eighteenth centuries.

Constant, or at least frequent warfare is not a complete answer to the question why the West progressed so quickly in gunpowder weapon technology while Asia and Byzantium did not, not least because it excludes or minimises cultural, political and operational considerations; but it was clearly important. In addition, Byzantium by the fifteenth century was a poor state, and this poverty may have been partly responsible for the failure to develop a significant gun-making industry.

A number of economic historians, particularly Eric Jones and Joel Mokyr, have also emphasised the importance of political fragmentation in ensuring the continued advance of technology in Europe. More specifically, if one centre of technological innovation ceased to set the pace, another would supplant it, and the same was true of commercial energy and financial enterprise.[3] From this point of view, the political and military factors that encouraged and sustained such fragmentation were in turn enhanced by the process of technological change. Thus, for example, printing helped to disseminate opinions and to encourage the development of national identities, while the pressure of international competition ensured emulation in military innovations, preventing the creation of long-term gaps in military capability.

The character of the international system in Europe therefore becomes an important variable that helps to explain the particular nature of warfare on the continent, both warfare as a function and expression of tactics, technology and techniques, and warfare

1. Jan Mostaert, *West Indian Landscape*. Spanish imperial power brought a new form of economic, political and social organisation to the New World as well as new forms of warfare.

as a pressure for governmental and social action and change. In multipolar Europe, societies did not have as large an option about mobilising resources for war as was the case with states elsewhere that lacked powerful neighbours. Instead, the pressure of international competition affected the nature of states, the conduct of politics, the culture of societies, the degree of military preparedness and the search for alternative means for security in diplomatic organisation and devices.

Balances of Power

A balance of power was, for Gibbon, a crucial device of and for collective security. He believed that it was self-correcting, prevented hegemony and permitted progress through emulation that was essentially competitive but that, within Europe, was tempered by 'the general manners of the times': the ethos and conventions of warfare and the international system. Far from adopting any timeless geopolitical systemic account, Gibbon, therefore, argued that the ideological context of international relations was important.

This stress on the balance of power in international relations matched a similar emphasis on the balance in domestic politics. Gibbon favoured a balance in the disposition and operation of power within communities, but it is clear that for him this balance reflected ideological-cultural as well as constitutional-structural factors: balance was most likely to work in virtuous communities. For Gibbon, 'the firm and equal balance of the constitution' of republican Rome somewhat confusedly 'united' the character of three different elements: popular assemblies, senate and regal magistrate (IV. 160), and 'legislative authority was distributed in the assemblies of the people by a well-proportioned scale of property and service' (V. 263). In contrast, in the post-Classical world, Theodoric the Great, King of the Ostrogoths, 471–526, failed to join, through balancing, 'Goths and Romans', and was thus unsuccessful in creating a stable state fusing Roman civilisation and barbarian vigour (IV. 187). The military ability of the 'barbarians' to overthrow the Western Roman empire was not matched by their political capability; an argument that could be echoed in the case of Nazi Germany and imperial Japan. In eighth-century AD Rome, the attempted re-creation of the 'rough model of a republican government', with its consultation and checks and balances, failed because 'the spirit was fled', so that 'independence was disgraced by the tumultuous conflict of licentiousness and oppression' (V. 263–4).

Gibbon's use of the concept of balance in both domestic and international policies, however, raises several questions. The apparent precision and naturalness of the image and language of balance greatly contributed to its popularity in an age in thrall to Newton and mechanistic physics. Furthermore, balance served as an appropriate *leitmotif* for a culture that emphasised the value of moderation and, in the eighteenth-century British context, 'politeness', the last understood as a moral and practical code of restraint. In military terms, it corresponded to an emphasis on discipline, drill and a science of war, although they were not necessarily designed to serve international or domestic equipoise.

However, the notion of balance of power offered little guide as to what criteria should be used to measure strength and military capability, assess intentions, or respond to change, while there was a central contradiction between the descriptive and normative possibilities of the theory. In international relations, it was also unclear how regional balances were related to a general balance; how the military-political system worked. Regional hegemonies could be seen variously as maintaining or threatening the balance. For example, Gibbon presented Theodoric as supporting, not threatening, international stability: '[Theodoric] maintained with a powerful hand the balance of the West . . . and although unable to assist his rash and unfortunate kinsman the king of the Visigoths, he . . . checked the Franks in the midst of their victorious career . . . the Alemanni were protected . . . an inroad of the Burgundians was severely chastised' (IV. 186). Gibbon noted that 'by the departure of the Lombards and the ruin of the Gepidae, the balance of power was destroyed on the Danube' (V. 53), but, although Avar dominance there threatened Constantinople, it is unclear what the wider significance of such regional balances was supposed to be.

As with other concepts, these limitations in terms of analytical rigour did not remove the value of the balance of power as a political and polemical tool. Indeed, its very openness to interpretation made the concept more flexible and thus widened its use in discourse:[4] the academic desire for precision is fundamentally misleading when considering the past use and development of concepts.

Gibbon's praise of the balance of power was in keeping with the assumptions of other eighteenth-century historians whose cultural emphasis was more strongly Eurocentric. They viewed the balance of power as characteristic of European political society, cause and consequence of European progress and strength. Non-Europeans were generally seen as lacking balance and balances. Furthermore, the balance was seen as a particular characteristic of a post-medieval world defined by the successful challenge to Papal authority and the pretensions of the Holy Roman Empire from the early sixteenth century. This matched a sense that warfare had changed from this period.

William Robertson, in *The History of the Reign of the Emperor Charles V. With a View of the Progress of Society in Europe, from the Subversion of the Roman Empire, to the Beginning of the Sixteenth Century* (1769), presented the balance as a product of political science . . . the method of preventing any monarch from rising to such a degree of power, as was inconsistent with the general liberty . . . that great secret in modern policy, the preservation of a proper distribution of power among all the members of the system into which the states of Europe are formed . . . From this aera [the Italian Wars of 1494–1516] we can trace the progress of that intercourse between nations, which had linked the powers of Europe so closely together; and can discern the operations of that provident policy, which, during peace, guards against remote and contingent dangers; which, in war, hath prevented rapid and destructive conquests.[5]

In one sense, Gibbon's account of the fall of Rome in the West and of the subsequent rise of Islam, the Mongols, 'Timour or Tamerlane', and the Ottoman Turks was of just such conquests, a vista of a world without balance. To Gibbon, barbarians and Orientals did not found states, only despotic empires which knew no balance. Robertson's very successful book, especially its closing sections, was an important source for Gibbon's thinking about international relations. It also provided empirical underpinning for the notion of contemporary Europe as a system that had devised a workable alternative to hegemonic power, and an alternative that was better, not only because it facilitated internal development, but also because competitive yet restrained emulation gave Europe a military and political edge over non-European powers. Gibbon argued:

It is the duty of a patriot to prefer and promote the exclusive interest and glory of his native country: but a philosopher may be permitted to enlarge his views, and to consider Europe as one great republic, whose various inhabitants have attained almost the same level of politeness and cultivation. The balance of power will continue to fluctuate, and the prosperity of our own or the neighbouring kingdoms may be alternately exalted or depressed; but these partial events cannot essentially injure our general state of happiness, the system of arts, and laws, and manners, which so advantageously distinguish, above the rest of mankind, the Europeans and their colonies (IV. 163).

Such a perspective – a European version of universalism – was in keeping with the views of the philosophical individuals praised in *Decline and Fall* who sought to keep values alive, despite the fall of Rome and the subsequent ebbs and flows of 'barbarian' power. For Gibbon, however, the balance of power ensured that the ebbs and flows of power would now take place in a beneficial manner and context, within a Europe that had progressed since the medieval period and that was now strong enough to resist 'barbarian' power.

Gibbon perhaps overstated the advantages of a multi-state system possessing balance and some internal competition, but the very concept was missed by most Chinese writers: they sought the *tat'ung* or great harmony/unity. This was feasible to a certain degree and China's size and strength imposed peace on much of East Asia for long periods over the last millennium, but it led to a far-flung territorial state with a degree of intellectual, political and governmental rigidity. As a consequence, in the nineteenth century the Chinese empire proved impossible to defend: there was no way to achieve both *saifang* (defence of the inner Asian frontier) and *haifang* (maritime defence), so choices had to be made. These were unsatisfactory and undermined the dynasty politically. Such political, and other non-military, reasons contributing to the weakness of the non-West help in the downplaying of technological determinism in explaining why the West triumphed.

The Sociology of Military Development

'Barbarians' played a major role in the *Decline and Fall*, not simply those that had laid Rome low, but, more generally, the migrant, mobile, fluid forces that had pressed on the settled peoples of Eurasia from the fifth to the fifteenth centuries. Gibbon presented barbarian energy and questing as a primeval force, comparing the 'rapid conquests' of Mongols and Tatars 'with the primitive convulsions of nature, which have agitated and altered the surface of the globe' (VII. 1). The military potential of barbarians was a function of the nature of their society, 'in which policy is rude and valour is universal' (VII. 2), and of their limited development:

> In the state of nature every man has a right to defend, by force of arms, his person and his possessions; to repel, or even to prevent, the violence of his enemies, and to extend his hostilities to a reasonable measure of satisfaction and retaliation. In the free society of the Arabs, the duties of subject and citizen imposed a feeble restraint.

The 'savage and simple rites' of the Roman festival of the Lupercalia 'were expressive of an early state of society before the invention of arts and agriculture'. For Gibbon, a differentiation of function was an important aspect of social development with clear military and international implications. Thus, he contrasted tenth- with eighteenth-century Western Europe. In the former, government was weak and

2. Armour of Sir John Smythe. English soldier and diplomat, probably Augsburg, *c.* 1585. Plate armour could offer little protection against gunpowder weaponry, but armour still had its value in hand-to-hand conflict. Helmets and breastplates were especially valuable.

the nobles of every province disobeyed their sovereign . . . and exercised perpetual hostilities against their equals and neighbours. Their private wars, which overturned the fabric
of government, formed the martial spirit of the nation. In the system of modern Europe,
the power of the sword is possessed, at least in fact, by five or six mighty potentates; their
operations are conducted on a distant frontier by an order of men who devote their lives
to the study and practice of the military art; the rest of the country and community enjoys
in the midst of war the tranquillity of peace, and is only made sensible of the change by
the aggravation or decrease of the public taxes. In the disorders of the tenth and eleventh
centuries, every peasant was a soldier, and every village a fortification (V. 358–9; IV. 33;
VI. 98).

Nomadic and primitive peoples were even more martial because, in their marginal habi-
tats, it was possible to recover 'the first ages of society, when the fiercer animals often
dispute with man the possession of an unsettled country'. In contrast, 'in the civilised
state of the Roman empire the wild beasts had long since retired from the face of man
and the neighbourhood of populous cities' (I. 93). Robertson made the same linkage of
martial commitment and energy with limited socio-political development. He wrote of
the barbarian invaders of the Roman empire, coming from lands much of which were

covered with woods and marshes; that some of the most considerable of the barbarous
nations subsisted entirely by hunting or pasturage, in both which states of society large
tracts of land are required for maintaining a few inhabitants; and that all of them were
strangers to the arts and industry, without which population cannot increase to any great
degree. If these circumstances prevented the barbarous nations from becoming populous,
they contributed to inspire, or to strengthen, the martial spirit by which they were distin-
guished . . . accustomed to a course of life which was a continual preparation for action;
and disdaining every occupation but that of war; they undertook, and prosecuted
their military enterprises with an ardour and impetuosity, of which men softened by the
refinements of more polished times can scarcely form any idea.[6]

The barbarians were thus a threat because they were naturally more warlike. For
European powers, singly or collectively, to confront and defeat them it was necessary to
compensate for this barbarian advantage. This was more than simply of historical interest because, for Gibbon, the clash between civilisation and barbarism, indeed between
European civilisation and barbarism, had not ended. It had, rather, been displaced, as the
barbarians had been driven back in, but not out of, Europe, and – although here Gibbon
was less clear – as the Europeans had become transoceanic colonists.

Asia

In Asia, however, the struggle between civilisation and the barbarians had not similarly
shifted. Gibbon wrote of the latter: 'In every age they have oppressed the polite and
peaceful nations of China, India, and Persia, who neglected, and still neglect, to counterbalance these natural powers by the resources of military art' (IV. 166).
    This scarcely made allowance both for the frequently symbiotic nature of the rela-
tionship between China and the nomads and, more generally, for Chinese dynamism in
the eighteenth century. Earlier, in 1449, the Chinese Cheng-t'ung emperor had been captured and his army destroyed in a Mongol ambush,[7] and in the 1640s the Ming dynasty

had been replaced by Manchu invaders, a conquest extended and consolidated in the 1650s and 1660s. The situation in the eighteenth century, however, was very different. Greater domestic stability from the 1680s and massive demographic growth served as the basis of a tremendous period of Chinese imperial expansion that brought control over large tracts of territory inhabited by non-Chinese people. The Russians were driven from the Amur region in the 1680s and an expedition against the Mongols in 1695 was followed by control over Outer Mongolia. There was military intervention in Tibet from 1718 and Ching-Hai from 1720, and they were brought under control from 1750 and 1724 respectively. In the 1750s, Chinese power was extended to Lake Balkhash; Kashgar fell in 1759. Rebellions by non-Chinese people were crushed in 1746–9, 1765, 1781–4 and 1787–8. In short, Gibbon was wrong in his notion that the prerequisite to the defeat of barbarism was a multiple state system, its internal competitiveness and external military effectiveness maintained by a balance of power.

One of the more puzzling features of *Decline and Fall* was that the well-read Gibbon revealed himself more aware of the Orient of the thirteenth century than of the contemporary world of East and South Asia. He created a misleading stereotype of an effete 'oriental' monarchy that was then borrowed in his treatment of the rest of the non-West. Gibbon also offered the misleading Eurocentric opinion that 'from the age of Charlemagne to that of the Crusades, the world (for I overlook the remote monarchy of China) was occupied and disputed by the three great empires or nations of the Greeks, the Saracens, and the Franks' (VI. 91). In addition, far from contemporary Asia being militarily inconsequential, there was in that region great interest in what Gibbon termed 'the resources of military art'. Indian rulers, such as Haidar Ali and Tipu Sultan of Mysore, and the Maratha Mahadji Shinde, were keen to train at least some of their troops on European lines and to acquire modern cannon and muskets. Indeed, it can be argued that, in part of Asia, the military process of competitive emulation seen as crucial by Gibbon was also occurring in the late eighteenth century. One distinction, however, is that in much of India from the mid-1760s, the principal threat was no longer nomadic (particularly Afghan) advances across the Hindu Kush, as in that and previous centuries, but rather the advance of imperial Britain.

Europe and the 'Barbarians'

In Europe, Gibbon explained the displacement of the clash between civilisation and barbarism by focusing on military development:

the military art has been changed by the invention of gunpowder; which enables man to command the two most powerful agents of nature, air and fire. Mathematics, chymistry, mechanics, architecture, have been applied to the service of war; and the adverse parties oppose to each other the most elaborate modes of attack and of defence. Historians may indignantly observe that the preparations of a siege would found and maintain a flourishing colony; yet we cannot be displeased that the subversion of a city should be a work of cost and difficulty, or that an industrious people should be protected by those arts, which survive and supply the decay of military virtue. Cannon and fortifications now form an impregnable barrier against the Tartar horse; and Europe is secure from any future irruption of Barbarians; since, before they can conquer, they must cease to be barbarous. Their gradual advances in the science of war would always be accompanied, as we may learn from the example of Russia, with a proportionable improvement in the arts of peace and civil

the *second* Motion

the *third* Motion being Aduanced

3. Detail from Pike Drill portrayed in Henry Hexam's *Principles of the Militarie*. The operation of a unit of pikemen required concerted actions that rested on drill. As with musketry, methodical training was required.

policy; and they themselves must deserve a place among the polished nations whom they subdue (IV. 166–7).[8]

Gibbon's argument, that military technology had permitted the European powers to break free from a cyclical process of growth and then collapse at the hands of barbarians, appeared justifiable in the eighteenth century. Earlier, not least in the 1650s to 1680s, the Ottoman Turks had remained very much a dynamic force. Indeed, insofar as there was what has been termed a 'military revolution' – a major shift in the way of making and organising war – either in the period selected by Michael Roberts (1560–1660)[9] or earlier, as argued by Geoffrey Parker with his emphasis on developments in fortification designed to thwart cannon, and by John Guilmartin with his stress on the Spanish creation of combined armed forces of pikemen, arquebusiers and cavalry,[10] it had not, hitherto, led to a decisive shift in the military balance or movement in the frontier between Christendom and Islam. By 1718, however, the situation had changed radically and the pressure on Christian Europe from the East, which was to be such a theme of *Decline and Fall*, was now reversed. The military balance between 'West' and 'East' had reversed.

The relationship was more complex than a simple one of gunpowder giving victory to settled peoples over nomadic hordes, and it was not one that was restricted to Europe. The Chinese tradition also had a stereotype of the nomad and the wilderness from which he emerges. The *hu* – the horse nomads – were an apparently intractable problem that posed a threat to China analogous to the European situation on which Gibbon concentrated. The Gibbonian analysis of the value of cannon and fortifications in halting the depredations of the nomadic hordes is rather like the Chinese solution of the wall, although the Chinese also used the crossbow as well as gunpowder weapons.

The two great nomadic empires of Genghis and Timur, and their light cavalry armed with compound bows, were exceptionally successful in extending their power in the thirteenth and early fifteenth centuries respectively. Until quite late, the 'West', China and the states of South and South-West Asia really had no answer to the sort of power they deployed. The Muslims introduced mounted archery to India. Indeed, it was the Mongol empires, which effectively controlled Eurasia, and their withdrawal and decay that offer an appropriate starting point for the military history of much of Eurasia from the thirteenth century. Such an approach provides a broad organising principle that puts the Europeans into a solid context, rather than having the European soldiers advance into a sort of dark void, full of 'others'.

The Timurid and other empires were vast and had more organisation than is often realised. But they lacked the kind of density of resources and expertise that the Europeans began to command from the fifteenth century. The political decay of these empires – owing to lack of legitimating principles, succession struggles, lack of common ethnic base and geographical challenges, rather than to military limitations or failure – provided the openings, at the margins, for European military success. The military technological factor can then be included by noting that the intensive military conflicts bred by the political division of Europe helped create a Western technological lead; not least in terms of a comparison between the fate of firearms in Europe and in Ming China.

The distinction between settled and nomadic and also between their respective military styles has to be employed with care. Western Europeans had been settled long before the 'military revolution', but without enjoying military superiority over their more mobile opponents: the Mongols had inflicted serious defeats on them in the mid-thirteenth century, the Ottomans from the late fourteenth. By 1683, when they were defeated outside Vienna,[11] the Ottomans had for centuries ceased being a nomadic horde and, instead, were a major empire. Gibbon noted the development of 'a regular body' of trained Ottoman infantry in the fourteenth century; this gave them a decided superiority over the Christians. Although the Ottomans were fairly late in acquiring gunpowder weaponry, they were using both cannon and hand-held gunpowder weapons by 1450.

Yet it was European superiority in gunpowder weaponry that was partly responsible for their advances at the expense of the Turks after 1683. However, this was more than simply a matter of technology. Ottoman discipline and skill, both crucial to the rate of infantry fire, were by then inferior. Gibbon wrote of the janizaries that 'their valour has declined, their discipline is relaxed, and their tumultuary array is incapable of contending with the order and weapons of modern tactics' (VII. 25, 32). The Turks never developed a comprehensive system of military institutions or behaviour that was truly independent of their nomadic steppe origins. By 1683 their advantage over the West was in numbers and ferocity, not discipline; and certainly not in cannon and forts. Their elite janizary infantry had lost its edge.

Qualitative European military changes, such as the bayonet, the flintlock musket and accurate and mobile grape- and canister-firing field artillery, opened up a major gap in capability among militaries supplied with firearms from the late seventeenth century. The introduction of close-order formations firing by volley was also very important: an individual on his own with a musket, and even a crowd of individuals, were of limited effectiveness. For a long period the rate of fire, accuracy and penetration obtainable with the compound bow of the steppe nomads was as good as those obtainable with muskets, but this situation changed, and, whatever the prowess of individual mounted archers,

4. Siege of Vienna, 1683. A rapid Turkish advance under the Grand Vizier, Kara Mustafa, led to the encirclement of the city on 16 July. While a relief force gathered, the Turks began building siegeworks and mounting assaults. The latter were increasingly successful, and the garrison suffered heavy casualties as well as losses from dysentery. The Turks suffered similarly and were outgunned, but, during August, the city's outer defences steadily succumbed. Lacking heavy-calibre cannon, the Turks depended on undermining the defences, which they did with some success. Nevertheless, on 12 September the relieving army descended from the hills surrounding Vienna, and attacked and defeated the Turks.

the aggregate firepower of units armed with muskets increased, although archers remained important, for example, on foot in Angola.

European land and sea tactics put a premium on drill, discipline and professionalism. This was a natural consequence of an emphasis on rapid, massed, close-range firepower, a situation that entailed the risk of high casualties, although there were also important medieval antecedents for military coherence and cooperation.[12] Indeed, these antecedents, the effective use of infantry across medieval Europe, and the creation of military structures and social and cultural practices that stressed discipline rather than individual heroism were all a necessary background to the successful adoption of firearms by European armies.

Military capability therefore was more than solely a matter of technology, and Gibbon's feel for the wider context of military development was pertinent. The European advantage in military technique and infrastructure rested on the foundations of centuries of European social and institutional change.[13] Technology and culture interpenetrate; they were, and are, not simple alternatives. Technology has to be understood in its social context.

In the period in which Gibbon was writing, the 'barbarians' did indeed appear to have been defeated. Thanks to successes against the Ottomans in the wars of 1736–9, 1768–74 and 1787–92, Russia came to control the lands to the north of the Black Sea, the traditional route of nomadic irruption into Europe from the East. In 1783, the Crimea was

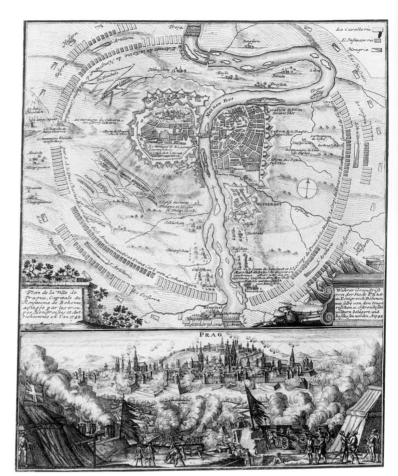

5. Siege of Prague, 1742. Having been stormed by the French and their German allies in November 1741, Prague was besieged by the Austrians the following July. The French abandoned the city in December 1742 in a gruelling winter retreat that prefigured Napoleon's from Moscow. Prague was crucial to control of Bohemia, and thus to hegemony in east-central Europe.

6. Battle of Fontenoy, 11 May 1745. A more stylised view than Blarenberghe's painting (see illus. 34), this illustration captures the geometric nature of formations, the orderly ideal of the battlefield and the proximity of the opposing forces.

annexed: the Khanate of the Crimean Tatars was no more. Until 1683 the Khan had received an annual tribute from Russia, and the cessation of this had only been accepted – by the Turkish overlord of the Khan – in 1700.[14] When Catherine the Great of Russia toured the Ukraine and Crimea in 1787, with the ruler of Austria, the Emperor Joseph II, among her guests, she used the tour to present Russia's military triumph as an advance for European civilisation.

Marshal Saxe, the leading French general of the 1740s, who had earlier served in the Balkans, drew a direct comparison between the Ottomans and the Gauls, and, therefore, by extension, the Austrians and Russians, and the Romans, in his *Rêveries* when he wrote of 'the number of years during which the Gauls were perpetually conquered by the Romans, without ever attempting to retrieve their losses by any alternation in their discipline, or manner of fighting. The Turks are now an instance of the same.' Saxe's comparison reflected a more general sense in Europe that knowledge of the Classical world was of great relevance, an attitude that encouraged interest in Gibbon's book.[15]

For Gibbon, European military advantage was a decisive one, as non-Europeans could only compensate for it if they ceased 'to be barbarous', as he argued Russia had done under Peter the Great (1689–1725). 'Progress' was a multi-stage process. Peoples who could not forge iron, for example most of the Siberians in the sixteenth century, could not produce firearms. Gibbon, however, was more concerned about socio-political development. To him, Europeanisation, 'the progress of arts and policy' crucial to greater Russian strength, had become the key to development, but to Gibbon this was more than a matter of simply borrowing military technology (IV. 120–1), a point that also emerges in David Ralston's recent study of the process.[16] Gibbon also shared Robertson's view that imitation and cultural transmission held the key to growing European homogeneity, and Gibbon presented this as a source of relative strength *vis-à-vis* non-Europeans.[17]

Gibbon noted that some military techniques were transferred to barbarians: 'The despair of a captive, whom his country refused to ransom, disclosed to the Avars the invention and practice of military engines; but in the first attempts they were rudely framed and awkwardly managed.' In the siege of Constantinople in 626, the Avars revealed 'some progress in the science of attack', and in the thirteenth century Genghis Khan was able to employ Chinese engineers to besiege successfully the fortified towns between the Caspian Sea and the Indian Ocean. Similarly, earlier Chinese knowledge of gunpowder from the ninth century did not prevent the Mongol conquest of China in the thirteenth century; the Mongols used both the techniques of siege craft and foreign experts (V. 56, 86; VII. 9, 11–12; VI. 141).

This theme of transferability was not probed. On occasion, Gibbon emphasised a gap in military technology between 'barbarians' and their more 'civilised' opponents. 'Greek fire', an inflammable substance that could be attached to projectiles such as arrows, which he described in detail (VI. 10–11), was presented as prefiguring gunpowder in giving the Byzantine empire a vital technological edge over its less civilised opponents, although Gibbon's account of 'Greek fire' was incorrect. In the earlier Arab siege of Constantinople in 668–75, Gibbon recorded that 'the Saracens were dismayed by the strange and prodigious effects of artificial fire'; and, in this and the second Arab siege of 716–18, 'the deliverance of Constantinople may be chiefly ascribed to the novelty, the terrors and the real efficacy of the *Greek fire*', the use of which continued until gunpowder 'effected a new revolution in the art of war and the history of mankind'. 'Greek fire' also stopped the Russian attacks on Constantinople in 941 and 1043 (VI. 3, 9, 12).

Yet Gibbon claimed 'Greek fire' was 'discovered or stolen by the Mahometans' and used by them against the Crusaders (VI. 11–12, 156). The implications of the adoption of

7. (*left*) Fiji Club. Such weapons were of great value in hand-to-hand conflict. There was no major change in warfare in the Pacific in this period prior to the arrival of the Europeans and their gunpowder weaponry.

8. New Zealand, Maori Bone Club. An example of the variety of weapons employed in hand-to-hand fighting. The advent of gunpowder weaponry brought a measure of standardisation.

first 'Greek fire' and later gunpowder by non-Europeans were ignored by Gibbon in his discussion of military factors in international relations. Transferability was not restricted to 'Greek fire' and gunpowder. Indeed, European military history in the eleventh to thirteenth centuries in part centred on how the Frankish development of knights, castles and siege techniques enabled the rulers who employed them to extend their power, against domestic opponents and on their frontiers, forcing the rulers of more peripheral regions, such as Scotland, Prussia and pagan Lithuania, to adopt these devices.[18] However, this process of transfer and diffusion entailed socio-cultural change unlike the use of, for example, 'Greek fire' by non-Europeans. An absence of a wider social transformation limited the impact of the adoption of weapons and specific military techniques thus returning the focus to Gibbon's emphasis on Europeanisation.

Gibbon's account is valuable for a number of reasons. His long-term and historical perspective ensured that he saw the military relationship between Europe and the outer world in terms of defence as well as aggression. A similar note was to be struck by Halford Mackinder, the leading British geopolitician at the height of empire, who in 1904 saw 'Europe and European history . . . subordinate to Asia and Asiatic history, for European civilisation is . . . the outcome of the secular struggle against Asiatic invasions . . . for a thousand years a series of horse-riding peoples emerged from Asia'.[19]

Gibbon was aware of the military dimension and problematic nature of European expansion. The knowledge of gunpowder weaponry was presented as responsible for the Europeans' 'easy victories over the savages of the new world' (VII. 82). These victories were discussed as an aspect of Europeanisation that would continue even if political control was lost; indeed, although Gibbon did not make the point, the Europeanisation was a necessary prelude to the successful rejection of European political control in the New World, and more generally, because only such a society and economy would have the military capacity to defeat such control. Gibbon argued that, in what was seen as the unlikely event of civilisation collapsing in Europe before new barbarian inroads, 'Europe would revive and flourish in the American world, which is already filled with her colonies and institutions'. He added a footnote that made reference to the contemporary American revolution against British authority (1775–83): 'America now contains about six millions of European blood and descent; and their numbers, at least in the North, are continually increasing. Whatever may be the changes of their political situation, they must preserve the manners of Europe' (IV. 166).

Yet Gibbon was also aware of the problematic nature of European expansion. He was convinced of its general benefit, 'since the first discovery of the arts, war, commerce, and religious zeal have diffused among the savages of the Old and New world these inestimable gifts . . . every age of the world has increased, and still increases, the real wealth, the happiness, the knowledge, and perhaps the virtue of the human race'. However, he added a perceptive footnote: 'The merit of discovery has too often been stained with avarice, cruelty, and fanaticism; and the intercourse of nations has produced the communication of disease and prejudice' (IV. 168–9).

Yet, despite his earlier contrast of the situation in Scotland in the first century AD, 'untutored Caledonians, glowing with the warm virtues of nature, and the degenerate Romans, polluted with the mean vices of wealth and slavery' (I. 130), Gibbon did not subscribe to modern notions, expressed recently by Parker and John Keegan, that non-European warfare was less violent and destructive and less intent on killing opponents.[20] This view is questionable and it has been argued that prehistoric warfare was more deadly, frequent and ruthless than its modern counterpart.[21] However, the notion of European warfare as more ruthless and destructive than non-European is supported by some research, including that on the situation in North America, Siberia and South-East Asia in the early modern period.[22] Native Americans sometimes fought for different motives than Europeans. Concern to preserve population levels caused them to be more interested in prisoners and to avoid heavy casualties. Therefore they sometimes defined battle success differently from Europeans.

The 'warm virtues of nature' could be militarily successful: although the Romans beat the Caledonians at the battle of Mons Graupius (AD 84), they failed to subdue Caledonia (Scotland). Gibbon recognised the harsh aspect of European expansion, an aspect that led to the Spaniards being termed *popolocas*, meaning barbarians, by the Aztecs;[23] and this recognition offers a suitable point for turning back to consider the beginning of the process.

3 Fifteenth- and Sixteenth-Century Expansion and Warfare

The Limitations of Christian Power

In the first three-quarters of the fifteenth century, Europe, understood as Christian Europe, was scarcely the most impressive political force in the world. The very term Europe is misleading as it implies a degree of cohesion that was absent. Instead, there were major conflicts within Europe, not least between England and France and between Burgundy and France, conflicts that were to limit the response to the Turkish advance. Irrespective of these divisions, there was also pressure on the European political space. Ottoman Turkish expansion in the Balkans entailed a loss of (Christian) European political control that also led to a movement in religious, ethnic, linguistic and economic frontiers. The fall of Constantinople to the Turks in 1453 after a two-month siege was symbolic as well as significant; and much of its importance lay in the symbolism. A centre of power that had resisted non-Christian attack for nearly a millennium had finally fallen, and fallen not to a 'barbarian' society, but to a polity that had assimilated techniques of statecraft very different from those of its origins.

Furthermore, the Ottoman Turks used gunpowder weaponry and did so effectively, thanks to the skilful direction of Sultan Mehmed II, although Ottoman numerical superiority was also crucial.[1] The artillery that drove off the Byzantine navy and breached the walls of Constantinople served notice on military attitudes and practices that had seemed to protect 'civilised', i.e. Christian, society. Relying on fortifications to thwart 'barbarians', to offset their numbers, dynamism, mobility and aggression, no longer seemed a credible policy.

The period between the fall of Constantinople in 1453 and that of Belgrade to Suleiman I, the Magnificent, in 1521 is not commonly seen as one of Turkish inroads in Europe. In 1456 Mehmed II was defeated outside Belgrade, which had earlier resisted Ottoman siege in 1440, and in 1480 he failed to capture Rhodes; but there were important Turkish gains, including in Albania, Serbia, Attica, the Morea (Peloponnese), and the Aegean. Lesbos fell in 1461 after the successful Turkish siege of Mitylene. The capture of key islands and bases in the war with Venice of 1463–79, for example Negroponte (1470) in Euboea, won the Turks the dominant position in the Aegean. Otranto in southern Italy was captured by an amphibious force of 12,000 Turks in 1480, but, after a lengthy siege, the Turks surrendered the following year.

The capture of Kaffa, which had earlier successfully resisted Tatar-Turkish attack in 1454, from the Genoese in 1475, established the Ottomans in the Crimea. Kaffa, Kinburn, Kerch, Ochakov, Azov and the southern shore of the Crimea came under direct Ottoman control. Akkerman at the mouth of the Dniester was captured by the Turks in

1484. From Anapa, the Turks dominated the Kuban and influenced the Caucasus. In Anatolia, the Greek kingdom of Trebizond (Trabzon) and the Islamic Isfandiyari principality to its west were brought under control, giving the Turks dominance also along the southern shore of the Black Sea: Sinope and Trebizond were both captured in 1461 and the Isfandiyari fortresses of Koyulhisar and Karahisar fell that year after bombardment by Mehmed's cannon.

The Black Sea was now controlled by the Turks and this gave them control or influence over the rivers that flowed into it, and thus over the lands around the sea. The Golden Horde, the successor state to the Mongol empire in its western conquests, had been divided into Tatar Khanates as a result of struggles for leadership in the first half of the fifteenth century; this left no dominant Islamic force north of the Black Sea. There was therefore no power able to stop both Ottoman advance – as Persia did and Mameluke Egypt sought to do elsewhere – and the advance of Christian powers. The Khanates of the Crimea, Kazan, the Golden Horde and Astrakhan were not strong enough to prevent Muscovite expansion, but in the late fifteenth century it was Turkey, not Muscovy, that dominated north of the Black Sea, and thus was the state best placed to recruit local protégés. The Crimean Khanate, which emerged in 1441, was from 1475–6 closely allied to the Turks, and a major source of slaves for them. This encouraged the Tatars to raid Muscovy, with whom relations became hostile from the 1470s. The Russians were made to pay an annual tribute, but that did not prevent raiding for slaves.

The Turks benefited, both in Europe and Asia, from the absence of any sustained and powerful opposing alliance. In 1458 Uzun Hasan, the head of the Aqquyunlu Confederacy in Iraq and Persia, joined a coalition with David Komnenos, King of Trebizond, and a number of Caucasian rulers. In 1460–1 this precarious alliance sought the support of European Christendom. However, no powerful anti-Turkish league able to concert operations was created. The failure of Turkey's Islamic opponents to unite was as serious as the comparable failure of the Europeans, and it proved impossible to create a viable league spanning the two spheres of opposition.

Global Reach

Aside from Turkish pressure, there is a more general absence of European global reach capability in the early fifteenth century. The contrast with the Chinese is instructive. A large Mongol-Chinese force had invaded Java in 1292. Under the following Ming dynasty, whose fleet carried cannon from the 1350s, a series of seven expeditions was sent into the Indian Ocean under Admiral Zheng He (1371–1433), a Muslim, and Chinese power was made manifest along much of its shores. The largest ships were 400 feet in length and carried nine masts. At the same time that they were pressing Burma and Vietnam on land, the Chinese, in a major show of force, reached Aden and Mogadishu and successfully invaded Sri Lanka in 1411 on the third expedition. South Asian trade patterns were greatly affected.[2]

In contrast, the Portuguese seized Ceuta in Morocco in 1415, but failed to take Tangier in 1437. However, the Iberians were increasingly important as maritime powers along and off the north-western coast of Africa. Portuguese settlement of Madeira began in 1424 and of the Azores in the 1430s; in the 1440s the Portuguese explored the African coast as far as modern Guinea. Castilian interest in the Canaries increased.

It is possible to use this situation as a background to the major rise in European power and presence from the close of the fifteenth century, to suggest a transformation that constitutes and reflects a military revolution. Such an analysis would focus on the dual process of the entry of Portuguese power into the Indian Ocean and the subsequent creation of a Portuguese maritime empire, and the Spanish overthrow of the Aztec and Inca empires in the New World.

These were very important changes, but it is also necessary to note the extent to which the Europeans were not the sole dynamic powers in the world and, more generally, to draw attention to the limitations of European military power. Both themes will be re-iterated throughout this book, and the question of where best to place an emphasis repays attention. At one level, the very ability to project power over a long distance is of greater consequence than its effectiveness in a given sphere. For example, in the six-teenth century a Portuguese presence was an issue for both China and Japan, but not vice versa. However, that is an argument that has to be handled with care: Viking power extended to Newfoundland, but to scant effect. There is also the question of how best to relate the projection of naval and land power, and also the relationship between naval strength and resistance on land. The Europeans were far more successful in projecting naval than land power.

More generally, the definition of naval power is an issue. It was a function of ships, manpower, bases and logistical support, each of which was intimately related to the others, and it is important not to adopt a single definition of naval power. In addition, the temp-tation to think in terms of violence as a form of seizure of resources, of the gains to be made through the use of power, has to be related to the symbiotic nature of trade and the need for maritime powers who developed a monopoly of regular long-range ocean transport to accommodate themselves to the demands and opportunities of land-based economic systems if they were to be much more than transient plunderers.

Issues of comparison, and the problems of comparing differing systems, therefore play an important role. First, however, it is necessary to appreciate the degree to which such comparisons have to be made. Thus, at the turn of the fifteenth and sixteenth centuries, it is valuable to focus on the number of dynamic powers in addition to those of Christian Europe.

The Advance of the Turks

One such power straddling the European and non-European worlds was Ottoman Turkey. Indeed, in crude geopolitical terms, there was an obvious contrast between the far-flung expansion of the Portuguese into the Indian Ocean and the more central control over important portions of south-west Asia and much of North Africa gained by the Turks. In military and political terms this was significant, because it was an expansion achieved at the expense not of inchoate nomadic polities, but by the defeat of one imperial system, Safavid Persia, and the overthrow of another, Mameluke Egypt. Although Gibbon argued that a failure to employ gunpowder was important in the Ottoman defeat by Timur in 1402 (VII, 59), already, by the late fifteenth century, the Ottomans had used their fire-power with great effect against other Islamic rivals, providing backing for modern schol-ars who focus on firepower. In 1473, at the battle of Baskent, the effect of Ottoman cannon and handguns on Türkmen cavalry led to victory over Uzun Hasan, the head of the Aqquyunlu confederacy that controlled Iraq and most of Persia. Hasan, in contrast, had a classic Central Asian army that centred on cavalry: the clans, armed with bows, swords and shields, and deployed in a two-wing cavalry formation, accounted for over 70 per cent of the army. However, battle was not simply a matter of technology. The

Ottomans also benefited from having a fortified camp from which to resist cavalry attack, and from both numerical superiority and better discipline.[3] The Ottomans had initially relied on mounted archers, but in the second half of the fourteenth century they developed an infantry that became a centrally paid standing army eventually armed with field cannon and handguns.

Under the Ottoman ruler Selim I, 'the Grim' (1512–20), grandson of Mehmed II, the greatest challenges and opportunities for the Turks came not in Europe but in Asia. This reminds us of the danger of adopting a Eurocentric approach, whether to Ottoman history and geopolitics or to that of the Roman empire and, subsequently, Byzantium. At one level, there was an essential stability in south-west Asia. With the exception of Alexander the Great's shortlived empire, no state based in the Mediterranean was able to conquer Persia, just as, indeed, the Sudan eluded control; similarly, after Alexander's destruction of the Persian empire, control over Anatolia, still more the Aegean, was outside Persian capability. Yet, there was a wide extent of land, much of it prosperous, between Anatolia and Persia, and rivalry for domination of this land between states controlling these areas was frequent.

In the early sixteenth century the dynamism of Safavid Persia was as apparent as that of Ottoman Turkey, although in Eurocentric accounts an emphasis on the Turkish threat to Europe ensures that the role and importance of Persia are generally minimised; a lesser parallel to the more general neglect of non-European powers. The Safavids were a militant Muslim religious order that developed a powerful military dimension. They conquered the province of Sharvan in 1500. In 1501 Shah Isma'il I (1501–24) and his nomadic Türkmen followers from Azerbaijan founded Safavid power in Persia when he defeated the Türkmen Aqquyunlu rulers of northern Persia at Sharur and captured Tabriz, where he had himself proclaimed Shah. The Aqquyunlu were totally defeated at Alme-Qulaq near Hamadan in 1503, one of the most decisive battles of the century. It led to the fall of most of the Iranian plateau, including Isfahan, Shiraz, Yazd and Kirman. Diyar-Bakr was conquered in 1507–8 and Baghdad fell without resistance to Isma'il in 1508. By 1510 modern Persia and Iraq were under Safavid control. They had benefited greatly from Aqquyunlu disunity and conflicts.

The Safavids operated in, and were threatened from, a number of directions. They were under pressure from another Central Asian steppe polity, the Uzbeks. Uzbek tribes from the steppes were highly mobile, and their successes reflected the potency of light cavalry. They repeatedly attacked Transoxania, seizing Bukhara in 1499, Samarkand in 1500, Tashkent in 1503, Farghana and Kunduz in 1504, Balkh in 1506, and Herat in 1507. In 1510 Isma'il defeated the Uzbeks of Turkestan in battle near Merv. The skull of the Uzbek ruler, Muhammad Shaybni, was set in gold, made into a drinking cup and sent to Isma'il's other major enemy, the Ottoman Sultan Bayezid II (1481–1512). Support for the Safavids and their millenarianism among the peoples of eastern Anatolia threatened both Ottoman security and its sense of religious identity, especially when that support prompted rebellions in the area in 1511–12.

Selim brutally repressed the rebels, and in 1514, five years before Hernán Cortés marched on the Aztec capital and with an incomparably greater army, Selim invaded Persia. The initial Safavid scorched-earth strategy, a strategy that the economic system, the role of distance and political culture encouraged, created serious logistical problems for the Ottoman forces, but Isma'il chose to fight his far more numerous opponents at Chaldiran on 23 August.

The Safavid army was of the traditional Central Asian nomadic type: archers on horseback who combined mobility and firepower, the ability to control vast spaces and to fight effectively on the battlefield. The Ottomans, however, had made the transition to a more mixed force and had innovative weapons systems. In addition to cavalry, they had infantry equipped with handguns, and field artillery. The availability of a mixed or combined arms force was very important; this was also to be shown by the Spaniards when campaigning successfully in Italy against the French in the early decades of the century.

Although the Safavids had used cannon in siege warfare, they had none at Chaldiran. Cultural factors were important: the Safavids thought firearms cowardly and, initially, adopted cannon with reluctance, preferring to use them for sieges not battles. Thanks to their numerical superiority and firepower, the respective importance of which is hard to disentangle, the Ottomans won a crushing victory over the Safavid cavalry. But the cannon were also important for another reason: chained together they formed a barrier to cavalry charges.[4]

Unlike Baskent, which was not followed by any significant Ottoman territorial advance, Chaldiran was followed by the capture of the Persian capital Tabriz in 1514. However, an Ottoman-supported advance by the Aqquyunlu leader, Sultan Murad, was defeated near Ruha weeks after Chaldiran and Murad was killed. Furthermore, logistical problems exacerbated by Persian scorched-earth tactics, meant that Tabriz was not retained. Nevertheless, there was a major eastward shift in the Ottoman frontier. The Safavids were pushed on to the defensive for most of the century, although their use of scorched-earth tactics again limited Ottoman gains when the Turks invaded in 1534, 1548 and 1554. The Safavids created a small unit of musketeers and gunners in 1516.

An opportunity for Ottoman expansion southwards had also been created. The defeat of the Persians was a crucial precondition of the Turks' subsequent advances against both Mamelukes and, later, Christians. The Emirate of Dhu'l-Kadr, between Anatolia and Mesopotamia, was annexed in 1515, and Selim then achieved the rapid overthrow of the Mameluke empire which had successfully resisted his father's expansionism in the indecisive war of 1485–91, a conflict largely restricted to a struggle over fortified positions in and near the Tauris mountains, and essentially won by the Mamelukes. In the new war firepower was decisive in the defeat of Mameluke heavy cavalry at the battles of Marj Dabiq (1516) and al-Rayda (1517). The former led to the capture of Syria and its centres of power in Aleppo and Damascus, the latter to the conquest of Egypt.

Ottoman power was thus established on the Red Sea, although there had been an important presence there since 1511 when the Ottomans had sent help in response to Mameluke requests for assistance in developing naval power able to resist the Portuguese. The Mameluke naval base of Suez was taken over in 1517 and the Ottomans acquired control of the Muslim holy places of Mecca and Medina, a vital source of prestige, and subsequently gained Aden (1538) and Massawa (1557), became committed in conflicts in the Horn of Africa and active in the Indian Ocean.

Like the Safavids, the Mamelukes put a premium on cavalry and did not associate the use of firearms with acceptable warrior conduct. Firearms were seen as socially subversive, as also in the case of samurai aversion to firearms in seventeenth- to nineteenth-century Japan. Hostility to the use of musketeers obliged successive Mameluke Sultans in 1498 and 1514 to disband musketeer units they had raised, although a foundry for cannon was established in the early sixteenth century and the Mameluke army used gunpowder against Shah-suwar of Dhu'l-Kadr. Like the Aztecs, who, however, did not use cavalry, the Mamelukes stressed individual prowess and hand-to-hand, one-to-one combat with a matched opponent, and this made them vulnerable to forces that put an emphasis on more concerted manoeuvres and on anonymous combat.[5]

The conquest of the Mameluke world was not the limit of Ottoman expansion. The

Persians were pushed back in 1534 when Suleiman I, the Magnificent (1520–66) invaded. The Safavids preferred to avoid conflict, so Suleiman abandoned operations in the harsh climate of Persia and, instead, overran northern and central Iraq. Basra and southern Iraq were later taken, expanding Ottoman power eastwards to the Persian Gulf. The Arabian port of Katif near Bahrain was captured in 1550. The conquest of the granary of Egypt and the vital port of Alexandria had already re-created a crucial link in Imperial Roman and early Byzantine history – the Constantinople-Alexandria axis – that helped to bring fresh strength to the Ottomans. This was seen directly in the growth of Ottoman naval power and in rising influence within the Mediterranean that led to Cyprus becoming a tributary in 1517, to the capture of Rhodes in 1522 and to the extension of Ottoman control along the North African coast. The Ottomans remained dominant in the Black Sea.[6]

The Ottomans had created a fleet to help prevent Constantinople from being relieved when they attacked it in 1453; an earlier fleet had been destroyed by the Venetians in the Dardanelles in 1416. The Ottomans subsequently developed their fleet for more distant operations and to carry cannon, which they used with effect against the Venetians at the battles of Zonchio in 1499 and 1500. In that war with Venice (1499–1503), the Ottomans successfully combined a strong fleet, intended to support amphibious operations rather than to seek battle, and heavy siege guns moved by sea in order to drive the Venetians from their bases in the Morea (the Peloponnese). Lepanto fell in 1499, Modon and Coron, 'the eyes of Venice', in 1500. The remaining Aegean possessions of Venice and Genoa were largely conquered in 1537–40 and 1566.[7]

The Ottoman state was the inheritor of important Euro-Asian and, to a lesser extent, trans-Saharan trading networks, and a crucial participant in the volatile contest for commercial hegemony in the valuable economic space between the Indian Ocean and the leading European entrepôt, Venice. Ottoman seapower was crucial to this process as it enabled the Turks to reduce other powers, such as Venice, to relationships in which they were subordinate. The Portuguese advance in the Red Sea and the Indian Ocean enhanced the position of the Ottomans in the Euro-Asian sphere because they were the only power with the artillery and naval resources to resist the Portuguese. The conquest of Iraq added another important axis to Ottoman power, that from the Mediterranean to the Persian Gulf, although the Ottomans were not able to maintain a large fleet in the Gulf.[8] However, they limited Portuguese penetration of the region.

A Multitude of Dynamic Powers

Other dynamic powers of note in the late fifteenth century included in Indo-China, Annam (Dai Viet), which in 1471 defeated Champa (southern Vietnam) and in 1476 annexed the capital, Vijaya, and extinguished the independence of the state; in South-East Asia, Malacca, which conquered or controlled much of southern Malaya and eastern Sumatra; in Sri Lanka, the Kotte kingdom under Parakramabahu VI (1411–66) although not subsequently; in West Africa, the Songhai empire of the middle Niger which pressed hard on the Hausa, exacting tribute from Kano; and, in the New World, the Aztecs and the Incas. In South America, after 1438, when Pachacuti Inca gained power, a strongly centralised Inca state was established. Inca dynamism was soon apparent with the defeat of the Chimú, who controlled the north coast of Peru, in 1476. Topa Inca (1471–93) expanded Inca authority far to the south, into modern central Chile and northern Argentina, although south of the Maule River in Chile the Mapuche blocked Inca advance. His successor, Huyana Capac (1493–1525), extended Inca territory north into modern Ecuador.[9] In Central America the Aztecs, with their militaristic culture and professional army,[10] defeated the hitherto stronger city state of Atzcaportzalco in 1428, and then conquered an empire that stretched from the Gulf of Mexico to the Pacific.

Similarly, in the sixteenth century, the Europeans held no monopoly of military dynamism. Important as they were, the Portuguese made less of an impact in India than the Mughals. Babur, the founder of the Mughal dynasty, was descended from Genghis Khan and Timur (Tamberlaine) and was another instance of the extraordinary military potency of Central Asia, Gibbon's source of 'barbarian' vitality. Babur inherited the Central Asian kingdom of Farghana, one of the successor states to Timur's empire, in 1494, captured Kabul and Ghazni in 1504, thus gaining control of eastern Afghanistan, invaded the Punjab in 1525, and on 20 April 1526, at the first battle of Panipat, decisively defeated the predominant power of northern India, the Afghan Lodi Sultanate of Delhi.[11] Buhlol Lodi (1451–89) and Secander Lodi (1489–1517) had themselves already extended the Lodi dominions east and south of Delhi. Babur's opium-addicted successor, Humayun (1530–56), was driven out of Hindustan, after defeats at Chausa and Bilgram, by the Afghan Sher Shāh Sūr in 1539 and 1540, but regained control of Delhi after victories in 1555. His son, Akbar (1556–1605), rebuilt and extended his grandfather's empire, his conquests including Gujarat (1572–3), Bengal (1575–6), Kabul (1585), Kashmir (1585–9), Tatta (Sind) in 1586–93 and Orissa (1592).[12] Some of these gains cut short other expanding politics. The Arghuns of southern Afghanistan had conquered the Sammas of Sind in 1518–22 and the Langas of the middle Indus in 1526.

Elsewhere in Asia, Altan Khan (1550–73) revived Mongol power and attacked Ming China, riding beneath the walls of Beijing in 1550. He also defeated the Oirat confederation of northern Mongolia, capturing Karakorum in 1552: 'barbarian' forces had to be able to fight each other, as well as the forces of more settled states. The Burmese kingdom of Toungoo overran Pegu in 1535–41, territory around Pagan in 1542 and the rival kingdom of Ava in 1555. The resulting dynamic state expanded considerably in the 1550s and 1560s, capturing Lan Na/Chiengmai in 1556 and the Siamese capital of Ayuthia in 1564 and 1569. Further east, after the *sengoku jidai*, 'the age of warring states', a protracted period of civil war that had started in 1467, Toyotomi Hideyoshi reunified Japan by 1590, and the new state launched invasions of Korea in 1592 and 1597–8.[13] In East Africa, Ahmad ibn Ibrihim al-Ghazi, the Islamic Sultan of Adal, routed the much larger army of Christian Ethiopia under Emperor Lebna Dengel at Shimbra Kure in 1528. In West Africa, the Songhai empire destroyed Mali in 1546 and itself collapsed after the victory of a Moroccan expeditionary force at Tondibi in 1591.

The Character of Conflict

The list of expanding powers accounts for the bitterness of much of the conflict of the period and can be extended, but it is more useful to advance some measure of categorisation. This can first be attempted in socio-political terms. States based on settled agrarian societies, such as those of Europe and China, were different from nomadic or semi-nomadic peoples, for example those of much of North America, Siberia, Central Asia and Australia. The agriculture of the former, especially the plough societies of the eastern hemisphere, supported larger populations, and thus possessed the resources for substantial armed forces and, thanks to money economies and taxation, for developed governmental structures. Relatively well-defined zones of control, although not precise frontiers in the modern sense, were an important aspect of such structures and they led to an emphasis on fortification, seen most obviously in the complex termed the Great Wall of China, some of which was constructed in the sixteenth century. The fortified lines constructed by Muscovy/Russia for protection against steppe nomads, for example the Belgorod Line of the 1630s to 1640s and the Izium Line of the 1670s, are other examples.[14] Settled societies developed communications systems: roads, bridges and relay stations for fresh horses. In South America, where there were no horses, the Incas nevertheless created an effective system of roads and bridges that sped not only trade, but also troops and commands throughout their extensive dominions.[15]

Nomadic peoples, in contrast, were less populous and their governmental structures less developed. They did not therefore tend to develop comparable military specialisation, either in fortification and, its corollary, siegecraft, or in terms of distinctive developed weapons or weapons systems. In war, nomadic peoples often relied on raiding their opponents, as with the advance of the Crimean and Kazan Tatars towards Moscow in 1521, which, combined with their limitations in siegecraft, lessened their capability to gain and retain territory.

This essential divide, between settled and nomadic peoples, interacted with general conditions affecting warfare throughout the world, leading to customary academic problems of where to place the emphasis, whether on similarities or differences. Alongside differences in social structure and practice, there were also important similarities. First, the conduct of war in all societies was very much the duty of men. Women were closely involved in warfare, not only as casualties, but also because their agricultural labour was crucial to the economic survival of societies at war; but their direct involvement in hostilities was exceptional.

The relatively low level of technology in even the most developed sixteenth-century societies ensured that all warfare remained subject to physical constraints which were common worldwide. The limited nature of industrial activity combined with low agricultural productivity restricted resources, wealth and taxable potential.

The deficiencies of the agrarian economy, and human vulnerability to a hostile environment, particularly the absence of any real understanding of infectious diseases and their vectors, ensured that population figures were low everywhere, and thus that the potential pool of warriors was restricted. This was less serious during periods of demographic expansion, especially the sixteenth and nineteenth centuries in Europe and the eighteenth in China, but was more serious in those of decline or stagnation, such as the seventeenth century across most of the world.

Disease and illness affected both specific operations and the general parameters of warfare, not least by establishing the seasons and environments in which forces could operate without heavy loss. Disease was a particular problem for troops moving into unfamiliar ecosystems. This was obviously a disadvantage for Europeans operating in what to them were the Tropics. For example, malaria led to the rapid abandonment of a Spanish colony established in 1526 near the mouth of the Pee Dee River in South Carolina, and in 1582 disease wrecked a Spanish expedition against Ternate in the East Indies. However, the need to adapt to different ecosystems also affected other peoples. Afghan and other Central Asian horsemen, who could operate effectively in the plains of North India, found Bengal, Assam and the Deccan less favourable. After their crushing victory over the Marathas at Panipat, north of Delhi, in 1761, the Afghans were reluctant to remain for long in the heat and humidity of India.

The military potential of all societies was also affected by the nature of energy sources and transmission, and of communications. Most labour was exerted by generally malnourished human or animal muscle, and other power sources were natural and, mostly, fixed: water and wind power and the burning of wood. There were no rapid communications on land or sea. However, the logistical difficulties of deploying large armies overland were reduced when it was possible to send supplies and cannon by river flotilla, for bulk transport was less difficult by water than overland. Thus, operating across the vast distances of the Russian steppe was made easier for Ivan IV when attacking Kazan and Astrakhan in the 1550s by his ability to use the Volga. The Don was used for Russian operations against Azov in the second half of the seventeenth century. Rapids on the lower Dnieper, however, prevented a comparable use of that river by the Russians.

The absence of rapid communications determined the movement of soldiers, supplies and messages everywhere in the world, with serious consequences for logistical, and command and control, capabilities. Modern maps can be deceptive when considering the strategy and tactics of the period, unless combined with a sense of historical real time, and military-time capability. In the Mediterranean, for example, the effects of prevailing wind patterns, currents and climate, ensured that voyages were easiest if they began near the northern shore. As a result, this ensured that shipping was generally restricted to a certain number of routes, thus affecting strategic options and leading to pressure to control nodal points on these routes.[16] Unseasonably severe weather helped to wreck the Spanish Armada against England in 1588.[17]

In addition to these constraints, there was an obvious contrast with modern warfare. At the close of the twentieth century, regular armed forces employ weapons which differ relatively little from those of their regular opponents, and their tactics are similar worldwide. This was not the case at the close of the fifteenth century. The cannon and firearms of the large Ottoman armies were a world away from the wood, bone or stone weapons of the aboriginal peoples of Australia or Siberia. Ottoman siege artillery played a decisive role in the successful siege of Modon in 1500: 22 cannon and two mortars fired a total of 155 to 180 shot per day. The Tungus of western Siberia would scarcely have been able to attack Muscovy with such resources.

Thus, very different military systems co-existed and even competed. This offers another opportunity for categorisation, one that concentrates on weaponry, rather than socio-political context. In many cases, decisive victory in the sixteenth century reflected a technological gap in different weapons systems, specifically the role of cannon at sea, and the advantage on land that gunpowder weaponry afforded infantry over infantry or cavalry relying on cutting and thrusting weapons: missiles over shock (cavalry that relied on firepower were different to those that emphasised shock). Technology does have a major impact when there is such a gap, though in both the short and the long term this impact may not be as important as other factors.

The Role of Firepower

The Portuguese navigator Vasco da Gama arrived in Indian waters in 1498, dropping anchor near Calicut on 20 May, with vessels carrying cannon that Asian warships, lacking cannon, could not resist successfully in battle. This technological gap gave the Portuguese victory over the Calicut fleet, although the latter was supported by Arab vessels, in 1502, and over the fleets of Japara and Gujarat in 1513 and 1528 respectively. South Asian trade routes were transformed.

Drawing on late fourteenth- and fifteenth-century developments in ship construction and navigation, specifically the fusion of Atlantic and Mediterranean techniques of hull

9. Primitive shooting armoured vehicle depicted in *The Temptation of St Anthony* by Jan Mandign. Such vehicles, visible here at far left of painting, were still very much in the realm of diabolical fantasy.

construction and lateen and square rigging, and advances in location-finding at sea,[18] the Portuguese enjoyed advantages over other vessels, whether they carried cannon or not. Thanks to the use of the compass and other developments in navigation, such as the solution in 1484 to the problem of measuring latitude south of the Equator, it was possible to chart the sea and to assemble and disseminate knowledge about it, to have greater control over the relationship between the enormity of the ocean and the transience of man than ever before.

Portuguese naval strength was based on full-rigged sailing ships which were strong enough to carry heavy wrought-iron guns capable of sinking the lightly built vessels of the Indian Ocean. Although the first recorded sinking of a naval vessel by shipboard guns did not occur until the early sixteenth century, fairly heavy cannon were carried on some European warships from the middle of the fifteenth century. These cannon were constructed with a particular concern for their use at sea in a fashion distinct from that of land-based weaponry: an important aspect of specialisation. In addition, large sailing ships with two masts required fewer bases than galleys, which relied on rowers: their crews were smaller and they could carry more food and water. Able, as a result, to transport a large cargo over a long distance at an acceptable cost, these ships, thanks to their cannon, could also defend themselves against attack.[19]

The heavier armament of the Portuguese warships was crucial in the face of the numerical advantage of their opponents, who had more ships and more men. The Portuguese initially relied on the caravel, a swift and seaworthy but relatively small ship, and the *nau* or 'great ship', a very large carrack-type vessel. They subsequently developed the galleon, a longer and

10. Bronze Culverin, English, dated 1542. Recovered from the wreck of the *Mary Rose*. Sixteenth-century European warships used three types of cannon: wrought-iron bombards; thin-walled bronze guns that fired stone shots; and thickly cast bronze guns thick enough to withstand the high pressure from large powder charges and able to fire iron shot with a high muzzle velocity and great penetrative force. From the 1540s, cast-iron guns were produced in England. The process of modification and improvement in naval ordnance helped to give the Europeans a major advantage.

narrower ship with a reduced hull width-to-length ratio that was faster, more manoeuvrable and capable of carrying a heavier armament. The cannon were fired from the side of the vessel, a change that owed much to the development of the gun port. Such cannon could inflict serious damage near the waterline and thus hole opposing warships.

Developments in gun founding and gunpowder made comparatively light guns more effective and increased the number of cannon that could be carried. As early as 1518, the standard armament of a Portuguese galleon was 35 guns and the Portuguese deployed their galleons in the Indian Ocean in time to confront the Ottoman naval challenge. When the Japanese ruler Toyotomi Hideyoshi planned his invasion of Korea in 1592, he unsuccessfully attempted to hire two Portuguese galleons.

Contrasts in firepower can also be emphasised in land warfare. The Spanish conquest of the two leading American states, the Aztec empire of Mexico and the Inca empire in the Andes, is often presented as the impact of a military new world, Europe, on an old world, for neither the Incas nor the Aztecs had firearms or horses. Their societies were reliant on wood and stone, not iron and steel. Slings, wooden clubs and obsidian knives were no match for the Spanish arms. The cannon, arquebuses and crossbows of the Spaniards all had a greater range and killing power than their rivals' weapons. In addition, the Aztecs probably could not use captured firearms, because they had no gunpowder and also lacked the necessary training, although it is not known whether the Aztecs did or did not use captured guns, or indeed when Indian units which were trained to fire guns began to be used by the Spaniards. In hand-to-hand combat, the Spaniards also benefited from the power and flexibility of their single-handed steel swords and from their steel helmets. In close combat, even without horses, these gave the Spaniards superiority over their Aztec and Inca opponents: metal weapons were more effective than stone; metal armour offered more protection than cotton-quilted.

Technological superiorities are widely held to explain the victories of tiny European forces. Hernán Cortés had only about 500 Spanish soldiers, 14 small cannon, and 16 horses when he landed at Vera Cruz in 1519. Francisco Pizarro had only 168 Europeans, 4 cannon and 67 horses, yet he overran the Incas in 1531–3: the latter referred to the shot fired by arquebuses as *Yllapas*, meaning thunderbolts. Spanish cavalry crushed an Inca rebellion in 1536: the Incas were very vulnerable in the open. Hernando De Soto, who had served under Pizarro and who between 1539 and 1543 brutally pillaged local peoples in what is now the southern USA, in 1541 won a battle with the Choctaws at Mabila (Selma, Alabama), in which his cavalry was able to dominate the open ground without competition. When Magellan arrived at Cebu in the Philippines in 1521 he showed off his firearms and armour in order to convince the population of his potency.

Firearms were also significant in the major battles in the eastern hemisphere. At Mohacs (1526) the heavy cavalry of Louis II of Hungary drove through Suleiman the Magnificent's lighter cavalry, but was stopped by his infantry and cannon whose fire caused havoc. The Hungarians were defeated. In the same year, at the first battle of Panipat, Babur employed both matchlockmen and field artillery successfully against the cavalry of the

11. Battle of Mohacs, 29 August 1526. Crushing defeat of the Hungarians under Louis II by the Turks under Suleiman the Magnificent. The Hungarian cavalry attacked, pushing back the Turkish cavalry, only to be stopped by the janissary infantry and cannon. Their fire caused havoc, and the Hungarians, their dynamism spent, were then attacked in front and rear by the more numerous Turkish forces. Louis and most of his aristocracy died on the battlefield or in the nearby Danube marshes.

Lodis, whose armies did not use firearms. In 1527 Mughal firepower also played a role in the defeat of the cavalrymen and armoured war elephants of a confederacy of Rajput rulers led by Sarga, Rana of Mewar, at Kanua, although the flexible enveloping tactics used by Babur's Central Asian cavalry were also effective, and mounted archers were more important than infantry matchlockmen in the battle. The following year, at the battle of Jam, Safavid artillery played a part in the victory of Tahmasp I of Persia over the Uzbeks. This was followed by the conquest of Khurasan.

Tactics were similar at Panipat, Mohacs, Kanua, Jam and Chaldiran. The winning side employed a technique known in Turkish as *tābūr cengī*: a row of carts linked by chains was arranged across the centre to block the advance of the opposing force, and behind it both artillery and infantry were deployed. Mounted archers were placed on the wings. At Baskent (1473) the Ottomans used a fortified camp, similar to the Timurid wagon fort, but also defended by artillery; their cavalry were initially in the fortified position. The vital Ottoman addition was firepower. The notion of a wagon fort was familiar to the Turco-Mongols of Central Asia, but it was greatly strengthened by firepower. Babur borrowed the tactic from the Ottomans.[20]

12. Indian printed and lacquered composite bow, eighteenth century. This is a decorated example of a deadly weapon. The composite bow was able to launch an arrow with considerable force.

Firepower played a major role in other battle. In 1556, at the second battle of Panipat, Akbar's Mughal army under the Regent, Bairam Khan, defeated a much larger insurrectionary force under Hemu, without the use of a *tābūr cengī*, or, apparently, artillery. Hemu relied on an elephant charge, but the Mughal centre redeployed behind a ravine and eventually prevailed thanks to their mounted archers.[21] At Haldighati (1576) a Mughal force defeated a Rajput army, because only the Mughals had musketeers, and they and the Mughal archers killed the elephant drivers who were crucial in their opponent's army.[22] At Tondibi in 1591, Moroccan musketry defeated the cavalry of Songhai.

Other factors, such as leadership, were also important, but access to firearms often enabled relatively small forces to destroy far more numerous opponents. This was true of the Spanish in their conquest of the Aztecs and Incas, of the Mughal defeat of the Rajput rulers and of the Moroccan victory at Tondibi, although precise figures are difficult to verify. At Kanua, Babur had only about 12,000 men; his Rajput opponents allegedly had 80,000 cavalry and 500 war elephants. At Jam, Tahmasp I had 24,000 men, his opponents allegedly about 120,000.

The Diffusion of Firearms

The use of firearms altered the balance of military advantage between states, peoples and areas. Possession of, and expertise in, firearms became the first priority in the struggle for military predominance, or even survival. The situation was far from static, because firearms, and training in their use, were exportable and, in some cases, were disseminated very quickly. Hungarian and German gunners helped Mehmed II at Constantinople in 1453. Concerned about Turkish pressure on their Greek possessions, the Venetians sought without success in the 1470s to provide Aqquyunlu Persia with firearms to use against the Turks. In 1472 Uzun Hasan requested cannon, gunners and arquebuses. Without them, he was defeated by Mehmed II at Baskent in 1473, but five years later the Aqquyunlu army had both field artillery and handguns, although their source is not clear.

In the early sixteenth century, the Portuguese, from their base at Ormuz on the northern shore of the Persian Gulf, were able to provide Persia with cannon to use against the Uzbeks, who understood the importance of artillery but, having no access to oceanic trade, found it difficult to acquire. Persia also obtained cannon from Russia. By 1600 the Safavids of Persia had about 500 cannon, while in mid-century Ottomans sent the Uzbeks a 300-strong janizary force armed with firearms and some cannon.

The Ottomans also provided firearms and light cannon for the unit of 1,200 janizaries, called *sekbans*, whom they provided as a bodyguard for the Khan of the Crimea. The *sekbans* also served as a control on the Khan's policy although their value for the diffusion of gunpowder weaponry was limited by the continued preference of the Crimean Tatars for fighting as light cavalry, most of whom were armed with compound bows and/or swords.[23] Further east, the Ottomans provided weapons to Caucasian supporters in the 1560s, in response to Russian intervention in Kabarda. In the 1580s the Russians offered their Caucasian supporters firearms.

Ahmad ibn Ibrihim al-Ghazi, an *iman* who conquered Adal in the Horn of Africa in the mid-1520s and launched a holy war against Ethiopia, trained his men in the new firearms and tactics introduced into the Red Sea region by the Ottomans after their conquest of Egypt in 1517. Better weapons were partly responsible for Ahmad's victory at Shimbra Kure in 1528, but he was unable to follow it up in 1529 because the tribal confederation he had built up collapsed. In 1530, however, Ahmad used loot from his 1528 campaign to buy seven cannon and recruited foreign experts to use them; although he also hired a force of Arabian archers. Ahmad's cannon helped him to victory over the Ethiopians at Antika in 1531. In 1541 the Portuguese, who had sent two cannon as a present in 1520, dispatched 400 musketeers to the aid of Ethiopia (where the first muskets had been bought from Turkish traders), and a joint Ethiopian and Portuguese army defeated Ahmad. He turned to the Ottomans, who provided him with 900 musketeers and 10 cannon, with whose help he defeated the Ethiopian-Portuguese army in 1542, only, in turn, to be defeated the following year.[24]

Idris Aloma, *mai* (ruler) of Borno (1569–*c*.1600), an Islamic state based in the region of Lake Chad, obtained his musketeers from Tripoli on the Mediterranean, which was captured by the Ottomans in 1551, and their assistance played a role in his success. The muskets were acquired either by diplomacy or through adventurers and mercenaries. The Ottomans similarly helped the Islamic Sumatran Sultanate of Aceh, providing gunfounders and artillerymen who increased Acehnese naval capability: several hundred men were sent in the 1530s; more help followed in the 1560s. Turks and Acehnese as well as Portuguese increased the military strength of the Javan state of Demak in the sixteenth century. In southern India, the Hindu state of Vijayanagara, under its dynamic ruler Aliya Rama Raja (1542–65), maintained its position by deploying armies equipped with artillery manned by Portuguese or Muslim gunners. Ibrahim Qutb Shah of Golconda (1530–80), who played a major role in overthrowing Rama Raja in 1565, relied upon both heavy cavalry led by his nobility and upon a European artillery corps. Golconda also provided arms and men to help Aceh attack Malacca.[25] In western India, Bahadur Shah of Gujarat developed a large army in the 1530s that was equipped with new cannon manned by Portuguese gunners. Bahadur Shah was himself killed by the Portuguese.

Portuguese auxiliaries using cannon and handguns played a major role in Arakan in the sixteenth century, and helped Tabinshweihti (1531–51) and Bayinnaung (1551–81) of Toungoo create a powerful Burmese state: Pegu was conquered in 1535–41 and Ava in 1555, large areas of Shan, Lao and Siamese population were overrun, including the Siamese state of Lan Na/Chiengmai, and the Siamese capital of Ayuthia was captured in 1564 and 1569.[26] Indeed, there were probably several thousand European renegades in south and east Asia by the early seventeenth century, some of whom forged cannon for local rulers,[27] although their military impact should not be exaggerated. Portuguese mercenaries helped in the introduction of new technology, but their role in Bayinnaung's army was less than that in the army of his predecessor. Similarly, two Muslim renegades were responsible for operating the first cannon in the Ethiopian army. The Ethiopians rewarded Portuguese musketeers with land in the 1540s in order to retain their services and these musketeers and their descendants continued to play an important role into the following century. Turkish musketeers and muskets were important in quarrels between Central Asian rulers.[28]

The issue of diffusion and, more generally, the possession of firearms serves as a valuable reminder of the fact that the Europeans neither invented gunpowder weaponry nor enjoyed a monopoly of its use. The same is true of earlier innovations in, for example, cavalry warfare. Accepting this, it is nevertheless possible to argue that the Europeans used such weaponry more effectively than other societies and that this was responsible for their military success. Similarly, the success of Muslim horsemen from Central Asia in medieval India 'points to [a] decisive edge in tactics and possibly in their *élan* as professional soldiers'.[29] Such an analysis, however, must confront the issues of the extent of European success in the sixteenth century, of the variety of reasons that can be advanced for the successes that were achieved, and of the limitations of firepower in the period.

European Expansion

Success is difficult to gauge. Drawing attention to the number of other dynamic powers necessarily limits any concentration on the Europeans as the definers of military activity and territorial expansion. Such an approach, however, does not aid comparison.

Here the first point is that of considering actual military clashes and confrontations between Europeans and non-Europeans. These encompassed a great variety of conflicts in the sixteenth century and a number of categorisations offer themselves, most obviously clashes on land and sea; or those with peoples using gunpowder weaponry and with those who did not do so; or those in Europe and nearby waters as opposed to those at a distance; or those with developed polities and those where state structures were less developed. There is also the problem of what standards to use in measuring success. It is all too easy to assume that the conquest of territory is the best measure, but that is to adopt a potentially misleading and anachronistic criterion. For example, the territorial imperative that was so important during the 'New Imperialism' of the nineteenth century, especially the 'Scramble for Africa', had far less weight 350 years earlier. Instead, the Portuguese, and from the close of the sixteenth century the Dutch and English, came to the Indian Ocean in large part in order to trade. Violence was employed in order to influence or even dictate the terms of trade, in particular by excluding rivals, rather than to gain territory. The Portuguese lacked the manpower to become a major Asian territorial power. The population of Portugal in the sixteenth century – about one million –

was not large, and there were many other emigration opportunities, especially to the less remote colony of Brazil. Tropical diseases killed many of the Portuguese who went to India, and there was a shortage of female emigrants.[30]

The gap in land warfare capability in South Asia was less than in the New World. Unlike the Incas and the Aztecs, Portugal's Indian opponents had gunpowder weaponry,[31] steel armour and swords, and war horses, and this was also true of some of their other Asian opponents. The Portugese found 3,000 firearms in the magazine when they captured Goa in 1510. The major entrepôt of Malacca, which fell to Portuguese attack in 1511, had numerous bronze cannon, although the decisive clash was between the Sultan's war elephants and a well-coordinated and determined Portuguese force relying on pikes as much as firepower. Portuguese cannon, however, were superior to those of their opponents. Nevertheless, the Asians were able to respond effectively to the Portuguese in both commercial and military terms in the sixteenth century so that the degree of control enjoyed by the Portuguese in the Indian Ocean should not be exaggerated.[32]

In simple and simplistic terms, the Europeans held the Ottoman advance in the second half of the sixteenth century, gained oceanic predominance and became the dynamic powers in the New World, but had only limited and largely coastal impact in Africa and Asia. Such a sentence can be glossed at length and variously, either to emphasise gains or to stress defeats and limitations. As attention commonly focuses on the gains, it is worth noting some of the failures.

The Europeans in the New World

From the outset, the Spaniards had encountered difficulties. They came to the West Indies via the Canary Islands where the native Guanches had mounted a vigorous resistance. In the sixteenth and seventeenth centuries the Spaniards never devoted military resources to the New World that in any way compared with their effort in European and Mediterranean struggles. In the New World, while the Spanish conquests of some areas like Cuba and New Granada (Columbia) were relatively swift (1511–13 and 1536–9 respectively), others took far longer. The reasons varied, but were typically a combination of local resistance, difficult environmental conditions, limited Spanish manpower and insufficient interest in expansion. Northward expansion in Mexico was impeded by the Chichimecas in 1550–90[33] and, further north, by the discovery that there was no gold-rich civilisation to loot.

The Spaniards also encountered problems in Central America. Cortés himself led a costly campaign in Honduras in 1524. Guatemala was conquered by 1542, but the Yucatán, the centre of Mayan civilisation, was not speedily overrun: although much of the Yucatán was conquered in 1527–41, the Itzás of the central Petén were not defeated until 1697, and the Lacandones to the west were never conquered.[34] Spanish control of jungle regions south-east of Mexico was limited, and the absence of major imperial states, similar to the Aztec or Inca empires, that could be overthrown ensured that the Spaniards had to consider whether and how to confront more groups. As in Africa in the late nineteenth century, the Europeans found it easier to conquer developed polities than acephalous peoples.

In South America, central Chile was conquered in 1540–58, Santiago being founded in 1541. However, the native people of Chile, termed Araucanians by the Spaniards, who relied on guerrilla warfare rather than pitched battles, were formidable opponents. They also benefited from a measure of diffusion, learning to ride horses and to use Spanish weapons which they captured.[35] Far from a continuous process of Spanish advance, the Spaniards were pushed back from the Southern Central Valley in the period 1598–1604 and, thereafter, the River Bió Bió served as a frontier beyond which the Araucanians were independent.

In Florida, although a number of coastal bases, most significantly St Augustine, were founded, Spanish control was limited. When they first arrived in 1513, the Spaniards had been obliged to withdraw by Timucua and Calusa archers. Pánfilo de Narváez's expedition of 1528 was repelled by Apalachees and Autes whose accurate archers used arrows capable of penetrating Spanish armour. The first fort at St Augustine, built in 1565, was burned down by the Timucua the following spring.[36]

In the Caribbean, the Kulinago of the Lesser Antilles and the Caribs and Arawaks of the Guianas thwarted Spanish attacks and mounted counter-raids with fast, manoeuvrable shallow-draft boats carved from tropical trees.[37] The Caribs of St Vincent kept the Spaniards out and were not indeed subjugated by a European power until a British campaign in 1772–3.[38] Warriors equipped with quilted cotton armour and carrying bows, slings, stone-tipped spears and flint or obsidian-edged swords, drove back a smaller Spanish force under Hernández de Córdova that in 1517 sought slaves on the Yucatán and Campeche coasts.

Similarly in Brazil, which they 'discovered' in 1500, the Portuguese made only slow progress at the expense of the Tupinambá and Tapuya,[39] although they were helped by rivalries between tribes and by the alliance of some.[40] Portuguese muskets were of little value against the nomadic Aimoré, mobile warriors who were expert archers and well adapted to forest warfare.[41]

Nevertheless, potential resistance to European control was lessened by enslavement and disease. Enslavement disrupted social structures and household and communal economies, leading to famine and population decline. The herding together of enslaved peoples, for example Arawaks brought from the Bahamas to work the gold mines of Hispaniola in the 1510s, exacerbated the impact of disease, both new and old. Smallpox decimated the population of Hispaniola in 1519.[42] Even without enslavement, disease imported by Europeans, particularly smallpox, led to a major fall in indigenous populations.[43]

Spanish conquest was not solely a matter of initial military success. It was followed by the arrival of colonists and their livestock, by Christian proselytisation and the destruction of rival religious rituals, by the introduction of administrative and tenurial structures, and by a degree of Spanish acceptance of local elites and local material cultures, and of local adaptation to the Spaniards. The quest by colonists for land encouraged an extension of Spanish control, while the importance of bullion to the Spanish economy and to Habsburg finances increased governmental supervision and commitment.

The Indian Ocean

Whereas for the Ottomans at their most ambitious, state policy meant aggressive territorial expansion on every possible frontier, Portugal had a different model, that of the Venetian Empire da Mar in the Mediterranean: a chain of islands and fortresses protecting entrepôts and enforcing monopoly or near monopolistic trading terms – a monopoly excluding other Europeans being the important point. This was the essence of the Portuguese empire: a global Empire da Mar.

In the Indian Ocean the Portuguese had made a great initial impact. Their chain of fortresses included Socotra at the approach to the Red Sea (1507), which was rapidly abandoned because there was little water, Ormuz at the mouth of the Persian Gulf (1507, and, having lost it, 1515), Cochin (1503), Cannanore (1505), Goa (1510), Diu (1534) and Bassein (1534) on the west coast of India, and Malacca in the straits of that name (1511).[44] From Muscat and Suhar, Portugal controlled the Arabian coast at the entrance of the Persian Gulf. A Mameluke counter-offensive was stopped in Indian waters: an Egyptian fleet, partly of galleys, sent from Suez in 1507 and supported by Gujarati vessels, initially defeated a greatly outnumbered Portuguese squadron at Chaul in 1508, but was largely destroyed by Francisco de Almeida at Diu (1509). Almeida, the first Viceroy of Portuguese India, had earlier served in the Spanish war against Granada. Affonso de Albu- querque, Viceroy (1509–15), appreciated the strategic importance of seapower in the region and applied it systematically. It is necessary to consider Portuguese achievements in order to make studies of the foundation of the modern world-system more concrete by focusing on the military foundations of European economic hegemony.

Yet this record of success can be qualified and was to be challenged. First, not all the Portuguese targets were gained. Albuquerque failed at Aden in 1513, an important setback given the role of the Red Sea as the primary route for Islamic naval counter- attack. The Portuguese sought to assault the walls using scaling ladders, not to breach them with preliminary cannon fire. Instead, cannon, firing stones, were used by the defenders. A second attempt, made in 1517, also failed; the Mamelukes had also been repulsed there in 1516. At Jeddah in 1517, a Turkish galley fleet checked a Portuguese attempt, under Albuquerque's replacement, Lopo Soares, to sail up the Red Sea by taking up a defensive position in the reef-bound harbour under the cover of coastal artillery. Fortifications in the region, not least at Jeddah, had been greatly improved by Mameluke forces sent to provide assistance against the Portuguese.[45]

Secondly, especially beyond Malacca, Portuguese bases were generally commercial centres, not major fortified positions like Elmina, Goa and Malacca, although their base at Ternate, established in 1522, only fell after a five-month siege in 1575, and other fortified posts were built at Solor (1562) and Tidore (1578). The Portuguese gained wealth from the trade routes they developed from Malacca to the Far East, with bases established at Macao in China (1557) and Nagasaki in Japan (1570), but they did not acquire any significant military capability in the region and were unable to thwart the establishment of Spanish power in the Philippines, despite attempts in 1568 and 1570, or to resist effectively the development of Dutch interests in the East Indies.

Portugal versus the Ottomans

Thirdly, the Portuguese encountered serious challenges further west. The expansion of the Ottomans into Egypt and Iraq gave this dynamic Islamic power a direct interest in the Red Sea and the Persian Gulf, although in the 1520s and early 1530s Suleiman devoted little attention to the area and, indeed, transferred cannon and munitions from Suez to the Mediterranean in 1532. The 72-strong Ottoman fleet sent to Diu in 1538, the largest fleet the Ottomans ever dispatched to the Indian Ocean, failed to win Gujarati support and was repulsed, but en route the Turks seized Aden, pre-empting a Portuguese expedition, creating the basis for the Ottoman province of Yemen and strengthening the Ottoman ability to defend the Red Sea and to intervene in the Horn of Africa. From bases at Aden, Basra and Suez, the Ottoman admirals Piri Reis and Seydi Ali Reis exerted much pressure in mid-century. In 1552, Piri Reis, with 30 warships and 850 soldiers, sailed from Suez, sacking the Portuguese base of Muscat and then besieging Ormuz. The latter, however, resisted successfully, leading to the execution of Piri Reis, and an Ottoman fleet under Seydi Ali Reis was heavily defeated there in 1554. Firepower played a crucial role in the engagements, but the 1552 expedition was also compromised by the loss of a vital supply ship.[46]

From the 1560s, Ottoman naval activity in the Indian Ocean declined, although in 1568 artillerymen and gunsmiths were sent to help the Sumatran Sultan of Aceh against Malacca; he had also requested specialists in shipbuilding and fortifications. As with Spain and the Ottomans in the Mediterranean after the mid-1570s, a rough division between areas of naval hegemony, or at least activity, was developed. Although the Portuguese had sent an expedition into the Red Sea in 1541, which unsuccessfully tried to destroy the Ottoman fleet at Suez, their hopes of influence there had to be abandoned, and, from the Red Sea, the Turks threatened the Portuguese position on the Swahili coast of East Africa in 1585 and 1589: fleets under Mir Ali Bey were able to force most of the coastal cities between Mogadishu and Kilwa to accept Ottoman suzerainty.

However, with the support of Persia, the Portuguese were able to limit the Ottoman presence in the Persian Gulf, and in addition Ottoman maritime power was essentially restricted to the Gulf and the Red Sea (as well as to the Black Sea and the Mediterranean). This was appropriate given the nature of their warships. Ottoman galleys were less suited to the Indian Ocean than Portuguese vessels. The Ottomans preferred to attack Cyprus in 1570 rather than send aid to distant Aceh. Frontiers stabilised. Ethiopian resistance led to the defeat of Turkish advances inland from their Red Sea base at Massawa from 1578.[47]

Challenges to Portuguese Power

Elsewhere in the Indian Ocean, the Portuguese were challenged by Asian powers. The Sultanates of Indonesia, especially Aceh, attacked Malacca on a number of occasions. Aceh, a Sultanate greatly expanded in 1520–4 when Sultan Ali Mughayat Syah overran much of the eastern and western coasts of north Sumatra, defeating a Portuguese fleet in 1524 and ending the Portuguese presence in the area,[48] was a centre of Islamic activity. An Aceh fleet of 300 ships with 15,000 troops attacked Malacca in 1553 and further attacks were launched in 1568, 1570, 1573 and 1595, while the north Javanese state of Japara mounted attacks on Malacca in 1513 and 1574, and Johor, where the ruling family of Malacca had moved after its capture by Portugal, launched attacks, including one in 1551. Peace was not made with Aceh until 1587.

Towards the end of the century, although they took the initiative in Sri Lanka, gaining the kingdom of Kotte in the 1590s,[49] the Portuguese were under increasing pressure in Asia. The protection costs of empire rose. Portuguese trade with India was attacked, and fell from 1580, ensuring that revenues declined at the very time that defence expenditure rose. As Islamic identity in the Moluccas increased, Portuguese relations with the Sultans of Ternate deteriorated. The Portuguese were driven from Ternate in 1575 after a lengthy siege of their position, and the Portuguese attempt to create a monopoly over the Moluccan spice trade was lost with it. In 1588 Philip II of Spain, from 1580 also King of Portugal, turned down a request from the Viceroy in Goa for forces with which to attack Aceh. In 1589 the Portuguese had to send a large force to the Swahili coast to check the advance of the Ottomans. The Portuguese felt it necessary to begin new fortifications at Muscat in 1587 and at Mombasa in 1593. In 1596 the first Dutch fleet reached Bantam in West Java, and in 1602 the Dutch first landed on Sri Lanka. Having suppressed a rebellion on the island of Solor in 1599, the Portuguese were expelled by the Dutch in 1613 and, after a Portuguese return, in 1636.[50]

These challenges contributed to and reflected imperial overstretch: the problems of an imperial power with great, but in the last resort limited, resources seeking to allocate its efforts between a number of overextended commitments. More generally, the course of Portuguese and Spanish transoceanic activity leads to the question of the reasons for successes and failures, and thus also to the limitations of firepower in the period.

As with earlier developments, such as cavalry warfare with the stirrup, success can be explained in military-technological terms, but this explanation can also be qualified by drawing attention to additional or alternative factors. Thus the creation of the Portuguese empire in Asia indicated what could be achieved with naval power when a substantial technological gap existed in military capability. Portugal's success, however, also reflected the advantage of seeking colonial gains in areas like the Moluccas and on the Swahili and Indian coasts, where there was considerable political fragmentation and so the possibility of creating new political links or entities with relatively little opposition and in cooperation with some local polities. The local political environment was important when, with 1,200 men and 17 or 18 ships, Albuquerque captured Malacca, the leading entrepôt in South-East Asia, in 1511. He played on divisions among the large, multiethnic mercantile community in order to win support against the Sultan. Bahadur Shah of Gujarat, whose navy had been defeated by the Portuguese in 1528, was attacked by the Mughals in 1535. He then made a defensive treaty with the Portuguese who built a fort at Diu.

In contrast, attempts by Asian rulers to consolidate political power, for example by Rama Raja of Vijayanagara on the Coromandel and Malabar coasts of India in 1544–54, hindered Portuguese penetration. Earlier, Albuquerque had had good relations with Vijayanagara and this had aligned the Portuguese against the hostile Muslim state of Bijapur and given the Portuguese an important entrée into local power politics. Similarly, the Turkish impact in the Horn of Africa was lessened by Ethiopian resistance. The Ethiopians gained firearms, not least by captures from the Turks, and by secret purchases.[51]

Portuguese action was relatively effective because it was supported by the resources of a state. Initially, the Portuguese had relied on more informal activity. Thus, for example, the Portuguese presence on the Gold Coast of West Africa began with the discovery of Mina in 1469 by the sea captains of Fernão Gomes, a wealthy financier. However, the Portuguese state soon came to play a much greater role. Indeed, Mina's gold trade was controlled as a royal monopoly.[52] Political ambitions and available resources tended to ensure that transoceanic intervention by European states was more effective and lasting than by pirates, although more concerted interventions by larger private entities, such as the Dutch East India Company, also led to territorial gains.

Most territory was seized by Spain. The original Spanish model of expansion was not too dissimilar to that of Portugal, one of islands and mainland fortress-ports, and this was applied from the Canaries and Ceuta on. Cortés, however, followed his own ambitious project, not that of the Spanish authorities, and in Mexico he was going against the letter and spirit of his authorisation. Success acquired a dynamism of its own and led to a shift in official Spanish policy towards extensive territorial conquest.

European Expansion and Local Divisions

There were also important non-military-technological reasons in the case of Spanish success in the New World, especially the weakness of Aztec and Inca leadership and their socio-political structures, and the Spanish ability to find local allies. In addition, as the Spaniards were most successful in the New World in regions where there was much for them to gain, their failures to expand were not necessarily military in nature. It is important not to exaggerate the role of technology in Aztec and Inca defeat. Spanish firearms were few and slow, and much of their impact was psychological. Aztec wooden clubs, studded with flint or obsidian, proved effective against Spanish horsemen thanks to the skill of the warriors. The Spaniards also adopted native quilted cotton armour: it was more appropriate for the climate than metal armour and offered protection against spears and bows; although the Spaniards retained their metal helmets which were useful against slingshots.

Mutual cultural incomprehension played a role in Aztec defeat. The panicky Aztec leader Montezuma was fascinated by Cortés and unwilling to act decisively against him, worried that he might be a god or an envoy from a powerful potentate. Cortés reached the Aztec capital Tenochtitlán without having to fight his way there. After Montezuma was killed in 1520, either by the Spaniards or in an anti-Spanish rising, the Aztecs lacked clear leadership. His energetic brother Cuitlahuac, who replaced him, was killed in an outbreak of smallpox in 1520: the disease, brought by the Spaniards to the Americas, killed at least half the Aztecs, and weakened the morale of the survivers. In India, similarly, the death of Sultan Ibrahim Lodi and most of the Lodi elite at Panipat in 1526 helped greatly in the establishment of Mughal power, while Babur's invasion had been encouraged by opponents of Ibrahim who provided him with important manpower.

Divisions also helped the Spanish gain allies. The Inca ruler Huyana Capac (1493–1525) left a disputed succession between the northern and southern sections of the empire, which were led respectively by his son Atahuallpa and his half-brother Huescar. Once captured by the Spaniards, Atahuallpa was used against his rival Huescar before being strangled in 1533. Reactions to the Spaniards were greatly affected by allegiance to one or other of the factions. Pizarro's seizure of power was in part a coup as much as an invasion. In addition, Aztec and Inca expansion in the fifteenth century left conquered peoples ready to ally with the Spanish. The Totonacs and the Tlaxcalans welcomed Cortés and he encouraged the rebellion of the ruler of Cempoala in 1519. Having been driven from Tenochtitlán in 1520, Cortés recouped his strength with the help of the Tlaxcalans, and his eventual victory in 1521 owed much to the role played by about 200,000 Indian allies. Native support was essential in order to match the massive numerical superiority of the Aztecs, who learned to alter their tactics to counter European arms, especially firepower.[53] Pizarro received help from the Canari Indians. In the conquest of Guatemala, the Spaniards benefited from disputes between Maya groups. The Spanish expedition sent to Pensacola Bay in 1559 helped the Coosa subjugate the formerly subordinate Napochies.[54]

The local political environment was also crucial in the establishment of Spanish control over much of the Philippines. Indicating the global range of European maritime power and the capacity of far-flung European military systems for independent or autonomous action and for mutual support between parts of the system, the first Spanish settlement in the Philippines was planted, not by an expedition from Spain, but by one that had crossed the Pacific from Mexico. Miguel Lopez de Legaspi established a base on Cebu in 1565 and, before he died in 1572, he had extended Spanish control over that island, as well as Leyte, Panay, Mindoro and the central plain of the largest island, Luzon.

The island nature of the Philippines facilitated Spanish action – this was a territory wide open to maritime attack. The limited nature of local fortifications was also important. When de Legaspi arrived in Manila Bay in 1572, the local communities were defended only by a bamboo stockade at the entrance to the Pasig River, and only one stone fort is known to have existed in the Philippines before the Spaniards arrived. Yet political circumstances were arguably more important. This was a conquest that involved relatively little warfare, for there was no strong political entity in the Philippines able to mobilise resistance. The *barangay*, a comparatively small kinship group, was the sole significant political unit, and this limited the organisation of resistance.

Furthermore, cultural assimilation was aided by the nature of Philippine religion – animist and without an organised ecclesiastical structure – and by the willingness of Spain to encourage effective Catholic missionary activity. It is significant that the Spaniards encountered most serious resistance in the Philippines from those areas where Islam had made an impact: Mindanao and Sulu. The first major Spanish attack on Sulu, begun in 1578, failed, as did a 1596 expedition to Mindanao. Fortunately for the Spaniards, the Philippines were at the edge of the Islamic world, distant from centres that might have provided support for co-religionists,[55] while those centres, for example Aceh, were also involved in conflict with local centres of Iberian power, especially Malacca. The Spaniards saw the Philippines as a base for further expansion. In 1589 Philip II instructed its governor to occupy Formosa (Taiwan) and in 1598 two Spanish warships were sent to seize the harbour of Keelung, only to be thwarted by the weather.

Opportunities for determined Iberian adventurers were arguably greater in Asia than, after the initial wave of conquest, in the New World, because royal power and sovereign pretensions were rapidly extended in the latter. Spanish-supported adventurers, led by a Portuguese mercenary Diego Veloso, attempted to take over Cambodia in the 1590s and in 1597 their candidate was proclaimed king. This endeavour came to an end in 1599, when the greatly outnumbered Spaniards were killed in a rebellion, but, the same year, a Portuguese adventurer, Philip de Brito, was given charge of the port of Syriam in Pegu by the ruler of Arakan, who had attacked the area. De Brito had been in the service of Minyazagyi of Arakan since the 1570s. The Portuguese Crown recognised de Brito's position by granting him the captaincy of Syriam and de Brito sought to play a role in the trade of the eastern Bay of Bengal and in Lower Burma.

The Russians, Kazan and Astrakhan

The expansion of Muscovite power to the east and south-east similarly benefited greatly from divisions among potential opponents. Ivan III (1462–1505) began to take the initiative in the longstanding struggle between Muscovy and the Tatars. He conducted a series of campaigns against Kazan in 1467–9 and then took advantage of dynastic strife within the Khanate, so that in 1487 his forces were able to make a sympathetic claimant Khan.

Vassily III (1505–33) initially maintained good relations with Kazan, but the Crimean Tatars organised a pan-Tatar league which ousted the pro-Muscovite ruler of Kazan in 1521, replacing him with Sahib, the Crimean Khan's brother. In the same year, the Crimean and Kazan Tatars advanced on Moscow from the south and the east, and the city was saved only by an attack on the Crimea by the Tatars of Astrakhan. In 1524, the Khan of Kazan acknowledged the suzerainty of Suleiman the Magnificent, but in 1532 Vassily succeeded in installing another pro-Muscovite Khan, Djan Ali. He, however, was murdered in 1535 and replaced by Sahib's nephew, Safa-Girey. Relations between Muscovy and Kazan deteriorated with frequent raids by Tatar cavalry. Contemporary

Russian sources speak of at least 60,000 Russian captives in the Kazan Khanate.

In 1545 Ivan IV, 'the Terrible' (1533–84), took the initiative, helped by divisions among the Tatars. He attempted two winter campaigns against Kazan in 1547–8 and 1549–50, but these failed because the Russian army had no fortified base in the region, had to leave its artillery behind because of heavy rains and ended up campaigning with an exclusively cavalry army that was of no use in investing the fortress of Kazan.

But for the third campaign a base was secured. In the winter and spring of 1551 the Russians prefabricated fortress towers and wall sections near Uglich and then floated them down the Volga on barges with artillery and troops to its confluence with the Sviiaga (25 kilometres from Kazan); here the Russian fortress of Sviiazhsk was erected in just 28 days. Sviiazhsk not only provided a base of operations against Kazan, but also protected the upper Volga towns from raids by the Crimean Tatars. That summer, siege guns and stores were shipped down the Oka and Volga to Sviiazhsk and, after a Crimean invasion of southern Muscovy, with artillery support probably from Turkey, was repulsed near Tula in mid-June, the Russian army advanced on Kazan, which it reached on 20 August. Including peasants levied as sappers and transport labour, the Russian army was allegedly 150,000 strong. It also had 150 siege guns.

Kazan stood on a high bluff overlooking the Kazanka and Bulak Rivers. It had double walls (cradle-built) of oak logs covered over with clay and partially plated with stones. There were 14 stone towers with guns and a deep surrounding ditch. The garrison consisted of 30,000 men with 70 cannon and was supported by over 20,000 cavalry outside the town.

The Russians constructed siege lines from which cannon opened fire and also used a wooden siege tower carrying cannon and moved on rollers. The supporting Kazan cavalry were routed on 30 August, the ditch surrounding the city was filled with fascines and sappers tunnelled beneath the walls. The mine was blown up on 2 October, destroying the walls at two of the gates, upon which the Russian army drawn up into seven columns attacked all seven of the town gates simultaneously. They soon broke through and Kazan fell after a 28-day siege. The campaign witnessed the first large-scale use of artillery and mining by Russians.

The Russians owed their success in part to more advanced weaponry, especially cannon, and the war demonstrated the effectiveness of Ivan's new infantry and artillery units, but there were other important factors. The demographic balance favoured Russia, and there was a clear difference in consistency and quality of leadership. Although during Ivan IV's minority the Russian government was weak and divided, there was little comparison with the situation in Kazan, where the throne changed hands six times between 1546 and 1552. This provided numerous opportunities for Russian intervention.

Once Kazan had fallen, there were several serious rebellions – in 1553, 1554 and 1556. These were repressed with great brutality: towns were destroyed, men slaughtered, women and children taken prisoner, the countryside devastated. Only in 1556 did organised resistance cease.[56]

The Russians were also helped by divisions between the peoples of the steppe. The Russians benefited greatly from the support of the Nogais who lived north of the Caucasus. In the late 1520s the centre for the Nogai trade in horses was moved from Constantinople to Moscow, helping to cement political links. In turn, the Russians provided goods, including some firearms. In 1563 the head of the Great Nogai Horde became Ivan IV's brother-in-law. The Nogai alliance was useful for a number of reasons. The Nogais made possible the Russian conquests of Astrakhan in 1556 and Sibir in 1582. Their supply of horses helped the Russians operate outside the forest belt of northern

Russia. In addition, after the fall of Kazan, the Russians were aided in the suppression of Tatar resistance by the support of many of the Khanate's former subjects.

The capture of Kazan opened the way for Russian expansion towards the Caucasus and across the Urals into West Siberia. Some of the Tatar military pressure on the south-eastern frontier was reduced and Muscovy was given greater access to the trade routes of the Transcaucasus and Central Asia. The Russian occupation of the southern Volga ensured that the Ottomans were cut off from Sunni co-religionists and trade partners in Transoxiana at the same time as the Safavids confronted them in the Caucasus. Rivalry between Russia and the Ottomans became more intense and was to become a major element in Eurasian geopolitics. However, the Russian policy of exploiting local divisions proved less successful in the northern Caucasus, where Russian attempts to create anti-Ottoman coalitions failed in the 1580s and 1590s, and Russian expeditions were totally routed in 1594 and 1605. Persia, not Turkey or Russia, became the dominant power in the region.[57]

Similarly, although the 1550s saw a marked development in Russian military capability, not least with the emergence of the central chancelleries and the appearance of military governors on Russia's frontiers, the Russians were unsuccessful in the Livonian War of 1558–83 against Sweden and Poland. The Russians were quite successful in driving out the Swedes and occupying the Baltic coast from Reval to Riga in 1575–7, but Ivan IV then made the mistake of failing to go on to capture Riga, the gateway to southern Livonia, perhaps because he thought he could receive favourable armistice terms from Stefan Batory, whose hold on the Polish throne he considered shaky. As a result, forces from Riga began recapturing fortresses as soon as the Tsar left Livonia; and Batory, once he had secured his rights to the throne, was able to use the union with Lithuania to mobilise much more power than previously possible for Polish kings. Batory was able to recapture Polotsk in 1579 in large part because his forces (41,000, along with 10,000 Swedes) outnumbered the Russians: 35,000 in total on the north-western front, in part because part of the Muscovite army had to be diverted to the southern frontier against the Crimean Tatars. However, the Poles fared less well when they besieged Pskov in 1581–2. The greatly outnumbered Russian defenders held on, exhausted the Polish army and thereby prevented further Polish invasion; a contributory factor was the Swedes' refusal of closer military cooperation with the Poles. Thus, as in the case of European expansion, the political context played a major role in determining or affecting the dynamics of alliance politics and strategy, while military resources alone did not guarantee success.

The Political Dimension of Conquest

As with so much else of the military history of the period, it is necessary to appreciate that a factor – political context facilitating conquest, which so helped Ivan IV against Kazan, but not, eventually, in Livonia – was not unique to European expansion, and that it is better understood if seen in a wider context. Thus, the success of Ahmad ibn Ibrihim al-Ghazi of Adal in conquering much of Ethiopia in 1527–40 owed much to half a century of political strife among the Christian warlords of Ethiopia, but also to the very nature of the state. Ethiopia was a very heterogeneous polity composed of numerous linguistic, ethnic and religious communities that lacked the cohesion normally achieved by cultural assimilation or political integration. Instead, unity was retained only if the military superiority[58] of the 'central government', to employ a modern reification, was apparent.

This was not only the case with Ethiopia, but was more generally true of the states of the period, for example Aztec Mexico, the Mughal empire,[59] Vijayanagara in southern India,[60] and states in the East Indies, such as Aceh in Sumatra, Gowa in Sulawesi and Mataram in Java. The Lodi Sultanate of Delhi was much weakened by civil war from 1518 and this greatly helped the Mughal invasion. The nature of the government and politics of these states helps to explain the speed with which they could be overthrown. It is not necessary to adopt a military-technological explanation in order to do so, and, indeed, it would be mistaken to see such rapid overthrows only in terms of the successes of European powers. However, a recent account of the fall of Granada that addressed the issue of the role of domestic divisions has suggested that they were less important than the Spanish use of largely German-manned artillery. It has also been argued that resourceful Moorish resistance obliged the Spaniards to adapt and adjust their tactics, providing them with crucial training that was to serve them in good stead in conflict against the French in Italy in the 1500s.[61]

Christian–Muslim Conflict in North Africa

The Europeans encountered serious difficulties in North Africa. Along most of the African coast this became an aspect of the wider struggle with the Turks, a conflict in which the Muslims took the initiative from the 1520s.[62] In 1492, the *Reconquista*, the centuries-long Christian reconquest of Iberia (Spain and Portugal), culminated in the capture of Granada, Spain's last Moorish state. This achievement owed much to the combination of greater military resources and the Spanish use of artillery. Their opponents were outgunned and the Spaniards benefited not only from more and better-supplied artillery, but also from shifting firepower 'to operational centre stage' and by adopting offensive artillery tactics. Malaga fell in 1487, followed by Baza, Almería and Guadix in 1489.[63]

The *Reconquista* had led to a militarisation of Iberian society. It was then extended by Spanish and Portuguese interest in gaining possessions in North Africa, more especially ports from which regional trade could be controlled; Ceuta had already been captured by the Portuguese in 1415. Spain's interest was further aroused by religious concern: the conquest of Granada raised anxiety about the loyalty of the Muslims in Spain and the spectre of foreign intervention on their behalf; indeed in 1487 Granada had appealed to both the Ottomans and the Mamelukes for assistance. The Mediterranean was not a barrier to action and intervention; instead, it encouraged and facilitated them. This concern led in 1502 and 1525 to decrees insisting on baptism or exile for Muslims, but Spain was left with a substantial minority of *moriscos*, converts whose loyalty was suspect.[64]

The Portuguese had similar expansionary ambitions in Morocco and established a network of bases along the coast. Proximity, opportunity and anxiety ensured that Portugal's commitment in Morocco was far greater than that made by her elsewhere. There were 20 ships on Vasco da Gama's second voyage to India in 1502, a larger fleet than any that had hitherto sailed that far from Europe, but still only 20. Affonso de Albuquerque, Viceroy of Portuguese India (1509–15), wanted a large fleet manned by 3,000 Portuguese, but none was sent to the Indian Ocean during the sixteenth century. He attacked Aden in 1513 with 1,000 Portuguese and 700 Malabar archers. In contrast, although the figures were probably exaggerated, the Portuguese allegedly used 400 ships and 30,000 men to capture Arzila on the Moroccan coast in 1471, while the force defeated in Morocco in 1515 was larger than that commanded by Albuquerque. Similarly, Philip II sent 98 ships and 15,000 men to capture Terceira in the Azores in 1583, a far larger force than that

13. *Battle of Pavia*, 25 February 1525. Artist unknown. Like many battles, this arose from an attempt to end a siege, in this case that of Pavia in Lombardy by Francis I of France. A Spanish relief army under the Habsburg Emperor Charles V attacked the French lines in the dark and, having placed themselves across French communications, adopted a defensive position – with arquebusiers on the flanks and pikemen and cavalry in the centre – to await French counter-attacks. The French cavalry defeated their Spanish counterparts, but were held by the Spanish pikemen and cut to pieces by arquebus fire. Then an advance by the Swiss pikemen in French service was thrown back by the arquebusiers. At the close of the day, Francis was captured. Pavia was a battle decided by the combination of pikemen and arquebusiers fighting in the open, rather than depending on field fortifications.

sent to the Philippines. The largest fleet sent by Portugal–Spain to the East Indies was that of 43 warships sent to Malacca in 1606.

Cannon played a major role in Portuguese gains along the Moroccan coast.[65] The Portuguese captured Alcacer in 1458, Larache and Tangier in 1471 (after failures to take Tangier in 1437, 1463 and 1464), Agadir in 1505, Safi in 1508, Azamor in 1513 and Mazagão in 1514, thus gaining control of most of the towns on Morocco's Atlantic coast. The Portuguese thus sought to seize the trade of the region.

Initially, the Spaniards enjoyed much success in North Africa. Their military machine had been well honed by the long war for Granada and their opponents were weak and divided. Melilla was gained in 1497, Mers-al-Kabir, where the Portuguese had failed in 1501, in 1505, Oran in 1509, and Bougie, Tripoli, and the Peñón d'Argel position dominating Algiers, in 1510.

The situation, however, deteriorated in the 1520s as the Habsburg Holy Roman Emperor, Charles V, the ruler of Spain, the Low Countries, the Habsburg hereditary lands (Austria, Bohemia, Silesia), and southern Italy, devoted more resources to war with Francis I of France, especially in Lombardy (the Milanese). This helped the Muslims in North Africa to seize the initiative. This process began with corsairs, especially Kemal Reis and, later, Oruc, and his brother Khair-al-Din, Barbarossa, but, after the conquest of Egypt in 1517 and the suppression of a Mameluke rebellion there in

1523–4, Suleiman the Magnificent began to take a greater interest in North Africa and the western Mediterranean. In 1516, the rulers of Algiers had called on the Barbarossas to recapture the Peñón. By the time Khair-al-Din did so, in 1529, he had also gained control of Algiers and its hinterland, displacing local Muslim rulers, especially the Zayanid Sultanate of Tlemcen. Oruc had captured Tlemcen in 1517, but was killed by the Spaniards in 1518. As elsewhere, an emphasis on the struggle between the Turks and Christian powers can lead to a failure to devote sufficient attention to Turkish conflict with co-religionists.

The Spaniards lost Bougie also in 1529. Suleiman appointed Barbarossa Grand Admiral of the Ottoman fleet and in 1534 he drove the Spaniards from Coron in the Morea which they had captured in 1532, attacked the coast of southern Italy, and also expelled Mulay Hasan, the pro-Spanish Moorish ruler of Tunis. Maritime links between Spain and Italy, and with them the basic axes of Habsburg power, were threatened.

Furthermore, the tightening of the frontiers between Europe and the Ottomans was linked, not only to the emergence of a Spanish interest in the Mediterranean, moving from West to East as the Ottomans moved from East to West, but also to an increase in religious tension. The seizure of Otranto in Italy by the Turks in 1480–1 with attendant atrocities had galvanised Europe to the threat from the East, making real something that Byzantine refugees had been pleading since the 1430s. In 1499, during the Venetian–Turkish war, Turkish raids reached the borders of Friuli in north-eastern Italy, and there were rumours of the Turks using mastiffs to hunt down Christian peasants. The ostensible purpose of Charles VIII of France's invasion of Italy to claim Naples in 1494–5 was to launch a great crusade. Crusades were proclaimed in 1500, 1517 and 1530. The various Holy Leagues in Western Europe saw their eventual project as being an assault on the Turks, and they did indeed gather and act to that end in 1538 and 1571.

In response to Barbarossa's capture of Tunis in 1534, a crusade was launched from Europe, and Charles V in person conquered La Goletta and Tunis in 1535. A pro-Spanish Muslim ruler was installed in Tunis. In 1541, with Cortés in his suite, Charles led another major amphibious expedition that was a considerable logistical achievement, on this occasion a crusade against Algiers, the leading corsair base, but his fleet was badly damaged by an autumnal storm and, thereafter, Charles turned his attention to France and the rising challenge of German Protestantism.

Barbarossa's successor, Dragut, captured Tripoli from the Knights of St John in 1551, and turned it into a corsair base under the authority of the Sultan. A Spanish force sent to recapture it by Charles' son, Philip II of Spain, was defeated at Djerba, a base on the route between Tunis and Tripoli, in 1560 with the loss of 10,000 men. The Turks were checked when they attacked Malta in 1565 and their fleet defeated by a Spanish–Venetian– Papal fleet at Lepanto in 1571, but they conquered Cyprus in 1570–1 and in 1574 captured Tunis and Biserta,[66] and by 1578 the Spanish held nothing east of Oran. Venice had already made peace with the Turks in 1573; Spain followed with a truce in 1578.

The active campaigning of the early 1570s was followed by a long period of strategic stasis that, in part, reflected alternative commitments for both Spain and the Ottomans – the Dutch Revolt and war with Persia respectively; but that was also a product of the absence of any gap in military capability. Both sides had effective fleets of cannon-bearing galleys, although their range was affected by prevailing wind directions and the presence of bases.[67] Unlike in southern Russia, where the abortive 1569 expedition against Astrakhan demonstrated the limitations of Ottoman operational effectiveness set by distance, the Ottomans had not exceeded their range of possible large-scale attack in the

Mediterranean in the 1560s and 1570s. Corfu, southern Italy and Malta still remained possible targets.

However, the Turks were affected by improvements in Christian fortifications and by the heavy expenditure made available to that end. Christian losses like Modon and Rhodes were made before the introduction of the new angle-bastioned military architecture, which the Venetians were very quick to use in their Empire da Mar. On Crete a castle was built at Candia (Iraklion) in the second quarter of the century and a major fortress at Rethymnon after 1573. The Turks found such fortresses difficult to capture, and although in 1570 they captured Nicosia in Cyprus, the first town to be encircled with an extended *enceinte* entirely constructed according to the most modern design, they only did so by brute force and guile. Nevertheless, they did capture it. There was little equivalent Turkish fortification re-evaluation, no large-scale equivalent to the new European fortifications, although the Turks scarcely required such a development in the sixteenth century: they were not under attack.[68]

In the following century, however, as external pressure on the Turks increased, they built some impressive fortifications, many of which only fell after lengthy sieges. These included Belgrade, Buda and Vidin on the Danube, Temesvár on the Tisza, Khotin and Bender on the Dniester, Ochakov and Kilburn controlling the Dnieper estuary, and Azov on the Don. Although technically not as impressive as the fortifications that Vauban designed for Louis XIV, the Turkish positions fulfilled the same purpose: in general, they absorbed considerable effort before they fell. They also reflected the resources available to the Ottoman state.

Defeat in Morocco

The single most important defeat for European expansion during the sixteenth century occurred in 1578. The young ruler of Portugal, King Sebastian, boldly sought to extend longstanding Portuguese interests in Morocco in order to make it a client state, and one, moreover, that was immune to the threat of expanding Ottoman influence. However, Moroccan military capability was much improved on the situation a century earlier when the Portuguese had developed a 'quantum superiority in operational versatility, tactical expertise and the types, numbers and technical currency of guns'.[69] Since then, the Wattasids of Fez had been driven from much of Morocco by more vigorous opponents, the Sa'dis. The years 1536–49 were crucial in Morocco. Firearms forces and artillery arsenals grew substantially as the native dynasty added more territory, widened contacts with European sources of munitions, and won victories. The Sharifs worked diligently to integrate arquebusiers and field artillery into their forces, and to develop combined infantry–cavalry tactics for their battles. Their light cavalry was more flexible than the heavier cavalry of the Mamelukes and of Western European armies.

The Sa'dis captured Agadir in 1541, and the Portuguese were driven to abandon Safi (1542), Azamor (1542) and Arzila (1549). By 1549 Muhammad ash-Shaykh had brought Morocco closer to unity than it had been in generations: that year he captured Fez from the Wattasids. The capture of Santa Cruz from Portugal was Morocco's first artillery victory in offensive operations and indicated that the technological gap in land warfare had been closed. Morocco ceased to be an arena of contest and, instead, became a potential contestant in Mediterranean warfare. Moroccan military capability increased as campaigns shifted from static sieges against Portuguese fortifications to the rapid manoeuvres of infantry–cavalry armies against Islamic foes, particularly the advancing

Ottomans in the 1550s. External success ensured that Morocco gained internal stability. This was challenged by Sebastian.

In 1578 he led a poorly prepared army of 18,000–20,000 men, crucially short of cavalry, into the interior of Morocco in order to challenge the Sharif, Abd al-Malik, and his force of about 70,000. Sebastian sought to benefit from division within Morocco by helping Muhammad al-Mutawakkil, the former Sharif, who had appealed for Sebastian's assistance, having been deposed by his uncle, Abd al-Malik. Thus Sebastian hoped to establish a client ruler. He also felt it necessary to displace al-Malik, who had been supported in his seizure of Morocco by the Turks and the Habsburgs.

Sebastian sought battle at al-Qasr-al-Kabir/Alcazarquivir on 4 August, believing that his infantry would successfully resist the Moroccan cavalry. He deployed his infantry units in a deep phalanx, with cavalry on the flanks and artillery in the front. The Moroccan army consisted of lines of arquebusiers, with cavalry, including mounted arquebusiers, in the rear and on the flanks. The Moroccans opened the battle with harrying attacks by horse arquebusiers; the unsupported Portuguese artillery was overrun. The Portuguese infantry fought well, however, and pressed hard on the Moroccan infantry. A second Moroccan cavalry attack pushed back the Portuguese cavalry on both flanks, but the Moroccans again lost impetus. A renewed attack by the Portuguese infantry allowed a gap to open in their left flank, which the Moroccans exploited with great effect. The Moroccan horse arquebusiers then succeeded in destroying the cohesion of the Portuguese rear right flank, and Sebastian's army disintegrated. Sebastian himself was killed and his entire army either killed or captured. The skilful, well-disciplined Moroccan force had won a crushing victory thanks to superior leadership and discipline, more flexible units and tactics, and the events of the battle. Their army had matured as an early modern gunpowder force and made particularly effective use of arquebusiers trained to fire from horseback.[70] Morocco was left free from European invasion until 1844.

The battle of Alcazarquivir is not generally given much, if any, weight in military history. It does not appear to fit in with the grand theme of the rise of the West. More specifically, study of the military struggle between Christendom and Islam in the sixteenth century concentrates on the Ottoman–Habsburg conflict to the detriment of other struggles, including those in the Horn of Africa and in Russia. In addition, Morocco has never received much attention from military (or indeed most other) historians. If Alcazarquivir is considered, it is dismissed with reference to Sebastian's folly.

This approach is misleading. Alcazarquivir is significant in any discussion of European military capability and expansion for a number of reasons. The specific point that it led to the end of European pressure on Morocco is not unimportant as a qualification to European expansion. More generally, the failure to conquer the so-called Barbary States of Morocco, Algiers and Tunis revealed the deficiencies of the European military system when it came to campaigns in the interior of countries, and, also, European limitations in coastal campaigning, both in amphibious operations against coastal positions and, subsequently, in defensive efforts to consolidate and retain gains.

These points do not relate only to North Africa in the sixteenth century, but are of more wide-ranging application, both chronologically and geographically. Alcazarquivir also directs attention to the specific question of the relationship between European military capability and that of other states making extensive and effective use of firearms. It raises the question whether the Portuguese entry into the Indian Ocean should, in part, be seen not only as a geopolitical outflanking of Muslim power, but also as, in effect, an outflanking of a more formidable military challenge and a search for easier and more readily exploitable spheres of activity.

The Portuguese Empire

Lastly, Alcazarquivir led to the end of Portuguese independence. Sebastian had no children. His successor, the Infante-Cardinal, was elderly, ill and childless, and when he died in 1580, Philip II was able to enforce a claim to the succession employing both widespread bribery and troops. Supported by a fleet from Cadiz, the Duke of Alba invaded in late June. Sétubal fell on 18 July, Lisbon in late August and Coimbra on 8 September. The Portuguese were defeated at Alcantara. This was one of the most rapid and decisive campaigns of the century. Although circumstances were very different, the Portuguese empire fell far more rapidly than those of the Aztecs and Incas. Longer Portuguese resistance was limited to the Azores, and it was finally overcome there by Spanish expeditions in 1582 and 1583 that defeated French warships supporting Don Antonio, the Portuguese claimant.

Portugal, one of the world's two leading transoceanic colonial empires, had been taken over by its rival empire, Spain, with relatively little fighting, an obvious contrast to the contest between Portugal and Islam. Yet this reflected the primacy of the dynastic theme within sixteenth-century European polities: the destruction and exhaustion of the dynasty (the death of Sebastian and the absence of effective claimants) entailed the end of an independent Portugal. The process of dynastic takeover, however, was eased by the willingness to maintain distinct institutions and separate practices and privileges, as with Scotland and England in 1603. Philip II became Philip I of Portugal. No new state was created.

However, from 1580 until 1640 Portugal was ruled by the kings of Spain. This compromised Portuguese imperial activity and expansion, although both had indeed encountered serious problems hitherto. First, after 1580, Portuguese resources were, in part, used to further Spanish interests in Europe and elsewhere, a process that had its most dramatic form in 1588. The Spanish Armada against England sailed from Lisbon and the brunt of the subsequent battles was borne by Portuguese galleons. Less dramatically, once Terceira in the Azores was captured in 1583, the fortress at Angra was strengthened in order to protect Spanish transatlantic trade.

This shift in the use of Portuguese resources was of great importance because, prior to that, Portugal had enjoyed a significant window of opportunity. It had not been involved in the Italian Wars and the Franco-Habsburg struggle for predominance of 1494–1559, nor in the 'Wars of Religion' that began with the Habsburg-German Protestant conflict of 1546–7 and that became more extensive from the 1560s, with the Dutch Revolt against Philip II's rule, the French Wars of Religion and confessional-related civil conflict in Scotland, England and Ireland. Thus, unlike other European states, Portugal, with its narrow demographic base, had been able to devote its military resources to extra-European activity, whether in Morocco or further afield, although the latter had led to tension with Spain. For example, concern about Spanish intentions led the Portuguese to construct forts in the Moluccas, at Ative (1564) and Hitu (1568). Portugal had thus achieved a military situation that prefigured the position of Britain for most of the century after Waterloo: it had been an expansionist power on the edge of Europe and relatively disengaged from that continent's struggles.

Secondly, when Portugal became part of the Spanish system, it was targeted by attacks on that system, and indeed became a tempting victim due to the wealth and apparent vulnerability of the Portuguese empire. Prior to 1580, Portuguese global military-economic organisation had already faced many difficulties. These became much more acute after 1580. Whereas English attacks on Portuguese trade prior to 1580 had been small-scale, thereafter Portuguese possessions were directly affected by the upsurge in English attacks on the Spanish maritime and colonial world. The Dutch also became a serious threat to the Portuguese. Philip II banned Dutch trade with Lisbon in 1594, encouraging the Dutch to seek spices at their Asian sources.

The first English ships in the Indian Ocean arrived in 1591. The *Edward Bonaventure*, captained by James Lancaster, who had earlier served the Portuguese, captured three Portuguese ships in 1592. Lancaster went on to command a fleet that captured the Portuguese base of Pernambuco in Brazil with great booty in 1595, and to command the first fleet of the English East India Company formed in 1600. He arrived at Aceh in 1602 and found that the English were seen as allies against the Portuguese. Furthermore, the Portuguese now lacked the diplomatic independence necessary in order to consider how best to respond to such attacks. Thus, paradoxically, although the Spanish–Portuguese union of 1580–1640 lessened the number of European powers engaged in extra-European activity, it actually served to increase, or at least exacerbate, rivalry between these powers.

Portugal and Sub-Saharan Africa

The Europeans encountered problems in sub-Saharan as well as North Africa. The Portuguese discovered early on that slave raiding met strong resistance from the kingdoms south of the Senegal river, many of which were far from weak. Instead, trade was a more successful means of access[71] and helped to finance further expansion. The profits from the trading base of São Jorge da Mina, founded in 1482, financed later voyages, such as those of Diogo Cão and Bartolomeu Diaz. Mina itself was a logistical achievement, prefabricated with stones, timbers and tiles all prepared in Portugal.

More generally, although it was possible to establish and seize bases, as for example the Portuguese did in East Africa with Sofala (1505), Kilwa (1505) and Mozambique (1507), in Angola with Luanda (1576), and in West Africa with Mina (1482), Axim (1495) and Accra (1515),[72] it proved difficult to expand into the interior. This was a particular problem for the Portuguese in Angola and in the Zambezi valley. An expedition of 700 musketeers sent in 1571–3 to the Zambezi valley to seize the gold of Mutapa lost most of its men to disease. No gold mines were discovered. The Portuguese had explicitly sought to emulate the achievement of the Spaniards in the New World. Instead, they revealed the total ineffectiveness of the European military system in land-based campaigns in sub-Saharan Africa. Both major sixteenth-century Portuguese attempts at conquest in Africa – in Mozambique in 1569–75 and in Angola in 1575–90 – were unsuccessful. Disease was as devastating for the Europeans in Africa as it was for their opponents in the New World. About 60 per cent of the Portuguese soldiers who served in Angola in 1575–90 died of disease. Most of the rest were killed or deserted. In addition, horses could not survive. More generally, the environment was much more savage than the New World. Whereas Mexico and Peru were populous and had a well-developed agricultural system that could provide plenty of resources for an invader, Africa lacked comparable storehouses, food for plunder and roads. Mexico and Peru were also more centralised politically, and thus easier to take over once the ruler had been seized. In contrast, Africa was more segmented, and new chiefs could emerge. The Portuguese also found the Africans well armed with well-worked iron weapons as good in some ways as Portuguese steel weaponry and certainly better than the wood and obsidian of the New World.

However, the Portuguese presence along the West African coast helped to divert the gold and other valuables of central West Africa towards coastal entrepôts, rather than across the Sahara to the more ancient entrepôts of the coastal Maghrib (North Africa). Thus, in terms of trade, possession of Morocco was less important than it would have been in the fifteenth century. Furthermore, the Portuguese impact was not solely a matter of conflict. In 1483 the Portuguese navigator, Diogo Cão, became the first European to set foot in the kingdom of Kongo. Peaceful relations were established and in 1491 the king was baptised as João I. A syncretic blend of Christianity and local religious elements spread rapidly, a syncretism that is a good model for much of the more general process of European impact in the non-European world.

The Limitations of Firepower

It is clear that not all battles in the sixteenth century were decided by firepower. At Alme-Qulaq (1503) the Safavids defeated the Aqquyunlu, in part because divisions among the latter undermined their attempt to unlimber cannon behind a wagon fort. In 1573 in order to crush a rebellion in Gujarat, the Mughal Emperor Akbar's 3,000 troops travelled by camel 500 miles (800 km) in just 11 days and then defeated 15,000 rebels in a cavalry engagement. Eight years later, Akbar's massive field army still included only 28 cannon in a force of 50,000 cavalry and 500 war elephants. The Mughal ability to control the supply of war horses in India ensured that they dominated mounted archery in the subcontinent in the sixteenth century, and this archery played a major role in a relative decline in the importance of elephants, which had hitherto been much more important in north Indian warfare. Mounted archers were as significant as artillery in this shift, and Babur's victories owed more to his use of such archers than to firearms. At Tukaroi (1575) the Mughal army in East India under Todar Mal defeated the Afghan Sultan of Bengal, Daud Karrani, by recovering from the initial shock of a successful elephant charge on the Mughal centre and wearing down their opponents in hard fighting in which archery played a major role.[73] When Shah Abbas I of Persia advanced on Herat in 1598, he defeated a slightly larger force of Uzbeks at the battle of Rabāt-i Pariyān, a battle decided by a charge by Abbas' mounted bodyguard led by the Shah himself.

Mounted horse archers of Central Asian origin were the most appropriate answer to the dangers facing the Islamic world in the twelfth and thirteenth centuries: the Crusades and especially the Mongols. In the early sixteenth century, the Turks revealed them to be technologically obsolete, but this was less the case in South and Central Asia.

In Africa, firearms had most impact along the savanna belt, where Islamic 'foreign' influence, from the Mediterranean littoral, was strongest, but it is important not to exaggerate their impact. The Moroccans overran the Pashalik of Timbuktu in 1591, but strong Songhai resistance prevented further expansion. Ibn Fartuwa's contemporary account of the wars of Idris Aloma of Bornu with Kanem makes no mention of guns playing a crucial role, and Fartuwa concentrates on other units of Aloma's army and on non-firearm tactics. In Ethiopia the use of firearms was restricted by the limited availability of shot and powder. In the early seventeenth century no more than 500 musketeers took part in any one expedition.[74]

Native African fighting methods could be very effective. African coastal vessels, powered by paddles and carrying archers and javelin men, were able to challenge Portuguese raiders on the West African coast. Although it was difficult for them to storm the larger, high-sided Portuguese ships, they were, nevertheless, too fast and too small to present easy targets for the Portuguese cannon. In 1535, for example, the Portuguese were once more repelled when they tried to conquer the Bissagos Islands off the West African coast.

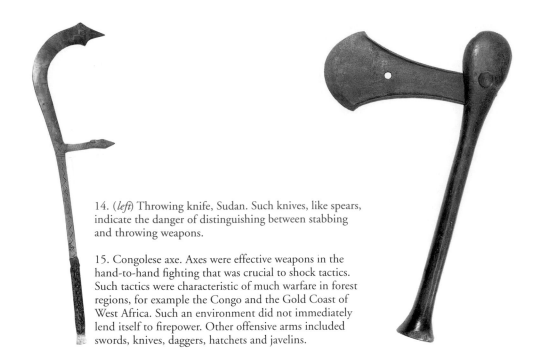

14. (*left*) Throwing knife, Sudan. Such knives, like spears, indicate the danger of distinguishing between stabbing and throwing weapons.

15. Congolese axe. Axes were effective weapons in the hand-to-hand fighting that was crucial to shock tactics. Such tactics were characteristic of much warfare in forest regions, for example the Congo and the Gold Coast of West Africa. Such an environment did not immediately lend itself to firepower. Other offensive arms included swords, knives, daggers, hatchets and javelins.

On land, Portuguese cannon proved to have little impact on African earthwork fortifications. In Angola the slow rate of fire of muskets and the openness of African fighting formations reduced the effectiveness of firearms, and the Portuguese were successful only when supported by local troops. In cavalry, the Portuguese were unable to deploy anything larger than a small force, and could not therefore counter their opponents' open order of fighting.[75] Similarly, to be successful, Chinese campaigns against the nomadic horsemen of the steppes to the north generally required nomadic allies and a willingness to understand the political and economic dynamics of nomadic society.[76] As far as interior West Africa was concerned, the spread from North Africa of larger breeds of horse, new equestrian techniques and new tactics of cavalry warfare, was more important than the use of firearms, although the process had begun in at least the fourteenth century.

Japan

In Asia the situation was more complex than any simple concentration on gunpowder weaponry might suggest. Firearms could indeed be important and were certainly so in Japan. Warfare on horseback with bow and arrow as the principal weapon had been the major mode of conflict until the fourteenth century, with increasing use of foot soldiers thereafter. The Japanese were exposed to gunpowder during the Mongol invasions of the late thirteenth century and received crude guns from China in the fifteenth century, but the first functionally effective guns were brought by Portuguese traders in 1543. They were widely copied within a decade as Japan's metallurgical industry could produce muskets in large numbers. Firearms certainly played an important role in war after the battle of Shinano Asahiyamajo (1555), and, at the battle of Nagashino (1575), 3,000 musketeers in the army of Nobunaga, of the Oda clan, used volley fire to smash the charges of Takeda cavalry, winning a decisive victory, a scene repeated in the famous 1980 film *Kagemusha* by Akira Kurosawa. Such firepower tactics were in use neither in China nor in Europe at this time, although their impact on the course of Japanese warfare and on the process of unification is a matter of controversy. Firepower led to a stress on defensive tactics in Japan, as at Shizugatake in 1583, and in Kyushu in 1587 where Hideyoshi's forces were deployed behind entrenchments. The Koreans had few muskets and were greatly at a disadvantage when the Japanese invaded in 1592.

Cannon were known in Japan from at least 1551, although they did not become important until the last quarter of the century. They were employed in sieges from 1582. The challenge of Korean warships and fortifications in the 1590s forced the Japanese to develop their artillery on sea and land, although by 1598 the Koreans appear to have had a lead in cannon, especially at sea.[77]

The most important changes in Japan occurred earlier, from the late fifteenth century, as the pace of warfare accelerated. These included larger armies, greater preponderance of infantry, increasingly sophisticated tactics and command structures, and changes in weaponry, especially the spear, and armour. The only major change introduced by the Portuguese was the gun. While this became an important weapon and had far-reaching effects on armour design, it did not revolutionise the conduct of battles to the extent that

16. Armour in flame and gold of an officer of the Daimyo of Sakai, *c.* 1550. Japanese body armour sought to combine flexibility with protection, but was affected by the introduction of firearms.

it did in Europe. The Europeans appear to have had less of an impact on Japanese warfare than that of the Mongol invasions. The Mongols had directly presented the samurai with an enemy that relied on more sophisticated tactics and utilised both novel forms of familiar weaponry, such as swords, bows and armour, and completely unknown weapons, such as exploding shells. The invasions appear to have triggered changes in Japan in styles of armour more suitable to fighting on foot, in swords with shorter, heavier blades, and in tactics, for example the use of more coordinated infantry movements. All these changes were beginning to show during the fourteenth century, but it is difficult to assess whether they were mostly the result of autonomous internal developments or largely caused by the Mongol experience and the resulting diffusion and emulation of techniques and tactics.

In Gibbon's terms, the struggle for predominance between the clans of Japan which occupied much of the sixteenth century helped to produce military development – the adoption of firearms and the extensive construction of fortifications – by competitive emulation. War with Korea in the 1590s also encouraged development by emulation. However, in the seventeenth century Japan chose not to embark on a similar course in international relations and her military capability did not develop either on land or at sea. There was considerable socio-cultural opposition to giving guns to ordinary people. No one outside the closed samurai elite was allowed to own any arms, including swords.

Firearms played a smaller role elsewhere in East Asia, and that itself is an indication of the danger of focusing too much on them, for not only can such a focus lead to an exaggeration of the role of military-technological factors but also, in so far as the latter are considered, of the specific role of gunpowder weaponry.

China

Gunpowder weaponry had developed first in China, where the correct formula for manufacturing gunpowder was discovered in the ninth century and effective metal-barrelled weapons were produced in the thirteenth.[78] The use of cannon and other firearms spread from China to Burma, Cambodia, Siam, Vietnam and elsewhere in the fourteenth century. When the Portuguese captured Malacca in 1511 they found many cannon, while the Spaniards captured 170 cannon from Brunei in 1579. Large cannon were also cast in Java in the sixteenth century.[79] However, although China was responsible for important advances, it lost the lead in hand-held firearms. Matchlocks were introduced into China, probably from both the Turks via the Muslims of Xinjiang, and from Portuguese merchant adventurers, either directly or via Japanese pirates. Furthermore, the Chinese did not develop flintlock muskets.[80]

The Chinese were pressed hard by the Mongols once the latter had recovered from internal conflicts in the first half of the sixteenth century. The Mongols raided every year from 1550 until 1566 and heavily defeated a Chinese army which they ambushed on the steppe in 1552. As a result, the Chinese, whose annual military expenses rose rapidly, returned to the defensive, relying on garrisons at strategic passes and walls, and taking successful steps to accommodate the Mongols. A treaty with Altan Khan was signed in 1571. Trade and gifts were used as effective means of defence.[81]

Mobile artillery was developed in China in the 1570s and the Great Wall was adapted for musketeers to resist the Mongols,[82] but the military strength of the Ming empire lay primarily in the size of its army – up to half a million in number – and, to a lesser extent, in fortifications, rather than in firearms. Although better firearms and fortifications helped, in the 1550s the Ming used large numbers of men armed with traditional weapons – bows, lances and swords – to capture the Chinese bases of the *wako* (Japanese pirates) who attacked the coasts of the Yellow Sea. Cannon were felt to be unreliable and/or inaccurate. In 1593 it was the size of the Chinese army sent to support the Koreans against Japanese invasion that was important, not its level of military technology. The Japanese were pushed back to a bridgehead near Pusan, but the Chinese were unable to destroy the bridgehead. In contrast, the 1582–3 and 1584 expeditions against the Burmese had been successful.

Numbers were also crucial in Chinese siege techniques. The earlier use of gunpowder in China ensured that their fortified cities had very thick walls capable of withstanding the artillery of the sixteenth century. As a consequence, assault rather than bombardment was the tactic used against fortifications. This was also appropriate to the large forces available. The risk of heavy casualties could be accepted, a matter both of pragmatic military considerations and of cultural attitudes towards loss, suffering and discipline, and sieges had to be brought to a speedy end because of the logistical problems of supporting large armies.

South-East Asia

Firearms also played a relatively minor role in South-East Asia and the East Indies, for example in warfare on Java. Again this reflected cultural assumptions. The emphasis was on the fighting qualities of individuals, and on warrior elites, not on large numbers. In general, handgunners were treated badly; they were not members of these elites. Effectiveness in the use of muskets, which were low-precision weapons, required their use in a regular manner in order to provide concentrated fire. The necessary discipline and drill did not match social assumptions about warfare in the region, because they subordinated individual skill and social rank to the collective, the disciplined unit. Furthermore, cannon were used as symbolic supports of authority rather than as killing machines. They were adjuncts of courts, and there was an emphasis on their size, not their manoeuvrability.[83]

In addition, the provision of a large number of similar, let alone identical, weapons was beyond local metallurgical capability. European-type matchlocks were manufactured in a number of countries, for example Burma and Vietnam, but flintlocks and wheel-locks had to be imported from Europe. Sieges played only a limited role in warfare because most cities were not walled – certainly true of Malacca, Johor, Brunei and Aceh. However, in response to European pressure, construction of city walls spread in the sixteenth century, for example in Java. Nevertheless, the notion of fighting for a city was not well established culturally. Instead, the local culture of war was generally that of the abandonment of cities in the face of stronger attackers who then pillaged them before leaving. Captives, not territory, were the general objective of operations. European interest in annexation and the consolidation of position by fortification reflected a different culture. Differing assumptions were as important as any technological gap: Portuguese cannon were swiftly captured by Indonesian competitors and the Portuguese lost their technological lead on land.[84] Unlike in much of South Asia, mounted archery did not play a role in South-East Asia, while war-elephants remained important. Kerala in southern India was more similar to South-East Asia than to northern India.

India

The need for a pluralistic interpretation of military success is apparent if Mughal India is considered. The great extension of Mughal territory under Akbar (1556–1605) reflected his energy and determination, the divisions among his opponents, the impressive demographic, economic and financial resources of Hindustan and the regions gained by conquest, and the strength of the Mughal military system. Firearms certainly played a role. Akbar took an interest in the improvement of his muskets, maintaining a special collection which he tested himself.[85] His infantry was equipped with muskets and his artillery was superior to that of rival rulers. Akbar's siege artillery was instrumental in the capture of well-fortified positions, such as the Rajput fortress of Ranthambor in 1569, although in the case of Chitor in 1568 mines dug by sappers in which gunpowder charges were placed were more important.[86]

Yet Mughal military force was not restricted to firearms. The Mughals also deployed heavy cavalry armed with swords and lances, horse archers and war elephants. In addition, Akbar anchored his position with a number of fortresses: Agra, Allahabad, Lahore, Ajmer, Rohtas and Attock. Furthermore, while gunpowder weaponry was important to Akbar, it also benefited his opponents and his victories were not easy. The sieges of Chitor and Ranthambor were both lengthy and difficult, as, more generally, was the deployment of cannon. Logistics played a major role in sieges, encouraging negotiations while they were in progress.[87] Much of Akbar's success was due to his military skill and to the strong organisation of his state. Furthermore, the successful combination of a number of arms was important. Thus, any concentration on firepower has to be qualified or, rather, set in context. Historians of technology would rarely see any development as a simple response to technology, while, from the perspective of military historians, it is apparent that tactics were changing for several reasons, of which advances in technology was only one.

The Naval Situation

While it is instructive to contrast other gunpowder societies when considering European use of gunpowder weaponry, there is no point of reference for ocean-going cannon-carrying warships. The Egyptian and Turkish vessels that sailed to the west coast of India or between the Red Sea and the Persian Gulf were different in their long-distance capability and were also less heavily gunned. Indeed, whereas there was considerable diffusion of new weapons and techniques in land warfare in the sixteenth century, there was no comparable diffusion of naval weaponry and techniques.

Nevertheless, this did not mean that European warships were invulnerable. In African, Indian and Indonesian waters, the heavily gunned Portuguese vessels, with their deep draught and reliance on sails, were vulnerable to shallower-draught oared boats. Some damage was done by Indian (Malabar) and Malay privateers. More generally, Portuguese warships, like those of other European powers, had only very limited value in inshore, estuarine, deltaic and riverine conditions, a situation that was not to change until the introduction of shallow-draught steamships carrying steel artillery in the nineteenth century. South-East Asian rulers responded to the threat posed by European warships not by copying them but by building bigger armed galleys whose oars gave them inshore manoeuvrability. A fleet of about 50 Cochin-Chinese galleys destroyed three Dutch warships in 1643.[88]

Yet large Portuguese vessels in deep waters were difficult to attack successfully, and the effectiveness of European warships as maritime cannon carriers increased with the

17. Malay kris. Such weapons remained important after the development of muskets. In general, the continued use of weapons for hand-to-hand combat has been unduly minimised by military historians whose customary emphasis has been on firepower.

development of gunports just above the waterline and of waterproof covers for them. This ensured that guns could be carried near the waterline as well as higher up, thus reducing top-heaviness and increasing firepower.

On the oceans of the world there was little challenge to European military technology, but, again, the situation is more complex than might be suggested by any technological determinism. In considering European transoceanic naval prominence it is appropriate to consider the dog that didn't bark in the night. China, the most populous and wealthiest state in the world, the state with the largest army and one that had in the early fifteenth century deployed long-distance naval power more than any other state, did not contest the Portuguese arrival in the Indian Ocean or in Indonesian waters, and did not resist the establishment of Spanish power in the Philippines. The great Chinese naval expeditions had been succeeded by a period of contraction that owed something to failure in Vietnam in the 1420s. This period was characterised by a hostility towards maritime trade. The move of the capital from Nanjing to Beijing in 1421 led to a diminished interest in South-East Asia, with which trade declined.[89] Shipbuilding was restricted. A Chinese naval squadron employing cannon defeated a Portuguese force off Tunmen (Tou-men) in 1522, but that defeat simply highlights the issue, for Tunmen (Tou-men) is near Macao. Chinese junks were sturdier than Indian ships. The Portuguese were fortunate they did not reach the Indian Ocean eighty years earlier. By the early sixteenth century, the Chinese had an inshore naval capability, but no longer deployed distant fleets, and their navy faced difficulties in dealing with Japanese piracy.[90] The Chinese were scarcely pacific in the late sixteenth century: they fought against the Mongols, sent a large army into Korea to repel Japan and launched campaigns against indigenous peoples in south-west China. However, there was no war with Portugal. Had there been, the Chinese would have had large numbers of warships, although they would have been lightly gunned.

A similar point could be made about those East Asian powers that did deploy formidable fleets in the sixteenth century. Unifying Japan, Toyotomi Hideyoshi used ships in his invasion of Kyushu in 1587 and his amphibious force that attacked Korea in 1592 was the largest armada of the century. In 1592 and 1597 he invaded with about 150,000 men. Although Chinese intervention on land on the Korean side in 1593 was crucial, naval operations were also vital. The Japanese fleet was defeated at the battle of the Yellow Sea (1592) by a fleet commanded by Yi Sun-Shin that included some of the more impressive warships of the age: Korean 'turtle ships', oar-driven, cannon-firing sailing boats that were apparently covered by hexagonal metal plates, in order to prevent grappling and boarding, and were possibly equipped with rams. However, the Japanese rapidly deployed cannon on their warships and used them with effect in 1593 and 1597.[91] In 1598 the Koreans were also supported by a Chinese fleet under an artillery expert, Ch'en Lin.[92] That year, the Japanese fleet was defeated by Yi at the battle of Chinhae Bay.

Yet neither Japan nor Korea developed a long-distance naval capability, or sought to challenge the Iberian presence in Asian waters. The Japanese took steps to develop ships protected with iron plates but, once ambitions for conquest in Korea died with Hideyoshi in 1598, these steps were abandoned. The Korean turtle ships fought no further battles. The Portuguese were to have a fleet defeated off Johor in 1603 and to have their principal bases in Sri Lanka taken, but by the Dutch, not by an Asian power.

Military historians need to consider the battles, campaigns and wars that did not occur as well as those that did; indeed, both in counterfactual terms and in trying to assess relative capability, the former are as important as the latter. Although the Portuguese clashed with the Turks in the Indian Ocean, they did not clash with the major Turkish naval forces in the Mediterranean.[93] The absence of a major European–East Asian clash in the sixteenth century is another crucial instance. Proposals for a Spanish conquest of China and/or Japan were rejected by the Council of the Indies in 1577, and their reiteration in 1583–6 was without effect.[94]

In the second half of the century a number of South-East Asian states, especially Aceh, Johor, Bantam and Brunei, developed substantial fleets of war galleys which were able to hold their own in the face of the then weakening Portuguese empire.[95] The situation was in part to change when the more assertive Dutch and English deployed their heavily armed sailing ships in the seventeenth century and, thanks to the autonomous structure of their East Indian mercantile enterprises, were able to use the profits of their East Indies trade to support their forceful stance.

Conclusions

In an influential recent work, Charles Tilly focused attention on what he saw as a mutually sustaining relationship between military development, capitalism and governmental power, and argued that the early modern period was especially important in this process:

... with the organizational and technical innovations in warfare of the fifteenth and six-teenth centuries, states with access to large numbers of men and volumes of capital gained a clear advantage, and either drove back the tribute-takers or forced them into patterns of extraction that built a more durable state structure.[96]

As already suggested in this chapter, Tilly's interpretation, which essentially repeats that of Gibbon, is of some value in explaining the greater long-term capacity of Europe to resist nomadic onslanght. Had there been a second Mongol onslaught, it is likely that the Mongols would have encountered more effective resistance than they faced in the thirteenth century. The Crimean Khan, Devlet Girei, sacked Moscow in 1571, but he was able to do so because Ivan the Terrible was concentrating on the struggle for domi-nance in Livonia on the eastern shores of the Baltic. Similarly, the major Tatar raid on Muscovy in 1633 was facilitated by the Russian concentration on the siege of Smolensk. However, Tilly's interpretation is less helpful in accounting either for military relation-ships between European states and other polities deploying regular forces equipped with firearms, or in explaining the growing transoceanic capability of a number of European powers, and of no other states.

Furthermore, an emphasis both on technological innovations in warfare and on their global impact in the sixteenth century is in part challenged by the argument that the changes in European warfare discussed by Michael Roberts and Geoffrey Parker were not in fact revolutionary, but long-term and evolutionary. New tactics, enlarged army sizes, increased military expenditures and the proliferation of the *trace italienne* fortresses, which the proponents of the Military Revolution theory argue occurred in the late fifteenth and sixteenth centuries, all had medieval precedents which were not caused by gunpowder weapon technology. Indeed, fifteenth-century sieges in Italy indicated the importance of the spirit and commitment of the combatants and the availability of good infantry for storming the breaches, rather than gunpowder weaponry. Conversely, the impact of gun-powder weaponry in Europe prior to the Roberts-Parker period can be emphasised.[97]

Moreover, the revolutionary character and consequences of the changes discussed by Roberts and Parker within Europe can be queried in terms of scope, scale, chronology and consequences.[98] A criticism of the Military Revolution theory more closely accords with the evolutionary theories of many historians of technology than with an emphasis on revolutionary leads. Any reassessment of European warfare has important implications for the understanding of the role of technological innovations in warfare in the sixteenth-century expansion of Europe's global power.

To turn to technological diffusion within Europe, it is clear that new developments were rapidly diffused. Gibbon's thesis of competitive emulation was well founded. The effectiveness of Swiss pikemen against Charles the Bold of Burgundy's army in 1476–7 led other powers to hire (France) or emulate (several German rulers) the Swiss. The pike was devastating *en masse* in disciplined formations, and its adoption led to a need for trained, professional infantry, far superior to most medieval levies. However, as so often with military innovations – tactical or technological – that created a capability gap, it is necessary to be cautious in assessing the causes, extent and nature of the gap. The Swiss benefited in their victories over Charles the Bold from their pikemen but also from his poor leadership and from cavalry provided by allies, and Swiss tactics were rapidly revealed as rigid. The cannon, arquebuses and pikemen of Charles V's army repelled a Swiss pike attack with heavy casualties at Bicocca in 1522.

Charles VIII of France invaded Italy in 1494 with iron cannon balls allowing smaller projectiles to achieve the same destructive impact as larger stone shot, and, therefore, with

18. *The Cannon* by Albrecht Dürer. The German artist had no practical experience of war, but he
published a treatise on fortification, *Etliche Underrich zur Befestigung der Stett Schloss und Flecken* in 1527.
He proposed walls dominated by massive, squat roundels, towers that would also provide gun-platforms.

smaller, lighter, more manoeuvrable cannon which were mounted permanently on
wheeled carriages. The artillery impressed most contemporary Italians, leading the
Aragonese in 1495 to begin to cast iron balls in the Naples arsenal, the Venetians to order
the new cannon (100 wheeled 6 to 12-pounders) in 1496 and the Duke of Ferrara to
begin new fortification construction the same year.[99] Cannon became more accurate, not
least because of the addition of trunnions on which the barrel could turn in a vertical
plane and the development of moveable carriages. These developments and the increased
use of quantification in European society for the understanding of space and time, encouraged the prediction and calculation of range, and thus the instrumentation of an important aspect of war.[100]

Technological change within Europe achieved a greater momentum than in Asia, certainly than in the Islamic world and, increasingly, more than in China.[101] This is important, but it is also pertinent not to treat warfare solely as an aspect of diffusionism and
acculturation. Such a model, usually Eurocentric in its application, leaves insufficient
scope for the vitality and success of different traditions of warfare.

More generally, there is the question of how best to emphasise the existence of other
expanding powers and cultures, while still stressing the overall and lasting importance
of a Europe that literally exploded on to the world stage from the 1490s to the 1590s,
from Columbus and da Gama to the Spanish adventurers trying to do to the Khmers
of Cambodia what Cortés had done to the Aztecs. Although it was the Mughals, not
the Portuguese, who conquered much of India, Europe's relative position had changed
completely: the Portuguese were on Deshima, the Japanese were not on the Isle of Wight.
Less far-flung, the Ottomans had tried and failed to hold Otranto, while the Spaniards
still retained Ceuta and Melilla. The major European power, Habsburg Spain, had

expanded both within and outside Europe. Although the Ottomans, Incas, Aztecs, Safavids, Mughals and Japanese had all been advancing for at least part of the sixteenth century, no non-European power had matched the range of the Habsburgs. The sixteenth was also the first century of global war, with the endemic and ancestral struggle of Cross versus Crescent[102] greatly expanding: clashes between the Ottomans and their allies and the Iberians and theirs extending from the western Mediterranean to South-East Asia. It would soon be followed by inter-European wars fought on a global scale.

4   The Seventeenth Century

The major themes outlined in the previous chapter were still apposite in the seventeenth century: the role of maritime and firearms technology in abetting European overseas expansion; the on-going conflict between nomadic and settled peoples; and the limits to any argument which posits the superior military effectiveness of settled peoples over nomads. Technical superiority rarely brought any benefits to Europeans, except on the high seas and in defence of fortified positions, and most conquest was in alliance with, and often partially subordinate to, local interests who had manpower and also 'arts of war' that could benefit from European participation, but were not overwhelmed by it.

There were also significant developments. In essence, the European powers were aggressively expanding on land and sea, taking with them their long-standing and more recent rivalries. Greater competition between European powers in oceanic trade, maritime control and colonial acquisition outweighed any transoceanic struggle with non-European powers, although the seventeenth century saw the beginning of large-scale European impact on North American peoples. A shift in military capability heralded the decline of some non-European forces and the start of a new European-dominated power balance, remaining in part to the present day.

In Europe the Ottomans were decisively defeated on land for the first time, and for the first time the frontier between their dominions and those of their European opponents moved permanently back towards Constantinople. In Siberia, Russia made an enormous acquisition of Asian territory, and thereby extended European control overland to the Pacific. This brought a European power into direct border contact with China, and indeed created the notion of a frontier in the region. Not all non-European powers, however, were in retreat: Russian expansion led to a short-lived conflict won by the Chinese, evidence not only of their own military potential, but also signalling the start of border tensions that were to persist into the late twentieth century. The expulsion of the Dutch from the Pescadores and Formosa (Taiwan) was also evidence of Chinese vitality.

The China of the 1680s, however, was a very different military power from the situation a half-century earlier when the Ming government was under mounting pressure from Manchu invaders. Mention of China allows us to make two points about seventeenth-century conflict. First, historians have identified a general 'seventeenth-century crisis', either one that is specific to the mid-century or one that is more generally associated with the century as a whole and with its varied and related demographic, economic, social and political problems. The crisis may have been triggered by a sudden change in global temperature with drastic effects on the food supply and stability of peoples across the world. In 1644 the Ming dynasty fell victim to this general instability and was replaced by nomadic forces from Manchuria. It was these forces that confronted Russia in the 1680s.

Secondly, the overthrow of the Ming dynasty and the accession of the Manchu can be seen as another stage in the incessant struggle between the nomadic and the settled world, one part of which Denis Sinor has recently referred to as 'the endemic conflict between peoples of Inner Asia and the sedentary populations'. However, the nature of the relationship between China and its neighbours varied. It is possible to present it in adversarial terms, but it has also been argued that most of the nomad rulers who controlled the northern borderlands wanted to extract resources from China rather than conquer it, that this extraction was most efficient if relations were peaceful and that intervention was usually a response to political fragmentation within China.[1]

For our purposes, it should be remembered that, while European expansion undoubtedly provoked conflict with competing non-European forces, there were also expansionist non-European forces, such as the Dzhungars of Xinjiang, and European expansion was arguably dependent on existing conflicts in other parts of the globe. By the 1690s a dynamic Manchu China was to be successfully expanding into Xinjiang, a reminder of the danger of smoothing out history in favour of long-range trends.

Naval Power

The principal technology behind European expansion was maritime. Aside from gaining control over more of the world's land surface in the seventeenth century, the Europeans strengthened their position on the major trading routes, not least by gaining or creating crucial maritime bases,[2] and were thus able to support and benefit from distant possessions. European naval power, however, was never absolute. European control over African, Indian and Indonesian coastal waters remained limited and their warships suffered in clashes in these waters through a lack of manoeuvrability and through their deep draught. However, the Portuguese developed coastal fleets at Goa, Diu and in the Persian Gulf. These fleets were composed of local oared vessels or small sailing ships.

There were important successes. In 1664 a fleet of Portuguese *feringhi* (adventurers), based at Chatgaon on the Arakan coast of the Bay of Bengal, sailed up-river towards Dacca, putting to flight a Mughal fleet of 260 ships and destroying more than half of them. The Maghs of Arakan also raided the coast of Bengal. However, in 1664 Shaista Khan, the new Mughal governor of Bengal, built a new fleet, responding to the external challenge. The *feringhis* quarrelled with the Maghs and some of them changed sides to support Shaista Khan whose fleet defeated its Arakanese rival and annexed the Chatgaon region. The existence of Mughal and Magh fleets exposes the error of assuming that, after the Portuguese successes of the sixteenth century, there was no large and potentially powerful South Asian navy.

Similarly, in 1629 Sultan Iskandar Muda of Aceh launched a major, albeit totally unsuccessful, land and sea attack on the Portuguese base of Malacca, utilising 236 vessels. Aceh's large galleys were capable of carrying over 600 men, and in 1614 he had already defeated a Portuguese squadron. After Sultan Agung of Mataram (1613–46) gained control of the major Javan coastal areas with their timber for shipbuilding, he created a navy to support his conflict with the rival state of Surabaya; although he also, unsuccessfully, sought Dutch naval support. The Mataram navy played a major role in the capture of the port of Sukadana in Borneo in 1622, but this was the extent of its range.[3]

Disparities in strength between European and non-European naval forces were most apparent on the open seas, where European warships were becoming more heavily

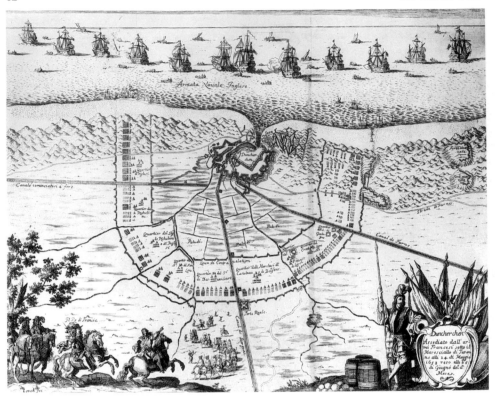

gunned. Instead of relying on converted merchantmen, the European Atlantic powers, especially the English, the French and the Dutch, used purpose-built warships, heavily gunned and, accordingly, with strong hulls. This led to a professionalisation of naval officership, senior ratings and infrastructure, but also ensured that less heavily gunned vessels, such as those of the Dutch in the First Anglo-Dutch War of 1652–4, were rendered obsolete.

Improvements in armaments, rigging and sail patterns helped to ensure that sailing ships rather than galleys became far more important in Mediterranean warfare. They thus freed warships from dependence on a network of local bases. This shift was widely diffused: the English and Dutch vessels that introduced new methods into Mediterranean naval warfare were copied by the Mediterranean powers, including the Turks and the North African Barbary states. The latter adapted Atlantic naval technology first – in the late sixteenth century – through the intermediary of English and Dutch privateers. The Turks were not confronted by the example, challenge and threat until later, and did not adopt sailing ships until the second half of the century. Even then, they continued to lack good gunners.

The range and role of warships increased. Although heavy cannon and cannon-carrying warships played only a minor role in the Iberian conquest of much of the New World, the nature of inter-European conflict meant they were crucial in the subsequent struggles between European powers for control both of the Iberian empires and of their maritime routes.[4] A breakthrough in European iron gunfounding in the late seventeenth century aided production of large quantities of comparatively cheap and reliable iron guns. These replaced the more expensive bronze cannon that had generally been used hitherto

AGOUSTA

Ville de Sicile fameuse par son port, elle est bâtie dans une petite Isle qu'elle occupe presque toute entiere il y a trois forts qui la deffendent, et elle a une citadelle assis reguliere: Le Marechal de Vivonne jugeant ce poste necessaire pour la Navigation, des François dans la Sicile, l'attaqua avec toute sa flotte, et s'en rendit maistre en huit heures le 17 Aoust 1675.

19. (*facing page*) Siege of Dunkirk, 1658. The most important Spanish naval base on the North Sea, Dunkirk was crucial to any supply of the Spanish Netherlands by sea. It was captured by the French in 1646, lost in 1652 and taken again, this time with English land and naval help, in 1658. Its fall followed the Battle of the Dunes, in which a Spanish relief attempt was defeated: the Spaniards were outnumbered, their artillery had not yet arrived, the terrain prevented them from exploiting their advantage in cavalry and their flank was bombarded by English warships. England was rewarded with Dunkirk in the peace, but Charles II sold it to Louis XIV in 1662.

20. Whereas naval confrontations in the central Mediterranean involved the Turks, in the 1670s there was a series of battles between European navies. The Sicilian port of Augusta was easily captured by the French in 1675 in an impressive display of naval firepower. The following year, the Dutch under Ruyter and the Spaniards sought to regain the position, but were thwarted by the French in an indecisive naval battle. Louis XIV commissioned celebratory paintings for both engagements.

and directly abetted the vast expansion of European battle fleets. Iron was heavier and less forgiving than bronze (which would swell or crack rather than explode), but weight was not so much a factor at sea as on land and the far cheaper cost of iron won out.

While there were few powers able to challenge European naval technology, it was, as in the sixteenth century, the absence of conflict that was most apparent. For example, from its stronghold in Manila in the Philippines, Spain established bases on Formosa (Taiwan) – at Keelung in 1626 and Tamsui in 1629 (in between which Philip IV claimed the island in 1627) – and became the dominant naval power in the Western Pacific, in so far as dominance can be ascribed to such vast bodies of water, without meeting serious resistance. Spanish authority also extended in some of the archipelagoes of the region: the Mariana Islands in 1668, and the Caroline Islands in 1696. Trans-Pacific trade developed between Manila and Acapulco on the Pacific coast of Mexico to the extent that Mexican silver dollars became the international currency of the region and had a major impact on the economies of China and Japan.

Such Pacific settlement and trade were not launched by the East Asian powers, although the successors to Coxinga, a Ming supporter who had established himself in Formosa, sent an expedition to the Philippines in 1673. The Japanese had considered an attack on Spanish Manila, but none was launched. Instead, the seventeenth century saw Japan withdraw from all long-distance maritime activity.

In part, this was a result of domestic power arrangements. Shimazu, of the powerful Japanese Satsuma clan, had obtained permission to restore the profitable trade with China via the Ryukyu Islands. His initial approaches were unsuccessful, so in 1609 an invasion force of 1,500 was sent to impose Satsuma suzerainty. Concerned about Satsuma strength, the new shogun, Tokugawa Ieyasu, responded by ordering the destruction of all large ships in south-west Japan.

A rogue fleet dispatched to conquer Formosa in 1616 suffered ignominiously; 13 junks filled with Japanese warriors were wrecked by a storm. Only one ship reached Formosa and the local population killed the crew. The attempt, mounted by a Japanese merchant-adventurer, was not repeated. Although his failure was due to a storm, the absence of any further attempt can be related to a more widespread restriction on the military activities of Japanese adventurers. In contrast, adventurers were given more leeway by European rulers and were, indeed, crucial to the system of military entrepreneurship by which troops were raised.

In Japan, the shogun's fear was in part also of domestic disorder fuelled by the contending rivalries of the recently arrived European missionaries and traders. By the 1630s these were mostly expelled, as were the Portuguese in 1639. Although the Japanese had traded with South-East Asia in the sixteenth century, in the 1630s they were forbidden to travel overseas. Ieyasu, who founded the Tokugawa shogunate in 1603, had risen through force. The battle of Sekigahara in 1600 brought him to power, and his position was sustained by violence: the two sieges of Osaka Castle in 1614–15 that ended Toyotomi opposition. However, he initiated a long period of internal stability and external peace, and did not seek foreign conquests. The Japanese still cast cannon, but they made no serious attempt to extend their control in Yezo (Hokkaido), where there had been rigorous Ainu resistance to Japanese power in the sixteenth century.[5] In 1647 the Russians established a base at Okhotsk and from there began exploring the North Pacific, a process not checked by Japan. This indifference to what lay to their north was to undergo a complete revolution from the nineteenth century.

The Dutch as World Power

While Russia had a free passage in the north-west Pacific, the Dutch were able to trade and establish bases in coastal areas of South Asia and the East Indies with no hindrance from the major Asian powers. The first Dutch expedition for the East Indies set sail in 1595 with four ships carrying 249 men and 64 cannon. Twenty-two ships followed in 1598, 14 expeditions in 1601. The profits made from shipping spices back to Europe led to the foundation of the United East India Company, which was granted a charter giving it political and military powers, including the right to make war, peace and treaties and to construct fortresses. Jayakĕrta, where the Dutch had a trading base from 1603, became the centre of Dutch power in the East Indies from 1619 after the town was stormed and the forces of Bantam defeated. It was renamed Batavia. In 1608 the Dutch appeared in the Bay of Bengal, establishing themselves at Masulipatnam and Pulicat and setting out to drive the Portuguese from the Bay.

However, when the Dutch approached too close to Chinese territory and tried to establish a base on the Pescadores islands west of Formosa from 1622, a Chinese army numbering tens of thousands, carried by a large fleet, invaded in 1624 and cut the 800-strong Dutch force off from their water.[6] The Dutch were allowed to withdraw to Formosa where they established Fort Zeelandia. While they failed to overrun the Spanish positions on Formosa in 1641, in 1642 a Dutch force of eight warships and 690 men forced the vulnerable Spanish deployments to surrender by placing cannon on commanding positions.[7]

The Dutch were the world's leading naval power in the first half of the century, their naval primacy closely linked to their maritime commercial position. In Europe, the Dutch

21. Fort Zeelandia, Taiwan, 1632. The principal Dutch base on Taiwan 1624–62, this position was taken by Coxinga in 1662 after a nine-month siege. The failure of the Dutch to sustain a military presence so close to China contrasted greatly with the situation two centuries later, when the British were able to force the Chinese to accept their establishment in Hong Kong.

were the premier trade brokers and their role as multiple commercial intermediaries promoted cheap bulk trading, much to their own profit and at lower cost than their rivals. In Asian waters, the Dutch East India Company similarly linked trading zones, thus enhancing economic specialisation and exchange. This further encouraged the Dutch to displace competitors and gave them the resources to do so: thus the Spaniards were driven from Formosa, the English from Ambon in the Moluccas, and the Portuguese from Sri Lanka,[8] Ambon, the Malabar coast of India and Malacca. However, the Dutch failed when they attacked Portuguese Macao in 1622 and, despite initial successes, also failed to drive the Portuguese from Brazil, Angola and West Africa. Until their European resource base and commercial position were badly hit by war with France in 1672–8 (and with France's ally England in 1672–4), the Dutch were the most globally expansive European power of the century, the power that best combined military force and commercial skill; but, thereafter, their overseas enterprise was reduced and, in relative terms, the Dutch declined in the face of rising English trade and naval power.[9] In this sense, expansion and empire were no substitutes for military strength at home.

The Rise of Oman

European naval strength was only seriously challenged in one region: the western portion of the Indian Ocean. There the Portuguese were affected by the rise of Omani naval power. In 1650 Sultan Ibn Saif al-Ya'rubi of Oman captured the Portuguese base of

Muscat and developed a fleet on the basis of the ships he seized in the harbour and the hybrid culture he took over in Muscat. The Omanis created a formidable navy with well-gunned warships: the largest fleet in the western part of the Indian Ocean. Benefiting from the use of European mariners and from the assistance of Dutch and English navigators, gunners and arms suppliers, the Omanis were also helped by the degree to which the extensive Portuguese overseas empire had already been weakened in its turn by persistent Dutch attacks. The Portuguese had a scant military presence on the East African coast: they were short of men, ships and money. In 1661, the Omanis sacked Mombasa, though they avoided Fort Jesus, the powerful Portuguese fortress there. In 1670 the Omanis pillaged Mozambique but were repulsed by the fortress garrison. The Omanis not only pressed the Portuguese in East Africa, but also in India: Bombay was attacked in 1661–2, Bassein in 1674 and Diu sacked in 1668 and 1676.[10]

Yet it is important not to exaggerate the scope and scale of Omani power. Aside from at Diu, the Omani impact on India was limited. Although the Omanis had links with the Marathas, who suggested they develop Anjedive as a base, these contacts did not lead to concerted action against the Portuguese. In addition, Omani campaigns on the East African coast scarcely revealed a major power. Pate fell, but it was barely defended. Fort Jesus fell in 1698, but the siege had lasted since 1696 and the Omanis had no siege artillery. The Portuguese, instead, were weakened by beri-beri and other diseases which killed nine-tenths of the garrison. Regained by the Portuguese in 1728, Mombasa fell to the Omanis again in 1729, but the besiegers still had no artillery and very few firearms; the garrison capitulated as a result of low morale and problems with food supplies.

The loss of Fort Jesus weakened the European presence on Africa's Indian Ocean shore-line, but the history of the fort had already indicated the difficulty of maintaining a foothold. It had fallen in 1631 to a surprise storming by Sultan Muhammad Yusuf of Mombasa, and a Portuguese expedition from Goa failed to regain it in 1632. They were able to return only when the Sultan abandoned the fortress under the pressure of Portuguese attack.[11]

In North Africa, there was no major revival of the Hispanic advance of the late fifteenth century. The Spaniards launched naval expeditions against the Barbary pirates, including in 1601, 1602 and 1609, but territorial gains were few, although Larache on the Moroccan coast was captured in 1610. In 1655 an English fleet under Robert Blake attacked a Tunisian squadron at Porto Farina, destroying both the fleet and the covering shore batteries.

The Portuguese in Africa

More generally, the Portuguese experience in Africa revealed the limitations of European land warfare outside its home continent. From Mozambique, Portuguese adventurers, barely operating within the sphere of the empire, who lived in the towns of the Zambezi, such as Sena and Tete, tried to gain control of the upper Zambezi, but there was no technological multiplier to give weight to their small numbers: Portuguese musketeers could not prevail against larger forces that were well attuned to fighting in the region. The adventurers raised private armies from among their slaves and offered their services as mercenaries in the civil wars in Mutapa (in modern Zimbabwe), sometimes with two adventurers serving on opposite sides. In exchange, they were given what amounted to revenue assignments, which they then represented in Portugal as land grants, and levered their way into having them recognised by the Portuguese Crown. The military multiplier was the recruitment of local people to serve in their forces. The adventurers never really operated independently in the local wars, but instead always in cooperation with an African ruler, whose authority they accepted and recognised. In 1693, Changamira of Butua drove the Portuguese from the plateau and they retreated to Tete on the lower Zambezi.[12]

In Angola, the Portuguese were effective only in combination with African soldiers; indeed, like most nineteenth-century colonial armies, the Portuguese army in Angola was essentially an African force, although its structure was different. Unlike the nineteenth-century pattern of European-organised units filled with African recruits, the Portuguese in seventeenth-century Angola were all organised together into a single unit with its own command structure, while the Africans, either mercenaries, subject rulers, or allies, were separately organised in their own units with their own command structure. It was only at the level of the army as a whole – control for entire operations – that Portuguese officers had command.

The effectiveness of Portuguese musketeers was reduced by their slow rate of fire and by the non-linear, open-order fighting methods of their opponents. Firearms diffused rapidly and Africans possibly even had them in equal numbers already in the 1620s, when quantities of them were reported in the first war against Queen Njinga of the Ndongo (1626–8). The Portuguese victory over the shield-bearing heavy infantry of the Kingdom of Kongo at the battle of Mbumbi (1622) was the result of overwhelming numerical superiority, not weapons superiority, and the Portuguese army withdrew very quickly and even returned captured slaves when the main Kongolese army reached the region. When they were left without African light infantry, Portuguese forces could well be destroyed, as by Queen Njinga at the battle of Ngolomene (1644).

In contrast, the combination of Africans and European infantry, with its body armour and swordsmanship as well as firepower, was effective, as in the Portuguese victories over Njinga at Cavanga (1646) and over Antonio I of Kongo at Ambuila (1665). Antonio's army included a small force of musketeers as well as two cannon. The Portuguese victory at Ambuila has attracted attention, but Kongo did not collapse rapidly: Portuguese efforts to overcome it had a long history. The Portuguese attempt to intervene in the Kongolese civil war led to a disastrous defeat at Kitombo (1670). This caused all hope of intervening in Kongo, even when it was severely divided in civil war, to be put aside. Since the civil war had only begun in 1665, after what many considered one of Portugal's greatest victories (Ambuila), it was unclear what openings were now available in a country that had previously been essentially invulnerable. Kitombo showed that there was little to be gained even against a weaker Kongo.

In addition, a long series of wars against the kingdom of Ndongo, begun in 1579, ended in stalemate for the Portuguese in the early 1680s. Portuguese policy throughout central Africa shifted away from large-scale wars aimed at conquest after, at considerable cost, they took Pungo Andongo in a heroic siege in 1672, and central Angola was not to be conquered by them until the late nineteenth century.[13] Portugal would have found if difficult to carry war much further east against any sort of organised and determined resistance because of the need for extended supply lines. The same was true of the north (into Kongo), and the period of quiescence from the 1680s in part reflected acceptance of the fact.

Europeans and Local Struggles

The Angolan example is more generally applicable to the use of European military force in the wider world. Far from being purely a European versus native situation, the West versus the Rest, the European forces involved were generally explicitly or tacitly allied with a group of native leaders, who used their European military connections for their own purposes. Often misunderstood by the Europeans, the use of these connections had very important consequences in the context of local politics.

Furthermore, Portuguese forces were not only defeated in Africa. In 1630, at the battle of Randeniwela, the army in Sri Lanka fell victim to an ambush by the troops of Kandy and the Captain-General was killed. In 1638 there was another defeat and the death of another Captain-General. Kandy itself allied with the Dutch in 1638 and in 1640 joint attacks led to the fall of Portuguese-held Galle and Negombo.

The direct impact of European military power, especially away from coasts and fortress ports, was not only limited in Africa. It was also restricted in Asia, other than in Siberia, and in South Asia the Europeans generally sought trade rather than territory. It was not possible to conquer the Mughal empire, but it was possible to trade there. The Dutch gained control over parts of the East Indies, although the process was far from easy. Gowa in Sulawesi (the Celebes), for example, was only subjugated in 1669 after protracted struggles. Dutch success owed much to the assistance of a local ruler, the Buginese leader Arung Palakka who handled much of the fighting on land, and his men inflicted most of the casualties. The Dutch, nevertheless, contributed 600 troops and used 30,000 musket balls in the attack on the Makassarese citadel. They also provided 21 ships under Cornelis Speelman that defeated the Makassarese fleet. The final peace awarded the Dutch the Makassarese fort of Ujungpandang, which they renamed Rotterdam.[14]

Similarly, the Dutch helped local powers against their European rivals. In 1605 in the Moluccas, Dutch support for the Hituese led the Portuguese to surrender their fort of Ambon, and Sultan Zaide of Ternate received Dutch assistance in driving the Portuguese from their forts on Ternate and Tidore, although in 1606 a Spanish expedition defeated the allies and left a garrison in Ternate. In 1639 the Portuguese and Dutch took opposite sides in the conflict among Vijayanagara grandees.[15] Although the Dutch, when their aid was sought by King Rajasimha II, ruler of the inland kingdom of Kandy, were able to drive the Portuguese from their coastal bases in Sri Lanka in 1638–42, they had no such success in the second half of the century against Kandy. Dutch forces moved into the Javan interior in 1678–81, but in alliance with Amangkurat II of Mataram against rebels. The Dutch were better armed, trained and disciplined than their Asian opponents, but they faced problems due to logistics, terrain, the number of their opponents and the reliability of their allies.[16]

European fortified positions in South Asia were generally strong enough to resist attack: in 1628–9 Dutch-controlled Batavia on Java survived two sieges by Sultan Agung of Mataram, and Portuguese Malacca a siege by the Sultan of Aceh. The defeat of Aceh owed much to the support provided to the Portuguese by the fleet of Abdul Jalil, Sultan of Johor. Malacca, however, fell in 1641 to the Dutch, who had won the support of Abdul Jalil. Portuguese Goa resisted attack by the Sultanate of Bijapur in 1510, 1654 and 1659, and by the Marathas in 1683. Goa and Chaul, which was also attacked in 1683, were saved because the Mughals attacked the Marathas the same year.

European fortifications, such as the major works begun by the Portuguese at Diu in 1634, were very expensive, even if local resources could be forcibly obtained. Philip de Brito, the Portuguese adventurer who had seized Syriam in Lower Burma in 1599, lacked the resources of a European state or trading company. The Burmese ruler Anaukpetlun who invaded Lower from Upper Burma was able to capture Syriam in 1613 after a long siege by land and water. Goa did not send a fleet speedily enough to relieve the post, and it was betrayed when one of the defenders opened the gates. De Brito was crucified or impaled – accounts vary – and the Portuguese and Eurasian inhabitants enslaved and employed as gunners.

Portuguese positions that were less well fortified than Goa fell to Asian attack: after a siege in 1632 Selim Shah of Arakan forced Portuguese adventurers to abandon their positions on Sandwip Island and at Chittagong and Dianga. The Mughal Governor of Bengal took Hughli in Bengal. In the 1650s Sivappa Nayaka of Ikkeri captured the Portuguese possessions on the Kanara coast of India: Honawar, Basrur, Gangolli and Mangalore. In 1662 Golconda took the Portuguese post at São Tomé. Hence, the Portuguese presence in the Bay of Bengal declined nearly as much as a result of Indian as of Dutch and English attacks. The Portuguese usually had tiny garrisons. They were expelled from Ethiopia in 1636.

More generally, although the Europeans were reasonably successful in maintaining their maritime position and their coastal bases, their situation was defined by their commercial interests. This ensured that relations with land powers that controlled overland communication routes, sources of goods and access to markets, were vital to the success of European projects and positions. The role of these Asian powers and the nature of the trading system ensured that much Indian Ocean trade remained outside European power. When the Europeans gained control of ports they found it difficult to retain their trade, let alone to create a monopoly. Thus Malacca was of limited value to the Portuguese and customs revenue from Goa fell in the early seventeenth century.[17]

European rivalries were exploited by Asian powers. Shah Abbas of Persia used the English desire to trade with Persia and English rivalry with Spain in order to obtain English support against the Portuguese base of Ormuz. Deprived of a friendly hinterland after the Safavids overran the mainland possessions of the indigenous ruler of Ormuz and of naval support by English action, Ormuz surrendered in 1622 after a siege. It had lacked adequate artillery. The Turks, in turn, sought Portuguese help against the Persians in 1624. The Sultanate of Gowa in Sulawesi in the East Indies turned to other European traders to evade Dutch attempts to create a spice monopoly, leading to conflict with the Dutch from 1615.

European military, economic and cultural penetration were limited even in regions generally seen as under their control. The Philippines are frequently presented in historical atlases as Spanish from 1570. Yet although Spanish expeditions reached northern Luzon before the end of the sixteenth century, specific documentary reference to a Spanish presence in what is now central Ifugao, an inland agrarian region, dates only from 1736, and Spanish military and missionary activity in that part of Luzon was still sporadic during the nineteenth century. The Spanish presence, as with most European empires, was more marked in coastal regions. Thus in 1635 Zamboanga on the coast of Mindanao was captured and a strong fortress constructed under the direction of the Jesuit missionary-engineer Melchor de Vera.

The Conquest of Siberia

In Luzon the European power faced peoples with looser governmental structures. This was also true of those areas where the Europeans made the greatest territorial gains in the seventeenth century: Siberia and North America. Siberia was a vast area inhabited by small numbers of nomadic and semi-nomadic peoples who were well attuned to the hunting, fishing and pastoral possibilities of their environment. Siberia was also the world's leading source of fur, a vital form of wealth and prestige. As a result, Russian merchants, especially the Stroganovs of Novgorod, came to take a greater interest in Siberia from the late sixteenth century.

Access to Siberia had long been blocked by the Islamic Tatar Khanate of Kazan, which was conquered by Ivan IV, the Terrible, in 1552 after nearly a century's conflict. Ivan had then enforced his power along the Volga by punitive expeditions, finally occupying Astrakhan without a struggle in 1556. In the same year, Ivan issued a Decree on Service which obliged the nobility to provide lifelong military or administrative service, thus greatly increasing his military resources. These, however, were devoted to struggles with the Christian powers to the west: Poland and Sweden. Expansion to the east received far less political attention and military support.

The capture of Astrakhan and, in particular, Kazan ensured that the Russians could advance to the Urals and then across the accessible southern Urals, where there were a number of low passes. Firearms played the most decisive role in the earliest stage of the conquest of Siberia, in 1581–2. An 800-strong Cossack force under Yermak Timofeyevich, in the service of the Stroganovs, advanced in 1581, conquering the Tatar Khanate of Sibir in 1582 after several battles. The Cossacks originally had three small cannon, but these had probably been abandoned en route some time before. Nevertheless, it was crucial in 1581–2 that the Cossacks had firearms, their opponents only bows and arrows. However, although this brought initial success, the Tatars had the advantage in numbers and mobility and in 1585 wiped out most of Yermak's force.

It required further expeditions, launched in 1586–98, for Russia to win control over the Khanate. The Siberian Tatars did not lose their will to resist until the defeat of Prince Kuchum in 1598. Although Russian firearms played a decisive role in battles, it was difficult to replace stores of powder and shot, and they had to be used with care.

The Europeans enjoyed a definite technological edge in the advance across Siberia and employed it brutally. Their opponents had no gunpowder weaponry and, indeed, many, especially in northern and eastern Siberia, existed at a very primitive level of military technology: there was no catalyst, such as continuous warfare or the availability of metals, for military innovation. The Cossacks in Russian service used firearms effectively against Siberian aborigines and also against the remnants of the Tatar Golden Horde along the Tobol and Irtysh rivers. The Buryats, a Mongol tribe, were defeated in the 1630s and 1640s by Russian firepower.

The native peoples were also subjugated by the Russian construction of forts. Bases were established, including at Samara and Ufa in 1586, and then, across the Urals, at Tyumen in 1586, and at Tobolsk on the Ob, near the site of Sibir, in 1587. From there, Russian power expanded eastwards across Siberia (rather than southwards against the more powerful steppe nomads), with bases established at Yeniseysk on the Yenisey in 1619, Yatuksk on the Lena in 1632, Okhotsk on the Sea of Okhotsk in 1647, and Irkutsk in 1661. The Pacific itself had first been reached in 1639 and a post then established at the mouth of the Ulya river. Russian towns were typically stockaded and each contained buildings of control and power: a fort, a barracks, a prison, a church and the governor's residence. Forts maximised the defensive potential of firearms and anchored Russian routes to the Pacific. Attacks on forts, such as that of the Tungus on Zashiversk in 1666–7, were thwarted by the use of defensive gunfire, though Okhotsk was stormed by the Tungus in 1654. It was speedily rebuilt by the Russians, and subsequently resisted local rebellions in 1665 and 1677; in the last, it was besieged without success by 1,000 men armed with bows and bone-tipped arrows.

Furthermore, as with the earlier Russian conquest of Kazan, resistance was weakened by local divisions. In the case of Siberia, several of the mutually hostile tribes provided

The Habitts of the Tungusen and Daurischn people.

22. Illustration from Adam Brand's *A Journal of the Embassy from their Majesties over Land into China* (London, 1698). Siberian tribes armed with bows and arrows were only able to offer limited resistance to the advance of Russian power, not least because they were weakened by divisions and by European diseases. However, some tribes proved intractable opponents.

the Russians with support. Thus, the Russians exploited conflicts on the Yenisey between Kets and Tungus, gaining the support of some of the former against the latter. Moreover, prominent Tatars and others who agreed to become vassals of the Tsar were allowed to retain their position in return for military service. Those who resisted were treated barbarously. This, plus the cruelty of Russian forced-tribute in furs, *yasak*, and the seizure of local women, as well as the introduction of new diseases, especially, from 1630, smallpox, led the native population to decrease dramatically. The demographic decline reduced native capacity for resistance and subsequent rebellion and thus exacerbated the weaknesses stemming from their small numbers and the limited governmental development of the indigenous peoples.[18] Eighty per cent of Yakuts perished due to smallpox. The Russians therefore had a demographic effect similar to that of the Spaniards in the Caribbean. However, successful resistance continued in the far north-east, especially among the Chukchi of north-east Siberia and the Koryaks of Kamchatka.

In south-west Siberia, where the Russian frontier of settlement advanced southwards, the Russians had to fight warlike nomadic horsemen, such as the Kalmyks, Yenisey Kirghiz, Khalkha Mongols and Dzhungars, for over a century. These nomads were also able to acquire firearms technology, possibly by capturing Russian guns. Yenisey Kirghiz were using guns against the Russians as early as the 1640s. The Russians found it necessary to construct fortified lines in south Siberia, such as the Ishim Line. The Kirghiz, who had delayed the Russian advance on the Upper Yenisey, were, however, heavily defeated in 1690–2 and 1701. The Russians again benefited from divisions among their potential opponents: in 1635 the Dzhungars, who were then allies of the Russians, defeated the Kazakhs.

The Russians versus the Chinese

Russian expansion was not only an effort to gain control of fur-producing regions; they also sought to expand into the Amur valley. The valley was seen as a source of food for their Siberian settlements, while, moreover, there was interest in developing overland trade routes with China.[19]

However, Russian movement into the valley in the 1640s led to a vigorous response from Ch'ing (Manchu) China, once the Manchus had completed their overthrow of the Ming dynasty. An initially successful Cossack force on the Amur was defeated by a Chinese fleet in 1658. In 1682 the Chinese ordered the Russians to leave the Amur valley, and in 1685 they successfully besieged the Russian fortress of Albazin. The Russians rebuilt it, only to lose it to a second siege in 1686. The Russian forces were heavily outnumbered by the Chinese, although estimates of the size of forces vary.[20] Both sides were equipped with cannon, but, in capturing Albazin, the Manchu allowed hunger, backed up by superior numbers, to do their work. In 1683–4 other Chinese forces attacked Russian positions to the north of the Amur basin, demolishing forts on the Zeya, Selemja and Tugur rivers and clearing the Russians from the maritime region.

In 1689 a large Chinese army advanced as far as Nerchinsk. By the Treaty of Nerchinsk in 1689, the Russians acknowledged Chinese control of the Amur valley, but Chinese demands for a withdrawal beyond Lake Baikal, so that the Russians would abandon their Pacific coastline, were unsuccessful. The Russians were ready to yield the Amur in order to obtain better relations with China, but they fully intended to retain Siberia for it offered resources, prestige and a link to the Pacific. Nevertheless, the Russian advance towards China had been stopped.

Seventeenth-century China was a militarily capable, expansionist, non-European power. Combined with success in Mongolia in the 1690s, the Chinese expulsion of the Russians from the Amur gave China its strongest and most advanced northern frontier since the beginning of the fifteenth century. By driving the Russians from the Amur valley in the 1680s, the Chinese improved their position as far as Mongolia was concerned. They were most concerned not about Russian expansion but with the danger that the Russians would form a military alliance with, and give guns to, the west Mongolian tribes, known collectively as the Oirats, and, from 1635, united in the dynamic new Dzhungar confederation; it was to forestall this that the Chinese signed the Treaty of Nerchinsk. Indeed, the Russians rejected the Dzhungar approach for an alliance in 1690.

Thus, both Chinese expansion into inner Asia and their policy towards Russia were dominated by the perceived threat from the Dzhungars; it is only in hindsight that the clash between Russia and China seems more important. In 1667 the Dzhungars had conquered the domain of the last Altan Khan in north-western Mongolia and in 1670 they overcame his former vassals in the western part of Tuva. Under Taishi Galdan Boshugtu (1671–97) the Dzhungars seized the Islamic oases near Mongolia from 1679: Hami and Turfan in 1679, Kashgar in 1680 and Yarkand soon after. In 1688 the Dzhungars overran the Khalkha regions of Mongolia. As the Khalkhas took refuge in China, many entering the Chinese army, this brought the Dzhungars into direct confrontation with China. In 1690 the two armies clashed at Ulan Butong, 300 kilometres north of Beijing: Galdan's defensive tactics, not least sheltering his men behind camels armoured with felt, limited the effectiveness of the Chinese artillery, and the Chinese commander was happy to negotiate a truce. It was by no means clear that the Dzhungars would be less successful than the Manchus. In 1696, however, the K'ang-hsi emperor advanced north, destroying Galdan's army at Jao Modo, a success that owed much to support from Galdan's rebellious nephew, Tsewang Rabtan. Sino-Russian enmity did not become central in the region until after the defeat of the nomadic peoples.[21]

In combination, the Russian advance into Siberia and that of the Chinese into Mongolia dramatically increased the amount of Eurasia under the control of states with developed governmental structures: much of Eurasia became colonies under the control of the political and military structures of distant settled peoples. For example, in response to Russian advances, the Manchus brought the area between the Amur and Argun rivers under direct control and organised the native population into banner armies designed to serve with their troops. In a related process in India, in successive campaigns in 1641, 1643 and 1661, Mughal forces conquered the chiefdom of Palamau, a sparsely populated, forested and hilly area south of Bihar occupied by a tribal people, the Cheros.

Present-day ideas of Russian greatness may be traced back to the seventeenth century. The advance to the Sea of Okhotsk gave Russia control of a vast territory, which was to be expanded over the following two centuries as pursuit of sea otter furs led Russia into the Aleutians, then Alaska, and from there down the western coast of North America. Although these activities surpassed those of any other East Asian power, the degree of Russian state commitment to the Pacific was limited. The concentration of population, resources and government in the European side of Russia, increased further in 1712 by Peter the Great's transfer of his capital from Moscow to his new city of St Petersburg, tended to marginalise Siberia. Conquests on the eastern Baltic were more important to the Russian leaders. However, during Peter's reign, state undertakings, such as mines, became more important than private enterprises in Siberia. The Russian population of Siberia rose from about 100,000 in 1701 to 700,000 by 1721. Mining and metallurgy developed first in the Urals and subsequently in the Altay, creating important concentrations of people and resources that had to be fed and protected.[22]

Nevertheless, the hostile Siberian environment only exacerbated the difficulties arising from the region's vast distances, and there was no warm-water sea route along the coast. Furthermore, Okhotsk was a poor port and the ships constructed there were inferior in quality. The Russians did not gain a good port on the Pacific until they founded Vladivostok in 1860. Seventeenth-century maritime technology was not always sufficient to promote European expansion.

There was also no river route across Siberia: the major rivers flowed south-north, not west-east. There was therefore no equivalent to the use of the Ukrainian rivers by the Russians, for example in flotilla expeditions down the Don against Azov and the Khanate of the Crimea from 1646, and even these faced problems. For example the Dnieper rapids limited the use of the river to supply expeditions against the Crimea in the 1680s. In the late seventeenth, eighteenth and nineteenth centuries, the Russians employed their military resources in wars in Europe and against the Turks. They were not to fight a major war in the Far East until the Russo-Japanese War of 1904–5, a struggle begun by the Japanese. Thereafter, despite conflict with Japan in 1939 and 1945 and confrontation with China in 1969, Russian attention was again focused on Europe.

North America

In seventeenth-century Siberia there was only a limited transfer of military technology from the Russians to strengthen opposition to the advancing Europeans. In North America, by contrast, both firearms and horses were acquired by the native peoples. A series of settlements was founded by Europeans, including Québec by the French (1608), Jamestown (1607) and Plymouth (1620) by the English, and New Amsterdam (1614) and Albany (1624) by the Dutch. One result of the growing presence of Europeans and the greater commercial opportunities they provided for the native peoples was an increase in warfare between the tribes as they sought to control contact with the Europeans, and growing European involvement in the warfare. The French originally refused to supply firearms, but, after an initial prohibition, the Dutch began trading, and, as warfare increased in scope, restrictions on the supply of firearms decreased. In the early 1640s, the French also began to sell muskets to baptised native allies to strengthen them against the Mohawks, who themselves traded freely for Dutch muskets after agreements in 1643 and 1648. By 1648, the Mohawks had amassed at least 800 muskets. In the 1660s the Swedes provided the Susquehannock of the Delaware valley with cannon and they used them against both Iroquois and the English. However, this transfer of artillery was unusual and, without cannon, the native Americans could make little impact on European forts.

Thus, the expansion of the European presence resulted in a heightening of war and military technology. As so often, divisions among the European powers increased their willingness to provide arms to non-Europeans, and in addition the Europeans were drawn into local struggles and their impact felt in large part through their role in them. The same was true of West Africa: the initial dominance of the European presence by Portugal was replaced in the seventeenth century by competition between the European powers. Whereas the Portuguese had refused to sell arms to the Africans in the sixteenth century, all the Europeans were willing to do so in the seventeenth. If the Europeans exploited African divisions on the Gold Coast, the Africans also benefited from European rivalries. Local struggles also played a major role on New Spain's northern frontier where crucial changes arose largely from hostilities between native American groups, rather than from Spanish intrusion.[23]

In North America, the native Americans were well attuned to fighting in the unmapped hinterland, and their general lack of fixed battle positions made it difficult for the Europeans to devise clear military goals and ensured there was no role for volley fire. Furthermore, as experts with bows and arrows the eastern American peoples were adept in missile warfare, and thus were more readily able to make the transition to muskets, which were easier to aim, and the bullets of which, unlike arrows, were less likely to be deflected by brush and could not be dodged. These factors combined to reduce any significant advantage in military technology the settlers might have possessed. In the Pequot War of 1637, it was first the overwhelming superiority in firearms of the English which brought them victory in the Connecticut river valley, but also the fact that their enemy was not supported by other tribes. However, from the 1640s, the spread of firearms among native peoples made them even more effective opponents of European colonists.

The rising in New England of 1675–6, King Philip's War, was suppressed with considerable difficulty, and in 1682 a French attempt to crush the western Iroquois led to a humiliating climbdown after influenza and logistical problems weakened the French force.[24] In spite of the ravages of disease, the Iroquois confederacy was in the seventeenth century able to function as a North American great power, a more or less equal contender with England and France in the military struggles of the region. New England native

Americans acquired the ability to cast bullets and make gunflints, although they were unable to make gunpowder. Some native American tribes learned to use bastions as early as the 1670s and by 1675 they were using flintlocks. Trained from at least the age of twelve, able to march at least 30 miles a day, experts at marksmanship and firing from cover, and reliant on merit for military leadership, the natives were formidable foes.

The military balance in the region was not to shift significantly in favour of the Europeans until the following century, by which time the native Americans were greatly outnumbered. European fortresses were important because their garrisons could resist and harass raiding parties, but they did not guarantee control. In 1658, the French garrison of Sainte-Marie-de-Gannentaha fled when warned of imminent attack. The British sent few regulars to North America until the 1750s, and the French regulars, first sent in 1665, had only a limited impact. The ability of the Europeans to travel by sea became less valuable once they moved away from coastal regions. As with the Portuguese in Angola, European success in frontier warfare in North America depended on native assistance or adaptation to the native way of war, as in the case of the defeat of King Philip's rising, when the English colonists moved in loose order, adapted to the available cover, and fired at specific targets.

The power balance between native and colonist was shifted less by weaponry than by demography. The Europeans came to North America to colonize rather than to trade and they came in increasing numbers. Although themselves in flux as new settlers, Anglo-French immigrants had settled ideas of government and social organisation. By contrast, native American numbers did not grow. The pre-colonisation population of New England was less than 150,000, possibly considerably so. The Five Nations (Iroquois) were devastated by smallpox in 1633, the Hurons in 1634, the Mohawks, one of the Five Nations, soon after.

Disunity among the native Americans, who frequently allied with Europeans, was also very important. In 1609 Huron and Montagnais native Americans joined with the French leader Samuel de Champlain against the Mohawks. He reported the use of wooden armour, flights of arrows and massed formations. In the Pequot War, the English were supported by the Narragansetts, while in 1675, in a battle known as the Great Swamp Fight, Pequot warriors in turn helped the English against the Narragansetts. 'King Philip', the English term for Metacom, the Sachem of the Pokanokets, was killed in 1676 by a native American in an ambush arranged by Benjamin Church, the head of a force of English and allied native Americans. Many native Americans converted to Christianity, and in both Canada and New England the converts tended to support the Europeans. Traditional cultural and religious beliefs and imperatives were lost with conversion.

However, it was the rising number of Europeans and their ability, thanks to advantages of mobility, logistical support and reinforcement, to concentrate forces at points of conflict, which proved crucial along the St Lawrence, which was under French control, and on the east coast of North America, which was increasingly under English control. This paralleled the situation in Eurasia where Denis Sinor has argued that

> The manner and the length of the process by which each Inner Asian attack was neutralised varied from case to case, but the sedentary people's victory was seldom achieved by brute force . . . almost invariably a superior fertility rate was the crucial factor in the outcome of the confrontation . . . the gradual expansion from the periphery towards the heartland was, first and foremost, the result of the increase – either from natural causes or by immigration – of the sedentary populations.[25]

This essentially gradualist argument is clearly more appropriate for some areas of the world than others. Russian expansion into the steppes was a matter of military success, but also of the related advance of the Russian peasant turning new land into tillage.[26] The creation of fortified defensive lines, such as the Tsaritsyn Line between the Volga and the Don constructed in 1694–1718, and their associated military colonies, covered the extension of the Russian cultivated area. Sinor's approach does not address the issue of political or military relations between sedentary or between nomadic peoples, but it does offer a new perspective on differences in success between different types of society, one in which military explanations play a modest role.

Such an overview raises the issue of demographic warfare. The destruction of peoples could appear necessary to contemporaries. In 1665 and 1666, for example, the French resolved to end the threat from the Iroquois confederacy; by burning the major Mohawk villages and their crops, they forced them to terms. Destructive raids, for example those of the French and their allies, such as the Ottawa, on the Seneca in 1687, or of the Iroquois on French settlements near Montréal in 1689, eliminated food supplies vital for campaigning. There were obvious demographic as well as logistical effects: the two are not properly separable. For example, about 7,900 of the 11,600 native Americans living in southern New England on the eve of King Philip's War, died through battle, disease or exposure, or were removed by being sold as slaves or becoming permanent refugees.[27] Thus the possibility of future resistance was lessened.

Restraints on the use of terror expected in European warfare were generally ignored outside Europe.[28] This was certainly the case with seventeenth-century Portuguese operations in Brazil: great brutality was used on many occasions. The leading eighteenth-century European writer on international relations, Emmerich de Vattel, did not feel that the laws of war need apply when fighting 'savage' peoples.[29] The brutality of twentieth-century warfare, often genocidal, was not without all too many precedents. However, in addition the Europeans were willing to lose a large proportion of their troops in order to win, and this gave them an advantage against societies such as those in North America where the native population had less extensive notions of the acceptable social limits of casualties.[30]

Societies and State Development

In considering warfare, one must therefore consider different types of society. This brings us back to Gibbon's paradigms. Can the sociology of development that he advanced be considered, not only in light of the specialisation of functions, but also in terms of certain forms of social organisation being more appropriate to different rates of demographic density and growth? Moreover, do these varied forms have different consequences in terms of military effectiveness, not least a willingness to sustain casualties?

The seventeenth century may be seen as a period of contraction on the part of 'nomadic' peoples, Gibbon's 'barbarians'. These were societies without powerful and far-flung governmental institutions. The importance of this period, consequently, is in terms of shifts in the relative capability of such societies as opposed to those with a stronger state apparatus. It is true that internal political crises in mid-century in a large number of states, including China, the Ottoman empire, Mughal India, Russia, France, Spain, Poland and Britain, affected their military strength in differing ways. Nomadic peoples benefited, although one major nomadic force, the Dzhungars, were affected by political turmoil from 1653. Another, the Don Cossacks, captured Azov from the Turks in 1637. They also undermined the Polish position in the Ukraine.

23. Night attack on the Citadel of Ypres, 24–25 March, 1678. Louis captured the fortress from the Spaniards, his great-grandson Louis XIV taking it from the Dutch in 1744. The French had already taken it in 1648 and 1658. They became increasingly adept at siege warfare, thanks in large part to the development of more systematic siege techniques under Sébastien Le Prestre de Vauban (1633–1707), a master of positional warfare. The vulnerability of fortresses underlined the importance of mastery in the field, but this vulnerability generally required the successful besiegers to deploy substantial forces.

Nevertheless, a worldwide process of recovery from economic problems and a consolidation of governmental power is perceptible in the second half of the century. This led, despite widespread demographic stagnation and continuing economic difficulties, to increased resources at the disposal of the state, and to an increase in the military activity of a number of powers, most obviously China, the Ottoman empire, Mughal India, Russia, France, Austria and England, but not Poland and Spain. Some of this activity was directed against peoples with looser governmental structures, as with the Chinese in Mongolia, the Russians in Siberia and the Europeans in the New World. The Don Cossacks were unable to retain Azov, and the Ukraine was partitioned between Russia and Poland, after war between them in 1654–67, although the power of both in the area remained limited. Most state military activity, however, was deployed against other states with comparable governmental structure, and the external military forces that were in part responsible for mid-century crises were generally those of settled states with comparable political structures. This was not true of Ming China, but was true of the European states. Thus, for example, the Russian 'Time of Troubles' at the beginning of the century (1598–1613) saw defeats at the hands of Polish and Swedish armies (such as the Swedish victory at Klushino in 1610), not at those of the Tatars or the peoples to the east of the Caspian Sea.

States that had a degree of coherence, continuity and bureaucratic development had several advantages in conflict with peoples with looser governmental structures. These included not only structures for tapping the demographic and economic resources of their societies, but also access to information technology denied societies that lacked widespread literacy and a printing and publishing industry. Such technology was of direct military value. Printed manuals on gunnery, tactics, drill, fortification and siege-

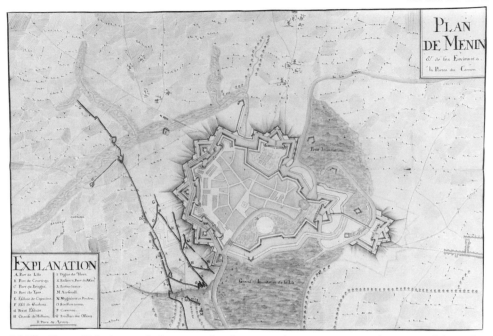

24. The Siege of Menin, 1706. Geometric fortifications and systematic siegecraft. A successful siege by the Allies under the Duke of Marlborough. Trenches were dug to provide cover for the artillery and, under heavy fire, the French surrendered as soon as the English batteries were established on the counterscarp.

craft spread techniques far more rapidly than word of mouth or manuscript, and also permitted and made possible a degree of standardisation that both helped to increase military effectiveness and was important for the successful utilisation of the military resources of developed and populous states. The role of printing in Europe gave its states an advantage in military potential lacking in other states where printing was absent or limited.

Another link between state development and military potential was provided by the need for a political-administrative structure capable of mobilising large numbers in order to sustain firepower tactics based on large, rather than elite, forces. This was definitely true of European states that created substantial forces in the second half of the seventeenth century, but was also the case elsewhere. For example on the Gold Coast (coastal modern Ghana) and the Slave Coast (coastal modern Togo and Benin), the replacement of shock by missile tactics was linked to a shift from elite forces relying on individual prowess to larger units, although in Dahomey there was an emphasis on a small standing army. It would be misleading to adopt a technological causation and argue that this shift was solely due to the spread of firearms. Instead, it has to be considered more widely, in the context of political, social and economic developments. The military changes outlined were linked to the rise of the states of Akwamu and Asante on the Gold Coast and Dahomey on the Slave Coast. There is a difference between the causes, course and consequences of the spread of firearms in an area where they had hitherto been rare or unknown, and in an area such as Europe, where they had been long in use.

The Mughals

The view that 'nomadic' peoples lost ground during the seventeenth century needs to be qualified. Most importantly, we must remember the rise of the Manchu in China, even though they became 'sedentary' as a result of their success. It is also worth noting that the Mughals (given Chinese problems in mid-century, then the leading land military power in the world) encountered serious setbacks, both within India and in neighbouring regions. This was especially the case in areas where the terrain was not suitable for Mughal forces. In the valley of the Brahmaputra, the Ahom, a Shan people originally from upper Burma, proved a serious challenge from 1612, not least because they mobilised all their resources for war. The riverine and jungle terrain were very different from the plains and hills of Rajasthan, where the Mughals had campaigned extensively and for which their weaponry and tactics were appropriate. Although the Ahom were outnumbered, their fighting techniques were well adapted to the terrain. They relied on infantry, armed with muskets or bows and arrows, used flexible tactics, including surprise night attacks, and rapidly created fortified positions based on bamboo stockades. A fierce war in 1636–8 led to a compromise peace, but in 1682 the Mughals were forced to retreat.

25. Mughal commander in the Deccan. The conquest of the Deccan by the Mughals was crucial to the geopolitics of early modern India. The Mughals greatly relied on cavalry. This commander was armed with spear, sword and bow and arrow.

Afghanistan also proved difficult terrain for the Mughals. They advanced against the Uzbeks in 1646, occupying Badakhshan and Balkh, but in 1647 their field artillery and musketeers were unable to defeat their more mobile opponents, and in addition they found it impossible to obtain adequate supplies from the harsh region. Local knowledge, supplies and military adaptability were essential to success there. In 1647 Prince Aurangzeb evacuated Balkh and retreated through the snowbound Hindu Kush mountains with heavy losses. The Amu (Oxus) was not to be the boundary of Mughal India. In 1672–4 the Afridi, a Pathan tribe near Kabul, successfully ambushed Mughal armies. Aurangzeb came to rely on bribes to keep the Pathans quiet.

Despite their military strength and determination, the Mughals, therefore, were unable to prevail in adverse circumstances in frontier zones. They also suffered greatly at the hands of the mobile, lightly armoured horsemen and musketeers of the Marathas in the western Deccan from the 1650s. The Marathas under Shivaji Bhonsle (1627–80) adapted well to the opportunities and problems of their environmental and political circumstances. They avoided battle, and, instead, concentrated on a strategy of 'bargir-giri': cutting supply links and launching devastating raids. The Marathas did not defeat the Mughals in decisive battles, but rather denied the Mughals victory and territorial expansion.

However, the centres of Mughal power did not collapse; no more than those of Spain or Turkey did during their seventeenth-century problems. There was no real rival for power at the time. Politically, the Mughals were more effective than the states of southern India, some of which, such as Vijayangara, found it difficult to control powerful provincial governors.[31] Indeed, a stress on some frontier problems should not detract from Mughal success in reducing the Deccan Sultanates of Bijapur and Golconda to vassalage in 1636. After they reasserted their independence, they were annexed in 1686 and 1687. Moreover, the Mughals pushed north into Baltistan and Ladakh (1637–9). Their ability to maintain dominance of northern India, even when Aurangzeb and most of his army were engaged in protracted conflict with the Marathas, was significant. Moreover, the Mughals triumphed against Maratha strongholds, Aurangzeb taking a whole series in 1689 and 1700–7, thus achieving more than the Sultan of Bijapur had done in 1659. The forts provided clear targets for the Mughals and their effective siege equipment. The Maratha advantage of mobility was lost when they defended positions, but they had been swayed by the wisdom that forts were necessary both for the symbol and for the reality of power.

The Fall of Ming China

The ups and downs of the seventeenth-century Mughals may be contrasted with the Ming and Manchu experiences in China. There the state collapsed and the dynasty came to an end. Originally based in the mountains of south-eastern Manchuria, the Jurchens expanded under Nurhachi (1559–1626) to dominate the lands to the north of the Great Wall in the early seventeenth century. Nurhachi both united the Jurchen tribes, by means of war, marriage alliances and exploiting the Chinese tributary system, and developed a strong cavalry army based on horse archers; this was organised into 'banners': units that incorporated tribal groups. He used this force to gain control of most of northern Manchuria by 1616. Nurhachi declared himself Khan in 1615 and founded the Manchu state. In 1618 he attacked the Chinese, capturing Fu-shun. Korean-supported Chinese attacks on Nurhachi failed disastrously in 1619; Chinese and Korean firearms and numbers could not counteract the tactical mobility of the determined, well-led and numerous Manchu cavalry. As a result, Chinese armies were defeated in a series of major battles including Siyanggiayan (1619), Niu-mao chai (1619) and Kuang-ning (1622).[32] Liaoyang fell to the Manchus in 1621, and Nurhachi, instead of making over the conquered territory for looting and division among his banners, left it outside the tribal system to be administered by Chinese bureaucrats. Thus a dual state, separately administering Chinese and Jurchens, was created.

The dynamic expansion by the Manchus continued, L'ung Taiji (Abahai; 1626–43), proclaiming himself Manchu emperor in 1636. After invasions in 1627 and 1636–7, Korea, China's most important ally, was reduced to vassal status: the Koreans surrendered within two months in the face of the Manchu winter invasion of 1636–7. Inner Mongolia became a Manchu dependency in 1633–4, a process helped by disunity among the Mongols: the Khalkhas refused to help both the Chahars and the Oirats. Lighdan Khan (1604–36), the leader of the Chahars, had allied with the Ming in 1618, but the Chinese cut off his subsidy and lost his support in 1628. Lighdan lost control of the steppe and was defeated by the Manchus in 1632 and 1634. The Chinese had failed in their long-established policy of manipulating their steppe neighbours, and, as so often, the struggle between 'barbarians' was crucial to that between 'barbarians' and settled societies. The Manchus also benefited from marriage alliances with the Mongol elite, from matching Ming tribute and from purchasing Mongol horses. Mongol banners were organised by the Manchus. The cooperation of the Mongols made it easier to attack China, not least by circumventing the Chinese defences at Shan-hai-kuan in north-east China. The Amur region was also conquered, and the area further north between the Amur and the Argun rivers brought under Manchu control by 1643.

Attacks on China in 1627 and 1630 were unsuccessful, but the fortress of Dalinghe fell in 1631 after Ming relief attempts were defeated, and plundering expeditions into northern China in 1629, 1632 and 1634 were followed by a major invasion in 1638–40 which captured many cities in Shantung and Chihli. Victory by Manchu cavalry at the battle of the Pass (Shanghai-Kwai) in 1644 was followed by the capture of Beijing. North and east China fell to the Manchu in 1644–5, Szechwan in 1646, Canton in 1650, much of the south by 1652 and Yunnan in the south-west in 1659.

Some would say this was a clear case of 'barbarian success', another episode in the struggle between nomadic and sedentary people, following the victories of earlier steppe peoples, most recently the Jurchen Jin and Mongols, at the expense of China: they had conquered much and all of it respectively. Manchu triumph can be seen as a victory for cavalry over the static military system and warfare of China. Moreover it indicated China's probable military inferiority to Europe, as it was in the seventeenth century that Europeans were able to defeat the Turks as they had earlier overcome Kazan.

Such an analysis, however, is misleading and underrates the complexity of the conquest. First, it is necessary to appreciate the lack of unity on the Chinese side and the degree to which this weakened resistance and in some cases directly abetted the Manchu advance. Secondly, it is clear that the process of civilising that Gibbon regarded as crucial if 'barbarians' were to challenge Europe successfully, and for which he gave the example of Russia under Peter the Great, can also be extended to the Manchu military challenge to China. The Manchus themselves should be seen as semi- rather than fully 'barbarian'; they were descended from the Jurchen Jin, who controlled all of China north of the Huai river from 1126 to 1234. The Manchu conquest resulted in a nomadic people taking over virtually without change the developed bureaucratic structure of China and themselves becoming settled in due course.

The China that fell to the Manchus had been gravely weakened by internal instability and disorder. From 1582, there were weak emperors, increasingly arbitrary central government, oppressive taxation and growing financial problems. These encouraged both rebellions and a quest for power among ambitious leaders. It was one powerful regional warlord, Li Tzu-ch'eng, who was responsible for capturing Beijing in 1644 and provoking the suicide of the last Ming emperor. He had established his base in Hunan in 1641 and benefited from the degree to which Ming forces and fortifications were concentrated further north and designed to resist attacks from the north. Li proclaimed the Shun dynasty, but his army was poorly disciplined and he lacked the supports of legitimacy, powerful allies and administrative apparatus. It was the collapse of the Ming dynasty, and thus of its frontier defence system, thanks to Li, that gave the Manchus their opportunity.

Other powerful Chinese figures directly assisted the Manchus. Wu San-kuei, who commanded the largest Chinese army on the northern frontier, refused to submit to Li and, instead, supported the Manchus. Wu and the Manchus together defeated Li at the battle of the Pass, forcing him to abandon Beijing in 1644. Wu pursued Li and was responsible for his death in 1645. Chinese units were reorganised by the Manchus and used to help conquer the rest of China. Hung Ch'eng-Ch'ou became a Manchu general, captured Hankow and Nanjing and pacified Fukien. Keng Ching-chung also became a Manchu general. The Manchus were earlier helped by fifth columnists when they gained Shenyang in 1619 and Liaoyang in 1621.

As with other expanding powers, the Manchus sought local allies. Cooperation with important Chinese elements strengthened the Manchus militarily. For example, in a battle near Dalinghe in 1631, the Chinese held off frontal assaults by Manchu cavalry, but were then disrupted by the artillery and fire arrows of the Manchus' Chinese allies. The Manchu cavalry therefore ultimately triumphed.[33]

The Manchus also demonstrated their adaptability and sought to benefit from the military technology of their rivals. A metallurgical industry developed in Manchuria by the end of the sixteenth century, so that the manufacture of munitions became a major activity. Cannon production was developed. In 1629 the Manchus captured Chinese artillerymen skilled in casting Portuguese cannon, and by 1631 had obtained about forty pieces from their captives. Their Ming opponents not only sought the advice of Portuguese artillery technicians, but also of Adam Schall, a European astronomer who produced smaller and more manoeuvrable cannon for them.

The Manchus did not only copy military technology. They also emulated the political techniques and administrative structures of imperial China, developing a system that was recognisably different from that of tribalism. This left the Manchus better able to benefit from the flux of 1644; in contrast the poorly organised Shun dynasty collapsed when Li was defeated.

As so often with history, therefore, certainties dissolve under scrutiny. The Manchu conquest becomes more complex as a process and, as a result, the question of military explanation becomes at once more elusive and more multifaceted. It is certainly clear from the campaigns of 1618–21 that the Chinese military system suffered the same problems and lack of effectiveness as Chinese politics and government. But, as with the 'decline and fall' of imperial Rome and the role of 'barbarians' both in defeating Rome and in fighting for it, it is less obvious that there were two clear-cut sides and the 'overthrow' that is to be explained is by no means apparent. It is necessary to be cautious about adopting ethnic or cultural accounts or explanations of the two sides. Instead, the process of Manchu conquest involved redefinitions of cultural loyalty in which distinctions between

Chinese and 'barbarian' became less apparent and definitions less rigid. This shift affected both the Chinese and the Manchus themselves. Cultural and political expressions of identity were far from fixed.[34]

These problems of definition were even more apparent when the new Manchu rulers encountered strong resistance in southern China.[35] Their position was challenged by Cheng Ch'eng-Kung (known to Europeans as Coxinga) who, with the profits of piracy and trade, had developed a large fleet based in Fukien and amassed a substantial army of over 50,000 men, some of whom were equipped with European-style weapons. In 1656–8, he regained much of southern China for the Ming. The success of Coxinga is a reminder of the danger of concentrating on gunpowder weaponry. The force of about 250,000 men he led to the siege of Nanjing in 1659 was mostly armed with swords – two-handed long heavy swords, or short swords carried with shields. The soldiers wore mail coats to protect themselves against bullets. Coxinga's army included cannon and musketeers, but also an archery corps that was more effective than his musketeers.[36] This army was defeated outside Nanjing by Manchu cavalry and infantry attacks, but its earlier success exposes the danger of judging military capability against a single global standard.

This was further demonstrated in 1661 when, deprived of his mainland bases after the Manchus advanced into Fukien in 1659, Coxinga turned his attention to Formosa. The island had not previously been under Chinese control and the Dutch had considerable influence. Coxinga invaded in 1661 with a force of 300 junks and 25,000 men and, after a nine-month siege, took the Dutch base of Fort Zeelandia, helped by the defection of some of the garrison who then explained how it could best be attacked.

Coxinga's success owed much to old- and new-style weaponry. He used his shield-bearers as an aggressive assault force, but several infantry attacks were beaten off. Coxinga also had 28 European-style cannon, some directed by Dutch renegades, and the fort surrendered after the walls of its Utrecht redoubt collapsed under heavy fire.[37] Dutch relief attempts from Batavia in Java failed due to poor leadership, bad weather and insufficient troops. Squadrons sent to re-establish the Dutch position in 1662, 1663 and 1664 were all unsuccessful.

Although Coxinga's use of artillery was important, his force was lightly gunned by European standards. Furthermore, like other Chinese armies, Coxinga's did not use flint-locks. However, the number of cannon in China increased in 1674–81 during the San-fan rebellion, the War of the Three Feudatories, a rebellion begun by powerful generals who were provincial governors: Wu San-kuei who controlled most of southwestern China, Keng Ching-chung and Shang Chih-hsin. The feudatories used bronze from temple bells to cast cannon, and, in response, the Emperor had Father Ferdinand Verbiest, the European Jesuit President of the Tribunal of Mathematics, repair the army's cannon and cast 152 new pieces. Verbiest improved the Chinese manufacture of light-weight cast-iron ordnance, rather than introducing new Western types of cannon. His cannon were also used in the campaigns against the Russians on the Amur in 1685–6, and his designs were still in use at the time of the Opium War in 1839.[38] Nevertheless, because of the Jesuits, the Chinese had access to nearly current Western technology in the seventeenth century.

The feudatories overran most of south China, but were driven back to the south-west by 1677 thanks to the use of Green Standard Troops: loyal Chinese forces. Manchu units had failed earlier to defeat the rebels, and this failure helped in the consolidation of a new political system in which Manchu tribesmen could no longer challenge the adoption of Chinese administrative techniques, personnel and priorities. Wu died in 1678, but the rebellion, which prevented Chinese opposition to Dzhungar expansion in Turkestan, did not end until 1681.[39] It was an important war, generally ignored in the history of warfare with its Eurocentric bias.

Asian Military Developments

Despite the situation in the 1670s the ratio of cannon to troops in China remained slight by European standards, and indeed in the 1620s the Chinese had turned to Portuguese gunnery instructors and cannon from Macao for assistance against the Manchus.[40] This position was not restricted to China. In terms of weaponry, seventeenth-century Indian warfare was hardly innovative. Adoption of the flintlock was slower than in Europe, and the bayonet was not used. No effort was made to centre battlefield tactics on firepower. Mughal India failed to keep pace with European advances in artillery, especially in cast-iron technology. Akbar's successors were not interested in firearms technology.

This failure can be approached in a number of lights. First, it can be asked whether it prevented success. It is possible to argue that more and better firearms would have enabled the Chinese to defeat the Manchus, or would have brought victory to Coxinga, but such an analysis ignores the wider 'political' context of such struggles.

Secondly, it can be suggested that attention should focus on other military dimensions and differences, including those between Asian powers. Thus, the use of conscript troops in Arakan, Burma and Nepal, rather than mercenaries as in northern India, can be regarded as more significant to the character of warfare than an emphasis on firepower. In addition, there were other important tactical differences, such as the skillful use of stockades in Arakan, Burma, Kerala and Nepal. The differences between warfare in Kerala and northern India are a reminder of the dangers of assuming that there was a common pattern or trajectory to warfare in India.

Thirdly, it can be argued that the external pressures on China and India were not such as to force the pace of military change and innovation, an argument that Gibbon employed to explain European military superiority. The crushing defeat of the Acehnese attack on Malacca in 1629 and the total failure of the second Mataram siege of Batavia the same year indicated that the European presence in the waters and coastal bases of the East Indies was proof against the most powerful of local powers. China and the Indian states experienced no such blows at European hands.

However, they did have other external challenges. While China after the end of the rebellion of the Three Feudatories did not face serious threats, the period 1618–81 was certainly one of crisis, and, thereafter, there was concern about the Dzhungars. In the case of India, there was continual external pressure. Conflict in adverse environments with Ahoms or Pathans might not encourage a premium on military technology, but there was no such environmental edge in the case of campaigns in the Deccan, whether against Ahmadnagar, Bijapur and Golconda, or against the Marathas.

In addition, the Mughals had a long-standing rivalry with Safavid Persia that owed something to Safavid influence in the Deccan Sultanates resisting Mughal advance, but that centred over control of Kandahar, the gateway for the Persians to southern Afghanistan and the Indus valley. Lost to Shah Abbas I of Persia in 1622, Kandahar had been regained in 1638, when the Persian commander, fearing execution by his sovereign, surrendered. Shah Abbas II recaptured Kandahar in 1649 and Mughal attempts to regain it in 1649, 1652 and 1653 all failed. It was difficult to campaign effectively so far from the centre of Mughal power, and success had to be achieved before the harsh winter.

26. Complete North-Indian armour, Lahore, late eighteenth century. This armour was of scant value against musketry volleys, but was more useful in hand-to-hand combat.

Mughal siege artillery was also of poorer quality and less accurate than the Persian cannon which inflicted heavy casualties on the besiegers. In 1653, three specially cast heavy guns made breaches in the walls of Kandahar, but the onset of winter and logistical problems made it impossible to exploit them.

Thus, the argument which applies in the case of Japan – that the absence of foreign rivals led to indifference to military improvement – cannot be applied to Mughal India. For similar reasons, it is also inappropriate in the case of Safavid Persia and Ottoman Turkey. Like Mughal India, they had to face powerful external enemies that could not be overcome; most obviously these were each other. Furthermore, these states clearly did develop their military capabilities. Persia exemplified the interaction between military capability and administrative reform. Shah Abbas I (1587–1629) created a large standing army based on Caucasian military slaves (*ghulams*), including a 12,000-strong corps of artillerymen with about 500 guns although most of the *ghulams* fought with traditional weapons. This force was supportable because of administrative changes allowing troops to be paid directly from the royal treasury, rather than from the revenues of provinces assigned to tribal governors. Abbas enlarged the amount of land he directly controlled, while increasingly *ghulams* became provincial governors, also strengthening the position of the Shah. This stronger government-military nexus contributed to a series of important Persian military successes. Herat was regained from the Uzbeks in 1598 and Kandahar from the Mughals and Ormuz from the Portuguese, both in 1622. Abbas took Tabriz from the Turks in 1603 and Erivan in 1604, defeated them at Sūfiyān in 1605, and took Baghdad from them in 1623.[41]

Iskandar Muda (1607–36) of Aceh in Sumatra had a smaller army than Abbas but he also had a substantial fleet, until much of it was destroyed by the Portuguese when he attacked Malacca in 1629. Nevertheless, Muda's army included many cannon, as well as infantry, cavalry and elephants. The army was well up to the task of dominating northern Sumatra, although it lacked the infantry coordination and increasing emphasis on firepower that characterised the leading European armies.

Although the Mughals paid insufficient attention to the quality of their firearms, they nevertheless maintained a formidable mixed-arms army. In 1647, the historian Abdul Hamid Lahori listed Mughal military strength as 200,000 stipendiary cavalry, 185,000 other cavalry and a central force of 40,000 garrisoned musketeers and gunners.[42]

A large cavalry force was not itself a sign of military obsolescence. Aside from the value of cavalry in India, Central Asia, China and the sahel (Sudan) belt of Africa and the spread of the horse in the New World, its continued role in Europe in the sixteenth and seventeenth centuries (like that of the pike) has been undervalued because of a concentration on firearms. However, the importance of traditional, close-quarter cavalry engagements for settling battles in Germany during the Thirty Years War (1618–48) has recently been emphasised.[43] The Catholic League's cavalry played a crucial role in the Danish defeat at Lutter in 1626.[44] Mughal heavy cavalry was more mobile and effective than its European counterpart.

The Ottoman Turks failed against Austria in 1683–99, but were scarcely ineffective militarily. Indeed, the Ottoman empire had recovered after its own mid-seventeenth-century crisis to display considerable vitality from the 1660s. After formidable losses, Crete was finally conquered from the Venetians in 1669, while the Poles were forced to cede Podolia in 1672, and in 1677–8 Turkish invasions of the eastern Ukraine pressed the Russians hard, although the war was indecisive. Nevertheless, the 1681 Russo-Turkish treaty of Bakhchisarai recognised Turkish rights to right-bank (western) Ukraine. The struggle with the Turks was far more important to Russia than the confrontation with the Chinese in the Amur valley. In 1682 Turkish forces, operating against the Austrian Habsburgs and in support of the Hungarian Imre Thököly, captured Kosice, and Thököly was crowned king of Hungary.

The Turks were beaten outside Vienna in 1683 and driven from most of Hungary in 1686–7, but in 1690 they mounted a successful counter-offensive, regaining Nish and Belgrade. Driven from Belgrade in 1717, the Turks regained it in 1739. Similarly, a modernisation of the Ottoman fleet was begun in the 1650s and pushed hard in the 1680s: the number of sailing vessels increased.[43] The Ottoman military system was particularly dependent on the quality of leadership. In 1657 a vigorous new Grand Vizier, Mehmed Köprülü, had broken the Venetian blockade of the Dardanelles, in 1690 an able and energetic new Grand Vizier, Fazil Mustafa, had restored order to the army and regained Nish and Belgrade, and in 1695–6 an active new Sultan, Mustafa II, took back the initiative in Hungary. Thus, it is necessary to be cautious in discerning an obvious problem – Asiatic military failure – that requires a clear explanation.

If India, Persia and Turkey all operated in an obvious context of pressure and rivalry, the same was also true of the European states. This encouraged a process of competitive emulation. The different weapons systems that characterised the armies of the considerable combatants in the Italian wars of the early sixteenth century had been replaced by a considerable degree of uniformity as each power sought to counteract the strengths of its rivals. Mercenaries helped to spread military practice, and there was a keen interest in foreign developments. Thus, in the early seventeenth century, Christian IV of Denmark looked to Dutch examples.[46] A measure of relative homogeneity came to prevail on the parade grounds and battlefields and in the dockyards of western Europe. This, in turn, helped to ensure that powers were able to prevent the development of lasting gaps in military capability, either in terms of new weaponry or new tactics, such as line-ahead tactics for warships. Such gaps, for example the exploding shells fired by Spanish siege mortars that led the unprepared French rapidly to surrender the fortresses of Capelle and Le Câtelet in 1636,[47] were swiftly countered. The absence of a gap in military capability encouraged an emphasis on building up the size of forces, both on land and at sea.

The Turks and Europe

The extent to which the process of military 'improvement' by competitive emulation and the use of resources increased European effectiveness *vis-à-vis* non-European peoples is difficult to assess. As already indicated, transoceanic operations by European forces were scarcely a measure of their technological capability in land warfare. It was only against the Turks that a measure of land warfare can be readily suggested. Here again, it is necessary to consider wider military-political contexts, including the determination of combatants,

27. The Turkish siege of Raab (Györ) in 1594. Raab was a crucial part of the Habsburg defence system on the Danube. The importance of artillery and the bastioned nature of the defences are readily apparent.

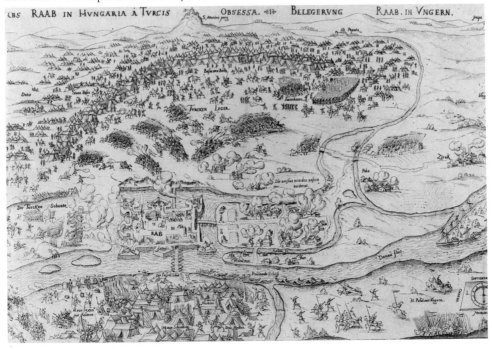

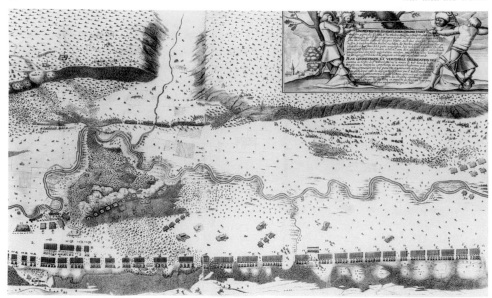

28. Section of a plan of the battle of St Gotthard, 1664. The battle was a major defeat of the Turks by the Austrians which prefigured a series of defeats from 1683. The Austrians were no longer dependent on fortresses in order to thwart the expansion of Turkish power.

not least in the context of alternative commitments, and the dynamics and problems of coalition warfare on the Christian side. Furthermore, the drag of logistics was especially important on the Turkish side, and, once the Christian powers began to advance, on their side also. It is anyway difficult to decide how best to assess military effectiveness in the case of Christian fortresses holding off Turkish attack but without any ability to inflict defeat. The problem of deciding how to assess sieges is especially complex because there were relatively few battles after the Turkish victory over the Hungarians at Mohacs in 1526.

In 1529 Suleiman the Magnificent had besieged Vienna, but he did not reach the city until 27 September and the city was able to resist assaults until the Ottoman retreat began on 14 October. Heavy rains reduced roads to mud, ensuring that the Turks lacked their heavy cannon. Campaigning at such a distance from their base caused major logistical problems, as troops and supplies had to move for months before they could reach the sphere of operations and the onset of winter limited the campaigning season.

There was no battle during Suleiman's next expedition, that of 1532, when the Ottomans besieged Güns. As with the Persians in 1534–5, 1548 and 1554, the Austrians had learned that the best policy was to avoid major battles, although it can also be argued that Suleiman failed to provoke such an engagement.[48] The Austrians, however, could not prevent Ottoman gains in areas within effective Ottoman operational distance. Thus, in Hungary, the Ottomans captured Gran in 1543, Visegrad in 1544 and Temesvár in 1552. When battles were fought, the Ottomans were successful, as at Szegedin and Fülek in 1552.

After 1566 there was no large-scale conflict until the 13-year war of 1593–1606. The outbreak of this struggle followed on from the end of the Ottoman – Persian war in 1590. As so often, the course of Ottoman pressure on Europe can only be understood if it is seen in the wider context of Ottoman commitments. In 1593 the Austrians defeated an Ottoman force besieging Sisak/Sissek in Croatia, but that Austrian army soon after collapsed due to logistical problems.[49] Ottoman logistics were more effective, although the permanent garrisoning of numerous border fortresses created financial pressures.[50]

The war saw more effective Austrian infantry firepower, but there was no total shift in battlefield capability, in part because the Ottomans recruited more musketeers.[51] When in 1596 Mehmed III took personal charge of the army, the first Sultan to do so since Suleiman, he demonstrated the continued effectiveness of the Ottoman army. Erlau was besieged successfully, and, at the battle of Mezö Kerésztés, Mehmed, with a significant advantage in artillery and cavalry, outflanked and defeated the Austrian infantry which had broken the Ottoman centre.

The Austrians under Count Raimondo Montecuccoli, however, won the battle of St Gothard (1664), a successful defensive operation against an Ottoman advance, the sole significant engagement during the next war of 1663–4. Starting with the 1683 battle of Kahlenberg that raised the siege of Vienna and decisively ended a run of Ottoman success, they also won a number of victories in the following war of 1683–99. This was not simply a matter of weaponry. Divisions among the Turkish commanders that reflected an absence of common purpose and reliable command structures appear to have played a major role in the Ottoman defeat in 1683. Murat Giray, the Khan of Crimea, distrusted the Grand Vizier and deliberately did nothing to prevent the Christian forces from crossing the Danube. The Turkish right flank abandoned the subsequent battle itself.[51]

29. Attack on Buda, 1684. The Austrians found it difficult to follow up the Turkish defeat at Vienna. Charles of Lorraine besieged Buda, the key to Hungary, but the fortress was a strong one with powerful cannon, and disease and supply difficulties hampered the four-month siege, which was eventually abandoned. In 1686, however, a shell landed on the main powder magazine, blowing open a breach in the walls, and repeated assaults then led to the fall of the city. This illustration indicated the importance of naval forces on the Danube.

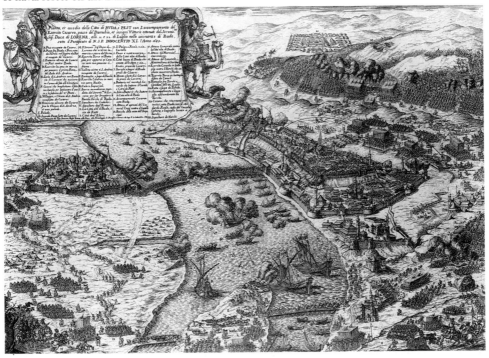

Later in the war, the Margrave of Baden's defeat of Mustafa Köprülü's army at Szalankemen (1691) and Prince Eugene's victory at Zenta in 1697 were especially important. An initial, very limited Austrian capability in siegecraft, that led to the failure of the siege of Buda in 1684,[53] was remedied: Nové Zamsky fell in 1685, Buda in 1686, Eger in 1687, Peterwardein and Belgrade in 1688.

A similar shift occurred to the north of the Black Sea as the Russians came to take the initiative. In the early sixteenth century, and indeed in 1633, the Tatars had raided Muscovy and captured large numbers of slaves. In 1659 the Tatars had joined Hetman Vyhovsky of the Ukraine and the Cossacks in heavily defeating a Russian army at Konotrop: a victory of steppe cavalry over the Russian cavalry. In 1672 the Turks forced Poland to recognise Turkish suzerainty over the western Ukraine and to pay a heavy annual tribute. Sultan Mehmed IV visited Kamieniec and prayed in its cathedral, which had been converted into a mosque. In 1677–8 the Turks had pressed the Russians hard in the eastern Ukraine.

However, in 1695, with an army of over 90,000 troops, Peter the Great besieged and in 1696, after a second siege, captured the important Turkish base of Azov. His success owed much to the construction of a fleet on the River Don. After capturing Azov, Peter created a naval yard at Taganrog. The balance of initiative had shifted, and this was crucial to Russia's emergence as a great power. Russia had waged war successfully against the Tatars and the Turks. By the Peace of Carlowitz (1699) and the Treaty of Constantinople (1700), the Turks lost much territory, including most of Hungary and Transylvania to Austria, the Morea to Venice and Azov to Russia. The Khan of the Tatar's claim to an annual tribute from Russia was also repudiated.

Austrian and Russian victories which continued, albeit with important reversals, during the following century, can in part be attributed to general European military technological developments, in particular, the shift to the socket bayonet and the adoption of flintlock muskets, both of which were important from the last decades of the seventeenth century, and the use of light cast-iron guns. The Russians used flintlock muskets from mid-century, but the bayonet only from the 1700s. This process was supported by an effective Russian metallurgical and arms industry that produced 125,000 handguns alone between 1700 and 1710. The use of the flintlock and of bayonets encouraged the Russian infantry to develop offensive tactics:[54] more effective infantry weaponry led European forces to phase out body armour, thus increasing the mobility of their troops. Russian artillery was organised into a regular branch in 1701, and in 1706 a permanent horse corps to pull cannon was created.[55] In contrast, the Turks were more conservative in weaponry and tactics. They lacked mobile field artillery, and were slow to adopt flintlocks and bayonets: they were used, and then only in relatively small numbers, from the 1730s. Turkish siegecraft failed to develop as that of their European rivals did. The Turks failed to standardise their artillery or to improve the quality of their artillerymen.[56]

At present, it is unclear how far this approach can be pushed, but the evidence suggests a vindication of Gibbon's thesis. Conflict between the European powers had led to a rapid diffusion of new weaponry that was then used effectively against non-Europeans, although in North America native peoples had gained access to such weaponry. Furthermore, the enhanced capability of new weaponry encouraged a stress on discipline and training, as in the French army under Louis XIV (personal rule 1661–1715). This combined with the demographic stagnation of the seventeenth century, when there was a more acute shortage of soldiers, and with domestic and international political shifts, to ensure that there was a greater emphasis on the continuity of military units and forces, as well as a partial change in the nature and perception of soldiering.

30. *Imperial musketeers supported by Pikemen.* Artist unknown, time of Thirty Years War (1618–48). These heavy muskets were rested on stands, rather like the swivel guns employed on some ships and in parts of Asia. Such muskets were of scant protection in hand-to-hand fighting.

European Developments

However, the shift in Eastern Europe could be conceptualised differently by arguing that, for both Austria and Russia, European military change was in part a product of the global military struggle. Rather than treating Eastern Europe, and more specifically Austria and Russia, as 'backward' powers that adopted the early modern European 'Military Revolution' discerned by Roberts and Parker only slowly, it is possibly more appropriate to think in terms of a multi-centred early modern European 'Military Revolution'. In addition to the *trace italienne* and other changes in land warfare in western Europe on which Roberts and Parker focus, it would be possible to discuss an Atlantic naval revolution and also changes in land warfare in eastern Europe that owed much to the stimulus provided by conflict with the Turks and the Tatars. Thus, adaptation to the external threat was as important as the example provided by inter-European conflict. In place of the Magyar cavalry destroyed at Mohacs in 1526, and in response to Ottoman infantry and cannon – an example that was more present and pressing than those provided by western European warfare – the Habsburgs deployed infantry and cannon in positional warfare that entailed support from field fortifications. Similarly, the Russians developed the nexus of infantry – cannon – fortifications. The Turks influenced the force structure and tactics

Contrafactúr der Stad Lintz/wie die von den Eurischen Bawren belagert beſtúrmbt und wieder abgetrien worden.j626.

31. The siege of Linz by the Austrian peasantry, 1626. Although eventually unsuccessful, the peasant army had been able to mount a regular siege. The rising was eventually suppressed by regular troops.

of the Russian army developed in the mid-sixteenth century, with the new streltsy infantry drawing on the example of the janizaries.

External pressure and opportunity and the circumstances of conflict in particular areas were certainly important, but, in addition, there was a process of diffusion of weaponry and tactics within Europe. Thus, sixteenth-century Russia was also influenced by developments elsewhere in Europe, not least by those in Italian military engineering and guncasting. Dutch shipbuilders were hired to help build up the Swedish fleet in the 1610s. In 1617 the Venetians recruited 4,000 Dutch troops to help them in operations against Austria, and in 1618 they sought to obtain the support of a Dutch naval squadron against Austria's ally, Spain.[57] Large numbers of English, Irish and Scots fought in foreign armies during the century – including 10 per cent of Scotland's adult males between 1625 and 1632. Many subsequently used their experience in warfare within Britain.[58] Montecuccoli, the victor at St Gotthard, had fought in the Thirty Years War; Eugene had fought Louis XIV.

The Russians had long experience of conflict with Poland and Sweden, and recruited foreign officers to help create western-style units. Peter the Great followed his father Alexis in this policy. Manuals and instructions were borrowed from Austria and Sweden.[59] Between 1651 and 1663, under the pressure of war with Sweden and Poland, the percentage of the Russian army consisting of 'new-formation troops' trained in western European methods dramatically increased. Such troops had earlier been used in the Smolensk War against Poland in 1632–4, although they proved less experienced than Poland's mercenaries. However, the principal reason for the failure to capture Smolensk was the delayed arrival of the Russian artillery due to poor weather and primitive roads. Despite the significant role of military example and diffusion within Europe, it is important to note that the adoption and effectiveness of technology and tactics reflected local conditions and circumstances, as was, more generally, the case with the spread of European weaponry and military methods elsewhere in the world. In 1685 the English Ordnance Office sent Jacob Richards to the Danubian war front:

'You are to set forward on your journey towards Hungary with all convenient speed, and there to survey, learn and observe the fortifications and artillery, not only of Hungary but of places in your way thither . . . and when you come into the next campaign in the Emperor's army to observe all the marching and countermarching and in the besieging of any town to observe their making approaches, mines, batteries, lines of circumvallation and contravallation . . . make . . . draughts of places and fortifications.'[60]

Richards did so, taking part in the siege of Buda. After returning to England, he served in William III's campaigns in Ireland and the Low Countries.

The degree to which the European borrowing of military methods from the Turks or other contiguous opponents declined is important. In the late fifteenth century, warfare in Italy had been affected by the Ottoman advance and the responses to it. In the War of Ferrara of 1482–4, Venice had used Albanian and Greek stradiots (light cavalry troops)

32. Manuscript map showing routes into the Valtelline. This Alpine valley was a crucial route between Lombardy and the Tyrol, linking the power of the Spanish Habsburgs in northern Italy with that of their Austrian cousins. Habsburg opponents such as France sought to block the route. In 1620 the Spaniards overran the valley. The mountainous terrain is a reminder that it was not only outside Europe that European forces encountered major operational difficulties. In 1635 the French forces in the Valtelline under the Duke of Rohan had to cope with waist-deep snows and lacked sufficient food, fodder and money.

who had initially been employed to fight the Turks in the Morea and Friuli. Venice's opponents used squadrons of Turkish cavalry captured and re-employed after the fall of Otranto in 1481. Stradiots were used against the French at Fornovo in 1495, although their value in a preliminary engagement was not followed through in the main battle.[61] Light cavalry units developed to fight the Turks were to be used for inter-European conflicts on subsequent occasions; the Austrian use of Hungarian cavalry in the War of the Austrian Succession (1740–8) was particularly effective. However, as the emphasis both in the Danube sphere of conflict between Austria and the Turks and, more generally, within Europe shifted towards the value of infantry firepower, the example and applicability of warfare with the Turks and of Turkish military methods became less generally valuable. Instead, the Turks increasingly employed Westerners, as in the design of new fortifications at Belgrade and the use of English and Dutch gunners and Italian gun founders at the siege of Candia.[62]

33. Reverse of a medal struck to commemorate the Anglo-Dutch taking of the Meuse fortress, 1702: a view of the bombardment of the positions. Venlo fell after a heavy cannonade that had been preceded by the storming of part of the fortifications. During the siege, 40,000 fascines were used.

Conclusions

Eurocentrism is not only involved in the issue of emphasis. It also plays a major role in what is to be covered or even mentioned. For example, the Uzbeks are generally ignored in books on global and military history. Yet they provide one of the more impressive examples of the continued vitality of Central Asian military power. Unable to manufacture their own, the Uzbeks had few firearms, and requests for them from the Turks yielded few, but, nevertheless, they were an important force. Invading Khurasan on a number of occasions in the sixteenth century, the Uzbeks were for long at war with the Safavids. They pressed hard the Dörben Oirats of Mongolia, although the Uzbeks themselves were under pressure from the Kazaks. The Uzbek nomadic system was politically fissiparous and much energy was spent on warfare between the tribes. In the late sixteenth century Abd Allah Sultan made the last real attempt to unite Transoxiana. He seized Balkh in 1573, Samarkand in 1578, Turkestan in 1582, Badakhshan in 1584 and Herat in 1588. However, he was unable to conquer Kabul, Khurasan and Kashgar, and in 1598 the Kazaks invaded the Uzbek lands. Abd Allah died that year, and the Uzbeks divided. Nevertheless, under the Janid dynasty, especially Shaybani Khan, the Uzbeks remained a major force with wide-ranging territories until about 1660, after which they lost control of their territories south of the Amu (Oxus). The Uzbek Khanate of Bukhara, still ruled by the Janids, was to be conquered by Persia (under Nadir Shah not the Safavids) in 1740, although it regained its independence after his death in 1747.[63]

As with the history in this period of, say, Madagascar or of southern India, in which battles could involve formidable forces,[64] that of Uzbekistan can appear of no long-term consequence to any bar its inhabitants, and it is easy to understand why it is generally omitted. Yet the teleology, Eurocentrism and bias that underlie such decisions are questionable. Similarly, North Africa is ignored. Yet under Sultan Muley Ismael (1672–1727), the Moroccan pressure drove the Spaniards from La Mamora (1681), Larache (1689) and Arzila (1691), and the English from Tangier (1684), Spanish-held Ceuta was unsuccessfully besieged (1694–1720) and Moroccan expansionism at the expense of Algiers was stopped as a result of a decisive defeat in the Chelif valley in 1701. These developments were both significant in themselves and indicative of more widespread trends, not least the vitality of Islamic powers.

Yet they are generally ignored. Instead, there is a disproportionate emphasis on the course of struggles within Europe; just as battle and sieges receive too much attention in work on early modern warfare and insufficient space is generally devoted to logistics, indecisive campaigns, vacillations among the high command and political contexts. To turn to the Uzbeks, their success in undermining Mughal expansion beyond the Hindu Kush in 1647 indicated the limitations of imperial power and the vitality of forces that were well attuned to the possibilities of difficult terrain. This lesson was to be repeated, on the same terrain, but with the British and Soviets as the defeated parties, in the nineteenth and twentieth centuries.

5 The Pre-Revolutionary Eighteenth Century

The eighteenth through to the early nineteenth century presents a classic example of Euro-centrism in military history thanks to the influence of Frederick the Great, King of Prussia (1740–86), and Napoleon, First Consul (1799–1804) and later Emperor (1804–14, 1815) of France. This is paradoxical because, unlike say Philip II's Spain, the Dutch republic in the seventeenth century, or Victorian Britain, neither Frederician Prussia nor Napoleonic France had much direct military impact outside Europe. Frederick II and his forces did not fight at all beyond Europe, and the Prussian navy was both small and of slight consequence.

At the very end of the eighteenth century, Napoleon famously campaigned in Egypt, but his reign saw France contract militarily as its overseas empire was lost. To begin an account of military history in the period by arguing that attention should not primarily be devoted to Prussia or France is to draw attention both to other regions of the world, to the European power most able at this time to achieve global capability, Britain, and to Russia, the European power that achieved most gains at the expense of the Turks.

As in the two previous centuries, the direct European military impact in Asia and the Middle East was limited and, in a marked reversal of the situation between 1560 and 1660, China itself was one of the most expansionist powers of the century. Yet elsewhere the European military impact was increasingly apparent. As far as Gibbon's clash between civilisation and the 'barbarians' was concerned, the traditional route of nomadic irruption into Europe came under European control, as Russia, thanks to its successes against the Ottomans in 1736–9, 1768–74 and 1787–92, seized the lands north of the Black Sea. In addition, the annexation of the Khanate of the Crimean Tatars in 1783 by Catherine the Great of Russia brought to an end a power that had once threatened Moscow and marked the extinction of one of the leading names among the 'barbarians'.

The Europeans made appreciable gains in North America, but there were also important signs of 'barbarian' resilience. This was particularly the case in south-west Asia, as in the successes of the Afghans against the Persians in the 1710s and 1720s, the rebellions of Arab and Kurdish tribes in Iraq against Ottoman rule in the 1730s and 1740s, threatening Basra in 1741, and an Arab revolt against Persian rule in 1741. As part of a programme of response, in 1753 the Turks attacked the Yezidis of Sinjar whose raids were threatening the caravan routes between Iraq and Syria.

Whereas China made major gains at the expense of the Mongols, the Türkmen of Xinjiang and the Tibetans, and the peoples between China and Russia were mostly brought under the control of one or the other, no such process characterised the situation in south-west Asia. Russia, Turkey, Persia and Mughal India were unable to subdue both the intervening peoples and other neighbouring tribes, and Persia succumbed to

Afghan attack. More generally, it has been argued that the period 1720–60 witnessed a tribal breakout, especially by Afghan, Persian, Türkmen and Arab tribes invading the neighbouring states and increasing the importance of tribal cavalry in the region.[1] Gibbon's sense that advances by nomadic peoples might not have ceased appeared justified.

Transoceanic initiatives rested with the Europeans, not least because their trading systems enabled them to acquire the naval stores, such as hemp, sailcloth and iron, essential for maritime power, while they also had techniques and systems for constructing, maintaining and supplying sizeable fleets of ocean-going warships. Indeed, in the eighteenth century, no non-European power emulated the seventeenth-century naval moves of the Omanis and of Coxinga which had both thrown the Europeans on to the defensive, albeit in a regional context. The Omanis had taken Mombasa not Luanda, Rio de Janeiro or Lisbon; Coxinga had captured Fort Zeelandia, not Malacca, Batavia or Amsterdam.

On land, the advances of the British in India from 1757 and the establishment of a British position in Australia in 1788 are well known, but there were also many other less prominent moves, such as the development of a French base at Cayenne in South America in the 1760s or the capture in 1785 by a Dutch fleet of Kuala Selangor and of Riouw, the island that controlled the eastern approach to the Strait of Malacca. In addition, the process by which European military experts and arms were used by non-European rulers continued. Both were important in the case of the Marathas of India. Kamehameha I, who fought his way to supremacy in the Hawaiian archipelago in the 1790s, did so in part thanks to his use of European arms. Guns replaced spears, clubs, daggers and sling-shots, leading to convincing victories, such as that of Nuuanu (1795) which made Kamehameha ruler of the archipelago.

34. *The Battle of Fontenoy, 11 May 1745*, by Louis-Nicolas van Blarenberghe. This battle contrasts with another punishing and long battle, that between the Afghans and Marathas at Panipat in 1761. At Fontenoy, which was mostly an infantry battle, cavalry played a far smaller role and cannon and field fortifications were more important. Although, like the Marathas, a coalition army, the Allies at Fontenoy fought in a more coherent fashion. In both battles, staying-power was crucial. Fontenoy was more a victory of the defence than Panipat.

35. (*right*) Infantry plug bayonet by Timothy Tindall. Developed in the seventeenth century, the plug bayonet, a knife with a tapered handle that could be placed in the muzzle of muskets, enabled musketeers to stand up against infantry and cavalry attack, but muskets could not be fired when they were in place and they also damaged the barrel. In the 1680s and 1690s, plug bayonets gave way to ring and socket fittings. Europeans embraced the use of the bayonet far more readily than other societies using gunpowder and this helped to make their infantry more effective.

36. Muskets, English or Flemish *c.* 1642 (*above*) and English *c.* 1640. Like the cannon, the musket was a weapon that experienced considerable modification in the early-modern period. The change related both to the weapons themselves and to their use. Disciplined volley fire was particularly important, not least because it compensated for the principal problems of the musket, its low rate of fire and limited accuracy.

This broad account is largely similar to that for the seventeenth century, and it is appropriate to seek greater detail in order to detect the nature and degree of change. The relative military capability of the Europeans was greater in the eighteenth than in the previous century, both on land and at sea. On land, pikemen were replaced by more musketeers, their defensive capacity improved by the bayonets on their muskets at the turn of the seventeenth and eighteenth centuries. Flintlocks replaced matchlocks. Both changes increased the firepower of European infantry. In addition, the essential standardisation of its weaponry improved the infantry's manoeuvrability. As drill and discipline were essential to firepower, the change in weapons system permitting more effective drill was also important. The development of the elevating screw and improvements in casting techniques increased the effectiveness of artillery.

In mid-century, Britain and France clashed for control of parts of India and North America. In the former, they both mostly employed Indian troops, but in North America, although native Americans and European settler militias were used on both sides, there was also a Europeanisation of the war, with the deployment of armies of hitherto unprecedented size for the region. Combined land–sea operations, lengthy sieges and broad-ranging strategic plans also came to play a major role.

Naval Developments

At sea, the large fleets of heavily gunned ships of the line employing line-ahead tactics developed by a number of European powers in the second half of the seventeenth century became more capable of long-distance operations in the eighteenth, thanks in part to changes in ship design.

No non-European power matched Europe's naval development. The British destroyed the base and fleet of the Angres of West India in 1756. This victory owed much to Maratha support. The Omani Arabs did not increase their naval range, although in 1717 or 1718 their fleet conquered Bahrain. Oman itself was the target of a military intervention by Nadir Shah of Persia, who sought to create a Persian Gulf navy based at Bushire, with a supporting cannon foundry at Gombroom. He forced the sale of ships by the English and Dutch East India Companies and by 1737 had a fleet that included four sizeable warships, two of which he had obtained from the English. After an unsuccessful attempt by the Persian fleet to capture Basra from the Turks in 1735, Bahrain was seized the following year. In 1737 the fleet carried 5,000 troops to Oman, in 1738, 6,000 men.

As more generally with many European expeditions, it is necessary to see the Persian campaigns not as a conflict between two clearly separated powers, but as a struggle in which elements of both sides cooperated. Thus, in 1737 and 1738 the Persians invaded in alliance with the Imam of Oman and were resisted by his rebellious subjects under Bal 'arab ibn Himyar Al-Ya 'riba, who was defeated in both years; but each year the allies fell out. The Persian expedition also suffered from a serious shortage of food and money, and in 1740 the navy, which had defeated the Arab fleet the previous year, mutinied.

A fresh attempt to build up the fleet was made from 1740. Nadir Shah sought to purchase foreign ships, ordered 11 from Surat in 1741, and more ships were built at Bushire from that year. After being reduced to a precarious hold on the port of Julfār in 1739–42,

37. The Battle of Sole Bay, 1672. In the Third Anglo-Dutch War, the Dutch under De Ruyter surprised the English under James, Duke of York, and their French allies, inflicting much damage and delaying a planned attack on the Dutch coast.

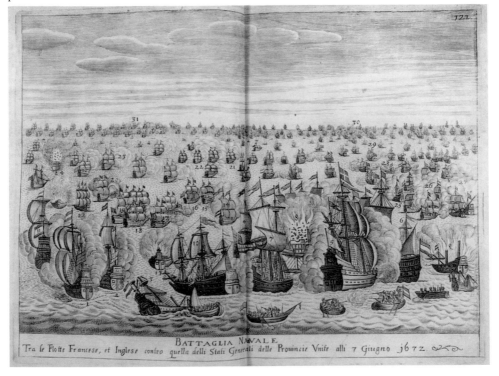

BATTAGLIA NAVALE
Tra le Flotte Francese, et Inglese contro quella delli Stati Generali delle Prouincie Vnite alli 7 Giugno 1672.

the Persians benefited from a fresh civil war in Oman in 1742. However, alternative commitments, especially against the Turks, led to a shortage of funds and provisions, leading the Persian troops to desert and surrender, and the Persian commander rebelled against Nadir.[2] A lack of reinforcements led to the abandonment of the Persian presence in Oman in 1744: wars with the Uzbeks and the Turks were more important. The Persians did not persist with their maritime schemes; pressure on the Mughals and Baluchistan was exerted overland, but not by sea.

The Ottoman Persian Gulf fleet based at Basra made even less of an impact than its Persian counterpart during the century. Ottoman naval power was far more important in the Black Sea and the Mediterranean, but the Turks were defeated by the Russians in the Aegean at the battles of Chios and Chesmé in 1770, with the loss of 23 warships, and in the Black Sea at the battles of the Dnieper (1788) and Tendra (1790): the Turks lost 12 warships in the latter two engagements, the Russians only one. The naval forces of the North African powers – Morocco, Algiers and Tunis – were essentially privateering forces, appropriate for commerce raiding, but not fleet engagements. The Sakalava and Betsimisaraka of Madagascar developed fleets of outrigger canoes that by the end of the century could raid as far as the mainland of northern Mozambique, but logistical factors limited their range, and these fleets were essentially for raiding. War canoes were used on the coastal lagoons of West Africa and in the 1780s a free Black from Brazil introduced brass swivel guns in the canoe fleets, but, again, the range of these forces was limited.

Greater European military capability, however, was of less effect in terms of the European/non-European balance than might otherwise have been anticipated. In large part, this was because the Europeans devoted most of their military resources to conflict with each other. Gibbon's account of European powers struggling with each other could be extended to encompass such conflict in different parts of the world, for example the Anglo-French wars in North America. Yet this did not generally lead to the deployment of substantial forces against non-Europeans, especially in the first three-quarters of the century. There was no attempt at this stage to use naval power to force the Chinese or Japanese to trade or to trade upon certain terms, no prelude to the gunboat commerce that was to come in the following century. Conflict with non-Europeans was more limited and was often a direct consequence of European rivalries, as in the Anglo-French struggle in India during the 1740s and 1750s which involved allied and client rulers.

If improved naval capability did not translate into new relationships with non-European powers, the greater effectiveness of European firepower was not without consequence. The British victory at Plassey in Bengal in 1757 might seem an obvious example of this process. However, such an analysis should not be pushed too hard. British victory at Plassey owed much to dissension among the Nawab of Bengal's army, while the Nawab had to divide his forces to meet a possible attack by the founder of the Afghan Durrani dynasty, Ahmad Khān.[3] Furthermore, Ottoman resilience was amply displayed in the Austro-Turkish war of 1737–9, and Russian victory over the Turks in 1768–74 involved more than simply better battlefield firepower.

European–Turkish Conflict

Nevertheless, and again clearly in contrast to the situation until 1683, the general trend in the struggle with the Turks was in favour of the Christian powers, although not initially. In 1710, concerned about Russian control in Poland and influenced by opponents of Russia, especially Charles XII of Sweden, the Ottomans declared war on Peter the Great and he responded by invading the Balkans. As with many other European assaults in the early modern period, this involved an attempt to divide his opponents. The common tactic was to gain support from peoples who had been forcibly absorbed into the rival state: Spain and the Aztecs, Adal and Ethiopia, the Austrians and the Balkans in the 1680s, are obvious examples. Peter, who had gained effective control of the Ukraine through force in 1708–9, was himself vulnerable to this tactic.[4] In 1711 he issued appeals for assistance to 'the Montenegrin People' and to 'the Christian People under Turkish rule'. Peter also signed a treaty with Demetrius Cantemir, Hospodar of Moldavia and thus, hitherto, client ruler for the Turks, providing for Russian protection over an independent Moldavia under his rule and Moldavian assistance against the Turks. If successful, this agreement would have taken Russian power to the Black Sea.

Peter's invasion was, however, a humiliating failure. The restructuring of army and state that had brought victory over Charles XII of Sweden at Poltava in 1709 did not have comparable results against the Turks: the ability to deploy strength effectively at a distance against them proved elusive. Advancing in 1711 from Kiev, the acquisition of which under Tsar Alexis had greatly improved Russian military capability in the region, the 54,000-strong army marched through Poland towards Moldavia, but was badly affected by supply problems and by Tatar harassment. Both had also seriously affected Prince Golitsyn's unsuccessful advances on the Crimea in 1687 and 1689, and indicated the problems of campaigning on what were in effect land oceans – regions without urban bases or a population from which supplies could be obtained.

38. The Battle of Naseby, 1645, seen from the parliamentarian side. Charles I had only 3,600 cavalry and 4,000 foot; Fairfax, the Commander-in-Chief of the New Model Army, 14,000 men. The royalist general Prince Rupert swept the parliamentary left from the field, but then attacked the baggage train, while Oliver Cromwell on the parliamentary right defeated the royalist cavalry and then turned on the royalist infantry in the centre which succumbed to the more numerous parliamentarian forces.

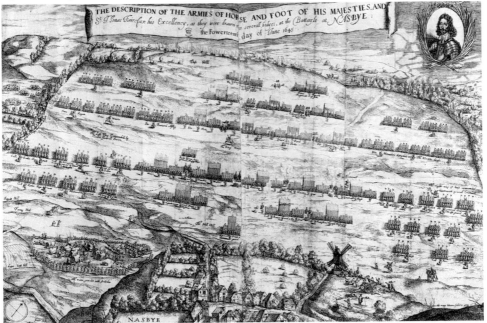

In 1711 Peter the Great received Moldavian support, but the speedy advance of a large Ottoman army dissuaded Constantine Brancovan, the Hospodar of Wallachia, from sending his promised forces, and he, instead, blocked the march of Peter's Serbian reinforcements. The failure of the Moldavian harvest further affected Russian logistics. The movement of a large army over a long distance into hostile territory was a difficult undertaking. Indeed, it was one in which naval power, where the ratio of force to manpower was higher, offered benefits if it could be employed. One of Russia's principal disadvantages as a power was that its access to water and its naval capability were limited, a problem that was to encourage Russian leaders to establish ports such as St Petersburg, Sevastopol and Vladivostok.

In 1711 Peter planned to reach the Danube before the Turks could cross and was encouraged by inaccurate reports that the Turks feared him. The Russians, however, advanced too slowly and lost the initiative. By advancing as one army they increased logistical pressures and made it easier for the Turks to encircle them. Far larger Turkish forces were already across the Danube and moving north along the right bank of the Pruth. Peter was surprised, outmanoeuvred and surrounded as he retreated. The mobile Tatars blocked the Russian avenue of retreat towards Jassy. Based on the hills dominating the Russian position, the Ottoman artillery bombarded the Russian camp. Ottoman attacks were repelled only with difficulty and, short of food, water and forage, Peter was forced to sign a peace agreement in July 1711.[5]

This was not the sole Ottoman success in the 1710s; indeed in 1711–15 the Ottomans enjoyed more military triumphs than any power in Europe. The Turks drove the Venetians from the Morea in 1715, although that was in part a product of weak resistance. But the situation was very different on the crucial Hungarian front where war resumed in 1716. The Ottomans besieged the Austrian general Prince Eugene in a fortified camp at Peterwardein (Petrovaradin). Eugene, however, sallied out on 5 August with 70,000 men and beat his 120,000 opponents. The Turkish janizaries had some success against the Austrian infantry, but the Austrian cavalry drove their opponents from the field, leaving the exposed janizaries to be decimated. Possibly up to 30,000 Turks, including the Grand Vizier, Silahdar Ali Pasha, were killed. As on other occasions, for example Rocroi in the Thirty Years War (1643) and Naseby in the English Civil War (1645), a strong infantry force, exposed and placed on the defensive by the loss of the cavalry battle, became vulnerable.

Eugene successfully combined battles and sieges, a strategic ability that often eluded early modern generals and one that reflected both his own skill and the capability of the Austrian army. After his victory, Eugene marched on Temesvár, which had defied the Austrians in the 1690s, and which controlled or threatened much of eastern Hungary. Well fortified and protected by river and marshes, Temesvár, nevertheless, surrendered on 23 October after heavy bombardment.

In 1717 Eugene advanced to attack Belgrade, crossing the Danube to the east of the city on 15 June. Belgrade had a substantial garrison of 30,000 men under Mustafa Pasha, and in August the main field army, 150,000-strong under the Grand Vizier, Halil Pasha, arrived to relieve the city. They commenced bombarding the Austrians from higher ground. In a difficult position, Eugene resolved on a surprise attack, and on the morning of 16 August, 60,000 Austrians advanced through the fog to crush Halil's army. This led to the surrender of Belgrade six days later and in 1718 to the Peace of Passarowitz which left Austria with substantial territorial gains: the Banat of Temesvár, Little (Western) Wallachia, and northern Serbia.

The battle of Belgrade was a confused engagement. It was not a matter of clear-cut

The Battle of CHIARI, between the Imperialists, Commanded by his Highness Prince Eugene of SAVOY, and the French and Spaniards, Commanded by M. de Villeroy, 1st September 1701.
1. Prince Eugene. 2. Chiari. 3. Hills & Eminces, refused by the Imperialists. 4. The French and Spanish Troops in Battle Array. 5. The Imperial Army in Battalia. 6. The Imperial Horse.

39. Battle of Chiari, 1 September 1701. The Austrians under Prince Eugene defeated the Franco-Spanish army under Villeroi. Eugene's career – fighting both Turks and Bourbons – indicated the variety of opponent faced by some European armies. Victorious at Zenta in 1697, Eugene then transplanted the mobility of warfare in Hungary to western Europe, displaying boldness of manoeuvre in north Italy in 1701–2 and 1706. He did not allow the French emphasis on the defence to thwart his drive for battle and victory.

formations exchanging fire, and great caution is required before judging it a triumph for European firepower. Yet it did show the battlefield quality of some European units in the face of superior numbers. The firepower deficit that had characterised the Hungarians at Mohacs in 1526 had been amply rectified.

The next period of conflict was in 1735–9. This involved two related struggles: Russo-Turkish[6] and Austro-Turkish. The former involved fewer battles, largely because the lands to the north of the Black Sea were marginal to the central area of Ottoman military concern in Europe: the Danube valley. Instead, the Russians took the initiative in their conflict and the war was therefore a matter of how far they were able to exert their force successfully in a hostile terrain and at a considerable distance. If it apparently centred on successful sieges – Azov in 1736, Ochakov in 1737 and Khotin in 1738 – the true operational challenge was in fact that of distance and terrain. When in 1736 the Russians invaded the Crimea for the first time, the Tatars avoided battle and the invaders, debilitated by disease and heat and short of food and water, retreated. Further invasions of the Crimea in 1737 and 1738 were also unsuccessful. In the 1737 Crimean campaign the Russians lost 34,500 to disease, but only 2,114 men on the battlefield. The logistical task was formidable, although Russian logistical capability had increased with the creation of the Commissariat of War in 1711 and improvements in provisioning in 1724. The force that advanced on Ochakov in 1737 was supported by supplies brought by boat down the Dnieper and thence by 28,000 carts.

Disease and logistical problems prevented further Russian advances in 1737, and in 1738 the same difficulties ended Field Marshal Münnich's hopes of crossing the Dniester to invade the Balkans. Ochakov was abandoned in the face of a major outbreak of the plague which killed thousands of Russians. Tatar irregular cavalry was also a formidable challenge, employing a scorched-earth policy in which crops and forage were burnt and wells poisoned; this had already been used in the Crimea in 1736. In 1737, the Tatars burnt the grass between the Bug and the Dniester, hindering Münnich's operations after he captured Ochakov. Münnich, a German who was also President of the College of War, was overly influenced by German tactics and methods. His preference for heavy cavalry and heavy guns was inappropriate for war with the Turks, and robbed his army of necessary mobility.

Yet it would be mistaken to stress failure, to argue that the Russian military machine was rendered useless by the combination of irregular or 'barbarian' opponents and a hostile terrain. The Russians were successful at siege warfare, so that, deprived of the cover of a field army, Turkish fortifications were vulnerable, as was shown at both Azov and Ochakov. In addition, in 1739 an advance across Polish territory was successful. Münnich avoided the lands and Tatars near the Black Sea, crossed the Dniester well upstream, and drove the Ottoman army from its camp at Stavuchanakh. The battle of Stavuchanakh initially looked like a replay of the 1711 débâcle. The Russians' forward advance road was blocked by 80,000–90,000 Turks dug in behind three lines of entrenchments, with 11 batteries totalling 70 guns; meanwhile Tatar cavalry had encircled the Russian flanks. However, the result was different. Münnich managed to extricate his forces by leading them over 27 pontoon bridges across the Shulanets River, with all their artillery and baggage. The Russians reassembled in one mass on the other bank of the river, placed their artillery on the heights, and advanced against the Turks, who broke and fled to Khotin. Russian losses were minor. Münnich ascribed his victory to his emphasis on aimed fire.[7]

Münnich then captured the major fortress of Khotin and the Moldavian capital of Jassy. The Moldavian nobility pledged loyalty to Empress Anna. Thus the Russian military system could deliver victory, although it was greatly helped by the degree to which the Turks concentrated on the Austrians. However, in 1739 this was also to let the Russians down, for the Austrians, having fared badly in the war, made a unilateral peace with the Ottomans.

Austria's poor performance in the war shows the danger of assuming either that the Ottomans were exhausted militarily or that military history moved and moves in terms of a smooth progression. The Austrian advance into Serbia in 1737 saw their most unsuccessful year of campaigning in the Balkans since 1695. Field-Marshall Seckendorf advanced into Serbia in 1737, but was then driven back, although Turkish attempts to subvert the Habsburg position in Transylvania were unsuccessful. The Turks ravaged Habsburg Wallachia and Serbia in early 1738, and in June they besieged New Orsova. Under their new commander, Count Königsegg, the Austrians set out to relieve the fortress, defeating the Turks nearby at Cornea. The Turks then lifted the siege but, in face of a second Turkish army, and, despite another victory near Mehadia, Königsegg retreated, abandoning both Mehadia and New Orsova. The Austrian army was decimated by disease: the Danube valley with its marshes was very unhealthy, especially in the summer.

Command in 1739 was entrusted to Count Wallis, an Irishman in Habsburg service, but at Grocka/Krozka, south-east of Belgrade, his advancing troops suffered heavy casualties when forcing their way through a defile in the face of the Ottoman army. Although the Austrians won control of the battlefield, Wallis erred on the side of caution

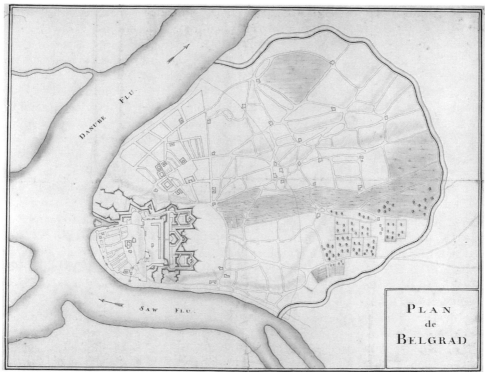

40. Plan of Belgrade *c.* 1720, showing proposed fortifications. Captured by the Austrians in 1717, after the Turkish relief army had been defeated, this crucial position on the Danube was then extensively refortified, with a new enceinte (perimeter) of eight substantial bastions. However, defeats in the field and a collapse of confidence led the Austrians to surrender the still unbreached fortress in 1739. In 1789 the Austrians regained Belgrade after a heavy bombardment, only to return it at the subsequent peace when under pressure from domestic disorder and the Anglo-Prussian alliance.

and withdrew. Taking advantage of the situation, the Turks besieged Belgrade. This had been refortified by the Austrians since its capture in 1717, but the local Austrian commanders, their confidence gone, surrendered, making peace at the price of Belgrade, Little Wallachia and northern Serbia. The Russians had to make peace also. Their gains in the southern steppe and the retention of an unfortified Azov still left them without a Black Sea coastline.

The Austrian army was in a poor state in 1737–9, badly led, and battered by the recent War of the Polish Succession with France, Sardinia and Spain (1733–5): competition within the European system did not in this case increase effectiveness at the expense of a non-European power. In addition, the standard formation employed by the Austrians – a linear deployment with cavalry on the flanks – was inadequate, both because the numerically inferior Austrian cavalry could not protect the flanks, and because the Turks, rather than attacking on a broad front, used separate attacks on parts of the Austrian front, which made the line formation very vulnerable.[8]

The crisis of the late 1730s illustrated the potential advantage enjoyed by the Ottomans: their central position enabled them to decide which enemy to concentrate on, and it was very difficult for their opponents to coordinate operations. This had a political as well as a military dimension. In the 1730s the Eastern Question emerged in the European policy of the leading East European Christian powers: at heart it was a struggle for the Ottoman succession between Austria and Russia. This greatly helped the Turks. Whereas, earlier on, European rivalry had facilitated Ottoman gains in the Balkans as well as further north and north-west, that same rivalry would delay the processes of de-Ottomanisation in the Balkans. The decline of Habsburg political pressure on the Balkans after 1739 helped to increase Russian influence and from the 1760s Russia replaced the Habsburgs as the crucial political hope of the Balkan Christians.[9]

Again, military developments have to be set in the wider international context. It is difficult to assess the relative development of Christian and Ottoman military capability because the two sides were not continually at war. Furthermore, as a widespread empire, the Ottomans faced problems on many fronts and their military system had to be able to respond. The Ottomans were greatly concerned about developments in Persia where Safavid rule collapsed in 1722 as a result of a successful invasion by Afghans. The Ottomans then overran much of western Persia, but were driven out in 1730 and forced in 1732–3 and 1743 to defend Baghdad from attacks by Nadir Shah, the new ruler of Persia. The Austrians similarly were under multiple threat and were drawn into a struggle to maintain their predominance in Germany when Frederick the Great of Prussia invaded Silesia in 1740, beginning the first of the four Austro-Prussian wars of his reign: 1740–2, 1744–5, 1756–63, 1778–9.

Indeed, war with the Turks did not resume for Russia until 1768, and, for the Austrians, until 1788. In the meanwhile two aspects of military change had occurred. On the Ottoman side there had been stirrings of Westernisation. The Turks achieved most success in developing their navy, altering their fleet from galleys to ships-of-the-line. They had made the change to a predominantly sailing battle fleet already in the late seventeenth century, at the same time as the Venetians built a sailing fleet. The Turks were indeed less conservative than most Italian navies which tenaciously kept several galleys until the end of the eighteenth century when the Turks had already practically abolished theirs, replacing them with small oared craft.

The lesser success of the Turks in modernising their army can be interpreted as a victory for conservatism, and a reflection of the more central role of the army in Turkish culture, society and politics. Conservatism, however, is a universal catch-all of military and other history, not least because it appears to be descriptive, analytical and explanatory as a concept. This is misleading. 'Conservative' societies have a dynamism and adaptability of their own and it is important not to neglect them.

In the case of the Turks it is difficult to show that their military system was obviously defective, and indeed without its strengths, in the mid-eighteenth century. They had captured Kirmanshah in 1723, although they were heavily defeated between Kirmanshah and Hamadan in 1726 and Nadir Shah drove the Ottomans from western and northern Persia in 1730, defeating their army at Nahavand. Nevertheless, the Mughals in 1739 and the Uzbeks in 1740 fared even worse at the hands of Nadir Shah, and the Ottomans successfully defended Baghdad and Mosul from him in 1732–3 and again in 1743. In 1744 Nadir Shah failed to take Kars, despite an 80-day siege, although the following year he routed an 100,000-strong Ottoman army near Erevan.[10] The Russians had made significant gains from the Turks in 1739, but these had been less important than the Turkish success in driving back the Austrians.

Despite a number of successes, there was some support for military innovation in Turkey at the very top. Claude-Alexandre, Comte de Bonneval, a French noble who had fallen out successively with Louis XIV and Prince Eugene, converted to Islam and sought to Westernise the Turkish army in the 1730s. He also attempted to modernise the manufacture of munitions and in 1734 opened a military engineering school. Other foreign advisers were brought in by Sultan Abdulhamit I (1774–89), who did not require them to convert and adopt Ottoman ways. Baron François de Tott, a Hungarian noble who had risen in the French artillery, was influential in the 1770s. In 1774 he established a new rapid-fire artillery corps, and he also built a modern cannon foundry and a new mathematics school. Such moves were aspects of the attempted diffusion of weaponry, tactics and military infrastructure, in this case aspects of Westernisation.

However, interest in Westernisation was resisted by sections of the official elite supported by the *ulema*, the religious judges, and an important section of the masses, leading at times to violent opposition, as in the Patrona Halil rebellion of 1730. There was a parallel with Petrine Russia, but there the elite offered less resistance, not least because it did not align with religious groups that opposed Westernisation. These groups were also less important within the structure of established religion, the Russian Orthodox church, than their equivalents in the Ottoman empire.

Aside from Westernisation, developments within a system, in this case the competitive emulation of European warfare, were also important. This emulation was at a high point at sea from the 1720s, as the French began to build a new fleet, and on land in the mid-eighteenth century, as Prussian successes led Austria, France and Russia to respond with major attempts to improve their military effectiveness. These responses to failure were matched more generally. Thus, for example, the French navy responded to defeat in the Seven Years War with a postwar programme of reconstruction and reform, and did the same after the War of American Independence.

Attempts to standardise weaponry were an important aspect of enhanced European effectiveness, a process that reduced the role of craft skills – knowledge of the characteristics and quirks of a particular weapon – and, instead, enhanced those of regularity. In this sense, arms manufacture heralded modern industrial techniques. It was part of the shift to modern industrial production, especially in terms of the declining role of the craftsman. In a similar way, American arms manufacturers were central to the industrialisation of American production in the nineteenth century. Thus, for example, José Patiño, the Spanish naval minister in 1718–36, sought to ensure that all six-pound cannon balls weighed six pounds.

Such standardisation was a counterpart to the emphasis on drill and discipline that was so important for the maximisation of firepower on land and sea. In the case of the Russians, a series of new cannon provided greater firepower, while exercises built up the speed and accuracy of the artillery so that it became more effective in battle. The Austrian artillery also improved greatly in mid-century. The daily rate of march in the Russian army improved. The Russians also made progress in the use of field fortifications, the handling of battle formations, and the use of light troops. The adoption of more flexible means of supply helped to reduce the cumbersome baggage train of the Russian field army, although logistics remained a serious problem until the development of railroads, not least because of the primitive nature of the empire's administrative system.[11] More generally, the Russians developed a professionalised officer corps concerned to transform Russian military capability through their own solutions rather than through the adoption of those of other European countries. This influenced strategic and tactical thinking and practice.

These improvements all helped the Russians against the Turks when war resumed in 1768, as, more generally, did the recent combat experience of the Russian army in the Seven Years War (1756–63), and their long tradition of adaptation to steppe warfare against Turks and Tatars. The aggressive, offensive tactics and strategy employed by the Russians in the Seven Years War and earlier conflicts were more successful thanks to the improvements in the army introduced in mid-century. Combined, they proved very potent. Russian strategic planning was far better than in previous Russo-Turkish wars. In 1769 Golitsyn captured Khotin and Jassy, the position Münnich had only reached in 1739. Golitsyn's replacement, Count Peter Rumyantsev, was a firm believer in the offensive, both strategic and tactical. This was a matter of temperament, but also reflected Rumyantsev's awareness of the logistical difficulties faced by a large army and his grasp of the need to take the initiative. In 1770, he advanced down the Pruth, successively storming the main Ottoman positions at the battles of Ryabaya Mogila, Larga and Kagul. The Ottomans sustained heavy losses, while Russian casualties were relatively low.[12]

In battle, Rumyantsev abandoned traditional linear tactics and, instead, organised his infantry into columns able to advance rapidly and independently, and reform into divisional squares, while affording mutual support in concerted attacks. The columns included mobile artillery, which played a major role, and relied on firepower to repel Ottoman assaults. A major role, however, was also played by bayonet charges: firepower was followed by hand-to-hand fighting. In both strategic and tactical terms, Rumyantsev took the offensive. His campaign on the Pruth in 1770 was a great improvement on that of Peter the Great in 1711. The Russian army had become more professional and effective.

Only those who have a blinkered view of *ancien régime* European warfare can deny its capacity for change and development. It is misleading to imagine that offensive tactics were invented by the French revolutionaries: the column did not have to wait for ideological developments. Warfare in Eastern Europe often seems more innovative than in the West, and yet in the eyes of eighteenth-century Western European intellectuals and much subsequent scholarship the powers of the region were allegedly more 'backward', politically, culturally, economically and militarily.

After his victories over larger forces on the River Pruth, Rumyantsev advanced to the lower Danube, where he rapidly captured the major fortresses of Izmail, Kilia and Braila. Akkerman and Bucharest also fell. Having sailed from the Baltic to the Mediterranean in 1769–70, the Russian navy defeated the Turks at Chesmé (1770), a victory primarily due to the effective use of fireships against the closely-moored Turkish fleet. In 1771 the Crimea was overrun, but in 1772 the Russians were distracted by the First Partition of Poland and in 1773 by the Pugachev serf rising.

In 1774 Rumyantsev again made significant advances: he seized the major Ottoman Danube fortresses of Silistria and Rushchuk and his advance guard routed the main Ottoman army near Kozludzhi. The Ottoman fortress system had been totally breached, the Russians had pushed south of the Danube, and the Ottomans had lost the major agricultural areas of Wallachia and Moldavia. The Turks hastily made peace by the Treaty of Kutchuk-Kainardji (1774), by which the Russians gained territory to the north of the Black Sea, including the coast as far as the Dniester, and in the Caucasus, as well as the right to navigate the Black Sea. Victory over the Turks ensured that the latter could not prevent Russian gains at the expense of Poland in the First Partition of Poland. This success marked the culmination of the process by which Russia became the dominant Christian power in the region, rather than Lithuania, and later Poland-Lithuania, which had seemed, and had often been, more powerful in the region for most of the period since the fifteenth century.

Russian success was not simply a matter of the effective use of weaponry. The Turks were also handicapped by poor leadership. In 1770, for example, the Grand Vizier, Mehmed Emin Pasha, lacked military competence, had no effective plan and was unable to arrange adequate supplies or pay for his army. Poor leadership was in part redeemable. Yet, whatever allowances are made, the Russo-Turkish war of 1768–74 was an impressive display of Russian military prowess, especially in contrast to earlier campaigns.[13]

Russian Expansion

Russian victories were possibly the most pointed example of European military success over non-Europeans in the pre-revolutionary eighteenth century. Yet they were by no means the sole example. In the case of the Russians, it is also pertinent to note continued expansion in Siberia. The poorly armed Itelmens of Kamchatka, who relied on bone or stone-tipped arrows and on slings, were brutalised in the Russian search for furs. They rose in 1706 but were suppressed. When they rose in 1731 the Itelmen had some firearms obtained from the Russians and were able to inflict many casualties as a result, but they were eventually crushed, while their numbers were further hit by the diseases that accompanied their adversaries. Another rising in 1741 was defeated.

The Koraks of Kamchatka were more formidable than the Itelmens, effective with bows and captured firearms, fierce and willing to unite against the Russians. Relations were murderous and the Russians sought to kill as many Koraks as possible, not least in the war of 1745–56. The Koraks then submitted. The Chukchi of north-east Siberia were also formidable, defeating a Cossack expedition in 1729, and resisting genocidal attacks in 1730–1 and 1744–7. The Russians eventually stopped the war, abandoning their fort at Anadyrsk in 1764, although it had successfully resisted siege as recently as 1762. Trade links developed and the Russians finally recognised Chukchi rights to their territories.[14]

The Russians also expanded at the expense of Persia. Peter the Great advanced along the Caspian Sea in 1722–3. He hoped to benefit from the disintegration of Persia in order to gain control of the silk routes, annex territory and pre-empt Ottoman expansion. Derbent fell in 1722, Baku and Rasht in 1723. The Russian advance was preceded by careful planning: naval and cartographical missions explored and mapped the coastline and an army officer examined the roads.[15] Yet aspects of the campaign were mismanaged: logistics were poor, especially the supply of food and ammunition. In this sense, more facets of warfare were becoming professionalised, but the key element of long-distance combat, logistics, remained poorly organised and arbitrary in part.

The Russians found their Caspian conquests of little use: large numbers of garrison troops, possibly up to 130,000 men, were lost through disease and, at a time of rising Persian power, the lands to the south of the Caspian were ceded by the Russians in 1732. The Russians also made gains to the north-east of the Caspian, although, further east, an expedition sent to discover gold sands in Dzhungaria was forced to retreat in 1715 in the face of superior forces that threatened their communications. A second expedition sent in 1719 was clearly defeated in spite of Russian superiority in firearms. Relations with the Dzhungars had already been exacerbated by the Russian advance into the upper reaches of the Ob. Biysk was founded as a base in 1709, but the Dzhungars responded by destroying it and besieging Kuznetsk unsuccessfully. This led to a standard Russian response: expansion and consolidation through fortification. In reply to the Dzhungars, a series of forts was built on the Irtysh, including Omsk (1716) and Ust'-Kamenogorsk (1719). Furthermore, the Russian position in the Altay foothills was protected by the Kuznetsk-Kolyvan' Line, designed to block Kalmyk raids.

Prince Cherkasskii, who founded two Russian fortresses on the eastern shores of the Caspian in 1715–16, was less successful when ordered to persuade the Khan of Khiva to accept Russian suzerainty and, thereafter, to investigate the route to India. His force was attacked by Khivans, Uzbeks and Kazaks in 1717, and, although protected within their camp by firepower, the army was annihilated when it left camp. Nevertheless, the Bashkirs were suppressed in the 1730s and 1740s. Relations with the Kazaks improved from 1731 and the Kalmyks provided assistance against the Bashkirs. Control over the latter was anchored by a new line of forts from the Volga to the new fort at Orenburg, built from 1733. The Usinskaya Line based at Troitsk (1743) was constructed along the River Uy to protect the agricultural zone to the east of the Urals. The Ishim Line was superseded as Russian settlement advanced southwards, and was replaced by Petropavlovsk (1752) and its Presnogor'kovskaya Line (1755). These southward advances of fortifications paralleled the offensive tactics of Russian infantry and artillery. Gibbon's 'cannon and fortifications' were employed not only in a defensive fashion against 'barbarians', but also in an offensive manner, matching their transoceanic use by Western Europeans.

By the second half of the century, a chain of forts, over 4,000 kilometres in length, extended from the Caspian to Kuznetsk in the foothills of the Altay. They were more effective than the Spanish *presidios* in North America, not least because the Russians devoted more military resources to the task; five regular infantry regiments alone were added to the Irtysh Line in 1745. Rivalries between the Kazaks, Kalmyks and Bashkirs played a major role in enabling the Russians to conquer the last. The Kazaks had turned to the Russians for military assistance against the Dzhungars in 1731 and the Kazak Younger Horde became a Russian vassal, followed by the Middle Horde in 1740.[16]

North Africa

If conflict along the Christian-Islamic 'frontier' in Europe was frequent and in Asia less so, there was little movement in North Africa. The Algerians had captured Oran in 1708 at a time when Spain was convulsed by civil war and foreign intervention. In 1732 a united and stronger Spain retook the port, but that attack was the only one mounted in the region in a period of Spanish activity and expansion. Instead, Philip V preferred to launch attacks on Sardinia (1717), Sicily (1718, 1734), Naples (1734) and Savoy (1743). Ceuta resisted Moroccan sieges in 1694–1720 and 1732, and Melilla another in 1774–5; but the Portuguese lost Mazagam to Morocco in 1765, and a French attempt to land at Larache in Morocco in 1765 failed in the face of heavy fire. In East Africa, the Portuguese regained Mombasa in 1728, but lost it again in 1729, and another attempt failed in 1769.

South-East Asia

In South Asia, with the exception of India, the Europeans were most effective on islands rather than on the mainland. The Dutch East India Company played an important role in Java, intervening in disputes in the kingdom of Mataram in the First and Second Javanese Wars of Succession (1704–8, 1719–23). However, the Dutch army was weak and its ability to operate successfully away from coastal areas was limited, as was shown in the Third Javanese War of Succession in 1746–57, and in operations against Bantam in 1750. Dutch garrisons were forced to withdraw from Kartasura, the capital of Mataram, in 1686 and in 1741. By a treaty of 1749, the Dutch acquired sovereignty over

Mataram, but this authority amounted to little in practice, and indeed the Dutch had little interest in conquering the interior. Instead, they sought to ensure that the rulers there did not contest their coastal positions and trade.[17] The Dutch had only a small regular force and used local troops extensively.

In 1759 Rajah Muhammad of Siak in Sumatra destroyed the Dutch post at Pulau Gontong, but in 1761 a Dutch punitive expedition avenged the massacre and placed the Rajah's brother on the throne. Victory over Kandy in 1761–6 led to Dutch control of all Ceylon's coastal regions. The Spaniards, however, had scant success in subduing and Christianising the southern Philippines.

On the mainland of South-East Asia, European power was of little consequence. British and French attempts to establish a presence in Burma in the 1750s were unsuccessful. Further west, the Portuguese were hard pressed in India in 1737–40 when they were involved in a disastrous war with the Marathas. Salsette was taken in 1737, Bassein fell after a siege in 1739 and Goa was nearly lost the same year. Chaul was taken in 1740. The Marathas benefited from the support of disaffected peasantry. The peasantry provided an infantry to complement Maratha cavalry, and this infantry was crucial to sucessful sieges. Also in India, the Dutch were defeated by Travancore in 1741. The Persian Gulf remained closed to European power, and the Dutch lost their last base there in 1765. The English left Bandar Abbas in the Gulf in 1763 due to commercial difficulties.

The British in India

Regional conflicts in India brought the Europeans more opportunity for expansion, and a major change in mid-century led to the Europeans developing important land forces there. Both Britain and France came to play an important role in the internecine disputes of the rulers of the Carnatic (south-eastern India) from the 1740s. The French Governor-General, Joseph Dupleix, was a skilled player in the field of South Indian politics, but he was outmanoeuvred by the British and lacked the resources to sustain his ambitions.

Dupleix's ally, Chanda Sahib, became Nawab of the Carnatic in 1749, but a rival claimant was supported by the British. Robert Clive led a diversionary force of 500 which captured Chanda Sahib's capital Arcot, and then held it against massive odds. In 1752 both the French and Chanda Sahib surrendered. A French attempt under Lally to regain their position in the Carnatic during the Seven Years War (1756–63) was initially successful, with the capture of Fort St David in 1758, but the siege of Madras ended after the French were defeated at Masulipatam (1759) and Lally was later routed by Sir Eyre Coote at Wandewash (1760).

The combination of French commitments to European hostilities during the Seven Years War and British naval victories in 1759 prevented France from sending further aid to its colonies. The French revival in India during the American War of Independence (1775–83), when Britain was otherwise distracted and France was not at war on the continent of Europe, bears this out. There was a growing interconnectedness of war around the world: conflict in Europe affected North America or India and vice versa. This was a feature of the eighteenth century, and one that was growing in importance. The connection depended on growing European dominance, although this was still tentative.

Rivalry with France also played a role in British intervention in Bengal, but Britain's opponent there was Indian, Nawab Siraj-ad-Daula of Bengal, who, in 1756, had captured the East India Company's trading base, Fort William, and harshly confined his prisoners in the 'Black Hole of Calcutta'. Clive was sent from Madras with a relief expedition of 850 Europeans and 2,100 Indian *sepoys*, an important deployment of British strength. Fort William was regained, largely thanks to the guns of the British naval squadron under Vice-Admiral Charles Watson. The Nawab then advanced on Calcutta, but was checked by Clive in a confused action fought in a heavy morning fog. This led to a peace during which Clive used fire from Watson's warships to force the French base at Chandernagore to surrender. Clive then decided to replace the Nawab, whom he suspected of intriguing with the French. He reached an agreement with one of the Nawab's generals, Mir Jaffir, and marched on his capital. The Nawab deployed his far larger force at Plassey to block Clive's advance, but the Indians made little attempt to attack, apart from two advances that were checked by artillery and infantry fire. Clive's men then advanced and stormed the Indian encampment. The British position in East India was consolidated by further victories at Patna and Buxar in 1764, in each of which grapeshot fire halted indian attacks and inflicted heavy losses.

The value of European artillery was further demonstrated by the fall of Manila to a British force that had sailed from Madras in 1762. This revealed the vulnerability of European 'artillery fortresses' to an attack conducted by superior artillery and contrasted with the difficulties of non-European powers in taking such fortresses. Colonel George Monson of the British forces recorded:

> An eight gun battery was finished about three hundred yards from the wall the 2nd of October at night, and opened the 3rd in the morning on the south west bastion which immediately silenced the enemy's guns and made a breach in the salient angle of the bastion, the fourth at night batterys were begun to take off the defences of the south east bastion and of the small bastions on the west side of the town; which were opened the fifth by ten o'clock in the morning and had so good an effect, that the general gave out orders for storming the place next day; which was done about seven in the morning, with very little loss, on our side.[18]

However, the fortifications were weak, the garrison small and attack was not anticipated.[19] At Havana, the same year, British artillery was effective against more impressive fortifications:

> our new batteries against the town being perfected (which consisted of forty four pieces of cannon) we all at once, by a signal, opened them and did prodigious execution. Our artillery was so well served and the fire so excessively heavy and incessant, principally against the defences of the place, that the Spaniards could not possibly stand to their guns.[20]

The scale of European firepower was dramatically on the increase. This was revealed in 1760 when the British captured Karikal, on the Carnatic coast of India, from the French. John Call, the British Chief-Engineer in the region, recorded, 'We found 94 guns . . . mounted, and about 155 altogether, 6 mortars and plenty of ammunition'. Call then began preparations to besiege the leading French base in India, Pondicherry, noting he would have '30, 24 pounders, and 20, 18 pounders, besides small guns, 6 large mortars, and 12 Royals or Coehorns [mortars], with ammunition for 40 days firing at 25 cannon [sic] per day'; it fell the following year. Call was inaccurate in his prediction that within ten years Europeans would intervene to determine who controlled Delhi,[21] but his career indicated the potential of European firepower. In 1762 he was responsible for the capture of the major Indian fortress of Vellore; British artillery could prove very effective against native fortifications. In January 1760 Sir Eyre Coote wrote from Chetteput in the Carnatic,

> I invested this place on the 27th at night. On the 28th the army encamped three miles from the garrison; the same night I raised a battery for two 24 pounders, and this morning at day light we began to batter the South West Tower of the Fort. About 11 o'clock beginning to make a breach, a flag of truce was flung out.[22]

Firepower was not the sole key to Britain's victories in India and elsewhere. Mir Jaffir played an important role in Bengal in 1757 where political and military factors interacted. Similarly, in 1774 the British destroyed the Rohilla state in cooperation with Awadh, and it was annexed by Awadh.[23] Nevertheless, firepower was important and it is clear that in this respect the Asians largely failed to match European developments. At Buxar (1764), for example, the Indian army had more cannon and used them to considerable effect,[24] but British firepower was superior. In the 1750s the British East India Company was pleased when Indians in the Carnatic entered their service with their own muskets, but they saw these guns as less satisfactory than European counterparts and replaced them as soon as possible.

One important reason was probably the greater role and prestige of cavalry in Indian armies and a resultant inattention to infantry. Mobile light cavalry was crucial in the Maratha forces, playing for example a central role in their defeat of the Nizam of Hyderabad near Bhopal in 1737. The role of cavalry in Indian warfare was amply displayed at the largest battle of the century, the third battle of Panipat fought on the plains north of Delhi on 14 January 1761. The Afghan victors under Ahmad Khān consisted largely of heavy cavalry equipped with body armour, swords and spears, as well as mounted musketeers armed with flintlocks: the latter had largely replaced mounted archers, and thus represented the transition of traditional Central Asian warfare to gunpowder weaponry. Afghan cavalry attacks, first by mounted musketeers and then by heavy cavalry, were instrumental in the collapse of the Maratha centre. The Afghans, who also had camel-mounted swivel guns, fought well, but their victory also owed much to a lack of coordination among the Marathas, specifically to the absence of an effective central command in what was a conglomeration of different armies; in short political-military factors played a crucial role in the sphere of command and control.[25]

Most of the cavalry of the Indian forces used horses far better than those of the British, and British generals were concerned about how best to respond to Indian cavalry. The Afghan role in supplying horses and cavalry gave them a military importance in India comparable to that of the British.[26] An effective use of light cavalry enabled Haidar Ali of Mysore to check the British in the First Anglo-Mysore War (1767–9).

Some of the Indian rulers undertook major efforts in the closing decades of the century to develop their artillery and to create effective infantry units after the European model. At Panipat the Maratha forces already included the trained infantry of one commander, Ibrahim Gardi. Prithvi Narayan Shah (1742–75), ruler of Gorkha, who unified much of Nepal, sought to adopt British methods of military organisation. In the late eighteenth century, after the combined introduction of flintlocks, bayonets and infantry drill, and under the impact of European challenge and the European example, gunpowder weaponry came to play a greater role in Indian battlefield tactics. Striking power came to replace the former emphasis on mobility.

Far less progress in adaption, indeed Westernisation, was made in South-East Asia. The use of firearms was extensive there, but the volley technique was not adopted. The war

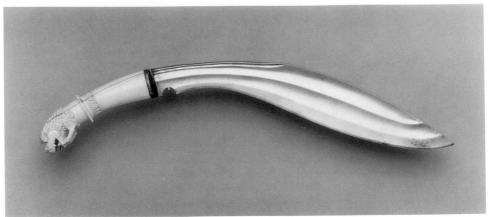

41. Gurkha sword (kukri), nineteenth century. The Gurkhas used both traditional and European weaponry. The terrain ensured that their armies were composed of infantry. Tactics involved extensive use of ambushes, ruses and temporary fortifications, especially stockades. In their war with Britain in 1814–16, the Gurkhas were initially successful, thanks to a combination of defensive positions, especially hill forts and stockades, with attacks on British detachments. British victories in 1815–16 that owed much to the effective use of bayonet attacks, luck, the skill of commanding officers, and the failure of the Sikhs and Marathas to support the Gurkhas, turned the tide.

elephant, pikes, swords and spears were still the dominant weaponry, and firearms made little impact on tactics. By the eighteenth century the South-East Asians had abandoned the attempt to keep pace with new developments in the production of both firearms and gunpowder. Thus, wheel-lock and flintlock mechanisms were not reproduced in South-East Asian foundries; only matchlocks were made.[27]

Again, this did not pose a problem for the states of the period. It was possible to be successful and dynamic without European-style firearms, as the new Burmese dynasty, the Konbaung, showed in the second half of the century. This did not mean complete indifference to European firearms: in 1787 King Bo-daw-hpaya sought firearms from the French at their Bengal base of Chandernagore.[28] However, without them in 1784–5, he had conquered Arakan, regained part of Laos, overrun the Kra Isthmus and advanced on Chiangmai in Siam.

China

Similarly in East Asia, in China and Japan, there was no attempt to transform armies, or indeed to develop naval power. The Chinese still used matchlock, not flintlock, muskets and scarcely seemed to need military modernisation. There was no maritime threat, and on land China expanded rapidly.

Having captured Formosa, driven the Russians from the Amur region and taken control of Outer Mongolia in 1690–7, the Chinese sustained the pace of their expansion. In part, they maintained the dynamic of their campaigns against the Mongols and moved into areas where Mongol power was at issue. Tibet had been under the partial control of the Mongols since 1642 when the last king was deposed, but their relationship with the Dalai Lama was not always easy. The important role Tibetan Buddhism played in Mongol politics encouraged Chinese intervention. A dispute over the succession to the Dalai Lama from 1705 led to Chinese diplomatic action. In 1717 the Dzhungars invaded Tibet hoping to enlist Tibetan support against China. They captured Lhasa and killed the Chinese client ruler, Lajang Khan. The Chinese sent an army of 7,000 troops in 1718, but this was destroyed by the Dzhungars. In 1720 the Chinese mounted more wide-ranging attacks on both Tibet and Dzhungaria; Lhasa was captured, the Dzhungars withdrew from Tibet and the Chinese established a protectorate. Perhaps not so dissimilar to Chinese policies in the twentieth century, Lhasa was occupied, its walls pulled down and a Chinese garrison installed. In 1730 the Chinese assumed suzerainty over Bhutan, a Tibetan vassal.[29]

The Chinese were also active elsewhere: Urumchi in Turkestan was occupied in 1722 and an invasion of Ching-Hai led to the Chinese assuming control from 1724. In 1727 Sulu resumed the practice of sending tribute to China, although that was not due to Chinese military action.

There was fresh fighting with the Dzhungars in the 1730s. A Chinese army was annihilated in 1731 and the Dzhungars then attacked Mongolia in 1731 and 1732. Peace was negotiated in 1739. However, succession disputes from 1750 led to civil war and the loss of Dzhungar unity. As a result, the Chinese found local allies. In 1755 Dzhungaria was overrun by the Chinese, without serious opposition: their opponents were defeated on the Ili River. Nevertheless, the Chinese were then faced by rebellions which were not finally suppressed until 1757 when the Chinese were greatly helped by a smallpox epidemic which is reported to have killed half the Dzhungars. The Chinese army killed most of the rest and deported some of the survivors to Manchuria, and the very name Dzhungar was proscribed.[30] In contrast, in Kashgar and Tibet, the Chinese left local government in the hands of the indigenous elite.[31] A Tibetan rising in 1750 and a Khalka rebellion in Mongolia in 1756–7 were also both suppressed.

42. The Potala, citadel of Lhasa, from Athanasius Kircher's *La Chine Illustrée* (Amsterdam, 1670). Lhasa was the seat of much conflict. In 1706 the Dalai Lama was deposed by Lha-bzan Khan, a Chinese protégé, in 1717 Lhasa was stormed by a Dzhungar army that overthrew him, and in 1720 the Chinese captured the city. It was not only European-style fortresses that were important and effective in this period.

In the 1750s, Chinese power was therefore extended over Xinjiang to Lake Balkhash and to Muslim east Turkestan; Kashgar fell to the Chinese in 1759. As with the Russians in the Ukraine, direct power was now being employed in regions where China had hitherto largely relied on the ability to play off local peoples and factions. The Chinese also advanced into the southern Altay, which the Russians had annexed in 1756. Conflict was avoided, although neither side recognised the claims of the other. Some tribes were made to pay tribute to both powers.

Risings by non-Chinese peoples within China were crushed, for example by the use of mortars against high stone fortresses in the Second Jinchuan War of 1771–6,[32] and, although Chinese invasions of Burma in 1766–9 made little progress, they did weaken the Burmese and there was no Burmese invasion of China. The Chinese were less successful when they intervened in Vietnam in 1788.

The rise in the Chinese population, combined with greater domestic stability, had thus supported widespread expansion. The Manchu dynasty can, in many respects, be seen less as the government of China than as an imperial authority ruling China, Manchuria, Mongolia, Tibet, Korea and, later, Xinjiang. The rulers consciously addressed themselves to different racial groups. Documents written in Chinese and Manchu, and originally thought to be simply translations, proved to say different things in the two languages. There was also an explicit use of Buddhism to control both the Tibetans and the Mongolians. Thus, characterising the conquests in Xinjiang in the 1750s as simply a Chinese conquest of Turkic people is problematic. Much of the army was composed of Manchu and Mongol bannermen, and their military system depended upon such innovations in organisation. The banner system enabled Mongols, Chinese and Manchus to work as part of a single military machine. In one light, it might be argued that the Manchus use of Chinese troops was much like the British use of *sepoys* (native troops) in India. However, the degree of acculturation and assimilation of the Manchus into Chinese culture was greater and therefore it is more appropriate to use the term China. Nevertheless, the strength of Manchu China owed a lot to the extent to which much of the territory that formed the initial Manchu homeland and acquisitions (the north-east, Mongolia) had been the source of intractable problems for the previous (ethnically Chinese) Ming dynasty.

Japan, in contrast to China, was not expansionist. There was some concern about Russia and consequently greater interest within Japan in seizing Hokkaido,[33] but Russian pressure remained minimal until the nineteenth century. In the meantime, the Tokugawa shogunate committed its energies to political consolidation at home. Neither China nor Japan had any immediate rival facing them or appeared to have any need to match European developments in military technology and, indeed, European efforts to increase trade with China were made solely by diplomatic means and not in the threatening fashion that was to be displayed the following century.

Any consideration of military capability in the case of East Asia relative to Europe thus has to relate to technology – how weaponry compared – or to be counterfactual – what would have happened had war occurred? Neither approach, however, is terribly helpful. As already indicated, the Chinese army, like that of Burma, was well able to tackle the tasks in hand. It was highly bureaucratised, and had a tremendously sophisticated logistics system supported by a centralised state. Preparing for hypothetical wars with European powers that had no serious military presence in the region was scarcely necessary, and thus the relative redundancy of firearms and cannon was not yet of consequence. The Kazaks repelled a Dzhungar invasion in 1726–9 without either side requiring 'advanced' European weaponry. It is of course reasonable for the historian to note, in light of events the following century, that developments or their absence in the eighteenth century later had detrimental consequences. However, this risks accusations of teleology, anachronism and chronological determinism. It is certainly unclear that the argument is appropriate as a means of judging eighteenth-century warfare and military technology in East Asia.

Persia

This approach is also appropriate for Persia. Campaigns such as that of 1730, in which Nadir Shah took Hamadan, Kirmanshah and Tabriz from the Turks, or 1735, when he defeated the Turkish general Abdullah Köprülü, or 1739, when Delhi was captured, rebut any suggestion of a redundant military system. Under charismatic leadership, *ad hoc* hosts of men whose traditions were warlike, but who essentially lacked formal training and discipline, were still capable of major achievements. Nadir Shah's artillery was adequate for his purposes. In advance of his cannon, he arrived at Ottoman-held Kirkuk in August 1743, and was unable to capture the town, but, once the artillery arrived, a day's bombardment led to the surrender of the fortress. Nadir Shah did encounter checks, but, significantly, they were similar to those that would have affected a European power. For example the harsh terrain of the Caucasus led to defeats and failures when he tried to conquer Daghestan in 1741–3, but the more militarily advanced Russians were also to find subjugation of the Caucasus difficult.

The situation changed after Nadir Shah's assassination in 1747. Divided and weaker, Persia became far less aggressive, although expeditions could still be mounted. Karim Khan Zand and an army of 30,000 men captured Basra in 1776 after a 13-month siege.[34] The eastern part of Nadir Shah's empire passed into the hands of Ahmad Khān (1747–73) whose Afghan Durrani empire, with its capital at Kandahar from 1748, included not only present-day Afghanistan but also much territory to the south, east and west, including Punjab, Sind, Baluchistan and Kashmir. These were gains from the Mughal world at least as important as the losses to the British elsewhere in India. Ahmad Khān also thwarted the Uzbek attempt to regain Balkh in 1768.[35]

Ahmad Khān organised his army on similar lines to that of Nadir Shah, not least with the use of mounted musketeers. There was a comparable stress on mobility which ensured that anything that was slow-moving was avoided, whatever its value for firepower. In place of heavy artillery, Ahmad Khān preferred to rely on mobile camel-guns: swivel-guns fixed to the saddle of camels, a device that the Afghans had successfully used against the Persians at the battle of Gulnabad (1722). The extent and nature of Afghan territories and campaigning were such that there was a stress on cavalry, not infantry. They captured Kirman in 1721 and Isfahan in 1722 by starvation, not bombardment.[36]

Africa

The use of firearms increased in some areas in Africa, but one must be cautious before comparing developments with a European context. In West Africa, for example, Europeans were restricted to a few disease-ridden coastal bases, and posed little military challenge to the local rulers. Indeed, European forts, many of which were small and poorly defended, could be taken by Africans: the Dutch base at Offra and the French one at Glehue were destroyed in 1692, the Danish base at Christiansborg fell in 1693. However, although the minor secondary English factory at Sekondi fell in 1694, the leading English base at Cape Coast Castle was never taken, and was successfully defended against African attack in 1688. British cannon drove off Dahomey forces that attacked their fort at Glehue in 1728, but these forces had already captured the Portuguese (1727) fort there and the French fort was partially destroyed by a gunpowder explosion in 1728.

In West Africa there was diffusion of European arms without political control, although the traffic in firearms developed more slowly at a distance from the coast. Muskets, powder and shot were imported in increasing quantities, and were particularly important in the trade for slaves. There is little evidence that Europeans provided real training in the use of firearms, although rulers showed a keen interest in seeing European troops and their local auxiliaries exercise in formation. The auxiliaries were crucial to the security of the European positions and to the offensive capability of European forces and were probably the key figures in the transfer of expertise. Since they often worked seasonally for the Europeans and were trained to use firearms, for example in the riverboat convoys on the Senegal, they had ample opportunity to sell their expertise to local rulers. There is evidence that the troops of some African kingdoms trained in formation. Further, there are a few cases of Africans capturing European cannon and putting them to use, but field pieces were normally not sold to them, although some were given as gifts. West African blacksmiths could make copies of flintlock muskets, which replaced the matchlock as the principal firearm export to the Gold and Slave Coasts from about 1690; but casting cannon probably exceeded their capacity.[37]

African firearms can be criticised by European standards, but they served their purpose and became the general missile weapon over much of Africa, for example in Angola[38] and on the Gold and Slave Coasts. The Kingdom of Dahomey owed its rise in the early eighteenth century under King Agaja (c. 1716–40) to an effective use of European firearms combined with standards of training and discipline that impressed European observers; weaponry alone was not enough. The Kingdom of Allada was overrun in 1724 and in 1727 Dahomey forces conquered Whydah, despite the widespread availability of firearms in that kingdom. Europeans on the Slave Coast had to take careful note of Dahomey views, not least in ensuring that their quarrels did not disrupt trade with that kingdom. Two French officers provided the Dahomians with military guidance in the 1720s, including instruction on how to dig trenches.[39]

The ability of Bekaffa of Ethiopia (1721–30) to regain control over rebellious provinces owed much to his recruitment of new units which he armed with muskets. In the 1760s, Mikail Sehul, the Ethiopian imperial Ras, built up an army, 8,000 of whom he equipped with muskets. In 1769 he defeated his master, the Emperor Iyoas. However, most Ethiopian soldiers were not equipped with muskets, and the majority of those who had them were from Tigre, the province nearest the coast. Ethiopian muskets, which were still matchlocks rather than flintlocks, were imported, mostly via Massawa, and were therefore relatively expensive and subject to interruptions in supply. Control of Tigre gave Ras Mikail a dominant position, but in 1771 another provincial potentate, Bäwändwässan of Bägémder, who had several hundred musketeers and also appreciated that shock tactics could disrupt their Tigre counterparts, defeated Mikail. The Tigre army was obliged to surrender its weapons, and this encouraged the diffusion of firearms. Thus, the weapons capability gap in Ethiopia was lost.[40]

In central Madagascar, the Merina expanded, making effective use of firearms. Similarly, Moroccan and Mauritanian armies successfully invaded the middle valley of the Senegal valley. However, as in India, the role of firearms should not be exaggerated. Cavalry remained more important in the Sudan, and it was largely thanks to cavalry that the Kingdom of Oyo (in modern north-east Nigeria) was able to defeat Dahomey and force it to pay tribute from the 1740s. The Lunda of eastern Angola who spread their power in mid-century relied on hand-to-hand fighting, particularly with swords.[41] Once again, military technology and tactics changed and continued according to local needs and conditions.

South America

In the Americas there was a rapid expansion of European territorial control in the eighteenth century. There was also some diffusion of European weaponry, although not of other aspects of European warfare. Moreover, the situation differed in North and South America. In South America there was an expansion of control from well-established colonies on both sides of the continent but there was little diffusion of technology. The Spanish made minor advances south in both Chile, where San Carlos de Ancud was founded in 1763, and Patagonia, where Carmen de Patgones was founded in 1779, but in Chile expansion was limited and warfare with the Araucanians, who themselves attacked in 1723, 1766 and 1769–70, decreased. The Araucanians also advanced across the Andes to challenge the Spanish position in Argentina. In territorial and economic terms, expansion into the interior of South America by the Portuguese in Brazil and by the Spanish east of the Andes and north from Buenos Aires, was more important. The discovery of gold and diamonds in Minas Gerais, in the interior of Brazil, led to extensive colonisation.

This European expansion was aided by superior numbers, firearms and the absence of large-scale organised resistance. Numbers and firearms also permitted the suppression of rebellions, of which there were over 100 in the Andes in 1742–82 alone, although major rebellions were rare.[42] However, the rigorous collection of taxes led to a general insurrection in Peru in 1780–1, headed by Túpac Amaru, who was a descendant of the last Inca rulers. He sought the support of local colonists, but was executed. Over 100,000 people died in the war began by Túpac Amaru's rising.[43] At Arequipa in Peru in 1780, superior firepower determined the defeat of local rebels armed with lances, sticks and the traditional Andean weapon, the sling. Similarly, firepower – cannon and muskets – were responsible for the victory of Caibaté (1756) by which a joint Portuguese-Spanish army smashed an Indian force, 'smothered in gunfire and shot', attempting to block their advance on the Jesuit missions of Paraguay and Brazil: the former claimed to lose only three dead compared to 1,400 Indians killed. The use of cannon fire led another Indian force to retreat.[44]

Yet firepower capability could only achieve so much. In some areas, hostile terrain, determined opposition or an absence of major European pressure ensured success for native forces. The Spaniards failed in the 1770s to subdue the Guajiros Indians, residents of the Guajiro Peninsula in modern Colombia.[45] Their control of Nicaragua, especially of the Mosquito Coast, was also very limited. In Amazonia, the Portuguese advance up the Tapajiós river was resisted by the Mawé, and in central Amazonia in the 1760s and 1770s the Portuguese were unable to resist guerilla attacks by the mobile Mura with their ambushes of Portuguese canoes and their attacks on isolated settlements. The Muras did not learn the use of firearms, but were very effective with their bows and arrows. Nevertheless, the Muras could never defeat the Portuguese and the peace they sought in 1784 appears to have reflected the need to reach an accommodation with colonial power.[46] In the Yucatán, where there was a major revolt in 1746, the thick forests limited Spanish control.

The European presence in South America in the eighteenth century was very different to that in South Asia. There was no major demographic imbalance; the Europeans were based in long-established colonies of settlement; they faced no powerful state structures in the territories they did not control; and within those that they did rule there had been an appreciable degree of interbreeding with the native population. As a result, the development of local military forces took place in a very different context to that of the French and Dutch, and still more the British, in South Asia.

Nevertheless, the essential military problem was the same. European governments and chartered trading companies were only prepared to afford a relatively small-scale deployment of troops anywhere outside Europe in the eighteenth century, especially in peacetime when there was no offensive goal that could justify a major deployment. Yet there were also reasons for such a deployment, not least policing of possessions and maintaining governmental authority, dissuading rebellion and deterring external attack.

The problem of external attack was especially serious for the Spaniards in Latin America, for the international context had already become more threatening for them. In the late sixteenth century, French and English privateers, such as Francis Drake, had raided Spanish possessions and on occasion launched more substantial expeditions. However, although they had inflicted damage, as when Drake's 1585–6 expedition had sacked Cartagena and St Augustine, the English and French were essentially unsuccessful. Although the French burnt Havana in 1552, their attempts to establish themselves in Florida had failed. In the Caribbean, Spanish defensive measures, including the organisation of effective convoys, improved in the sixteenth century[47] and Drake's last Caribbean expedition in 1595–6 was a failure. English attacks on Spanish interests were generally a matter of raiding, the search for profit rather than permanent control, and accordingly most English forces were small. The English lacked the infrastructure of bases and permanent land and naval forces necessary for a serious challenge to Spanish control.[48]

By the eighteenth century, the situation was very different. The British had bases in the Caribbean, including Jamaica captured from Spain in 1655, and deployed substantial forces there in wartime. Attacks were mounted on the coasts of Latin America, for example Admiral Vernon's seizure of Porto Bello in 1739. This encouraged the development of defensive systems, as indeed did clashes between Spain and Portugal. Already, in 1672–87, in response to an unsuccessful attack in 1668 by Robert Searles, an English pirate, the Spaniards had constructed at St Augustine the Castillo de San Marcos, a massive stone fortress with a permanent garrison.[49]

In the eighteenth century, Spain created a system based on regular army units and fortifications, supported by militia, to which Blacks were increasingly recruited from 1764.[50] This was a method well adapted to the logistical, environmental and ecological problems of warfare in the tropics; and when Spain gained Louisiana from France after the Seven Years War, the colony's defences were reorganised accordingly. Defence of the interior of the French colony of Cayenne was entrusted to native Americans and free Negroes who were organised into a company of soldiers.[51] In the 1760s and 1770s auxiliary cavalry and infantry regiments were raised throughout Brazil, and black and mulatto Brazilians were recruited into companies of irregular infantry.[52] However, these units were to serve as potential bases for hostility towards the mother countries, not least because in Latin America regular regiments brought in from Europe absorbed large numbers of native recruits and were increasingly officered by natives.

North America

The military experience of British colonists in North America was also to have ambiguous long-term political consequences. The British colonists acquired military experience fighting both native Americans (Indians) and other Europeans: the French in Canada and the Spaniards in Florida.[53] Both were formidable opponents. The native Americans resisted European advance with determination. There was resistance against the British near the eastern seaboard, along the northern border of French expansion from Louisiana, and against Spanish expansion north from Mexico. In the first, the Yamasee, with Creek support, nearly destroyed the British colonies in the Carolinas in 1715, while guerrilla warfare by the Abenaki in the 1720s kept British settlers out of Vermont.

Yet the native Americans were harmed by their rivalries. In 1711 the Yamasee helped the North Carolinians defeat an attack by the Tuscaroras; in 1715 the Cherokee helped the Carolinians defeat the Yamasee. Defeats had a crucial demographic impact on the native Americans. Tuscaroras' numbers fell from 5,000 to 2,500. Many took refuge with the Iroquois and those who remained, in a prelude of things to come, were grouped by the colonists in a reservation which, by 1760, contained only about 300 people. In 1715 most of the Yamasee were killed or enslaved. Such losses helped to ensure permanent moves forward in the frontier of European control.

As with the US army of the nineteenth century, the Europeans sought to anchor their presence with fortresses, the French, for example, expanding west with forts at Michillmackinac (1700), Detroit (1701) and Niagara (1720). This process accelerated with time, so that the British built more forts in the 1720s to 1740s than earlier. These forts were more formidable than the defences created by the native Americans, although the fort of the Fox (or Mesquakie) on the Illinois Grand Prairie had a heavily fortified palisade and maze of trenches that protected the Foxes from French gunfire in 1730. However, the Foxes lacked cannon.[54]

In contrast, the British fort of Fort William Henry at Pemaquid had an outside circumference of 737 feet, 28 gun ports and a complement of 18 cannon. Nevertheless, there was a major difference between the forts designed to fend off native American attacks, which were based on simple palisade designs, and the more elaborate fortresses built to resist European-style sieges, such as Charleston and Halifax where the British followed the models of Vauban's fortifications.[55]

The British and French forts built in the interior had, however, in the 1750s to face not just the prospect of native American attack, but also that of attack by Europeans.[56] French regular forces under Louis, Marquis de Montcalm (1712–59), a veteran of the War of the Austrian Succession, supported by cannon and by native American allies and taking advantage of surprise, attacked British interior forts during the Seven Years War. In 1756 they drove the British from Lake Ontario and captured Forts Bull, George, Ontario and Oswego. In the following year, the French advanced towards the Hudson, capturing Fort William Henry after heavy bombardment by 30 cannon hauled over land to the siege. In turn, the British deployed far larger forces and captured Louisbourg and Fort Frontenac (1758), Niagara and Québec (1759), and Montréal (1760).

The French developed Louisiana, founding settlements at Biloxi in 1699, Mobile in 1710, New Orleans in 1718 and Baton Rouge in 1722. An 800-strong French force in Louisiana savagely crushed the Natchez in 1729–31, in a campaign of systematic extermination. Most of the prisoners were shipped to Santo Domingo in the Caribbean, where they became slaves. The Natchez were weakened by their failure to win support from other tribes. The French suffered defeat at the hands of the Chickasaw in the late 1730s, and were hit by Chickasaw raids in 1747–8 and 1752. However, the use of extreme methods, destroying native villages and crops, forced the Chickasaw to terms in 1752.

The value of fortresses for European control was mixed. They could reduce a potentially mobile force to a fixed-point defence, and the latter could be of limited value. The Spanish, who had been forced out of the Santa Fe region of New Mexico between 1680 and 1692 by the Pueblo rebellion, attempted to create an impregnable cordon of *presidios* (fortified bases) to protect their northern possessions, but native American war parties bypassed them without difficulty. Santa Fe itself had resisted siege in 1680, but had then had to be evacuated. Population shifts on the Great Plains, especially the southward movement of the Comanches and the Utes, put pressure on the Spaniards. The Apache, Comanche and other Plains tribes were well mounted and armed, their firearms coming from trade with British merchants and with Louisiana when it was under Spanish rule (1763–83): there the established policy was to win them over through commerce. The spread of firearms and houses among the natives forced the Spaniards to reconsider their military methods. The native tribes were able to respond with considerable flexibility to Spanish tactics. Spanish expeditions, such as those against the Apache in 1732 and 1775, were hindered in turn by the lack of fixed points for them to attack. Punitive expeditions, which were dependent anyway on support drawn from a shifting pattern of native alliances, were, at best, of limited value. In 1751 the Pimas of Arizona rebelled. In 1758 the Comanche attacked the San Sabá mission, eighty miles north-west of modern Austin, killing all bar one of the missionaries and most of the population. This led the Spaniards to abandon efforts to convert the Apaches and by the end of the century most of the missions and *presidios* in the north had been abandoned. The Yuma rebellion of 1781, in which Spanish positions were destroyed, thwarted plans for expansion through the Colorado valley and into central Arizona.

However, it would be misleading to concentrate on Spanish–native hostility as there were important rivalries between the native Americans. These had helped the Spaniards reoccupy Santa Fe in 1692. The Comanches defeated the Penxaye Apaches in the 1700s and in the second half of the century had a lengthy struggle with their former allies, the southern Utes, who had themselves defeated the Navajos in the 1710s to 1750s.[57]

If differences between native American tribes hindered resistance, there were also European rivalries, although there was a crucial difference in the number of powers among which the two 'sides' were divided: there was only Britain, France and Spain on the European side. Furthermore, these intra-native and intra-European rivalries were inevitably connected. This further compromises any attempt to approach the question in terms of European versus non-European. Looked at differently, such rivalries should be seen as a crucial aspect of the opposition between Europeans and non-Europeans and a means by which the Europeans furthered their interests and influence as well as an important cause of the diffusion of firearms. The British and French colonisers actively competed for trade in the interior, and this exacerbated or incited conflict. For example, suspicious that the Fox tribe from the Mississippi-Illinois region was plotting with the British, the French, with native American support, launched five attacks on them in 1712–34, finally breaking Fox resistance, particularly thanks to a victory on the Illinois grand prairie in 1730. In 1721, Governor Shute of the British colony of Massachusetts sent an expedition into modern Maine to destroy the mission of the French Jesuit Sebastian Râle, and thus French influence among the eastern Abenakis. French attempts in the 1740s to prevent their native allies from trading with the British led to British-incited resistance: the Miami people sacked Fort Miami (1747) and Fort Vincennes (1751), while the Huron burnt Detroit. The French responded vigorously, forcing the Miami back into alliance (1752) and establishing new posts in the Upper Ohio (1753–4), which helped to provoke the Seven Years War with Britain, a conflict known in North America as the French and Indian War.[58]

Indeed, it was the French determination to rely upon forts, rather than on alliances with native Americans held together by trade, that led to the war. As was to be repeatedly the case with European expansion, the attempt to increase the degree of control over native peoples, and to make it concrete through fortified positions, led to a reaction not only from these peoples but also from other European powers. This was to be more the case in Africa, Asia and Oceania in the nineteenth than in earlier centuries, but in North America it was in the eighteenth century that this process occurred; although in the nineteenth there was competition between the USA and other European powers, and in the case of Spain and Mexico war.

In 1755 a force of British regulars and Virginia militia under General Edward Braddock was defeated at the Monongahela River when it marched on Fort Duquesne. The well-aimed fire of a smaller French and Indian force using forest cover proved devastating to a column that simply did not know how to respond. The absence of native American allies and of experience in forest warfare were crucial to Braddock's defeat.

The Seven Years War was followed by renewed British–native American tension. The peace had not taken note of native American views and tension rose as the British failed to provide the native Americans with anticipated presents, while British American settlers moved into native lands. This led to Pontiac's War (1763–4), which involved a number of tribes, especially the Ottawa under Pontiac. Successful attacks were made on a number of British forts while the British were forced to abandon several others; British field forces were also ambushed. The British were less effective at fighting in the woodlands of the frontier zone than their opponents, and British dependence on supply routes made them more vulnerable to ambush. However, owing to the British conquest of Canada in 1758–60, the natives had no access to firearms other than those they captured. The Anglo-French rivalry that had given a measure of opportunity to the native Americans, providing for example arms and ammunition to the Abenakis of Vermont, had been ended. Native Americans opposed to the British had lost their French supporters.

Furthermore, in 1763–4 major British positions with sizeable garrisons and artillery, such as Detroit, Niagara and Fort Pitt, successfully resisted attack. The British also planned to distribute blankets infected with smallpox, an early example of biological warfare, and the tribes were indeed affected by an epidemic of the disease. In the late summer and autumn of 1764, the native Americans, who found it difficult to sustain long conflicts and were probably short of gunpowder, settled the conflict. They were also threatened by a British advance towards the Ohio native American towns in the Muskingum valley, and affected by smallpox.

The problems created for the native Americans by their dependence on European munitions were not new. The 'Achilles heel' of the Iroquois in the second half of the seventeenth century, when they were the most powerful military force in the interior of North America, had been their increasing dependence on European firearms and iron weapons, and, in particular, gunpowder.[59] This indicated a major limitation to the argument that the diffusion of European arms lessened the military advantage enjoyed by

Europeans. This was only the case if there was a combination of unlikely circumstances. First, it was necessary to be able to develop the capability to make and repair the arms and to make any ammunition that might be required. Secondly, it was important to acquire proficiency in their use, either by emulating European tactics or by integrating the weapons with tactics developed for the particular societies and environments in question. Otherwise, the very adoption of European weaponry would weaken the states and peoples that were impressed by them.

In the eighteenth century, native Americans were under great pressure in the eastern states of what was to become the USA, not least because of the greater European-American numbers. After the Peace of Paris, European-American settlement increased west of the Appalachians, while in northern New England the western Abenaki of Vermont were threatened by spreading settlement after New Hampshire militia cut a road through the Green Mountains.

This pressure was not yet the case, however, in the west. Indeed, the diffusion of European weaponry increased the military potential of the native Americans. Tribes which acquired firearms in quantity, such as the Cree and Chipewayo, were able to establish trading and fur-trapping empires at the expense of rivals. Once the Chipewayo had matched the armaments of their rivals the Cree, they could block Cree expansion northward to the west of Hudson Bay.

One of the most important European transfers of military technology to America was the horse. Native peoples living near Spanish settlements in the early seventeenth century had first acquired the animal, and it spread northward, by trade and theft, to the Rocky Mountains and the Great Plains. The Apache and Comanche had the horse before the end of the century, the Cheyenne and Pawnee by 1755. In the eighteenth century, more were acquired from Europeans trading from the St Lawrence Valley. A major equestrian culture developed on the Great Plains. The native Americans had therefore become more mobile, and the combination of firearms and horses made the tribes of the Plains a formidable military challenge.

By contrast, the native Americans on the distant Pacific coast lacked both guns and horses. In the first clash for control of Lower California, the battle for Loreto Conchó of 13 November 1697, a missionary party drawn up in a position protected by a barrier of thorny mesquite branches was attacked by Californians armed with bows and arrows. The victorious defenders had a stone-throwing mortar that blew up, a pair of tripod-mounted swivel guns and muskets. In a second, smaller-scale clash the Spaniards lost no men while the natives had six casualties.[60] Victory was followed by the spread of Christianity; as elsewhere during the Iberian conquest of Latin America, smaller, weaker native groups proved more receptive to conversion.[61] Spanish power expanded rapidly from Mexico into California in the 1770s, although in 1775 the Ipais burnt the mission at San Diego.

Thus, in North and South America a relatively small deployment of European troops had a much greater effect in terms of territory gained than was the case in Africa or South and East Asia, and that despite the greater willingness of the native population in North America to adopt European weaponry. The principal reason was demographic, not military. European colonists went in considerable numbers to the Americas, but not to Africa or South Asia. In the Americas the settlement of land took priority over trade: seizure over symbiosis. In addition, North America supported a much smaller native population than South Asia. The only point of comparison was with the Russian conquest and consolidation of Siberia. There the number of settlers was lower, but the native population was only 200,000–240,000.[62] Furthermore, the native Americans were divided, their politics often factionalised, and they lacked the infrastructure as well as the demography for a sustained, large-scale, organised opposition to the European advance.

Yet it is necessary to be cautious before assuming that the overrunning of, say, North Carolina represented success, while the failure to make any territorial impact on China was a sign of weakness. In practice, more wealth was derived from trade with Canton than from settlement in Carolina. The bullion Europeans had seized from the New World most contributed to European economic hegemony by buying Europe's way into the lucrative Asian trade, although, in addition, from 1757 the British territorial presence in India drained bullion from it to the benefit of Britain. Gibbon referred to India's 'riches . . . now possessed by a company of Christian merchants, of a remote island in the Northern Ocean' (VII. 71).

Nevertheless, the India Act passed by the British Parliament in 1784 declared that 'schemes of conquest and extension of dominion in India are measures repugnant to the wish, the honour, and policy of this nation'.[63] The European powers were more concerned with fighting each other, both in Europe and overseas, than with conquering non-Europeans. The British sought to capture the French base of Québec, rather than Kentucky. The Spanish naval bases in the New World, Havana, Guayaquil in Ecuador and, from 1776, Montevideo, were designed to enable Spain to confront other European powers, not native resistance or rebellion.

Britain as the Global Power

The struggle between the Europeans led in the Seven Years War (1756–63) to one power – Britain – gaining a position of global control only previously attained by Philip II of Spain after taking over the Portuguese empire in 1580. This Spanish position had been challenged by Dutch attacks on the Hispanic world, and the seventeenth century had seen Britain, France, Spain and the Dutch all powerful, but none enjoying a position akin

43. Battle of Toulon, 11 February 1744. The role of politics. It was not easy to decide how best to engage a Franco-Spanish fleet when Britain was not at war with France. The British pressed the Spaniards hard, while the French exchanged fire at a range from which they could not inflict much damage. The rear did not engage due to Vice-Admiral Richard Lestock's determination to keep the line. The British squandered their numerical advantage and their commander, Admiral Thomas Matthews, was cashiered.

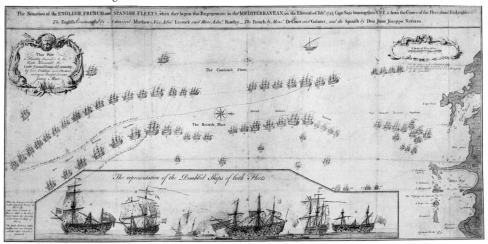

44. *The Action between the Centurion and the Nuestra Señora de Covadonga, 20 June 1743*, by Samuel Scott. The British assault on Bourbon trade was world-wide. Anson captured the treasure-laden Manila galleon off the Philippines.

to that of Philip II in the early 1580s or of Britain in the mid-1760s. The British overran French bases in West Africa in 1758, conquered French Canada in 1758–60, French positions in India in 1760–1, and seized Havana and Manila from Spain in 1762. British successes exposed the vulnerability of French overseas bases in the face of regular attack. In 1744 the British diplomat Robert Trevor wrote of the Dutch barrier fortresses in the Austrian Netherlands:

> I dare not preach up the doctrine of putting their fortresses into an impregnable condition . . . I had rather see the places secured by an army in the field, and opposed to the enemy; than the army secured in the places. I confess, I am one of those, who cannot understand how a country is the weaker, in proportion to the number of fortified places, it has; which must however be the case, if they are to absorb, instead of ekeing out, the troops of a state.[64]

In the imperial context during the Seven Years War, the French and Spaniards found themselves unable to protect bases, whether they relied on armies (or navies) to cover the positions, or simply on the defences of the bases themselves. In the former case, the French were defeated, on land outside Québec (1759) and at Wandewash in India (1760).

Britain's triumphs rested on secure control over the home base once the Jacobite challenge had been defeated at Culloden (1746), and on naval power and success. Thanks to captures and shipbuilding, the British navy in 1760 had a displacement of about 375,000 metric tonnes, at that point the largest in the world. Gibbon's thesis that a similarity in weaponry would prevent any one European power from achieving a position of hegemony was completely inaccurate as far as the maritime and extra-European world was concerned. Indeed, the British navy was very similar to its opponents in the weaponry it employed. Sir Thomas Slade, Surveyor of the British Navy 1755–71, worked from Spanish and French warships captured in the 1740s, to design a series of two-decker 74-gun warships that were both manoeuvrable and capable of holding their own in the punishing close-range artillery duels of line of battle engagements. Fourteen were in service by 1759 and they played a major role in the British victories of the Seven Years War.

This was part of a system in which European powers copied each other's developments, including both the 'sailing battle fleet concept and the bureaucratic form of warfare at sea'.[65] This copying could take the form of hiring foreign shipwrights and designers, as with Peter the Great's reliance on the Dutch and English, and of purchasing foreign warships. Jean Orry, the chief minister of Spain 1714–15, sought to rebuild the Spanish navy after the War of the Spanish Succession by buying ships from abroad. In 1749–50 Jorge Juan travelled from Spain to study English naval design and construction. He was responsible for *Examen Marítimo* (1771), a guide to both subjects, became Director General of Naval Construction, and hired three English specialists, creating the English school of Spanish naval architecture. One, Mathew Mullan, was sent to Havana where he was responsible for the *Santissima Trinidad* which, when launched in 1769, was the most heavily armed ship in the world.[66]

45. Battle of Blenheim, 13 August 1704. The scale of victory. A hard-fought engagement with over 30,000 casualties out of the 108,000 combatants. Victory was largely due to the tactical flexibility of John Churchill, in particular to his ability to retain control and manoeuvrability. The decisive factors were mastery of terrain, the retention and management of reserves and the timing of the heavy strike. Having pinned down much of the French infantry in defensive engagements, Marlborough launched the substantial force he had kept unengaged in the centre.

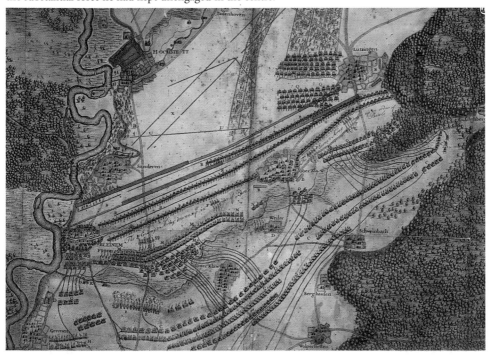

In overseas conflict, the British used weapons and tactics similar to those of their European rivals, although they benefited from a greater capability to apply force at particular points. A gap in weaponry capability was not therefore responsible for British success. The British navy was more effective than its opponents, but this was largely due to more ships, to its extensive and effective administrative system, to the strength of public finances, to a more meritocratic promotion system and more unified naval tradition than that of France, to good naval leadership, and to the greater commitment of national resources to naval rather than land warfare, a political choice that reflected the nature of public culture and national self-image. The last contrasted greatly with China, and thus the two strongest powers of the period, both of which greatly expanded territorially around 1760, were very different politically, geopolitically and militarily.

Sir Horace Mann, a British diplomat, pointed out the particular basis and economic context of British power when he told the House of Commons in 1779,

what has been and is looked upon to be the source of our power and greatness: our trade and commerce, the consequent number of our seamen, and our naval superiority, which all inseparably give us riches and power, and everything derived from an extensive commerce, numerous dependencies, and transmarine dominions; and the means of retaining and protecting them. Strip us of our marine pre-eminence, and where must we find ourselves? Not among the first powers of Europe, far from it. Many countries exceed us infinitely in extent of dominions, others in native produce, and perhaps manufactures. If, therefore, we should ever even come to an equality upon our proper element, with any other power, our importance must go; every thing we possess out of this island will be held by a very precarious tenure, and our influence and consequence among the great powers of Europe must depart with the cause which chiefly created it.[67]

6 An Age of Revolution and Imperial Reach, 1775–1815

The military history of the period 1775–1815 is open to various approaches, whether the overall perspective is Eurocentric or not. If it is Eurocentric, it is possible to concentrate on French revolutionary and Napoleonic warfare, and to treat other aspects of the period as less consequential adjuncts. Alternatively, or in addition, it is possible to devote considerable attention to the American Revolution (1775–83) and to the beginnings of the Latin American wars of independence. These can be approached as part of the same process of military change as French revolutionary warfare, especially as instances of the people under arms, and/or as an aspect of a novel military development: the victory by people of European descent, using European weaponry and military techniques, over European regulars.

Again, it is possible to adopt a Eurocentric approach, but to direct attention away from Europe by concentrating on the extension of European power overseas. The expansion of the British empire is the obvious subject here, an expansion achieved at the expense both of other European imperial powers and of non-European peoples. Such an approach would also invite inclusion of Russian success and expansion, both against the Turks and in the Caucasus. Thus, European military power could be better understood by considering its activity and potential within and outside Europe. In the case of Britain, this invites the interesting contrast of failure to deal with the American Revolution, but success against other opponents armed with firearms, especially Tipu Sultan of Mysore and, even more, the Marathas. This contrast raises questions about military potential in different spheres and about relative military capability. Yet it is also possible to adopt a less Eurocentric perspective. A consideration of the situation in East Asia and Africa would lead to less of a concentration on the European powers. However, it is pertinent to note that the expansion of British power in South Asia and Australasia made this less true than a century earlier.

The Events of 1792

It is possibly best to begin with four events in 1792, each of which points to a different conclusion or suggests a specific image. The first is the Prussian advance on Paris. The old and new in military terms are generally seen as the competing forces at Valmy in eastern France on 20 September 1792, and the result is seen as the first military triumph of the French revolutionaries and thus of a new military order. The battle is usually cited as a revolution in the history of warfare: the first victory by a 'popular' or national army over a dynastic one. The campaign was in fact more complex. The experienced Prussian

46. Pressure on the Turks, the siege of Khotin, 1788. Khotin, a key fortress on the Dniester, fell to Austrian and Russian forces. It had also fallen to the Russians in 1739 and 1769. Turkish failure in battle was matched by the vulnerability of their fortresses. The fortresses that protected the Balkans fell rapidly in 1788–90.

commander, the Duke of Brunswick, a pupil of Frederick the Great, had encountered serious problems in his advance from the French frontier, thanks to the intractable terrain of the Argonne, logistics, the effect of rain on the roads, and sickness, especially dysentery, in the army. More seriously, French resistance did not collapse and Brunswick's army was not prepared for a major campaign. Valmy was not a full-scale battle. The outnumbered Prussians were checked by the strength of the French position, especially the French artillery, which came from the *ancien régime* army, and retreated.[1]

The second episode took place thousands of miles to the south-east. The Gurkhas, who had failed to conquer Nepal in 1736–48, gained Katmandu and the Nepal Valley in 1767–9 and then overran much of the Himalayan chain, including Sikkim in 1789 and Kumaun in 1790. Concerned about this activity and about Gurkha interest in Chinese-ruled Tibet encouraged by the aggressive regent, Bahadur Shah, the Chinese responded from 1788 with military pressure, culminating in an invasion in 1792, commanded by one of their most successful generals, Fukang'an. Marquis Cornwallis, British Commander in Chief and Governor General in India, approached Nepal in 1792 seeking the development of trade with the dominions of the East India Company. This approach was countered with a request for military aid against the Chinese, but the cautious Cornwallis would go no further than offering mediation.[2] The Chinese were able to penetrate Nepal as far as Katmandu. It was not surprising that the Chinese adopted an aloof approach to the Macartney embassy which left England in 1792 in order to obtain commercial advantages; the mission, which reached Beijing in 1793, failed, although the emperor, Qianlong, was fascinated by the model of the 110-gun *Royal Sovereign* presented to him and asked a series of technical questions about warships.[3]

47. Battle of Martinestie, 22 September 1789. In place of the linear tactics they had adopted against the Turks in 1737–39, the Austrians now used infantry squares arranged so as to offer mutual support. Hard-pressed also by the Russians, the Turks were unable to mount effective opposition and in late 1789 they were driven from Belgrade and Serbia.

The third episode took place in southern India. To the south of Hyderabad, another regional power emerged when Haidar Ali usurped the throne of Mysore in 1761. In 1763 he conquered Kanara, gaining Mysore a coastline. In 1780, with his substantial cavalry-strong army, Haidar Ali invaded the Carnatic, destroying a British force of 3,720 men under William Baillie at Perumbakam. Haidar's son, Tipu Sultan, who succeeded in 1782, pressed the British hard, capturing Mangalore in 1784 after a ten-month siege. After Britain and Tipu negotiated peace in 1784, Tipu used his cavalry, trained infantry and artillery to press Hyderabad and threaten the Marathas.

War between Britain and Tipu revived after he attacked a British ally, the Rajah of Travancore, late in 1789. In the 1790 campaign General Medows made little impact and in 1791 Cornwallis took charge. He was convinced that Tipu's destructive raids on the Carnatic could only be stopped if Mysore was invaded, and he succeeded in combining the firepower that was so effective against Mysore's fortresses with a reasonable degree of mobility. Cornwallis stressed the importance both of cavalry and of bullocks to move the artillery. He wrote,

> Large iron guns are certainly not convenient travellers, but I have always thought that unless we could carry a sufficient number of heavy guns and a good supply of money, with us, we might be disappointed of gaining any material advantage from ascending the Ghats.[4]

Cornwallis was well aware of logistical problems and he proposed seizing Bangalore to improve communications with the Carnatic, thus creating a reliable supply system for an

48. Prussian officers' uniforms, 1789. Uniform was important to the cohesion of armies. It represented both control and standardisation, and each was focused on the sovereign. The use of European-style uniforms elsewhere in the world was a testimony to the impact of the European military model. Many uniforms were in practice of limited utilitarian value for moving and fighting, but the image of state power and unit cohesion was important.

advance on the Mysore capital of Seringapatam. The citadel of Bangalore was stormed on 21 March 1791, and Cornwallis defeated Tipu close to Seringapatam. However, as the city was well-defended and Cornwallis short of supplies, he fell back on Bangalore.

Late in 1791 Cornwallis captured a series of hill forts hitherto thought impregnable, and in 1792 he advanced rapidly on Seringapatam, being joined there by British forces from Bombay who had already occupied the Malabar coast. Cornwallis's resupply columns were protected by Maratha light cavalry. This was important, because, in earlier conflicts, the British had lacked an adequate response to the Mysore cavalry which ranged widely but did not attack positions unless in overwhelming strength.[5] The rapid progress of the siege led Tipu to surrender and cede much of his territory.[6] As well as Britain, her allies gained territory.

The fourth event in 1792 was the Treaty of Jassy between Russia and Turkey, at the end of a war that Russia had clearly won. The treaty tacitly accepted the annexation of the Crimea in 1783 and gave Russia Ochakov and the territory to the Dniester conquered in 1788, and undisputed mastery over the entire northern coast of Black Sea, and deprived the Ottoman empire of its control over Black Sea trade, which had been a crucial source of revenue and resources. The military situation had clearly changed: in 1792 Captain Sidney Smith was sent to Constantinople by the British government to report on how best a possible future Russian amphibious attack on the city might be resisted. The 'Eastern Question' – the fate of the Ottoman empire – was to play an increasingly important role in European diplomacy over the following century.

These four events all revealed different facets of warfare at the close of the eighteenth century: changes in warfare within Europe, the continued vitality of non-European powers, and the successful deployment of European power, both across the globe and overland, against strong states. The last was the most important, for on their southern borders with Turkey and Persia in 1768–1813, and in India in the period 1775–1815, the Russians and British, respectively, overcame powerful polities with substantial populations and armies that used firearms extensively and effectively. This was very different to the Portuguese maritime expansion in the Indian Ocean in the sixteenth century.

The British impact in India was therefore qualitatively different to earlier European military pressure in South Asia. It was also more significant in global terms than developments within Europe. The most important war in the European world was the American Revolution. A crucial episode in global history and development,[7] it invites the question of whether British defeat was inevitable. This throws light on a struggle that was of great military significance as the first defeat of a European power by a colony of settlement (a colony inhabited by Europeans). It was also a defeat of the strongest military power in the world and as such has led to comparisons with the American failure in Vietnam in 1965–73.

Counterfactual history has always had its critics, and has generally been presented as trivial if not misleading. However, it has much to offer as an approach. The past was far more complex than is generally presented and historians need to guard against the processes and methods that suggest or imply a degree of inevitability. Instead, the past cannot be understood if the elements of chance and contingency are ignored. In re-creating the world of choice in uncertainty that affected decisions and developments, scholars, teachers and students alike are restoring the element of free will, a moral dimension, to history – one which invites us, in considering how people in the past chose, to reflect on what we might have done, and do, in similar circumstances. The uncertainties of the past restore a human perspective to an historical imagination too often dominated by impersonal forces.

Military history is the most obvious field in which it is dangerous to adopt the perspective of hindsight. War-gamers devote their time to an entirely reasonable pastime, asking whether battles, campaigns and conflicts could have had different results. Could the Jacobites have won, the British have defeated the American revolutionaries or the Confederates triumphed in the American Civil War? The role of chance and contingent factors of terrain, leadership quality, morale, the availability of reserves and the unpredictable spark that ignites a powder magazine, appear crucial when explaining particular engagements. War is not always won by the big battalions and the determinist economic account that would explain success in international relations in terms of the economic strength of particular states, the approach essentially adopted in Paul Kennedy's influential *Rise and Fall of the Great Powers* (London, 1988), is open to serious question.

The American War of Independence

To ask if the British could have won the War of Independence might appear foolish given the outcome of the struggle. It may also appear offensive to an American readership, though possibly less so in the South where there is much interest in the American Civil War and in why the Confederates lost. Any reappraisal may seem irrelevant. The familiar image of the war – of British redcoats advancing slowly in rigid formation only to be shot down by brave and camouflaged American riflemen aiming purposefully from behind the shelter of trees and walls – would suggest that the result of the conflict was a foregone conclusion. Furthermore, there is the argument of anachronism: that British warfare was an instance of the rigid, outdated *ancien régime* military system, bound to fail before the onset of revolution and revolutionary warfare, especially mass politicisation, enthusiasm, élan and energy.

Yet such an account is misleading. It ignores the nature of the conflict and indeed, by making the result of the war appear inevitable, underrates the American achievement. Instead, it is useful to consider the revolution in its ideological aspects alongside other struggles within the English-speaking world. It is helpful to ask the question why did the Americans win and the Jacobites, supporters of the exiled Stuart dynasty who rebelled, especially in Highland Scotland, in Britain in 1715–16 and 1745–6, lose?

The classic answer to this question is a clear one. The Americans represented, indeed were, the future, a future of liberty, freedom, secularism and individualism. The Jacobites were the past, reactionary and religious, the products of a hierarchical society motivated by outdated dynastic loyalty. This difference was supposedly reflected in their military methods in a way that explained their respective success and failure. Thus the mass charge of the Scottish Highlanders was seen as anachronistic, bound to fail before the disciplined firepower of British infantry. Conversely, the individually aimed shooting of patriotic American riflemen was seen as superior to the mindless, mechanistic methods of disciplined British and Hessian soldiers.

This contrast reflects potent national myths, but it is flawed. It expresses an arrogant hostility to the Jacobites, and particularly the Scottish Highlanders, that is misleading. The analysis also adopts a teleological reading of the American War of Independence that is inaccurate. Several comparative points are worth underlining. First, the eighteenth-century British state controlled a formidable war machine, arguably the strongest in the world at that point and Jacobite failure is no more discreditable or evidence of anachronism than is George Washington's inability to regain New York. Britain controlled the largest navy in the world, had the best system of public finance, was the strongest commercial power and had recent experience of successful transoceanic operations.

Secondly, the British state had a good recent record in defeating internal insurrections and winning civil wars. Aside from defeating the 1715–16 and 1745–6 Jacobite risings, the British state had also crushed Monmouth's rising in 1685 and Irish opposition in 1690–1, and was to smash the Irish rising of 1798.

The American Revolution, therefore, was the only successful rising within the eighteenth-century British world. This was not thanks to French participation alone, for the French intervened to assist Scottish and Irish rebels, without bringing victory to either. Nor was the factor of distance necessarily crucial. The British had managed to conquer Canada in 1758–60 and were able to act effectively in India which was then far more distant, as all troops had to move there by sea and there was no Suez Canal. Indeed, the factor of distance helped the British in one important respect. However unsuccessful the British might be in North America, there was no danger of the Americans seizing London, as the Jacobites threatened to do in December 1745, although after France entered the war in 1778 there was concern about French naval plans, and in 1779 France and Spain jointly tried to mount an invasion of southern England. Nevertheless, thanks to British naval strength, the American threat could be contained, as it was again to be in the war of 1812. The American privateers were irritants, capturing British supply ships, but no more. The flow of British supplies and soldiers to North America was not cut.

The Continental Navy was a failure; it could not become large enough to fend off the Royal Navy with its own resources.[8] Thus, when the ice on the St Lawrence broke in early 1776, the British were able to relieve Québec without hindrance, and in 1778, when the

British commander, General Sir Henry Clinton, withdrew from Philadelphia he was able to sail to New York from the New Jersey shore after the battle of Monmouth Courthouse without any interruption. Lieutenant General William Skinner, Chief Engineer of Great Britain, recommended in 1779 'that all garrisons or large forts should be as near to the shore as possible, that they may be relieved by our fleets'.[9]

Indeed, the inability of the Americans, the Jacobites and, for that matter, the Indian opponents of Britain, to mount an effective naval challenge to British maritime supremacy was fundamental to the potency of Britain's power and helps to explain the importance of French intervention, for France was the second strongest naval power in the world, and was closely allied to the third strongest, Spain. The combination of naval strength and fortified maritime bases, developed by the Portuguese in the sixteenth century, was crucial to British power, not only in North America but also elsewhere, especially in the West Indies and on the coasts of the Indian Ocean, but, as with the earlier Dutch challenge to the Portuguese, the British were affected by the fate of their and their opponents' maritime bases. In 1782 Major-General Sir John Burgoyne commented on the French capture of the Sri Lankan port of Trincomalee, which Britain had earlier seized from the Dutch: 'I really believe the fate of the whole Carnatic to be involved in the loss of it. Had this remained in our possession, with such a fleet as the Admiral now has, we could have had nothing to fear.'[10]

War in the colonial hinterland was different from the struggle over maritime bases. In America, Britain's opponents could trade space for time, crucially so in the middle colonies from 1778 and in the South from 1780. The Jacobites and the Irish lacked that space for retreat and manoeuvre. America was also a more prosperous and populous society, better able to support the strain of protracted conflict than the often harsh terrain of Ireland and Scotland.

Yet it is clear that victory for the Americans was no more inevitable than it was for the royal army over the Jacobites in 1715–16 and 1745–6. The heavy casualties that the Americans suffered were a testimony to the severity of the conflict. Although American deaths in battle amounted to about 6,000, the number of probable deaths in service was over 35,000, as a result of casualties in camp and among prisoners. This was 0.9 per cent of the American population in 1780, compared to nearly 1.6 for the Civil War, 0.12 for the First World War and 0.28 for the Second World War.

These heavy casualties reflected the fact that there were two stages to the War of Independence. Driving the British out in 1775–6 proved relatively easy, not least because the British, short of men and believing that a show of force in Massachusetts was necessary and would bring success, concentrated their troops in Boston, leaving royal authority to collapse elsewhere with scarcely a struggle: the Loyalists were undermined by this foolish policy. In Massachusetts itself the high British casualty rate at the battle of Bunker Hill (1775) discouraged further offensive operations, so that the British lost both the strategic and the tactical initiative.

However, in 1776 the British sent a major army to crush the revolution and thus began a second stage that was more widespread, bitter and sustained than had at first seemed likely. This was equivalent to the British riposte after the Jacobite advances into England in 1715 and 1745, but the Americans had space and resources to cope, whereas the Jacobites did not. On the other hand, the British base in the British Isles was not exposed to American attack.

The struggle was more close run than is sometimes made clear in the American public myth which, paradoxically, underrates the challenge posed by Britain and treats its defeat as inevitable, and thus both minimises the American achievement and detracts attention from the actual details of the conflict. By 1780 the Americans faced growing exhaustion and war-weariness. The limited credit-worthiness of Congress and the reluctance of the states to subordinate their priorities and resources to Congress ensured that the army had to live from hand to mouth. In January 1781, short of pay, food and clothes, and seeking discharge, both the Pennsylvania line and three New Jersey regiments mutinied. The Pennsylvania mutiny was ended only by concessions, including the discharge of five-sixths of the men. The entire episode was a salutary warning to the revolutionary cause and cannot but give rise to speculation as to what would have happened had the army been obliged to endure another harsh winter without the prospect of a victorious close to the conflict created by Cornwallis's surrender of a besieged British army at Yorktown on 19 October 1781.

The rifle did not make American victory inevitable, as is generally believed in the American public myth. The rifle carried no bayonet, took one minute to load and an expert to fire it, of which there were relatively few. More generally, rifles in the age of muskets were more common than is often appreciated, but they had little impact on warfare, mainly being used by sportsmen and target shooters, and in combat only by specialised infantry.[11] British muskets could be fired faster than rifles and were fitted with bayonets. Only a minority of American soldiers were riflemen and the Americans were in general armed with muskets, including Charleville muskets supplied by the French which were every bit the equal of the British Brown Bess musket.

This absence of a technological gap can be paralleled in the Jacobite case by the suggestion that the Highland charge should not be dismissed as an anachronistic system of warfare.[12] On 21 September 1745 the Highlanders crushed a royal army at Prestonpans, to the east of Edinburgh. A Highland charge, the formation unbroken by the fire of Sir John Cope's opposing infantry, led the royal forces to flee in panic a few minutes after the first impact of the charge. They only fired one round before the Highlanders, with their broadswords, were upon them. Cope's army was destroyed, taking heavy casualties during the retreat.

49. Siege of Barcelona, 1714. A Franco-Spanish force under the Duke of Berwick launched three storming attempts that were repulsed but the outnumbered defenders then accepted terms.

The Jacobites were again successful at the battle of Falkirk (17 January 1746). A Highland charge was again decisive, although the royal troops were also hindered by having to fight uphill, while the heavy rain and growing darkness of a late winter afternoon both wet their powder so that it would not ignite and hindered their aim, thus diminishing the role of firepower. Highlanders were fighting to win and the charge demonstrates that they were willing to gamble all for a decisive victory. In contrast, George Washington, and in most cases other American commanding officers, was predisposed not to engage in aggressive offensive attacks that could bring the destruction of their army. Thus, American commanders fought limited engagements generally designed not to lose rather than to win.

It is misleading to separate Jacobite from Western European warfare. Other armies relied on the attack, tactical and/or strategic. Frederick the Great was a bold general.[13] In 1745 Prussian infantry attacks brought victory over Austro-Saxon forces at Hohenfriedberg, Soor and Kesseldorf. These victories appeared to vindicate the commitment to cold steel that had led Frederick in 1741 to order his infantry to have their bayonets permanently fixed when they were on duty. Marshal Saxe, the leading French general of the mid-1740s, was also an exponent of the strategic offensive and close-quarter tactics. The rapidity of his campaigns in Flanders in the summer of 1745 and in Brabant in early 1746 can be compared to the speed of the Jacobite advance. Similarly, Franco-Spanish forces advanced rapidly in northern Italy in late 1745.

Western European warfare is often typecast as slow, limited and indecisive by reference to lengthy sieges. The Jacobites who lacked heavy artillery, in contrast, are not associated with sieges. Yet, again, the contrast should not be pushed too far. Western European armies could rely on storm, as Bavarian, French and Saxon forces did at Prague in 1741 and the French at Charleroi in 1746 and Bergen-op-Zoom in 1747, the last the best-fortified position in the Low Countries. Thus, it is misleading to see Jacobite warfare as totally different from Western European conflict, as alien, for example, as that of the Africans in the late nineteenth century. Instead, Jacobite warfare should be regarded as an aspect of Western European warfare; placed on a continuum, rather than contrasted with a rigid model.

The royal forces only won one of the battles in the '45, but it was decisive. At Culloden (16 April 1746) the terrain suited the defending Duke of Cumberland as did the failure of the Jacobite plan for a night attack. His artillery and infantry so thinned the numbers of the already outnumbered advancing clansmen that those who reached the royal troops were driven back by bayonet. The general rate of fire was increased by the absence of any disruptive fire from the Jacobites, while the flanking position of the royal units forward from the left of the front line made Culloden even more of a killing field.[14]

The Americans never suffered a defeat as severe as Culloden, although they did suffer serious blows. Charleston surrendered, with 5,500 continentals, militia and armed citizens and what was left of the Continental Navy, on 12 May 1780. At Camden on 16 August 1780, Horatio Gates's army was smashed, with the loss of about 800 dead and wounded, as well as 1,000 taken prisoner and the loss of their supplies. Cornwallis had only 300 casualties. These were serious blows. They established the British position in coastal South Carolina and the Americans were not to regain Charleston during the war.

Yet neither blow was fatal. A major part of the strength of the American cause was that it was based on the free association of different communities. War cannot be divorced from its ideological character and socio-political context. Each colony/state had a

50. *Map of New York, showing British and American troop positions* by Charles Wilson Peale, 1776. The map shows British forces landing on Long Island. In the battle there on 27 August, the American failure to guard Jamaica Pass on the left of their line was exploited by the British, who outflanked the outnumbered Americans, while the left of the British army engaged the American front. The Americans there mounted a rearguard action, but were captured or dispersed as their main force fell back on positions on Brooklyn Heights.

political organisation and military and economic resources of its own, and a British victory in one part of America had only a limited effect elsewhere. The fall of Charleston did not make that of Boston much more likely.

Clearly, the middle colonies were more crucial than South Carolina, because of their geographical position. Here again, however, the Americans suffered severe blows, but without their proving fatal. In 1776 they were defeated at Long Island and lost New York; in 1777 at Brandywine and lost Philadelphia. Yet in neither case did this lead to the collapse of the revolution. The lack of any strategic centre in the American colonies was a problem for the British. Not even the capture of Philadelphia could bring the rebellion to an end.

In large part the Americans were helped by the fact that their defeated forces were generally able to retreat. There was no total loss, as the British suffered when they surrendered at Saratoga (1777) and Yorktown (1781), and the Americans likewise at Fort Washington (1776) and Charleston (1780). Yet, even had the British achieved a more decisive victory at either Long Island or Brandywine, they would still have had to face an undefeated New England and South. Compared to the Jacobites, the Americans benefited from having a more divided leadership, more military and political autonomy, and more space. After Culloden there was not a vast interior with defensible positions such as Washington had, for example his Watchung Mountains position in western New Jersey. In Scotland bleak, bare and unproductive hill country could not provide support for reorganising the Jacobite army.

However, the colonies also suffered from divided leadership. Each colony, although British in origin, had a different tradition and heritage. As such, the colonies found it difficult to achieve any sense of unity. It was only the fear of a British presence that brought the colonists together.

There is also an instructive contrast with the French Revolution of 1789. Unlike the Jacobites, but like the Americans, the French revolutionaries were successful in carrying through a seizure of power and then defending it from domestic and external forces. However, there were major contrasts between the two revolutions. Although American revolutionary councils and militia could be quite harsh in their dealings with Loyalists, their treatment of Loyalists was less savage than that of Royalists in France: in America the tumbrels never rolled carrying victims to execution. American society was less mobilised for war than that of revolutionary France was to be, and more respect was paid to private property and pre-existing institutions. This was in part because there was less of a social contest in the American Revolution than in its French counterpart.

In addition, French local government was reorganised institutionally and geographically, provincial assemblies being a major casualty. In America there was no equivalent centralisation; in fact, avoidance of centralisation was a principle of American revolutionary ideology. Before their respective revolutions, America lacked a strong identity, other than as part of the British world, certainly nothing comparable with that which France enjoyed, and in America, unlike France, there was to be no source of revolutionary activity able to terrorise those who supported the revolution, but had alternative, less centralist views of how the new state should be organised. Nor was there any comparable attempt to export the revolution, certainly not outside North America. The Americans were free of many of the illusions of the possibility of and need for universality that were to affect so many of the politicians of revolutionary France, and therefore did not mobilise an opposing coalition. France and Spain felt able to ally with the Americans. The ideology and practice of the American Revolution thus helped it to win crucial foreign support and this support was vital to the course of the war.

The conservatism of the American Revolution emerges clearly in contrast with that in France. It can be seen as crucial both to the success of the American cause – allowing the often differing American regional political cultures to combine and cooperate – and to the definition of the political character of America. Yet, despite this conservatism, the war created a new nation in America.

The French revolutionaries adopted a harsher attitude toward the rights, responsibilities and property of individuals and institutions. They also felt it entirely proper for the state to try to change society with the creation of a new calendar and the attack on Christianity. Had the Americans emulated this attitude towards government in order to win, the consequence might have been a very different American public culture, one that stressed the national state more than the individual, obligations more than rights. The ideological underpinnings of the American Revolution were so strong, that it is possible that it would have been abandoned by many, if not most, Americans in the face of such a compromising of their principles.

The Jacobite risings were similarly conservative in contrast to the French Revolution and, in addition, in contrast to the American ideology and practice of freedom. The total failure of the Jacobites, however, stemmed not from their conservatism, but both from the particular geographical circumstances of the conflict and from contingent political and military factors. The Jacobites were badly weakened by their failure to coordinate effectively with French invasion plans in 1744–6. They were also hindered in late 1745 by the lack of substantial support in England when Bonnie Prince Charlie marched south. Furthermore, unlike the situation in American waters in the face of the French navy in 1781, the British navy did not lose its maritime superiority.

Against these factors must be set Jacobite success prior to Derby where, on 'Black Friday', 5 December 1745, the decision was taken not to march on for London. In addition to the victory at Prestonpans, the Jacobites had also been victorious when they invaded England: Carlisle Castle, with its weak defences and small garrison, surrendered on 15 November, and, thereafter, the Jacobites encountered no resistance on the march south. As Penrith, Kendal, Lancaster, Preston, Manchester and Derby fell without resistance, the fragility of the Hanoverian state was brutally exposed, as it was to be again when royal authority collapsed so readily in America in 1775. As in America, the defence of the Hanoverian regime in 1745–6 had to rely on regulars, who were outmanoeuvred both in Scotland and in England in 1745.

That the Jacobites could have won is one of the interesting conclusions to emerge from a consideration of the strategic situation in December 1745. Separately, both a Jacobite advance from Derby and the invasion of southern England that the French were planning[15] were serious challenges. In combination, they could each contribute to the threat posed by the other. Jacobite forces in the London area could have handicapped any attempt to mount coherent opposition to a French advance. The French could offer the Jacobites what they lacked: siege artillery, regular infantry able to stand up to British regulars in a firefight, and a secure logistical base.

The failure of the French invasion attempt on southern England in 1744, thwarted by the weather, did not mean that their naval power and amphibious capability were not threats in 1745–6. The sole naval battle hitherto in the war, off Toulon in 1744, had been indecisive, leading to bitter disputes between the British admirals and savage parliamentary criticism. Unlike during the next French invasion attempt, in 1759, which was to be smashed by Hawke's victory at Quiberon Bay, there was no British close blockade of Brest, the principal French naval base, in 1744–6; while Forbin's success in taking a French invasion squadron from Dunkirk to the Firth of Forth in 1708[16] indicated the problems of blockading that port successfully. Had Marshal Richelieu's force embarked at Dunkirk on 17 December 1745, as he considered, it could probably have reached England. Amphibious operations in this period were far from easy – ships were dependent on wind and tide, there were no specialised landing vessels and few docks – but William of Orange had landed successfully in Torbay in 1688, and Richelieu, like William, would have had an unopposed landing. Richelieu was to be successful with his, and France's, next amphibious operation, the 1756 invasion of British-ruled Minorca.

Thus, the role of contingency repeatedly emerges when considering Jacobite failure, and is a powerful counter to any argument about technological determinism in the conflict. Contingency can also be seen in the case of American victory. What if Admiral Howe had cut off the American retreat from Long Island or Washington had failed to achieve surprise at Trenton? What if Burgoyne had not plunged south towards Saratoga in 1777 or if General Howe had taken Philadelphia earlier? What if France had not entered the war or had failed to block the Chesapeake in 1781? The list can readily be extended. Each hypothesis can be weighed and none disproves the strength of the American, and weakness of the British, position. Yet, each reminds us of the role of chance in war and of the folly of assuming an inevitable outcome. As with discussion of 'Could the South have won the American Civil War?', it is misleading to dismiss speculation on this theme as pointless or as revisionist obscurantism and nostalgia. The past, and therefore the present, can never be understood if the options facing individuals in the past are ignored. It is wrong to assume not only that the path of history is preordained and obvious, but that the past belongs to the victors and that they should also own the present and the future. This is especially true of military history.

Piers Mackesy has emphasised the possibilities of counter-insurgency and argued that British pacification in the South was possible. Furthermore, he drew attention to problems affecting the French, a theme that emerged subsequently in the work of Dan

Baugh,[17] and argued that had France withdrawn from the war, the 'rebels' in the state they were in in 1781 could probably not have continued to support regular armies in the field. This, Mackesy argued, would have facilitated pacification.[18] He concluded, 'to me it seems that if the British had persevered a little longer, they could have won the war'.[19] However, Mackesy's argument about the pacification of essentially coastal South Carolina does not seem to extend to New England. In addition, a degree of 'pacification' that may have been possible in, say, 1776 was less feasible after several more years of politicisation and bitter conflict. Nevertheless, if the middle colonies had been pacified and placed under Loyalist authority, the combination of blockade against the New England coast with control of the line of the lower Hudson (by forces based on New York, not Canada) would have made it hard to sustain resistance in New England (through loss of political will, not by British invasion).

Viewed as an episode in overseas rebellion *within* the European world, in other words by European colonists rather than the indigenous population, the American Revolution appears as the first in a victorious series that led to the expulsion of direct European political control from the bulk of the continental New World. There might therefore appear a ready contrast between the failure of European states in the Europeanised colonies in the period 1775–1835 and their success in the same period in expanding their territorial control at the expense of non-European peoples, most obviously with the British in Australasia and India, but also, for example, with the French in Algeria from 1830 and the Dutch in the East Indies. This analysis could be given greater force by including American expansion at the expense of native Americans, for example in the Ohio country and in Florida, as an aspect of the expansion of the European or at least Europeanised world.

If such an analysis is to be adopted it would lead to a conclusion that the crucial factor was the European military system: that this ensured victory over peoples who lacked it, but not over rebellious Europeanised colonies. The slave revolt on San Domingo, that began in 1791 and was led by Toussaint L'Ouverture (1743–1803), is an interesting variation. There were important African echoes in the rising and the subsequent warfare, but the rising also drew on European practices and on the ideology of revolutionary France. Toussaint seized the Spanish side of the island in 1800. His forces were defeated by the French under Charles Leclerc, in part because Toussaint was treacherously seized during negotiations in 1802, but Toussaint's successor, Jean-Jacques Dessalines, drove them out in 1803, establishing the independent state of Haiti on 1 January 1804. Dessalines proclaimed himself Emperor Jacques I, but was assassinated two years later. The experience of the British West India Regiments indicated that Blacks were far better than Europeans as warriors in the Caribbean, especially because their resistance to malarial diseases was higher,[20] and this was also demonstrated in Haiti. The conflict on the island also indicated both the strength of ideological factors and the role of other commitments affecting the colonial powers.

In general, the military infrastructure and techniques that multiplied European force against non-Europeans, enabling relatively small numbers of men to defeat far larger numbers, did not have the same impact against Europeanised settlers. As a consequence, without a clear margin of superiority or an obvious gap in relative military capability, warfare was more obviously affected by other factors that were always present: first, the customary features of warfare, especially determination, morale, leadership and fighting quality; secondly, the problems, particularly logistical, of waging war at a great distance, especially the contrast between an imperial power aiming to deliver force and exert control effectively and a rebellion seeking to develop rapidly an effective military infrastructure;

and, thirdly, the attritional nature of conflict, more particularly the military and political attrition involved when the conflict centred on rebellion and civil war. That first Britain and then Spain were defeated might suggest that these three factors were such as to make defeat for the European power by its Europeanised colony at least probable; whereas, in contrast, European success against non-European peoples in the half-millennium from the late fifteenth century on, could lead to the conclusion that technological, organisational and other elements summarised in the phrase European warfare were decisive.

This analysis can, however, be qualified. First, it is by no means clear that European powers enjoyed a decisive military advantage on land, certainly until the nineteenth century. For example, the casualties incurred and difficulties faced by the British in their victories over the Marathas in India in 1803 scarcely suggest any easy superiority. Secondly, both the British and the Spaniards enjoyed more success in their wars with rebellious colonists than might be suggested by such an analysis. This was true both of conflict in the field, for example victories at Huaqui (1811) and Sipe Sipe (1815) which led to Spanish reconquests of Upper Peru (Bolivia) and of Rancagua (1814) which led to that of Chile; and also of the degree of local support for the British and the Spaniards during what were in effect civil wars. Thirdly, the adaptability and resilience of the *ancien régime* military methods displayed by the powers resisting revolution qualify any suggestion that revolutionary forces were bound to win. The Spaniards employed commanders who had been effective in the irregular warfare of the Peninsula War.

Fourthly, American expansion was not so much at the expense of native Americans as to the detriment of weaker neighbours. In 1790–1820 Americans took land from native Americans in the old north-west, and from native American and Maroon communities in Florida after the War of 1812; but also from the weakened Spanish in the Gulf South during the French revolutionary and Napoleonic Wars. Poorly defended Baton Rouge was captured by an unofficial American force in 1810, and then annexed. Andrew Jackson successfully invaded Florida in 1818 and it was ceded by Spain the following year. Thus, the United States seized on the weaknesses of a European nation in order to secure her objectives along the Gulf coast. The Americans also attempted to seize Canada during the War of 1812, but British Canada was strong enough to fight them off.

The Spaniards were weakened more by political than by military problems, not least by the weaknesses arising from the repeated blows struck by France against continental Spain. The royalists (Spanish supporters) in Latin America were badly divided, and their divisions interacted with contradictions within Spain's incoherent policies. Civil and military authorities, metropolitan and provincial administrations, clashed frequently. In New Granada, the Viceroy and the Commander in Chief were bitter rivals. Financial shortages forced the royalist army to rely on the local economy, which proved a heavy burden on the population. Forced loans and seizures were not the best way to win 'hearts and minds'. The royalist forces sent from Spain were also hit by disease, especially yellow fever and dysentery, and they were forced to recruit locally, leading to fresh political problems. Whereas New Granada had largely welcomed the royal army in 1816, by 1819 there was widespread support for an independent Colombia.[21]

Spain did not possess any technological advantage. On the contrary, Spain was universally regarded as militarily backward by the other European powers. The insurgents, for their part, were largely supplied by arms dealers in the United States. Spanish governments sent relatively few weapons to their troops in the Americas. Most of the weapons used by the royalists were acquired locally. If anything, the various insurgent groups were at some slight advantage in weaponry. For example, in Colombia, the republicans made good use of the equestrian skills of the *Llanero* cowboys who inhabited the vast plains between Colombia and Venezuela. The *Llaneros* were highly skilled in the use of the lance, and the royalists never developed a very satisfactory response to a mounted *Llanero* attack. A cavalry charge was also crucial to the insurgents' victory at Chacabuco (1817) in Chile.

Political not technological factors were crucial. The Spanish American wars of independence were not a replay of the Spanish conquest, where technological advantage was long held to be a determining factor. But then, as indicated in Chapter 3, that view of the conquest is questionable too.

In the case of Britain, it is the range and multifaceted nature of military power that is most impressive. Between 1740 and 1783 the British state destroyed the Jacobite rising, fought well against French forces on the European continent, conquered the bulk of the French overseas empire, and, in what could be described as the War of the British Empire (1775–83), held off the attempt by France, Spain and the Dutch to partition the British world, suffering heavy but not crippling blows. Between 1783 and 1815, the British state defeated Mysore and the Marathas, the most dynamic Indian powers, crushed the Irish rebellion of 1798, and fought off the challenge of revolutionary and Napoleonic France, eventually defeating the latter.

This scarcely suggests a state that was militarily weak or rigid. Instead, Britain was more effective than any other state in integrating land and sea power. This success is generally minimised in accounts of the War of American Independence because the focus is on the failure to relieve Cornwallis by sea in 1781, and, more generally, because the failure of the Americans to mount a serious challenge at sea has led to a lack of attention to the naval dimension in general studies of the war by American scholars. As with the case of the Portuguese and the East Asians in the sixteenth century, the battles that did not occur have conditioned the general impression of the military situation.

Again, the military dimension cannot be separated from political considerations. Determination to win is a crucial element in military capability. If only for that reason, it is somewhat idle to ask what would have happened if the War of American Independence had continued for several more years. Although militarily the British could have fought on in 1782, and were indeed to fight without a break for longer during the war with Napoleonic France, this was less credible politically. Unlike earlier conflicts, Britain, now isolated, did not need to consider the exigencies and problems of alliance politics and the danger of being left isolated as allies abandoned the conflict – instead the British government was able to exploit divisions among its opponents. However, the absence of victory had a wearing impact on morale. There was no equivalent to the years of victories over France in 1759–61 and Spain in 1762 that helped to sustain enthusiasm in the Seven Years War. Instead, the absence of victory – in India, Africa, the West Indies, the Mediterranean, home waters and in North America – sapped morale and, it could be argued, encouraged both a sense of opportunism that led to Cornwallis's risky march into Virginia and a sense of concern that ensured that setbacks, such as Yorktown and the loss of the Mediterranean base of Minorca in 1782, were magnified and led to pressure for peace, arguably more so than in the French revolutionary and Napoleonic Wars.

In 1775–8 defeats and setbacks in North America could be faced. They were arguably at least as serious as Yorktown: the loss of control over all the Thirteen Colonies by the end of March 1776, the initially successful American invasion of Canada in late 1775, the surrender at Saratoga (1777), the abandonment of Philadelphia (1778). By 1781–2, however, the domestic political and geopolitical situations were different: possibly any of the above would have led to a policy shift comparable to that which followed Yorktown.

It would have been best for the British to have avoided the revolution, possibly by offering the colonists prior to 1775 the terms suggested by the Carlisle Commission in 1778 or legislative independence comparable to that granted to Ireland during the war: both measures that indicate the flexibility of the government in a crisis. Once the revolution had broken out *and* the Loyalists had lost the initial struggles so that royal authority was expelled from the Thirteen Colonies, it would arguably have been best for the British to have cut their losses. Had they 'won' the conflict, they would have needed to deploy a large force to maintain their position, and thus would have exceeded the military and financial resources of the British state and created fresh pressures in North America, jeopardising possibilities of reconciliation.

This argument should not be pushed too far. Scotland after 1746 and Ireland after 1798 did not present insuperable problems of control, and the British government would have been able to turn to the Loyalists in many regions of America. Yet there would have been tension, and this leads to a 'silver lining' conclusion. Britain faced two major challenges between 1775 and 1815, a defining period in British history, first the American Revolution and secondly the wars with revolutionary and Napoleonic France. She was very fortunate that they were distinct, and separated by a period of governmental, financial and military revitalisation. America did not challenge Britain again until 1812 and, by then, the serious challenges of 1795–8 and 1805–11 had been surmounted, the French navy had been defeated and Napoleon had turned to attack Russia; although the British could not have known that the Americans would not bring their resources to bear against Britain earlier. Had America still been part of the British empire, another revolution there in the 1790s or 1800s would have been very serious indeed.

Secondly, and more specifically, the large number of warships built during the War of American Independence was used to defeat the navies of France and her allies and clients in the later conflicts. Had there not been this earlier challenge, the British navy would have been both smaller and composed of more elderly and less seaworthy vessels, with possibly fatal results; although it is also true that the French navy built a large number of ships as a result of the American war.

It may appear paradoxical to emphasise the benefits of defeat, but that is a reminder of the unintended consequences of history, especially military history. The British could have won had they averted the revolution, and a successful military solution appeared close in December 1776. Thereafter, victories were possible and, indeed, gained, but, with the possible exception of a decisive victory had the British successfully advanced in New Jersey in 1780, victory seemed increasingly less likely whatever the problems on the American side. With the benefit of hindsight, it was also arguably undesirable, but in the 1770s British statesmen were not to know that an independent America would not join France in overthrowing the British world.

The newly created America was to become the first and foremost of the decolonised countries, best placed to take advantage of the potent combination of a European legacy, independence, and the new opportunities for expansion. Although it failed, in the face of Canadian resolve, to conquer Canada during the Anglo-American War of 1812–14, the USA successfully resisted British attack at New Orleans in 1815, and also expanded at the expense of Spain along the Gulf of Mexico in the 1810s. The victory at New Orleans was the basis of Andrew Jackson's subsequent career as President and was very important in the development of American nationalism, a vital source of identity and pride. America was a nation framed in a cult of violence, and the questioning of authority was crucial to its identity.

British Imperialism

Yet in terms of the projection of power and the shifting of global relationships in the closing decades of the eighteenth century, it was the terms imposed by the British on Tipu Sultan in 1792 that were the most significant development of the period. The British not only made substantial territorial gains. They were also responsible for their allies – the Marathas and the Nizam of Hyderabad – gaining territory. In short, relations between Indian rulers were increasingly at the behest of Britain.

In some respects the British were just another non-Indian people winning Indian wealth and territory, as, for example, the Lodis and Mughals had earlier done, and as the Afghans sought to do in the second half of the century. However, they were less willing than earlier conquerors to absorb Indian values,[22] and the distance of their home country helped to preserve their distinct identity.

It would be a mistake to think that British military reach, or that of other European powers and peoples, was effective all over the non-European globe. Japan and China were still closed worlds. The Russians had not attempted to reverse their expulsion from the Amur region by the Chinese. Much of Africa, Australasia and the Pacific was as yet unaffected by Europeans. There were also blows at the expense of particular European powers. For example, the British settlement of Balambangan in Borneo was destroyed in 1775 by a local uprising.

More generally, there was a sense of necessary limitation in commitment on the part of the European powers. Thus, in the early 1790s, the British decided not to respond to requests from the Rajah of Kedah (in modern Malaysia) for assistance against Siam, even though the British had obtained Penang in 1786 by offering the prospect of such assistance.[23] In 1782 Chakri, a dynamic Siamese general later known as Rama I (1782–1809), had seized the throne of Siam and begun to resume Siamese pressure on Burma and the northern Malay rulers. The Burmese countered with unsuccessful expeditions against Siam in 1785 and 1786 for which 200,000 men were conscripted – a force far greater than any that Britain could deploy in South Asia; about 40 per cent were lost to disease or desertion.[24] In the 1790s and 1800s Siam increased its influence in Cambodia and the northern Lao states, and regained territory from Burma. Britain did not control or influence this conflict.

Necessary limitation on the part of Britain reflected not only concern about the strength of local powers, but also caution about territorial expansion. In 1790 the far-from-radical Earl of Fife noted, 'I have no ambition for extended dominions but only to manage what we have'. Two years later, after some opposition politicians had been shown a draft of the royal speech, one, Lord Loughborough, wrote to the Prime Minister, William Pitt the Younger: 'It would be a satisfaction to many to find some distinct intimation that the value of these acquisitions was estimated rather by their importance as a safeguard to our old possessions than as an extension of territory, and that security not conquest was the object of our military operations.'

In July 1786 the Board of Control for India sent the Secret Committee of the Court of Directors instructions that clearly outlined the priorities of official policy: 'one universal principal . . . either in the present condition of the native powers, or in any future revolutions amongst them . . . that we are completely satisfied with the possessions we already have, and will engage in no war for the purpose of further acquisitions'.[25] The Board added an important caveat, namely that if any native prince accepted European aid, Britain would back rival native rulers, but that also was a defensive provision.

Accused in the French National Assembly in May 1790 of seeking '*la monarchie universelle*',[26] the British government was in fact far more cautious about territorial expansionism, and this reflected and affected Britain's nature as a military system, and was more generally true of European maritime powers in the eighteenth century. Alongside undoubted interest in transoceanic commercial expansion, there was also a certain reluctance to extend territorial control, and definitely to take on major commitments. Aggressive British officials and traders could, however, compromise the defensive orientation of policy. A similar contrast between national policymaking and more aggressive private initiatives was also true of the United States, albeit with the additional complication of migration.[27] Furthermore, if, as in Australia in 1788 and the Andaman Islands in 1789, no native state was acknowledged, then Britain could act in a bold fashion, taking advantage of established conventions relating to land seen as waste or desert.[28]

Forward defence as a motive for territorial gain was to become far more important for Britain from 1793, as the resilience and ambitions of first revolutionary and later Napoleonic France became apparent, and as the defeat or loss of independence at the hands of France of formerly anti-French imperial powers led to concern about their navies and colonies. France conquered the United Provinces (Dutch) in 1795, leading Britain to seize her colonial bases: Malacca, Trincomalee, Galle, Padang and Cape Colony all being captured or occupied that year. Napoleon's invasion of Egypt in 1798 threatened not simply the status quo in the eastern Mediterranean, but also the route to India. Within five years, there were to be French plans for expeditions to India, the West Indies and Louisiana, the last acquired from Spain in 1801. Concern about French and Russian intentions led to greater British interest in the Near East. It is in these years that 'forward defence' can be seen clearly,[29] and that there was an emphasis on territorial acquisition, although it had also been a factor in the previous years of peace between Britain and other European powers (1784–92). The principal thrust of empire, however, was war, war both as a means of gaining power and territory, and as a precipitant of fear. It was only therefore from 1793, when Britain went to war with France, that forward defence took on a new immediacy. This shift had been prefigured in British policy in India by governmental and popular willingness during the Third Mysore War (1790–2) to support what became a war of conquest.[30]

The Pacific

Although, therefore, it is mistaken to assume that the Europeans were set on a course of world territorial domination, it was, nevertheless, the case that the areas outside European influence were shrinking. The eighteenth century was the great age of European exploration of the Pacific, much of it conducted by warships. In 1784–9 France sent ten naval expeditions into the Indian and Pacific Oceans, charting the coast of Asia from Suez to Korea. The expedition of La Pérouse in 1785–8 indicated the range of European interest. Having reached the Pacific, he first followed the American coast south from Alaska to Monterey, before crossing to Macao; en route, he was the first European to discover what he named Necker Island in the Hawaiian archipelago, part of the process by which Europeans appropriated the rest of the world by 'discovering' and naming it. In 1787 La Pérouse explored the north-western Pacific, following the coast of Korea, Sakhalin, Hokkaido and Kamchatka. On 24 January 1788 he reached Botany Bay, six days after the British had arrived in order to found a penal colony there. Although scientific aims played a part in La Pérouse's expedition, political and economic competition stemming from rivalry with Britain, were also very important.[31] Exploration, particularly the charting of waters, was an aspect of military competition and capability.

The British established bases: Diego Garcia on the 'Middle Passage' to India in 1785, Penang off Malaya in 1786, Botany Bay in Australia as a penal colony in 1788 and Port Cornwallis in the Andaman Islands in 1789 as a naval base. In the waters of the south-west Pacific, the British added to their empire Lord Howe Island (1788), the Chatham Islands (1791) and Pitt Island (1791). Captain William Bligh made intelligible charts of Fiji, the Banks groups and Aitutaki in the Cooks, Captain Lever discovered the Kermadecs and Penrhyn Island, Captains Gilbert and Marshall discovered the islands that bear their names, and in 1789 Lieutenant John Shortland explored the shores of Guadalcanal and San Cristóbal. Commander George Vancouver explored part of the coast of New Zealand, discovered the Chathams and charted the Snares.[32]

The Spaniards, from their bases in Mexico and the Philippines, had been very active in Pacific exploration,[33] but the French revolutionary and Napoleonic Wars in which Spain was defeated, conquered and then fought over, brought that process to a close. The same was true of the French. The French expedition that set off under D'Entrecasteaux in 1791 circumnavigated Australia, named the Kermadecs, discovered the D'Entre-casteaux Islands and explored the Solomons, but, due to the wars, the French added nothing to their empire in the south-west Pacific.

Instead, the British made substantial gains in the transoceanic European world, certainly as far as areas exposed to naval power were concerned. Although some of the conquests were handed back at the eventual peace, the Congress of Vienna of 1815 left Britain with Ceylon (Sri Lanka), the Seychelles, Mauritius, Trinidad, Tobago, St Lucia and the 'land-islands' of Cape Colony, Essequibo and Demerara (British Guyana).

The Russians also made a greater maritime impact in the period. The Russian-American Company was chartered in 1799, the first Russian circumnavigation of the globe achieved in 1804–6, a Russian base, Fort Ross, established in California in 1812, and in 1815 an independent initiative by George Sheffer, an employee of the company, nearly led to the acquisition of Hawaii.[34] Russian naval raids and 'gunboat diplomacy' off Hokkaido and Sakhalin from the 1780s convinced some Japanese commentators that Japan needed a navy and coastal artillery.[35]

Further east, although the Russians had made progress against the Aleuts of the Aleutian Isles and the Eskimos of Alaska, they found the Tlingit Indians much more formidable opponents.[36] The Russians met their first organised resistance in the early 1760s when they reached the eastern Aleutian Islands. Effective resistance on the Fox Islands began in 1761 when traders on Ilmnak were killed. However, five years later, Ivan Solovief, a merchant from Okhotsk, organised a fleet that successively attacked the islands. Cannon proved effective against the Aleut villages and resistance was overcome. Massacre and European diseases led to a dramatic fall in the Aleut population. Mass conversions of the Kodiak Aleutians began in 1794.

The Tlingits opposed the Russians from the 1790s until Alaska was sold to the USA in 1867. The acquisition of British and American firearms made the Tlingits more formidable foes and they launched frequent attacks on Russian fur-hunters and their bases. The settlement of New Archangel on Sitka, wiped out by the Tlingit in 1802, with the loss of 20 Russians and 130 Aleuts, was re-established in 1804: after a long bombardment of the island by Russian warships, the post was recaptured. The following year, however, the Russian base at Yakutat was attacked, and in 1818 the Russians had to send a warship to the area. Further south, the Pomos who lived near Fort Ross reacted violently to the Russian arrival, but disease and Russian firepower cut their numbers.

Naval Power

As since the 1490s, it was naval power that was the most impressive feature of European military capability. Fleets of warships were complex, powerful military systems, sustained by mighty industrial and logistical resources, which was one reason why the Continental Navy of the American revolutionaries, which lacked such an infrastructure, was so weak. In the late eighteenth century, the major European powers were able to support still larger fleets. In the years between 1775 and 1790, formidable numbers of vessels were launched: the combined displacement of the British, French and Spanish ships of the line rose from 550,000 to 730,000 metric tonnes. Spain, for example, launched massive 112- and 120-gun three-deckers, as well as 74-gun two-deckers of high quality. The French navy was 60 per cent larger in 1790 than in 1775, the British 40 per cent, the Spanish almost 30 per cent, ensuring that the conflicts of the period 1792–1815 – the French revolutionary and Napoleonic Wars – were crucially important to the naval ranking of the powers. The Russian navy was about 130 per cent larger in 1790 than in 1773, the increase coming in the 1780s.[37]

This huge naval scale dwarfed that of non-European powers even more decisively than it had in the late fifteenth century. The Omanis and Barbary states continued to build ships, but at nowhere near the same rate. The East Asian powers did not develop a naval capability. The Turks, however, began a large programme of naval construction from 1790, so that in the early nineteenth century Turkey was the fourth largest naval power.

During the French revolutionary and Napoleonic wars, the situation altered as there was a concentration of European naval strength and thus of transoceanic amphibious capability and military potential. Seizure by the French and attack by the British combined to weaken, and in large part destroy, the Danish, Dutch and, in particular, Spanish navies.[38] The French navy was badly hit by successive defeats at the hands of the British, although in Napoleon's last years as emperor an active building programme, especially at Antwerp, which the French had held since the early stages of the French revolutionary wars, led to an increase in the number of French warships. He sought to make full use of the continent's shipbuilding industry against Britain. For example, ten ships of the line and a number of frigates were laid down at Venice, lesser numbers of warships at Naples and Trieste. At least in the Mediterranean, shipbuilding projects initiated by the French affected the regional balance of naval power for years to come; as late as 1832, the Austrians launched a frigate originally laid down by the French at Venice.

However, the net effect of the problems besetting other navies and of the growth of the British navy was that the hegemonic power Gibbon had regarded as unlikely within the European system emerged anew at sea even more clearly than it had done in the Seven Years War. By 1810 Britain had 50 per cent of global naval forces, up from 29 per cent in 1790. Her proportion of world mercantile shipping also increased, ensuring that the mercantile manpower and commercial wealth on which naval strength rested were sufficient for Britain to be the world's leading naval power. In *The Sailors Advocate* (London, 1728) James Oglethorpe had written,

> Our trade and power are so linked that they must stand or fall together. Suppose us once
> inferior in force to any nation which rivals us and our trade is gone. Suppose our trade

lost, and there is an end to our force; for money is the support of the navy, and trade the source of riches.[39]

Thanks to her naval strength, Britain was able to block attempts at invasion, with the exception of Ireland in 1796 and 1798, and to subvert and circumvent the trading blockade that Napoleon sought to introduce with his Continental System of 1806–13. The British were also able to cope with wars on two fronts without serious danger. Thus, war with France could be combined with conflict with Indian opponents, such as Tipu Sultan in the Fourth Mysore War of 1799, and also with war with the United States in 1812–14. In both, British reinforcements were able to move without danger and there was no serious military threat of any concerted action by Britain's opponents, even if they could have achieved political cooperation. In addition, the British navy was large enough to maintain offensive capability in a number of spheres simultaneously, and that in a period in which it was impossible to move warships speedily across the world. In 1812–15, for example, British warships supported operations on the coasts of Spain and maintained links with the Duke of Wellington's army there, while other ships took part in amphibious operations in North America, reinforcing Canada, and attacking Baltimore, Washington and New Orleans.[40]

The British navy was stronger than those of its opponents. This was not so much a matter of the superiority of individual warships as weapons systems – although British fire discipline was better than that of the French – as of the strength of Britain as a naval state and the professionalism of the navy that reflected widely diffused qualities of seamanship and gunnery, a skilled and determined corps of captains, able leadership and an effective and global naval infrastructure. The resources and effort that the British navy represented were amply demonstrated in 1779 when the decision was taken to sheath the bottom of warships with copper in order to reduce the need for dockyard work against fouling and shipworms.[41] Aside from having the largest fleet of ships of the line, the British were also foremost with smaller warships. For example the number of their frigates greatly increased during the 1790s and the 1800s.[42]

The British navy was the best example of the type of military force that enabled the Europeans to transcend their position as a minority of the world's population (about 190 out of 900 millions in 1800), and to dispatch armies all over the globe. Systematic planning, like Cornwallis's in the Third Mysore War, and the concerted operations by independently moving columns with which the British overcame the Sri Lanka kingdom of Kandy in 1815, were not exclusive to European societies – Chinese military activity required much organisation, but governmental and military organisation combining such scale and sophistication was absent in Australasia, Africa and the New World, with the significant exception of the United States. Combined with future advances in military capability, both on and off the battlefield, this deficiency was to ensure that, whereas in the early modern period a number of military systems had co-existed, in the nineteenth century that of Europe was to prevail.

Tropical Environments

Naval strength did not, however, ensure that British forces could win battles on land. The Europeans, for all their advanced weaponry, were still unable to campaign with safety in much of the world: tropical diseases devastated their troops from Africa to the West Indies and had an especially ruinous impact on British forces campaigning in the Caribbean in the 1790s.[43] The British were thwarted in their 1803 war with the kingdom of Kandy by inhospitable terrain and disease, logistical problems and guerrilla attacks. In addition to the general problem of disease, battlefield capability was not such that the Europeans enjoyed an automatic victory in engagements elsewhere in the world.

Nevertheless, despite problems with local environments, there were still important advances by Europeans, and by people of European descent who had adapted to fighting in these environments, for example Boers in South Africa, and Americans and Latin Americans of European descent. For example, there was a fair amount of fighting between native and European Americans in Brazil during the late eighteenth and nineteenth centuries. Despite the absence of big set-piece battles such as Caibaté in 1756, the European Americans did win most of the fighting, although native Americans, especially the Mura tribe, fought very effectively during the Cabanagem rebellion. The elusive Canoeiro used guerrilla tactics well along the Tocantins River in the early nineteenth century. However, there was violent suppression of some Kaiapó tribes and of the tribes who 'rebelled' in Rio Branco in the 1780s as well as massacres of native Americans during the nineteenth-century Brazilian rubber boom.[44]

Egypt

There were some spectacular European battlefield victories in the period 1775–1815. Possibly the most striking occurred when Napoleon invaded Egypt in 1798. In some respects the battles repeated the Ottoman triumph in 1517, especially the victory of al-Rayda, when firepower was decisive in the defeat of heavy cavalry. In 1798 at Shubra Khit and Embabeh, the latter better known as the battle of the Pyramids, Napoleon did not use the linear formation common to European battlefields. Instead, he deployed his infantry in squares, rather as Rumyantsev had done against the Turks in 1770. This enabled the Emperor to combine the firepower of densely packed infantry with a tactical flexibility of formations that could not be put at a disadvantage by being attacked in flank or rear by more mobile cavalry. In the battles French cannon and musket fire repelled cavalry attacks, inflicting heavy casualties. These battles were significant triumphs of infantry over cavalry and also reflected the weakness of the Egyptian military system, which had little experience of sustained warfare and, in particular, of European-style conflict. The French won further victories at Sadiman (1798) and at Mount Tabor (1799), in the last of which troop deployment in squares was again decisive: the French force, outnumbered by 17 to 1, held off the Turks for eight hours before being relieved by Napoleon.

Non-European forces tended to be most effective when able to rely on their mobility. In defensive positions, whether on the battlefield or in fortresses, they were vulnerable to the firepower and tactical flexibility of European units. Thus Napoleon was able to capture the fortresses of El Arish and Jaffa with little difficulty when he advanced into Palestine in 1799. Significantly, he was unsuccessful at Acre, which he besieged from March to May 1799, a setback which owed much to a shift in the firepower equation. Napoleon's siege artillery, sent by sea, had been captured by British warships, and his field artillery was an inadequate substitute. Acre itself was a strong fortress with numerous cannon, ably defended by a French *émigré* colonel supported by British warships.

Unsuccessful at Acre, Napoleon retreated to Egypt, but he then won another victory over a Turkish force that had been shipped to Egypt by the British. At the battle of Aboukir (1799) he combined firepower and tactical control. The French successfully assaulted fortified lines using their artillery to clear a section through which the cavalry were able to storm. The Turkish army collapsed with heavy casualties, while French losses were few.[45]

Yet not all victories were so easy and the Europeans encountered serious problems. In 1807, 5,000 British troops under Alexander Fraser were sent to Egypt. Poorly defended Alexandria was taken without difficulty, but a detachment sent to seize Rosetta was forced to retreat with heavy losses in the face of Mehmet Ali's Albanian soldiers after an unsuccessful attempt at storming the narrow streets of the city, and the British evacuated Egypt. Poor intelligence and determined opposition had thwarted Fraser, and, overall, the British lacked the resources to make a determined attempt on Egypt: the troops sent were simply too few. Nevertheless, the British failure underlined what was already apparent from experience in India, that well-led and motivated non-Western forces armed with firearms could mount formidable opposition.

India

In India the British fought numerous wars between 1790 and 1815, but they were greatly helped by their ability to engage their opponents separately, and thus to use their sepoy forces effectively. As so often, divisions among the non-Europeans were very important. In 1792 Cornwallis's operations against Tipu Sultan were supported by Maratha and Hyderabadi cavalry. In northern India Cornwallis had very good relations with Awadh (Oudh).[46] Furthermore, in the case of India, the ability of the British to monopolise the European military presence ensured that there was no countervailing division.

The Third Mysore War of 1790–2 was followed by the Second Rohilla War of 1794, in which Cornwallis's successor as Commander-in-Chief, Sir Robert Abercromby, with a small force, won the battle of Battina against a far larger army under Gholam Mahommed, although the victory was hard fought. The battle led to a satisfactory peace settlement for the British. In the Fourth Mysore War (1799), Tipu Sultan's capital of Seringapatam was successfully stormed, Tipu dying in the defence. This marked the end of Mysore as an independent force.

Four years later, a wider-ranging and more serious conflict, the Second Maratha War, broke out in west and north India with the British fielding 60,000 men on a number of fronts. A series of crucial engagements was fought in 1803. At the battle of Assaye (23 September), Sir Arthur Wellesley, later 1st Duke of Wellington (1769–1851), with 4,500 men, 17 guns and 5,000 unreliable Indian cavalry successfully confronted an army composed of 30,000 cavalry as well as 10,000 infantry trained by European officers but weakened by the defection of many of them to the British and the dismissal of the rest, and over 100 cannon, although the cavalry took little part in the battle. The cannon, which had been organised by Pohlmann, a German mercenary, moved fast, were well served and laid, disabled the British guns, and inflicted heavy casualties. In response, Wellesley demonstrated what he believed essential for campaigning in India: speedy attack. His success at Assaye owed much to a bayonet charge, a manœuvre scarcely conforming to the standard image of European armies relying on defensive firepower to destroy advancing troops relying on cold steel. Casualties accounted for over a quarter of the British force, comparable to the percentage lost at Bunker Hill near Boston in 1775. A bayonet charge had also played a crucial role in the victory of European American forces under Anthony Wayne over native Americans at the battle of Fallen Timbers (1794), a victory that broke the native American position in the old North West, allowing European American expansion into the region. The native Americans were malnourished and, in part, taken by surprise.[47]

British losses were less in their victory at Argaon (Argaum) on 29 November, but, again, the Maratha artillery, which checked the first British attack, was effective. Wellesley eventually succeeded with a second attack supported by light artillery. This victory, and Wellesley's ability to retain mobility and take the initiative, were instrumental in leading to a successful peace that December. A recent study has concluded that the 'Maratha artillery was more advanced than the British on several counts', but that their 'command structure was in shambles' and that the absence of regular pay destroyed discipline and control.[48] In short, it was not military technology but rather other factors of military-political effectiveness that were crucial. Wellesley's seizure of the initiative on the battlefield was also vital to British success.

Operations in northern India were also successful for the British. They were directed by the Commander-in-Chief in Bengal, General Gerard Lake (1744–1808), like Wellesley a bold general, who defeated French-officered forces at Delhi (11 September 1803) and Leswari (1 November 1803). At Delhi, the British lost 838 killed and wounded, the Marathas 7,000. The following year, Lake defeated Jaswunt Rao Holkar at Farruckhabad (17 November) and forced him to surrender in 1805. Like Wellesley, Lake was a firm believer in mobility. Indeed, it was only through strategic mobility, and by exploiting their command of the sea in order to mount attacks from several directions, that the British could hope to counter the Maratha cavalry[49] and impose themselves on such a large area.

This was one of the crucial operational problems of European warfare overseas once it moved beyond the stage of seeking to control the coastal forts and trading bases of European rivals. Lake was interested in developing light forces: horse artillery, native light cavalry and native infantry skirmishers, in short, in responding to Indian methods of warfare. The situation was more complex than the argument that British effectiveness with gunpowder weaponry and tactics led to inevitable victory might suggest. Apart from anything else, such an interpretation places excessive weight on battles.

The fusion of European and Indian manpower, skills and resources that the British achieved in India helped to create an imperial state of hitherto unprecedented range in South Asia, a new type of power in the region. The army was able to operate successfully throughout India, both in the north and in the Deccan, and, in addition, there was a crucial amphibious component to British strength. There was an impressive growth in British power. The mostly native Indian army under British control was 18,200 strong in 1763, numbered 115,400 in 1782, 154,500 in 1805 and nearly 230,000 by 1820. Their maintenance was expensive, and the cost led to concern on the part of the East India Company and to tension between it and its governor generals and commanders in India, such as Wellington's elder brother, Richard, Marquis Wellesley.

Nevertheless, the British could afford the effort because their unprecedented military system was supported by an unprecedented economic system. The resources of the fertile areas of India under British control – Bengal and the Carnatic – were combined with payments or contributions from other regions, sometimes extorted as the price of protection, and with a global trading system that enabled the British to establish and control profitable new commercial links.

These resources underpinned an army capable by the 1800s of defeating the most powerful of Indian forces. During the Napoleonic Wars, expeditions were sent from India to Sri Lanka, Egypt, Mauritius and Java. There were 5,770 Indian as well as 5,344 British troops in the expedition that took Batavia, the leading Dutch position in the East Indies, in 1811. Four years later, Sir Robert Brownrigg conquered the Sri Lankan kingdom of Kandy with 900 British and 1,800 Indian troops. Thus Britain's Indian army offered a larger-scale and more systematic example of what had already been seen repeatedly in European expansion: cooperation with or co-option of non-Europeans in order to offset the demographic and environmental problems of campaigning outside Europe. In some cases, as with the British in North America, the Portuguese in Angola and the British use of Maratha light cavalry in India, this was an example of using forces that offered a military capability that the British lacked. However, in the case of the sepoy regiments, the British trained Indians to fight like them, a sign of confidence in their own military system. Cornwallis wrote in 1790 that it was

> absolutely necessary for the public good that the officers who are destined to serve in those corps should come out at an early period of life, and devote themselves entirely to the Indian service; a perfect knowledge of the language, and a minute attention to the customs and religious prejudices of the sepoys being qualifications for that line which cannot be dispensed with.

He presciently noted, 'how dangerous a disaffection in our native troops would be to our existence in this country',[50] but there was to be no such rebellion until the Indian Mutiny of 1857.

European Expansion

Although there were examples of European failures at the hands of non-European forces (i.e., excluding those of European descent) armed with firearms in the period 1775–1815, there were also major successes. Aside from those already mentioned in Egypt and India, important victories included the British storming of the Javan Sultan of Yogyakarta's *kraton* (royal residence) in 1812, despite its far larger garrison and numerous cannon,[51] and Russian successes against the Turks in 1787–92 and 1806–12. The deficiencies of the Russian army, which included inadequately developed support services, did not prevent it from being an effective force. In 1806–12 the Russians occupied Moldavia and Wallachia, operated south of the Danube and, as a result of Kutuzov's victory at Ruschuk (1811), gained Bessarabia at the peace. Similarly, the Austrians developed tactical formations to counter Turkish cavalry superiority, especially infantry squares arranged in supporting checkerboard pattern, helping them to defeat the Turks in 1789.[52]

The Russians also made gains in the Caucasus. In 1783 Erekle II, ruler of Kart'li-Kakhet'i, the principal Georgian state, placed himself under Russian protection, and Russian troops entered Tbilisi. In 1784, a military road through the Dariel Pass, linking Russia and eastern Georgia, was completed.

Such initiatives were typical of an important aspect of the military capability of settled societies, their ability to carry out major works that altered their logistical, and thus operational, potential. Road, canal, harbour and dockyard construction were important examples of this. They were to be joined in the nineteenth century by the creation of railway systems, a process that fused technical advance, the ability to plan, the desire for a system and the resources to achieve one. On occasion, as with the construction by the French of an ambitious artificial harbour at Cherbourg, begun in 1783, such schemes encountered major difficulties, but the continual and increasing attempts to alter the environment and parameters of life were important to military capability.

The Russians, however, were initially unable to maintain their presence in Georgia. War with Turkey led to the withdrawal of Russian troops in 1787 and Catherine II refused to send them back in 1791 when Erekle was threatened by Persian attack. In 1795 Persian cavalry overran Georgia and sacked Tbilisi.[53] Nevertheless, the Russians captured Derbent in 1796 and annexed much of Georgia in 1801. A Georgian revolt in 1812 was unsuccessful.

The Russians also developed their naval capability. Catherine II revived the thrust of Russian naval power developed under Peter I, and was thus able to make Russia a force either on which hopes were built or one to be feared, in the Baltic and the Mediterranean. The annexation of the Crimea in 1783 was followed by the development of naval bases, especially Sevastopol. The Russian Black Sea fleet played an important role in the capture of Ochakov in 1788 and in 1790–1 defeated its Turkish rival, decisively so in the battle off Cape Kaliakra south of Varna in 1791. The Black Sea increasingly became a Russian sea. These geographical commitments were maintained in the 1800s.[54] Russian involvement in the Mediterranean between 1799 and 1807, including brief control over the Ionian Islands, played a major role in the international relations of the period. A Russian Mediterranean presence of comparable strategic magnitude would not come until the Arab-Israeli Yom Kippur War of 1973, when the American fleet in the eastern Mediterranean was shadowed by a Soviet fleet of almost equal size.

Westernisation

The military shift between European and non-European powers had direct territorial results in the period, more so indeed in 1775–1815 than earlier in the eighteenth century. These developments led a number of non-European powers to try to westernise their forces. Sahin Giray, who became Khan of the Crimea in 1777, sought to build up a regular army that would follow his orders, so that he was no longer dependent on the goodwill of the Tatar clans. Seeking an army of 20,000 regulars, Sahin introduced conscription: one soldier from every fifth household, with the arms and horses provided by the household. The soldiers were to wear western military dress, and to drill and organise in the Russian manner. He also began plans for constructing a powder factory and a foundry.

Sahin's westernisation policies led to rebellion in 1777, and Sahin was only able to resume control in 1778 thanks to Russian military assistance. He repeated his attempts to form a Russian-style army, but this was now a matter of 1,000 guards only. He also sought to purchase arms, and in 1781 acquired 30 cannon and mortars. However, his plans were again cut short by rebellion, during which much of his army proved unreliable, and in 1783 by Russian occupation.[55]

Selim III attempted to introduce changes in the Turkish army. He developed a new force, the *Nizam-i Cedid* (new order army), organised and armed on European lines. However, the overthrow of Selim in 1807 when he sought to reform the janizary auxiliaries, the dissolution of Selim's new model force, the *Nizam-i Cedid*,[56] and the failure of Mahmud II to re-establish control over the janizaries in the 1810s, indicated the deeply rooted ideological, political and social obstacles to Turkish military reform. Although military improvements played a role, the Turkish empire owed much of its survival in the nineteenth century to intervention and diplomatic pressure by European powers concerned about the possible international consequences of its collapse. For example, in 1807 French advisers helped the Turks deploy cannon to prevent a British fleet seeking to force the Turks to accept British mediation of their war with Russia. In those pre-steamship days, the British navy was also held back by contrary winds. In Japan, where centuries of peace had brought a transformation and bureaucratisation of the samurai class, there was virtually no pressure for military modernisation.[57]

Military change was introduced more successfully in India. This was true both of the forces of Mysore and also of the Marathas. Although his army was dominated by cavalry, Haidar Ali of Mysore used French experts to create an artillery force and to establish foundries. The Marathas increasingly emulated the infantry and artillery combinations of European armies. In response to the new weapons and tactics introduced to India by the Europeans in the mid-eighteenth century, Maratha armies became larger and more professional, so that a strategy based on living off the land became less possible. Military developments had administrative consequences; moreover the new infantry and artillery units proved expensive. This forced developments in revenue administration, banking and credit. The greater effectiveness of both Maratha and British forces placed considerable burdens on their respective logistical and financial systems.

Mahadji Shinde (Sindhia) was the Maratha leader most determined to train his infantry and artillery along European lines in order to complement the traditional Maratha cavalry. Benoit de Boigne, a Frenchman whom he hired in 1784, initially raised a force of 2,000, but, under a new contract in 1790, he was given a large personal estate that enabled him to raise a far larger force. The forces he trained in European methods were 27,000-strong with 130 cannon in 1793, and the cannon were used to destroy the military effectiveness of opposing fortresses. As well as muskets, gunpowder and shot, the cannon were produced in five factories established by a Scotsman, Sangster. The officer corps was nearly entirely European. Thanks to their commander, Shinde, who died in 1794, and Tukoji Holkar, who died in 1797, were able to dominate Rajastan in the 1780s and 1790s, and this in turn produced the resources for their military build-up. Their armies were eventually to be defeated by the British in 1803–4, but they offer important examples of forces that, at least in part, adopted European military technique as well as technology.[58]

The Gurkhas used British deserters to teach them British drill and how to manufacture European-style muskets. They also learned how to cast cannon, although in battle the Gurkhas did not act tactically like a European force. Ranjit Singh, who united the Sikh clans and in 1799 established Sikh dominance in the Punjab, began in 1803 to create a corps of regular infantry and artillery on the western model to complement the Sikh cavalry. In 1807 he set up factories in Lahore for the manufacture of guns.[59]

The Spread of Firearms

More generally, the diffusion of firearms continued. They were introduced to the northwest of North America by European and American traders in the 1780s and the willingness to trade firearms led the native Americans to substitute them for bows and arrows, although the limitations of the former and the nature of native warfare were such that firearms were not necessarily superior to traditional weapons. The use of the former was then spread by inter-tribal trade, and the native Americans, who rapidly became expert in their use, using them for warfare among themselves and against Whites as well.

Indeed, further east in north-east North America, native American warfare was particularly sophisticated. Battlefield manoeuvring made expert use of flanking movements proceeding from a half-moon starting position. These flanking movements could incorporate firepower and be used for advance or retreat. The native American rank and file was disciplined and led by capable officers. The military potency of native Americans was

51. A battle between Captain Robert Gray's Boston-based *Columbia* and some Kwakiuts (Native Americans) in Queen Charlotte Sound, 1792. European and European-American traders brought firearms to the Pacific Coast, and, more generally, to the Pacific. Their introduction changed warfare both in Hawaii and in New Zealand.

increased by the development of a stronger sense of common identity that owed much to religious revival. European-American expeditions into native America, for example John Sullivan's campaign against the Iroquois in 1778, were often unsuccessful and during the American War of Independence the native Americans were neither outfought nor defeated. However, their economies were disrupted and the cumulative pressure of sustained conflict was damaging.[60]

Firearms were introduced to New Zealand by European traders, and then used extensively by the Maoris in inter-tribal warfare in the early nineteenth century. The direction of influence was shown by the visit of Hongo Hika, a Maori chief, to Britain in 1820, in order to obtain muskets and a double-barrelled gun.[61] The power of Kamehameha I was based on the west coast of the island of Hawaii, a coast frequented by European ships, and he used Europeans as gunners and ship handlers. Some of the Xhosa who fought the Boers in South Africa in 1793 had firearms. In Indo-China, with the help of French merchants, Nguyen Anh (1762–1820) hired French advisers to train his troops in European methods in 1789–92 in order to conquer Cochin China. They continued by capturing the Tay Son capital at Hué in 1801, and by 1802 the whole of Vietnam was united under one ruler for the first time in its history. Nguyen Anh proclaimed himself Emperor Gia-Long.[62] Although a number of factors were responsible, this was a dramatic example of the value of European military techniques.

Emulation reflected a strong sense of relative capability. This was not always a matter of 'objectivity' or scientific observation. The possession of firearms also had a totemic significance. As such, they vied with horses, which also had both a totemic and practical value; although, as with firearms, this varied greatly by region and combatant. The complexity of warfare in Africa brings out the dangers of assuming any pattern or teleology in the role of firearms. It was not a matter simply of the diffusion of firearms, parallel, for example, to the advance of European cartographic knowledge presented in Edward Quin's *Historical Atlas in a Series of Maps of the World* (London, 1830), in which the clouds and darkness that shrouded much of the world progressively retreated before the Europeans. Instead, it was the case that, even where firearms were introduced in Africa and elsewhere, their impact was far less in some areas than in others. In addition, far from there being progressive diffusion, smooth or otherwise, there were societies where firearms were dispensed with. This was true, for example, of Japan and the African state of Bornu in the seventeenth century. Neither suffered as a consequence, although it was true that neither adopted an expansionist policy in the seventeenth or eighteenth centuries. The successful forces in the *jihad* (holy war) launched by Usuman dan Fodio and the Fulani against the Hausa states in modern northern Nigeria in 1804 initially had no firearms and were essentially mobile infantry forces, principally archers, able to use their firepower to defeat the cavalry of the established powers, as at the battle of Tabkin Kwotto in 1804. Their subsequent acquisition of cavalry, not firearms, was crucial in enabling them to develop tactics based on mobility, manoeuvre and shock attack. The powerful Hausa fortified positions were isolated and fell to the irregular insurgents, so that by 1808 all the major Hausa states had fallen. In 1808 the Gobir capital of Alkalawa fell to a coordinated three-pronged pincer attack,[63] proving that firearms and/or 'European warfare' were not prerequisites for sophisticated offensive strategies. The *jihad* resulted in the creation of a new state, the Sokoto Caliphate.

Military Capability in Europe

In 1775–1815, at the same time that the use of firearms by non-Europeans was increasing in some parts of the world, for example India, Madagascar and the Great Plains of North America, European warfare was not standing still. On the eve of the outbreak of the French revolutionary war in 1792, European military systems were very different to the situation in the late fifteenth century, but still, essentially, the same as in the early decades of the eighteenth century. In contrast to the late fifteenth century, there was a heavy emphasis both on infantry and on firepower: the pike had gone and heavy cavalry was less important. With the exception of operations involving the Turks, both weaponry and tactics were essentially standardised. There was an emphasis on linear tactics and on volley fire, rather than individually aimed shots. Cannon were far more numerous, both on the battlefield and in fortresses. The small British island of Guernsey alone had 253 cannon in position in August 1780, to help protect it against French attack. In the Seven Years War the battlefield use of artillery had increased not least in the form of massed batteries. This was to be taken far further during the French Revolutionary and Napoleonic wars.

After the Seven Years War there were tactical debates that prefigured the innovations of the revolutionary period. These were important, but possibly even more so were the demographic and economic shifts of the time. After a time of demographic stagnation that had lasted across most of Europe since the early seventeenth century, the population began to rise rapidly from the early 1740s. The continent's population rose from about 118 million in 1700 to possibly 187 million a century later. Territorial gains helped to

52. Woolwich Dockyard, part of the powerful infrastructure of British naval strength, by Nicholas Pocock (*c.* 1741–1821), who in a series of paintings of naval engagements acted as a chronicler of British victory.

push Russia's figures from 15 million in 1719 to 35 million in 1800, a figure that put her ahead of France whose population had risen, again partly due to annexation, from 19 or 20 million in 1700 to 27 million in 1789. Such growth played a major role in enabling rulers to raise and maintain large armies. About 35 per cent of the total population increase in the Russian empire in the eighteenth century can be attributed to the acquisition of new territories. Russian average annual population growth peaked at 1.02 per cent for the period 1762–82 and her standing army expanded from about 200,000 to 450,000 over the course of the century.[64]

Economic development was also important in permitting the maintenance of large armies. Although there was scant qualitative improvement in agriculture across most of Europe, production increased, not least in the frontier lands of Hungary and the Ukraine now incorporated within the Austrian and Russian empires. Cereal cultivation spread in both areas, and their economic development contrasted markedly with their earlier situation under Turkish control. For Russia, the economic development of the steppe lands was as important as the conquest of the Baltic provinces, not least in helping to make her politically a great power by increasing the resources at her disposal. The mid-eighteenth-century wars opened up new markets for Hungarian agriculture, as did growing governmental interest in purchasing Hungarian products for the Austrian army.

Industrial growth in Europe was also important, providing the basis for the production of large quantities of armaments and the possibility of rapidly implementing new advances in weaponry. Significant developments occurred in metallurgy, where the smelting of iron and steel, using coke rather than charcoal, freed an important industry from dependence on wood supplies. Britain led the way, but the technology spread. In Liège, a major munitions centre, coke replaced charcoal in the manufacture of high-grade iron in 1770. Friedrich von Heinitz, head of the Prussian mining department from 1776, built the first Prussian coke furnaces. Buoyant metallurgical industries underlay British and

Russian military activity and the scale of demand was considerable. In 1760 the munitions to be sent to South Carolina, not a major centre of British military activity although then involved in conflict with the native Americans, included 36,000 musket cartridges and ball and 3,600 flints. In 1780, when the British had many other commitments in the War of American Independence, truly a world war, Major General Vaughan's force on St Lucia submitted a request for 1,800 spades, 800 pickaxes, 800 handhatchets, 500 wheelbarrows, 600,000 musket cartridges, 200,000 flints, 2,400 cannon shot, 12,000 barrels of powder, 50 tons of musket balls, 366 reams of musket cartridge cases and four light six-pounders on travelling carriages. In five days in 1809, 46 British guns fired 4,000 shot and 10,000 shells at Martinique.[65] Such requirements were far greater than those of three hundred years earlier and they were being expected by forces at a great distance from their home base.

Yet the European economies were able to support such demands. The 1780s was a great age of naval construction in Europe, while the warfare and military preparations of 1787–92 revealed and sustained a high level of activity. Programmes of naval construction displayed some important features of European military capability. In 1786 the French imposed standard designs of ship construction for their fleet, evidence of the standardisation that was increasingly apparent in the period. After the War of American Independence, the French incorporated British naval innovations such as coppersheathing and carronades, while the Swedo-Russian war in the Eastern Baltic in 1788–90 saw each side try to match or thwart the naval capability of the other,[66] instances of Gibbon's concept of progress through competitive emulation. The Swedish ship designer, Fredrik Henrik af Chapman (1721–1808), who designed the archipelago fleet of frigates, had studied in France and Britain.

It would be mistaken to see this activity as taking place within a conservative context that was about to be swept away as redundant by revolutionary warfare. The Russians, under Rumyantsev and Suvorov, revealed an adaptability to the problems of warfare against the Turks that scarcely suggests rigid conservatism. Frederick II considered new, more flexible tactical ideas in 1768, in particular an advance in open order, although in general there was little change in Prussian methods after the Seven Years War.

Instead, it was in France, largely in response to failure in the war, that there was most experimentation in theory and practice. In his *Essai Général de Tactique* (Paris, 1772), which influenced Napoleon, Guibert stressed movement and enveloping manoeuvres, advocated living off the land in order to increase the speed of operations, criticised reliance on fortifications and urged the value of a patriotic citizen army. In France the concept of the division, a unit composed of elements of all arms and therefore able to operate independently, developed. Such a unit could serve effectively both as a detached force and as part of a coordinated army operating in accordance with a strategic plan. The divisional system evolved from 1759 and in 1787–8 army administration was arranged along divisional lines.[67]

There was also interest in France in different fighting methods, a development of earlier ideas by writers such as Saxe. His *Mes Rêveries*, written in 1732 but posthumously published in 1757, criticised reliance on firepower alone and instead advocated a combination of firepower and shock:

the insignificancy of small-arms began to be discovered, which makes more noise, than they do execution . . . the effects of gunpowder in engagements, are become less dreadful, and fewer lives are lost by it, than is generally imagined: I have seen whole volleys fired, without even killing 4 men; and shall appeal to the experience of all mankind, if any single

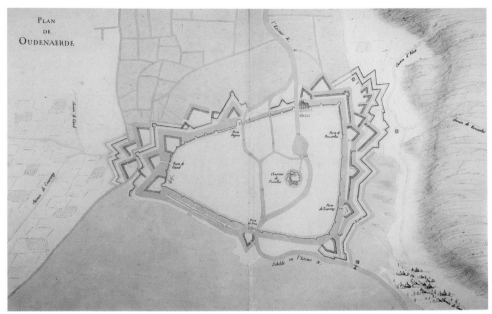

53. Plan of Oudenaarde. Easily captured by the French in 1667 and 1674 and the site of an Allied defeat over the French in 1708, Oudenaarde guarded a crossing over the Scheldt and was an example of the close relationship between rivers and the locations of fortresses.

discharge was ever so violent, as to disable an enemy from advancing afterwards, to take ample revenge, by pouring in his fire, and at the same instant rushing in with fixed bayonets; it is by this method only, that numbers are to be destroyed, and victories obtained.

Saxe was unhappy with 'the present method of firing by word of command, as it detains the soldier in a constrained position, prevents his levelling with any exactness'; he preferred individually aimed fire. Though advocating shock action and willing to consider different formations to the customary thin line, Saxe noted problems with columns:

if it happens, that the files are once disordered, either by marching, the unevenness of the ground, or the enemy's cannon, which last must make dreadful havoc amongst them, it will be impossible to restore them to good order again; thus it becomes a huge, inactive mass, divested of all manner of regularity, totally involved in confusion.

Columns were in fact to be more effective in the French revolutionary war, but Saxe was important because he encouraged fresh thought about tactics and strategy. Saxe's observations found application in the tactical innovations of Rumyantsev and Suvorov, although they did not depend on him for their ideas.

Saxe was not alone. In contrast to the customary emphasis on firepower and linear tactics, two other French writers, Folard and Mesnil-Durand, emphasised the shock and weight of a force attacking in columns. Manoeuvres in 1778 designed to test the rival systems failed to settle the controversy, but the new tactical manual issued in 1791 was able to incorporate both.[68]

Jean de Gribeauval (1715–89), who served during the Seven Years War with the Austrian artillery, then the best in Europe, standardised the French artillery from 1765, being appointed Inspector General of Artillery in 1776. He used standardised specifications: 4, 8 and 12-pounder cannon and 6-inch howitzers in 8-gun batteries. Mobility was increased by stronger, larger wheels, shorter barrels and lighter-weight cannon, and better casting methods. Accuracy was improved by better sights, the issue of gunnery tables and the introduction of inclination markers. The rate of fire rose thanks to the introduction of prepackaged rounds. Horses were harnessed in pairs instead of in tandem. Thanks to Gribeauval's reforms, revolutionary France had the best artillery in Europe.

As France did not take part in a European war between 1763 and 1792, the success of her *ancien régime* army in adopting new ideas was not tested until the special circumstances of the Revolution make comparison difficult. In several significant respects the army of revolutionary France was a product of pre-revolutionary changes. Even if its former commander-in-chief, Louis XVI, was executed, Gribeauval's guns remained standard. Napoleon, who was taught to use them, also read Guibert. The regular army was disrupted through desertion and emigration, but it played a major role in the successes of 1792.[69] These have often been ascribed to revolutionary enthusiasm, but weight has also to be placed on military capability.

It is possible to present European warfare in the period 1792–1815 in two lights. On the one hand, continuity, indeed conservatism can be stressed. This might appear paradoxical in an age of revolution, not least because the successful counter-revolutionaries in Europe prevailed in part because they introduced change themselves. Nevertheless, if the context for judgment is late nineteenth-century warfare, then, indeed, it is possible to stress continuity rather than change for the period 1792–1815; to argue that there was a use of yet greater resources of people, *matériel* and funds to pursue familiar military courses. Greater use of light infantry was certainly a characteristic of Napoleonic warfare, but much else that it is noted for had been anticipated in earlier conflicts: large armies, a strategy of movement, a preference for battles over sieges, a greater emphasis on artillery. In this context, Napoleon was more of a consolidator than an innovator.

However, if the political and social context is to be seen as crucial, then the revolutionary and Napoleonic period was more of a departure than would appear if attention was concentrated, instead, on weaponry and naval conflict. Large conscript armies, organised into corps, were a new development in western Europe.

Possibly the greatest tactical difference was that of scale and the resulting organisational, operational and logistical problems. At Leipzig on 16–19 October 1813, 560,000 men took part in the 'Battle of the Nations' by the time both sides were fully engaged, and the campaign of 1813 was subsequently to be considered by the German general staff as a crucial stage in modern warfare. More men fought there than in any battle until Königgrätz in 1866. Napoleon had invaded Russia in 1812 with half a million men, and 233,000 troops and 1,227 cannon were deployed at the battle of Borodino as the Russians sought to block the French advance. Waterloo in 1815 was a smaller-scale affair, but still involved 140,000 men aside from the Prussians, and Wellington had argued that Napoleon's opponents should not begin their offensive until they could ensure overwhelming superiority by deploying 450,000 men.[70]

Furthermore, even if the warfare of the period was still fundamentally a matter of 'more of the same', especially in the perspective of the late nineteenth century, there were, nevertheless, important qualitative differences. Partly this was a matter of the operational experience that troops and officers acquired during the conflict, an important development in a period when training, whether with large numbers or in the field, was far less

54. *Napoleon Crossing the Alps* by Jacques-Louis David. After meeting Napoleon in 1798, David became an enthusiastic Bonapartist. Napoleon was attracted by a heroic military image and aware of its propagandist values. Paintings such as this and *Napoleon at the Bridge of Arcole* by David's friend Antoine Gros provided crucial images for the Napoleonic legend.

common than a century later. Partly it was also a matter of small qualitative improvements in military methods, the cumulative impact of which was impressive. This was not particularly a matter of new weaponry, although there were important changes, especially in artillery. Flintlocks were applied to cannon in the British navy from 1778, leading to faster, more reliable and better-controlled fire. The shrapnel shell, a spherical hollow shell filled with bullets and bursting charges, was first used, again by the British, in 1804. There were also developments with balloons – first used on the battlefield in a reconnaissance role in 1794 – rockets[71] and submarines, the first screw-propelled vessels.[72]

The development of light infantry was more important than any of the above as far as the campaigning of the period was concerned. The build-up of fire discipline was also crucial, especially for the British navy and infantry. Thus, to return to Gibbon's analysis, it can be argued that the effectiveness of European military systems increased in relation to non-Europeans in part because the extensive warfare of the period led to the fine-tuning of already effective military practices.

The warfare of the period was also important in the development of the military effectiveness, in the widest sense, of European states. Thus, formidable resources were devoted to warfare and the practice of the mobilisation of a large proportion of national manpower and wealth became more insistent, not least because of the length of the period of warfare and military preparedness. The French raised about 800,000 men for active service in January 1794. Napoleon raised 1.3 million conscripts in 1800–11 and one million in 1812–13 alone. Similarly, large quantities of munitions were produced. The need to equip the French revolutionary armies led to the creation of a large powder factory at Grenelles, producing 30,000 pounds of gunpowder daily, while in 1793–4 nearly 7,000 new cannons and howitzers were cast by the French. In August 1813 Napoleon had a reserve of 18 million musket cartridges.[73]

The massive resources raised and created could also be deployed rapidly and effectively, as in 1805 when Napoleon speedily moved 194,000 men and about 300 cannon from northern France, where they were preparing to invade Britain, eastwards to attack the Austrians in south-west Germany, although the logistical basis of the campaign in 1805 was inadequate and the French were forced to resort to ravaging the countryside. Better roads and better map-making facilitated the swifter movement of troops.

No non-European state had a metallurgical capacity comparable to that of the leading European powers. Furthermore, the practice of standardisation of weaponry that was so important to the effectiveness of European fire discipline on land and sea was either not matched elsewhere or not matched to the same degree. At sea, there was nothing to compare with the heavily gunned specialist warships that the European powers could build and maintain.

The rapid development of an armaments industry in North America during the American War of Independence indicates the speed with which such a capability could be built up and yet also suggests that its creation was an aspect of the European, or in this case European-American, industrial nexus. In 1775 gunpowder mills were established in Hartford and Rhinebeck. Armaments plants were established at Fredericksburg, Virginia and Providence. Foundries were constructed at Easton, East Bridgewater, Lancaster, Principio, Springfield and Trenton. Nathanael Greene, Quartermaster General of the Continental Army, argued in 1777 that an important reason for the defence of Philadelphia was the degree to which its industries were important for the army,[74] an interesting, early example of what was to become a more common feature of European strategy: the need to protect industrial capacity.

The independent United States was to be capable of producing sufficient weaponry for its needs. In 1799 the Washington Navy Yard was founded to construct warships, although the US had no ships of the line in service until 1816. Nevertheless, in the 1800s smaller warships launched by the yard were to be able to mount attacks on the Barbary states of North Africa, a range of military activity that no other non-European state could match. In the nineteenth century the Russians purchased warships in the USA, including the *Kamchatka*, the second Russian steam warship of major size.[75] The first steam warship ever, *Demologos* (Voice of the People), later renamed *Fulton*, was built in the United States by Robert Fulton in 1814. She was intended for the defence of New York Harbour and carried 30 guns. However, in the Anglo-American War of 1812–14 the Americans were unable to match British naval power, and, instead, relied on privateering. The British blockaded the USA and mounted amphibious attacks in the Chesapeake and on New Orleans.

Thus, alongside an emphasis on continuity, it is also appropriate to stress aspects of global potency and potential in the efforts and changes that the European powers made in 1775–1815 in response to the struggles of the period. They reflected the extent to which states that adopted only a minor role in, for example, issues of social welfare, nevertheless played a much greater part in aspects of society focusing on military capability. This situation was not restricted to European states, but their greater relative effectiveness owed much to more insistent practices of governmental intervention and also to the development of a culture in which planning and the measurement, understanding and control of time and space played a greater role. These cultural and psychological attitudes and procedures enabled the Europeans to take particular advantage of technological changes, and also ensured that they were better able to analyse and systematise military practices, to discuss new options and to consider war in its political and social contexts.[76] As long as the European powers were busy with what was in effect the long European civil war of 1792–1815, their armed forces responding to the challenge of French power and its use,[77] and subsequently with political disorder that peaked in 1848, the resulting global military capability of the European states was restricted in its consequences. However, this situation was to change later in the century.

7 The Nineteenth Century

I'm Captain Corcoran, K.C.B.
I'll teach you how we rule the sea,
And terrify the simple Gauls;
And how the Saxon and the Celt
Their Europe-shaking blows have dealt
With Maxim gun and Nordenfeldt
(or will, when the occasion calls).
If sailor-like you'd play your cards,
Unbend your sails and lower your yards,
Unstep your masts – you'll never want 'em more.
Though we're no longer hearts of oak,
Yet we can steer and we can stoke,
And thanks to coal, and thanks to coke,
We never run a ship ashore!

Captain Sir Edward Corcoran R.N.,
from Gilbert and Sullivan's *Utopia Limited* (1893), Act 1.

Speed, Steam and Evaporated Milk

During the post-Napoleonic nineteenth century, the processes of military change that were already in evidence prior to 1815 continued, but with greater intensity and more impact. Given the dramatic shifts in territorial control in Africa and in influence in East and South-East Asia that marked the period 1815–1900 it is very tempting to look for new developments in warfare and to present them as crucial. Although useful, that approach underrates the degree to which the period saw the continuation of earlier processes. What was novel was the degree to which European (and European-American) military control could now be enforced on the ground, across the world, and across a great variety of terrains and climates.

This owed much to changes in the understanding of disease and its vectors, to improvements in the scientific aspect of logistics, and to a revolution in communications. The first of these reduced casualty rates and increased the effectiveness of surviving troops: this, for example, enabled European troops to operate more successfully in the Tropics. Improvements in logistics were also of great importance in the Tropics, but had an even more widespread impact.

Developments in comprehension and engineering were both important in tackling disease. The germ theory and a stress on prevention, rather than cure, provided the background for an emphasis on clean water, adequate nutrition and sewage disposal. Sanitary engineering made a major difference and tropical medicine and hygiene developed rapidly in the 1870s, 1880s and 1890s. In 1821 a Persian advance on Baghdad had been stopped by a cholera epidemic. In 1837–8 the French naval blockade of Veracruz in Mexico was wrecked by yellow fever; but, later in the century, tropical blockades became easier. Malaria, yellow fever and cholera ceased to be so deadly, although the role of the mosquito as the carrier of malaria and yellow fever was not identified until the close of the century.[1] British troops serving in India's Madras Presidency in 1836–47 had a death rate of 41.50 per thousand; the comparable figure for India in 1909–13 was 4.87 per thousand. Similarly, medical services improved so that, for example, the Russian mortality rate for sick and wounded personnel in the Russo-Turkish War of 1877–8 was only about one-third of that in the Crimean War (1854–6).[2]

The invention of canned meat, dried milk powder, evaporated milk and margarine in the 1840s to 1860s changed the perishability and bulk of provisions.[3] Such inventions, like progress against disease, were of importance for naval as well as land warfare. They made it easier to operate for longer periods between revictualling, and thereby increased the territorial range of forces and the time they could devote to engagements. Mechanical water distillation was also important.

However, it is necessary not to exaggerate the impact of these changes. The British army in the Boer War in South Africa (1899–1902) and the American army seeking to 'pacify' the Philippines in 1900–1, both examples of the range of imperial power, nevertheless suffered heavily from disease: the British lost 13,000 men to typhoid, compared to 7,000 killed by the Boers: Lord Roberts rested his army in Bloemfontein for nearly two months in 1900 because of the impact of enteric fever. Two years earlier, the Americans in Cuba had lost over three times as many men through disease as in battle with the Spaniards. The French suffered very badly from yellow fever in Madagascar in the 1890s. However, the scale of losses was very different to that in the eighteenth century: death rates were lower and armies no longer wasted away.

Improvements were not restricted to the Tropics. Medical knowledge and application increased greatly. The first military use of anaesthetics was in 1847 and post-operative infections – tetanus, gangrene and septicaemia – declined. Medical treatment became more rapid (thanks in part to horse-drawn ambulances), professional and predictable.

Progress in communications was also crucial. The new technologies of steam and iron provided major opportunities on sea and land, most obviously steamships and railways. It was not until the development of extensive railway systems, and, later, of mechanised road transport, that military operations ceased to depend almost entirely on the speed at which soldiers marched, and that the very movement of troops ceased to be a debilitating experience; although an emphasis on railways brought a new military inflexibility, not least by tying armies to railheads. In addition, with the exception of forces lucky enough to find supplies in the campaign areas, operations hitherto had also been dependent on the availability and speed of draught animals and vehicles. Railways transformed logistics. The American Civil War (1861–5) proved the importance of both railways and the telegraph. The creation of the Prussian railway network and the use made of it for mobilisations, helped Prussia to achieve the victories that led to the unification of Germany, although that was by no means the sole factor.[4] At sea, steam power freed warships from dependence on wind strength and direction, although the presence of coaling stations now became important, and figured heavily in the strategies of expanding powers. Steamships and railways helped to reduce the cost of deploying force. This was as important as technological improvements in weaponry. Furthermore, reduced transport costs made it possible to benefit more extensively from colonial gains.[5]

Command and control capability was also revolutionised by communications. Earlier the semaphore had resulted in change. Introduced from 1794 in France, the system was extended by Napoleon to reach Venice, Amsterdam and Mainz. The semaphore had a capacity of 196 different combinations of signs and an average speed of three signs a minute; code could be employed. In favourable weather, one sign could be sent the 150 miles from Paris to Lille in just five minutes.[6] Yet semaphore systems had their limitations: fog, poor weather and darkness rendered transmission impossible, and the absence of mobile semaphore stations was a further handicap. Most orders and reports in the Napoleonic period were still sent by mounted messengers or by ship, with all the problems such practices entailed. Not least of these was the difficulty of establishing whether instructions had actually been communicated, and the absence of a speedy response.

No better system of communications was to be devised until the electric telegraph, which offered both rapidity and range. The latter was of great value in the coordination of far-flung resources, while, more generally, the telegraph facilitated the practice of strategy. During the Crimean War (1854–6), the European telegraph network was extended to the Crimea, allowing Napoleon III of France to intervene in allied strategy and William Russell of *The Times* to send home critical reports. From 1859, the Prussians sent orders for mobilisation by telegraph.

In 1899 an Italian, Guglielmo Marconi, transmitted by wireless (radio) across the English Channel, and so began a new stage of technological development in communications, one that was not dependent on fixed links. In 1901 Marconi sent radio signals over 3,000 miles across the Atlantic. The British navy, which needed to control and coordinate widely separated units, was to be his best client. Radio networks were created. In 1912–14 the Germans built a network of radio stations in their colonies: at Duala, Windhoek, Dar-es-Salaam, Kamina, Tsingtao, Yap, Apia, Rabaul and Nauru. The seizure or destruction of wireless towers was to play a role in the opening stages of the First World War outside Europe. In 1914 the British navy cut German cable routes and began the attack on German East Africa (now Tanzania) with the shelling of the wireless tower at Dar-es-Salaam. Other naval units that year destroyed German wireless stations in the Pacific.[7]

Steam at Sea

Technological changes also had a rapid impact on warfare, most obviously at sea. The first steamship in the British navy, the *Comet*, built in 1819, was a towing vessel for men-of-war, and early steamships suffered from slow speed, a high rate of coal consumption and the problems posed by side and paddle wheels, which included the space they took up.

However, the potential of steampower for naval operations was rapidly developed. In the introduction to his *On Naval Warfare under Steam* (London, 1858), General Sir Howard Douglas claimed, with reason, that 'the employment of steam as a motive power in the warlike navies of all maritime nations, is a vast and sudden change in the means of engaging in action on the seas, which must produce an entire revolution in naval warfare'. Now able to manoeuvre in calms and make headway against contrary winds, the operational independence of individual warships in a fleet action was greatly extended.

In addition, steam increased the manoeuvrability of warships as far as coastal positions were concerned, while long-range artillery and armour plate made them more effective against coastal forts. Steamers played a useful role when the British fleet bombarded Acre in November 1840 and towed into position the British warships that breached the forts defending the Pearl River below Canton in January 1841. In contrast, within the 'European' world, the well-fortified Confederate position at Vicksburg was not reduced when bombarded from the Mississippi by Farragut's Union fleet in 1862. Increased manoeuvrability made it easier both to sound inshore and hazardous waters and to attack opposing fleets in harbour, and so destroy them, and therefore led to much fortification of harbours and dockyards. Steam power led to new senses of vulnerability and opportunity. British governments felt Britain vulnerable to an invasion by French steamships.

The ability of ships to operate in rivers and during bad weather was also enhanced. Steam was extremely important for interior navigation. This was demonstrated in the First Burmese War of 1824–5, when the 60 horse power engine of the British East India Company's steamer *Diana* allowed her to operate on the swiftly flowing Irrawady. The *Diana* towed sailing ships and destroyed Burmese war boats and was crucial to the British advance 400 miles up-river; this led the Burmese to negotiate and accept British terms. Iron ships were more useful than their wooden predecessors: far less vulnerable to tropical parasites, less prone to catch fire, lighter and stronger. Gunboats played a major role in the American Civil War, for example Union boats on the Cumberland and Tennessee Rivers in the critical campaign in central Tennessee in February 1862. The Russians used steam-driven launches for their crossing of the Danube in 1877 in the face of Turkish opposition. Although liable to damage and technical problems, the French used steam gunboats on the rivers of West and Equatorial Africa, the Dutch in Borneo. The French used two gunboats when they advanced on Timbuktu in 1894 and in 1898 five British gunboats took Kitchener to Fashoda on the Upper Nile. The Portuguese used gunboats on the Limpopo and the Zambezi.

Steamships were also able to cope with bad weather. The *Nemesis*, a British iron steamer that sailed through the winter gales off the Cape of Good Hope to China in 1840, was the first such warship to reach Macao, although two lesser warships had crossed the Pacific from Chile the same year.[8] In 1842 the *Guadalupe* and the *Montezuma*, iron-hulled steam frigates, were built in Britain for Mexico.

The process by which steam technology revolutionised naval warfare after 1815 was not one of instantaneous change. Instead, there was a series of innovations, each with its own chronology and pattern of diffusion. These included the paddle wheel and more powerful naval ordnance in the 1820s, the screw propeller in the 1840s, followed by the combination of the screw propeller and armour from about 1860, and the ensuing development of ever more lethal guns countered by ever thicker wrought-iron armour.[9]

In the early 1820s Colonel Henri-Joseph Paixhans had constructed a gun and a gun-carriage steady enough to cope with the report produced by the explosive charges required to fire large projectiles and to give them a high enough initial speed to pierce the side of a big ship and explode inside. Paixhans used exploding shells, not solid shot. His innovations were demonstrated successfully in 1824, and their impact was increased by his publications including *Nouvelle Force Maritime et Artillerie* (1822) and *Experiences faites sur une Arme Nouvelle* (1825). Nine years later, Giovanni Cavalli, a Sardinian, was the first to construct an effective rifled gun. In 1837 the French established the Paixhans shell gun as a part of every warship's armament; the British adopted a shell gun as part of their standard armament the following year. Such developments were to lead to armoured warships.[10]

Anglo-French rivalry pressed forward the development of new technologies. From 1879 the British pioneered steam torpedo boats. The French responded. In this way, typical of many fields, one breakthrough prompted another as powers sought to maintain and extend their technological lead.

Steam transport increased amphibious capability. In addition, the possibilities of using steam warships to destroy enemy commerce were grasped by Stephen Mallory, the Confederate Secretary of the Navy in the American Civil War, and he, accordingly, ordered speedy raiders built in Britain. Ships laid down in British and French yards, which the Confederate states ultimately could not pay for, ended up in the navies of those countries, as well as in Denmark, Prussia and even Japan.

Industrialisation

Improvements in weapons capability were matched by a greater ability to manufacture in large quantities and to consistent standards. In 1798 the American Eli Whitney pioneered the mass production of weapons by manufacturing muskets with interchangeable parts. Weapons manufacture played a major role in industrialisation, not least because the scale of demand and the size of some individual weapons created pressure for new facilities and processes. Industrialisation ensured that more weapons were available, both for warfare within Europe and for the overseas projection of European power. The adoption of new technologies, for example wooden-hulled iron-clad ships and longer-range guns, led to the real or apparent obsolescence of entire weapons systems and thus to the need to replace them; this was a test not only of industrial capacity, but also of political and financial willingness.

Shell-fire and the ability of iron-hulled ships to carry at sea furnaces capable of filling shells with molten iron, spelled the end of wooden ships. The purpose of the shell gun was to fire a round shell at relatively slow velocity so that it would lodge in the hull of an opposing ship, then explode, and actually have a chance of sinking it. Solid shot simply passed through, caused human casualties, but rarely sank a vessel, as holes were easily patched. The British were only reluctant converts to the new technology of warfare at sea because they had the most to lose: by far the largest wooden sailing fleet in the world.

The widespread impact in the nineteenth century of industrial technology and equally of intellectual and institutional forms for mass industrial society were characteristic of the American Civil War (1861–5),[11] and of subsequent conflicts within the European (and European-American) world. The fall of shipping costs made it easier to apply European power overseas. The Europeans also benefited from their accumulation, systematisation and application of knowledge. Thus, for example, information about depths, currents and ice conditions increased the effectiveness of naval operations.

'Modernisation'

These developments necessarily increased the relative military capability of American/European to non-European, industrial to non-industrial societies. The developments were not matched to the same extent elsewhere, although there were attempts to adopt European weaponry and other related aspects of 'modernisation', such as institutionalised military education. This was true, for example, of Mehmed Ali who from

55. Matchlock musket (toradar), South Indian, eighteenth century. The rate of adoption of flintlock muskets was lower and slower in Asia than in Europe. This ensured that European-armed units had a battlefield advantage. Flintlocks were lighter, more reliable, easier to fire, and more rapid. In the flintlock, powder was ignited by sparks produced by a flint striking a steel plate.

1815 organised an impressive military system in Egypt. This included an officer training course established at Cairo in 1816 and the introduction of conscription in the 1820s. A ministry of war was the first permanent department of state to be instituted. Relatively well-equipped Egyptian forces operated successfully from 1824 against Greeks revolting against Ottoman rule, while in 1839 the Ottomans themselves were heavily defeated by the Egyptians at Nezib.[12] In Turkey, Mahmud II (1807–39) pressed forward Selim III's reforms, suppressing the janizaries in 1826.

Elsewhere, a similar process affected Sikh and Persian forces. In 1822 the Sikh leader Ranjit Singh recruited several European officers. Two of them, both French, raised a model unit of regular infantry and cavalry, the *Fauj-i-Khas*, designed to act as a pattern for the rest of the army. By 1835 the regular army was organised on brigade lines and armed with flintlocks. At Ranjit's death in 1839 the army was about 150,000 strong, including 60,000–65,000 regulars. Many of the officers were Sikhs trained in European drill and tactics.[13] After defeating the Sikhs in the First Anglo-Sikh War of 1845–6, the British by the Treaty of Lahore forced the Sikhs to reduce the size of their army.

In Persia, Crown Prince 'Abbās Mīrzā (d. 1833) developed a European-officered, armed and trained *Nizam-i-Jadid* (new army), in response to Russian victories in the wars of 1804–13 and 1826–8. By 1813 it was 24,000 strong and with 20 cannon. Two of his European officers, Claude August Court and Paolo di Avitabile, went on to do well under Ranjit Singh. Other Persian princes also developed European trained units. Muhammad 'alī Mīrzā had one such force at Kirmānshāh and it was linked to a park of artillery created for him in the mid-1810s by a Russian renegade named Yūsuf Khān. Yūsuf also established a foundry for casting brass cannon and a factory for manufacturing gunpowder. However, the success of these measures was limited. Muhammad 'ali Mīrzā's innovations did not prevent defeat at the hands of Russia in 1826–8, and in 1838 the Persian siege of Herat was poorly handled and the new units were regarded by observers as less impressive than traditional-style mounted levies led by Persian commanders.[14]

There were to be other, parallel, attempts at industrialization later in the century, especially in Japan. By 1840, however, the process of military Europeanisation was still restricted geographically, while even by 1860, although more efforts at change had been made, its scope remained limited. Consequently, as European weaponry and techniques were becoming more effective from 1815, other peoples had less ability outside Europe to match or resist them. This was especially serious in territorial terms, because it interacted with a clear shift in the official and popular attitudes of Europeans, in particular Western Europeans, towards territorial gains. A belief in the need, duty and right to control territory and rule over different peoples came to play a major, or at least more prominent, role in the European (and European-American) psyche. Thus, opportunity and mission converged, rather as they had done in Spain after the conquest of Granada in 1492.

British Expansion 1815–45

Opportunity was especially apparent in the case of Britain which played a relatively limited role in continental European politics after 1815. The Portuguese monarchy was backed by British warships, marines and finally by troops from 1824, the climax occurring in 1826–7 when the government was threatened by a Spanish-supported insurrection. Largely thanks to superior British gunnery, an Anglo–French–Russian fleet under Sir Edward Codrington destroyed the Ottoman and Egyptian fleets at the battle of Cape Navarino on 20 October 1827, the last great battle of the Age of Fighting Sail. However, in general, the British were hesitant about involvement in continental power politics. They refused both to join and to oppose the Holy Alliance of 1815 and although the government protested in 1823 when French troops helped suppress a liberal revolution in Spain, there was no willingness to launch a liberal crusade there or elsewhere. The Peninsular War was refought in memoirs and other books, but certainly not by British troops.

Britain neither intervened greatly in continental politics nor apparently needed to do so. Turning away from Europe's conflicts gave Britain the opportunity to expand and campaign elsewhere. Equilibrium in Europe provided opportunity abroad. In the three decades immediately after 1815, a period in which other European states made only modest colonial gains, the British empire expanded across several continents. India was the most important area of expansion with important acquisitions, such as Maratha dominions in western India in 1818, after British victories at Kirkee (1817), Sitabaldi (1817), Mahidpur (1817), Koregaon (1818) and Satara (1818);[15] lands acquired from Burma in 1826: Arakan and Tenasserim; Mysore in 1831; Karachi to amphibious attack in 1839; and Sind in 1843, after British victories at Umarkot (1843) and Mirpur Khas (1843). The British showed that they were capable of conceiving and sustaining strategies and logistics that spanned all of India. They were also helped by the failure of potential opponents to cooperate. Thus, when the Nepalis sought support from China, Bhutan, the Marathas and the Sikhs in 1814 they received none.

The British also expanded in Malaya, gaining Malacca and Singapore, and annexed Aden in 1839, the first time it had been captured by a European power. British successes in the Opium War of 1839–42, including the capture of Amoy, Chusan, Canton, Ningpo, Shanghai and Chinkiang by amphibious forces, led China to cede Hong Kong by the Treaty of Nanjing of 1842. British warships moved into the Persian Gulf to stop what they saw as the piracy of the Qasimi Arabs. Argentinian and American interest in the Falkland Islands was countered by their reoccupation by the British in 1832–3.[16] In South Africa, the British expanded inland from the appropriately named Cape Colony. British naval action against Mehmed Ali in 1840 – the occupation of Sidon and Beirut and the bombardment and capture of Acre – limited Egypt's northward advance. The British were also an example to other powers, especially in naval technology. Thus, after spending two years visiting dockyards in Britain and the Netherlands, the engineer Mikhail Grinval'd returned to Russia in 1835 in order to lay down Russia's first steam frigate, the *Bogatyr*.[17]

The World 1815–45

No other European state could compare with Britain's transoceanic gains, although the French began their second (post-revolutionary/Napoleonic) colonial empire when they occupied Algiers in 1830, the Marquesas and Tahiti (proclaimed a protectorate) in the

Pacific in 1842, and Gabon in West Africa in 1844. Accusing Sultan Abd er-Rahman of Morocco of helping opposition in Algeria, the French under Bugeaud invaded Morocco from Algeria in 1844 and defeated the Sultan's forces at Isly.

The Russians were more concerned about resisting rebellion in Poland than in making gains in Central Asia, although in and around the Caucasus they made important advances at the expense of Turkey and the local peoples, and they also made major gains in Kazakstan. In the Russo-Turkish war of 1828–9 the Russians captured Anapa, Akshaltsikhe, Kars and Erzurum,[18] and by the Treaty of Adrianople (1829) the Turks abandoned their position on the Circassian coast. Nevertheless, the subsequent Russian effort to subdue Circassia proved very costly, despite major commitments of troops, naval blockade, fort construction and attempts both to pursue pacification and to adopt more brutal tactics. However, the Russians were helped by ethnic and religious divisions among the Caucasian peoples. Chechnya and Daghestan were not conquered until 1859, Circassia until 1864.

In 1822 the Russians annexed the lands of the Middle Kazak Horde, restructuring its organisation and leadership and introducing Russian administrative control based on a number of forts built in 1824–31. New fortified lands – the Ilek and the New Line – brought much of the best pastureland under Russian control. The Kazaks revolted, capturing the Russian fort of Akmolinsk (1838), but their opposition was weakened by divisions: the rebels had to help the Elder Horde fight off the Khanate of Kokand, while the Russians subsequently gained the allegiance of the Elder Horde (1846) and allied with Kokand. Kirgiz, loyal to Kokand, then destroyed the rebels. Meanwhile, the inexorable advance of Russian forts and farmers continued. The Chinese, who had largely controlled the Elder Horde and had a considerable impact on the Middle Horde the previous century, were no longer strong enough to intervene in the region.[19] The Russians also advanced in Turkestan. A campaign launched in 1839 against the Khanate of Khiva for robbing Russian caravans was unsuccessful, but, thereafter, fortresses were constructed, beginning with Aleksandrovskiy in 1840.

In North America, the native Americans were repeatedly defeated. The Creeks were attacked in 1813 and defeated at Tallasahatchee and Talladega. The following year, Andrew Jackson attacked the centres of Creek power and stormed their fortified camp at Horseshoe Bend, although his victory owed much to his native warriors. The natives were also defeated in the Seminole wars in Florida (1817–18, 1837–43). In the first war Andrew Jackson was helped in his 1818 invasion of Florida by a force of Lower Creeks. In the second war the government deployed large numbers of troops. The outnumbered Seminole generally avoided fighting in the open and eventually took shelter in the more inaccessible parts of the Everglades. Having driven them to these refuges, the government wound down the war. The frontier of European American settlement also moved west of the Mississippi, a move made possible by the defeat of tribes in the old north-west with close ties to the British in Canada: the Shawnees at Tippecanoe (1811), and at the battle of the Thames (near London, Ontario) in 1813 during the war of 1812, and Black Hawk and the Sauk and Fox peoples in the Black Hawk War in Illinois and Wisconsin in 1832, a war rapidly ended with Black Hawk's crushing defeat at Bad Axe River. Boer firepower smashed a Zulu attack on their wagon circle in the battle of Blood River in Natal in 1838.

Although the period 1815–45 is not one of many European military defeats, apart from the Latin American Wars of Liberation, the British did lose an entire British-Indian division in a disastrous evacuation of Afghanistan in 1842, and the Russians suffered defeats in the Caucasus in 1842 and 1845. The British disaster of 1842 was due to poor decision-making, a failure to understand the Afghan political situation and 'General

Winter'. The commander in Kabul, the elderly, infirm and poorly prepared Major General William Elphinstone, who had fought with great credit at Waterloo, hardly knew whether to retreat or to stay. When he finally decided to go, the winter had set in, and his army (by now deeply demoralised) faced serious logistical problems as they tried to cross passes deep in snow, with a lot of camp-followers. It was 116 miles from Kabul to Jalalabad where a British garrison waited, and the first day the column marched only five miles. The British were ambushed by Ghilzni tribesmen, but it was a classic case of the importance of terrain and generalship in warfare. In 1878–9, in contrast, Sir Frederick, later Lord, Roberts was besieged outside Kabul, but he knew he had to stay, prepared a strong position, laid in food supplies for winter, and survived. Having used up its ammunition, a small British force under Colonel Sir Charles McCarthy, Governor of Sierra Leone, was destroyed by a much larger Asante army in 1824. The governor's head became a war trophy. Elsewhere in Africa, the Gaza Nguni of southern Mozambique destroyed a Portuguese army in 1834 and the Zulus sacked Lourenço Marques the previous year.

The contrast between Russian success against French, Persian and Turkish armies in the first half of the century, and the length of time it took them to conquer Chechnya and Daghestan,[20] reflected the limitations of military force in the face of popular opposition, and the error of assuming one common hierarchy of military capability and success. In addition, there were difficulties and setbacks for the Americans, especially in subjugating the Seminole of Florida in the 1830s. The Seminole won several battles in 1835 in the initial stages of the second Seminole war. They were able to take shelter in the Everglades.

Furthermore, Dutch expeditions against Palembang in Sumatra were defeated in 1819 and, at first, in 1821, but the Dutch were eventually victorious in 1821. Also on Sumatra, the Dutch only won the Padri War (1821–38) after defeats, including a serious one at Lintau (1823). The Java War, which began in 1825, was brought to a successful conclusion by the Dutch only after five years of hard fighting. The Dutch were short of troops, but they benefited from Indonesian allies, including the Sultan of Yogyakarta. Initially, the Dutch were thwarted by the mobility and guerrilla tactics of their opponents, but they developed a network of fortified bases from which they sent out mobile columns that policed the local population, prevented the consolidation of rebel positions and attacked the rebels.[21] In contrast, in 1831–2, the Dutch were unable to reconquer Belgium, which had rebelled against Dutch rule in 1830.

The French encountered strong resistance in Algeria in the 1840s from troops employing firearms led by Abd el-Kader (1807–83), who had proclaimed a *jihad* in 1832. One poorly led French column was destroyed at Sidi-Brahim (1845). The seizure of land for French settlement made it more difficult for the French to fit into existing power structures. At the outset, the French commanders of the Army of Africa sought to employ familiar tactics: those of Napoleonic conflict, namely mass manoeuvre and large columns, and the holding of territory by posts creating a front. However, this policy was changed by General Bugeaud in the 1840s as the French came to emphasise a more fluid strategy: many posts were abandoned in order to free troops for a more aggressive strategy in which rapidly moving columns and cavalry units attacked the Algerians. These tactics were supported by overwhelming force: by 1846 the French had 108,000 effectives, one-third of their regular army, in Algeria – one soldier for every 25 to 30 Algerians and a force that greatly outnumbered that of Abd el-Kader. The latter surrendered in 1847. Further west the British navy found it difficult to deal with Moroccan pirates, not least because their muskets were better.[22]

56. *The Thin Red Line* by Robert Gibb (1881). The painting depicts an incident at the battle of Balaclava (1854) and is based on a battlefield dispatch by William Howard Russell: 'a thin red streak tipped with a line of steel'. The painting shows the Russian cavalry far nearer the 93rd Highlanders than was actually the case, for the Minié rifles of the latter drove the enemy off and the Highlanders began firing at about 600 yards.

Despite difficulties, the overall impression is one of an increasingly apparent European-American effectiveness in battle and campaign. A further demonstration was the British victory in the Opium War. In part this was due to a repetition of the familiar: to a victory of small European units over larger non-European counterparts. More significantly, however, this was the first time a west European state had waged war on China, the first European victory over the Chinese and one achieved in China itself. In addition, Java was brought under control and came to serve as the basis for an expansion of Dutch power, comparable to, although on a smaller scale than, that of Indian-based British power. Both states took a more direct role than when their presence had been controlled by their East India Companies. Furthermore, naval power was deployed effectively. The threat of naval bombardment led the Dey of Algiers to capitulate to British demands in 1824; the city had already been bombarded by an Anglo-Dutch fleet in 1816, leading to an agreement to end the taking of Christian slaves. The British naval bombardment and capture of Acre was a decisive blow in the expulsion of Egyptian forces from Syria in 1840. A fortuitous shell caused the main magazine to explode, but the whole operation was an impressive demonstration of western power against the modernising and empire-building Egyptians.

Weaponry

The principal innovations in infantry weaponry in the early decades of the century were all European. They improved the reliability and rate of fire. In 1807 Alexander Forsyth, a Scottish cleric, patented the use of fulminates of mercury in place of gunpowder as a primer for firearms. Mercury fulminates ignited when struck: there was no need for external fire and thus detonation. The resulting use of the percussion cap, coated with fulminates of mercury, produced a reliable, all-weather ignition system. Joshua Shaw developed the mass-produced metal percussion cap in 1822. Positioned over the fire hole, it ignited the main charge. Percussion muskets were introduced into European armies, for example that of Austria from 1836. The dramatic reduction of misfires resulted in a great increase in firepower. However, a lack of government support delayed the use and development of Forsyth's invention, and its impact was minor until after 1815.

The percussion cap was to be followed by Captain Claude Minié's cylindro-conoidal lead bullet (1849) which expanded when fired to create a tight seal within the rifle, thus obtaining a high muzzle velocity, and by Johann von Dreyse's 'needle' rifle. The Minié bullet made for rapid fire (due to its easy loading) and accuracy and it was adopted by the British army in 1851.

The Minié bullet contained an iron plug in its base and was cast with a diameter slightly less than that of the gun bore. When fitted in the muzzle it slid easily down the bore. When the gun was fired the charge pushed the iron plug into the base of the bullet, causing it to expand and grip the rifling of the bore. Thus it was fired on an accurate trajectory. A later form of the Minié bullet had a hollow base, which had the same effect of expanding when the charge went off and sealing the bore. This did away with the need for the iron plug. The charge was fired by an external percussion cap, and this system married up the reliability of fire of the latter with the greater accuracy of the Minié bullet.

Warfare 1845–75

The three decades from 1845 witnessed a continuation of the trends already mentioned, but with the important addition of a protracted period of war within the European and European-American world. The first of these conflicts centred on the nationalist uprisings of 1848 and the subsequent wars of German (1864, 1866, 1870–1) and Italian (1848–9, 1859–61, 1866, 1870–1) unification; the second on the Mexican-American war (1846–8) and later the American Civil War. Casualties were heavy, over one million dead and wounded in the American Civil War alone, in part because of the use of new firearms, especially the percussion-lock rifle to which close-order linear and column attacks, such as Pickett's Charge at Gettysburg (1863), proved very vulnerable.

Developed in the 1840s, the rifled barrel of the percussion-lock rifle gave bullets a more reliable trajectory and far greater effectiveness than the balls fired by muskets with their smooth barrels. The combination of the percussion-lock rifle and the Minié bullet was deadly. The effective range of infantry firepower increased and the casualty rates inflicted on close-packed infantry rose dramatically. Attacking Russian columns took major losses at the hands of the British and French in the Crimean War of 1854–6. The Crimean War was followed by the public, thanks to newspaper reports, and also by military observers. Thus the American War Department drew up a *Report on the Art of War in Europe, 1854, 1855, and 1856* (3 vols, Washington, 1857–61), based on the reports of American army officers, including George B. McClellan who was to be prominent in the Civil War, being appointed Union General-in-Chief in 1861.

The hard-fought battles of the wars of German and Italian unification, especially the Franco-Piedmontese victory over the Austrians at Solferino (1859), saw very heavy casualties and the impact of improved artillery: the new French rifled cannon were superior to their Austrian smooth-bore counterparts and destroyed most of them with highly accurate counter-battery fire. Although developed in the mid-seventeenth century, optical sights on cannon only became common in the mid-nineteenth. In 1859 both sides employed railways in the mobilisation and deployment of their forces; the French moved 130,000 men to Italy by rail.

However, the muzzle-loaded rifle could fire only one to three rounds a minute, compared to the longer-range breech-loading Prussian Dreyse *Zündnadelgewehr* or 'needle' rifle (named because of its needle-shaped firing pin) that could be loaded lying down and that fired four to seven a minute. The Dreyse was fired largely from the hip because of the problem of escaping gases. First used, with great effect, by the Prussians against German revolutionaries in Baden and Hesse in 1849, breech-loading rifles were employed by the Prussians to deadly effect in the Danish War of 1864 and the Austrian War of 1866. Both these conflicts were sweeping victories for Prussia, with important victories at Duppel (1864) and Sadowa/Königgrätz (1866). It was the volume of fire rather than its accuracy that was important at Sadowa, although the Prussians trained all their soldiers to be skirmishers, able to fire their rifles accurately. Soldiers who could load and fire their rifles lying down were more readily able to benefit from cover and this encouraged the digging of trenches.

Prussia's success in 1866 led other European powers to adopt breech-loading rifles and also the tactics of concentrating their strength on the skirmishing line, thus adopting extended formations that were more dispersed than columns or lines and less vulnerable to infantry and artillery fire. In 1866 the French adopted the *chassepot* rifle which had a more gas-tight breech and a greater range than the Prussian needle rifle; but, despite their better infantry weaponry that inflicted heavy casualties on a foolish Prussian frontal attack at Wörth, the French lost the Franco-Prussian War (1870–1). This reflected the superiority of the Prussian artillery, in contrast to the French who were still using muzzle-loading artillery; and also of Prussian strategy, in particular the use of dispersed forces that outmanoeuvred the more concentrated and slower-moving French armies.

Prussian strategy and tactics countered the mid-century developments in rifled weapons and the scale of conflict that had given the defence many advantages, as shown in Italy in 1859, Denmark in 1864 and Virginia in 1865; although these advantages did not prevent the Austrians, Danes and Confederates from being defeated. Instead of a war of attrition, Helmuth von Moltke, the Chief of the Prussian General Staff, adapted Napoleonic ideas of the continuous offensive to the practicalities of the industrial age, including railways.[23] In place of frontal attack, he sought to envelop opposing forces and to oblige them to mount such attacks in an effort to regain freedom of manoeuvre. Prussia's victory led to her gaining Alsace-Lorraine and a substantial indemnity from France and enabled her to transform her hegemony within Germany into a German empire ruled from Berlin, an achievement greater than any aimed at by Frederick the Great.

These various conflicts, in combination with periods of military confrontation and preparation, ensured that only a small portion of Europe's forces was devoted to expansion at the expense of non-Europeans. For example, the new iron-clad warships were used, or their use planned, against other European military powers, as in the Austrian victory over a larger Italian fleet in the Adriatic at the battle of Lissa in 1866, the largest naval battle since Trafalgar in 1805 and prior to Tsushima in 1905, and one in which the two fleets were in part composed of steam-driven ironclads. Arms races, such as that between Italy and Austria in the Adriatic in the 1860s,[24] were between European powers. Similarly, the Americans deployed far more troops in the Civil War than in operations against the native Americans.

Latin America

The Latin American powers did not take part in transoceanic expansion: they lacked the resources, especially naval strength and finance, and the tradition, and were under the economic influence of Europe and the USA. Instead, their nationalist passions led to conflicts within Latin America, such as the War of the Triple Alliance (Argentina, Brazil and the Uruguayan *colorados*) against Paraguay (1864–70), and the War of the Pacific (1879–83), in which Chile, Bolivia and Peru fought to control the valuable nitrate deposits in the Atacama Desert north of Chile. Outnumbered Chile won, thanks in part to the victory of its ironclad warships over the Peruvian ironclad *Huascar* off Punta Angamos (1879), captured Lima (1881) and gained Bolivia's Pacific coastline.[25]

These South American conflicts were major wars. In the Paraguayan war, 330,000 died, many in savage battles in 1866, and Paraguay was devastated: the allies occupied the capital, Asunción, in 1868 and the Paraguayan leader, Francisco López, was killed in 1870, bringing hostilities to a close. Infantry tactics relied heavily on frontal attacks, and logistical capability played a major role in campaigns in difficult terrain. The availability of European weaponry was also important.

During the war of the Triple Alliance, raiding Native tribes made inroads on Argentinian ranches, as troops were diverted to the war. After the war ended, the government regained the initiative, building forts that were linked with railways, and, in 1877, launching a major offensive in which Natives were defeated in a number of engagements and tribal lands were seized.

The American Civil War

The American Civil War (1861–5) was very different to the Napoleonic Wars in strategy, tactics and logistics. The railway made a major difference, helping the North mobilise its greatly superior demographic and economic resources, and playing a role in particular battles. Reinforcements arriving by train helped the Confederates win at Bull Run (1861). Rail junctions, such as Atlanta, Chattanooga, Corinth and Manassas became strategically significant and the object of operations. Furthermore, man-made landscape features, such as embankments created for railways, played a part in battles. The North's dependence on railways led to the South raiding both them and the telegraph wires that were their counterparts.

On the battlefield, firepower, especially new, high-powered rifles such as the Enfield, proved more deadly than hitherto in North American conflict. American weapons production was already at a sophisticated level by contemporary standards. After the Crimean War the British acquired American machinery for weapons production: a team of inspectors was sent out by the Board of Ordnance to bring equipment back from Colt and other manufacturers. The Gatling gun, an early, hand-cranked multi-barrelled machine-gun patented in 1862, was used in the American Civil War, following on from the use of Colt's machine-gun in the Mexican War. The Model 1855, the standard infantry weapon in use in the American army in 1861, fired the Minié bullet and had a muzzle velocity of 950 feet per second. By 1863 much of the Union cavalry was equipped with breech-loading repeating carbines, which they used in clearing eastern Tennessee, and by 1865 some of their infantry had repeating rifles.

Due to defensive firepower, massed frontal attacks on prepared positions became more costly and unsuccessful, as the Union, for example, discovered at Second Manassas (1862)

57. *The Battle of Fredericksburg, 13 December 1862*, by Carl Rochling. The assault of the Union forces under Ambrose Burnside on the entrenched positions of Robert E. Lee's Confederates was an expensive failure that indicated the potency of defensive firepower.

and Fredericksburg (1862) and the Confederates at Corinth (1862) and Stones River (1862–3). Most of the casualties inflicted by rifle fire in the Civil War resulted from long-range accurately aimed defensive fire from behind entrenchments and log breastworks. Both sides learned the necessity of throwing up entrenchments as a consequence of fighting each other to a costly draw at the battle of Antietam (1862). Bayonets and rifled muskets were increasingly supplemented by, or even downplayed in favour of, fortifications and artillery, a sign of the future character of war between developed powers. Heavy casualties and the near-continuous nature of the conflict from Ulysses Grant's advance in May 1864, gave the war in the Virginia theatre an attritional character. This ground down the South, which had a smaller army. Although entrenchments became more important in the centre of hostilities, Virginia, further west and south the war was more mobile, as with William Sherman's destructive 'March through Georgia' in 1864, and cavalry had a greater role.[26] The South also suffered from serious economic problems, including food shortages. The Civil War witnessed an application of devastation as a means of conflict in a 'European' context: Sherman considered that he was fighting 'a hostile people' and set out to destroy the will of the civilian population, to 'make Georgia howl!' South Carolina was devastated in 1865.

At sea, ironclads played an important role, but one that was lessened by the ability of both sides to deploy them, as in the inconclusive duel between the *Monitor* and the *Merrimac* (renamed the *Virginia* by the Confederates) in Hampton Roads on 9 March 1862, the first clash between ironclads in history, and the manner in which both sides had ironclads when David Farragut's Union fleet successfully fought its way into Mobile Bay in August 1864. The use of ironclads encouraged their construction in Europe: an example of diffusion between the European-American and European world. The first successful torpedo boat attack occurred in Albemarle Sound, North Carolina in 1864, when the Union sank the *Albemarle*, a Confederate armoured vessel similar to the *Merrimac*, with a spar torpedo fitted to a launch. Earlier that year the first effective attack by a submersible was mounted in Charleston Harbour when the *Hunley* sunk the Union corvette

Housatonic but was herself destroyed by the force of the explosion. The *Hunley* was one of a number of hand-propelled screw-driven Confederate craft, known as Davids, designed to do battle with Goliath – the Union navy. In 1863 Rear Admiral Samuel F. du Pont commanded nine Union ironclads in an attack on Charleston, but they were hampered by mines and five of the ships were badly damaged by shore batteries.[27] Larger Union naval forces ultimately prevailed. In January 1865 an amphibious operation covered by 58 Union warships, the largest fleet hitherto assembled in the war, captured Fort Fisher, and thus closed Wilmington, the Confederacy's last major port.

As with Gibbon's model of competitive military emulation between the European powers, so the American Civil War led during the conflict to a tremendous growth in military and naval capability. Thus, having been defeated at First Manassas/Bull Run in 1861, the Union reorganised its forces into the Army of the Potomac, developing a well-disciplined, well-equipped and large army. Yet organisation and resources were of limited value without able leadership. George McClennan, who became General-in-Chief in November 1861 and who organised the new army, was indecisive, cautious and defence-minded, allowing the Confederates to gain the initiative in the eastern theatre for most of 1862–3. Grant, in contrast, understood what it took to win.

European Expansion 1845–75

Despite the wars between European and European/American powers, expansion at the expense of non-Europeans continued, not least because the two European powers best placed to gain territory, Britain and Russia, were not deeply involved in European conflict in this period, with the exception of the short-lived Crimean War of 1854–6.

India again served as the basis of British expansion from the late 1840s. Campaigns there provided the British with crucial experience of operations outside Europe, and the Indian army was the leading British strategic reserve on land. Kashmir became a vassal in 1848. The Punjab was annexed in 1849, after a series of hard-fought British victories in the First (1845–6) and Second (1848–9) Anglo-Sikh Wars against Sikh forces armed with effective firearms and cannon, culminating in the battle of Chillianwalla in which the British army fielded 106 cannon. The Sikh Wars encouraged an emphasis on more and heavier cannon.[28] The Sikhs were weakened by serious divisions.

Lower Burma was annexed by the British in 1852, although it was not 'pacified' until 1857; Nagpur, Jhansi and Berar followed in 1853 and Awadh (Oudh) in 1856. The Indian Mutiny of 1857–9 was violently suppressed by British and loyal Indian troops, especially Sikhs and Gurkhas, in the largest deployment of British forces since the Napoleonic Wars and before the Boer War of 1899–1902. Victory in this lengthy conflict was seen as crucial to British prestige and power in India. The challenge was exacerbated by the presence of numerous trained artillerymen among the rebels. They also had new Enfield rifles. The important role of Indian military manpower was indicated by the trigger of the Mutiny: the British demand that their Indian soldiers use a new cartridge for their new Enfield rifles greased in animal tallow, a measure that was widely unacceptable for religious reasons.[29]

Elsewhere, native resistance was overcome in Australia and, though less easily and completely, in 1860–72 in New Zealand. The Maoris, under Titokowaru and Te Kooti, used well-sited trench and *pa* (fort) systems that were difficult to bombard or storm, and inflicted serious defeats on the British.[30] In Africa, Cape Colony expanded with the acquisition of British Kaffravia which had been annexed in 1847; Natal had already been annexed in 1845. Lagos was annexed in 1861. The British used Gatling guns and seven-pounder artillery in 1873–4 in Garnet Wolseley's well-organised and successful punitive expedition against one of the more militarily powerful of all African people, the Asante (Ashanti) of West Africa. They also benefited from the assistance of other African peoples, especially the Fante. The Asante were outgunned by the British breech-loading rifles – shot from their muskets could only inflict minor wounds – and defeated at Amoafu (1874), the advancing British square firing repeatedly into the surrounding vegetation. The Asante capital, Kumasi, was seized and burned down.[31] The previous expedition – in 1864 – had been wrecked by disease.

The French expanded their strength in the Senegal Valley from 1854, developing an effective chain of riverine forts linked by steamboats.[32] The French also expanded their control in Algeria and began a territorial presence in Indo-China, Somaliland and the Ivory Coast. They annexed New Caledonia in 1853.

The Dutch made gains in the East Indies – in Borneo, the Celebes, Bali, Sumatra and New Guinea – although the process was a slow one, in part because of the problems of campaigning – logistics, disease and native opposition – and in part because of only limited political will and resources.[33] The Dutch devoted fewer troops and less attention to imperialism than did the British and French: there was certainly nothing to compare with the French in Algeria or the British in India.

In North America, the pace of expansion of native Americans resumed after the disruption of the American Civil War. The native Americans suffered from a lack of unity, and from the replacement of the weak presence of Mexican control and the accommodating views of the British in the Oregon Territory, by the more insistent territorial demands and military activity of the burgeoning American state. Nevertheless, it was the demographic weight of the European-Americans that was crucial, combined with their willingness to migrate from regions already settled to those occupied by native Americans.

The railway played a major role, not only in speeding American troops but also in developing economic links between coastal and hinterland America and integrating the frontiers of settlement with the exigencies of the world economy. This was important, both in the spread of ranching, with the cattle being driven to railheads, and of mining, for example for silver. Thus, as with the Russians in the Ukraine in the eighteenth century, the spread of politico-military control has to be seen alongside that of settlement and economic exploitation. Not all native American tribes fought the European-Americans. The Utes, Crow and Pawnees, for example, were generally friendly, and, indeed, provided the army with scouts. Nelson Miles, a veteran of the Civil War, used Crow assistance when he attacked the Sioux and northern Cheyenne after Custer's defeat at Little Bighorn.[34]

Although the Crimean War checked Russian ambitions on the Turkish empire in Europe, between 1845 and 1875 Russia's frontier expanded greatly. The Crimean War arose from a Russo-Turkish war that began in 1853. Although the Russians were defeated by the British and French in the Crimea, they fought well, forcing their opponents to abandon their initial war goals. The Russians were more successful against the Turks, though in 1853 the Russians were driven out of Wallachia and Moldavia. A wooden Turkish squadron was surprised and destroyed at Sinope on 30 November 1853 by Russian warships using shells. 3,000 of the 4,400 Turks present were killed. The main Turkish army in the Caucasus was defeated at Kurudere in 1854, and in 1855, after an initial attempt to storm it had failed to win Kars, the Russians took the city.

Further east, the shifting balance of advantage between Russia and China enabled her to gain the Amur region in 1858 and the Ussuri region in 1860. The Treaty of Beijing of 1860 delimited the new frontier. Vladivostok was founded in the Ussuri region in 1860, providing Russia with a warm-water Pacific port. In Central Asia the Russians made important advances. A line of fortresses against Turkestan was constructed in 1864–5, and Kazakstan, now isolated from outside intervention, was brought under increased Russian administrative control and opened to further settlement by the code of 1868. A revolt by the Younger Horde in 1869 was put down. Extensive settlement followed.

In Turkestan the Russians advanced up the Syr Dar'ya in the 1840s and made gains at the expense of Kokand in the 1850s. In the early 1860s extensive conquests were made in what was organised in 1865 as Turkestan. Tashkent was gained in 1865 and Samarkand in 1868. Kokand (1866) and Bukhara were defeated, as was Khiva (1873),[35] the latter two becoming Russian protectorates. The Russian empire was an extension of its frontier, rather than, as with Britain and France, the creation of an overseas empire. Russian expansion owed much to the disunity of the Khanates. Bukhara itself was weakened by rebellion.

Japan

Yet this was also a period that was to herald major changes, in that it saw greater efforts on the part of some non-European powers to adopt European technology, military techniques and institutions. The most important was Japan. Outside pressure, particularly from the expeditions of Commodore Perry in 1853 and 1854 onwards, changed Japan, although only as a result of the domestic response: pressure on China was greater but the domestic context was less conducive to westernisation. From 1867 the Tokugawa shogunate began a serious effort to remodel its army along French lines.[36] Already domains such as Choshu had begun to introduce military reforms, and, as a consequence, the shogunal army was defeated in 1866. This was followed in 1868 by civil war and the overthrow of the Tokugawa shogunate in the so-called Meiji Restoration.

The civil violence of the period had demonstrated the superiority of western weaponry and the political shift made it easier to advocate and introduce a new military order. The privileged, caste-nature of military service was replaced by conscription, which was introduced in 1869. The two systems, one traditional, one European and modern, were brought into conflict in 1877 with a samurai uprising in the south-western domain of Satsuma. This brought a substantial samurai force armed with swords and matchlock muskets into combat with the new mass army of conscripted peasants. In what was in some respects a repeat of the Ottoman and Napoleonic defeats of the Mamelukes in 1517 and 1798 respectively, individual military prowess and bravery succumbed to the organised, disciplined force of an army that on an individual basis was less proficient. Conscription was a crucial process, breaking down the division between a small, and sometimes westernised, regular army and very differently armed levies that were often tribal in character, a division that affected Turkey, Persia and China.

Japanese military development was supported by policies of education and industrialisation, and was enhanced by the institutionalisation of planning. In 1874, the Sambōkyoku, an office to develop plans and operations, was created within the Army Ministry and this became first the Staff Bureau and subsequently the General Staff Headquarters.[37] The organisational transformation of the Japanese army was linked to an institutional professionalisation and, also, to the creation of a capacity for overseas operations. In the 1880s, thanks not least to the creation of a system of divisions, the army was transformed from a heavily armed internal security force reliant on static garrison units into a mobile force.

A European-style navy was also developed. While French and, later, German models and military missions influenced the Japanese army, the navy looked to Britain for warships and training. Thus in 1871 Heihachiro Tōgō, who was to defeat the Russian fleet at Tsushima in 1905, arrived in Britain for training. Masajirō Ōmura translated German military theory. Thanks to the progress of both army and navy, the Japanese developed an amphibious capability.

Japanese military activity also highlighted what was to become a more important theme in global military relations: increasing confrontation between European and Europeanising military powers. The defeat of the Emperor Maximilian's attempt to take over Mexico in the 1860s was an example of the deficiencies of European military power in the face of a Europeanised power. Maximilian, the younger brother of the Austrian Emperor, Francis Joseph I, had far less success than Cortés had had in 1519–21, but the issue was more complex: the intervention was mishandled and met a strong nationalist response. There was a long guerrilla war with few conventional battles, and French support was both insufficient and not maintained. Napoleon III had persuaded Maximilian to accept the offer of the Mexican throne, but, after the American Civil War, American pressure led Napoleon to withdraw his forces and Maximilian was defeated and shot in 1867.

The pressure for military change in Japan owed much to the aggressive use of European and American naval power to open the country to trade in mid-century. In addition, a territorial clash between Japan and Russia developed over the islands to the north of Japan, Sakhalin and the Kuriles. Opportunity and concern over the possible ambitions of other European powers led Russia to occupy Sakhalin in 1853, so brushing aside an earlier Japanese presence. The issue was settled, initially by a condominium over Sakhalin and a partition of the Kuriles and, subsequently, in 1876, by a treaty by which Russia obtained Sakhalin and Japan the Kuriles.[38] These treaties reflected the degree to which military development and territorial expansion led to clashes between states with strong forces. The buffer zones provided by peoples and polities that had less military power were progressively occupied in the second half of the nineteenth century. The world was increasingly divided by frontiers drawn by European powers, and these frontiers were implemented by force.

China

China was affected by the same processes of westernisation as Japan, but the political context was very different, and the response to western examples more uneven and hostile. China's capitulation to 30,000 or so British and French troops in 1860 is one of the starkest contrasts of most Asiatic military performances in the nineteenth century compared with the post-1945 era. It was followed by the British expansion of Hong Kong to include the Kowloon Peninsula. However, although the Chinese army certainly lagged behind western forces in technology, this gap was not large enough to explain the tremendous victories the western powers won. Instead, a failure of leaders to unite the country behind them was crucial. The Chinese could fight well; the British found Chinese fire as accurate as their own at the mouth of the Peiho in 1859 and British warships were badly damaged by the Chinese artillery, while the earthern Chinese fortifications absorbed British shot. The British landing at Taku was defeated, although the port fell the following year. Canton had already been occupied in 1857.[39]

An important aspect of western military example was the mercenary forces that were recruited to fight the Taiping revolution in the early 1860s, the mainly Filipino Foreign Rifle Corps organised by the American adventurer Frederick Townshend Ward, the French-commanded Ever-Triumphant Army and the British-led Ever-Victorious Army.[40] The French artillery of the Ever-Triumphant Army breached the Taiping positions at Fu-Yang (1863) and Hangchow (1864) and that of the Ever-Victorious Army, under Charles Gordon, had the same effect at Soochow (1863); but artillery was not enough: once breached, the positions still had to be stormed. These forces served as an inspiration and a challenge to a number of Chinese leaders, encouraging the formation of Western-style armies towards the end of the century. The defeated Taiping forces themselves relied heavily on spearmen, halberdiers and matchlock muskets,[41] although they also acquired several thousand small arms.[42]

Persia and Turkey

The Qājār Shahs of Persia devoted relatively little attention to improving the armed forces, and compared to Japan, Turkey and even China, there was only a limited attempt to westernise the army in the period 1848–1922. Instead, as in Ethiopia, the small regular army was greatly outnumbered by tribal forces that fought in a largely traditional fashion. In Persia there was a strong conservatism that restricted reform initiatives and, unlike in Turkey, China and Ethiopia, only limited conflict with foreign enemies. Nevertheless, visiting Russia in 1878, Nasir al-Din Shah was impressed by Russian Cossack forces, and thereafter used Russian officers to command and train the Persian Cossack Brigade founded in 1879. Similarly, the first modern police force in Teheran was established in 1879 with the advice of an Austrian officer. An instrument of Russian influence, the Cossack Brigade was also a crucial support to the Shah, being used by Muhammad 'Ali Shāh when he suppressed the popular national government in a coup in 1908.[43] The 1870s was a decade of military modernisation for the Turks, not least with the adoption of the breech-loading Peabody-Martini rifle, a highly effective weapon, and the acquisition of 48 Krupp steel cannon. The Turks had a steam navy, including ironclads on the Danube. However, Acehnese appeals for Turkish support against the Dutch in 1869 and 1873 were unsuccessful. The age of Suleiman the Magnificent was long past.[44]

In Siam under Rama IV (1851–68) and especially Rama V (1868–1910) a degree of modernisation included significant changes in the army, communications and finances. Siam also benefited from being situated between spheres of British (Burma, Malaya) and French (Indo-China) expansion, and served as a buffer state.

European Expansion 1875–1900

The last 25 years of the nineteenth century saw the rapid allocation among the European and European-American powers of much of the world's surface, particularly in Africa. This was achieved at the expense both of developed states with substantial armed forces using firearms, such as Madagascar, which the French annexed in 1896, and of peoples who lacked such forces, for example in New Guinea, which was divided between Britain,

Germany and the Netherlands. Native American resistance was crushed, the Sioux being defeated at Wounded Knee (1890), the last major clash in more than 350 years of 'European'-native American conflict. Less a battle than a policing operation gone amiss, it arose from a scuffle during an attempt to disarm the Miniconjou Sioux. The outnumbered Sioux lost most of their men, in part to shells from the four Hotchkiss guns deployed by the Seventh Cavalry.[45]

At another scale of conflict, a war between France and China in 1883–5 that arose as a result of French expansion into Indo-China was a victory for the French and was followed by their annexation of Tonkin. Elsewhere, historic centres of resistance to European power were captured: Aceh in Sumatra fell to the Dutch in 1873–4, although bitter guerrilla resistance continued in the hinterland, and the Dutch were unable to force their leading opponents to surrender until 1903. Oman became a British protectorate in 1891. By 1900 the British had an empire covering a fifth of the world's land surface and including 400 million people; France one of six million square miles and 52 million people.

European expansion, however, was not achieved without considerable difficulty including some important defeats.[46] These included 'Custer's Last Stand' at Little BigHorn (1876), the defeat of a rashly led and outnumbered American force by the Sioux; the British defeat by the Zulus at Isandlwana (1879); the French defeats in Indo-China at Lang Son (1885), a Chinese victory which destroyed the political career of Jules Ferry, and in the Yen The Massif (1892); the French loss to a surprise night attack of a force near Timbuktu (1895); and the Italian defeat by the Ethiopians at Adowa (1896). At Isandlwana, a 20,000-strong Zulu force defeated a British force of 1,800 (of whom only 581 were regulars). The British had only two seven-pounder guns and their camp was not entrenched. The Zulus enveloped the British flanks and benefited from their opponents running out of ammunition, but, thanks to the British Martini-Henry rifles, Zulu casualties were very high.[47] The Zulus, who did not want rifles, referred to the British as cowards, because they would not fight hand-to-hand. Near Timbuktu the French lost only 82 men, but at Adowa, the outnumbered and badly led Italians lost 10,000.[48] The Italians had already lost 430 men at Dogali north of Asmara in 1887 when the Ethiopian use of enveloping tactics destroyed an Italian column. In 1880 an 11,000-strong Afghan force under Ayub Khan, armed with British Enfield rifles and 30 well-handled cannon, including three rifled 14-pounder Armstrong guns, defeated a 2,500-strong British brigade under George Scott Burrows at Maiwand, killing 962: the British artillery was outgunned and part of the infantry gave way after five hours, leading to a harrowing retreat.[49]

Isandlwana and Adowa are reminders that it was not only the European and European-American states that were expanding and had expanded during the nineteenth century. In Africa, Egyptian control moved southwards. Massawa and Suakin on the Red Sea were occupied by Mehmed Ali in 1818, and Nubia (northern Sudan) in 1820. Egyptian expeditions were also sent into Arabia in 1811, 1815 and 1818. Fashoda, the Sudanese site of an Anglo-French confrontation in 1898, was established as an Egyptian base in 1855 and a strong fortress was built there in the mid-1860s.[50] Equatoria (southern Sudan) in 1871, Darfur (western Sudan) in 1874 and Harrar (later British Somaliland) in 1874 were subsequently gained by Egyptian forces, under Mehmed's grandson Ismail. Artillery played a crucial role in two important victories that Egyptian forces gained over the Shāyqiyya in the eastern Sudan in 1820–1. The Egyptian army was 60,000 strong in 1875 and equipped with modern weaponry: Remington rifles, Gatling machine-guns and 80 mm Krupp artillery. It was, however, disrupted by political instability in 1879–81 and routed by the British under Wolseley at Tel el Kebir in 1882. As a prelude, a British squadron had silenced the forts near Alexandria.

The Zulu under Shaka, their chief in 1816–28, proved dynamic, leading other peoples in South Africa to migrate in the *Mfecane* (Time of Troubles) of the second quarter of the century. Far from drawing on European methods, Shaka changed Zulu tactics, replacing light throwing *assegais* (javelins), by the *i-klwa*, a heavier thrusting spear, and emphasising speedy assault and shock tactics. The success of the Zulu crescent formation was made possible by brave and disciplined troops led by effective officers. Shaka forced defeated peoples to become Zulus: their clans were absorbed.[51]

A number of powerful short-lived polities developed. First, Hadji Omar, from 1848, and later, in the 1870s and 1880s, Toure Samory, the 'Napoleon of the Sudan' according to the French, established states on the upper Niger. The cavalry élite of Hadji Omar's *jihad* created the Tukolor empire, but French mobility and firepower proved superior in the late 1850s. Samory, the leader of the Mandinke people, relied on the *sofa*, professional troops, trained along European lines and equipped with modern firearms, who were supported by a larger militia. The firearms were bought in part from British traders in Sierra Leone, but also manufactured in Samory's own workshops; he had placed agents in the French arsenal in Senegal to learn how to make rifles and cannon.[52] Samory's forces fought a mobile and, frequently, guerilla war that delayed the French conquest of the western Sudan. The Hova kingdom of Merina conquered most of Madagascar by 1880.

Calling himself the Mahdi (divinely guided one), Muhammad Ahmad-Mahdi took over much of the Sudan from 1881, destroying Hicks Pasha's European-commanded Egyptian army at the battle of Shaykan on 5 November 1883, capturing Khartoum and killing 'Chinese Gordon' in 1885, and cutting the land communication routes on which Egypt's far-flung empire depended. The Mahdists saw spearmen as crucial, although they also had an infantry force armed with western rifles, the *jihadiyya*. This played a crucial role at Shaykan. The Mahdi died of typhus in 1885 and his successor, Abdullahi, then attacked Ethiopia: as Christians, the Ethiopians appeared the obvious enemy to the fundamentalist Mahdists. An Ethiopian army was heavily defeated near Lake Tana in 1887. At al-Qāllabāt in 1889 a Mahdist army of about 100,000 men defeated an Ethiopian force of comparable size, after the Emperor, Yohannis, was shot dead.[53]

Longer-lasting states also expanded. Gezo of Dahomey (1818–58), whose troops were armed with firearms, defeated the Kingdom of Oyo, ended payment of tribute to it in 1823 and expanded Dahomey to its furthest limits in the 1830s and 1840s, conquering the Mahi to the north-east who had successfully resisted Dahomian attack in the 1750s. The Mahi were politically fragmented and their warfare based on bows and arrows as Dahomey prevented the sale of European firearms to interior peoples.[54]

The Ethiopians developed a successful army thanks to the leadership of three emperors, Tewodros II, Yohannis IV and Menelik II. It increased from fewer than 15,000 men in the 1860s to 150,000 in 1896, by which time nearly half were armed with modern weapons. Tewodros (1855–68) tried to create a national army, attempted to import large numbers of muskets, and sought to cast cannons and mortars. For him, as for his successors, modernisation centred on military enhancement,[55] although Tewodros committed suicide after he failed to repel a British expeditionary force under Lieutenant-General Robert Napier. Napier led a force from India that was instructed to rescue British hostages. In a methodically planned campaign, Napier's force advanced into the mountains from the Red Sea, defeated the Ethiopians at Arogee and stormed the fortress of Magdala, rescuing the hostages.[56]

The Ethiopians were to be more successful in resisting the Italians. Victories over Egypt at Gundet (1875) and Gura (1876) provided cannon and captured gunners who by 1880 had trained a force of Ethiopian artillerymen. French and Russian advisers improved the Ethiopian artillery in the 1890s, helping to defeat Italy at Adowa in 1896. The Ethiopians used Hotchkiss machine-guns in the battle, although victory over the far smaller Italian army owed more to poor Italian tactics, not least the failure to co-ordinate operations. Menelik II had already expanded his domains of Shoa southwards from the Ethiopian highlands from 1881, and made further gains after he became Emperor of Ethiopia in 1889. After the Italian threat had been disposed of, Menelik made a really big push to the south. Although victory at Adowa earned Ethiopia a reputation as a leader of the liberation struggle in Africa, the neighbouring Somalis saw her in a different light. Ethiopia formally joined the Italians, Britain and France in dividing up Somaliland, the Ethiopians' share of the spoils being the Ogaden region, a gain that was to poison relations between the two states in the 1970s and 1980s.[57]

However, the spread of European military technology in Africa was often limited. Although firearms were eagerly adopted, wheeled gun-carriages made little impact. Furthermore, weapons that were received or copied from Europeans were not always used for military purposes or used, by European standards, effectively. For example, King Tenimu of Zinder (1851–84) developed the local manufacture of cannon, powder and shot and constructed wheeled gun-carriages, but the latter were not put to practical use and the cannon were only employed to fire salutes.[58]

In Asia, although the Russians defeated the Turks in 1877–8, fighting their way to within 15 kilometres of Constantinople, the latter fought hard and well. Thus, for example, the Russians successfully besieged Kars and Plevna, but the siege of Plevna proved both long and costly and the Russians were unable to capture Erzurum and Batumi. The Turks defeated the Serbs in 1876 and the outnumbered Greeks in 1897. They were to defeat the British when they tried to force the Dardanelles in 1915.

In the Far East, Japan heavily defeated China on land and sea in the Sino-Japanese war of 1894–5, acquiring Formosa (Taiwan), which they had unsuccessfully attacked in 1874, and the Pescadores islands as a consequence. The Japanese fleet had won the battle of the Yalu River (1894) over the less speedy and manoeuvrable Chinese. Despite problems with logistics and transport, Japanese forces had advanced through Korea into Manchuria and had captured the major bases of Port Arthur and Weihaiwei, but they were obliged to limit their gains due to pressure from Russia, Germany and France.[59]

In Africa and Asia, as in eighteenth-century India, it was a case of European powers expanding not into a passive world of decrepit states and undeveloped societies, but rather of the Europeans as an increasingly important aspect of a dynamic world, although more prominent than hitherto due to their military force and improved disease control. Precisely because these societies were not decrepit, primitive, undeveloped or weak, the European success in conquering large areas represented a formidable military achievement. This was a mixture of logistics and firepower, not least the use by the 1890s of Maxim (machine) guns, which were introduced in 1883. Hilaire Belloc observed,

'Whatever, happens we have got
the Maxim-gun; and they have not.'

Across much of Africa, it would have been more appropriate for him to mention the breech-loader rifle.

Single-shot breech-loaders such as the British Martini-Henry and the French Gras were in turn replaced by magazine rifles, such as the Lee-Metford, the Kropatschek and the model 1886 Lebel. The British used machine guns in Africa, but the French did not, and the Germans were slow to do so. In Africa, the Boers defeated the Ndebele in 1837, the British defeated the Zulu at Gingindlovu, Khambula and Ulundi in 1879, and Samory was captured by the French in 1898. At Gingindlovu, Khambula and Ulundi heavy defensive infantry fire from prepared positions, supported by artillery, stopped Zulu attacks before the Zulus could reach the British lines, and British cavalry then inflicted heavy losses as the Zulus retreated. The British launched successful campaigns against the Asante of West Africa in 1873–4 and 1895–6, and in 1896 defeated the Matabele and Mashona in Zimbabwe. The following year Benin fell after a rapid British response made possible by telegraph and steamships. The Yorubas were defeated in Nigeria; the British there benefited from the locally raised West African Frontier Force.

In Senegal and Algeria the French used artillery to breach the gates of positions and then stormed them. The Treuille de Beaulieu rifled mountain gun, a mobile, light mortar, was first tested by the French in Algeria in 1857. Artillery, especially 95 mm siege guns using more powerful explosives, played a crucial role in the conquest of the Tukulor forts by the French in 1890–1 and the walls of Kano in Nigeria were breached within an hour by British cannon in 1903. Nevertheless, bayonets, rather than cannon, were crucial to the French conquest of most of West Africa, and the French did not use machine-guns in the colonies. They could jam and early types, such as the Mitrailleuse, were heavy. One of Samory's *sofa*, captured by the French in 1891, shown a Lebel rifle and asked by Lieutenant-Colonel Humbert if he knew what it was, answered, 'When this touches me, this death'. Shown next an artillery piece, he replied, 'This much noise, but never kills anyone'.[60]

At Tel el Kebir the British attacked the Egyptian earthworks without any preliminary bombardment. Wolseley preferred to try to gain the advantage of surprise and his infantry attacked using their bayonets. In India the British found it difficult to use artillery effectively in mountainous terrain, and their field-guns were also of little value against buildings and trenches, both of which were used in the Second Afghan War. Mobile screw-guns were found best. These guns were light, carried in sections and then screwed together for firing. From 1896 high-angle howitzers were also used, for example by Kitchener at Omdurman.

In the 1890s the Belgians used Krupp 75 mm cannon and machine-guns to help overcome opposition in the Congo, while further east the Germans used their Krupps against the Unyamwezi: the latter's rifles were outgunned.[61] The Sudan was conquered by the British: Dongola was captured in 1896; at Atbara in 1898 advancing British troops outgunned the Mahdists, who had no artillery; at Omdurman (1898) British artillery, machine-guns and rifles devastated the attacking Mahdists, the Sudanese brigade in the British army playing a crucial role; and, lastly, the Mahdi's successor, the Khalifa Abdullahi, was defeated and killed by a cavalry force at Um Debreika in 1899. Churchill, who was present, wrote of Omdurman, 'It was a matter of machinery'.[62]

The Russian advance continued in Central Asia with the capture of Tepe (1881), Askhabad and Merv (1884), and the Afghans defeated at Panjdeh (1885), by a Russian force largely composed of Central Asian troops armed with breech-loading rifles. Kokand was absorbed into Turkestan in 1876. The Tekes, defeated in 1881, had already totally defeated Khivan (1855) and Persian (1861) attacks. An earlier Russian offensive in 1879 had also been repulsed.

In contrast to earlier periods of transoceanic expansion in Asia and Africa (although not America), there was now a greater emphasis on territorial control. Sovereignty became more crucial than influence, and the profit motive was subordinated to geopolitics. Much imperial expansion from 1880 arose directly from the response to the real or apparent plans of other European powers, although the search for markets was also important. Imperialists such as Cecil Rhodes and Frederick Lugard, who developed British power in Southern Africa and Nigeria respectively, were proponents of both business and great power rivalry.

Continental Europe was, from *c.*1885 to *c.*1903, locked in an effective balance of power or diplomatic stalemate: Germany, Austro-Hungary and Italy versus France and Russia: confrontation, but not war. Hence there was both impetus and opportunity to seek extra-European expansion, and increasing military professionalism and capability interacted with a growing sense of imperialist military mission. The military came to be a bigger element in, and often play a greater role in, national and international politics.

The major powers shifted their competition, in part by expanding their influence and power in non-European areas of the globe, a sphere where rivalries could be pursued with a measure of safety and without too substantial a deployment of resources. Indeed, relatively few troops were sent, ensuring that there was a heavy reliance on local soldiers. The Spanish-American war of 1898 was unusual in that the ambitions of the major 'European' powers were generally pursued without direct conflict with each other. It is significant that the Spanish-American war, as with the Russo-Japanese war of 1904–5, involved one combatant (Japan, USA) unconstrained by European power politics and alliances, and convinced, instead, that force was necessary to achieve a position in a world where its territorial options were limited by its latecoming to international military competition and territorial expansion. Nevertheless, the Americans were in general not disposed to conflict with European powers. Alaska was purchased from Russia, not conquered. War with Britain was avoided after 1814 despite tension over a number of issues including the Canadian frontier. Having created a major army during the American Civil War, the American government then rapidly demobilised it, much to the relief of Canada.

Instead of direct conflict among themselves, European powers often tried to pre-empt their rivals. The doctrine of 'effective occupation' developed at the Berlin Congress of colonial powers in 1884–5 encouraged a speeding up of the process of annexation. Suspicion of Russian designs on the Turkish empire and French schemes in North Africa led the British to move into Cyprus and Egypt, although Britain's invasion of Egypt in 1882 was also a classic case of imperial expansion taking place as a response to danger-ous instability at the periphery, in this case the threat to the Suez Canal (and European bondholders) posed by the nationalist revolt of Arabi Pasha. Concern about French ambitions led to the British conquest of Mandalay (1885) and the annexation of Upper Burma (1886), although much of it, for example the Shan and Wa States and Karenni, was only under limited control. Russia's successes in Central Asia led to attempts to strengthen and move forward the 'north-west frontier' of British India and the devel-opment of British influence in southern Persia and the Persian Gulf. The campaigns of the Second Afghan War (1878–81), in which the British relieved besieged Kandahar and eventually defeated Ayub Khan (1880), were followed by the construction of forts and cantonments by the British and eventually by their annexation of the frontier region in 1893.[63]

French and German expansion in Africa led Britain to take counter-measures, although economic factors, such as the search for markets and the wish to secure raw materials, for example palm oil, also played an important role. Having abandoned the Sudan in 1885 the British invaded it in 1896 in order to pre-empt the French. The British advanced rapidly in West Africa, with the occupation of the interior of the Gambia in 1887–8, the declaration of the protectorate of Sierra Leone in 1896, the establishment of the protectorates of northern and southern Nigeria in 1900[64] and the annexation of Asante in 1901 after a rebellion had been crushed.

In 1884 Germany claimed protectorates over Togo, the Cameroons, South-West Africa and Western New Guinea, and in 1885 followed with Tanganyika. German moves in East Africa led to the establishment of British power in Uganda in the 1890s. Coastal Kenya was conquered in the early 1890s, its Arab rulers defeated by British troops from India.

The French conquered Indo-China, spending about 500 million gold francs to get established in Tonkin in 1882–96[65]. Annam became a French protectorate in 1883, Laos a decade later. They also conquered most of North and West Africa, including Tunisia in 1881 and Dahomey in 1892–4. The French benefited from earlier experience of fighting in Africa and Senegal. Their European troops were supported by well-equipped and trained African light infantry, especially the *Tirailleurs Senegalais*, who were organised as a separate force in the 1850s.[66] Madagascar was also conquered in 1894–5, with Tananarive falling in 1895.[67]

The King of the Belgians' Congo Free State (modern Zaire) was conquered for Leopold I of Belgium by the *Force Publique* commanded by Francis Dhamis: Belgian-officered Hausa mercenaries from West Africa who defeated Arab rivals. The Congo, however, took many years to conquer. The Katanga was successfully invaded in 1891, but in 1892 much of the eastern Congo was overrun by Swahili forces and in 1893 the Tetela rebelled. The Yaka rebellion was not crushed until 1906.[68] The Italians established themselves in Eritrea in 1885, declared a protectorate over Ethiopia in 1891 and, when this was rejected, the Italians invaded in 1895 using Eritrean *askaris* (auxiliaries). The Portuguese overran much of modern Angola and Mozambique. The Pacific was also divided up by the imperial powers.

All of these actions were made possible by a variety of factors including superior weapons, medical improvements and local rivalries. European forces, especially the British, came to the task of fighting in Africa with considerable experience of treating with and fighting peoples outside Europe. This experience vitally encompassed the recruitment, training and use of local levies and allied forces, logistical capability and combined operations using coastal and river vessels. Local rivalries were of great importance in many cases. Thus, the Portuguese were able to defeat the Kingdom of Gaza in southern Mozambique in 1895 in large part because they benefited from rebellions against the Kingdom by its subject peoples. In battle Portuguese squares used their Kropatschek magazine rifles to defeat Gaza charges.

European expansion was also supported by a global network of bases, which were necessary for the coaling of steam ships; although they were to become less necessary when oil replaced coal in the twentieth century as oil could be transferred from oilers to warships at sea. Thus, French bases included Martinique, Guadeloupe, Dakar, Libreville, Diego Suarez, Obok, Saigon, Kwangchowwan, New Caledonia and Tahiti. In 1898 even an incomplete list of British naval bases included Wellington, Fiji, Sydney, Melbourne, Adelaide, Albany, Cape York (Australia), Labuan (North Borneo), Singapore, Hong Kong, Weihaiwei (China), Calcutta, Bombay, Trincomalee, Colombo, the Seychelles, Mauritius, Zanzibar, Mombasa, Aden, Cape Town, St Helena, Ascension, Lagos, Malta, Gibraltar, Halifax (Nova Scotia), Bermuda, Jamaica, Antigua, St Lucia, Trinidad, the Falklands and Esquimalt (British Columbia). Such bases served as nodal points for the movement of military resources – men, munitions, ships – which was such an important aspect of imperial success, permitting the concentration of resources when required and, more generally, the transfer of such resources in a planned fashion as part of a system of power. Thus in 1837–40 the Dutch moved recruits raised on the Gold Coast in West Africa to the East Indies. Outflanking the Taku Forts in China in 1860, Anglo-French forces were attacked by Mongol horsemen near Sinho, but the latter were routed by Sikh cavalry supported by Armstrong cannon, a combination of imperial manpower and home industry in support of British power.[69] In 1867–8 the British used troops from India in their successful invasion of Ethiopia. Whereas the Portuguese had sent 400 musketeers to the aid of Ethiopia in 1541, Napier invaded with 13,000 troops in 1867. The Ethiopians were outgunned, their matchlocks and smooth-bore shotguns less effective than the British rifles whether muzzle-loading or the more recent breech-loaders.[70] Forces from India were also sent to Aden, Cyprus and Malta. They suppressed the 1875 Perak rising in Malaya.

Napier's career itself illustrated the range of empire. Born in Colombo in 1810, his second name, Cornelis, commemorated the Javanese fort where his father was fatally wounded. Napier was commissioned into the Bengal Engineers, served in the Sikh Wars, and was also responsible for canals, roads and public buildings in the Punjab in 1849–56. Severely wounded in 1857 in the relief of Lucknow during the Indian Mutiny, he served in China in 1860 and was Commander-in-Chief in India, 1870–76.[71]

Britain as the World Power

European overseas bases, and imperial expansion in general, were supported in turn by a global economy that was organised by and to the benefit of the European powers. This was most apparent in the case of Britain because she was the leading global trader. Force was used to support trading interests, as in British policy towards China,[72] and the profits of that trade helped to sustain force. This was a basis for successful expansion: it was related to the commercial profits obtainable to fund the resulting extra burden of defence.

Between 1860 and 1914, Britain, the leading producer of steam engines, owned approximately one-third of the world's shipping tonnage. In 1890–1914 she launched about two-thirds of the world's ships and carried about half of its marine trade. In his poem *Cargoes*, published in 1903, John Masefield was able to present the three ages of marine trade through a 'quinquireme of Nineveh', a 'stately Spanish galleon' and lastly a 'dirty British coaster' carrying a cargo of British exports. The warships launched by the British included vessels for the Chinese, Japanese, Ottoman and Persian navies. It was from Britain that the Japanese ordered their first battle cruiser in 1910. The British were building for states that came to need defence from Euro-American imperialism (including that of the British). When in 1914 the British sequestered all foreign warships being constructed in British yards, that included two large battleships, the *Sultan Osman* and the *Reşadiye*, being built for the Ottoman navy. Most of the warships were built on the Tyne and, in the Northumbrian stately home of Wallington, the painting of industry on the Tyne by William Bell Scott chosen to depict the contemporary period in the region's history carried the maxim 'In the Nineteenth Century the Northumbrians show the World what can be done with Iron and Coal'. Painted in 1861, it included a 100-pound, 7-inch breech-loading gun and shell produced by William Armstrong's ordnance factory on the Tyne.

The global economy was further integrated during the century by developments in communications and finance. The former were important for trade and military capa-

58. *Iron and Coal on Tyneside in the Nineteenth Century* by William Bell Scott. A celebration of British industrial activity. The leading Tyneside entrepreneur William Armstrong (1810–1900) made his Elswick Ordnance Company one of the largest engineering and armaments concerns in the world. The 110-ton, nearly 44-foot long, Armstrong breech-loaders manufactured for HMS *Victoria*, which was launched in 1887, were the largest and most powerful guns in the world. Warships were also built for a host of foreign powers, including Argentina, Chile, Italy and Japan.

bility. This was true not only of railways, but also of improvements to shipping routes. The latter included the apparently mundane, but in fact very important, charting of the world's coastlines, and the more obvious digging of trans-isthmus canals: the Suez Canal opened in 1869 and the Panama Canal, for which excavations began in 1881 but which was not finally opened until 1914. In 1913 the Suez Canal carried over 20 million tons. An important link on the route between Western Europe and India had been created. In 1898 a powerful Spanish squadron left Cadiz for Manila via the Suez Canal. The same year Admiral George Dewey's squadron of American warships was ordered from Hong Kong to Manila by telegram.[73] The Panama Canal enabled the Americans to move warships between the Atlantic and Pacific more rapidly. New routes also entailed military commitments. Thus, in 1906 the British confronted the Turks over the Sinai frontier of Egypt, and during the First World War protection of the canal from the Turks became an important British goal.

Maritime expertise and commercial wealth helped to sustain British naval power. On land, the Crimean War (1854–6) was the sole European conflict in which Britain was involved between the Napoleonic and First World War. On the part of Britain, the conflict was characterised by administrative incompetence, heavy manpower losses and a series of military misjudgments, most famously the Charge of the Light Brigade into the face of Russian cannon at Balaclava in 1854. Ironically, the loss of the Light Brigade, and the care of British casualties by Florence Nightingale, ensures that the war is largely remembered for the British role, but their French ally had a far greater military presence in the Crimea.

The Russian army was also found wanting in the conflict,[74] and the war indicated Britain's ability to project her power around the world, naval attacks being mounted on

Russian coasts as far as Kamchatka in East Asia.[75] In this, the British navy was assisted by technological advances: the warships sent to the Baltic in 1854 were all fitted with steam engines, and they also benefited from Isambard Kingdom Brunel's work on gun-carriages. By the end of the decade the British and French had launched the first ironclad warships: the armoured frigates *Warrior* (1860) and *La Gloire* (1858); the first, which had armour-plating four and a half inches thick and a 6,109 tonnage, was more significant as she had an iron hull (i.e. was all iron rather than ironclad) and was generally more powerful. The *Warrior* was a revolution in ship design, actually a true iron ship with watertight compartments below, the first large seagoing iron-hulled warship. *La Gloire* was merely a wooden ship fitted with metal plates, but the French were handicapped by a lack of iron-working facilities.[76] Both ships retained sail rigs, as did most early steamers.

Britain's most difficult transoceanic conflict in the period was significantly, as earlier in the case of the War of American Independence, with people of European descent. This was the struggle with the Afrikaner republics of Southern Africa, the Orange Free State and the Transvaal: the Anglo-Boer Wars of 1880–1 and 1899–1902. The British were defeated in the first war at the battle of Majuba Hill (1881) and forced to accept Boer independence. The second war proved more difficult than had been anticipated by the British, because they were initially outnumbered and poorly led, while their opponents' superior marksmanship with smokeless, long-range Mauser magazine rifles, and the effective combination of the strategic offensive and a successful use of defensive positions on the tactical defensive by the Boers, inflicted heavy casualties. British artillery was still sited in the open, it being believed that this was the only way to get range; enemy infantry and their fire on the crews was ignored, despite the vastly improved rifles available to the Boers. The gunners were therefore shot down. In addition, the use of trenches, for example at Magersfontein, also meant that artillery fire was often useless. Training manuals were of scant help. In December 1899 the British were defeated at Stormberg, Magersfontein and Colenso, and their positions at Mafeking, Kimberley and Ladysmith were besieged; the following month they were defeated at Spion Kop. The use of cover and accurate firing which the British army had learnt on the North-West Frontier of India did not seem to be employed in South Africa. Theoretically, the British should have been adept at tactics of move and fire. Their contrasting fortunes probably owed much to bad generalship and to a failure to disseminate the specific tactical skills devised for hill warfare by frontier regiments, but possibly also to a habit of indifference in much of the army to the risk of frontal assaults, since they cost so little normally. The British had had relatively low casualty rates in, for example, the Afghan war of 1878–81. However, the effective use of modern rifles by the Pathians in their rising on the North-West Frontier in 1897–8 led to the development of a training regime for hill warfare by the Indian army.[77] Boer firepower forced a more general rethink in tactics. The British developed an appropriate use of cover, creeping barrages of continuous artillery fire, and infantry advances in rushes, coordinated with the artillery.

More effective generalship under Lord Roberts and his Chief of Staff and later successor, Kitchener, changed the situation in 1900, and the ability of Britain to allocate about £200 million and deploy 400,000 troops was a testimony to the strength of both her economic and imperial systems; the systems that had led to the conflict, although the dispatch of so much of the regular army left it far below normal strength in the British Isles. Other colonies, such as Australia and New Zealand, also sent troops. Britain's unchallenged control of the South African ports allowed her to bring her strength to bear and ensured that foreign intervention was not possible; the Boers lacked the coastline and naval power that made the USA and Japan such formidable opponents respectively to Spain and Russia. The navy also provided more direct support in the shape of naval artillery mounted on wheels and used to help the British army. In addition, the railways that ran inland from the ports facilitated the deployment of the military resources brought into Southern Africa, an obvious contrast with British campaigning in North America during the War of American Independence. However, it proved necessary to supplement the railways with less cumbersome wagon trains.

Once the Boer republics had been overrun in 1900, with a successful advance, via Bloemfontein, to Johannesburg and Pretoria, Boer forces concentrated on dispersed operations in which their mounted infantry challenged British control. In response, the by now vastly more numerous British relied on an extensive system of fortifications – the blockhouse system of barbed-wire fences and small positions, scorched earth policies and reprisals, a system that led in 1902 to the Treaty of Vereeniging, a bitter but conditional surrender on the part of the Boers.[78] Similar policies had been used by US forces against native Americans.

The Boers had tried in 1901–2 the strategy of wearing the other side out, or winning by avoiding defeat. This had been the strategy advocated by Charles Lee, and eventually adopted by Washington, in the American War of Independence, and, arguably, the strategy the outnumbered Confederates should have followed in the Civil War.[79] Such a strategy was to be developed with considerable success by guerrilla movements after the Second World War, but it was anticipated in the nineteenth century, not least by the Cuban insurgents resisting Spain in 1895–8. In 1895 they decided that it was best to harass Spanish forces through guerrilla attacks, and to avoid holding territory that would expose them to conventional attack.[80]

Military Developments in the Late Nineteenth Century

Competition on land and sea helped to enhance the combined military strength of the European powers, although it was to be used collectively on a large scale only in World War one, and then for self-destruction. The pace of the resulting change in military capability owed much to the size and flexibility of the industrial base of the major powers, while the very process of industrialisation exacerbated social divisions and created a situation in which war appeared as a viable solution to domestic crisis. It was possible to take new concepts and turn them relatively rapidly into new or improved weapons. It was possible, thanks to mass-production, to have such weapons adopted in large quantities. Thus, in 1900 the Russians ordered 1,000 quick-firing field-guns from the Putilov iron works. Prussia doubled the complement of field-guns to 144 per infantry corps between 1866 to 1905, and the guns were more powerful.

The availability of steel weaponry owed much to improvements in steel production methods, especially the Bessemer steel converter and the Gilchrist-Thomas basic steel process. As a result, output of steel rose dramatically from the 1870s. Steel was used by the Essen industrialist Alfred Krupp for the breech-loading artillery he produced from the 1850s for Prussia, Russia and other powers, such as Belgium or Turkey, helping the Prussians in 1870–1 to defeat France, which had turned down an approach from Krupp in 1868. There were continued innovations in rifles and cannon, including in the 1880s the adoption of smokeless powder, which burned more efficiently and permitted an increase in the range and muzzle velocity of bullets, and the development of an efficient system of magazine feed, permitting reliable repeating rifles using spring action to feed cartridges at a rapid rate.[81] Two of the other major advantages of smokeless powder were that the field of vision of infantrymen was not now blocked by their own fire, and the enemy had a harder time figuring out where fire was coming from. Among the clip-fed breech-loading rifles were the French Lebel (1886) and the German Mauser (1889). Having successively adopted Enfields, Sniders and Martini-Henrys, the British armed their troops with Lee-Metford magazine rifles. The development of the spitzer or boat-tail bullet provided a smaller, more aerodynamically stable and longer-range bullet. In contrast, cavalry came to play a smaller role in armies and military planning, although there was much resistance to this process. In 1866 and 1870 heavy cavalry attacks by Austrians and French respectively on Prussian infantry and cannon had been bloodily defeated.

Economic growth and the existence of empires produced more resources and revenue for military activity, permitting very high rates of peacetime expenditure on military preparations. For example, in 1907–13 Russia spent heavily on both army and navy, defence spending increasing from 608.1 million roubles in 1908 to 959.6 million in 1913, a figure far above inflation. The percentage of Russian government expenditure on defence rose from 23.2 per cent in 1907 to 28.3 per cent in 1913, in part because of a programme of naval expansion.[82]

More generally, budgetary competition with other states played a major role in military expenditure as[83] states scrutinised the spending plans of their rivals. In the nineteenth century the British took careful account of the state of Russia's finances in the Great Game and other crises. Growing Russian military strength led to pressure for a pre-emptive war in Germany.[84] By the eve of the First World War, the Russians were outspending the Germans. Russian spending on the military, combined with the development of her strategic railroad net, was one reason why the younger Count Helmuth Moltke, Chief of the General Staff 1906–14, pressed for war in 1913–14; he feared that Germany might not be able to win a war with Russia later.

Planning was involved not only in the provision of weaponry but also in preparations for conflict, both strategic and tactical. One famous example is the German Schlieffen Plan of 1905 for an offensive envelopment of the French army, followed by the use of the same strategy against France's ally Russia. A veteran of the Austro-Prussian and Franco-Prussian wars, Field-Marshall Alfred von Schlieffen was Chief of the General Staff in 1891–1906. European armies became more institutionalised and professional. The Prussians developed a system of general staff work and training at a general staff academy that was given much of the credit for victory over Austria in 1866 and over France in 1870, and that was copied elsewhere. The *École Supérieure de Guerre* was founded in 1878 in order to provide France with a staff college. It concentrated on conflict in Europe, especially Napoleonic warfare, rather than colonial wars. In 1890 Spenser Wilkinson, then a leading writer for the influential *Manchester Guardian*, and later the first Professor of the History of Warfare at Oxford, published *The Brain of an Army*: a call for the formation of a British general staff on the German model; it was formed in 1904.

Training of staff officers gave the Prussian army a coherence its opponents lacked and ensured that its large numbers and reserves could be mobilised successfully. This was achieved in 1866 and 1870, in part thanks to an effective exploitation of the railway network in order to achieve rapidly the desired initial deployment and thus gain the strategic initiative. The French had failed to match this.[85] General staffs were created elsewhere, including in Italy in 1882 and in the USA in 1903, but none had the efficiency or independence of the German model.

Contingency planning developed and interacted with arms races. Military plans, such as the Schlieffen Plan, drove policy. Campaigns were analysed at length in military institutions and publications in order to prepare better for the future, but this was not always helpful. Mistaken analysis of the French failure at Prussian hands in 1870 by officers such as Colonel Louis Loizeau de Grandmaison, Director of Military Operations 1908–11, led to a doctrine of *offensive à l'outrance,* the offensive at all costs. Pursued by the French against Germany in 1914, this led to heavy losses and failure. The 'spirit of the offensive' was seen by the French as a necessary counter to German strength. It also seemed the only way to regain Alsace-Lorraine from Germany.[86] Thus, political objectives played a role in framing strategy and tactics.

However, the concept of offensive at all costs was not unique to the French. The conflict of 1870–1 was dissected for 'lessons' by the generation of officers ultimately to hold high command positions in the First World War, for example Franz Conrad von Hötzendorf, Chief of the Austrian General Staff 1906–16, his French and Russian counterparts, and the Germans. The Prussian campaigns were also studied in American staff colleges.[87] Prussia's victory made Clausewitz's *On War* (1832), hitherto relatively obscure, an internationally known work.[88] It was used at the French *École Supérieure de la Guerre.* Victory also encouraged the use of German military advisers; from the 1880s by Japan and Turkey. Field-Marshal Iwao Ōyama, the commander of the Japanese forces in Manchuria during the Russo-Japanese war of 1904–5, had served as an observer in the Franco-Prussian war. The Austrian determination to emulate Prussian strategy led to disastrous offensives against Russia and Serbia in 1914.[89] Throughout Europe, military planners drafted blueprints for offensive action, which was seen as the only way to achieve victory.[90]

Ironically, the older Moltke himself became increasingly sceptical about the potential of the strategic offensive after 1871.[91] It has subsequently been argued that the war plans, with their dynamic interaction of mobilisation and deployment, made war 'by timetable' difficult to stop once a crisis occurred, although this interpretation has been challenged by an emphasis on the role of politicians in affecting the development of the crisis of 1914.[92]

All the continental armies sent observers to the second Anglo-Boer War (1899–1902), but, afterwards, there was considerable disagreement over whether to consider it just another colonial war (therefore, in contemporary views, the source of no lessons relevant to Europe), or as a war between two opponents of European stock, and thus somewhat less irrelevant. German and Austrian commentaries used the Darwinian language in vogue at the time in reference to the 'racial characteristics' of the Boers, praising them as warriors while at the same time underscoring their uniqueness as opponents. Most continental military experts saw little in the conflict that was relevant to European warfare. Many analysts observed (quite correctly) that factors such as the long-range marksmanship of the Boers and their tenacious guerrilla warfare of 1900–2 were not likely to be duplicated in clashes on the Continent among the great powers.

However, the war in fact had important implications for the European battlefields of the First World War, including the use of indirect artillery fire, smokeless powder, long-range rifle fire and camouflage. Nevertheless, machine-guns, which, arguably, should have dominated the battlefield in the Boer War, did not; yet in the First World War, alongside artillery and rifles, they were to dominate the field. This contrast owed much to the notorious unreliability of the Gatling gun for some time after its invention. A technological leap forward was made between the wars, like that from the early string-tied airplanes of the 1900s, to the nippy, useful planes of 1914–18.

Use of camouflage became more widespread from the 1900s. It involved cover and concealment on the battlefield, and, also, a shift towards camouflaged uniforms and a new, functional view of war rather than an emphasis on display. The British army had first adopted camouflaged (khaki) uniforms in the Indian Mutiny, but, thereafter, tradition reasserted itself. Nevertheless, such uniforms were subsequently used in Ethiopia, New Zealand and the Sudan. The British emerged from the Second Boer War with red replaced by khaki (Urdu for dust-coloured) as its primary colour, even for insignia of rank, which Boer marksmen were keen to notice. In 1910 the German army abandoned Prussian blue in favour of field grey; Hötzendorf wrote an article on the Anglo-Boer war advocating camouflaged uniforms for his army based upon the British experience in South Africa. By 1909 the Austro-Hungarian regular infantry wore pike grey rather than blue. However, the Austro-Hungarian cavalry resisted the trend, and went to war in 1914 with blue jackets and red trousers. The French were equally reactionary, only introducing horizon blue in 1915 and khaki generally in 1918. Lack of funds in Austria-Hungary prevented the second- and third-line infantry from getting the new uniforms by 1914; thus the Russians – simply by looking through their binoculars – were able to tell which Austro-Hungarian infantry were the regulars and which the reserves.

Naval Technology

New technology and new weapons systems pushed up the cost of military preparedness. At sea, a number of new ship types were developed, including the big armoured battleship, the battle cruiser, the torpedo boat destroyer and the submarine. The race between armour and armament, the problem of warship weight and manoeuvrability, led to a revolution in armour from the mid-1870s to the early 1890s, culminating in the nickel-steel plate patented in Germany by Friedrich Krupp: the iron navy was followed from the 1870s by the iron and steel navy (compound armour plate), and, from the early 1890s, by nickel-steel warships. These gave added protection without added weight, encouraging the construction of bigger ships, a process that required a shipbuilding industry and much expenditure: armoured warships were very expensive.

From the 1860s until the battleship proponents (bolstered by the works of Alfred Thayer Mahan) carried the day in the 1890s, the increasing size and cost of armoured battleships played into the hands of the advocates of cruiser warfare and torpedo boats. Admiral Aube and the French *Jeune École* provided an ideology for battleship opponents which gained at least some support in every navy. Instead of battleships, they pressed for unarmoured light cruisers that would use less coal and be more manoeuvrable, able to protect sea lanes and attack the commerce of opponents.

Some commentators wondered if battleships had a future in the face of torpedoes. The modern self-propelled torpedo originated with an Austrian invention of 1864 of a small vessel driven by compressed air and with an explosive charge at the head. When adopted by the Austrian navy in 1868 it was capable of a speed of 16 kilometres an hour. Britain and most European powers bought the right to manufacture it. In addition, the British even reverted for a while to muzzle-loading artillery because they found the new Armstrong breech-loaders too unreliable: their screwed breech-blocks blew out. No other nation was particularly menacing to the British, once the Americans demobilised their Civil War fleet and the French were defeated in 1870–1, until the mid-1880s, and, in the meanwhile, the British were able to muddle along, reasonably secure in their naval primacy. Despite the earlier appearance of steam, iron armour and breech-loading guns, the true ocean-going modern (all-steam) battlefleet did not really emerge until the 1890s and in between there was much experimentation, and some spectacular failures. The absence of conflict between the major powers ensured that technologies and theories of naval war could not be adequately tested.

In the 1890s the British built battleships of the class of the *Magnificent*, the first ships carrying cordite-using big guns. In 1906 the British launched HMS *Dreadnought*, the first of a new class of all big gun battleships, and the first capital ship in the world to be powered by the marine turbine engine, invented by Sir Charles Parsons in 1884. Completed in one year, her construction reflected the industrial and organisational efficiency of British shipbuilding. More sophisticated equipment led to a need for better-trained officers and sailors and, therefore, to the creation of new colleges and training methods. The Americans founded a Naval War College at Newport, and the naval strategist Alfred Thayer Mahan (1840–1914) lectured there from 1885 and was twice its president. It also became more important to ensure continuity of service in navies and this led to the development of career conditions and structures.

Advances in machine tools, metallurgy and explosives ensured that more accurate guns, capable of longer ranges and supported by better explosives, could be produced. The development of optical range-finders improved accuracy. The net effect of technological change was to ensure the need for frequent retooling in order to retain competitive advantage which placed a serious burden on government finances. In the nineteenth century warships became obsolete far more rapidly than in the past. The *Dreadnought* revolution, for example, led to a spiralling of costs as each naval power rushed to acquire the expensive new warship.[93] Similarly, on land technological change created problems as well as opportunities.[94]

Greater naval capability was designed both to meet actual threats from other European powers and to overawe them so that actual conflict was prevented. The balance of naval power changed significantly in the last decades of the century, and the traditional ranking of Britain, France, Russia was challenged by the emergence of Germany, the USA and Japan; even Italy and Austria-Hungary developed naval strength significant enough to matter in the global balance. Yet this balance remained focused on Europe, although the first successful attack with a Whitehead torpedo occurred in January 1878 when the Russians sank the Turkish harbour guardship at Batumi with two torpedoes fired from launches. The first recorded successful day attack using torpedoes was by the French at Foochow in 1884 when two Chinese warships were sunk by spar torpedoes.

However, until the 1890s, even the strongest navies employed fully rigged screw steamers to show the flag on non-European stations. Navies were faced with the dilemma of maintaining fairly distinct forces in home waters (an armoured battleship-centred fleet) and on colonial/overseas stations: a hodgepodge of unarmoured ships and gunboats whose fighting value was relatively far less.

Yet, inshore and river steamers could play a major role on such stations. River steamers were certainly very important on Chinese and African rivers, such as the Yangtze, the Niger and the Nile. Often relatively small European warships similarly played a major role in inshore waters. In 1849 three British warships destroyed 23 Chinese pirate junks in two battles, and one of them, a sloop, went on that year, without any British casualties, to destroy 58 pirate junks mounting about 1,200 guns.[95] Similarly, small forces of gunboats enforced European interests in Melanesia[96] and on the coast of British Columbia, destroying canoes and villages in punitive actions.[97] Britain's Australian colonies acquired gunboats in 1882 – the origin of British colonial navies.

European Military Capability

The concentration of naval resources on confrontation in European waters was also true of most of the enhanced land capability of the European powers. Analysis of investment in fortifications is instructive. Major fortified positions were developed outside Europe, but were generally coastal and intended to protect naval bases and ports from attack by other European powers. Thus, in Australia, a fort was erected in Sydney harbour to guard against possible Russian attack; nothing comparable was spent on defence against the Aborigines.

Expenditure on defensive positions outside Europe was minimal compared to the major sums spent on fortifications in Europe. In the 1850s the British had constructed forts along the Channel coast, especially near Portsmouth, for protection in the event of French invasion.[98] The effectiveness of traditional fortifications was affected by advances in artillery, especially the development of rifled steel breech-loaders and improved pneumatic recoil mechanisms that obviated the need for re-siting. They led, in response, to more extensive fortress complexes, offering defence in depth, such as the heavily protected detached forts circling Antwerp, Liège and Namur that were designed by Henry Brial-mont, 'the Belgian Vauban' (1821–1903). After 1871 the French created an extensive defensive belt to prevent further German advances from the east in the event of another war: the French had less space to trade than hitherto. Military bases, such as Belfort and Verdun in France, were surrounded with fortified positions.

Unable to appreciate the defensive potential of trenches, powers such as Russia spent too much on fortresses and fortress artillery, which were essentially static, and not enough on field artillery.[99] The latter was mobile while trenches themselves could be readily dug and were therefore more dynamic than fortresses as a defensive system. The strategy of relying on fortresses to protect frontiers and positions was revealed as unwise in the First World War: Antwerp, Liège and Namur all fell in 1914 after the bombardment of their forts by 305 mm Austrian and 420 mm German heavy howitzers. The pentagonal Fort Douaumont at Verdun was captured by the Germans in 1916, only to be recaptured by the French a little over six months later.

Although Britain was the leading colonial power, her military thinking was dominated not by the experience of colonial warfare, but by consideration of Napoleonic campaigns and the Wars of German Unification.[100] The same was true of France. At the turn of the century British military thinkers were also very interested in the American Civil War.

Yet, even if the military build-up of the European states was primarily made with reference to European power politics, the resulting strength was more mobile and more transferable outside Europe than had been the case in earlier centuries. The Italians who occupied Eritrea in 1885 used telegraph lines, steamships, barbed wire, electric mines, bridge, road and fortress construction to anchor their presence.[101] Steamship, railway and telegraph combined to facilitate transfer and return, permitting a greater integration of the European and transoceanic military structures of individual states. This was a process that was to become even more pronounced after 1945, as air power came to play a role in the movement of troops and supplies. Its origins and impact, however, can be traced to the nineteenth century, although mixed railway gauges, insufficient rolling stock and poor organisation all created serious problems.

Faced by the Métis rebellion in Saskatchewan in 1885, the Canadian government sent several thousand militia west over the Canadian Pacific Railway, achieving an overwhelming superiority that helped bring victory. This was followed by a new increase in government subsidy for the railway that enabled its completion that year.[102]

Communication links were sought by imperial powers and seen as a way to strengthen them politically and militarily. In 1896 the Russians obliged China to grant a concession for a railway to Vladivostok across Manchuria and this Chinese Eastern Railway was constructed in 1897–1904. The Russians also developed a naval presence in Manchuria, building ports at Dairen and Port Arthur on the Liaotung peninsula which was leased to them. Also in 1896, the British army under Kitchener invading the Sudan built a railway straight across the desert from Wadi Halfa to Abu Hamed. It was pushed on to Atbara in 1898, and played a major role in the supply of the British forces in the Sudan.

By 1900 the British had constructed 20,000 miles of railways in India,[103] an aspect of the technological transfer from Europe to the non-European world in which the colonial experience played a major role,[104] but for which it was not necessary.[105] Rail links came to play a greater role in geopolitics, strategy and logistics. In 1897 the British in India moved troops by train against the Waziris on the North-West Frontier. Three years later in China the Boxer destruction of part of the track between Tientsin and Beijing forced the abandonment of the initial attempt to relieve the foreign legations in the capital. Across the Pacific, the building of a railway across the rebel area in 1900 helped to end long-standing Mayan resistance to the Mexicans, although the effects of cholera, smallpox and whooping cough were also important. Fear of an invasion of Canada during the Anglo-American Venezuela crisis in 1904 led to surveillance of nearby American railways. In Russia the capacity of the Trans-Siberian Railway, and its uncompleted section round Lake Baikal, were important in Russia's attempt to defeat Japan in the war of 1904–5: the railway could move about 35,000 men a month. The Russians were determined not to repeat their position in the Crimean War; then the absence of rail links had greatly limited the movement of reinforcements and supplies.

The German Berlin-Baghdad railway project was designed to create a new geopolitical axis in Eurasia. The French embarked on extensive railway construction projects in Africa and Indo-China from 1898. Described as 'the geometric principle of imperial thought',[106] the railway was crucial to the support and supply side of operations as well as to the expanding mental geography of imperialism. However, railways were of less direct use in operations. No railways were built in Afghanistan, a country that was not brought under European control.

Greater flexibility in the deployment and support of force did not necessarily lead to battlefield success. That owed much to the increase in the firepower capability of European forces, as seen for example in the British victory over the Mahdist forces at Omdurman in 1898.[107] In the Sudan a company of 100 British troops could fire ten shots per yard per minute across its 100-yard front if armed with Martini-Henry or Remington rifles which were effective from 1,500 yards. Firepower increased with the adoption of magazine rifles, multiple-barrel machine-guns, such as the Gatling, Nordenfeldt and the French Mitrailleuse, single-barrel machine guns, such as the Maxim, dum dum bullets,[108] and rapid-fire artillery with effective recoil mechanisms, such as the French 75 mm gun, so that at Omdurman the Sudanese casualties were 31,000; those of the Anglo-Egyptian troops only 430. The ratio of casualties in the British victory over the Zulu at Ulundi and in the British victory over the army of Sokoto (in Nigeria) at Burmi in 1903 were similarly striking. In the second, the Caliph and his two sons were killed, and resistance in northern Nigeria came to an end.[109]

The Maxim gun, patented in the USA in 1884 by Hiram Maxim, used recoil energy and was both reliable and readily transportable. It was water-cooled and fully automatic. The Vickers-Maxim machine-gun, adopted by the British army in 1912, fired 250 rounds per minute.[110] Such guns equalled the fire of many riflemen. The machine-gun, a repeated/automatic weapon, was a metaphor of the application of industry to war.

Although the decision of the Berlin Conference of 1885 banning the export of modern weaponry to Africa was ignored, political circumstances and resource availability limited exports. Most African soldiers were still armed with traditional weapons which were of limited effectiveness against rifles in open country. African firearms were generally outdated, for example single-shot breech-loading rifles not repeating magazine rifles. There were similar deficiencies in African gunpowder and artillery although the weaponry at the disposal of some African states improved in response to European developments.[111]

Communications and firepower were both important in the extension of European military power on land, but so also was the development of tactics and strategy that were appropriate for colonial conflict. Far from being 'small wars', some (although not all) colonial conflicts were major struggles that tested the effectiveness of European military machines and methods. There was a need to adapt to factors of distance and to force-space ratios that were very different to those encountered in European conflict (or in the crucial campaigning zones in the American Civil War). This led to an emphasis on mobile columns of light infantry, rather than slow-moving position warfare, an emphasis seen in French operations, including Bugeaud's campaigns in Algeria in 1841–7, Louis Faidherbe's campaigning in Senegal in the 1850s and 1860s, and Joseph Gallieni's in Indo-China and Madagascar in the 1890s, and in advances by other European forces.[112] In battle, European forces relied on volley firing, hollow squares, close-packed lines – the traditional response of infantry to cavalry. These techniques were effective on African battlefields, but were to be of little relevance in Europe in the First World War.

Indeed, colonial warfare can be seen as having a regressive effect on European preparedness for war in 1914. Bush fighting in Africa gave a new lease of life to the square formation and to volley firing, and encouraged belief in the decisive shock value of cold steel. Squares were valuable against enveloping forces, for example Zulus. There was also a tendency to discount the impact of artillery, in part because heavy artillery could play little role in colonial conflicts, and even to see the machine-gun as more useful for frightening 'savages' than for discouraging assaults by European infantry. Furthermore, the traditional cavalry, including the lancers, emerged from the colonial wars and victories such as the British over the Egyptians at Kassassin (1882) with faith in their efficacy as the *arme blanche* restored. Despite its limited effectiveness in the Boer War, the British cavalry remained committed to shock tactics.

Imperialism and Darwinism

Aside from victories in the field, the greater political will that underlay late nineteenth-century imperialism led to a determination to persist even in the event of setbacks. A sense of mission, often linked to or expressed in racial and cultural arrogance, was a characteristic of European imperialism and of the imperialism of expatriate Europeans, such as the Australians in their interior and in the south-west Pacific, the Canadians in the Arctic, and Americans in their interior and in the Pacific. Successful imperialism was used as 'evidence' for this arrogance. The jingoistic strains of popular culture reflected this sense of adventure and commitment.[113]

The persistence, sense of mission and racial/cultural arrogance that characterised imperialism beyond Europe also affected strategic and tactical thought within the European realm, and was reflected further in the willingness of the average citizen to acquiesce in the ever-greater burdens of military and naval spending and (except in Britain) peacetime conscription. The Social Darwinism of the 1870s and beyond, with its emphasis on natural competitiveness, encouraged interest in aggressive military planning and coincided with the revival of Clausewitz. Especially in Britain, the two phenomena became intertwined, as Clausewitz was read through Darwinian eyes and used to support notions of Social Darwinism. Academics, scientists, artists, clerics and intellectuals also played a major role in formulating rationales and objectives for expansion and conflict. War was seen as a glorious means to renew peoples and escape decadence. Most intellectuals were convinced nationalists; internationalism was of only limited appeal. A concept of triumphant will linked Romanticism to international relations.[114] Millenarian theology in Germany and elsewhere contributed to this mental world, as did the notion of providentialism. Thus, educated elites came to believe in the moral value of war. This was a 'rationality' centred on themes of sacrifice and ideas of vitalism. In addition, and contributing to the same end, industrialists pressed the economic and social utility of weapons programmes.

With the offensive in vogue, Clausewitz's chapter on defensive warfare (the longest chapter in *On War*) was largely ignored; some translations omitted it altogether. To sustain the offensive and achieve victory in the face of ever more lethal technology on the battlefield, strategists and tacticians called for ever larger armies and emphasised the value of conscription and the substantial reserve forces that universal military training permitted. Pressure for larger armies led to a concern about population size and birthrates, especially in France where they were lower than in Germany. Exacerbated by the French conscription system, this had ensured that the French were greatly outnumbered during the Franco-Prussian war. An alliance with the vast Russian army came to appear crucial to French politicians. Over a million strong in 1900, excluding reserves, the size of the Russian army had grown by 25 per cent between 1826 and 1912.[115] British military thinkers with the British tradition of volunteer service faced the dilemma of how to fight a future mass-army war without conscription.

In Britain, there was a turn-of-the-century fascination with the American Civil War. Army staff candidates studying at Camberley were expected to study Colonel George Francis Robert Henderson's *Stonewall Jackson and the American Civil War* (London, 1898; 3rd edn, London 1902) and to know the minutiae of Stonewall Jackson's Shenandoah valley campaign of 1862, in which a mobile Confederate force had outmanoeuvred and defeated larger Union forces. Henderson also produced a study of the Fredericksburg campaign of 1862.

Only a small number of European thinkers anticipated the horrific casualties that the expansion of army size and change in military methods were likely to produce in any future war, although, in his *Future of War* (first published 1897, New York, 1899), the Polish financier Ivan Bloch suggested that the combination of modern military technology and industrial strength had made Great Power European warfare too destructive to be feasible, and that if it occurred it would be won when one of the combatants succumbed to famine and revolution. Friedrich Engels had earlier argued that the American Civil War indicated the likely destructiveness of future intra-European conflict and he thought that this would undermine existing state and class hegemonies and make revolution possible. However, the impact of the American Civil War on European military thought was negligible on the Continent, where the leaders of professional armies and officer corps saw no lessons in a war fought by mass militia armies. The broader relevance of trench warfare at Petersburg in Virginia in the winter of 1864–5 became apparent only 50 years later.

The same was true of the defence of Plevna in 1877 in which entrenched Turkish riflemen had inflicted very heavy casualties on Russian frontal attacks. In the battle of

Second Plevna, Russian casualties amounted to 23 per cent of their rank and file.[116] Similarly, the Turks lost heavily in their unsuccessful assault on Russian positions covered by integrated fire zones in Shipka Pass in 1877. The successive attempts to storm Plevna also prefigured other aspects of the First World War, including the difficulty of destroying trenches by artillery fire, the employment of machine-guns, and the heavy use of munitions, both rifle rounds and shells. Plevna only surrendered when encircled and starved out, but the Russians failed to appreciate the limitations of direct infantry attacks. However, this preference for direct attack was not simply due to a cultural preference for glorious action, but also reflected Russian logistical limitations and the need to maintain the initiative in order to prevent counter-attacks. Furthermore, Plevna had fallen and the Turks had lost the war.

Despite the experience of the Civil War, the American army continued to emphasise the offensive. Field service against native Americans provided education neither in the manner in which firearms became far more deadly in the decades after the Civil War nor in the problems of handling large numbers of troops. Instead, there was an emphasis on morale, on spiritual qualities, rather than massive firepower support or the indirect approach, as the means to get across the killing zone provided by opposing firepower. The Spanish-American war of 1898, however, in which the Americans faced a European opponent, albeit a weak one, indicated the importance of entrenchments and the firepower provided by magazine rifles firing steel-jacket, high-velocity, smokeless bullets. German-Spanish Mauser rifles proved particularly effective.[117] The war was a more obvious triumph for the newly developed and powerful American fleet than for the army.[118] Already, in 1894, a powerful American naval demonstration had had a major impact on a civil war in Brazil, and had marked a blow to British influence.[119]

The heyday of European imperialism reflected in part a major gap in military capability between Europe and the rest of the world, but it was also the product of politico-cultural shifts that arose from a number of factors, including rapid demographic growth which continued across most of Europe until the First World War. These politico-cultural shifts put an emphasis on transoceanic European territorial control. European demographic expansion played a crucial role in making such control more concrete and in lessening an identity of land and people that could serve as the basis for indigenous resistance. This was particularly true in Australasia, Canada and Kazakstan, and also with independent states such as the USA and Brazil. Long-distance European emigration was greatly eased by steamships and railways.

European imperialism also reflected an international conjuncture that led the powers to compete actively for transoceanic territorial gains, but without pushing their hostility to the point of war, either in Europe or overseas, although there were moments of high tension, such as the Fashoda crisis between France and Britain in 1898 caused by competing interests in the southern Sudan and the deployment of small rival forces there.[120] The British won the dispute without fighting, in part by manipulating information about it thanks to their control of the telegraph links[121] and in part by a major display of naval strength in European waters.

In general, however, the threat of hostilities was avoided. Thus, the powers seeking to open Japan to their trade in the 1850s competed rather than clashed. The anti-foreigner Boxer uprising in China was put down by an international force, most of whom were Japanese troops, that occupied Beijing in 1900. It arrived in time to relieve the besieged legations which were under pressure from Chinese equipped with a Krupp quick-firing cannon.

Cooperation, or rather a willingness to seek a negotiated settlement to disagreements, led to a series of European negotiations and conferences that between them divided up much of the Old World and some of the New, for example the Anglo-Dutch Treaty of Sumatra (1871), the Congress of Berlin (1884–5) and Anglo-German agreements over East Africa in 1886 and 1890. In 1887 Britain and France agreed to form a mixed commission to maintain their interests in the New Hebrides, and in 1885 Germany and Britain agreed a delimitation of their spheres of expansion in New Guinea and the Pacific. This cooperation reflected an important aspect of the strength of the European system, namely that, alongside the fears that led to states viewing each other as threats, there were conventions and mechanisms for establishing compromise settlements. Indeed, the massive extension of competing empires in the late nineteenth century without sustained conflict with each other was an ample demonstration of the strength of this system. Its breakdown in the twentieth century was to help doom European power.

8   Warfare and the State, 1450–1900

War as the cause, course and consequence of state-building is an established and currently fashionable means of approaching history among both historians and political scientists: war equals state-building and state-building equals war. In place of an organic, or alternatively episodic, account that might focus on socio-economic trends or constitutional-political developments centring on domestic situations, war offers an explanatory model that makes it possible to relate international and domestic spheres and to align state-building – a central, structural feature of contemporary political society – with chronological specifics: the details of conflicts.

The State Monopolisation of Violence

The relationship between war and the state has a number of dimensions. The expansion of the state in order to improve its effectiveness for the conduct of war, more specifically the alterations in administrative organisation, political ethos and economic policy required to support military change, is a major theme. Also important is the degree to which the state increasingly became *the* expression of organised violence. This owed much to the ambition of governments to monopolise the use of such violence, at the expense, for example, of stateless pirates and mercenaries. Indeed, the monopolisation of violence became a definition of statehood as a functional rather than a legitimist understanding of rulership became more common.

Thus, in the nineteenth century there was a decline in a number of practices hitherto common in the European system. Military entrepreneurship, the practice of hiring and being mercenaries, became less frequent, and this influenced relations between states and those between states and non-state bodies. Subsidies and indirect recruiting were replaced by foreign aid and direct recruiting. The Crimean War was the last in which the British government recruited units of European foreign mercenaries for war service.[1]

Authorised non-state violence, for example by privateers, such as the government-supported and government-supporting Barbary corsairs of North Africa, and by mercantile companies with territorial power, for example the British East India Company, was eliminated in a piecemeal fashion, mostly in the nineteenth century. The elimination of such practices owed something to the degree to which they provoked interstate conflicts by being outside full state control. The elimination also reflected a sense that they were anachronistic to states and societies that increasingly placed a premium on and identified themselves through rationality, conceived of in terms of system, that is, a

59. The glory of the Royal conqueror. Statue of Louis XIV on the Place des Victoires in Paris commissioned by Marshal Feuillade. The Austrian envoy complained to the French foreign minister in 1686 'that the Emperor was not in the condition of a slave with his hands tied in chains, other than in the fancy of Monsr. de la Feuillade. This he thought fit to take notice of, upon occasion of one of the figures under the new statue, representing a slave in chains, with the arms of the Empire, the spread-eagle by him'.

clearly defined organisation and explicit rules of conduct, and state-directed systems. The territorial and military roles of the companies were ended. Thus in 1882 the Italian government took over the coaling base at Assab in Eritrea near the mouth of the Red Sea purchased in 1870 by the Rubattino Steamship Company. In 1898 the British government bought the properties and claims of the Royal Niger Company. This brought them control of southern Nigeria and of the company's army, the Royal Niger Constabulary.

There were exceptions, but they became more uncommon. One latter-day adventurer, James Brooke (1803–68), a veteran of the First Burma War, where he had formed a body of native volunteer cavalry in Assam, helped suppress a rebellion in Sarawak, and was rewarded by the Prince of Brunei with its governorship (1841). That became the basis of a territorial position that led to him and the nephew and grand-nephew that succeeded him being termed the 'white rajahs' of Sarawak: the last did not cede Sarawak to the British Crown until 1946. However, opportunities for such activity became less common.

Aside from authorised non-state violence, unauthorised non-state violence, particularly piracy and privately organised expeditions designed to seize territory, was also in large part stamped out in the nineteenth century. This both demonstrated and enhanced the ability of states to monopolise power,[2] although in Sarawak it was Brooke who played the major role in suppressing piracy. Nevertheless, the European powers, particularly Britain, devoted much effort to suppressing piracy, especially off China, in the East Indies, off British Columbia, in the Pacific and in the Persian Gulf. In 1819 a British naval force from Bombay destroyed the base of the Qasimi pirates at Ras al Khaima in the Persian Gulf and wrecked their fleet. This forced an agreement to end piracy signed in 1820. The British capture of Aden in 1839 owed much to the desire to end local piracy.[3]

The banning of the slave trade and the subsequent measures taken to extend and enforce the bans were important examples of moves designed to end authorised, and then unauthorised, non-state violence. The British navy was active against the traffic in slaves, particularly from Africa to the Middle East, employing violence to stop the destructive trade.[4]

The European powers sought to monopolise military force, both within their European territories and in their colonies, on land and at sea. The gradual bringing of the Cossacks of both Ukraine and south and south-east European Russia under state control (*c.* 1650–1800) was an important example of a state establishing a monopoly of violence.[5] The red-shirted volunteer force with which Giuseppe Garibaldi conquered Sicily and Naples in 1860 was absorbed into the Italian army, and in 1862, when he subsequently formed a private army to capture Rome, then an independent Papal state, it was defeated by the Italian army.

60. The battle of Glenshiel, 10 June 1719. British victory over a Spanish-Jacobite force in the Scottish Highlands. European warfare was not uniform. There were major differences between British and Jacobite forces. At Glenshiel, the government forces, assisted by mortar fire, took the initiative and successfully attacked the Jacobite flanks. Lacking resolve while it remained on the defensive, the Jacobite army disintegrated.

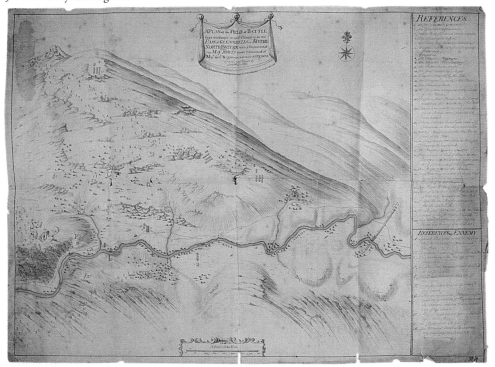

61. *The Siege of Münster* by Erhard Schoen, 1535. This woodcut illustrated the siege of Anabaptist-held Münster by an army combining numerous pikemen with batteries of cannon. Münster's fortifications had not yet been modernised; the city fell and the Anabaptists were killed.

Monopolisation of violence was also linked to the internal pacification, and thus control, of societies. This was a gradual process, the scale and scope of which varied greatly, and one that was to be challenged and, in part, reversed after 1945 with the rise of terrorism and other violent challenges to the authority of the state. Essentially, however, European states sought to prevent the use by partisan groups of organised violence for the pursuit of domestic political objectives. They also took steps against feuds. At the personal level, the activity of the state was less insistent, but measures were, nevertheless, taken to abolish, or at least limit, duelling, and to restrict the ownership of arms.

The last was a crucial aspect of social specialisation and the professionalisation of warfare. If, paradoxically, moves to restrict the ownership of arms were pursued in the nineteenth century, at a time when there was an increasing emphasis on conscription and the availability of military reserves, that, nonetheless, underlined the determination of governments to control both the practice of mass recruitment and its consequences.

More generally, there was a distinction between arms that had a battlefield capability and others whose value was largely restricted to personal violence. The first were monopolised by governments. This was true both of artillery from its initial development, and of flintlock muskets in the eighteenth century. The diffusion among civilians of hunting rifles and other personal firearms was of little military consequence. By the sixteenth century most sophisticated fortifications were under central governmental control, and by the eighteenth they all were; only states had the resources to maintain such fortifications. Cannon were used against the fortresses of recalcitrant cities and aristocrats, as in Scotland in 1456 when the Earl of Douglas's castle at Threave surrendered in the face of a 'great bombard'.

Outside Europe, the pattern of control over weaponry and fortifications varied considerably. Among the native Americans, for example, there was considerable individual control, while this was not the case in China, and, still less, in Japan. Personal ownership of weaponry was a feature of the societies deemed barbarian by Gibbon, and was indeed crucial to their military character. It can be argued that such ownership and the limited control wielded by tribal authorities made the Europeanisation of warfare by such societies highly unlikely. 'Barbarians' are definable as militarised but individualistic; the 'civilised' as members of states, created by war, and in which arms, certainly battlefield arms, are centrally organised.

The extension of European colonial control entailed the spread of European practices and views on the ownership and use of weapons. This was an aspect of Europeanisation that proved unpopular. Furthermore, it was compromised by the delegated nature of much colonial power and the use of native military units that were not part of the regular colonial army.

Within Europe a highly competitive and combative international system led to pressures for governmental change,[6] although this process was not restricted to Europe. To take a few prominent examples from the sixteenth and seventeenth centuries, Mughal India under Akbar (1556–1605), Burma under Bayinnaung (1551–81), Mataram under Agung (1613–45), Persia under Abbas I (1587–1629) and the Ottoman empire under the first two Köprülü Grand Viziers, Mehmed (1656–61) and Fazil Ahmed (1661–76), also demonstrate the interaction between international ambitions, enhanced military capability, especially the development of permanent forces, and administrative reform. However, such 'reform' often centred on the search for a new consensus with the socially powerful, rather than on bureaucratic centralisation, not that the latter process was without its ideological tensions, legal difficulties, administrative limitations and political problems. The pursuit of a new consensus was centralising – in that it focused the attention of regional elites on the centre – but not centralised.

Competitive military systems that put a premium on the size of armed forces and the sophistication of their weaponry enhanced the position of centralising rulers, while those

62. *Landscape with Ruined Castle of Brederode and Distant View of Haarlem* by Jan van der Croos, 1655. Thanks both to cannon and to the concentration of military strength by sovereign rulers, most medieval fortifications became obsolescent. Furthermore, new fortified positions were concentrated in frontier regions, such as Breda, which fell to the Spaniards in 1625 and was regained in 1637.

international and military systems that were not dominated by such armies and navies did not lend themselves to control by such rulers. Consensus was less necessary if rulers employed foreign mercenaries.

War and Government

However, stronger government was not simply a function of the nature of warfare. Political and religious cultures were important, as was the role of individuals. For example, royal authority in Aceh (north-west Sumatra) was greatly increased under two Sultans, Alau'd din Ri'ayat Syah al-Mukammil (1589–1604) and Iskandar Muda (1607–36), both of whom terrorised the nobility. Iskandar Muda created a new nobility that was responsible for raising a new army, and used a standing force of foreign slaves, akin to the Turkish janizaries, to control the capital. This situation reflected the ambitions of the rulers, not a competitive international situation or changes in the nature of warfare. There was a reaction against Iskandar Muda's policies, but, irrespective of the domestic situation, a Dutch blockade in 1647–50 led to the Dutch gaining control of the crucial West Sumatran dependencies that produced the pepper and tin on which Aceh's prosperity rested.[7]

Teleology is so tempting in military history because of the apparent objectivity of technological progress. However, the nature of this progress can be queried and the role of other factors in military history can be emphasised. If the emphasis in military capability is to be placed on administrative sophistication and, more generally, on the nature of the state within its various contexts, rather than on firearms, then the course of military history becomes considerably more complex. In essence it becomes an aspect of general history. Competing powers are competing systems; consequently, the potential for and the impact of war are strongly mediated by pre-existing structures, both administrative and social. In addition, the question of the nature of the state leads to a wider-ranging enquiry about the character of societies and their cultures. However effective a given state might be in raising resources, that does not explain the degree to which its people are willing to accept deprivation and risk death for its ends, whether defence or expansion, and yet that was, and is, crucial to its military character and capability.

The states with the most effective global range during this period (1450–1900) were western European. The willingness and ability of these societies to organise their resources for maritime enterprise were combined with a degree of curiosity about the unknown world, a wish to question rather than to accept received knowledge. This independence of mind and action was especially manifest in the explorers: they sought governmental support but were not constrained by it. Yet the global links that individuals established could only become a sustainable military reality with resources and institutional support. The willingness of western European governments to decide that such a goal was important reflected views on space and on the acceptance of new developments that were not shared by all states.

Governments not only set goals, they also realised them by altering political parameters and allocating resources. To these ends some states developed what were, by earlier, although not nineteenth-century standards, impressive bureaucracies that sustained far-ranging patterns of activity and action, although elsewhere war could trigger a reversion to more primitive military arrangements, with private entrepreneurs organising and local populations paying. While it is true that in the early seventeenth century structures for the financing, supply and control of European armies were inadequate to

63. *Battle of the Spurs.* This battle of 1513 earned its name from the speed with which the French fled from Henry VIII's cavalry. The French were exposed to archery fire when their advance was checked and this led them to fall back, eventually in disorder. The battle itself arose from an attempt to get supplies into besieged Thérouanne. The painting concentrates on the cavalry engagement, although it was the English archers who played a crucial role.

the burdens that the sustained warfare of the Thirty Years War (1618–48) was to create, it would be inappropriate to paint too bleak a picture. By global standards, European military administration was well developed, and had been so for centuries, and, in addition, accounts of deficiencies in army administration are not too helpful as a guide to the situation at sea, where the introduction of numbers of specialist warships led to a development of admiralties.[8]

European warriordom, its ethos and practices, depended heavily on clerks and, after an initial stage of partly free enterprise conquest in the sixteenth century, this was especially true of overseas military activity. Although affected by internal disputes, the 'centralised and systematic authority structure' of the Dutch East India Company gave it a continuity and stability in the seventeenth and eighteenth centuries that many indigenous states lacked. Despite waging war in Europe, Spain in the 1620s and 1630s was also committed to conflict around the world, and its bureaucracy showed remarkable agility, dedication and inventiveness in keeping the fleets supplied. Private contractors and public officials worked fruitfully together: forest legislation sought to conserve timber stocks; efforts were made to provide sailors and soldiers with nutritious food and good medical care. Severe discipline was enforced on erring fleet commanders and bureaucrats alike.[9]

The last was a crucial aspect of state control of warfare: the enforcement and acceptance of discipline. Martial elite culture was transformed as knights became officers. This helped to ensure the continuation of ancestral political and social privilege, but their technically different battlefield roles required a more predictable and disciplined response. As a result, the relative effectiveness of European forces improved. Both officership and generalship became more professional, or rather professionalisation increasingly entailed a greater measure of bureaucratisation and discipline than had been the case with the autonomous forces that had been characteristic in European warfare till the seventeenth century and that, thereafter, were still typical of armies elsewhere. Successful European generals, such as Oliver Cromwell, frequently displayed a painstaking attention to detail,

64. Defeat of Spanish army near Canal of Bruges, 31 August 1667. Attacked by larger French forces, the Spaniards, already at war with Portugal, were unable to offer successful opposition. The major fortress of Lille had fallen three days earlier. The rapidity of the French advance in 1667 indicated the decisiveness of European conflict under propitious circumstances.

especially with regard to the recruitment, training and organisation of their forces. Training was crucial to the effective use of weapons, because it was only thanks to training and discipline that different types of troops could combine effectively in battle tactics. For example, early handgunners were vulnerable to infantry and cavalry attack and therefore needed to combine with troops, such as pikemen, who could provide protection against hand-to-hand attack: advances in technology themselves were of limited use.

The European states were also able to utilise a wide-ranging resource base, one that was enhanced by transoceanic expansion. Within Europe there was heavy forest cover and abundant mineral resources; both essential for naval construction and metallurgy. Europeans probably had access to larger quantities of cheaper metal than was available elsewhere: some of this metal, in the form of nails, was used to hold European ships together. In contrast, the planks of Indian Ocean ships were sewn together with rope and therefore vulnerable to the recoil of heavy guns and to storms at sea. It has also been argued that by the close of the Middle Ages Europe contained the most advanced industrial technology and organisation in the world, with water mills, windmills, heavy forge work and mechanical clocks.[10] Such an argument may underrate the Chinese achievement, but, at the very least, Europe had one of the most advanced industrial systems of the time, and European primacy increasingly became the case. Along with a relative openness to new ideas, this economic strength helped Europeans in their adaptation and improvement of technology developed elsewhere, such as gunpowder or ship design.

This lead over the rest of the world was also true of European governmental administration, although there were many and important limitations by the standards of modern bureaucratic ideology. These affected the process of technological and scientific development and application.[11] Furthermore, the Europeans were well advanced in the field of international finance, enabling states, such as Spain in the sixteenth century, the United Provinces in the seventeenth and Britain in the eighteenth, in part to finance their activities through an international credit system.

Conflict led to pressure for improvement. For example, Dutch naval operations in the first half of the seventeenth century were affected by the autonomous nature of their five admiralties, but in the second half of the century, as a result of war with England and France, naval activities and administration were better coordinated. The Dutch navy was then well manned: the supply of seamen on the labour market and the regulations during wartime were such that all available and required men-of-war could always sail and could be commanded by qualified and motivated officers. The protection of economic interests and the political situation in Europe constantly compelled the Dutch ruling class to ensure that it had a strong navy.[12]

If European attitudes set the context for transoceanic activities, because such activities were launched by European states, the situation concerning inter-European conflict was less distinctive on the world scale, although the propinquity of a number of competing states was important. What is clear is that the use of force was expensive. It cost the British government £6.8 million to conquer and suppress opposition in Ireland in 1649–52. The incessant nature of competition between European states in very close proximity placed heavy burdens on governmental structures and led to attempts not only to utilise the resources of society, a traditional objective, but also to a wish to understand those resources and to appreciate the wealth-creating nature of economic processes and social structures. Such an appreciation was seen as a basis for the pursuit of measures to increase wealth.

65. The Dutch War, 1572. Drawing made for Gaspar de Robles. The Dutch War involved amphibious operations, a type of conflict too often ignored by studies concentrating on land warfare. The Dutch ability to gain naval superiority gave them a vital advantage in the provinces of Holland and Zeeland. In 1572 the Sea Beggars, a force of Dutch privateers, seized the Zeeland towns of Brill and Flushing. The Duke of Alba was unable to regain these positions and in 1574 the Dutch captured Middleburg.

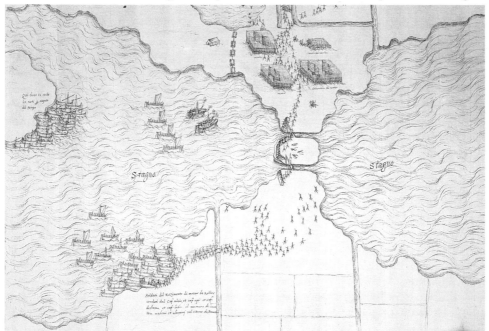

These attitudes are sometimes described, in a seventeenth-century context, as mercantilism or cameralism. They required planning, information and a notion of secular improvement: the capacity of and need for humans to better their condition on earth and one that could be achieved through state action. Attitudes to the goals and practices of European states were greatly altered in the sixteenth and seventeenth centuries. The notion developed of the state as an initiator of legislative and administrative rules designed to improve society and increase its resources: the theory and policy of cameralism. These two goals were also seen as directly linked. A central role was envisaged for the state, represented by an absolute sovereign authority assisted by a corps of professionalised officials. The state's legislative scope was universal, covering the mores of subjects as much as their economic activity, because the ability of a subject to participate in the latter was held to be dependent on the former. In this sense, the equation came to be: disciplined culture, rich resources, strong military.

Regulatory aspirations were not always successful in practice – far from it, but they indicate the degree to which eighteenth-century European Enlightenment attitudes towards government and the purposes of the state were in fact prefigured by and in large measure based upon the goals, and in part policies, of sixteenth- and seventeenth-century governments. These in turn drew on the corpus of legislation passed by medieval European towns: there was an important continuity of regulation and planning in Europe. Europe's broad urban development led to an expansion of state authority, likewise of resources, and thus of military power.

However, it is important not to adopt too black-and-white a picture and to overstate the conflict between cameralism and traditional institutions and views; not least because it seems clear that cameralists sought to work through such institutions. Rather than seeking to monopolise power, European central governments co-opted subordinate institutions, which issued ordinances as well as implementing them. Similarly, sovereign is a problematic term: early modern European sovereignty – theoretically irresistible and limited at the same time – was different to the modern sense of the term.[13]

The potential of European government, especially as a means to mobilise the resources of society in order to maximise the public welfare, however defined, was increasingly grasped. Pressure for stronger and more centralised administration had universalistic implications that clashed with traditional conceptions of government as mediated through a 'system' reflecting privileges and rights that were heavily influenced both by the social structure and by the habit of conceiving of administration primarily in terms of legal precedent. European rulers varied in their willingness to exchange the traditional foundations of royal absolutism in legal precedent and a particularist social order for a new conception of government. Potentially there was a clash between a mechanical/unitary/natural law concept of monarchy and one that was traditional/sacral/corporate/confessional. But this did not became apparent in Europe until the mid-eighteenth century. Previously the former was very much in check, except in Russia under Peter the Great: corporate and intermediate institutions were generally lacking there.

Many of the reforms in early modern European government can often be understood in habitual terms, both the response to new problems and the attempt to make existing practices work better. Nevertheless, even if rulers were dependent on the consent, assistance and often initiative of local government and the socially powerful, especially the aristocracy, the ability to raise formidable armies and navies and to conduct aggressive foreign policies reflected the strength of political-administrative structures and practices.

66. *The Siege of La Rochelle by Louis XIII* by Claude Lorrain. The leading Huguenot (Protestant) stronghold in France was besieged and starved into surrender in 1627–28. An English relief attempt was beaten off in 1627. Thus, although the French royal army of the period was relatively small and weak by the standards of neighbouring Spain, it was able to bring an effective end to a major challenge to the military, political and religious authority of the crown.

European rulers viewed the government machinery as a source of funds for war and foreign policy, and increasingly looked to it to tackle the administrative complexities of warfare, such as recruitment. Thus, the growing role of the European state gradually replaced the semi-independent military entrepreneurs of earlier days. Indeed, it would be mistaken to separate administrative and legislative reform from the political and fiscal background. The relationship between states, military forces (land and sea) and societies was different in the early eighteenth century to the situation a century earlier, although there were also important elements of continuity.

War finance was as important in forcing the pace of reform as changes in intellectual views or political culture were in providing the opportunity. However, it is important not to lose sight of the cultural aspect of warfare. The martial rituals and ceremonies at court played an important part in defining elite social roles and in maintaining elite cohesion. The rituals and ceremonies remained traditional and stressed the monarch's role as the head of the feudal hierarchy.

Enlightened absolutism, the term used to describe the governance of several of the leading European states in the period 1740–90, especially Austria, Prussia and Russia, encompasses two separate emphases on governmental aims and policies. One stresses the influence of new ideas on the purpose of society – the Enlightenment – and concentrates on a relatively idealistic approach to domestic reform. The second approach emphasises the role of war, not least the need to maximise state resources in order to prepare for it. Thus, for example, Peter the Great's reform programme in Russia was in part a consequence of the demands posed by the lengthy struggle with Sweden in the Great Northern

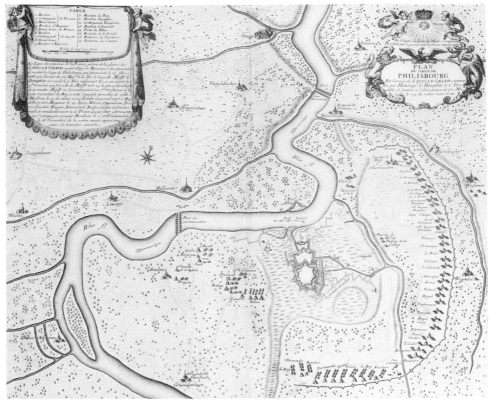

67. The siege of the principal Imperial fortress on the middle-Rhine, Philippsburg, 1688. Taken by a large French army under the Dauphin after the French cannon had prevailed over those of their opponents, and the outworks had been taken by storm. A crucial accretion of prestige for the Dauphin.

War of 1700–21, while Catherine the Great's governmental reforms of 1775 are explained as a consequence of the problems of resource mobilisation and control revealed in the Russo-Turkish war of 1768–74 and the Pugachev frontier rebellion by a variety of dis-affected people who lived in the south-east borderlands of European Russia. Austrian policies in the early 1750s were a consequence of the loss of Silesia to Prussia and a prelude to an attempt to regain it in the Seven Years War (1756–63). The war was followed by a widespread attempt throughout Europe to tackle the financial burdens arising from the conflict and to prepare for what appeared to be another inevitable round of warfare.

More generally, the states of continental Europe were militarised (and with a matching social structure), and, therefore, very responsive to changes in military circumstances; although in western Europe there was far less serfdom, labour control and conscription than in eastern Europe. Conscription, with its concomitant regulation and data gathering, was crucial in changing the relationship between state and people in eastern Europe.

Failure in international relations can be related to an inability to adopt a necessary level of militarism, militarism understood as implying an effective politico-governmental system, a militarised social structure and a militaristic ethos. Poland, which was partitioned out of independent existence in 1772–95, can be seen as lacking the first, while the United Provinces (Dutch Republic), which was successfully invaded by Bourbon France in 1747–8 and conquered by revolutionary France in 1795, lacked the last. Poland fell victim to Austria, Prussia and Russia, each of which, by Polish standards, was a centralising monarchy. Resistance to attempts to increase royal power in the 1650s and 1660s prevented political support for the development of a more effective Polish army.[14] The control that the Polish landlords wielded over their peasantry was matched in the partitioning powers, but, unlike Poland, their social structures and political practices served the pursuit of military strength.[15] The Partitions were the most significant territorial redistribution in Europe since 1718, when the Turks had ceded extensive territories to Austria, and, with the exception of gains at the expense of the Turks (1718, 1774, 1792), the most significant since the partition of the Spanish empire by the Peace of Utrecht of 1713.

However, the dialectic of war and reform also created political tensions that could lead to military weakness. Joseph II's attempts to reform Austria in the 1780s and French attempts in the same period to strengthen the state through the process and contents of reform, can both be seen in this light; as, indeed, can the attempts to widen the tax-base of the British imperial system after the Seven Years War: the last led, especially in the Stamp Act crisis of 1765–6, to a marked deterioration in relations with the American colonies. After *c.* 1750 monarchs were more prepared than hitherto to risk abandoning traditional norms, a shift due to a different ideology, not to changes in military technology.

Britain

Britain was clearly different in some important respects from the other major European powers, not least in self-image. It was of course a formidable military power, with the strongest navy in the world throughout the eighteenth and nineteenth centuries. The British state was able to deploy its strength effectively: in 1762 British forces captured both Havana and Manila. In addition, the English state was able to dominate the British Isles. The achievement that had eluded Charles I, that is secure military control over the British Isles, had been realised in 1649–53 by Parliament's leading general, Oliver Cromwell, whose New Model Army was the first to conquer Scotland. This control was strengthened later, by William of Orange (William III) in 1689–92, and was sustained by the Hanoverian dynasty.

Nevertheless, the social context of military power was very different in Britain to the rest of Europe, not least because of the large role of the navy, the small size of the British army and the absence of a system of conscription for the army. After 1690, army finances depended on Parliament, not the Crown. Compared to Austria, Prussia and Russia, Britain was not a militarised society, although it was still a militaristic one.

In the military dimension, it would be unwise to emphasise exceptionalism. Instead, Britain was more akin to the other major European Atlantic powers in devoting much of its military expenditure to naval and colonial forces. These were spheres that did not lend themselves to a nexus of control by aristocratic proprietorship (control, indeed ownership, by aristocratic commanders), as was commonly the case with army units, but rather to state- controlled enterprises such as the great naval bases at Brest, Cadiz, Havana, and Portsmouth, or institutional corporate control, as by East India Companies. Naval infrastructure and warfare demanded a professionalism that was lacking from land conflict. Civil war and, later, industrial capitalism undermined the status of a 'warrior' aristocracy in England and indeed most of Britain; the defeat of Jacobitism encouraged this process in the Scottish Highlands. In addition, the combination over much of Europe of large armies, with aristocratic proprietorship, was a limitation on the effectiveness of the expansion of state monopolies over violence, in so far as a large aristocratic role in the military might invite corruption and inefficiency, and also a possibility of aristocrats contesting state decisions.

The somewhat crude dialectic of war and reform, of war leading to reform, the latter understood in an ambiguous and contested light, can be applied to eighteenth-century Britain as well as to continental states. Thus, wartime increases in the British national debt were followed by major post-war readjustments. The extensive warfare of 1689–97 and 1702–13 – the periods of British participation in the Nine Years War and the War of the Spanish Succession – led directly to such steps as the Triennial Act of 1694 which ensured that there would be parliamentary elections at least every three years, the foundation of the Bank of England and the funded national debt in 1694, the Act of Union with Scotland in 1707, and interest in political arithmetic: social analysis and planning using statistics. The wartime and post-war dislocation of the War of the Austrian Succession, in which Britain participated in 1743–8, was followed by a post-war period of attempted social reforms. The Seven Years War (1756–63) was followed by an attempt to reorganise imperial relationships, not least fiscal responsibilities, by measures such as the Stamp Act of 1765. The War of American Independence (1775–83) led to new constitutional arrangements with Ireland, and was followed by attempts to reorganise the

68. The siege of Cork, 1690. During the war in Ireland between James II and William III, an English expedition under John Churchill, later Duke of Marlborough, attacked Cork. It surrendered after its fortifications were breached by a bombardment from higher ground, and the Jacobites' outworks were overrun.

69. *Battle of the Boyne*, here in a painting after Jan Wyck, was the decisive battle that delivered Ireland to William III on 1 July 1690. The outnumbered James II, his forces drawn up behind the Boyne, was outflanked and then under heavy pressure the Jacobites were pushed back. Dublin fell five days later.

government of British India, pressure for parliamentary reform, and by William Pitt the Younger's policies for fiscal regeneration and new commercial links.

In this context, it becomes possible to view the French revolutionary-Napoleonic period as another stage in the dialectic of war and state development. For Britain there was the introduction of income tax (1797), parliamentary union with Ireland (1800–1), the first British national census (1801), the mapping of the country by the newly created Ordnance Survey and the abolition of the slave trade. These moves scarcely constituted social revolution, but they did not really conform to the organic model of change discerned and advocated by Edmund Burke, the leading conservative polemicist of the 1790s. Instead, individually, each was a decision for change and, collectively, these steps represented a new age of political arithmetic. Britain was moving from a pre-statistical age to a period when the provision and control of information could serve as the basis for government action and reform agitation.

Reform and Warfare

The chronology and specifics were different, but similar processes were at work on the Continent. The Napoleonic enterprise was defeated not by an unreconstructed *ancien régime*, but by polities that had absorbed many of France's developments. Across much of Europe, the modernisation of political structures and administrative practices was influenced by French occupation or models, or by the need to devise new political and administrative strategies to counter the French. The changes introduced in the Prussian army and society after defeat at the hands of Napoleon in 1806 are an obvious example, although these changes were not limited to Prussia and, while Prussia did accept French ideas, there was also considerable continuity with the enlightened reforms of the pre-revolutionary period. Clausewitz's thinking reflected the impact of the Napoleonic challenge.

It is also mistaken to see any simple correlation between 'reform' and enhanced military capability. Political and administrative confusion and disjunctions frequently accompanied reform, and a lack of bureaucratic continuity was especially serious in the case of naval power. Thus, the French Revolution reduced a navy that had recently been expanding in size and improving in organisation and construction, to chaos. It led in 1793 to the surrender of the Mediterranean fleet at Toulon to the British and to the mutiny of the Brest fleet. To reassert the authority of central government in the navy and create a republican navy, the revolutionary Committee of Public Safety used terror. Sent to Brest in 1793–4, Jeanbon Saint-André restored order and subordination in the fleet by destroying alternative claims to represent the nation. The notion of popular sovereignty expressed in the direct democracy of sailors was curbed, as was the independence of local administrtions. He also dramatically improved the navy, for example by ensuring that naval conscripts received appropriate training.

Nevertheless, on 1 June 1794 in the battle of the Glorious First of June, the Brest fleet was defeated by the British. The French lost seven warships and had over 5,000 men killed, wounded or taken prisoner, while the British suffered fewer than 1,100 casualties and returned to Portsmouth with all their vessels. The battle revealed the continued superiority of British gunnery, and the inexperience of French crews, and was followed by the dismissal and arrest of several captains. Only the fall of Robespierre saved two captains from the guillotine. French naval authority remained weak and its leadership divided, and, thanks to the Revolution, professional disagreements were given ideological significance. Despite defeats, the navy furthered the Republic's war aims simply by continuing to pose a threat to Britain, but chronic shortages of construction materials, money and sailors greatly weakened it. It was clear from the experience of the 1790s that navies required effective executive power.[16]

It is unclear how far the thesis of reform under the stress of competition and war can be extended further afield. An acutely competitive international context was not restricted to Europe and nor was the European international context thus restricted. Napoleon invaded Egypt and negotiated with Persia. The British impact on South Asia had parallels with its Napoleonic counterpart in Europe. It is, therefore, unclear how far and how best the analysis of modernisation in the context of the international situation can be extended. Must one include the reform policies in Turkey under Selim III, the attempts by Maratha leaders to develop Europeanised military systems; or, indeed, pressure to create or extend federal institutions in the USA, for example agitation in favour of a national bank to be better able to finance the state?

In the case of the USA, it can be argued that its very distance from a bitterly contested international sphere enabled it to dispense with strong armed forces and the politics and practices of state and military centralisation. The USA thus represented an aspect of what certain British political thinkers, such as Bolingbroke and John Stuart Mill, would have liked for Britain: a state where, thanks to an ability to avoid international commitments, government was limited in authority and power and constrained by checks and balances. Although defeats at the hands of native Americans prompted military reform, as in the 1790s, the native Americans were not in a position to challenge the centres of American power and by the 1820s their strength east of the Mississippi was limited. The American lead in hand-held weaponry over the native Americans was minimal, but the Americans benefited from greater numbers and from a socio-economic system that permitted the development of a standing army. The army was able to remedy its initial incompetence in its conflict with the native Americans by developing training, discipline and effective operational techniques.[17]

War and Resources

Throughout the world, warfare required resources, and the major tendency in the early modern period was for an increase in military costs.[18] This owed much to the new equipment required by firearm forces on land and sea, changes to fortifications necessary to limit the impact of cannon, and the increase in the size of armed forces that was general in the sixteenth century and, not least in relation to population stagnation, also over the following 150 years. This increase was true of both land and sea warfare. It pressed on a European economic system that benefited from direct access to South Asian trade and from the benefits of New World bullion, but that did not have high growth rates.

War or, more specifically, military capability, increasingly became a matter of the intersection of capitalism and the state. This was central to the ability to marshal resources, and was focused and symbolised in institutions such as the Bank of England, which was founded in 1694. Thus the military-financial combination of the early modern period preceded the military-industrial complexes of the nineteenth and twentieth centuries. An economic system stressing values of labour, thrift, efficiency and accumulation enjoyed a military advantage over a large, settled state such as China in which capitalism and trade enjoyed only low esteem. The claim that 'European armed forces were not yet backed by an overwhelmingly more productive industrial system'[19] than those in Asia may be questioned. In addition, European forces do appear to have been supported by more effective financial systems, at least by the eighteenth century, and their industrial system appears to have been better adapted to producing and supporting a large number of warships. Resources were crucial not only for the creation of European forces, but also in order to maintain political and operational control over them. For example, in 1581 the Duke of Alençon captured Cambrai in the Netherlands, but his unpaid army then disintegrated.

Yet it was not only the Europeans who could afford, or be made to afford, the greater expenditure that was required. In southern India in the sixteenth century, for example, the state of Vijayanagara under Aliya Rama Raja (1542–65) combined expenditure on military modernisation with monetisation and increased customs revenue. Also in southern India, Sultan Ibraham Qutb Shah of Golconda financed an artillery corps in the 1560s and 1570s, thanks to his monopoly of diamonds, a newly discovered source of wealth in the region. In the 1530s, Bahadur Shah of Gujarat in western India used his state's maritime wealth to finance a large army equipped with new cannon. To a certain extent, India may be seen as a variant of Europe, consisting of a conglomeration of states, some of similar size and strength, perhaps with mutual influences in culture, and developing militarily in response to each other. However, in Europe there was no equivalent to the seventeenth-century hegemony of the Mughals.

Unfortunately no global indices exist for potential military expenditure and, therefore, it is not possible to assess the effectiveness of particular states in raising resources for warfare. This effectiveness was a matter not only of governmental efficiency, but also of socio-cultural attitudes to the state and to warfare. In short, the power of the state has to be understood in terms of consent as well as coercion. If government at one level was a means of extorting resources for the pursuit of policies that reflected the interests of rulers,[20] the willingness to contribute resources rested in part on ideological considerations, such as patriotism and religion. Furthermore, the vitality of intermediate bodies, such as town councils, whether representative or oligarchic, was also important. They could mediate between and reconcile the interests of central government and localities in

70. *Battle of Lowestoft*, 3 June 1665 by Hendrik van Minderhout. The English, under the Lord High Admiral, James, Duke of York, later James II, defeated Jacob van Wassenaer-Obdam, whose flagship was destroyed by an explosion. Fleet actions of this type were a feature of naval warfare in European waters, but they did not become more common between European navies outside Europe until the following century.

a way that could not be done by centralised bureaucracies and their local agents. This was exceptionally important in imperial/multiple monarchies, in which local elites were successfully integrated through voluntary coalescence. The traditional dualistic model of rulers versus estates (parliaments) can be challenged.[21]

Political Cohesion

Indeed, compromise emerges as a theme, not only in internal politics within European states, but also in their territorial expansion within Christian Europe. Thus, for example, the expansion of French interests in Picardy in the late fifteenth century was achieved in part by means of compromise. Alongside the role of force in extending French authority, the winning over of a wide range of local notables by peaceful means was also crucial. Their continued local power was complemented by the extension of the royal 'affinity' (following) into the region.[22] Repeatedly praised in sixteenth-century France as an ideal monarch, 'the Father of the People', Louis XII (1498–1515) combined an aggressive foreign policy with stability within France. He used consultative assemblies, indeed created several *parlements*, and avoided any active policy of reducing the power and autonomy of the nobility. Louis did not feel threatened by the latter as a group.[23]

These consensual elements were put under great pressure within Europe during the period of religious and civil war, which was most intense from 1560 until 1648. Religious divisions lent new intensity to conflicts between and within Christian powers; indeed religion, earlier the prime force for social and ideological cohesion, came to play a major role in a culture of violence within Christian Europe.[24]

Domestic tensions in this period channelled and exacerbated the role of war in creating policy and financial pressures that weakened Crown-elite ties. These pressures also wrecked military effectiveness. For example, Charles I (of England and Scotland) sought to suppress opposition in Scotland without the support of the Westminster Parliament. The English army was poorly prepared and deployed and its logistics wrecked by inadequate finance. As a result, the army collapsed when attacked by the Scots in 1639 and 1640. Equally, in the Far East religious divisions were clearly important, although serious and sustained internal conflict in sixteenth-century Japan and seventeenth-century China indicated that civil breakdown did not require such divisions.[25]

In Europe, in the second half of the seventeenth century, as domestic, especially religious, tensions eased, consensual elements in political structures, culture and practice helped better to elicit support for governments. Indeed, the greater military strength of the leading European powers in the century from 1660 can be seen as a product of this cooperation, however restricted in social scope it might be.[26] It is significant that during this period rulers and governments seeking to acquire territory generally sought to do so with the cooperation of the local elite. Thus, Louis XIV of France maintained the distinct identities of Artois and Franche Comté when he acquired them through war (1659 and 1678); William III accepted that Scotland and England should have different established Churches; and Peter the Great of Russia guaranteed the privileges of the local German Protestant nobility when he overran Estonia and Livonia in 1710.

The aristocracy officered the new standing armies that rulers instituted, and did so even if there had been initial concern about their creation. Armed forces strengthened the control of the social elite over their labour force. Towns, where people were most concentrated and least under traditional patterns of social control, were brought under political control. Paris had defied and expelled royal forces in 1588 and 1648, but, thereafter, did not do so again until 1789. Responding to a riot by weavers in London in 1719, a senior official wrote, 'I could not help wishing that the Guards here were in barracks as they are at Dublin, where upon such an emergency, the best part of the garrison may be got under arms in half an hour'.[27] The Royal Barracks in Dublin had been constructed in 1705–9.

It is unclear how far similar themes of Crown-elite cooperation and intermediate institutions as a means to forge consent, are appropriate in many other regions of the world. Ethnic and religious divisions between rulers and populace were a major problem in some regions, although this was also true of parts of Europe, especially eastern Europe. Such divisions did not prevent successful conquest, as the Mughals showed in northern India in the sixteenth and southern India in the seventeenth century, the Manchus in China in the seventeenth century, and the Chinese demonstrated in Xinjiang and Tibet in the eighteenth century. Nevertheless, they weakened the cohesion of states and left them scant powers of resilience when they were defeated.

An ability, both of elites and populace, to accommodate to the demands of new invaders, in, for example, India, did not translate into a system of mass consent that maintained the strength of government, although at the elite level there was such consent and cooperation. Thus the Hindu Rajput nobility adapted to Islamic Mughal rule under Akbar, and this extended to the raising of troops.[28] Nevertheless, there were important

71. Plan of Charleroi. Captured by the French in 1667, 1677 and 1693, Charleroi was crucial to control of the Sambre. The 1693 siege was masterminded by Vauban who claimed that the success of his systematic siege gave Louis XIV 'the finest frontier which France has enjoyed for a thousand years'.

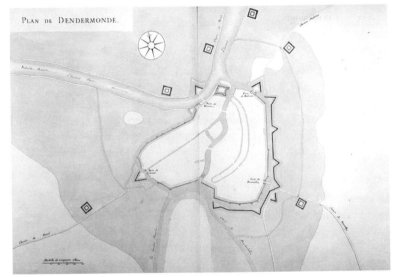

72. Plan of Dendermonde. Part of the Scheldt defensive system, Dendermonde relied on its riverine surroundings to enhance its defences. The low countires were the most fortified part of Europe, and siege warfare played a major role in operations there.

73. Strategic advantage and siegecraft: Plan of the Fortifications and siegeworks at Roermond, 1702. Captured by Anglo-Dutch-German forces under John Churchill, then Earl of Marlborough, 7 October 1702. This was part of a campaign in which Marlborough rapidly captured Venlo, Roermond and Liège, winning the Grand Alliance an important strategic advantage. The French would not be able to threaten the United Provinces from Germany, as they had done in 1672.

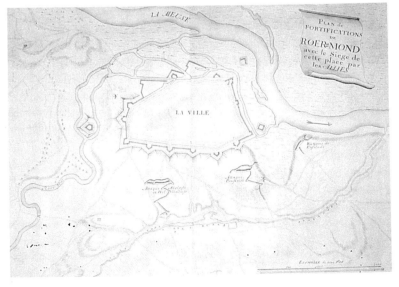

rebellions by distinct ethnic-religious groups in the Mughal and Chinese empires in the seventeenth and eighteenth centuries. However, it would be difficult to argue that several European 'states', especially Austria, but a group also including Britain and Russia, were more ethnically homogeneous than their major Asian counterparts.

Aside from the obvious point of their variety, it would be foolish to exaggerate the deficiencies of non-European governments, while, more generally, it is necessary to be cautious in developing views of the 'East' as backward and in presenting its institutions and cultures as static and hostile to modernisation and capitalism.[29] In his discussion of the transience of Timur's empire, Gibbon referred to the failure to maintain or create governmental structures (VII. 70). This was not, however, true of invaders such as the Ottomans, Mughals and Manchus, and, indeed, Gibbon contrasted the Ottomans with what he termed 'the transient dynasties of Asia' (VII. 78). One such transient state was the pan-Mongol confederation created by the Dzhungar leader Ba'atur in 1640, a bold alliance designed to provide unity, not least by declaring an official religion – Tibetan Buddhism – but one that lasted less than 120 years.[30]

In the late seventeenth century, however, Ottoman Turkey, Mughal India and Manchu China all ruled populations that were larger than any European state, and each state had been able to cope with serious problems in mid-century and then to revive in strength. It is all too easy to minimise the dynamism of systems categorised as conservative, although it is clear that, by European standards of military progress, there were deficiencies. Thus, for example, Akbar's successors failed to match his interest in muskets and cannon, particularly in research and development.[31]

Yet, while true of the late seventeenth century, this dynamism was less apparent a century later, although, as a recent study of elite politics and military society in Egypt has indicated, it is important not to ignore signs of significant change. Alongside their failures, Ottoman Turkey, Persia and the Barbary states of North Africa were each able to achieve defensive successes, but they failed to regenerate their domestic structures and political processes. Whereas in the sixteenth and seventeenth centuries, the Ottomans, Safavids and Mughals had been generally successful in linking their frontier areas with their imperial objectives and also in controlling interregional trade routes, in the eighteenth century they were to suffer at the hands of Afghan, Arab, Persian and Türkmen tribes.[32] Their armed forces lacked the degree of standardisation, order and training that the Europeans increasingly achieved. The gaps between elite and non-elite, regular and non-regular armies that affected non-European forces were much greater than those in their European counterparts. The Ottomans used their period of peace in the 1750s and most of the 1760s to improve revenue collection and reserves, in order to build up a stronger army for future war in the Balkans, but this army lacked the effectiveness of its Russian rival.

Furthermore, the Mughal state collapsed: provincial governors became autonomous and at the centre imperial power was taken over by nobles. This helped to ensure a weak and divided response to the Persian invasion of 1739, and some key Mughal figures refused to take part in the battle of Karnal that year. In response to the defeat, an attempt was made to raise a new imperial central army, but in 1743 this was abandoned due to financial problems, and by 1748 the empire was totally bankrupt.[33] Already, in 1724, the Nizam of Hyderabad had defeated a Mughal army and gained effective control of the Deccan. Mughal India disintegrated into warlordism over a century before China did so. Although some individual Indian rulers displayed considerable dynamism, especially Haidar Ali and Tipu Sultan of Mysore, the parts did not amount to the sum of power wielded by Akbar, Jahangir and Aurangzeb, effective Mughal rulers in the seventeenth century.

74. The Capture of Mons by Louis XIV, 1691. The surrender of the Spanish garrison, heavily bombarded by a large siege train and greatly outnumbered, provided a fresh triumph for a monarch who gloried in his victories. Louis XIV saw victory as a crucial source of *gloire*. The iconography of kingship, the theatre of display and ceremonial, within which monarchs lived, and through which they sought to have their role perceived, stressed martial achievements.

The imperial Islamic states – Ottoman Turkey, Safavid Persia and Mughal India – were challenged by other Islamic states, and in Persia the Safavids were replaced. Although the successor states in Persia and Afghanistan deployed considerable power in the eighteenth century, patrimonial autocracy – the style of government in much of Asia – seemed increasingly unable to produce a scale and regularity of resources sufficient to sustain military competitiveness in the context of mounting European pressure; such pressure was of increasing importance in India from the 1750s. It was also more serious for the Turks from 1683 and for Persia from 1723, although the process of increasing pressure was not continuous. Furthermore, it was of limited importance for China, Burma, Siam and Indo-China until the nineteenth century. Nevertheless, the relationship between structures of command and longer-term developments affecting resource mobilisation were no longer favourable to non-European societies.

Furthermore, whereas similar processes did not take place elsewhere, in Europe the era from 1660 to 1760 witnessed the important linkage of Newtonian science to military engineering, artillery and military thought. This was most dramatically demonstrated in European ballistics which was revolutionised between 1742 and 1753 by Benjamin Robins and Leonhard Euler. Robins invented new instruments enabling him to discover and quantify the air resistance to high-speed projectiles. His other achievements included an understanding of the impact of rifling. Euler solved the equations of subsonic ballistic motion in 1753 and summarised some of the results in published tables. These theoretical and empirical advances greatly increased the predictive power of ballistics, and helped turn gunnery from a craft into a science that could and should be taught.[34]

The Limitations of Imperial Cohesion

Christopher Bayly has argued that the years 1780–1820 witnessed a 'world crisis', that 'the European "Age of Revolutions" was only one part of a general crisis affecting the Asian and Islamic world and the colonies of European settlement . . . when the long-term political conflicts unleashed by the decline of the great hegemonies of the Ottomans, Iran, the Mughals and the monarchies of the Far East and southeast Asia came to a head'.[35] Certainly, the conflicts of the period absorbed formidable quantities of munitions and other resources, and thus posed a challenge to governments and economies alike. Even the relatively brief naval bombardment of Algiers in 1816, designed to ensure the abolition of Christian slavery, cost the British 40,000 round-shot and shell.[36] It is unclear whether the crisis described by Bayly was as widespread as he claims – the description is inappropriate for China and Japan, while earlier peaks of crisis can be given for Persia, Burma and Siam – but Bayly's argument directs attention to an important aspect of the political context of military power, namely the tension between, on the one hand, empires, imperial structures

75. *Royal Artillery in the Low Countries, 1748* by David Morier. The number, manoeuvrability and use of European field artillery increased in the eighteenth century, far more so than in non-European armies. The tactical integration of artillery with both infantry and cavalry was also further advanced and this gave the Europeans an important advantage when units were deployed outside Europe.

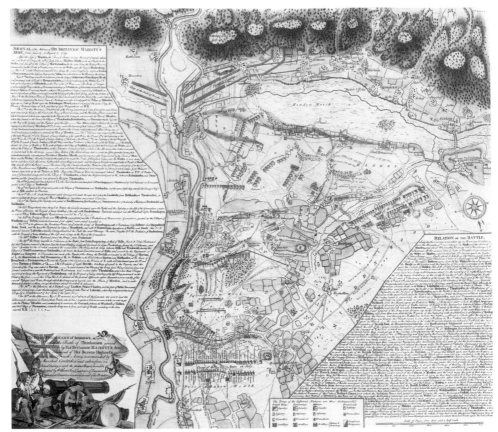

76. The battle of Minden, 1 August 1759. An Anglo-German army under Prince Ferdinand of Brunswick, a protégé of Frederick the Great, defeated the French under Broglie and Contades, inflicting 7,000 casualties while suffering 2,762. The courage and fire-discipline of the British infantry won the battle, six battalions defeating sixty squadrons of French cavalry by misunderstanding orders, advancing across an open plain, and then repulsing two charges by French cavalry. Most of the cavalry casualties were caused by musket fire, but those who reached the British lines were bayoneted. These charges were followed by a French infantry advance that was stopped by British cannon fire, and then by another French cavalry attack, which concentrated on the British flanks and rear, only to find the rear flanks turn about. The French did not fight well: their planning was poor and their artillery out-gunned, but the British cavalry failed to cement the victory by charging.

and ambitions, and, on the other, smaller, more compact states and their policies. Such a tension had also been discerned by Fernand Braudel when he contrasted imperial Spain in the late sixteenth century with England, France and Tuscany.[37]

   If global, or at least extensive, reach is held to be a characteristic of empires, indeed a definition of them, then any systemic change against imperial power would diminish such reach and the reach capability that is and was an important aspect of military strength (although imperial overreach directly weakened the military strength of Britain and France in the twentieth century). Thus, in one respect, the history of global, or at least extensive, military strength is a history not of the military ability to enforce and extend power, but of the politico-socio-cultural factors that inhibited support for such power. In the absence of traditions of large-scale organised autonomy, or a powerful ideology, resistance to imperial power was often gravely weakened by a lack of unity.[38] However, nationalism from the nineteenth century and international ideologies in the twentieth, especially

Communism, were powerful subverters of imperial military range, not only because they resisted its further extension, as with, for example, the Americans in Vietnam, but also because they challenged the internal cohesion of imperial states, as nationalism did in the Soviet Union. In the early 1990s, the latter lost more power and military strength as a consequence of the disintegration of the state resulting from nationalism than it had done in the unsuccessful attempt to control Afghanistan in 1979–89.

Prior to the nineteenth century, there were other sources of subversion. Religion was the most potent because it was crucial to the creation and sustaining of senses of identity: religion was both structure and agency, practice and discourse. Yet, in each polity, the Church or its equivalent as a national institution was potentially divisive because of the pluralistic confessional nature of most states: identities were multiple and often contradictory and atavistic. Identity seen as a process of definition by inclusion was challenged by religious heterodoxy.

Military strength could be employed to impose such senses of religious identity, but in the eighteenth century inclusive and secular notions of identity centred on allegiance to a ruler or state were increasingly adopted within Europe. Toleration was endorsed by 'enlightened despots', such as Frederick the Great of Prussia (1740–86) and Joseph II of Austria (1780–90), as well as by 'liberal' states where monarchical authority was absent or weak, such as the United Provinces (Dutch Republic) and Britain. Inclusive, secular notions of identity and allegiance were central to the ideologies and constitutions of new states, such as the United States of America, revolutionary France, and Poland under the Polish Constitution of 1791.

Nationalism

Nationalism added a further dimension of inclusion to some, but by no means all, European and European-American states in the following century. Nationalism as a term implying a socially comprehensive and insistent mass movement cannot reasonably be applied to most European states prior to the nineteenth century, for it was the changes of that period – stronger states, improved communications, national systems of education, mass literacy, industrialisation, urbanisation and democratisation – that were crucial preconditions, although important ideological and intellectual changes were also involved.[39] National consciousness became nationalism across Europe, the latter more politically potent and energising than the former. Nationalism channelled and fulfilled the ritual aspects of community. More than accommodating the rise of the universal male franchise in the nineteenth century; it could also welcome and benefit from it.

Nationalism also had a direct impact on military capability. Although systems of conscription did not require nationalism, they were made more effective by it, as was seen by the large numbers raised by both sides in the American Civil War. The Confederacy introduced conscription in 1862, the Union in 1863. Nationalism facilitated conscription without the social bondage of serfdom, because conscription was legitimated by new revolutionary and nationalist ideologies. It was intended to transform the old distinction between civilian and military into a common purpose.[40] The traditional republican preference for militia over mercenaries, a disciplined populace, not foreign troops,[41] was given a new political context. However, conscription could be unpopular, especially if introduced with exemptions that were seen as discriminatory. Major riots in New York greeted the introduction of conscription in 1863, while the Confederate forces were badly affected by desertion.[42]

77. (*left*) Medal struck by the Dutch to commemorate the capture of Bonn by John Churchill, 1703. About 300 light or 'cohorn' mortars, named after their inventor Menno van Coehoorn, were employed in the siege. First used the previous year, at the siege of Kaiserwörth, the rapid increase in the number employed – from 74 then – indicated the metallurgical and organisational capacity of European states.

78. Medal struck to commemorate battle of Blenheim. Such medals testified to the range of propaganda devices employed by the governments of the period. Blenheim led to the expulsion of French forces from Germany. It saved the Austrian Habsburgs and pushed Louis XIV back onto the defensive. It indicated the potential decisiveness of battles in *ancien régime* Europe.

Conscription, nevertheless, helped nationalism. Young men at an impressionable age were exposed to state-directed military organisation and discipline and this state direction was centralised: the sub-contracting of military functions to entrepreneurs and the autonomy of aristocratic officers were both ended or, at least, greatly eroded. Conscription was less expensive than hiring soldiers, at home or abroad, but it required a structure of training and authority that was under government control, and did not guarantee a high degree of preparedness, a situation that helped to account for the frontal attack tactics of the First World War.[43] Although the inclusive nature of conscription should not be exaggerated, especially in Russia, it helped in the militarisation of society,[44] so that the major social changes in nineteenth-century Europe did not lead to more pacific societies: competitive governing elites were able to draw on greater economic resources and patterns of organised and obedient social behaviour. Austria, France, Germany and Russia developed large reserve armies: conscripts served for about two or three years and then entered the reserves, ensuring that substantial forces of trained men could be mobilised in the event of war, and that the state did not have to pay them in peace. Combined with demographic and economic growth, this increased the potential size of armies. Troops were frequently stationed away from their localities. This practice, found for example in France and Italy,[45] delayed mobilisation, but it helped to break down the local identity of soldiers and encourage an awareness of the nation. Moreover, the practice was greatly assisted by the spread of the rail network.

Due to nationalism and the attendant increase in the scale of mobilisation of resources in the nineteenth century, it became more apparent that war was a struggle between societies, rather than simply military forces. Thus, Robert E. Lee, the leading Confederate general in the American Civil War, was a keen supporter of conscription, advocated the subordination of state rights to the Confederate cause, and believed, as a member of his staff testified, 'that since the whole duty of the nation would be war until independence should be secured, the whole nation should for the time be converted into an army, the producers to feed and the soldiers to fight'.[46]

Victory in the American Civil War and the mid-nineteenth-century European wars – all wars of national creation and identity – owed much to superior resources, not only military equipment, but, more especially, manpower. This led to an emphasis on larger regular armies and on reserve forces, on the Nation in Arms,[47] although the absence of external threat ensured that the USA escaped this development. The demobilisation of the massive land and naval forces created to wage the American Civil War was one of the most important military-political developments of the century.

Force in the nineteenth century was increasingly concentrated at the disposal of authority, especially the authority of the state. Thus in Spain the Carlists were suppressed in 1839, and in the 1860s a large army and the use of terror subdued peasant opposition in southern Italy. This process was seen even in the USA where traditions of individualism were strong and the ownership of personal weapons widespread. Lawlessness was brought under control, although the recently settled nature of the West, an open frontier only lately closed, ensured that this process was still an issue in the early twentieth century. For example, in California's 'Little Civil War' over water rights, ranchers in the Owens Valley blew up the aqueduct to Los Angeles and seized the aqueduct's principal diversion works in 1924. When, three years later, the bombing of the aqueduct was resumed, the City of Los Angeles sent trainloads of guards armed with submachine-guns and this show of force proved effective.

Nationalism was also a crucial aspect of the process by which the expression and manipulation of public opinion came to play a greater role in political culture. This influenced the context within which decisions were taken for war, and the manner in which wars were conducted. Thus the brutality of Spanish counter-insurgency measures taken against the nationalist rebellion in Cuba that began in 1895 outraged important sections of American public opinion and this was exploited by the yellow press, especially William Randolph Hearst's *New York Journal*.[48] War became an expression of nationalism, rather than dynasticism. This was obviously the case with the republican states of the Western Hemisphere,[49] but was also, increasingly, the case in Europe as dynasties adapted to the mass politics and increasingly urbanised and articulate societies of the states they ruled. Nationalism also made it easier to rally support against invaders deemed foreign. Religion fused with patriotism in the Ethiopian resistance to Egypt in the war of 1875–84, and in Egyptian opposition to the British in 1882.

An increasingly important element in the dialectic of war and reform, nationalism affected many states. Defeat led to political pressure for change, both in Europe and outside, for example in China and Japan. The failure of the Prussian mobilisation against Austria in 1850 led later that decade to a drive to improve the army, organised by Moltke, who was appointed Chief of Staff in 1857. The deficiencies revealed in the Crimean War of 1854–6 led to post-war pressure for change among the combatants. Russian defeat by Japan in 1904–5 was followed by a period of reform, including the establishment of a Council for State Defence in 1905, a major increase in military expenditure and the introduction of very modern artillery. Turkish defeat in the First Balkan War in 1912 led to pressure for military reform; a German military mission arrived at the start of 1914. Competing for influence and contracts, the British sent a naval mission.

However, nationalism did not strengthen all states. If it did so for France, or even, in the case of Germany and Italy, helped create states, nationalism also undermined imperial states, such as Austria-Hungary, by giving their mix of peoples a sense of new nationhoods, although some historians would question just how much damage internal

79. Plan of Québec, showing the principal encampments and works of the British and French armies during the seige by General Wolfe in 1759. Québec, the major French base in North America, surrendered to the British 18 September 1759 after British victory on the Plains of Abraham outside the city five days earlier.

nationalism was doing to Austria before and after 1914. Its forces stood up to the strains of war fairly well until 1918, although their campaigning depended in part on German reinforcements and resources.

Yet, while nationalism weakened empires within Europe, challenging the Austro-Hungarian empire, the Russian position in Poland and the relationship between Britain and Ireland, it did not undermine the European position in the Old World. The British in India and the Dutch in the East Indies were not affected in the nineteenth century by the internal and external pressures and defeats that shattered Iberian authority in Latin America; although the British faced a major mutiny in India in 1857 and there were rebellions against the Dutch.

The pattern of Crown-elite cooperation that was so important in Europe was, in part, replicated in the colonies, although there power was delegated, rather than shared: certainly there was no sharing at the level of the central government of the colonies. Thus, in India, and later Nigeria, the British cooperated with local rulers, as, to a certain extent, did the French in Morocco.[50] The British made few attempts to disrupt existing patterns of social and political authority or religious belief. Thus on the North-West Frontier of British India the tribal system was left in place and its leaders rewarded with payments, while Islam was respected; the Indian Mutiny of 1857 was in part suppressed by loyal Indian forces.

In colonies of settlement, where large numbers of Europeans migrated, the colonial powers came to rely on them to provide most of their own defence. In Canada, after 1871, there were no British bases apart from the coastal positions of Halifax and Esquimalt, although this was more than a matter of just leaving it to the colonists. By 1871 the British were convinced that they could not defend Canada in the light of the extraordinary military efforts made in the American Civil War. The United States could have taken Canada if it so desired. Gladstone and other British ministers also welcomed the opportunity to make defence savings and reduce imperial overstretch. The British were to appease the US at the expense of the Canadian periphery in the settlement of frontier disputes in the 1900s. However, Canada was vulnerable to the US, a state that had western military technology and vast resources. In the nineteenth century there was no equivalent challenge to European power anywhere else in the world.[51]

The combination of nationalism, a sense of imperial mission and global range capability, helped to make nineteenth-century European states particularly effective abroad as power systems. They controlled and benefited from the relationship of technology and capitalism. European states not only benefited economically from their global effectiveness; they also gained military strength. The core–periphery model of economic development can be extended to the military, and indeed it can be suggested that the two were closely related. Thus, for example, in the early modern period Spain drew on Italian, German, Irish and Netherlandish manpower, while in the eighteenth century France drew on Irish, German and Swiss. Subsidy treaties helped Britain to have a freer use for her own labour and affected the states that produced troops for Britain, especially Hesse-Cassel.[52] Such a model can be extended in the eighteenth century to note the extensive recruiting for the British army in the Scottish Highlands after the suppression of the Jacobite risings in 1746, and, although on a smaller scale, in Ireland later in the century; as well as the results of the massive expansion of the recruitment of local soldiers for the army of the East India Company from mid-century on.

In the nineteenth century the European powers were able to use this model and the weakness of Asian-African nationalisms to create large and effective imperial armies, such as the KNIL, the Royal Netherlands-Indies Army, and particularly the British Indian Army. Similarly, the Ottoman army in Iraq was composed of locally recruited rank and file commanded by Turkish officers trained in Constantinople. The Irish contributed more soldiers than their population warranted to the British army; indeed, in 1830 there were more Irish than English in the army.[53]

However, as with weaponry, gaps in capability proved difficult to sustain. The global diffusion of European notions of community, identity and political action, and of practices of politicisation, were to help subvert imperial structures in the twentieth century. In 1885 the Indian National Congress was formed; in 1897 the Egyptian National Party. This subversion was not simply a matter of the introduction of European concepts – it is important not to underrate indigenous notions of identity and practices of resistance, many of them central to a peasant culture of non-compliance[54] – but such concepts were disseminated within the very empires they undermined. 'Modernisation', understood as an imperial project, proved difficult to control, rather as subsequently, after 1945, the USA was on occasion to find unwelcome the consequences of the introduction of democratic practices it advocated around a world now more heavily militarised and structured by powerful states than at any time in its history. Changing practices of political behaviour and ideological cohesion were to lead to a situation after 1945 in which the incidence of internal relative to interstate wars rose.[55] The combination of nationalism and the mass mobilisation of people and resources that characterised industrialising nations in the nineteenth century[56] spread to the non-European world and helped to undermine the logic and practice of colonial control. Imperialism became ideologically and politically bankrupt, and this factor was to be more important in the collapse of European control over most of the world than the changes in economic resources and military capability.

9 Twentieth-Century Reflections

European Strength

In 1900 Europe and the USA dominated the economy of the globe, possessing more wealth and using more energy than the rest of the world. The military primacy and global reach capability of the industrialised European and European-American powers appeared, and indeed was, unprecedented at the beginning of the twentieth century. Most of the earth's surface was under the control of these powers, and their ability to deploy military force was illustrated in such episodes as the American conquest of the Philippines. The quantity and character of the force that could be deployed, as well as its range, were important. On a cold day in January 1904, the influential Royal Geographical Society in London heard Halford Mackinder, the pioneer of geopolitics in Britain, argue that, thanks in part to technology, the nature of the military challenge in Eurasia had altered:

> Russia replaces the Mongol Empire. Her pressure on Finland, on Scandinavia, on Poland, on Turkey, on Persia, on India, and on China, replaces the centrifugal raids of the steppemen . . . the camel-men and horse-men are going . . . railways will take their place, and then you will be able to fling power from side to side of this area.

Thanks to railways, Mackinder saw a heartland power in Eurasia, able to deploy its strength more effectively than the nomads had done. Technology thus enhanced, indeed created, geopolitical axes; indeed geopolitics was a function of technology. Mackinder's interpretation was challenged, however, by the young Leo Amery, who emphasised the onward rush of technology and the role of industrial capacity. He told the meeting that sea and rail links and power would be supplemented by air, and then

> a great deal of this geographical distribution must lose its importance, and the successful powers will be those who have the greatest industrial basis. It will not matter whether they are in the centre of a continent or on an island; those people who have the industrial power and the power of invention and of science will be able to defeat all others.[1]

European Colonialism

In the early decades of the century the frontiers of European control that were clarified through negotiation were generally frontiers between areas claimed by European powers, and such clarification was followed by the imposition of control over native peoples. In

1904 for example the Dutch and the Portuguese agreed to divide the East Indies island of Timor and settled the borders. This was followed in 1912 by the Portuguese suppression of the independent Timorese nobles and then by an extension of Portuguese law and administration.[2] The Dutch imposed control on their side of the border.

Rebellions against European rule were defeated. In 1905 the Germans suppressed the Maji Maji rising in German East Africa (Tanganyika), in part by the use of a scorched-earth policy against guerrilla warfare: about 250,000 Africans died. In 1907 the rebellion by the Nama and Herero of south-west Africa, which had begun in 1904, was finally crushed with great brutality. It had cost the Germans nearly 700 million marks to suppress, and this success led the government to call an election, the 'Hottentot election' of 1907. The Social Democratic Party, which had attacked colonial atrocities and mismanagement, substantially lost votes in the face of imperialist sentiment. The Germans used machine guns in suppressing both risings. Acehnese resistance to the Dutch in Sumatra was largely quelled by 1903, although fighting continued. Anti-French revolts in Madagascar in 1898–1904 and in Tunisia in 1915–16, and an anti-British Zulu revolt in Natal in South Africa in 1906, were all defeated, as was the revolt of the Beni Snassen in north-east Morocco in 1907. European imperialism did not therefore rest on placid consent, but rebellions were defeated. Similarly, the Japanese suppressed a guerilla uprising in Korea in 1907–9.

The boundaries of European imperial power were also extended, including in areas where the Europeans had never hitherto sent troops. In 1900 the French seized the Touat oasis in the Sahara, the first loss of territory by Morocco to a Christian power for over a century. They went on to make significant gains.[3] On 31 March 1904 a British force under Colonel Francis Younghusband advancing towards the Tibetan capital of Lhasa opened fire at Guru on Tibetans who were unwilling to disarm. Due in large part to their two Maxim guns, four cannon and effective rifles, the British killed nearly 700 Tibetans without any losses of their own. Younghusband then proceeded to Lhasa. Thanks to the resources of the British imperial state, his advance had been supported by 10,000 coolies (human porters), 7,000 mules, 5,000 bullocks and over 4,000 yaks.

The submission of the Ahaggar Tuareg in 1905 ended effective resistance to the French in the Sahara; five years earlier, the fall of In Rhar, after French artillery had breached its walls, had broken the resistance of the Tidelkt.[4] The Dutch seized and enforced control of more of the East Indies. In 1906 they intervened in South Bali. At Den Pasar and later at Paměscutan, the two *raja* families ritually purified themselves for death and fought their final battle (*puputan*): armed only with daggers and lances they were all slaughtered as they advanced in the face of Dutch firepower, killing their own wounded as they did so. In 1908 the Dutch attacked the Dewa Agung of Klungkung, and he staged his own *puputan*. In 1905–6 the resistance of the Bugis, Makasarese and Torajas of Sulawesi was broken: Dutch power was effective both against developed states (the first two cases), and against the head-hunting Toraja. The last resistance to Dutch rule in Banjarmasin in Borneo ended in 1906. On Sumatra, Jambi was brought under control in 1907.[5]

In 1911 Italy conquered Tripolitania and Cyrenaica from the Turks, and called their conquest Libya. The Italian navy and an expeditionary corps of 34,000 men captured the major coastal positions, such as Benghazi and Tripoli, but, in the face of determined resistance by Senussi tribesmen in the interior, found it more difficult to expand and consolidate their position, a situation that repeated much of the history of European military expansion, including the earlier Italian experience in the Horn of Africa. Although the Turks were defeated, the Libyans fought on. The Libyans first used traditional cavalry charges, but they were defeated by European firepower as at Asaba (1913). The Libyans then resorted to guerrilla tactics. In 1915 an Italian force of 4,000 troops was largely destroyed after its Libyan auxiliaries turned against it and the Italians were driven back to the coast.[6] The previous year, at El Herri in Morocco, a French force was largely killed or wounded when it was attacked from all directions by a far larger force. Earlier that year at El Bordj the French faced Moroccans armed with rapid-fire rifles. The Italian invasion of Libya was the first war in which aeroplanes and armoured cars were used. Hand-grenades were dropped on a Turkish army camp on 23 October 1911. Giulio Douhet (1869–1930), the commander of the Italian aerial bombardment unit, was to be a major theorist of aerial warfare.

Russo-Japanese War

Yet there were also important indications of shifts in political consciousness that were to lead to challenges to these hegemonic positions. The development of Japan as a major military power was to be dramatically revealed, on both land and sea, in the Russo-Japanese war of 1904–5, a war that was carefully followed by European and American military attachés; for example John Pershing, the Commander of the American Expeditionary Forces sent to France in 1917, had been an observer with the Japanese army. In one respect, this war was a triumph for Europeanisation in the form of western military organisation. The Japanese had won by employing European military systems and military technology more effectively than their opponents. The Japanese army was modelled on that of Germany, their navy on that of Britain. They used torpedoes for their surprise attack at the outset of the war on the Russian squadron in Port Arthur. The battle of Tsushima (1905) was the only example of a decisive clash between modern battleships in the twentieth century. Both sides lost battleships to mines. The war also saw the use of field telephones and electric searchlights.

Yet the Japanese victory was also a shock, in part because of European racialist assumptions, and in part because the USA – the major non-European nineteenth-century power that had a European-style military capability – had not challenged these assumptions or pursued an active imperial policy in Africa or Asia or waged war with any of the leading European empires; its short and successful war with Spain in 1898 was at the expense of a weak empire. The Japanese had gained great confidence in their military system as a result of their victory over China in 1894–5 and the Japanese contingent had been by far the largest in the international force that suppressed the Boxer rising of 1900; but those had been moves against China, not against a European power.

Other factors also played a role in the Japanese victory over Russia. Russia was fighting 6,000 miles from its political base, the government had domestic revolution to consider in 1905, a revolution in part fostered by Japanese military intelligence, and the Japanese would probably have been defeated if, as threatened, the Russians had committed new forces in mid-1905. The Japanese, however, used the victory in later years to bolster myths of cultural uniqueness through a peculiarly Japanese aptitude for war, the *bushido* spirit. Russia's defeat also encouraged anti-European movements elsewhere in Asia, for example the Chieu conspiracy against France in Indo-China.

The rise of American economic and naval power challenged Britain, just as that of Japan threatened Russia, but conflict between the two powers was avoided. In part this reflected a British willingness not to oppose American pretensions.[7] In addition, although far from pacific, the Americans were less aggressive than the Japanese. Relative American indifference to formal imperialism rested in part on the popular view that American foreign policies should be distinct from those of the *anciens régimes* of Europe and, therefore, rely more on informal than formal control, although the American role in the Pacific and the Caribbean was far more direct, leading to acquisitions, such as Hawaii (1898), and to the occupation of Haiti (1915) and the Dominican Republic (1916).[8] Despite the victory over Spain in 1898, the Americans were not prepared for a major war. In 1900–2 Filipino nationalists mounted a guerrilla war to resist American annexation, leading the latter to add counter-insurgency methods to their ideology of racialism and divine purpose. Prisoners were killed and prison camps created in which 11,000 died. The Americans were successful, but lost 4,200 troops and although in 1902 they claimed that resistance had been crushed, it continued.[9]

If Japanese victory indicated the potential military consequences of Europeanisation, there were other suggestions that the political processes associated with Europeanisation would spread. The overthrow of the Manchu empire in China in 1911 and the Young Turk movement in Turkey were both significant developments in political and military systems prior to the First World War. In Turkey it was disaffected army elements under Enver Pasha who rebelled against Sultan Abu ul-Hamid II in 1908, deposing him the following year after a rising by a section of the army linked to anti-western strict Muslims had been suppressed. The Turks were beaten in the First Balkan War, being especially heavily defeated by the Bulgarians at Kirk Kilesse (1912) and Lulé Burgas (1912), and lost most of their European empire. The Young Turks seized power in a coup in 1913 and Enver, appointed Chief of Staff, recaptured Edirne from Bulgaria in the Second Balkan War. Enver was helped by Otto Liman von Sanders, a German general sent in 1913 to head a military mission intended to reform the Ottoman army after the failures of the First Balkan War. He became Inspector General of the Ottoman army in late 1913, while Enver became Minister of War in 1914. Other non-Western powers sought to acquire European weaponry. In the Ethiopian Emperor's review of his nearly 100,000-strong army in 1902, elite units had demonstrated the use of machine-gun and artillery fire.

The Russo-Japanese war of 1904–5 anticipated some aspects of the First World War (1914–18) and was influential in framing the military ideas held at the outset of the latter. Japanese gunners at Tsushima (1905) scored hits on Russian battleships from unprecedented distances. This led many to conclude (correctly) that future battleship engagements would be fought at great distance, reinforcing the case for the heavily armoured, 'all-big-gun' battleship soon to be embodied in the *Dreadnought*, and causing more attention to be directed towards fire control in the years before 1914. A cult of powerful battleship fleets developed. This owed something to the impact of Alfred Thayer Mahan, an American naval officer who from 1885 lectured on naval history and strategy at the Naval War College in Newport. His lectures, published as *The Influence of Sea Power upon History, 1660–1783* (1890), and his other works emphasised the importance of control of the sea and saw the destruction of the opponent's battle fleet as the means to achieve this. Mahan's views were widely disseminated and encouraged the process of big-ship construction, one which affected many states, including some not generally seen as naval powers, such as Austria. The United States navy developed a concept of offensive sea control by a battle-ship fleet and pressed successfully for the launching and maintenance of an offensive battle fleet in peacetime. It also developed a military-industrial complex and a chain of protected bases from the Atlantic to the Pacific via Panama in order to be able to support a large fleet in the Pacific.[10]

Competitive emulation set the pace. The British-built *Dreadnought* was faster and more heavily gunned than any other battleship then sailing. It encouraged the Germans to respond with the construction of powerful battleships. The Austrian Navy League, founded in 1904, was instrumental in the increase of the Austrian naval budget and in a programme of *Dreadnought* construction that touched off a naval race with Italy. The Japanese laid down their first two *Dreadnought*-type battleships in 1909. With the arrival of the *Dreadnought*s, battleship architecture reached a new period of relative stability. The USS *New York* (BB-34) of 1914, *Texas*'s (BB-35) of 1914, and *Nevada* (BB-36) of 1916 participated in the D-Day bombardment on 6 June 1944. The *Texas* ten 14-inch guns could fire $1\frac{1}{2}$ rounds per minute; each armour-piercing shell weighing 1,500 lb.

On land, observers from all major European armies witnessed a campaign that featured many elements that were to be seen in the First World War: trench warfare with barbed wire and machine-guns, indirect artillery fire, artillery firing from concealed positions, a conflict that did not cease at nightfall, and the first war ever fought with continuous front lines, albeit only a fraction of the length of the English Channel to Switzerland front or the Baltic to Black Sea front of the First World War. Advocates of the offensive argued that the Russians stood on the defensive and lost, while the Japanese took the initiative, launched frontal assaults on entrenched forces strengthened by machine-guns and quick-firing artillery, as at Port Arthur and Mukden in 1905, and prevailed, despite horrific casualties. In fact, in the battle of Liaoyang (25 August to 3 September 1904), the Russians were attacked by a larger Japanese force on three successive occasions and repulsed them all, but their commander, Aleksei Kuropatkin, believed himself defeated and retreated. The tactical superiority of the defence over the offence revealed in the American Civil War was not seen as the problem that the First World War was to show it to be. Observers came away from the Russo-Japanese War reassured that frontal assaults were still feasible, and the bayonet still relevant, the latest technology notwithstanding. The bravery of Japanese infantry and their innovative tactics, such as night attacks, impressed everyone.

Given the Darwinian racialist mental attitudes of the period, many European experts concluded that if Japanese (i.e. non-'White') infantry could achieve victory under such battlefield conditions, surely the infantry of the superior races of Europe would be capable of similar, if not greater, heroic deeds, albeit at the cost of many lives. While no one before 1914 expected a general European war to be a long war, one of the great myths of First World War literature is the old truism that the army leaders did not expect heavy casualties. From 1905 onward, based upon the lesson of the Russo-Japanese War, they fully expected to suffer one-third casualties. This expectation dramatically changed thinking on manpower requirements and provided the impetus for programmes in all countries to expand the size of their armies before 1914. These programmes interacted with an increase in armaments to produce a growth in military preparedness.[11]

The Russo-Japanese War was not really an example of technological success: if anything, the Japanese risked catastrophic defeat because their political ambitions led them to overreach. If Kuropatkin had been able to fight as he had wanted to, luring the Japanese deep into Manchuria while bringing to bear the overwhelming Russian superiority in numbers, they would have been defeated. Kuropatkin came closer to success than is sometimes appreciated, not least at Sandepu (26–27 January 1905). Political weakness in St Petersburg was crucial to Russian defeat.

The First World War

The First World War (1914–18) is often remembered in terms of the trench warfare of the Western Front in France and Belgium, where very large numbers fought, and considerable numbers died to no purpose, certainly without major gains of territory. The war has been seen as the epitome of military futility and incompetence. This is in a way deceptive. The European powers and their colonies made hitherto unprecedented efforts and deployed armies and navies that represented a hitherto unknown aggregation of power. These forces were integrated fighting machines that were able to act effectively, although the swift victory, the railborne, or at least sustained, *blitzkrieg*,[12] that had been anticipated in 1914, proved elusive, as, subsequently, did hopes of decisive victory. The *blitzkrieg* concept predated mechanised warfare, and indeed fell within traditional German concepts of operations of envelopment and annihilation. The German and Austro-Hungarian general staffs were thinking in such terms in the First World War, relying on rail transport and forced marches.

The euphoria of the war's outbreak and the general confidence in its speedy conclusion were followed on the Western Front by the emergence of stalemate by October 1914. The concentration of large forces in a relatively small area, the defensive strength of trench positions (particularly thanks to machine-guns, with their range and rapidity of fire, and quick-firing artillery, but, also, helped by barbed wire and concrete fortifications), and the difficulty of making substantial gains even if opposing lines were breached, ensured that, until the collapse of the German position in the last weeks of the war, the situation there was essentially deadlocked; the Germans still maintained a continuous front in November 1918. It proved very difficult to translate local superiority in numbers into decisive success. It was possible to break through opponents' trench lines, but difficult to exploit such successes; as yet, aeroplanes and motor vehicles had not been effectively harnessed to help the offensive. Cavalry was the only arm of exploitation available and its potential was limited.

When in 1914 the Germans did advance on an open front through Belgium and France in a variation on the Schlieffen Plan, they were slowed down by the need to transport food and ammunition for their formidable numbers, and this gave the French an opportunity to regroup, counterattack and wreck the German plan. The absence of a speedy military victory and the fact that France was part of a powerful coalition ensured that the political collapse of an opponent that had enabled the Prussians to derive lasting success from their military, given victories in 1866 and 1870–1, was not repeated in 1914.

Artillery, rather than the machine-gun, was the great killer of the First World War; estimates claim artillery fire caused up to 70 per cent of battlefield deaths. The Italians, not the strongest or most industrialised of powers, deployed 1,200 guns for their attack on the Austrians in the Third Battle of the Isonzo in October 1915. The British used 2,879 guns – one for every nine yards of front – for their attack near Arras in April 1917.[13] Artillery bombardments inflicted devastating losses, especially at the outset of offensives before shell fire produced the cover of shell-holes, as when the Germans attacked French-held Verdun in 1916. In the British army, 58 per cent of battlefield deaths were from artillery and mortar shells, and slightly less than 39 per cent from machine-gun and rifle bullets. German machine-guns, which were concentrated by deployment in companies rather than dispersed among the infantry, were especially devastating against the British troops advancing slowly and in close order on the Somme in 1916. Although the French, who had not envisaged trench warfare, lacked heavy artillery at the outset of the war, their 75 mm field gun could fire over 15 rounds a minute and had a range of 9,000 yards, while German 150 mm field howitzers could fire five rounds per minute. Air-burst shrapnel shells increased the deadly nature of artillery fire. The spread of steel helmets offered scant protection. Reacting against colleagues who put an emphasis on the attack, General Pétain coined the maxim 'firepower kills'.

Attacks, for example by the British at Neuve-Chapelle and Loos (1915), the Somme (1916), and Arras and Passchendaele (1917), the Italians on the Isonzo (1915), the French in Champagne (1915) and the Germans at Verdun (1916), led to unprecedentedly heavy losses. This kind of frontal attack was used at the same time across the Atlantic in the Mexican Revolution by the revolutionary general Francisco Villa. It won him victory at Torreón in 1914, but the tactic was costly even there, and could be unsuccessful, as with Villa's defeat by Álvaro Obregón in 1915 at Celaya, a battle in which trenches, barbed wire and machine-guns thwarted the attack.

In Western Europe, where the ratio of troops and firepower to space was far higher, such methods were much more costly. The Americans, who entered the war on the Allied side in 1917, were to discover this when they launched human-wave assaults on the Western Front. Nevertheless, sometimes such attacks could prove amazingly successful. The British gained some initial successes in the 1915 battles, but then lost them as the high command dithered. Once troops had advanced it was difficult to recognise, reinforce and exploit success: until wireless communications improved in late 1917 control and communications were limited.

The unimaginative nature of most contemporary generalship, British, French, German, Austrian, Russian and Italian, with its preconceived ideas and strategy of attrition, did not help. Most generals were slow to adopt different approaches. The German attack on Verdun in 1916 was designed to do little more than inflict heavy casualties on the French. It served no strategic purpose, and cost the Germans almost as many men.

Verdun, like the British attack on the Somme in 1916, was larger in scale than earlier battles on the Western Front. This reflected the success of the combatants in raising troops and concentrating resources, especially their ability to sustain large numbers of men in the same area for long periods, as well as the pressure on commanders to break through. In Eastern Europe, however, the force-to-space ratio was lower and it was easier to smash through opposing lines and advance rapidly, as the Germans demonstrated at Russian expense in 1915.

Nearly 9 million troops died in the war. Casualty rates were high. On the French side; 27 per cent of all young men between the ages of 18 and 27 died in the war. Of the 8 million soldiers mobilised by Austria, 1,106,000 died. Subsequently, this form of warfare served as a potent image not only of the destructiveness and barbarity of war, but also of its apparent futility. The bitter criticisms of some leading war poets, such as Wilfred Owen and Siegfried Sassoon, attracted considerable attention. Following the débâcle of 1914–18, the victorious powers sought to resolve disputes without war. The League of Nations was established in 1919 as a body to maintain international peace.

However, the horror of what appeared to be military futility in the First World War distracted attention from the effectiveness of the European military system. Despite the nature of the conflict on the Western Front in 1915–17, the First World War was not an impasse made indecisive by similarities in weapons systems. The Germans defeated the Russians, seized large portions of Russia, and their victories played a major role in the collapse of Tsarist power within Russia in 1917. The Germans also conquered Belgium (1914). In the blitzing of Serbia (1915), the Central Powers used an Austro-German-Bulgarian army in which the Bulgarians were the largest contingent (although not a majority). Because German field marshals commanded the conquests of Serbia and Romania, these victories (especially the latter in 1916) usually appear in the literature as 'German' victories, much to the chagrin of Austrian military historians. Both conquests demonstrated the ability of contemporary armies to achieve decisive victories: large forces were ably deployed and coordinated over difficult terrain.

What were later called *blitzkrieg* tactics began in 1916. The so-called (although not by the Germans) Hutier tactics built on a captured French manual and on the Russian General Brusilov's successful, surprise 1916 offensive against the Austrians, were first used by the Germans in 1917 on the Eastern Front at Riga and then by the Austrians and Germans on the Italian Front at Caporetto. The Austrians and Germans advanced rapidly, with machine-guns and light artillery on lorries, avoiding Italian strongpoints as they advanced, and destroyed the coherence and communications of the Italian defence. The German emphasis was on speed, not attrition. The Italian collapse indicated the potential effectiveness of the offensive in the First World War. The Italians lost possibly as many as 600,000 men and were pushed back 80 miles. Italy was nearly knocked out of the war. The Germans first used these tactics on the Western Front on 30 November 1917, regaining most of the ground near Cambrai the British had recently gained thanks to their first use of massed tanks. This new approach to tactics was adopted more generally in 1918 and transformed the stalemate that had characterised the Western Front since late 1914. German 'storm troopers' advanced in dispersed units under cover of artillery barrages and broke into Allied trenches.

The effectiveness of the European military system was also demonstrated outside Europe; this was indeed a world war. The Allies, especially the British, overran all the German colonies, bar German East Africa, rapidly, while the British guarded their oil supplies in the Persian Gulf by advancing into Turkish-held Mesopotamia (modern Iraq), and in 1917–18 drove the Turks from Palestine. The British used both tanks and aeroplanes, although cavalry played a major role in the breakthrough. The Russians occupied northern Persia in 1915: Persia was unable to protect her neutrality, and Turkish, British and Russian forces all operated in the country.

In contrast, although defeated by the Russians in the Caucasus, the Turks fought well against the British, defeating their attempt to force the Dardanelles in 1915, and forcing an outmanoeuvred British force advancing on Baghdad to surrender at Kut the same year, both major defeats for a European force. The Japanese, who fought on the Allied side, captured Germany's Chinese base of Tsingtao in 1914 and German bases in the Pacific, escorted British convoys from Australia, hunted German surface raiders, and in 1917 sent warships to assist the Allies in the Mediterranean. The Germans in Tsingtao were outnumbered more than 13 to one, and outfought by a successful Japanese use of combined operations.

The British retained control of their home waters and were, therefore, able to avoid blockade and invasion, to retain trade links that permitted the mobilisation of British resources, and to blockade Germany; although the impact of the last was limited by Germany's continental position and her ability to obtain most of the resources she required from within Europe. The British and French also benefited from the support of empire. This was true at sea, but more so on land. The French deployed African troops on the Western Front. More than 800,000 Indian soldiers fought for the British in the war, so that, far from the British having to garrison the country, this most important of colonies proved a crucial source of manpower. The British used very large numbers of them on the Western Front, as well as a substantial Canadian force. Australian and New Zealand troops played the major role in the unsuccessful attempt to force the Dardanelles, and were also sent to the Western Front. Imperial forces were also important elsewhere. South African troops played the major role in the conquest of South-West Africa in 1915. Indian troops captured Basra in 1914, protecting British oil interests in south-west Persia, and advanced into Mesopotamia the following year. The greater use of oil by the British navy from 1907 increased strategic concern about the Middle East. This was to have a greater effect in the Second World War, by which time oil was also used more widely for land and air transport.

The nature of imperial power was demonstrated in 1914 when Gurkha and Indian units, supported by British and French warships, defeated Turkish attacks on the Suez Canal. Without the empire, the British would have been unable to mount offensive operations in the Middle East, would have been largely reduced to the use of the navy against German colonies, and would have been forced to introduce conscription earlier than 1916. The use of imperial forces was helped by the absence of an enemy in Asia. The situation was to be very different in the Second World War.

Germany was defeated in 1918 because of, first, the defeat of her army on the Western Front, secondly, the collapse of her principal ally, Austria-Hungary, and, thirdly, the degree to which the exacerbation that year of the military, economic and domestic problems facing the Germans destroyed their will to fight. The strain that the attempt to mobilise the resources for total war imposed upon German society was exacerbated and focused by the failure of the 1918 spring offensive. Army morale collapsed after the offensive did not bring the victory promised by Erich Ludendorff, the powerful German Deputy Chief of Staff.

The Western Front was very important. The blocking of German offensives in 1914, 1916 and 1918 was an essential precondition of Allied victory, and in 1918 the Germans were dramatically driven back in the theatre of operations where their strength was concentrated. This was a victory for the British, who played the major role in the advance, and also for their allies. The British recovered swiftly from the German advances in March–April, in which the Germans had used both human-wave frontal assaults and the more flexible tactics of storm trooper units, only to outrun their supplies and be blocked by Allied reinforcements. Using forces from the Eastern Front freed by the Russian collapse, the Germans had gained territory but had failed to destroy their opponents' fighting ability.[14] A last Austrian offensive on the Piave in northern Italy in June 1918 also failed.

In July–November 1918 the British, and to a lesser extent the French and Americans, launched a series of attacks in which they outfought the Germans, overrunning their major defensive system in September 1918. Tanks played a more important role in the advance than when first used by the British at the Somme on 15 September 1916, and by the French the following April, and the British use of them en masse was a shock to the Germans. On 8 August 1918 no fewer than 430 British tanks broke through the German lines near Amiens. Tanks could be hit by rifle bullets and machine-guns without suffering damage; they could smash through barbed wire and cross trenches. The Germans also deployed tanks in 1918, but they did so in far smaller numbers and to less effect than the British: these tanks, some captured from the British, did not influence the outcome of the spring battles. Their industry was unable to manufacture them in sufficient quantities. More generally, the Germans had lost their superiority in weapons systems. British gunnery, for example, inflicted considerable damage on German defences. The impasse of trench warfare was broken, although, in battle, tanks rapidly became unfit for service and there was a reaction against the use of armour by the British after August.[15]

American intervention from 1917 was also important. The American military machine moved on from the unpreparedness and administrative shortcomings revealed by the Spanish-American War of 1898, partly because the Americans had several years to prepare for conflict. In April–October 1918 over 1,600,000 American troops crossed the Atlantic, transforming a German superiority on the Western Front of 300,000 men

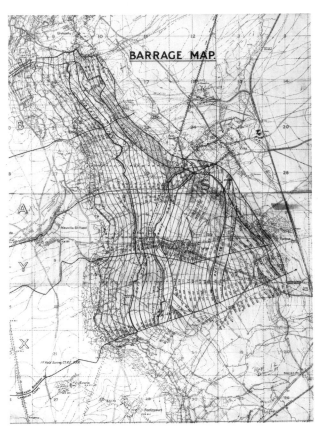

BARRAGE MAP.

80. Artillery barrage map, Vimy Ridge, April 1917. An effective creeping barrage helped the Canadians capture this position on the Western Front. The Canadians deployed 1,130 guns, an artillery concentration more than double the density employed the previous year at the Somme.

in March 1918 to an Allied superiority of 200,000 men four months later.[16] This was the largest movement of troops across an ocean hitherto. The Americans were fresh troops, and had the war continued they would have been decisive. The Americans also made a significant contribution to the war in the air and at sea.

Important as American troops were on the Western Front, American financial resources and industrial capacity were even more crucial.[17] Provoked by unrestrained German submarine warfare, America entered the war in 1917, but her industrial resources and technology were available to the Allies from the outset. They were crucial, because in 1914 neither Britain nor France had an industrial system to match that of Germany. For machine tools, mass-production plant and much else, including the parts of shells, the Allies were dependent on the USA. Thus, in 1915–16 shells from the USA and Canada were necessary for the British on the Western Front. For their transportation, as for other reasons, routes across the Atlantic were fundamental to the Allied war effort. However, by 1917, the British production of munitions had greatly increased, and a war economy had been prepared. German industrial capacity was itself crucial to the Central Powers. The Turks, for example, relied on German ammunition and the improvement of communications between the two powers was one reason for the overrunning of Serbia in 1915. The Austrians had only limited industrial capacity and their production of munitions was below that of other major European combatants. The rapid spread of advanced weaponry within the European world owed much to the pre-war and wartime alliance systems, although purchase was also important. In 1914 the Serbs had very effective Mauser rifles purchased from Germany, as well as French and Russian rifles, and also had 328 modern Schneider Creusot field-guns. Montenegro had Italian-made artillery.

New and recent technology played a major role in the war, especially aeroplanes, submarines, tanks and gas. Submarines and aircraft were introduced into combat rapidly, and swiftly affected the conduct of operations, although the potential of each was grossly underestimated by commanders in 1914. Even Admiral Tirpitz was a late convert to submarines. Nevertheless, in 1914 the threat of submarine attack forced the British Grand Fleet to withdraw from the North Sea. Submarines benefited from an increase in their range, seaworthiness, speed and comfort, from improvements in the accuracy, range and speed of torpedoes, which by 1914 could travel 7,000 yards at 45 knots, and from the limited effectiveness of anti-submarine weaponry. In November 1916 the Germans risked an entire squadron of capital ships to salvage a single submarine. The following February they introduced unrestricted submarine warfare and inflicted serious losses on Allied, particularly British, commerce. These losses owed much to British inexperience in confronting submarine attacks.

Aeroplanes also had an effect at sea. In July 1918 Britain conducted the first raid by land planes flown off an aircraft carrier and in the following month German seaplanes eliminated an entire naval force – six coastal motorboats. The following month HMS *Argus*, an aircraft carrier capable of carrying 20 planes with a flush deck unobstructed by superstructure and funnels – the first clear-deck aircraft carrier – was commissioned by the British, although she did not undergo sea trials until October 1918.[18]

Gas, used first by the Germans in 1915 (its first organised use was at the Second Battle of Ypres), and by the British later that year, was deadly at times, but had less effect than submarine warfare, although its psychological effect was considerable. Gas could be blown back by the wind, as happened to the British at Loos in 1915. Mustard gas, which harmed by contact, as well as by the ingestion which had brought death with the earlier chlorine gas attacks, was first used in 1917 by the Germans at Passchendaele.[19] Mustard gas was first and foremost an incapacitant, burning and blistering its victims, and so compounding the problems of medical and support services.

However, although aeroplanes, tanks and, in particular, submarines, were important, the crucial technologies were rather older: the machine-gun and steel artillery played a

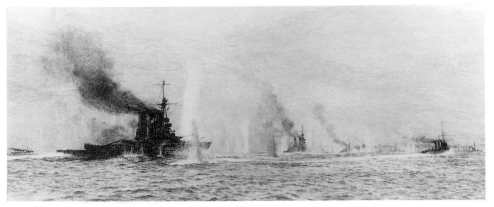

81. (*facing page*) *HMS Merope in action with a U-boat* by William Wyllie. *Merope* was a 'Q' ship, disguised as a vulnerable vessel to lead submarines to surface in order to sink them by shell-fire. The 'Q' ships would then open up with their hidden guns.

82. *The Battle of Jutland* by William Wyllie, 1916. The celebrated marine artist depicts *Tiger, Princess Royal, Lion, Warrior* and *Defence. Lion* was the flagship of Vice-Admiral Beatty's battle-cruiser squadron which took much damage from the Germans in the first stage of the battle.

greater role in the character and course of the conflict. Developments with radio were important on land and sea and in the air. Directional wireless equipment aided location and navigation, while radio transmissions changed from a spark method to a continuous wave system. At sea, mine barrages limited the options for surface and submarine vessels: the Allies laid massive barrages across the English Channel, the North Sea and the Straits of Otranto in order to limit the operational range of German and Austrian forces. The British naval attempt to force the Dardanelles in 1915 was stopped by mines after three battleships were sunk and three more were badly damaged. By the end of the war magnetic mines had been developed and were being laid by the British. The introduction in May 1917 of a system of escorted convoys by the British cut their shipping losses dramatically and led to an increase in the sinking of German submarines: convoys were more effective than mines in limiting the potency of German attacks, although mines sunk more submarines than other weapons.

Less spectacular developments were also important. The British produced new weapons, such as the Stokes mortar, and evolved more effective artillery techniques, which helped them in their advances in 1918. The flame thrower was first used in 1914 by the Germans, who then introduced the weapon to their Austrian allies. Technological advances were widely diffused and copied. This was true of tanks, gas and air warfare, for example the synchronising or 'interrupter gear' developed by Fokker for the Germans which was modelled on a French aircraft shot down by the Germans and, in turn, copied for Allied aeroplanes.

Stalemate had its analogue on the home front in terms of policies and strategies for war mobilisation. The ability to mobilise resources, both men and munitions, was crucial; 37 million shells were fired by the French and Germans in their ten-month contest for Verdun in 1916. Such a use of artillery ensured that the cost of offensives soared. The availability of shells became a political issue in Britain in 1915, and a serious problem in France. By the end of the war, the British Royal Arsenal at Woolwich employed over 80,000 people. Governments extended their regulatory powers in order to increase economic effectiveness and ensure that resources were devoted to war, a move which helped to deal with the pre-war crisis of European heavy industry. Armaments had an obvious appeal as an escape from over-capacity. The annexation of competitors offered another apparent solution. Even in the early stages of the war, governments felt it necessary to abandon pre-war practices in order to mobilise resources. The Germans passed war finance laws on 4 August 1914. The British government took over the control of the railways (1914), the coal mines (1917) and the flour mills (1918); a powerful Ministry of Munitions developed from 1915 and a Food Production Department was created in 1917. County agricultural committees oversaw a 30 per cent rise in national cereal production. The war effort was underpinned by a major expansion not only of the size of government administration but also, more specifically, of military administration.[20]

In France the government controlled bread prices, although the production of munitions was left to entrepreneurs, and state-supervised consortia directed the allocation of supplies in crucial industries. A government-directed shoe industry was created, as was a chemical industry.[21] Bread rationing began in Germany in January 1915 as the British blockade had its effect. The major German industries were taken under government control and, although not publicly owned, the economy was publicly controlled: in practice this entailed an alliance between big business and the military. Rationing was widespread.[22] The Russian economy, in contrast, was poorly managed, with industrial production and transport both in grave difficulties by 1915. The War Industries Committees that had been set up were found wanting and in 1916 state monopolies took over coal and oil production in Russia. Russia was short of shells.[23] The control of industries became a political issue both there and elsewhere. More generally, the mass management of resources, manufacturing and society became more important. War gave the states power and enabled them to circumvent many of the constraints and exigencies of pre-war politics. This was certainly so in financial terms: governments were now able to tax and borrow as much as they thought necessary. Income tax in Britain doubled in the first year of the war. War was a catalyst both for state power and modernisation.

Conscription systems were introduced in countries that lacked them, such as Britain (1916), Canada (1917) and the USA (1917), or expanded, although conscription was rejected by Australia in two divisive referendums. Universal military training and service was seen as both crucial to the war effort and a central expression of national identity.[24] The war effort was underpinned by government-directed or supported propaganda. This became more important in 1916 as demoralisation increased and opposition to the conflict spread. The war led to an extension of the female role in economy and society, much of it under the auspices of such organisations as the Woman's Land Army in Britain. Female employment rose and new roles were played by women. This extended to the armed forces, where they filled ancillary roles in order to free men for battlefield duties.

The pressure of war increased tensions within both the military and society. The former led to widespread demoralisation and to some acts of mutiny; the latter were especially acute in the French and Russian armies in 1917. The refusal of the St Petersburg garrison to fire on strikers was instrumental in the fall of the Tsarist government in 1917. There were German and Austrian naval mutinies in 1918, and the failure of the last Austrian offensive against Italy in June 1918 was followed by mutinies and mass desertion.[25]

Nevertheless, prior to 1917 there were few signs of widespread and sustained opposition to military service or the conduct of the war. Instead, it was noteworthy how far millions of men were willing, and often eager, to serve in what was already from late 1914 clearly a conflict involving heavy casualties. Habits of mass mobilisation acquired prior to the war thanks to industrial labour, trade unions and the organisation of democratic politics contributed to this willingness to accept discipline and order, but so also did passive acceptance of the social order. In addition, many wanted to fight and some wanted to die.

More generally, war was a major force for social change in Europe. Traditional assumptions were questioned, and social practices were affected by higher inflation, greater taxation, rationing and the spread of female employment and trade unionism. In Italy, for example, in 1915–18 inflation increased by over 300 per cent and the national debt by 500 per cent. The political, social and economic privileges and status of established elites and middle classes were qualified or challenged, and the stability of a number of important countries, never complete, was made more precarious. The war also left a series of unmet territorial claims and a sense of dispossession among the defeated, especially in Germany and Hungary.

The World Outside Europe in the 1920s

The defeat of Germany and its allies ensured that European and European-American control over the world's surface reached its maximum extent. Although the redistribution of Germany's colonies led to gains by Japan under a League of Nations mandate, the partition of the Ottoman empire led in 1920 to the gaining of effective rule, under League of Nations mandates, over Palestine, Transjordan and Iraq by Britain and over Syria and Lebanon by France. In 1914 the British had annexed Cyprus and gained a protectorate over Egypt, both of which had already been under their control: since 1878 and 1882 respectively.

Yet this position of European strength was soon challenged in a general crisis of imperial strength and military overreach. The war had exhausted the economies, public finances and societies of Europe. Aside from the lives and resources lost and damaged, there were important shifts in the relationship between Europe and the rest of the world. There was a growing dependence on extra-European finance and resources that were not under European control, especially those of the USA, a situation exacerbated by the consequences of financing much of the war through the issue of debt. The disruption of trade routes also led to the loss of European export markets and to the growth of industrial production in Asia and Latin America. Social exhaustion in the form of a loss of confidence in the future was indicated by the end of a long period of demographic expansion. The death of a large percentage of the young men of Europe during the First World War contributed to the situation. Thus economic demand within Europe was depressed, as, in the long term, was the availability of manpower.

Overreach was at once demonstrated in Russia. Intervention in the Russian Civil War (1917–20) by Britain, France, Japan and the USA, on behalf of the anti-Communist forces, was unsuccessful, in part because only limited resources were committed, not least thanks to the general unpopularity at home of intervention. Post-war demobilisation and the financial burdens left by the First World War limited interventionist options; unrest within the army led the British government to demobilise more rapidly than it had originally intended. The British Prime Minister, Lloyd George, argued in 1919–20 that Britain could not afford the intervention demanded by Winston Churchill, the Secretary of State for War and Air.

However, foreign intervention was not central to the struggle. There was a lack of agreed aims among the intervening powers, and a lack of resolve shown by those intervening: the forces actually committed were very small. The failure of the anti-Communist forces also owed much to their divisions and their underestimation of Communist tenacity, to Communist determination and use of terror and to their central position, in control of the vital populous and industrial areas, including key arms factories around Moscow, and rail links. As a result the Communists fought on interior lines. By retaining control of St Petersburg and Moscow, the Communists also benefited from whatever administrative continuity existed, most obviously from the ex-Tsarist officers who remained in the War Commissariat directing the administration of the Red Army from Moscow.

Thanks to the size of Russia, the Communists could afford to trade space for time in what was very much a war of movement in which cavalry played a major role. Neither side showed much strategic skill, instead choosing essentially to fight opponents where they found them: success usually came to the side that mounted the offensive. This included frontal assaults on fixed positions, such as Frunze's successful storming of the anti-Communist defences of the Crimea in November 1920. The Communists, who had destroyed the coherence of the Tsarist army in 1917 by challenging the disciplinary authority of officers, were greatly helped by the raising of a large conscript army in 1918; their numerical superiority was of great importance. Morale and logistics played a major role in engagements.[26]

Overreach was also a problem elsewhere. Revolts in Egypt (1919) and Iraq (1920–1) led to Britain granting their independence in 1922 and 1924 respectively, although Egypt remained under effective British control. British influence collapsed in Persia (1921) and the confrontation with Turkey in the Chanak Crisis (1922) caused a political crisis in London that led to the abandonment of the confrontation. The new British Prime Minister, Andrew Bonar Law, a Canadian, argued in 1922 that Britain 'cannot be the policeman of the world'.[27] This reflected the drift of British policy since the conclusion of its first alliance with Japan in 1902, the background to which was Britain's reliance on Japan thereafter to police the Far East. The British also lost control of the bulk of Ireland after a guerrilla war with Irish nationalists in 1919–21 led to the British granting dominion status to the Irish Free State.[28]

Other European powers faced growing problems in controlling overseas dominions. In 1919 the Italians recognised Libyan self-government. The French and Spaniards encountered opposition in Morocco, while the Druze rebelled against the French in Syria. The Greek advance on Ankara was blocked by Kemal Atatürk at the battle of the Sakkaria (24 August–16 September 1921) and the Greeks were driven out of Anatolia by the Turks in 1922: Smyrna fell to Atatürk on 9–13 September. On 21 July 1921, 10,000 Spanish troops were killed when General Fernández Silvestre's army was annihilated at Anual in Spanish Morocco by Abd el Krim. He captured 25,000 rifles and 150 guns, a crucial addition of strength. In 1924, despite air support, a Spanish offensive failed and the Spaniards were defeated at Sidi Messaoud. The mobile Riff fighters, armed with modern firearms including machine-guns and mountain howitzers, were not dependent on the cumbersome supply routes of their opponents. In 1925 French Morocco was attacked and a number of posts fell after Riff artillery bombardment. The PKI (Indonesian Communist Party) was responsible for a rebellion against Dutch rule in Java (1926) and Sumatra (1927). The rising in Syria in 1925–7 was a reaction to attempts by the French governor to introduce what he considered modernising reforms in the Jebel Druze area. They alienated the notables, the crucial intermediaries in successful imperialism.

Due to their continuing military superiority, however, the colonial powers were generally successful in reimposing control. The rebellion in Morocco was crushed by

Franco-Spanish forces in 1926, a conflict in which the Spanish officer Franco made his name. The Riff had constructed fortifications which were vulnerable to Franco-Spanish artillery, and their opponents were present in overwhelming force and able to mount simultaneous attacks. This was not an imperial victory obtained by small, lightly armed, mobile units.[29] The French regained control in Syria and the Dutch in Indonesia in 1926–7. The French had used heavy artillery bombardments to thwart Druze progress in Damascus in 1926. Employing great brutality against civilians, of whom over 50,000 were probably killed, the Italians subdued Libya in 1928–32. Their tactics, which included the use of columns of armoured cars and motorised infantry, the dropping of gas bombs and the employment of Eritreans rather than Libyans as auxiliaries, were accompanied by a ruthless suppression of the population: wells were blocked, flocks slaughtered, the Libyans disarmed and resettled in camps.[30] However, opposition to and risings against colonial powers testified to the more general problems created by anti-imperial feeling and sometimes nationalism for the European colonial empires.

Although not a colonial power, the Americans enjoyed a quasi-imperial position, supported by extensive and growing trade and investment in the Caribbean and Mexico. In both they intervened to protect their interests, but they encountered nationalist resistance in Mexico and parts of the Caribbean, especially Haiti.

In 1920 the Soviet Union hosted a Congress of Peoples of the East at Baku. The Communists' initial attempts to exploit anti-imperialism, as in Indonesia, were of limited success, but Communism benefited from having a base in Russia. Having gained control in Russia in the Russian Civil War, the Russian Communists also ensured that Tsarist imperial gains in the Caucasus and Central Asia were retained. Soviet forces occupied Armenia in 1920 and overran Georgia in 1921. A major rising in Georgia in 1924 was suppressed. The Basmachi rising, a Muslim attempt in the early 1920s to organise a government in Turkestan, was crushed by the local Russians, who had more modern weapons as well as the benefit of control over the major towns and railways. A widespread Muslim revolt in Central Asia against the introduction of conscription had already been defeated in 1916 by the Tsarist government, with great brutality and heavy casualties. In 1920 the autonomous Central Asian Islamic states of Bukhara and Khiva, which had been Tsarist protectorates, were subjugated. In 1921 first White (anti-Communist) and then Communist forces subjugated Outer Mongolia, and a pro-Soviet government was established. Thus, whereas the Soviets lost some European areas that had been under Tsarist control, including Estonia, Latvia, Lithuania and Finland, and their advance on Warsaw in 1920 was defeated, they gained a large area that had hitherto been a largely autonomous part of China. This can be attributed to technological factors, in particular the gap in firepower between the Mongolians and their invaders, but other elements played a role, including the small size of the local population. Overwhelming force, the use of artillery against mountain villages, and the support of local partisans were crucial in the Soviet crushing of the Islamic uprising in Daghestan and Chechnya in 1920–1, and subsequent uprisings in 1924, 1928, 1929, 1936 and 1940 were defeated.[31]

The Communists, who saw war as the continuation of politics by other means and an inevitable part of the historical process,[32] also sought to modernise their armed forces, establishing, for example, at the Frunze Military Academy a high-powered training course for future generals. Nevertheless, the Soviet Union did not develop a strong ocean-going navy. The major powers were able to decide on preferable levels of naval strength without worrying about any Soviet naval threat.[33]

China

As a result of an 1923 agreement between Sun Yat-sen and the Soviet diplomat Adolph Joffe, Soviet advisers began to arrive in China that year and Chinese were sent to Russia for training, including Chiang Kai-shek, an officer who, on his return, was appointed Commandant of the Whampoa Military Academy which had been founded by Sun Yat-sen in 1923. Subsequently, as commander of the Kuomintang (Chinese Nationalist) forces, Chiang Kai-shek commanded the 'Northern Expedition', the drive north from Canton against the independent Chinese warlords that began in 1926. He reached the Yangtze that year, defeating Wu P'ei-fu in Hunan and Sun Ch'uan-fang in Kiangsi. In 1927 Chiang captured Nanjing and Shanghai, and defeated the northern warlord Chang Tso-lin. Chiang's forces occupied Beijing in 1928 and defeated two powerful warlords, Yen Hsi-shan of Shansi and Feng Yü-hsiang of Shensi in 1929–30.

In China, the Communists formed the Red Army in 1927. Initially it suffered from a policy of trying to seize towns: this provided the Nationalist army under Chiang Kai-shek with targets. Thus in 1927 the Communists were swiftly driven out of the port of Swatow after they captured it, and were defeated when they attacked Ch'ang-sha. They captured the latter in 1930, only to be rapidly driven from it with heavy losses.

However, the Red Army was more successful in resisting attack in rural areas. There it could trade space for time and harry its slower-moving opponent, especially as the Nationalists lacked peasant support. Thus Chiang Kai-shek's 'Communist bandit extermination campaigns', launched in December 1930, February and July 1931 and March 1933, to destroy the Communist control of much of Kiangsi, failed. These were major operations: in the fourth campaign Chiang Kai-shek deployed 250,000 men. In 1933 Chiang was persuaded to modify his strategy by German military advisers provided by Hitler. In place of the frontal attacks which had proved so costly in the spring, there was a reliance on blockade in the fifth campaign which began in October 1933. The Communists tried and failed to thwart this strategy by conventional warfare, and, instead, in October 1934, decided to abandon Kiangsi in the Long March to Shensi. One of Chiang's sons, Chiang Wego, was trained by the German army and took part in the German occupation of Austria in 1938.[34]

Opposition to Imperialism

Militant opposition to the imperial powers continued in the 1930s. The French crushed an uprising at Yen Bay in Vietnam in 1930 and had pacified the tribes of the Moroccan Atlas by 1933. An anti-Soviet rebellion in Mongolia was defeated in 1932. The British faced Greek Cypriot nationalist riots in 1931 and Arab violence in Palestine in 1936–9, while they were opposed by the Nationalist Party in Malta and by the growing strength of the non-violent Indian National Congress in their most important colony. The British left India as quickly as they did after the Second World War in part because of numerous weaknesses which had been building up for some time.

There were also specific problems in parts of India. In the 1920s a permanent garrison of 15,000 men, supported by 10,000 Pathan militia, had been assigned to Waziristan on the mountainous North-West Frontier of India after the suppression of the 1919 rebellion there. The effective modern rifles used by the tribes had led to heavy British casualties in the winter of 1919–20. In 1936 rebellion resumed under the Faqir of Ipi and the following year the British deployed over 60,000 men to crush it: the Faqir's peak strength was 4,000 men, and, although his men had effective, locally produced rifles, they lacked artillery and machine-guns. Nevertheless, the British subdued the region as much because of tribal rivalries and financial inducements as superior numbers and firepower. The British success was consolidated by new roads, but guerrilla opposition in Waziristan continued until 1943.[35] In 1938 the British deployed 50,000 troops to suppress the Arab rising in Palestine, which had begun in 1936.[36] These were not rebellions that could be suppressed by small forces supported by air power.

Yet, despite political strains, imperialism worked increasingly effectively as a military system. Regions that had been conquered in the late nineteenth century came to yield soldiers for the colonial power, and both they and troops from areas that had been ruled for longer were trained in European methods of warfare and organised accordingly. Hitherto independent armies of local allies were similarly organised or were integrated into imperial forces. During the First World War, 750,000 Punjabis served in Britain's Indian Army; in the Second World War, one million. 65,000 Indian troops died in the First World War, the first protracted, large-scale overseas war for the Army in India.[37] Although the climate affected their operational capability in France, the Indian army fought well in Palestine and in the second Mesopotamian campaign. At the end of the war, Indian troops were deployed in Iraq, Palestine and the Caucasus, and, in response to the Arab rising in Iraq in 1920, four divisions were sent from India.

In the First World War, 250,000 West African soldiers served in the French army in Europe; over one million African and Indo-Chinese soldiers served the French as front-line troops, in construction battalions or as war factory guards during the conflict.[38] Locally raised troops helped the French suppress the Druze rebellion, and Eritreans bore much of the fighting when the Italians invaded Ethiopia in 1935–6. French military control of Syria and Lebanon substantially rested on the *Armée du Levant*, 70,000 strong in 1921, a force largely composed of colonial troops from Africa, and on local military and police forces: the *Troupes Spéciales du Levant*, 14,000 strong in 1935, and the Gendarmerie. Both had a strong element of local minority groups, such as Christians, that could be relied upon in the event of clashes with the rest of the population.[39] Divide, recruit and rule was the crucial object and process of imperialist control. Although, due to concern about Germany, the French did not concentrate military resources on extra-European commitments and their navy, their empire was still militarily effective.[40]

Nationalist movements were not without their successes. Popular guerrilla movements in Haiti and the Dominican Republic in the 1920s proved able to limit the degree of control enjoyed by occupying American marine forces who found that ambushes restricted their freedom of manoeuvre. American bombing was no substitute, particularly in face of guerrilla dominance of rural areas at night. However, the Americans were not defeated in battle, and in 1922 the guerrillas in the Dominican Republic conditionally surrendered. American troops sent to Nicaragua in 1927 failed to defeat a rebel peasant army under Augusto Sandino. The subsequent American withdrawal from Haiti in 1934 owed much to a sense of the intractability of the conflict;[41] the Americans were unwilling to devote resources comparable to those of the French in Syria.

In military terms, the European and European-American powers remained dominant, with the addition of Japan, although Japan was technologically well behind in the 1920s in aspects of military innovation such as weaponry, for example tanks. This led in Japan to a greater stress on 'spirit' as superior to material. European and European-American states controlled both the developing traditional technologies of warfare, weapons and weapons systems, such as warships and artillery, and new technologies, such as air power and flexible mobile land power following the introduction of the internal combustion engine to the battlefield in the shape of tanks and lorries.

Air Power

The most revolutionary change in twentieth-century warfare resulted from the development of aviation. The first successful powered flight, by the American Wright brothers in 1903, led the British press baron, Lord Northcliffe, to remark, 'England is no longer an island'. Powered, controlled flight impacted on a world prepared by imaginative literature, such as that of H.G. Wells. In 1908 one of Count Zeppelin's airships flew 240 miles, and in 1909 Louis Blériot made the first aeroplane flight across the English Channel.

Aviation rapidly became a matter for international competition and military interest. There was grave concern in 1909 and 1913 about the possibilities of an airship attack on Britain, with the bombing of defenceless strategic targets and cities. France, Germany and the USA took the lead with air power, but other states had to respond. In 1911 the British established an air batallion, in 1912 the Royal Flying Corps.[42] In 1910 an American admiral, Bradley Fiske, felt able to propose that the defence of the Philippines should be left to air power. Fiske sought to develop torpedo carrying planes.[43]

Aeroplanes were used in the First Balkan War (1912–13): Turkish-held Edirne (Adrianople), besieged by the Bulgarians in 1913, was the first town on which bombs were dropped from an aeroplane. Some military leaders and thinkers, for example General Ferdinand Foch, Director of the *École Supérieure de la Guerre*, in 1910, argued that air power would only be a peripheral adjunct to the conduct of war, but others thought it would play a more central role. Increasingly, military leaders and schools felt obliged to recognise air power. By 1914 the European powers had a total of over 1,000 aeroplanes in their armed forces: Russia had 244, Germany 230, France 120, Britain 113.

In the First World War aerial warfare involved aeroplanes and hydrogen-filled airships, especially the German Zeppelins, which attacked Antwerp, Liège and Warsaw in 1914. On 19–20 January 1915, Germany carried out its first aerial bombing raid on Britain, using Zeppelins. The largest raid was against London on 13 October 1915. However, the material damage inflicted by Zeppelins was relatively modest. A total of 51 Zeppelin attacks (208 sorties) during the war on the British Isles dropped 196 tons of bombs, killing 557 people and wounding 1,358. British sources estimated that the raids caused £1,500,000 in property damage.[44] Such attacks on civilians were a preparation for total war. Zeppelins were also capable of long-range missions. The longest was that of L59 sent in 1917 from a base at Jamboli, Bulgaria in order to carry supplies to German forces in German East Africa. When recalled by radio, L59 had almost reached Khartoum in Sudan, and it returned safely to Jamboli.

Aeroplanes were to be of most use for aerial reconnaissance and artillery spotting, for example reporting the change of direction of the German advance near Paris in 1914; but, in September and October 1914, the British Royal Naval Air Service conducted the first effective strategic bombing raids of the war when planes carrying 20-pound bombs flew from Antwerp to strike Zeppelin sheds at Düsseldorf and destroyed one airship.[45] In 1917 twin-engined German Gotha bombers flew over the North Sea, beginning aeroplane strategic bombing of Britain with attacks on London.

The military effectiveness of aeroplanes increased considerably during the war, enabling them to destroy airships with incendiary bullets, and to attack ground targets successfully: thus in 1917 German aeroplanes destroyed moving French tanks in Champagne, and the British used air strikes in their advance in Palestine. Supply links came under regular attack, inhibiting German and Austrian advances in 1918. Aeroplanes increas-

83. *Marham Aerodrome*, by William Wyllie, 1918. Wyllie's son Harold served in the Royal Flying Corps. Most of the planes are F.E.26s. Harold, a squadron commander, wrote in 1916 'sending out F.E.'s in formation with Martinsydes for protection is murder and nothing else. But flying men are very cheap and those who send them out get DSO's instead of a slip knot'.

ingly helped to influence campaigns on land and were also used at sea, including against submarines, one new weapon against another.

Aeroplanes came to fly in groups and formation tactics developed. Synchronising gear, developed by Anthony Fokker, modelled on a French aircraft shot down by the Germans, used by the Germans from 1915 and copied by the British, enabled aeroplanes to fire forward without damaging their propellers. They were also very useful for reconnaissance, the role for which they had initially been intended. As such, aeroplanes replaced cavalry. The Turkish columns advancing on the Suez Canal in 1915 were spotted by British planes.

Aerial photo-reconnaissance also developed, leading to the production of accurate maps. When the British Expeditionary Force (BEF) was sent to France in 1914 one officer and one clerk were responsible for mapping and the maps were unreliable. By 1918 the survey organisation of the BEF had risen to about 5,000 men and had been responsible for more than 35 million map sheets. No fewer than 400,000 impressions were produced in just ten days in August 1918.[46]

Aeroplane production rose swiftly. In 1914 the British Royal Aircraft Factory at Farnborough could produce only two air-frames per month, but their artisanal methods were swiftly swept aside by mass production. Air power also exemplified the growing role of scientific research in military capability: wind tunnels were constructed for the purpose of research; strutless wings and aeroplanes made entirely from metal were developed.

84. Aerial reconnaissance cameras mounted on a plane, First World War. The impact of air power on warfare was not only a matter of the projection and delivery of force, but also of improved command and control and intelligence. Reconnaissance cameras permitted a mapping of the battlefield that included the disposition of troops and *matériel.*

Engine power increased and size fell. The speed and rate of climb of aeroplanes rose. By 1918 the British had 22,000 aeroplanes, and that September a combined Franco-American-British force of 1,500 aeroplanes was launched against the Germans in the Saint-Mihiel Salient, the largest deployment of aeroplanes hitherto.

Air power was soon to be used by European powers not only to strengthen imperial links,[47] creating a new global strategic network that re–oriented geopolitical relationships, but also for policing duties within and beyond the boundaries of empire. Thus the British used air power to deal with opposition in both Iraq and Afghanistan, while the Italians employed it in Libya. The British air force bombed Jalalabad and Kabul during the Third Afghan War in 1919, tribesmen in Central Iraq in 1920, and Wahabi tribesmen who threatened Iraq and Kuwait in 1928. British air power played a role in ending long-standing resistance in British Somaliland in 1921, and was successfully used against Yemen in 1927–34.[48] Air power also played a part in Ethiopia's civil disputes: in 1929 imperial forces made bombing runs with a triplane flown by a Frenchman over a terrified rebel army causing it to flee in disorder.[49]

The use of air power in Ethiopia was an example of the diffusion of the military 'advances' made during the First World War. This was a rapid process in the 1920s and 1930s. The British trained a tank force in 1919 for General Denikin's anti-Communist army in the Russian Civil War. A tank was used to help thwart a coup in Ethiopia in 1928, and Chevrolet trucks equipped with machine-guns were used in Arabia.[50] Features of First World War warfare, such as air power, were introduced to China during the civil wars of the mid-1920s.[51] Extensive use was also made of trains and heavy artillery in China, although the warlord armies lacked the bureaucratic regularity of European counterparts. In the 1920s the Italians provided the Imam of Yemen with aeroplanes and the British supplied them to Ibn Saud of Arabia and the Afghans. The Afghans also received planes from the Soviets and the Italians in the interwar period, although they were handicapped by a shortage of mechanics.[52]

In Europe, in the 1920s, aerial attack was only feared from other European powers, not from non-European states. Interest in strategic bombing increased during the First World War, although it ended before the British could use the large Handley Page V/500 bombers they had built to bomb Berlin. In 1923 there were plans for the construction of an aerial defence system to protect London against possible French attack. The British feared an aerial 'knock-out-blow': in the 1930s, it was believed, in the words of the ex- and future Prime Minister, Stanley Baldwin, in 1932, that 'the bomber will always get through'. Air defence came to be a major issue in the 1920s and 1930s, with its own doctrine, technology and organisation.[53] Colonel Fuller, a leading British advocate of tank warfare, incorrectly predicted that air attacks on London would lead the people to demand that the government surrender.

Theorists such as Giulio Douhet and William Mitchell claimed that war could be won through air power. In his *Il Dominio dell'Aria* (*The Command of the Air*; 1921), Douhet, who had been appointed head of the Italian Central Aeronautical Bureau in 1917, claimed that aeroplanes were the best offensive weapon and that there was no effective defence against them. He pressed for air forces to be independent, rather than under army or naval command, and argued that air power could be used to attack enemy communications, economies and populations. Mitchell, Assistant Chief of the American Air Service, 1919–25, also pressed for an independent air force. He claimed that air power had made battleships obsolete and to try to prove his point sank the former German dreadnought *Ostfriesland* in $21\frac{1}{2}$ minutes' bombing in 1921. Mitchell was also interested in strategic bombing and large-scale airborne operations.[54] The creation of air forces was a major institutional change in the organisation of war, and a cause of greater expenditure.

Nevertheless, concentration on air defence led to a misapplication of scarce resources. The terror bombing of civilian targets, for example of Madrid and Guernica (1937), by German planes sent by Hitler to help Franco's Nationalists in the Spanish Civil War of 1936–9, did not play a significant role in the result of the conflict. However, they captured the imagination of many, sowing fears that strategic bombing would be decisive in a future war.

The potential of air power was developed in other ways in the inter-war period. There was a growing interest in jet aircraft, rocketry and space flight, especially in Germany, where the Space-Flight Society was founded in 1927, and in the Soviet Union. Konstantin Tsiolkovsky (1857–1936) developed a theory of rocket flight which encouraged the use of liquid propellants for them, while other work led to the development of the Soviet Katyusha multiple rocket launcher. Air power also led to interest in the use of airborne troops. A number of powers, especially Germany, trained parachute and glider-borne units. There were also developments in air transport: in 1935 the Soviets moved a 14,000-strong rifle division by air from near Moscow to the Far East while in 1937–8 they practised dropping artillery and tanks by parachute.

At sea, air power was restricted in the 1910s and 1920s by the difficulty of operating aeroplanes in bad weather and the dark, by their limited load capacity and range and by mechanical unreliability, but improvements were made, especially in the 1930s. The

Americans and Japanese, although not the British, made major advances with naval aviation and aircraft carriers.[55] Air spotting for naval gunfire also developed in the 1930s.

The 1930s

The development of mechanised forces on land was accompanied by discussion about their operational employment, in particular concerning new tactics of combined arms operations involving armour (tanks), infantry and cavalry. In the last stages of the First World War, a British colonel, J.F.C. Fuller, devised 'Plan 1919', a strategy based on a large-scale tank offensive. Following Fuller, Basil Liddell Hart, an ex-army military correspondent, developed notions of rapid tank warfare. He was particularly keen to advocate advances that did not entail frontal attacks: the 'indirect approach' that emphasised manoeuvre, not attrition. Although Liddell Hart was to exaggerate his influence, these ideas were to influence German *blitzkrieg* tactics in the Second World War. The tactics were a development of mechanised warfare and the offensive tactics employed by the Germans in 1917.[56] German forces sent to aid Franco in the Spanish Civil War (1936–9) indeed used armoured columns.

However, British tanks did badly in the early campaigns of the Second World War, in part because of flawed tactics; for example, inadequately supported tank charges were vulnerable to German anti-tank guns,[57] and there was a failure to appreciate the need for innovation on the battlefield that owed much to a poor choice of commanders.[58] The war was to reveal the need for combined operations (for example by tanks and infantry or tanks and aircraft) against forces with similar equipment.[59] As so often in military history, combined forces and the tactics and discipline necessary for their effective use were more important than technological developments in isolation.

In the 1920s and 1930s military thinkers had to adapt to new capabilities in firepower and mobility, and new relationships between force, space and time.[60] They had to do this in the context of a three-dimensional battlefield, considering, for example, how air power and armour could best cooperate. Yet, as with the submarine, this new technology was designed for and best suited to conflict between major powers using European military systems, rather than for imperial operations, whether aggressive or policing. Thus, German and Soviet thinking in the 1930s about mechanised warfare with aerial support was focused on conflict with other European powers, with the exception of Soviet interest in the possibility of war with Japan.

Nevertheless, the new military technology was employed with brutal effectiveness when the Italians successfully invaded Ethiopia in 1935–6. Motorised columns were supported by aeroplanes, and mustard gas was also used. The new technology compensated for Ethiopian bravery, for the ineffectiveness of much Italian generalship and for the logistical problems of campaigning in the harsh mountainous terrain; the last forced the Italians to devote much energy to road-building. Fortunately for the Italians, the Ethiopians chose to engage them in battle, rather than to avoid engagements and rely on guerrilla tactics. The Ethiopians were defeated at the battle of Mount Aradam in 1936. The ignominy of Italian defeat at Adowa was wiped out. Although subsequent guerrilla attacks had some effect, Emperor Haile Selassie did not regain Ethiopia until British and British Commonwealth forces defeated the Italians in 1941. Thus in Ethiopia native strategy, as well as Italian technology, played a major role. As in Morocco in the 1920s, numbers were also important. The Italians deployed nearly 600,000 men, of whom about 1,000 died in combat.[61]

The British also used new technology in land conflict outside Europe. Their forces deployed to deal with rebellion in Waziristan in 1937 included about 50 to 60 armoured cars which were used mainly to escort road convoys. The armoured cars proved quite effective in that limited role. A handful of light tanks went for an occasional trundle on open ground, but could get nowhere near the kind of mountainous terrain on which the principal engagements took place. The campaign also revealed the limitations of Western communications. The tribesmen cut telegraph lines. As wireless was still in its infancy in the British forces, most signalling below brigade level was carried out using old-fashioned coloured flags, the heliograph and despatch riders. Only the largest bases and head-quarters had reliable wireless communications. The British also used aeroplanes, but their effectiveness was probably exaggerated as their novelty wore off and tribesmen learned how to evade their attacks.

The scale of conflict in the First World War and the challenge of new technology led states in the 1920s and 1930s to devote considerable attention to their military-industrial capability. However, investment policies were challenged by alternative commitments, not least social welfare, and by the fiscal consequences of economic downturns in the 1930s. Thus, military build-up was easiest for states that were autocratic and lacked powerful representative institutions and practices of political consensus. This was true of Fascist Italy, Nazi Germany, the Communist Soviet Union and Japan.

Mussolini benefited from the failure of the Italian armed forces to resist his seizure and consolidation of power and developed their strength. He was interested in air power, describing Italy as a natural aircraft carrier in the Mediterranean, and believed that the adoption of advanced military technology would serve to enhance Italy's international position. However, although Mussolini was Minister of Marine for most of the period, his control of the armed forces was limited. The Fascist programme of 1919 had called for the creation of a National Militia, which was to have been the basis of a popular army under party control, and for the nationalism of all armaments factories, but this programme was not pushed through when Mussolini gained power. Although in 1938 Mussolini appointed himself 'First Marshal' of the empire, with a military rank at least equal to that of the king, Victor Emmanuel III,[62] the Italian armed forces, which had not suffered the traumatic experience of revolution like their Russian and Hungarian counter-parts, or defeat and enforced reduction like their German, Austrian and Hungarian counterparts, were not brought under Fascist control, and continued to owe allegiance to the Crown. Mussolini had little power over senior appointments.[63]

In contrast, in both Germany and the Soviet Union in the 1930s, dictators, who relied on force, felt it necessary to terrorise the very armed forces they built up in order to ensure that they were loyal to them personally rather than to a notion of national interests. Thus, in 1934 Hitler had the German army swear an unconditional oath of obedience to him as their commander, and in 1938 he removed the Minister of War and the army Commander in Chief, himself succeeded to the former post and took effective control of the entire military high command. In 1934 the German army uniform was altered to include the Nazi Party badge.

In the Soviet Union, Stalin moved with greater violence, claiming to discover a conspiracy between the Soviet and the German armies. Marshal Mikhail Tukhachevsky, the talented commander of the Red Army, who was interested in mechanised warfare and had been responsible for the creation of tank corps, was shot, over half the generals killed (the rank itself had been abolished during the Revolution), and the officer ranks heavily purged: over 35,000 were killed or dismissed. An alternative basis of political power was thus ruthlessly crushed. Party control of the armed forces was imposed with the reintroduction of political commissars in 1937; they were not noted for their military ability. Despite the purges, the Russians heavily defeated Japan in fighting on the Manchurian-Mongolian border at Nomonhan in 1939. However, the loss of talented officers and the promotion of men whom Stalin could trust, many of whom were mediocre and unwilling to challenge his views, ensured that the Soviet army was poorly led when it attacked Finland in 1939–40.

No such civilian control was imposed on the Japanese armed forces. They owed allegiance to the Emperor, but tended to follow their own views. Although the Japanese had been undefeated in their clashes with Germany in the First World War, the nature of the conflict had made Japanese equipment and tactics appear obsolete and in the 1920s this led the Japanese military to seek new resources in order to introduce new military technology.[64]

The Japanese army developed Manchukuo (Manchuria), which they seized in a five-month campaign in 1931–2, as a military and industrial base that was outside civilian control, and used it as a basis for expansionism in China and for greater strength in the event of possible war with the Soviet Union: something greatly feared in Japanese army circles. Developing it as a major coal- and iron-based zone of heavy industry, the Japanese invested more capital in Manchukuo than the British had in India over the previous century. A military–industrial complex served as the basis for a system of planning that sought to encompass industrial capacity. The War Ministry established the Kokusaku Kenkyukai, a consultancy, to prepare five-year plans and advise the army on economic matters.[65]

Helped by this resource base, the absence of hostile foreign intervention and the lack of other conflicts to absorb their attention, the Japanese made further advances in China. Jehol was overrun in 1935, and in 1937 the Japanese launched an all-out war of conquest. Shanghai and Nanjing were captured in 1937, Canton and Wuhan in 1938 and the island of Hainan in 1939. However, the Japanese lacked the manpower to conquer all of China and, even within occupied areas, their control outside the cities was limited. It was far easier to destroy the Chinese navy in 1937 and to deploy overwhelming force against cities, the nodes of the transportation system, than it was to fight in rural areas where the ratio of strength and space told against the Japanese, especially if their opponents employed guerrilla tactics. As with European expansion in Asia and Africa in the sixteenth, seventeenth and eighteenth centuries, it was easier for Japan to develop island bases in the Pacific, such as Truk, Kwajalein and Saipan, and to hold coastal positions in China, than it was to conquer a large area of mainland. The Japanese also failed to incorporate local elites into their imperial system on any large scale. Conflict with China led to an increase in government authority, in part designed to produce more resources for the war: the National Mobilisation Act was passed in 1938.

Resources played a role in the Chaco War between Bolivia and Paraguay in 1932–5, but the defeated Bolivians spent nearly twice what Paraguay could afford, and were also more populous and had the latest weaponry, including aeroplanes. However, the Paraguayans were better led, militarily and politically, benefited from better communications and understood how to fight a war of manoeuvre in a harsh, largely waterless, scrub terrain. Bolivian positions were encircled and their supply lines over-long, and the Bolivians lacked the water for their larger army and its tactics of the mass offensive. Bolivian invading forces were defeated and pushed back into Bolivia, leading to the overthrow of President Salamanca in 1934 and a truce in which Paraguay was left in control of the Chaco.[66] Elsewhere in the 1930s, bold expansionary initiatives using overwhelming force or the threat of it led to gains, as with the German intimidation of

Czechoslovakia in 1938, and subsequent German, Hungarian and Polish seizures of Czech territory, the German occupation of Austria in 1938 and the Italian annexation of Albania in 1939.

Although military preparedness was easier for autocratic states, the general development in the European economy in the interwar period ensured that other states also had relevant industrial facilities. The mass manufacture of high technology products, especially of electronics and engineered goods such as aeroplanes and cars, provided a resource and skills base for military strength.

The Second World War

The Second World War (1939–45) yet again saw not only a concentration of resources, force and technology in the hands of a few powers, but also their ability both to campaign around the world and to subsume other regional struggles and interests to their views. Thus, Australian forces were used in North Africa in 1941–2, despite the concern of the Australian government about Japan: a theme voiced by Australians from 1895. By the end of the war most of the world was involved in the conflict, even if in some Latin American cases this was largely a formality.

The Second World War began in 1939 when Hitler's Germany invaded and rapidly overran Poland; Stalin's Soviet Union took its share of Poland after, in cooperation with Germany, having also attacked the country. The Germans lost fewer than 10,000 dead in a *blitzkrieg* that led to the defeat of a state with armed forces totalling over 3 million men, although all bar 370,000 were reservists. The Germans greatly outnumbered the Poles in aeroplanes, tanks and other mechanised vehicles, enjoyed the initiative and benefited from the long and vulnerable character of the Polish frontier and the dispersed nature of the Polish army, most of which was infantry. Thus, by forcing the conflict as a war of manoeuvre, the Germans put the Poles at a tremendous disadvantage. The Polish air force was destroyed and German armoured forces then outmanoeuvred and isolated their opponents, for example leaving a large Polish force trapped in and near Poznan and Lodz. The cohesion of the Polish army was destroyed. The successful German campaign helped to consolidate the position of generals who favoured rapid armoured advance. It also signalled the end of cavalry. Poland's 11 cavalry brigades had contributed nothing. Despite brave resistance, the German victory was total and rapid. Poland was invaded on 1 September, Warsaw surrendered on 27 September and the last Polish troops stopped fighting on 6 October.

Britain and France entered the war against Germany in 1939 in support of the Poles, but were unable to provide assistance: their failure to attack Germany, during the Phoney War of 1939–40, was a matter of limited preparedness and military and political caution. In contrast, the numerically superior Soviets attacked Finland in 1939–40, using their superior artillery to smash their way through the fortified Mannerheim Line and winning territory after some serious defeats. The Soviets also occupied the Baltic states of Estonia, Latvia and Lithuania in 1940, with scant resistance from their vastly outnumbered forces, imposing a Communist tyranny.

In 1940 the Germans conquered hitherto neutral Denmark and Norway, using air power to counter the intervention of British amphibious and naval forces in Norway. Then the Western Front was rolled up in a German *blitzkrieg* that overran the Netherlands, Belgium and France and brutally exposed the military failure of the Anglo-French alliance. The French Maginot Line, a powerful fortification line directed against Germany that represented the lessons learned from strengthening the defensive in the First World War, was outflanked when the Germans advanced through the supposedly impenetrable Ardennes and pushed across the Meuse. The Germans made effective use of their mechanised forces, especially tanks, and of tactical air power, particularly Ju-87 (Stuka) dive- bombers, gaining the strategic initiative against forces that were collectively larger in number. The Allies had no equivalent to the Stuka, and the French air force was outclassed by its German counterpart. The German panzer (tank) divisions proved operationally effective as units that maximised the weapon characteristics of tanks.[67]

Expelled from the European continent – although able by bravery, skill and luck to save much of the army in the evacuation from Dunkirk – Britain had the valuable support of its empire and control of the sea, but this was challenged by German air power and U-boats (submarines). The blunting of German air power by British radar, effective and growing numbers of fighter aeroplanes, able command decisions and high fighting quality in the Battle of Britain led Hitler to call off Operation Sealion, his planned invasion of Britain (1940). However, Greek success in repelling attack by Germany's Italian ally and British successes against Italy in North Africa that winter were followed in 1941 by a successful German offensive in Libya, leading to an advance into Egypt, and by their rapid conquest of Yugoslavia and Greece, the latter entailing the defeat of British forces in Greece and Crete.

The loss of Crete in May 1941 was the last major defeat for an isolated Britain; her subsequent defeats occurred when she had powerful allies. The German assault on the Soviet Union (June 1941) and the Japanese attack on Britain and the United States, followed by the declaration of war on the Americans by Japan's ally Germany (December 1941), totally altered the situation. The Germans lost the support of Soviet resources and were forced to fight on two fronts. There were still to be serious blows for the Allies, especially in early 1942 as the Japanese made major advances. The surrender of 'impregnable' Singapore to the Japanese on 15 February 1942, after a poorly conducted campaign in Malaya, destroyed British prestige in Asia: 130,000 British troops were taken prisoner. The British in Malaya had considerably outnumbered the Japanese, but the latter were better led, had the strategic initiative and enjoyed air superiority. Twelve days later the Japanese used torpedoes with effect to crush an Allied fleet in the battle of the Java Sea, sinking five ships. On 29 February, five warships that had escaped were destroyed by more powerful Japanese forces.

Japanese success appeared to threaten a racial as well as a geopolitical recasting of the globe. Urging that the USA concentrate its resources not against Germany, but on offensive operations to stop the Japanese advance, Admiral Ernest King, Chief of Naval Operations, wrote to President Roosevelt in March 1942 that the USA could not permit the 'white man's countries' of Australia and New Zealand to be conquered by Japan 'because of the repercussions among the non-white races of the world'.[68] By the end of May the Japanese had conquered the Dutch East Indies, Burma and the Philippines. That summer both Chinese and Russian collapse appeared possible.

The Battle of the Atlantic against German U-boats was not won until early 1943, when escort carriers and long-range aeroplanes brought a decisive gain in aerial support. Despite inflicting heavy losses of merchantmen and escorts,German submarines had failed to break Allied maritime links. Nevertheless, already thanks to the accession of the Soviet Union, and, still more, the USA the Allied system was far stronger economically than that of Germany. Furthermore, the British conquest of Iraq, Lebanon and Syria in May–July 1941, the Anglo-Soviet occupation of Persia from August 1941, and the British conquest of Madagascar in May–November 1942, ensured that the worlds of German and Japanese would be kept well apart and that the Allied world would not be fractured. Lebanon, Syria, Madagascar and French North Africa had all been controlled by the French government acceptable to Hitler and based in Vichy that had been established after the defeat of France in 1940.

As German and Japanese offensives were blunted in late 1942, the long and stony path to victory appeared clearer: the American defeat on 3–5 June 1942 of a Japanese fleet seeking to capture the Midway atoll in the Pacific with the loss of all four Japanese carners present, and the Soviet encirclement of the German Sixth Army at Stalingrad in November 1942, were especially important. A Japanese move towards Port Moresby, that would have increased the threat of an attack on Australia, had already been blocked at the battle of the Coral Sea on 4–8 May 1942, the first battle between carrier groups. The Germans were also defeated by the British in North Africa: their advance into Egypt was halted at the Gazala-Bir Hakeim Line in July and pushed back in the battle of El Alamein in October–November 1942. French North Africa was successfully invaded by Anglo-American amphibious forces in Operation Torch in November 1942. Going into the First World War, strategists and field commanders had expected to bring matters to a head in 'one big battle' on each front, only to find this quest elusive. Going into the Second World War, the decisive 'big battle' was not anticipated, and yet there were clear turning-points at Midway, El Alamein and Stalingrad.

The Allies moved over to the offensive. Their insistence on an unconditional German surrender and the fanatical nature of Hitler's regime both ensured it was a fight to the finish. The war in part took on the character of attrition that had marked the First World War, attrition on land, at sea and in the air. In May 1943 the Germans surrendered in North Africa; in July the British and the Americans landed in Sicily, and in September in Italy. Massive resources, in the air and on land and sea, and the development of amphibious vehicles and training and of aircraft carriers, helped to make amphibious operations viable. Italy surrendered unconditionally in September, although the Germans still occupied much of the country.

The Japanese were pushed back at crucial points of their Pacific perimeter in 1943, losing Guadalcanal and New Guinea. In June 1944 the American Pacific fleet covered an amphibious attack on the Marianas, leading to a naval-aviation struggle that devastated the Japanese carrier force. Saipan fell, and the Japanese cabinet resigned on 18 July. The collapse of the Japanese Pacific empire was inexorable: without air superiority, Japanese naval units were vulnerable and the Americans could decide where to make attacks and could neutralise bases, such as Rabaul, that they chose to 'leapfrog'. Troops on the ground, such as the large garrison at Rabaul and the substantial German forces in Norway, were of limited value to the power that lacked the strategic initiative. In Burma, the Japanese were outfought on the ground, the simplicity of their determined offensive tactics no longer adequate against a better-trained Indian army able to control battles carefully and benefiting from high unit quality, superior logistics, air power and artillery.

In Europe, the initiative was also crucial. Soviet advances led Romania to surrender in August 1944 and Bulgaria the following month. In June 1944 Anglo-American forces landed in Normandy, although the speedy liberation of France and Belgium was followed by tough German resistance that prevented further advance in late 1944. After a German counter-offensive in the Ardennes was defeated in the Battle of the Bulge, Anglo-American forces advanced across the Rhine in early 1945. The Soviets fought their way into Berlin, and Hitler committed suicide.[69] In May 1945 the Germans surrendered unconditionally. As with the campaigns against Napoleon in 1812–14, Russian strength had played a crucial role and the numbers involved on the Eastern Front indicate that it was the decisive theatre in the war against Germany. However, the Anglo-American achievement had also been considerable, not least because they were also bearing the brunt of the war with Japan, a conflict that ended with Japanese surrender in August 1945 just a few days after the dropping of two American atom bombs.

Air Power

The impact of technology on warfare was important in all spheres in the Second World War, but was most novel in the air.[70] This in turn affected conflict not only on land, not least by providing a long-range form of artillery, especially useful against communications and concentrations of vehicles, but also at sea.

In the Second World War the Germans and Soviets stressed the tactical employment of air power. This proved to be far more important on the Eastern Front than long-distance bombing. Indeed, Germany did not have a strategic air arm, while the Soviet air force was largely an extension of the army. Earlier, Germany led in the development of the four-engine bomber (the 'Ural' or 'Amerika' bomber), but had only prototypes. Progress was halted after the death of the bomber's proponent, General Walter Wever, in 1936: the Spanish Civil War suggested that strategic bombers were not required, and, instead, the Germans practised dive-bombing tactics on behalf of Franco's forces. Furthermore, the Germans were affected by a lack of raw materials and engine-manufacturing technology. The *Luftwaffe* – the German air force – fought the Battle of Britain with a tactical air force, and therefore with aeroplanes with limited range, which was a key reason why she lost that battle.

However, overall, German resources were better spent on a tactical force geared to the needs of the army. This is a reminder of the role of choice in the use of resources and thus of the danger of simply quantifying the latter. *Blitzkrieg* tactics were not forced on Germany by circumstances; they reflected a choice of policy. The extent to which air power played only a supportive role on the Eastern Front reveals the limited effectiveness of air power on ground operations conducted on a massive scale. Nevertheless, the use of bombers in both a strategic role over France prior to D-Day and a tactical role over Normandy thereafter was a clear example of airpower working.

Land-based aeroplanes could weaken the control of inshore waters by warships, as when Japanese bombers sank the *Prince of Wales* and the *Repulse* off Malaya on 10 December 1941, thus ending British plans to intervene against the Japanese invasion of Malaya. Carrier-based planes became crucial in naval actions. This was true of the British pursuit of German warships in the Atlantic and nearby waters. More generally, air power played a central role in opposing German submarine operations. It was also vital to the conduct of war in the Pacific, a war begun when Japanese carrier aircraft sank five American battleships at Pearl Harbor on 7 December 1941, both in conflict between fleets and in support of amphibious attacks.

Air power was also used for airborne operations, both glider and parachute attacks, as in the German attacks on Denmark, Norway, Belgium and Holland in 1940 and on Crete in 1941, and the capture of the Sumatran oil fields by the Japanese in 1942. Air power also created opportunities for the supply and reinforcement of land and sea forces by air. This was particularly valuable where road links were unreliable and where units were isolated. Thus, the British in Burma in 1944, and, in the 1960s, the Americans in Indo-China benefited greatly from aerial resupply.

Air supply and reinforcement became even more important after the Second World War. Communist cutting of rail links in the Chinese Civil War of 1946–9, for example, forced the Nationalists to rely on aerial supplies for their major bases in Manchuria, Changchun and Mukden in 1948. American-supported units in Laos in 1964–72 relied on the mobility provided by CIA aeroplanes.[71] Airports became points of strategic importance: Soviet tanks were flown into Prague airport in 1968 when the Czech government was overthrown. Although the logistical capability of air power is easily exaggerated, air power could also be used to move large numbers of troops overseas more rapidly than ships. Thus, in 1936 German transport aircraft helped Franco transport troops from Morocco to Spain; the first American troops to arrive in South Korea in 1950 did so by air; and in the spring of 1965, in response to disorder in the Dominican Republic, the USA airlifted to Hispaniola 23,000 troops in less than two weeks. Soviet airlift capacity was seen in Angola in 1975 as well as in Ethiopia in 1977–8. In 1983 helicopter-borne American marines and US paratroops conquered the Caribbean island of Grenada, although the operation was poorly handled and led to a reshuffling of the American military, especially in inter-service cooperation. Once the British had recaptured the Falkland Islands from the Argentinians in 1982 they began construction of an airstrip capable of handling large long-distance planes, so that aerial reinforcement would be easier.

Air power was also useful for the rapid transport of troops overland, countering the propinquity of opponents. Thus in 1947 the Indians sent troops by air to Kashmir. Thirty years later, Moroccan soldiers were sent to Zaire aboard French transport planes in order to help resist an invasion of insurgents from Angola.

Air power was also used in the Second World War to try to destroy the economic capability and civilian morale of opponents. German terror bombing of undefended cities, such as Warsaw (1939), Rotterdam (1940) and Belgrade (1941), deliberately caused heavy civilian casualties. For Britain, the preservation of national independence had traditionally required a strong and successful fleet, but in 1940 the impact of new technology was highlighted with insistent German air attacks far more serious than those mounted by the Germans in the First World War. Aeroplane and, with the coming of the V1s, missile attack revealed that command of the sea could no longer protect Britain from bombardment, even if it could still thwart or inhibit invasion. The Germans also bombarded Dover with long-range guns from the other side of the Channel. The defensive perimeter of the country was thus extended. Although the Germans did not develop a long-distance heavy bomber force in the Second World War, their bombers attacked Britain from bases in north-western Europe, including Norway, while the ground-to-ground V2 missiles, which could travel at up to 3,000 mph, could be fired from a considerable distance. In strategic terms, Britain, which was bombarded by V2s in 1944–5, was no longer an island.

Long-distance American bombing had a similar effect on Japan. By early 1945 the systematic destruction of Japanese cities and infrastructure was seen as the sole alternative to a costly invasion and a much longer conflict. Strategic bombing, made more feasible by four-engined bombers, such as the American B-29 'Super Fortress', and, against Germany, the British Lancaster, by heavier bombs, developments in navigational aids and the introduction of long-range fighter escorts, especially the American P-38s, P-47s and P-51s (Mustangs), caused heavy civilian casualties in Japan and Germany. Despite the limited precision of bombing by high-flying aeroplanes dropping free-fall bombs, strategic bombing was also crucial to the disruption of German and Japanese logistics and communications, and prevented an increase in their production of weaponry that had important consequences for operational strength. The Germans diverted massive resources to anti-aircraft defence forces.

The British and Americans lost 21,900 bombers over Europe, suffering casualty rates among air crew that would have been considered unacceptable for infantry; but the German economy, especially the oil industry, aircraft production and communications, was savagely hit. This directly enhanced the Allied war effort. For example, thanks to strategic bombing, the construction of a new, faster class of U-boat – type XXIII – was delayed, so that it did not become operational until April 1945, too late to challenge Allied command of the sea. By 1943 Anglo-American bombing had wrecked 60 per cent of Italy's industrial capacity. Bombing was linked to long-distance photo-reconnaissance missions, which provided information to identify targets and success. Photo-reconnaissance also helped in planning land operations, as with the German attack on the Soviet Union in 1941, which was preceded by long-range reconnaissance missions by high-flying Dornier Do-215 B2s and Heinkel He-111s.

Part of the rationale for area bombing, such as the British bombing of Hamburg and Lübeck and the American raids on Tokyo, was that heavy casualties would terrorise the civilian population and put pressure on their governments. Over 30,000 people were killed in one British raid on Hamburg in 1943. However, efforts to break civilian morale through air bombing did not work in Germany or Britain during the Second World War or against North Vietnam in the Vietnam War (1965–8). British Bomber Command under Sir Arthur Harris ignored intelligence reports that stressed the limited value of the area bombing of German cities. British morale and industrial production were not badly damaged by aerial attack, certainly less so than had been feared before the war: then large numbers of cardboard coffins had been prepared and there was widespread preparation for airborne gas attacks, but they were not mounted. During the war, air-raid precautions, drill and shelters came to be important to civilian life in Europe and Japan.

The Japanese government was put under greater pressure during the closing stages of the Second World War, unable to mount an effective response to heavy air raids. In 1944–5 American bombers destroyed over 30 per cent of the buildings in Japan. Over half of Tokyo and Kobe was destroyed, and in the first major low-level raid on Tokyo, on 10 March 1945, more people were killed than in the atomic bomb attack on Nagasaki (upwardly revised figures for Hiroshima are greater). The dropping of free-fall atomic bombs on Hiroshima and Nagasaki in 1945, as a result of which over 280,000 people died, at once, or eventually through radiation poisoning, speeded up the process of terrorising the enemy into surrender by making clear the destructive potential of American air power. The Germans had not pursued their research into the atom bomb because they thought it would take too long to develop. They felt that the war would or could be finished using 'conventional' weapons long before the bomb would be ready; an example of over-confidence affecting the development of technological options.

In the aftermath of the use of nuclear weaponry it is easy to appreciate why an ideology of technology came to play a greater role in military history. Hitler's genocidal policies, the Soviet deportation of alleged hostile minority peoples from the Crimea and the Caucasus and the post-war expulsion of over 10 million Germans from their homes in Eastern Europe, were other aspects of the treatment of civilians as an important element in war and geopolitics. Japanese biological warfare experiments reflected the desire to test the effectiveness and practicality of means of waging war.

Technology and the Second World War

The impact of aerial force in terms of power politics was limited by the fact that no one state enjoyed a monopoly, although this was not true of long-range rocketry. Furthermore, as with submarines, there was an active pursuit of counter-measures, one to which technology and industrial capacity greatly and quickly contributed. Thus the British used radar to provide information about German aerial moves during the Battle of Britain in 1940 and against submarines in the Battle of the Atlantic. The capacity of technology to enhance human capability was amply demonstrated. Not only could human beings now fly, they could also 'see' what was not visible to the eye.[72] The interception and deciphering of German messages by the ULTRA system, one of the major developments in the gathering and processing of intelligence information, was also important in 1940; but so also was the Royal Observer Corps, a more traditional means of collecting information. Signals interception also played a major role against the Japanese, helping the Americans, for example at Midway.

More generally, during the Second World War, anti-aircraft weaponry and systems developed rapidly to counter advances in aerial capability. Under the pressure of war, technological advances were introduced rapidly. For example in 1943 the Germans recalled their submarines in order to fit *schnorkel* devices which allowed them to recharge their batteries while submerged, thus reducing their vulnerability to Allied air power, while the Allies introduced more powerful depth-charges, ship-borne radar and better asdic detection equipment. In 1943 the Germans introduced the T5 acoustic homing torpedo, at once sinking three escorts. However, counter-measures were soon in place.

Similarities in technology between the combatants in the First and Second World Wars can not disguise important disparities, but, compared, for example, to the contrasts in weaponry displayed by the opponents in the Sudan in 1898 or on the North-West Frontier and Afghanistan in 1919, they were minimal. As a result of the limited nature of the technology gaps in the world wars, the strength of resource and industrial bases and their implications for the quantity of weaponry available were of great significance in obtaining victory, but in combination with operational, strategic and political considerations. Thus, resources played a major role in the greater success which the Allies enjoyed in preserving sea links across the Atlantic during the Second World War compared to the Japanese failure in the same period to protect routes within their new maritime empire: the Japanese were also less effective at convoy protection and anti-submarine warfare and devoted fewer resources to them. In addition, the Japanese achieved little with submarine warfare, partly because they insisted in hoarding torpedoes, aboard submarines as well as surface ships, for use against warships rather than merchantmen. Naval blockade worked against the Axis powers; not as decisively, despite submarines, against the Allies. Despite initial problems with their torpedoes, American submarines sunk 1,114 Japanese merchantmen, and forced the Japanese to abandon many of their convoy routes in 1944. The Japanese failed to build sufficient ships to match their losses, their trade was dramatically cut, and the Japanese imperial economy shattered. The Americans thus became the major successful practitioner of submarine warfare in history.

New technology also shifted the balance between attack and defence. In both air combat and mechanised warfare on land, the tactical superiority of the offensive over the defensive became readily apparent. This was clear in tank combat and gave the Germans a major advantage when they invaded Belgium and France in 1940. Tanks could move across country, limiting the need to tie forward units to roads. The French actually had more tanks than the Germans in 1940, and their tanks were for the most part heavier gunned and had more effective armour protection, although they were somewhat slower. However, the French failed to develop an effective doctrine for their armour. They persisted in seeing tanks as support for infantry, and most French tanks were accordingly split up into small groups for use as mobile artillery, rather than being used as armour divisions for their shock value. Tactics and operational control and coordination were more important than the technological capabilities of the weapon.

Thanks to developments in weaponry and road and bridge building, an army taking the offensive could advance more rapidly than ever before, especially, as with the German invasion of the Soviet Union in 1941, if tank units were able to operate with open flanks and unconstrained by the need to wait for support and thus by the lower speed of supporting artillery and infantry. However, in the face of strong opposition it was necessary to cooperate with the latter, and thus make them mobile, as the Soviets did well in 1943–5.

In contrast to the relatively small size of the crucial field of operations in Poland and northern France, the Germans were handicapped in the Soviet Union by the length of the front and the area they had to advance across. Their logistical support, much of which was horse-drawn, not mechanised, could not keep up. The Americans and British had the same problem with logistical support after the breakout from Normandy in 1944, but not on the same scale or with effects so dire. On the other hand, the extent of campaigning territory and greater operational mobility, certainly compared to the Western Front in the First World War, ensured that the destructive defensive firepower of that war played a smaller role in the Second World War.

However, it is possible that some commentators remain excessively under the spell cast by the sheer shock and drama of the first *blitzkrieg* campaigns in 1939 and 1940, and therefore have overrated the impact on war of German military methods that represented more of an improvisation than the fruition of a coherent doctrine even among the Germans. Some hold that the German army walked rather than *blitzkrieg*ed through France in 1940; that the key element was tactical use of resources, rather than grand slam. Morale counted as well: when the British counter-attacked, as they sometimes did, they disrupted the German army considerably. But they were poorly commanded and, for many, their heart was not in the fight; to get the army out of France became paramount. French morale was on the whole poor.

Once the psychological shock of the *blitzkrieg* had been overcome, and effective anti-tank weapons reached the battlefield, then the defence could again cope with the offensive, beginning with the Red Army even in 1941. The German attack on the Soviet Union was presented in terms of rapidly advancing armour, but most of the Germans were slow-moving infantry dependent on horse-drawn transport, the German leadership was dangerously over-confident and the Soviets responded rapidly in order to rebuild their forces. At Stalingrad in 1942 the attacking Germans were fought to a standstill despite a massive commitment of resources. The Second World War reverted to a prolonged struggle of attrition not all that unlike the First, and subsequently it could be argued that there have been only two *blitzkrieg* campaigns, in the Arab-Israeli War of 1967 and in the Persian Gulf War of 1991. Liddell Hart greatly praised Israeli strategy and tactics in the former.

The range and effectiveness of less spectacular weapons also improved in the Second World War. The Vickers machine-gun used by the British had a range of up to 4,000 yards and could fire 500 rounds a minute. Radio was increasingly used for short-range communications. Fitted in army vehicles, it increased tactical flexibility and operational control. Radio made the use of artillery and air support more effective, and enabled the transfer of radar information.

The Second World War indicated the role of military diffusion within the 'European' world. This was especially so on the Allied side as munitions were provided to allies – for example by the British and Americans to the Soviets;[73] and technology shared, as when the British provided the Americans with information about radar. Anglo-American cooperation was also very evident in the development of the atomic bomb. However, the innovations of opponents were also copied. In 1930 Frank Whittle, a British air force officer, patented the principles that led to the first gas turbine jet engine which he first ran under control in 1937. Yet it was the Germans in 1939 and the Italians in 1940 that beat the British jet into the air.

State Power and Resources

The First and Second World Wars were also of tremendous importance in the development of state power. War gave a great boost to the role of the state and the machinery of government. The mobilisation of national resources led to state direction of much of the economy. It was necessary to produce formidable amounts of equipment, to raise, train, clothe and equip large numbers of men, to fill their places in the workforce and to increase the scale and flexibility of the economy. Free trade and largely unregulated industrial production were both brought under direction. Economic regulation and conscription were introduced more rapidly and comprehensively than in the First World War. The experience of state intervention in the First war ensured that it was more effective in the Second.

In Britain, where conscription of men began in 1939 and of women in 1942, rationing was introduced early on in the conflict. Food rationing began in January 1940 and the Ministry of Food encouraged consumption patterns and recipes that would make the best use of scarce foodstuffs; whale meat was one preferred food. Clothes rationing followed in 1941. Government regulation became ubiquitous and the Men from the Ministry a term used to explain much. A national government was also formed in May 1940 after defeat in Norway. Government-directed import reduction policies helped defeat the German submarine challenge.

During the Second World War the resources, commitments and pretensions of the federal government grew greatly as the USA became the most powerful country in the world. Phenomenal quantities of weapons and weapons systems were produced and the USA surmounted the divisions of the 1930s in order to create a productivity-oriented political consensus that brought great international strength. Taxes and government expenditure both rose substantially.[74] The attitudes and techniques of the production line were focused on war. The Americans produced formidable quantities of munitions – $186 billion' worth – and an infrastructure to move them.[75] In 1941–5 the USA produced 297,000 aeroplanes and 86,000 tanks. Despite losing oil tankers with a total tonnage of 1,421,000, the tonnage of the American oil tanker fleet rose from 4,268,000 tons in 1942 to 12,875,000 tons in 1945. The global scope of Allied power depended on American shipbuilding. Most of the 42 million tons of shipping built by the Allies during the war was constructed by the Americans: many were Liberty ships built often in as little as ten days, using prefabricated components on production lines. All-welded ships replaced riveted ships, speeding up production. Social flexibility aided the process. By 1944, 11.5 per cent of the workers in the American shipbuilding industry were women. Conscription was reintroduced in 1940 and by May 1945 the conscript army (including the army air force) was just short of 8.3 million men, all of whom had to be paid, fed, clothed, housed and organised. This was an unprecedented administrative challenge for the USA.

From the late 1920s, the Russians developed industrial production and mining in or east of the Urals, outside the range of German air attack. The Ural metallurgical industry was of especial importance. In addition, during the Second World War there was a widespread relocation of industries to the Urals and further east. Similarly, American aeroplane production increased greatly in California, and shipyards developed there and in Washington State.

Aside from industrial capability, there was also a major increase in communications networks, and these were seen as crucial both to realising industrial strength and to utilising military power. Thus, after the Japanese creation of Manchukuo, the Beijing-Mukden railway was equipped with large military yards and an exclusively military telegraph.[76] The enhanced role of communications ensured that attack upon them became a prime objective in wartime, much more, for example, than in early modern and eighteenth-century conflicts. Such attacks became especially important for air power and partisan (guerrilla) activity.

Not all states, however, responded with a similar level of effectiveness. In both world wars, the Germans knew that they were most likely to win in a rapid, offensive war because they could not match the industrial, financial and demographic resources of their opponents, hence their emphasis on surprise, 'will power' and knocking a major opponent out of the conflict. But none of this worked once the Allies had extended to include the USA and had mobilised their superior capacity to produce and overwhelm the enemy with military hardware. As a consequence, the Germans lost, as did the Japanese in the Second World War.

In this war, the Germans tried to mobilise their massive industrial base for a long period of fighting from 1939, an extensive conversion of industrial capacity to war production beginning with the outbreak of hostilities. However, they faced many difficulties, especially in 1939–41. Their highest levels of armaments production did not come until September 1944, towards the close of the war, when the plans of Albert Speer, who had been appointed Minister for Armaments in 1942, came to fruition. Unlike their opponents, the Germans failed to mobilise female labour. They preferred to use slave labour, an inefficient as well as cruel policy.

Furthermore, the Germans failed to exploit mass-production techniques as successfully as their opponents, because they put a premium on responding to military requests for specific weapons, rather than on production of a more limited number of weapons in bulk.[77] In part this reflected a culture, reminiscent of the monarchical 'absolutisms' of the seventeenth century, in which there was a reluctance to understand the exigencies and potential of the economy and a simple expectation that it would produce resources as required without consultation and to order. The Germans were also fascinated with potent weapons – moving towards bigger and bigger tanks and guns – rather than with weapons that were less effective individually, but easier to mass-produce. Hitler's interventions in the allocation of resources for weapon production and, subsequently, in the use of weapons were frequently deleterious. For example, he squandered the German lead in jet-powered aircraft, ordering that the Me262 should not be used as a fighter, despite its effectiveness in the role. Like Stalin, Hitler was fascinated by battleships to the detriment of smaller, frequently more effective, warships.[78] Rockets were another example of questionable German military policy. Although the V2 could travel 200 miles in five minutes, the technology then available was too limited to enable it to be aimed accurately. The rocket programme was neither cost-effective, nor did it display much insight into the psychology of Germany's opponents.[79] As with the British use of the new decyphering technology of ULTRA, the crucial issue was the use, rather than simply the potency, of new technology.[80] Although they lacked outward impressiveness, in the Second World War many of the real technological 'revolutions' occurred in the 'micro'-field, especially radar, and they did make a difference.

The Germans, like the Japanese, gained control over the resources and labour forces of areas they conquered or which were allied to them, for example the coal and industry of north-east France, and the oil of Romania and the Dutch East Indies. However, their value was diminished by the destruction wrought by retreating forces, especially in the Soviet Union and, subsequently, by Allied air raids; by the lack of adequate and flexible central planning; and by the cruel nature of Axis control, which dissipated support and, instead, encouraged resistance and labour non-cooperation, for example policies of compulsory labour including the deportation of workers to work in Germany, which met with opposition, as, for example, in Belgium.

Large numbers of German troops were deployed in order to limit resistance operations or to prevent their possible outbreak. Furthermore, the vicious programmes of genocide pursued by the Germans absorbed resources that might otherwise have been devoted to the war. Thus, trains were used to transport victims to the concentration camps, rather than to move military supplies. Similarly, hostility to 'Jewish physics' affected the German atomic bomb programme, although there were also practical problems, and initial German successes in 1939–41 had suggested that the bomb would not be necessary.[81]

Ideology thus played a decisive role. More generally, the alliance dimension was crucial to both wars and, although ideological factors only played a partial role in the alignments, these alliances underline the non-technological aspects of military history.

The value of conquests was also limited by the very fact of war, which disrupted the trading systems within which these economies, and indeed those of Germany and Japan, operated most effectively. Oil was crucial to warfare on land, at sea and in the air. The Japanese in particular suffered from oil shortages, but these also affected Germany, leading Hitler to try to advance on the Soviet oilfields at Baku in 1942. The oilfields which Germany overran were those they had been able to tap prior to the war. Thus in 1941 the Germans overran Estonia when they attacked the Soviet Union, but after 1935 they had already been the largest purchaser of oil from Estonia's oil-shale fields. Under the Nazi-Soviet pact of 1939, the Germans had enjoyed access to Soviet raw materials.

In contrast, the Allies dominated the world production of oil, especially after Iraq and Persia were occupied in 1941. The Allies controlled or had access to the economy of most of the world, including the western and most of the southern hemisphere and West Asia. Latin American involvement reflected the development of US hemispheric leadership, as exemplified by the Good Neighbor Policy during the 1930s. This led to political, economic and military cooperation during the war.

As a result of differences in resources, economic bases and managerial attitudes between the two sides, there were major differences in weapons production. Faster-firing weapons greatly increased the quantity of ammunition used. By late 1940 the British were producing more than twice as many fighters as the Germans, helping them to defeat German air attacks: the planes, especially the fast and manoeuvrable Hurricanes and Spitfires, were also effective. In 1942, even before the American economy had been put on a full war footing, the Allies produced 58,000 tanks and 101,000 aeroplanes; the Axis 11,000 and 26,000. Soviet tank production rose to 29,000 in 1943, American bomber production to 29,365 the same year. The construction of large numbers of American aircraft carriers transformed the air, naval and land war in the Pacific. The Soviet Union and the Americans concentrated on weapons that were simple to build, operate and repair. The scale of operations is indicated by the size of the force the Soviets deployed for their operations against Japanese-held Manchuria in 1945 once the war in Europe was over: 1.5 million troops, 4,370 aeroplanes, 5,500 tanks and 28,000 pieces of artillery. Earlier that year, the Soviets had sent $2\frac{1}{2}$ million men to storm Berlin.

The Allies had achieved overwhelming superiority in the *quantity* of resources. This affected the conduct of the war in many ways. For example, as the Americans advanced across France in 1944 after D-Day they did not storm villages and towns where they encountered resistance. Instead, they stopped, brought in aerial support, heavy armour and artillery, and heavily bombarded the site before moving in with scant loss of American life. The importance of industrial resources lent point to strategic bombing, and also ensured that victorious powers sought to seize industrial plant. Of the 2,690 tanks in the German armoured divisions that attacked France in 1940, 381 were Czech T-38s, good light tanks that the Germans had gained as a result of annexing Bohemia in 1939. The Czech AZNP-Avia factories at Cakovice and Kunovice were taken over and used to produce Messerschmitt fighters. Furthermore, the morale of labour forces became more important. The number of weapons was itself not instrumental in victory, especially if weapons were obsolescent, as, for example, were many of the pre-war Polish and Soviet aeroplanes and tanks. However, under the pressure of war an improvement in weapons effectiveness occurred.

State control or influence over the means of propaganda ensured that the greater access of the public to information, through mass literacy and ownership of radios, helped to create national views, or impressions of them, in accordance with the view of the state. The Second World War was not only a 'total war'; the populations involved were also told it was a total war. Thus, for example, the BBC played a major role in supporting the British war effort, not least by encouraging a sense of common purpose. Greatly influenced by the success of British propaganda in the First World War, Hitler used propaganda effectively in Germany, although it helped mobilise people for only so long.[82] Television did not play a role, but cinema newsreels were important.

The development of the mass media in the twentieth century altered the parameters of debate about military methods. Protagonists of particular weapons systems or strategies sought public platforms in order to influence government policy. This was true for example of the naval leagues and air enthusiasts of the early years of the century. In Britain, the Aerial League of the British empire and Lord Northcliffe's newspapers, such as the *Daily Mail,* pressed for the development of air power.

The Collapse of Empire

The Second World War left the USA by far the dominant economic[83] and military power in the world, with the European colonial powers, excepting the Soviet Union, considerably weaker. The European powers had not only suffered heavily in the conflict, but, after the war, they now faced a confrontation with a Soviet state that controlled most of Eastern Europe and maintained its grip on Siberia, Central Asia, the Caucasus and Mongolia. In 1944 the hitherto ostensibly independent 'people's republic' of Tannu Tuva, formerly a vassal state of Mongolia, was incorporated into the Soviet Union.

Some losses by the colonial powers were rapid. Italy forfeited her colonial empire as a result of Mussolini's alliance with Hitler, while the British renounced control over India

(1947), Burma, Ceylon and Palestine (1948), and Newfoundland (1949). Returning to Indonesia after the Japanese withdrawal, the Dutch were unable to suppress nationalist resistance in 1947, although they did limit the extent of Java and Sumatra controlled by the nationalists. However, anti-colonial American pressure, post-Second World War weakness, guerrilla warfare and nationalist determination forced the Dutch to accept Indonesian independence in 1949.

Nevertheless, Britain was still a major imperial power and sought to act like one in the late 1940s and 1950s in Africa, Malaya and the Middle East. The limited decolonisation of the late 1940s was part of a strategy designed to ensure the maintenance of Britain's position as a great power. Conscription was continued. However, in the 1950s a series of crises – the Abadan crisis of 1951, the Suez crisis of 1956, and the overthrow of the pro-British Iraqi government in 1958 – revealed the limitations of British strength and encouraged a new attitude towards empire that led to rapid decolonisation and an attempt to join the European Economic Community, now the European Union. Independence was granted to Ghana and Malaya in 1957, and to British Somaliland, Nigeria and Cyprus in 1960, the last being especially significant as it had been said that Cyprus would 'never' be independent, and because, with a population of only half a million, it set the precedent for cession of independence to small states within the Commonwealth. British withdrawal was in part a response to the failure to overcome nationalist pressure. Sierra Leone, southern Cameroons (as part of Cameroon) and Tanganyika followed in 1961, Jamaica, Trinidad and Uganda in 1962, Sabah, Sarawak, Singapore, Zanzibar and Kenya in 1963, Nyasaland, northern Rhodesia and the major naval base of Malta in 1964, Gambia and the Maldives in 1965, Bechuanaland, Basutoland and Barbados in 1966, Aden in 1967, Nauru, Mauritius and Swaziland in 1969, Tonga and Fiji in 1970, the Solomon Islands, Ellice Island and Dominica in 1978, the Gilbert Islands and St Vincent in 1979, New Hebrides in 1980, Antigua and British Honduras in 1981, St Kitts in 1983 and Brunei in 1984.

The French made a major effort to retain their colonies and expanded their army to do so, leading to bitter conflicts in Indo-China (1946–54) and Algeria (1954–62), which the French lost, despite deploying 400,000 men in Algeria in 1956 and winning control of Algiers in 1957 through tough anti-insurrectionary measures, including torture.[84] Many Algerian and Indo-Chinese troops fought for the French in the 1950s, and the Portuguese also made extensive use of colonial troops. In order to concentrate on Algeria, which had been declared an integral part of France (and thus not a colony) in 1848, the French granted Tunisia independence in 1956, although nationalist guerrilla activity there since 1952 had made only limited impact in the towns. The French protectorate in Morocco also ended in 1956; guerrilla activity there had been widespread since 1955. Although undefeated in battle and making effective use of helicopter-borne units, the French, who had been unable to suppress the guerrillas in an intractable and costly struggle, conceded independence to Algeria in 1962. France granted independence to most of its African possessions in 1960, including Madagascar where a rebellion had been suppressed in 1947–8. Belgium abandoned the Belgian Congo in 1960 and Australia and New Zealand granted independence to their colonies: Papua New Guinea (1975) and Western Samoa (1962).

The structure of foreign bases underlying European imperial range was destroyed, and replaced by bases supplied by allies. Thus, under the North Atlantic Treaty Organisation (NATO) established in 1949, the Americans developed a structure of bases in Western Europe. Economic support, provided directly through Marshall Aid and, indirectly, through the financial stability produced by the Bretton Woods system, helped to increase

Western European prosperity and to keep it in the American system. American bases in the Pacific, especially the Philippines, supported American operations in East Asia. Japan served as a major American logistical base in the Korean War.[85]

In contrast, the Europeans lost control of bases located in colonial territories. This was a consequence of the rise of nationalism in a Third World no longer under European control, but also a product of the Cold War in Europe which ensured that Western European military priorities centred on defence against possible Soviet attack. This was particularly important for British defence expenditure. Thus, the process of competition within Europe helped to weaken the global role of European military power. British military viability 'east of Suez' was lost when, in response to sterling crises from 1966, forces were withdrawn from Aden in 1967 and Singapore in 1971.[86] In contrast, a large force was maintained in West Germany to deter Soviet attack. The French, however, retained rights to use bases in some of their former colonies, such as Djibouti.

Equipped with tactical air support, helicopters and advanced rifles, the Portuguese fought on against guerrilla movements in their African colonies which began in Angola in 1961, Guinea-Bissau in 1963 and Mozambique in 1964, until a left-wing revolution in Portugal in 1974, which owed much to military dissatisfaction with the war. Due to military commitments in Angola, the Portuguese reduced their presence in Goa to 4,000 troops and in 1961 the Indians overran it with 71,000 men in one day. The Americans, although allied to Portugal in NATO, refused appeals for help.

Domestic political cultures and the structure of international relations both left little role for colonialism. Morale is crucial in warfare, but it proved difficult to sustain once confidence in the purpose and domestic support for imperialism was lost.

Guerrilla Warfare

The beginning of the wars of decolonisation are an appropriate point to underline a major theme of this work, the need not to exaggerate the potency of military technological advantage. If that was to be amply demonstrated by the American experience in the Vietnam War, it was already apparent well before. Although damaged by the experience of defeat and, sometimes, occupation in the Second World War, and with their economies and finances gravely weakened, the European colonial powers enjoyed better weaponry than their opponents. The British had the nuclear bomb and strategic bombers, but found it difficult to control Cyprus during the state of emergency in 1955–9. There was a major distinction between the importance of technological advantage in wars between states, and the lesser role of such advantage between, on the one hand, states and armies and, on the other, guerrilla forces. In the latter case, technological superiority in part only won the ability to confront the problems of facing guerrilla warfare.

Guerrilla forces in turn could compromise their advantages if they adopted more conventional methods of fighting. This helped to ensure the defeat of the Communist guerrillas in the Greek civil war of 1946–9. The Greek army was also helped by American aid from 1947, by the replacement in 1948 of their policy of static defence, by that of a systematic clearance of guerrilla forces out of particular areas and by the decision of President Tito of Yugoslavia, once he had broken with the Soviet Union in 1948, to stop sending the Communists assistance. Guerrilla forces could become vulnerable if they sought to attack strongly defended positions or to hold particular sites. Thus, in 1946 the French defeated a Viet Minh uprising in Hanoi. The Portuguese crushed a rising in the Angolan capital Luanda in 1961, but found it impossible to suppress subsequent guerrilla operations. An absence of adequate foreign support gravely weakened anti-Communist guerrilla movements in Eastern Europe in the late 1940s and 1950s, for example in Albania, the 'Forest Brethren' in the Baltic republics, and in Bulgaria and Yugoslavia.

Chinese Civil War

In the Chinese Civil War (1946–9), however, the Communists under Mao Tse-tung made the successful transfer from guerrilla warfare to large-scale conventional positional warfare. This was despite the greater size of the Nationalist forces, their superiority in the air and American support for the Nationalist cause. In 1948 the Nationalist forces in Manchuria were isolated and then destroyed, and the Communists conquered most of central China. Most of the rest of China, including Beijing, Nanjing and Shanghai, was overrun the following year. Technology did not triumph: the Communists were inferior in weaponry, and, in particular, lacked air and sea power, but their strategic conceptions, tactical skill, army morale and political leadership were superior. The Nationalist cause was weakened by poor civilian and military leadership and inept strategy, and, as the war went badly, by poor morale. The largest war, in terms of number of combatants and area fought over, since the Second World War had been won without reference to technological superiority. The Nationalists were left only with Formosa (Taiwan), where they were protected by American naval power and the limited aerial and naval capability of their opponents. A rising by the native Taiwanese had been suppressed in 1947.

Korea and Vietnam

The Chinese Communists were not so successful when they intervened in the Korean War (1950–3), a conventional conflict, and one where they faced the strongest power in the world. Although they drove the American-led coalition from North Korea in late 1950, capturing Seoul in January 1951, the Chinese forces were fought to a standstill that spring as American supply lines shortened and as Chinese human-wave frontal attacks fell victim to American firepower.[87] The Chinese were supported by the advanced MIG-15 fighters of the Manchurian-based Soviet 'Group 64'. The war encouraged a massive increase in American military expenditure: as a percentage of total government expenditure it rose from 30.4 per cent in 1950 to 65.7 per cent in 1954.[88]

The Chinese-supplied Viet Minh, having pushed the French back from their border posts, were defeated in mass attacks on French positions in the open areas of the Red River delta in North Vietnam in 1951 and 1952, for example at Vinh Yen (1951) and Mao Khé (1951), and in the Day River campaign (1951). Nevertheless, the Viet Minh succeeded in 1954 in defeating the French in position warfare at Dien Bien Phu. This was a forward base developed across Viet Minh supply lines by French parachutists, in order to lure the Viet Minh into a major battle. Thanks to their mass infantry attacks, the Viet Minh suffered more casualties, but the isolated French stronghold, denied air support due to artillery bombardment of the airstrip, fell after a 55-day siege: the Viet Minh had American 105 mm cannon, captured by the Chinese in the Chinese Civil War, and also Chinese anti-aircraft weapons. Despite their superior weaponry the poorly led French finally proved unable to combat their opponents effectively in either guerrilla or conventional warfare and they abandoned Indo-China. From 1949 the French had greatly

85. Airpower on the battlefield. Helicopters played a major role as mobile artillery and troops transports in the Vietnam War. Only the Americans used airpower, and it enabled them greatly to extend the range of their forces. This photograph shows Marines scrambling aboard a helicopter at Khe Sanh, 18 April 1968.

suffered from the Communist Chinese presence to the north of Vietnam. The Chinese provided automatic weapons and artillery, helping to transform the Viet Minh into a force able to act as a conventional army.

Vietnam was partitioned and the Viet Minh left in control of North Vietnam, where they ruthlessly suppressed a rebellion in Nhge An in 1956. An American-supported government was established in South Vietnam, but from 1959 it faced a Communist rebellion by the Viet Cong that led to more overt and widespread American intervention. From 1964 units of the North Vietnamese army were infiltrated into the South. The Americans found that air power could not defeat their Vietnamese opponents in 1965–73; bombing of North Vietnam did not lessen their resolve and it proved impossible to block their supply routes. In 1966 the weekly number of American air sorties frequently exceeded 25,000; in 1956–8, in operation Rolling Thunder, 643,000 tons of bombs were dropped on North Vietnam. Seeking a war of mobility and firepower, the Americans made extensive tactical use of helicopters, usually the Huey and the Chinook. Over 2,300 American helicopters were shot down during the war, but the Americans were able to manufacture and deploy vast quantities of arms. However, their initial success led to somewhat inflexible tactics, while the Viet Cong learned how to respond to the American use of helicopters.

Viet Cong attacks on American positions were generally held, for example at Plei Me in 1965, and in the Tet offensive and at Khe Sanh and in the A Shau Valley in 1968, and the Viet Cong suffered heavy casualties, especially in the Tet offensive of 1968; but the Americans proved unable to deny the countryside to their opponents. The Viet Cong enjoyed cover from view and this gave superior technology little to aim at, an obvious contrast to the capability of such technology elsewhere: at sea, in the air and in the desert.

Furthermore, although counter-insurgency policies worked in some parts of Vietnam, they were generally unsuccessful. The pacification programme also involved a 'battle for hearts and minds' involving American-backed economic and political reforms, but these were difficult to implement, not only due to Viet Cong opposition and intimidation, and the effectiveness of their guerrilla and small-unit operations, but also because the South Vietnamese government was half-hearted and the American army, lacking a reliable political base in South Vietnam, preferred to seek a military solution.[89] Financial and economic problems were also important, helping in 1968 to lead President Johnson to reject a military request for an additional 205,000 men in Vietnam.[90] Their leadership divided on policy, the Americans lost the strategic initiative.

The Communists were well led and organised and their political system and culture enabled them to mobilise and direct resources and maintain a persistent effort. The North Vietnamese and Viet Cong were more willing to suffer losses than the Americans, for whom the war was probably unwinnable. Limited war theory is a Western concept and American strategy was wrongly based on the assumption that unacceptable losses could be inflicted on the North Vietnamese in the way that they could on the Americans.[91] Vietnam demonstrated that being the foremost world power did not mean that a state could beat, say, the 60th, because power existed in particular spheres and circumstances. This problem of defining relative power suggests that concern with the ranking of world powers is unrealistic.

Political Will and Post-war Insurrections

In the Nigerian Civil War of 1967–70, the balance of military firepower was very important. The Biafrans, who fought a conventional war with front lines, had no answer to the air power of their Federal opponents, and little response to their armoured vehicles. After the initial stages of the conflict, they were also heavily outnumbered. Unlike the Viet Minh and Viet Cong, the Biafrans were swiftly cut off from foreign land links and this exacerbated their lack of food and military supplies. In contrast, in Cuba in 1958, when Batista's government launched its army against Castro's guerrilla forces, the offensive was poorly coordinated and lacked both adequate air power and foreign support. Once the campaign had failed the government suffered a crucial loss of nerve and lost the initiative, with fatal consequences.

Political will also played a major role in the Malayan Emergency of 1948–60 and the confrontation between Indonesia and British forces supporting Malaysia in 1963–5. In the former it took 300,000 men to defeat a Communist force that never exceeded 6,000. The British made effective use of helicopters, carefully controlled the food supply, resettled much of the rural population and used counter-guerrilla forces skilled in jungle craft. They also did not allow the Emergency to deter them from moves towards independence. Their opponents lacked adequate Chinese and Russian support.[92]

In 1963–5 the Indonesian government restricted its military attacks, and Anglo-Malaysian firmness, plus the effective use of helicopters by the British in 1964, prevented the situation deteriorating until a change of government in Indonesia in 1965 led to negotiations. The Indonesians had good weapons, especially anti-personnel mines and rocket launchers, but the British and Commonwealth forces, who deployed up to 17,000 men, were well led, had well-trained, versatile troops, and benefited from complete command of sea and air, a good nearby base at Singapore, excellent intelligence and an absence of significant domestic opposition in Britain.[93]

The political context was also crucial in the defeat of the peasant-backed Communist guerrilla movement on Luzon in the Philippines in 1950–5. The government benefited from American arms, but their counter-insurgency operations were also supplemented by land reform to win over the peasantry and by a programme of rural settlement. In Oman, the Sultan suppressed rebellious tribesmen in the extensive Dhofar region in 1965–75, in part thanks to foreign, particularly British and Iranian, assistance, but also because Sultan Qaboos, who deposed his father in 1970, was a more adept politician. Insurgency warfare was also defeated in Bolivia and Kenya. Indeed, it could be argued that the costs and shortcomings of this form of warfare spurred recourse to low-risk, low-cost, low-manpower terrorism in the 1970s, 1980s and 1990s.

Civilian Attitudes

There was a major cultural shift affecting warfare after the Second World War. With the exception of the Communist bloc, the most powerful military states in the world came to enact policy within a context in which civilian views played a greater role, and these views no longer centred on the desirability of rule over large sections of the world, let alone on the moral value of conflict, as the British government discovered when it attacked Egypt in the 1956 Suez Crisis. The situation was very different to when the British had attacked Egypt in 1882, and this difference was political, not technological. In addition, there was a greater unwillingness to accept casualties for anything but defence of the homeland. Indeed, it was in part precisely because post-1945 wars were not fought in or over the homelands of the great powers – that they were fought in Algeria, Vietnam, Afghanistan and the Falklands, not in France, the USA, the USSR and Britain – that shifts in the domestic context and culture of war in these powers occurred. Far from being total, war became a spectator sport for the bulk of the population and one for which they were unwilling to accept prolonged hardship.

Failure in war, at the very least an inability to secure victory, had sapped military and civilian morale earlier in the century. This was especially true of the First World War, for example with the Russians[94] and French in 1917 and the Germans in 1918. Domestic and military hostility to the continuation of conflict played a far smaller role in the Second World War, in large part because it was presented both in ideological terms and for the defence of homelands. In post-war Britain conscription was seen as a just return for social welfare, and as a measure necessary to show national resolve in the Cold War.[95]

However, the process of opposition to war, and the military and political effects it had, were readily apparent with the American involvement in Vietnam and became more marked later. Opposition to involvement in Vietnam rose because of the duration of the conflict and because the goals seemed ill defined. By denying the Americans victory in the field, the Viet Cong helped to create political pressures within America. The conscription necessary to sustain a large-scale American presence in an increasingly unpopular war played a major role in this process. A majority of the Americans who went to Vietnam were volunteers, not draftees, though in 1965–73 about two million Americans were drafted, and draftees accounted for a third of American deaths in Vietnam by 1969.

In contrast, the French had not sent conscripts to fight the Indo-China war in 1946–54. French law since the nineteenth century had forbidden the use of conscripts anywhere in the French empire except Algeria, which was considered a *département* of France. This ensured that the Indo-China war had to be fought by colonial troops and the Foreign Legion. Conscripts were sent to Algeria from 1956, with the same general result as the Americans experienced when they used draftees in Vietnam.

The draft had been a collective experience of American manhood. By 1958, either as draftees or draft-induced volunteers, 70 per cent of eligible young American males had served under the colours. Yet in 1969 President Nixon decided to quiet middle-class anxieties and improve his prospects for re-election by eliminating the draft. His withdrawal of American ground troops required a 'Vietnamization' of the war. This led from 1973 to an all-volunteer force that pushed manpower costs up and reduced popular identification with the military.[96] The Vietnam War led to a massive increase in anti-war sentiment in the USA, the world's strongest military power. Opposition to the war was widely voiced and 'draft dodging' was common. Indeed, in 1992 and 1996 the Americans elected Bill Clinton as President in spite of the fact that he had avoided military service in Vietnam. The war also accentuated the decline of deference that was a common feature of Western societies from the 1960s. An anti-heroic ethos came to characterise much artistic work about war, for example the savage British film indictment of the First World War, *Oh What a Lovely War!* and the popular American series *M.A.S.H.* (Mobile Army Surgical Hospital) that offered a sardonic account of the Korean War on American television screens in 1972–83. The fashionable British television comedy series *Blackadder* closed in 1989 with programmes presenting the First World War as futile, cruel and unheroic. In 1992 the Canadian Broadcasting Corporation showed *The Valour and the Horror*, a tendentious television series that heavily criticised Canada's role in the Second World War. In addition, military and political strategies were freely challenged by journalists. By the Gulf War of 1990–1, media coverage of a war in which the USA was involved had become almost constant.

Abandonment of conscription helped to ensure that the military came to play a smaller role in the politics of most Western countries than was the case in most of the rest of the world. The Nation-in-Arms approach of Israel, with its collectivist ethos, universal conscription and a long reserve obligation, was not matched elsewhere in the West, although a major degree of short-term mobilisation was achieved by peoples determined to win independence. Thus in 1991 about 70,000 men out of a population of only two million Slovenes mobilised in order to resist Yugoslav attempts to prevent Slovene independence. The Yugoslav army did not push the issue to widespread conflict, but in Bosnia, Croatia and Serbia extensive mobilisation was indeed linked to bitter and sustained fighting.

Fighting for survival and independence was not, however, a task that other Western powers faced. The military were increasingly seen as forces for national defence not foreign intervention, other than for crucial and short-term national or humanitarian reasons. Opposition to militarism remained strong in postwar Germany and Japan even after the occupying powers had withdrawn their forces. Britain phased out conscription in 1957–63. France, where discontent with national service grew from the late 1960s,[97] reduced conscription to a year in 1970 and announced in 1996 that it would be abolished by 2002. The Portuguese coup in 1974 and the subsequent abandonment of the overseas empire was followed by a dramatic fall in the armed forces: from over 200,000 men in 1974 to under 40,000 in 1991. Military expenditure was cut in Portugal, and in many other states, especially if considered as a percentage of government spending. Smaller armies encouraged the nuclearisation of military policy in the 1950s by those powers that possessed the nuclear bomb.

Even within a relatively controlled society like the Soviet Union, there was criticism of losses in Afghanistan in the 1980s where the Soviets lost about 15,000 men. By the 1990s sensitivity to any losses had become more acute, as American involvement in Somalia revealed. American weapons, such as M-16 rifles, were used by the Indonesian army to massacre civilians in East Timor, from 1975 on, but the Americans, in Somalia and elsewhere, were not prepared to use such methods and any killing of civilians was criticised. The terminology used to describe war – terms such as armed conflict and police action – reflects a reluctance to endorse war. Once the Soviet Union had collapsed, there was openly expressed hostility within Russia to the policy of suppressing the Caucasian region of Chechnya begun in 1994 and to the resulting losses.

This softened attitude was very different to the brutal Soviet suppression of the sailors of the Baltic Fleet who demanded reform in 1921: their base at Kronstadt was stormed, the defenders massacred and their reputation blackened. Similarly, European Communist governments used force to suppress demonstrations in East Germany in 1953, in Poznan, Poland in 1956 and in Czechoslovakia in 1968–9, but were unwilling to do so in Poland and elsewhere in 1988–92. In 1956 the determined use of Soviet armour crushed popular opposition in Hungary. In 1968 the Soviet Union sent 250,000 men, supported by Bulgarian, Hungarian and Polish forces, to occupy Czechoslovakia in order to thwart the liberal Communism of the government. The situation was entirely different in 1989 as Communist governments collapsed in the face of domestic agitation for change in Eastern Europe, although the Soviet army was used to resist nationalist pressures, including in Georgia (1989), Lithuania (1991), Moldova (1992) and Chechnya (1994–).

In contrast, the conquest in 1950–9 and subsequent retention of Tibet in the face of widespread guerrilla opposition posed no domestic political problems for Communist China, and in the 1980s and 1990s dictatorial regimes in Iraq and Burma were willing to use considerable force to gain and retain control over dissident minorities, for example the Kurds of northern Iraq. Although the notion of war as an instrument of policy has become less acceptable in Europe and North America, this is not the case in many other areas. In the Nigerian Civil War of 1967–70, the Nigerian government felt no hesitation in bombing Biafran towns with Ilyushin 28s and in using starvation to force their opponents to surrender. The Indonesian army used force to suppress the Republic of the South Moluccas in 1952, annex western New Guinea (as West Irian) in 1963, to invade East Timor in 1975, and subsequently to suppress demands for independence by the Fretilin movement in East Timor and the Free Papua Movement in Irian;[98] all without appreciable domestic criticism within Indonesia. About 200,000 Timorese – one-third of the population – have died. In the 1980s and 1990s China sought to combine the professionalism that characterised Western military systems in the period with coercive and centrally directed mobilising strategies; a combination of technology and organisational sophistication with massive manpower that other states did not seek to emulate.

Armies and Politics

Armies proved the focus of political unity in many Third World states. This was due to a number of reasons. In 'artificial' states whose boundaries had been dictated by imperialist powers, post-colonial national armies were frequently the major alternative to fissiparous tribalism. Armies could be open to radical ideas and to notions of national identity. They also offered a means of social mobility for able and ambitious individuals.

There was a militarisation of politics in many states.[99] Lastly, armies were able to seize power: they had administrative experience, manpower, arms, communications and transport.

This process did not begin with the retreat of imperialism. The seizure of power by the Young Turks in 1908–9 owed much to military desire for change; in 1903, a military coup had replaced one king of Serbia by another. Soldiers under Yuan Shih-k'ai took control of the Chinese republic from 1912 and subsequently China went through an extended period of civil war – especially, after Yuan's death in 1916, the warlord era of 1916–28, but in essence lasting up to the Communist victory of 1949. In 1921 Riza Khan, a Russian-trained colonel in the Persian Cossack Brigade, suppressed rebellions and seized power in Persia (Iran). He created a new national army, the loyalty of which he gained by better equipment, regular pay and success, and used it to crush opposition. Campaigns in 1922–5 spread governmental power throughout Persia. The disunited tribes were defeated and Riza Khan became Prime Minister (1923) and Shah (1925). Thereafter, the position of the tribes was weakened by disarming them and forcibly introducing conscription so that tribesmen could be used against other tribesmen. Major tribal rebellions were crushed in 1929 and 1932: the tribesmen suffered from the new mobility of their opponents, a mobility produced by armoured cars and lorries operating on new roads, and supported by the automatic weapons and observation planes of government forces.[100] In 1919 Mustafa Kemal, a general backed by the army, was able to organise Turkish nationalism against foreign control and partition. Army expansion was supported by Iraqi nationalists in the 1920s and 1930s as a means of integrating the new state and conscription was introduced in 1934, broadening the social basis of the officer corps. In 1933 the tribes had about 100,000 rifles, the Iraqi army only 15,000, but the army was able to break the military power of its disunited opponents. In 1933 the Assyrians (Nestorian Christians) were defeated, and in 1935 tribal uprisings were suppressed. The following year the army staged its first coup.

In 1930–1 Japanese officers, angered by what they felt was the failure of the government to defend national interests, planned a coup and the creation of a military government. Instead, they found it easier to seize control of Manchuria. There were also military coups in Europe: for example in Portugal in 1917 and 1926, Bulgaria in 1923, and Greece, Poland and Lithuania in 1926. The Spanish Civil War began with a military coup in 1936; there had earlier been a coup in 1923.

The military played a major role in Latin America. In 1930, for example, in order to end an incipient civil war, the Brazilian army removed the president and prevented the inauguration of the President-elect, instead, putting his defeated opponent, Getúlio Vargas, into office. Supported by the army, Vargas was able to crush the 'Constitutionalist Revolt' of 1932 and Communist risings in 1935, and in 1937 used troops to suppress the constitution.[101] He controlled Brazil until the military forced him out, first in 1945 and then in 1954, when he committed suicide.

In Chile the army forced out the President in 1924, and in 1927 Carlos Ibáñez, an ex-colonel then Minister of War, was elected unopposed with army support. The army intervened again in 1932 to guarantee the election of the President they had forced out in 1924. An army coup overthrew the peasant-backed government of El Salvador in 1931 and the subsequent peasant revolt was smashed with much slaughter in 1932. There was a coup in Cuba in 1933, the 'Sergeants Revolt'. The Argentine President was overthrown by the Grupo de Oficiales Unidos in a military coup in 1943,[102] the same year in which a military junta seized power in Bolivia.

In multi-ethnic states, such as Burma, India and Indonesia, the army has been the most effective national institution and has acted to prevent separatist tendencies, for example by Mons and Karens in Burma and by Nagas, Sikhs and Kashmiris in India. In 1984 the Indian army stormed the Golden Temple of Amritsar, the leading Sikh shrine, which had become a major terrorist base. In the southern Philippines the army resisted a Muslim separatist movement.

Sometimes, this use of the army has been linked to an attempted demilitarisation of other groups, a traditional policy used for example by the Soviet Union in the North Caucasus in the 1920s. In South Yemen the army, a national force, was seen as a crucial control on the power of often autonomous tribes and measures were taken against tribalism. In 1969 the wearing of arms was banned. Similarly, in Oman from 1970 the tribal militia was reduced in favour of the army. Conscription introduced in North Yemen in 1979 weakened tribal elements in the army.

More generally, armies have been used to maintain and enforce the cohesion of states. In the late 1930s the Afghan air force using British-supplied light bombers helped ground forces to suppress rebellions.[103] The walls of most Chinese cities, including the outer walls of Beijing, were demolished after the Communists won the Civil War. In 1969 the army and police in Guyana stopped a Venezuelan-backed secessionist rising in the Rupununi region,[104] while in Argentina that year the army suppressed an insurrection in Córdoba. In the 1990s the Georgian army used force to resist separatism by the Muslim province of Abkhazia, but the latter received Russian military assistance.[105] Troops have been used where the civil authorities have failed to maintain order, for example by the British in Northern Ireland since 1969, by the French in Corsica and by the Mexicans in their poor southern states such as Guerrero and Chiapas in the mid-1990s.

Where the army has fallen under the control of particular ethnic and religious groups, as in Nigeria, Pakistan, Sri Lanka and Sudan, its activities, including its opposition to separatism, have been associated with ethnic violence. In 1946 the Shah led the Persian army into Tabriz, producing a blood-bath that cowed Azerbaijani separatism. Attempts by the Pakistani army, which was dominated by troops from the Punjab in West Pakistan, to suppress the Bengali nationalism of East Pakistan provoked rebellion in 1970.[106] The Pakistani army was more successful in quelling a tribal uprising in Baluchistan in 1972–6 that arose from attempts to limit autonomy and tribal power. In Syria the Alawite-dominated regime and army brutally crushed a rising by Sunni Muslims at Hama in 1982.

Furthermore, military notions of national interests have sometimes entailed moves against democratically elected governments, as in Persia in 1953, Pakistan in 1958 and 1977, Turkey in 1960, 1971 and 1980, South Vietnam in 1963, Brazil in 1964, Peru and Greece in 1967, and Chile and Uruguay in 1973. Coups were also staged against non-democratic governments: monarchy was overthrown in Egypt in 1952, Iraq in 1958 and Libya in 1969; although in Iran in 1979 the Shah fell as a result of a revolution despite enjoying the support of the armed forces.

The seizure of power by military groups became more common after 1960, especially after the decolonialisation of Africa. Between December 1962 and March 1966 the governments of 11 African states were overthrown by their armies, including those of Togo, Congo (Brazzaville), Dahomey, Zanzibar, Algeria, Congo (Kinshasa), the Central African Republic, Upper Volta, Nigeria and Ghana. Libya and Sudan followed in 1969, Uganda in 1971 and Ethiopia in 1974. The process continues: the government of Sierra Leone was overthrown in 1997. The Indonesian army, which never regarded itself as apolitical,[107] seized power in 1965, and there was an attempted coup in China in 1971.

In response to the threat of military coups, many governments built up other forces as a control on the army. Thus in South Yemen, where the army grew in size after independence and played a role in struggles between politicians, for example in 1986, a militia was developed. In Saudi Arabia the National Guard was built up in the 1970s as a counterbalance to the army. The political and governmental role of military and quasi-military forces has been, and is, such that the institutions and processes of military training have been of great political importance. Thus, in Indonesia the Military Academy established in Magelang in 1957 and the Army Engineering Academy have been more than training grounds for military methods.

The Arms Trade

The shift in attitude towards casualties and towards control over foreign peoples within the European world was to be of greater potential importance as non-European states acquired enhanced military capability. As in the sixteenth, seventeenth and eighteenth centuries, when the English, French and Dutch had been willing to arm the opponents of their European rivals, so, after 1945, the arms industries of the Soviet Union and of other Communist states, such as Czechoslovakia, China and Cuba, were used to support anti-Western movements and states. The major differences were of scale and ideology. Arms industries based on mass production were used to support an enormous export of armaments. As a consequence, movements and states opposed to Western interests found it easier to obtain arms.[108] Military assistance is the modern equivalent of the seventeenth- and eighteenth-century subsidy treaties, but the key difference is the ideological dimension. The modern assisted ally is generally expected to behave *domestically* as well as internationally in accordance with the wishes of the sponsor.

The North Koreans invaded South Korea in June 1950 with T34 tanks and Yak aeroplanes sold by Stalin that gave them an advantage over their lightly armed opponents. The South Korean capital of Seoul rapidly fell to this *blitzkrieg*. It was not regained until September 1950, and then by American forces. The same year the Soviet Naval Advisory Mission to China was established. Soviet training, supplies and ship designs were important in the development of the Chinese navy.[109] The Viet Minh used Soviet Katyusha rockets in their final attack on Dien Bien Phu in 1953. The scale of war was such that in the 55-day siege of the position the Viet Minh fired 350,000 shells. The newly established Castro government was sent large quantities of Czech small arms in 1960. The Czechs also armed non-Communist states, including Israel and Ethiopia. Indeed, the Skoda works in Czechoslovakia provided much of the Communist world's export arms. The supply of Czech small arms and, to a lesser extent, aeroplanes, was crucial to Israel when it was attacked by its Arab neighbours in 1948.[110] The North Vietnamese and Viet Cong were armed by China and the Soviet Union. Soviet surface-to-air missiles inflicted heavy casualties on American aircraft bombing North Vietnam in 1965–8. Similarly, the Soviet Union and China armed the guerrilla organisations that sought from the 1960s to overthrow the minority white governments of Rhodesia, Namibia and South Africa, and to force the Portuguese to abandon their African colonies. For example, SWAPO (the South West Africa People's Organisation), which began guerrilla attacks in 1966, received Soviet assistance. The Soviet Union's Cuban surrogate sent substantial forces to Angola, ensuring that South African intervention was unsuccessful.

The provision of large quantities of modern arms helped to lend added destructiveness to regional conflicts. This was especially apparent in the Middle East, where from the late 1960s the USA armed Israel and from the 1950s the Soviet Union armed its opponents. In 1955 the Soviets, through Czechoslovakia, agreed to provide 200 MiG-15 fighters, 50 Ilyushin-28 bombers and hundreds of tanks to Egypt. In 1956 an Egyptian-Soviet arms agreement led to the sending of 800 Soviet advisers. In the Six Day War in 1967, Soviet T54 and T55 tanks used by the Egyptians were beaten in the Sinai desert by US Patton and British Centurion tanks used by the Israelis, although this owed much to Israeli operational flexibility, their successful use of the strategy of the indirect approach, their exploitation of the situation once they broke through into the Egyptian rear, and the air superiority that followed the destruction of the Egyptian air force on the ground in a surprise attack at the outset of the war. After the war, the Soviet Union rushed to make up for Egyptian and Syrian losses of equipment, and also provided military advisers. In 1968 the USA decided to provide Israel with Phantom F4 jets.[111] Soviet troops were sent to Egypt in 1970.

The quality of the arms supplied to the respective sides did play a role in the Arab-Israeli wars, sufficiently so for the conflicts to be seen as advertisements for the manufacturers. Thus, in the Arab-Israeli War of 1973 American M48 and M60 tanks supplied to the Israelis had double the rate and range of fire of the Soviet T55 and T62 tanks, ensuring that they were far better for offensive operations. In contrast Israel's American aeroplanes and tanks proved vulnerable to Soviet ground-to-air (SAM 6) and ground-to-ground missiles, although the Israelis argued that the best anti-tank weapon was another tank: Israeli tank losses were 75 per cent to other tanks and only 25 per cent to missiles, air losses 5 per cent to other aircraft, 40 per cent to conventional anti-aircraft guns and 55 per cent to missiles. During the war, the Americans rushed supplies to the Israelis by air from the USA via their air base in the Azores. The pattern of arms supplies by the superpowers in 1973 helped to ensure that neither side won or lost. In the Gulf War of 1990–1 the Iraqis relied on their Soviet tanks including 500 T-72s.

Similarly, in the Horn of Africa in the early 1970s the Soviet Union armed Somalia, the USA its opponent Ethiopia. When Soviet-armed Somalia attacked Ethiopia in 1977 with weapons including 50 MiG fighters and a squadron of Il-28 bombers, the USSR offered arms to Ethiopia if it abandoned its American alliance, which it did. By the end of 1977 Soviet surrogates – 13,000 Cuban and 4,000 South Yemeni soldiers – had arrived to help Ethiopia, the latter training the Ethiopians in the use of Soviet tanks. Deprived of Soviet help, the Somalis, who had earlier hosted a Soviet air base, communications facility and missile store, were defeated. Other African states that received Soviet military aid in the mid-1970s included Guinea, Mali, Mauritania, Nigeria and Uganda.

States that saw their rivals armed by foreign powers sought arms from the rivals of the latter and from other interested parties. After President Nasser of Egypt concluded a big arms deal with the Czechs in 1955, replacing France which had sent arms in 1954–5, Israel turned to France, which was opposed to Nasser's support for Algerian rebels, and the French armed Israel until 1967. A French–Israeli arms agreement in June 1956 encouraged Israeli bellicosity. When China briefly and successfully fought India in 1962, the USA provided the latter with arms. In Yemen the Egyptians and the Saudi Arabians armed different sides in the civil war of 1962–70. The Egyptians also sent up to 60,000 men to help the republicans, while the Jordanians sent military advisers and the Saudis money to their royalist opponents. In the 1980s the Indians were armed by the Soviet Union, their Pakistani opponents by the USA.

The provision of arms helped to consolidate military cooperation, making training and joint exercises easier. This was true both of armed forces that received American arms, such as Indonesia, and of their counterparts that were armed by the Soviets. Thus, in Eastern Europe, the forces received Soviet equipment, uniforms and training. Pakistan turned to both America and China for military assistance and in each case the source of arms helped to determine national policy.

Arms sales were seen to bring influence and this, plus the pressure to gain revenues for military-industrial complexes, encouraged large-scale sales. Such complexes were developed in states that had not hitherto been arms exporters, such as Argentina, Brazil and Israel.[112] In 1996 North Korea was reported to have provided Egypt with Scud ground-to-ground missiles, mobile launching vehicles and material necessary for the manufacture of the missiles.

Once states gained independence from the colonial powers, the latter rushed to provide military assistance. Faced with guerrilla opposition in 1964, the Congolese army received American and Belgian aid, and eventually help from Belgian paratroopers. In the Nigerian Civil War, Britain, Czechoslovakia, the Soviet Union and Spain supplied the Nigerians, France their Biafran opponents. The Nigerians obtained Iluyshin 28 bombers and MiG-17 fighters from the Soviet Union, Saladin and Saracen armoured cars from Britain, bombs, rifles, mortars, shells and grenades, as well as pilots and technicians to service the planes. An ideology of military modernisation encouraged the adoption of Western technology even by states that prided themselves on being anti-Western. Successive rises in the price of oil, in themselves evidence of Western weakness, provided resources for massive arms purchases, both in the Middle East and by states such as Indonesia and Nigeria. In Indonesia the army plays a major role in oil production. The massive rise in the price of oil in 1973 gave the Shah of Persia the means to finance a major programme of arms acquisition.

In 1972 President Nixon had agreed that the Shah could purchase whatever he wanted from America bar nuclear weapons. The Shah proceeded to do so, creating an arsenal that threatened his Arab neighbours, but did not bring domestic stability: the use of troops against rioters willing to take casualties proved ineffective in 1978–9 and the Shah fell in the latter year.

The Use of Force

Border disputes arising from the departure of colonial powers were responsible for many conflicts between regular forces and led to demand for advanced weaponry. Thus, for example, there were border clashes between Morocco and Algeria in 1963, Kenya and Somalia in 1963–7, Guyana and Venezuela, and Uganda and Tanzania in 1978, Mali and Burkina Faso (Upper Volta) in 1985, and, more seriously, between India and Pakistan in 1948–9, 1965 and 1984–5.

Such border clashes were sometimes intertwined with insurrectionary movements. Bulgarian support for the anti-Yugoslav and anti-Greek Internal Macedonian Revolutionary Organisation (IMRO) led the Greeks to send forces into southern Bulgaria in 1925. Libya intervened in Chad in the 1980s both in order to pursue a territorial claim to a northern strip of the country and in order to support protégés seeking to control the entire country. Overt Libyan military intervention in 1983 led to a military response by Zaire and France and the Libyan advance was halted. Once independent of Soviet control, Armenia and Azerbaijan went to war over the Azeri-controlled enclaves of Nagorno-Karabakh and Nakhicheven within Armenia.

As direct Western military intervention became less common in the era of decolonisation, so Western powers encouraged allies or protégés to fulfil their military goals, either by maintaining stability or by overthrowing unfriendly regimes, as with American pressure on Nicaragua in the 1980s via Central American surrogates. In 1973 the American government, through the CIA, supported the Chilean army under General Pinochet when it overthrew the Marxist Allende government. American forces were not themselves involved.

More generally, the perceived Communist threat in Latin America led to close links between the USA and Latin American military and authoritarian rulers and, from the mid-1950s, to the Americanisation of Latin American military establishments. They were restructured in accordance with American views, and many officers were trained in the USA.[113] The reconstitution of a significant Japanese navy and an even more significant German army, albeit each with specific regional responsibilities as Cold War supplements of American military might, was one of the ironies of post-1945 military history.

In addition to the use of surrogates by Western powers, non-Western powers took an active military role in their neighbours' affairs, as when Syria unsuccessfully invaded Jordan in 1970 in support of Palestinian guerrilla forces, Turkey invaded Cyprus in 1974, and India sent 100,000 troops to help Sri Lanka against Tamil insurgents in 1987. Such intervention could lead to the overthrow of governments, as with the Vietnamese conquest of Kampuchea (Cambodia) in 1978–9, and the Tanzanian overthrow of President Amin of Uganda in 1979. Vietnam, Tanzania, Iran and Turkey were examples of powers that benefited from Western weaponry and the removal of the constraints of Western control or hegemony to pursue regional territorial and political interests, often using force to that end. Thus, India sent troops into Kashmir in 1947, overran the princely state of Hyderabad in 1948, occupied the Portuguese possessions of Diu and Goa in 1961, conquered East Pakistan in 1971, creating the state of Bangladesh, annexed Sikkim in 1975, and intimidated Nepal in 1995.

The Pace of Technological Change

The technology of warfare became ever more sophisticated after the Second World War, in part as weapons and techniques developed in the latter stages of the war, such as jet aircraft, rockets, atomic bombs and the underwater recharging of submarine batteries, were refined. The Americans transferred most of the German rocket programme from Peenemünde to Huntsville, Alabama. The Cold War ensured that the process of technological change increased. Competition hastened the development and acquisition of advanced weapons such as jet fighters in the late 1940s and 1950s. Weaponry in which machinery played a major role, including, for example, complex automatic systems for sighting, ensured that skill rather than physical strength became more important for soldiering.[114] This had huge implications for the internal structure of armed forces, especially their internal systems of command and control. Such systems were not new – Arthur Pollen had developed a mechanical computer as part of the fire-control system he invented for the British navy in the 1900s[115] – but became far more common. Computers transformed operational horizons and command and control options from the 1960s. The notion that the navy mans equipment, while the army equips men, became an increasingly limited description of modern armies. The premium on skill led to greater military concern about both the quality of troops and training, and encouraged military support for a professional volunteer force rather than conscripts.

Weapons and weapons delivery systems both became more destructive and effective. For example, aeroplanes moved from free-fall to guided bombs. In the Gulf War of 1990–1 thermal-imaging laser-designation systems were employed to guide the bombs to their target. Pilots had to launch the bombs into the 'cone' of the laser beam in order to score a direct hit. However, the bombs had to be launched two or three miles from target, making them vulnerable to ground-to-air missile attack. In response, in the mid-1990s, air-launched Cruise missiles that could be deployed up to 300 miles from the target were developed: less vulnerable, but more expensive. Laser anti-missile defence systems were also tested in the 1990s.

Technology affected the condition, as well as the weaponry, of the soldiery. For example, military medicine became more effective. Helicopter evacuation of the wounded permitted more rapid surgery. Blood grouping enabled transfusions to compensate for blood loss. Antibiotics and anti-bacterial sulphonamides fought infections.[116]

The pace of technological change accelerated. Thus, for example, in submarines there were major advances in design, construction techniques, propulsion, communications, weaponry and surveillance. Weapons were able to alter the physical environment of conflicts. In Vietnam the Americans sprayed defoliation chemicals, such as Agent Orange, to deny their guerrilla opponents leaf cover. On the battlefield, infra-red viewing devices, such as those used by Syrian tanks against Israel in 1973, altered the night, while new warheads were able to pierce armour, and experiments with lasers and nerve gases threatened to change the sensory nature of combat and add new dimensions of vulnerability. Real-time, look-down, multi-sensor surveillance limited the nature of cover both on the battlefield and in guerrilla operations. The Iraqis used chemical weapons against Kurd insurgents in the 1980s and 1990s. Experiments with lightweight materials led to the reintroduction of a measure of body armour.

Enhanced weaponry affected the conduct and course of the conflicts of the 1980s and 1990s. Jump-jets that did not require large aircraft carriers were used by the British in their successful reconquest of the Falklands/Malvinas following an Argentinian invasion in 1982. The conflict was one of the rare occasions when a former imperial power was directly and openly at war with a state rather than engaged in a counter-insurgency struggle. The unexpected need to fight a war over one of the leftovers of nineteenth-century British expansion probably encouraged the British government to accommodate a rapidly militarising China over a speedy and complete exit from Hong Kong: this was carried out in 1997.

Enhanced weaponry also played a role in the Gulf War of 1990–1. Iraqi ground-to ground Scud missiles caused problems for the American-led coalition and there were fears about the possible Iraqi use of germ weapons (warheads), although in the end none was used. The Americans employed satellite surveillance, Patriot anti-missile missiles against Iraqi missiles, Cruise missiles to bombard Iraq precisely and guided bombs to the same end. The Iraqis were defeated with heavy casualties, while their opponents lost few men. The Iraqis surrendered mobility and the initiative by entrenching themselves to protect their conquest of Kuwait. Though blooded by a lengthy war with Iran, that was very different to the Gulf War: the Iranians lacked tank and, more crucially, air superiority, and the war had been mostly fought in mountainous and marshy terrain, not in the flatter desert of western Kuwait.

The Gulf War seemed to resurrect popular confidence in the impact of air power[117] following its apparent failure in Vietnam. B-2 Stealth bombers able to minimise radar detection bombed Baghdad – one of the most heavily defended cities in the world – and did so with total impunity and considerable precision, while risking far fewer air crew than the Americans had put at risk over Hanoi. However, the Stealth bombers and fighters, Tomahawk cruise and Patriot missiles and laser-guided bombs did less well than was at the time claimed. In particular, their much-praised accuracy was less manifest in combat conditions than had been anticipated, especially that of the Patriot which had a crucial role to play in the missile-to-missile war, protecting American bases in Saudi Arabia from Scud attacks. British runway-cratering bombs were less effective than had been envisaged.

This limited accuracy and effectiveness of some lavishly praised modern weapons was doubly serious because the nature of modern anti-aircraft and anti-missile weaponry depends on its accuracy: the speed and destructive capacity of the attacking weapon is far greater than in the Second World War. In addition, modern high-tech weaponry is very expensive. Tomahawk cruise missiles cost more than $1 million each. As a result, vast stores do not exist and the period in which conventional forces can sustain continual large-scale operations is very limited compared to the situation during the Second World War.

Sophisticated weaponry was expensive, in both nominal and real terms. Industrial mass-production capacity and the ability to fund it were crucial, not only to the two world wars, but also to the Cold War. Metal-bashing processes remained important, but a greater role than hitherto was played by advanced electronic engineering. The high costs of the Cold War, especially of the missile race and deployment of the 1980s, bankrupted the Soviet Union.

Finance and industrial capacity were crucial to the changing balance of naval power. Before 1914 Britain had mobilised unprecedented financial and industrial resources to fend off the challenge of the second-ranking naval power, Germany (while at the same time accepting the rise of American naval power, assuming that an Anglo-American conflict would be unlikely). After the Armistice and the surrender of the German fleet to the British, the Germans ceased to be a significant naval power, but in the early 1920s the British accepted naval parity with the Americans, the leading industrial and financial power in the world, and both powers accepted the fact of Japanese naval power in the Pacific: the 5:5:3 battleship ratio was agreed in the Washington Naval Treaty of 1922.

After 1945 the Americans dominated the world's oceans like no other naval power in history: technology gave their fleets a strength and capability that the British navy had lacked at the height of its power. From the Second World War on the British navy gradually descended to small-power status. The fleet sent to recover the Falkland Islands after they were captured by Argentina in 1982 had a makeshift quality, although it successfully supported and covered the recapture of the islands, limited disruption by Argentinian air power and, to an even greater extent, warships. In the same period, Russia, hardly a factor in the naval balance of power after its defeat by the Japanese in 1905, quickly became the world's number-two naval power after the Soviet fleet build-up began in the 1950s. By the 1980s the Chinese ranked third and the Japanese fourth among the world's navies. They could afford the cost, but also saw naval power as important in the competitive sphere of East Asian international relations. The Soviet navy, however, became increasingly obsolescent in the 1980s and 1990s as it proved impossible to sustain the cost of new units and in the 1990s it was affected by the break-up of the Soviet Union.

The greater sophistication and cost of weaponry in Western countries accentuated the long-term disparity between military and personal weaponry. This was linked to a further professionalisation of the military that led to the abandonment in most Western countries of systems of conscription and thus to a degree of alienation between general social mores and the military. The frequent movement of Israeli military commanders into politics was not matched in other Western states. On the other hand, the military was placed under greater pressure to conform to social mores. This was seen both with political pressure that the exclusion of homosexuals be abandoned, an issue that caused controversy in the USA in 1993 and in Britain in 1996, and with the spread of women into front-line units. Thus, for example, in 1996 the French air force decided to allow women to become fighter pilots; prior to that they had only been allowed to fly transport aircraft or non-combat helicopters. They were also still banned from submarines and front-line army units.

The Limitations of Technology

Cultural shifts after the Second World War and changes in arms availability made clashes between Western and non-Western states more problematic for the former. Sensitivity to losses, the abandonment of the notion that conflict was beneficial to individual character and national destiny, concern about public opinion, the greater cost of conflict and anxiety about its economic consequences all combined to place an emphasis on speedy success. This might be possible if the opponent had a state structure that could be rapidly destroyed by the effective use of force, but the situation was very different if the administrative structure of the opponent was more inchoate and its military infrastructure simpler. Furthermore, if the opponent was operating within an ideological and cultural context that made heavy losses acceptable, indeed could even idealise martyrdom, then the situation became very difficult for the 'Western' power. This had been apparent in the Second World War where the Japanese were willing to sacrifice themselves in a manner that was outside the general Western military experience. On Saipan and Iwo Jima 120 Japanese died for every one who surrendered, a ratio totally different to that of their opponents.[118]

A willingness to accept loss, indeed to welcome martyrdom, was also amply demonstrated in the 1980–8 war when Iran successfully resisted attack by Iraq with its western weaponry and military assumptions and in the Lebanon after the Israeli invasion of 1982. In September 1983 the American Sixth Fleet bombarded Druze positions in the hills near Beirut in support of the Lebanese army, firing shells the size of small cars; yet the following month neither the Americans nor the French could prevent the destruction of their headquarters in Beirut by lorries full of high explosive driven by guerrillas willing to give up their lives. As a result of their losses, and a more general sense of political impotence, the American marines sent to Lebanon in 1982 were withdrawn in 1984. Their presence had been far less successful than the earlier US marine intervention in 1958 and the difference reflected shifts in the political and military contexts of power in the region.

Despite using the military hardware of the most technologically sophisticated power in the world, the USA, the Israelis repeatedly found it difficult to deal with popular Islamic resistance movements that lacked the full range of high technology weaponry, especially air power, but were, nevertheless, able to maintain a continuous pressure, to inflict losses and to survive counterattack. The Israelis were able to eliminate the Syrian missile sites in Lebanon when they invaded in 1982, but found it harder to deal with less 'high-tech' opponents, both in Lebanon and in the Israeli-occupied Gaza strip and West Bank of the Jordan. The remarks of a Hizbullah spokesman in April 1996 are interesting: 'Do not say because we are weaker we should give in. Israel is not so strong. Look at the Vietnamese. Did they stop because America was stronger?' As if to indicate the worldwide dissemination of Western weaponry, the spokesman was guarded by a fighter carrying an American M16 assault rifle.[119]

However, this was not simply a problem for the USA and its allies, as the Soviets discovered in Afghanistan in 1979–89[120] and the Ethiopians in Eritrea and Tigre in the 1980s. The Soviets were able to overthrow the Afghan government in 1979, in part by the use of airborne troops, but, thereafter, they found it impossible to crush guerrilla resistance and finally withdrew their forces in 1989. The guerrillas benefited from ample foreign support, especially sophisticated American ground-to-air Stinger missiles, rocket launchers, mortars and radios, Chinese weaponry, Saudi money and the backing of neighbouring Pakistan. The Stingers reduced the effectiveness of Soviet helicopter gunships. Yet, foreign military assistance alone does not explain Afghan success. The bellicose nature of Afghan society and the fissiparous nature of its politics also made the country difficult to control, and the Soviets held little more than the major towns. Their use of land communications depended on convoys.

The Syrians occupied West Beirut in 1987, but had to deploy considerable force and to operate in alliance with local protégés in order to maintain control. Similarly, the Russians found it difficult to crush the attempt by the Caucasian region of Chechnya to become independent, although, given the number of Chechens they did better than is generally appreciated.[121] An invasion was launched in December 1994 and the capital, Grozny, fell in 1995, but success in crushing resistance thereafter proved elusive. The Chechen President Dzhokhar Dudayev (1944–96) represented an interesting combination of military traditions. He had risen through the Soviet air force, becoming its first Chechen general and commanding strategic nuclear bombers in Tartu, Estonia. In Afghanistan Dudayev had developed a new bombing strategy against the Mujahideen, the Afghans resisting Soviet control. Yet he had also come to be impressed by the nationalism of the Afghans and Estonians and adopted the guerrilla tactics of the former. In Chechnya he issued a decree giving every man the right to bear arms.

In Israeli attacks on the Hizbullah movement in southern Lebanon in April 1996, the very use of European and American technology, such as American Bell AH-1 Cobra helicopter gunships by the Israelis and Soviet Katyusha rockets by their opponents, indicated the degree to which modern weapons systems are employed throughout the world. The earlier use of Stinger missiles by Afghan rebels was an example of a small, technologically advanced weapon in the hands of relatively unsophisticated fighters that helped decide a war. Modern conventional weapons since 1945 have shown not only massive growth in their destructive capacity; they have also become widely available.

The role of technology can also be queried by asking how far weapons and tactics have been standardised worldwide. Westernisation can be regarded as more marginal than might be suggested by an emphasis on weaponry and its globalisation. Western-style uniforms, fighter jets and the like give a superficial impression of Western military ability, but there is a degree to which this often involves only the mimicking of the Western way of war and the adoption of Western trappings: core underlying principles remain unaffected. Thus, in Iraq in the Gulf Wars against Iran and the United Nations, the uniforms and equipment may have been Western. However, underlying and perhaps more fundamental ways of organising for and behaving in war were unaffected by Western standards of effective military behaviour. For example, the failure of Iraqi officers to stay with their troops in the field, and the command structure of the military being based more on tribal and family connections than service ability, may show the true colours of that regime's armed forces more than all the jets money can buy.

86. *Death on a Pale Horse, No. 1* by Benjamin West, c. 1787. An Italian-trained American who rose to be president of the Royal Academy in Britain, West depicted the drama, glory and terror of war. His works included *The Death of General Wolfe* (1770), *The Battle of the Boyne* (1780), *The Destruction of the French Fleet at La Hogue* (1780) and *The Death of Lord Nelson* (1806).

Nuclear Weaponry

The extent to which the Israelis have to consider the attitudes of their American patrons, and are dependent on them financially, demonstrates the global range of modern military power, and its instantaneous quality. So also does concern that Middle Eastern opponents of Israel will be armed by China, although Chinese technology remains relatively backward and supplies of the most needed or desired armaments both now and in the foreseeable future will be obtained elsewhere – from Europe and the USA. Nevertheless, the role of China underlines the extent to which European and American states no longer control the production and distribution of advanced weapons systems. This has also been indicated by the development of atomic weaponry by a number of Asian powers, especially China, India, Iraq and Pakistan, and by the advancing Chinese nuclear submarine, rocket and satellite programmes. The first atomic powers were all 'European' – the USA (1945), the Soviet Union (1949), Britain (1952), France (1960) – but in 1964 the Chinese exploded their first atomic bomb, and the Indians followed in 1974.[122] Competition between the nuclear and near-nuclear powers was also very important and encouraged the latter to acquire nuclear weaponry. The period of American nuclear monopoly was very brief, although while China lacked the bomb President Eisenhower had felt able to threaten its use in order to bring an end to the Korean War.

The Soviet Union launched the first satellite, Sputnik I, into orbit in 1957, revealing a capability for intercontinental rockets that brought the whole of the world within strike capacity. Investment in expensive rocket technology appeared an option thanks to the strategic threat posed by nuclear-tipped long-range ballistic missiles.[123] Prior to 1957, whereas the Soviet Union had been within range of American bombers based in Britain, the USA had appeared out of range of Soviet nuclear attack and the Americans had been prepared to develop the theory of massive nuclear retaliation in response to any Russian use of their larger non-nuclear forces, in Europe or elsewhere. The Berlin Crisis of 1948 led to the stationing of American B-29 strategic bombers in Britain. In 1950 Brendan Bracken, a British Conservative MP, wrote.

What a wonderful thought it is that President Truman can ring a bell and give an order that American aircraft can load their bombs and fly from London to Moscow! The interest of their visit will not be returned on Washington, it will be returned on poor old London. All this talk about giving up national sovereignty doesn't mean much when the President of the United States of America can use England as an aircraft carrier without the knowledge of the Ship's Company.[124]

There was a twofold response from 1957 to the enhanced Soviet capability. Notions of graduated nuclear retaliation through the use of 'tactical' (short-range) nuclear weapons based in Western Europe were complemented by a policy of developing an effective retaliatory second-strike capability. This entailed replacing vulnerable manned bombers by more inaccessible submarines equipped with Polaris missiles and by land rockets based in reinforced silos. The range and invulnerability of American nuclear weaponry were thus enhanced. The Americans fired their first intercontinental ballistic missile in 1958, and in 1960 followed with the first successful underwater firing of a Polaris rocket. Submarines could be based near the coast of target states. In 1965 Robert McNamara, the American Secretary of Defense, felt able to state that the USA could rely on the threat of 'assured destruction' to deter a Soviet assault. That did not prevent further attempts by the nuclear powers to enhance their nuclear attack and defence capabilities. For example, in 1970 the Americans deployed Minuteman III missiles. They were equipped with MIRVs (multiple independently targeted re-entry vehicles), thus ensuring that the strike capacity of an individual rocket was greatly enhanced. In 1977 the Americans tested a neutron bomb: an 'Enhanced Radiation Weapon'.

The capacity to destroy this planet in a few seconds, and the changing means of destruction (fission and fusion bombs) and of delivery have dramatically altered the potency of military technology. Nuclear weaponry provided a small number of powers with the capacity to inflict tremendous loss, but since 1945 none has been willing to do so. This reflects a balance of deterrence, concern about domestic and foreign opinion, and the degree to which the range of rocket-delivery systems has left no areas immune from attack. This in turn has increased tension about the military plans of often distant powers, while attention has also been focused on the deployment of rockets. Thus, in 1962 the USA came close to war with the Soviet Union when the latter began to deploy ballistic missiles in Cuba. The Americans considered an attack on Cuba, and imposed an air and naval quarantine to prevent the shipping of further supplies. The Soviet Union agreed to remove the missiles,[125] but the gap between decision, use and strike had been shown to be perilously small. Furthermore, the destructive power of nuclear weapons increased.

The atom bomb was followed by the hydrogen bomb, first exploded by the USA in 1951, and subsequently by the Soviet Union in 1953, Britain in 1957, China in 1967 and France in 1968. The hydrogen bomb employed an explosion to heat hydrogen isotopes sufficiently to fuse them into helium atoms, a transformation that released an enormous amount of destructive energy. The bombs were tested in territories gained in the age of imperialism: the views of the local population were ignored. Thus the first American H-bomb test was in the Marshall Islands in the Pacific, its Soviet, British and Chinese counterparts in Siberia, near Christmas Island and at Lop Nor in Xinjiang. The French exploded their first A-bomb in the Sahara, and, after the loss of Algeria, developed a test site in the Pacific on Muratoa atoll.

The spread of nuclear technology to Asia was initiated by the Soviet Union, which in 1957 signed an agreement with China to provide a prototype atom bomb and the technical data necessary to produce one. The Soviets, however, did not fulfil the agreement and, after the Sino-Soviet split of 1960 and the ending of Soviet technical assistance, the Chinese began an independent nuclear programme. This owed much to engineers trained in the West, especially Tsien Hsue-shen, who had played a major role in the American rocket programme in the 1940s, before losing influence when the outbreak of the Korean War led to suspicion of Chinese-Americans, and being deported in 1955. In China, Tsien was appointed Director of the Institute of Mechanics of the Chinese Academy of Science, and he developed a Chinese missile programme with other compatriots educated in the USA and Britain. Those on the bomb programme had been trained in Britain, France and the USA.

Rocket and satellite technology are especially important not only because rockets are effective long-range delivery systems, but also because satellites offer advanced command and control facilities in the shape of global communications and surveillance facilities. Improvements in command and control capabilities since 1970, such as information-display systems, owe much to developments in computer technology, not least the invention of the integrated circuit and the miniaturisation of parts, developments that are widely accessible throughout the global economy. The information deficit that non-Western societies suffered from in global terms in the nineteenth century has been considerably decreased. In any future major war it is likely that top priority will be given to destroying opponents' computer and communication capabilities, possibly by the use of electromagnetic pulses.[126] An American Defense Department panel on Information Warfare-Defence reported on 3 January 1997 that the American economy and military were very vulnerable to attacks on their information systems and that current precautions against such attacks were inadequate.

Looking Ahead

Looking ahead is always difficult. Yet some suggestions may be made. The massive global increase in population that has recently taken place will continue for at least several decades as current children age and have children of their own. This has tremendous resource implications, not least because the move of much of the world's population into urban areas increases their exposure to consumerist pressures. These pressures are also increasingly present in rural areas, not least thanks to the massive extension of access to television in countries such as India, and the role of advertising. The American-based consumerist model of society is all too exportable. Demands for goods and opportunities from predominantly young urban groups will increase the volatility of many states, particularly those that cannot ensure high growth rates, and will exacerbate problems of political management, encouraging interest in the politics of grievance and redistribution. The percentage of the world's population living in Europe and the USA will continue to fall, as will their role in global production and consumption. This is especially marked in Europe. European demographic and economic growth rates have been lower than those of the USA throughout the twentieth century and this will continue to be the case. Europe contained about a quarter of the world's population in 1900 but only 9 per cent in 1995, and by the 1990s her economy could not generate either full employment or economic growth rates to match the USA or East Asia.

At the global level, the exhaustion of oil reserves is one major problem. Another is posed by China's prosperity and declining food productivity which will cause it to become a major consumer of global foodstuffs and may make it more assertive in regional conflicts. It is unclear whether China will learn how to operate, balance and advance its interests within the international community (as powers seeking a long-term position must), or whether it will adopt the overly centralised goals and militarised means of a Genghis Khan or a Napoleon, and elicit a counter-hegemonic alliance, or even war. Furthermore, there is continuing political (and therefore military) instability in states which, relatively speaking, are only just emerging.

This situation will interact with a world in which the availability of resources, and population pressures, vary greatly.[127] Although the most sensible ways to maintain and enhance resources require international cooperation, it is likely that confrontation and conflict will arise from unilateral attempts to redistribute resources, for example water. Britain and Iceland clashed over fishing limits in the Cod War of 1972–6, and fishing has led to other outbreaks of fighting. The most obvious points of tension at the moment are the Middle East, where the distribution of land, water and oil lead to tension as with the Iraqi invasion of Kuwait in 1990, and oil-rich waters off South-East Asia. In 1996 Turkish construction of dams on the Euphrates that would provide irrigation and hydroelectric power for Turkey and deny them to Syria, led to armed confrontation between the two states.

Wherever these tensions develop, they are likely to involve the potent combination of resource demands and the politics of envy. Resulting conflicts will test military effectiveness. They may lead to a clash of conventional weaponry that is rapidly resolved: the speed, range and destructive capacity of modern weapons, especially rockets, aeroplanes and surface warships, make protracted conflicts in the air and at sea unlikely. However, it is far from clear that modern Western military systems are ready for long-term policing operations of recalcitrant populations, especially if the social infrastructure of occupied areas has been destroyed during the conflict. Technological advances, in, for example, explosives and communications, have enhanced the potential effectiveness of terrorism. In the 1980s the Israelis in Lebanon and the Indians in Sri Lanka learned the limits of effective intervention by technologically superior forces.

Nevertheless, the range of readily available modern weaponry is such that it is difficult for any state to ignore hostile developments in areas that may be several hundred miles away. American aeroplanes based in Britain bombed Libya in 1986 in response to apparent Libyan involvement in the terrorist killing of American soldiers in West Berlin. The Israelis bombed the Iraqi nuclear plant at Osirak in 1981, claiming that the Iraqis were manufacturing nuclear weapons: the Israelis used American-supplied F-16 aeroplanes. More generally, the notion of environmental and social threats also leads to military interest in distant regions, as with the American concern to prevent the production and movement of narcotic drugs in Latin America. Long-range, and even universalist, conceptions of national interests interact with the global pretensions of the United Nations and the sense that the settlement of international problems is a responsibility for neighbouring and other powers. A premium on order will encourage concern, insecurity and intervention.[128]

The twenty-first century will offer echoes of earlier military history. The major global states will be able to project their power around the globe thanks in particular to their control of sea and sky, but will find it difficult to achieve military and political objectives against recalcitrant peoples whatever disparity exists in the formal firepower capability of the two sides. There is unlikely to be a revival of interest in ruling distant territories. Innovations in military technology and in the capabilities of weapons systems will be disseminated rapidly, but their adoption will depend on institutional characteristics,[129] resources, and cultural, social and political receptivity.[130] Political rivalries within the 'developed world' and among its opponents will be as important as clashes between the former and the latter, if not more so. However, thanks to the globalisation of the economy and of information, and the role of global environmental issues, the notion of barriers against potential or real opponents, against those seen or presented as barbarians, will be increasingly suspect. To return to Gibbon: technology will not be able to provide barriers to protect 'civilisation'; for the nature of human society is now such that barriers are increasingly porous.

Notes

1 Introduction

1. Edward Gibbon, *The History of the Decline and Fall of the Roman Empire*, ed. J.B. Bury (7 vols, London, 1896–1900), IV, 166–7.
2. The role of military technology also emerges in McNeill's *The Rise of the West* (Chicago, 1963) and in his brief *The Age of Gunpowder Empires 1450–1800* (Washington, 1989).
3. J.M. Black, *A Military Revolution? Military Change and European Society 1550–1800* (Basingstoke, 1991) and *European Warfare, 1660–1815* (London, 1994), pp. 3–11; C.J. Rogers (ed.), *The Military Revolution Debate: Readings on the Military Transformation of Early Modern Europe* (Boulder, Colorado, 1995).

2 Gibbonian Strategies

1. J.E. Norton (ed.), *The Letters of Edward Gibbon* (London, 1956), III, 61. On Gibbon, see R. Porter, *Gibbon* (London, 1988) and R. McKitterick and R. Quinault (eds), *Edward Gibbon and Empire* (Cambridge, 1996).
2. Edward Gibbon, *The History of the Decline and Fall of the Roman Empire*, ed. J.B. Bury (7 vols, London, 1896–1900), IV. 165–6. For the limited battlefield impact of advances in military technology, G. Raudzens, 'Firepower Limitations in Modern Military History', *Journal of the Society for Army Historical Research*, 67 (1989), pp. 151–2.
3. McNeill, *The Pursuit of Power. Technology, Armed Force, and Society since AD 1000* (Oxford, 1983), p. 98 and 'European Expansion, Power and Warfare since 1500', in J.A. de Moor and H.L. Wesseling (eds), *Imperialism and War. Essays on Colonial Wars in Asia and Africa* (Leiden, 1989), p. 14;

E.L. Jones, *The European Miracle. Environments, Economies and Geopolitics in the History of Europe and Asia* (Cambridge, 1981), pp. 45, 123–4; J. Mokyr, *The Lever of Riches. Technological Creativity and Economic Progress* (New York, 1990), pp. 206–7; I. Wallenstein, *The Modern World-System: Capitalist Agriculture and the Origins of the European World-Economy in the Sixteenth Century* (New York, 1974).

4. Black, 'The Theory of the Balance of Power in the First Half of the Eighteenth Century: A Note on Sources', *Review of International Studies*, 9 (1983), 855–61.
5. William Robertson, *The History of the Reign of the Emperor Charles V. With a View on the Progress of Society in Europe, from the Subversion of the Roman Empire, to the Beginning of the Sixteenth Century* (London, 1769; London, 1782 edn), I. 134–5. Robertson and Gibbon are discussed in W. Nippel, 'Gibbons "philosophische Geschichte" und die schottische Aufklärung', in W. Küttler et al., *Geschichtsdiskurs* (Frankfurt am Main, 1994), II. 219–28.
6. Robertson, *Charles V*, I. 5–6.
7. T.J. Barfield, *The Perilous Frontier: Nomadic Empires and China, 221 BC to AD 1757* (Oxford, 1989); F.W. Mote, 'The T'u-mu incident of 1449', in F.A. Kierman and J.K. Fairbank (eds), *Chinese Ways in Warfare* (Cambridge, Mass., 1974), pp. 243–72. See, more generally, D.O. Morgan, 'Edward Gibbon and the East', *Iran*, 33 (1995), pp. 85–92.
8. 'Historians' is a reference to Voltaire's account of the siege of Turin in 1706.
9. M. Roberts, *The Military Revolution 1560–1660* (Belfast, 1956), reprinted in Roberts (ed.), *Essays in Swedish History* (London, 1967), pp. 195–225.
10. G. Parker, *The Military Revolution. Military Innovation and the Rise of the West, 1500–1800* (2nd edn, Cambridge, 1996),

pp. 9–12; J.F. Guilmartin, 'The Military Revolution: Origins and First Tests Abroad', in C.J. Rogers (ed), *The Military Revolution Debate. Readings on the Military Transformation of Early Modern Europe* (Boulder, 1995), pp. 307–8.

11. T.M. Barker, *Double Eagle and Crescent: Vienna's Second Turkish Siege and its Historical Setting* (Albany, New York, 1967) and 'New Perspectives on the Historical Significance of the "Year of the Turk"', *Austrian History Yearbook*, 19–20 (1983–4), pp. 3–14.

12. D. Showalter, 'Caste, Skill, and Training: The Evolution of Cohesion in European Armies from the Middle Ages to the Sixteenth Century', *Journal of Military History*, 57 (1993), pp. 407–30.

13. Black, *European Warfare 1660–1815* (London, 1994).

14. A. Fisher, *The Russian Annexation of the Crimea, 1772–83* (Cambridge, 1970) and, more generally, *The Crimean Tatars* (Stanford, 1978); B.W. Menning, 'Russian Military Innovation in the Second Half of the Eighteenth Century', *War and Society*, 2 (1984), pp. 23–41; W.C. Fuller, *Strategy and Power in Russia 1600–1914* (New York, 1992), pp. 158–66.

15. Saxe, *Rêveries* (London, 1757), p. 47; F. Gilbert, 'Machiavelli: the Renaissance of the Art of War', in E.J. Earle (ed.), *Makers of Modern Strategy* (Princeton, 1943), pp. 3–25; G.E. Rothenberg, 'Aventinus and the Defense of the Empire against the Turks', *Studies in the Renaissance*, 10 (1963), pp. 62–5.

16. D.B. Ralston, *Importing the European Army: The Introduction of European Military Techniques and Institutions into the Extra-European World, 1660–1914* (Chicago, 1990).

17. K. O'Brien, 'Between Enlightenment and Stadial History: William Robertson on the history of Europe', *British Journal for Eighteenth-Century Studies*, 16 (1993), p. 60.

18. R. Bartlett, *The Making of Europe* (London, 1994).

19. H.J. Mackinder, 'The Geographical Pivot of History', *Geographical Journal*, 23 (1904), pp. 423, 429.

20. Parker, *Military Revolution*, pp. 118–19; J. Keegan, *A History of Warfare* (London, 1993), pp. 387–92. See also McNeill, 'European Expansion, Power and Warfare since 1500', in Moor and Wesseling (eds), *Imperialism and War*, pp. 19–20.

21. L.H. Keeley, *War Before Civilization: The Myth of the Peaceful Savage* (Oxford, 1996).

22. W.J. Eccles, *The Canadian Frontier 1534–1760* (New York, 1969), p. 6; P. Malone, *Indian and English Military Systems in New England in the Seventeenth Century* (Ann Arbor, 1971), pp. 30–1; D.K. Richter, 'War and Culture: The Iroquois Experience', *William and Mary Quarterly*, 40 (1983), pp. 528–59; J. Forsyth, *A History of the Peoples of Siberia. Russia's North Asian Colony 1581–1990* (Cambridge, 1992), pp. 19, 51; A. Reid, *Europe and Southeast Asia: The Military Balance* (Townsville, Queensland, 1982), pp. 1, 5; re India, H. Macedo, 'Recognizing the Unknown: The Discoverers and the Discovered in the Age of European Overseas Expansion', *Camões Center Quarterly*, 4, nos 1 and 2 (1992), p. 13. For the ruthlessness of the French at the expense of their Italian opponents, A. Santosuosso, 'Anatomy of Defeat in Renaissance Italy: The Battle of Fornovo in 1495', *International History Review*, 16 (1994), pp. 240, 245–7.

23. N. Wachtel, *The Vision of the Vanquished. The Spanish Conquest of Peru through Indian Eyes 1530–1570* (Hassocks, 1977; translation of 1971 French original), p. 20.

3 Fifteenth- and Sixteenth-Century Expansion and Warfare

1. K. DeVries, 'Gunpowder Weapons at the Siege of Constantinople, 1453', in *War, Army and Society in the Eastern Mediterranean, 7th–16th Centuries* (Leyden, 1996). On the defeated, M.C. Bartusis, *The Late Byzantine Army: Arms and Society, 1204–1453* (Philadelphia, 1992).

2. J. Lo, 'The Decline of the Early Ming Navy', *Oriens Extremus*, 5 (1958), pp. 149–68; R. Finlay, 'The Treasure-Ships of Zheng He: Chinese Maritime Imperialism in the Age of Discovery', *Terrae Incognitae*, 23 (1991), pp. 1–12; L. Levathes, *When China Ruled the Seas. The Treasure Fleet of the Dragon Throne 1405–1433* (New York, 1995).

3. H.R. Roemer, 'The Safavid Period', in P. Jackson and L. Lockhart (eds), *The Cambridge History of Iran VI* (Cambridge, 1986), pp. 179–80; J.E. Woods, *The Aqquyunlu, Clan, Confederation, Empire: A Study in 15th/9th Century Turko-Iranian Politics* (Minneapolis, 1976), p. 122; on Baskent, ibid., pp. 132–44.

4. R. Savory, *Iran under the Safavids* (Cambridge, 1980), pp. 41–4.

5. S. Har-El, *Struggle for Domination in the Middle East: The Ottoman-Mamluk War, 1485–1491* (Leyden, 1995); D. Ayalon, *Gunpowder and Firearms in the Mamluk*

Kingdom. A Challenge to a Medieval Society (London, 1956); H. Inalcik, 'The Socio-Political Effects of the Diffusion of Fire-arms in the Middle East', in V.J. Parry and M.E. Yapp (eds), *War, Technology and Society in the Middle East* (London, 1975), pp. 195–217; A.R. Zaky, 'Gunpowder and Arab Firearms in the Middle Ages', *Gladius*, 6 (1967), pp. 57–8; S. Christensen, 'European-Ottoman Military Acculturation in the Late Middle Ages', in B.P. McGuire (ed.), *War and Peace in the Middle Ages* (Copenhagen, 1987), p. 234; C.F. Petry, *Protectors or Praetorians? The Last Mamluk Sultans and Egypt's Waning as a Great Power* (Albany, 1994); I. Clendinnen, 'The Cost of Courage in Aztec Society', *Past and Present*, no. 10/ (May 1985), pp. 60–1.

6. A.C. Hess, 'The Evolution of the Ottoman Seaborne Empire in the Age of Oceanic Discoveries, 1453–1525', *American Historical Review*, 75 (1970), pp. 1892–1919, and 'The Ottoman Conquest of Egypt and the Beginning of the Sixteenth Century World War', *International Journal of Middle East Studies*, 4 (1973), pp. 55–76; Q. Hughes and A. Migos, 'Rhodes: The Turkish Sieges', *Fort*, 21 (1993), pp. 3–17; C.M. Kortepeter, 'Ottoman imperial policy and the economy of the Black Sea region in the sixteenth century', *Journal of the American Oriental Society*, 86 (1966), pp. 86–113.

7. F.C. Lane, 'Naval Actions and Fleet Organisation, 1499–1502', in J.R. Hale (ed.), *Renaissance Venice* (London, 1973), pp. 149–54; J.H. Pryor, *Geography, Technology, and War: Studies in the Maritime History of the Mediterranean* (Cambridge, 1988), pp. 177–83.

8. P. Brummett, 'Kemal Reis and Ottoman gunpowder diplomacy', in S. Deringil and S. Kuneralp (eds), *Studies in Ottoman Diplomatic History V* (Istanbul, 1990), pp. 1–15, and *Ottoman Seapower and Levantine Diplomacy in the Age of Discovery* (Albany, New York, 1994); S. Özbaran, 'Ottoman naval policy in the south', in M. Kunt and C. Woodhead (eds), *Süleyman the Magnificent and His Age. The Ottoman Empire in the Early Modern World* (Harlow, 1996), p. 66. On Islamic trade, P. Risso, *Merchants and Faith. Muslim Commerce and Culture in the Indian Ocean* (Boulder, Colorado 1995).

9. M. Pärssinen, *Tawantinsuyu: The Inca State and its Political Organization* (Helsinki, 1982).

10. R. Hassig, *Aztec Warfare: Imperial Expansion and Political Control* (Norman, Oklahoma, 1988).

11. M. Hasan, *Babur, Founder of the Mughal Empire in India* (Delhi, 1985); D.E. Streu-sand, *The Formation of the Mughal Empire* (Delhi, 1989). On the earlier situation, J.N. Sarkar, *The Art of War in Medieval India* (New Delhi, 1984). The role of nomadic attacks is emphasised in K.N. Chaudhuri, *Asia before Europe: Economy and Civilisation of the Indian Ocean from the Rise of Islam to 1750* (Cambridge, 1991).

12. I. Prasad, *The Life and Times of Humayun* (Calcutta, 1955); Streusand, *Mughal Empire*.

13. M.E. Berry, *Hideyoshi* (Cambridge, Mass., 1982).

14. A. Waldron, *The Great Wall of China: From History to Myth* (Cambridge, 1990); D.J.B. Shaw, 'Southern Frontiers of Muscovy, 1550–1700', and I. Stebelsky, 'The Frontier in Central Asia', in J.H. Bater and R.A. French (eds), *Russian Historical Geography* (London, 1983), I, 117–73.

15. J. Hyslop, *The Inka Road System* (New York, 1984).

16. Pryor, *Geography, Technology and War*.

17. The role of the weather is emphasised in F. Fernández-Armesto's *The Spanish Armada: the experience of war in 1588* (Oxford, 1988).

18. R.C. Smith, *Vanguard of Empire: Ships of Exploration in the Age of Columbus* (Oxford, 1993); J.H. Parry, *The Age of Reconnaissance* (London, 1964), pp. 113–14; C.M.Cipolla, *Guns and Sails and Empires. Technological Innovation and the Early Phases of European Expansion, 1400–1700* (London, 1965); P. Chaunu, *L'Expansion Européenne de XVIIIe au XVe siècle* (Paris, 1969), pp. 268–88; F.C. Lane, 'The Economic Meaning of the Invention of the Compass', *American Historical Review*, 58 (1963), pp. 605–17; D.W. Waters, *The Art of Navigation in England in Elizabethan and Early Stuart Times* (London, 1958).

19. K. DeVries, 'A 1445 reference to shipboard artillery', *Technology and Culture*, 31 (1990), pp. 818–29; P. Padfield, *Guns at Sea* (London, 1975), pp. 19–29; J.F. Guilmartin, 'The Early Provision of Artillery Armament on Mediterranean War Galleys', *Mariner's Mirror*, 59 (1973), pp. 257–80; K.N. Chaudhuri, 'The Containment of Islam and the Background to European Expansion', in F. Fernández-Armesto (ed.), *The Global Opportunity* (Aldershot, 1995), p. 308.

20. Streusand, *Mughal Empire*, p. 52; R.K. Phul, *Armies of the Great Mughals* (New Delhi, 1978), pp. 271–7; Woods, *The Aqquyunlu*, pp. 131–2; Inalcik, 'Socio-Political Effects', p. 204.

21. Streusand, *Mughal Empire*, p. 53; J. Sarkar, *Military History of India* (Bombay, 1960), pp. 65–9.

22. Streusand, *Mughal Empire*, pp. 56–7.
23. Woods, *The Aqquyunlu*, p. 128 and unpublished piece 'Firearms in Iran and Central Asia'. I would like to thank him for sending me a copy. A.W. Fisher, *The Russian Annexation of the Crimea 1772–1783* (Cambridge, 1970), pp. 14–15.
24. H.G. Marcus, *A History of Ethiopia* (Berkeley, 1994), pp. 31–4; R. Pankhurst, *A Social History of Ethiopia: The Northern and Central Highlands from Early Medieval Times to the Rise of Emperor Tewodras II* (Trenton, New Jersey, 1992), pp. 16, 277–8; R.S. Whiteway (ed.), *The Portuguese Expedition to Abyssinia in 1541–1543 as related by Castanhoso and Bermudaz* (London, 1902).
25. A.R. Reid, *Southeast Asia in the Age of Commerce 1450–1680. II. Expansion and Crisis* (New Haven, Conn., 1993), pp. 146–7, 226; S. Subrahmanyam, *The Political Economy of Commerce: Southern India 1500–1650* (Cambridge, 1990), pp. 151–3.
26. V. Lieberman, 'Europeans, Trade, and the Unification of Burma, c. 1540–1620', *Oriens Extremus*, 27 (1980), pp. 208–14.
27. M.A. Lima Cruz, 'Exiles and renegades in early sixteenth-century Portuguese Asia', *Indian Economic and Social History Review*, 23 (1986), pp. 249–62; S. Subrahmanyam, 'The *Kagemusha* effect: the Portuguese, firearms and the state in early modern South Asia', *Môyen Orient et Océan Indien*, 4 (1989), pp. 97–123; G.V. Scammell, 'European exiles, renegades and outlaws and the maritime economy of Asia, c. 1500–1700', *Modern Asian Studies*, 26 (1992), pp. 641–61; C.R. Boxer, 'Asian Potentates and European Artillery in the 16th-18th Centuries', *Journal of the Malaysian Branch of the Royal Asiatic Society*, 28 (1966), pp. 156–72.
28. Parker, 'Europe and the Wider World, 1500–1750: the Military Balance', in J.D. Tracy (ed.), *The Political Economy of Merchant Empires* (Cambridge, 1991), pp. 177–8; Reid, *Southeast Asia*, II, 224–5; Pankhurst, *Ethiopia*, pp. 278–9; Inalcik, 'Socio-Political Effects', p. 209.
29. B. Stein, *The New Cambridge History of India. 1.2 Vijayanagara* (Cambridge, 1989), p. 22.
30. C.R. Boxer, *The Portuguese Seaborne Empire, 1415–1825* (London, 1969); B.W. Diffie and G.D. Winius, *Foundations of the Portuguese Empire, 1415–1580* (St Paul, 1977).
31. I.A. Khan, 'Origin and Development of Gunpowder Technology in India, AD 1250–1500', *Indian Historical Review*, 42 (1977), pp. 20–9, and 'Early Use of Cannon and Musket in India AD 1442–1526', *Journal of the Economic and Social History of the Orient*, 24 (1981), pp. 146–64.
32. Diffie and Winius, *Foundations of the Portuguese Empire*, p. 259; P.J. Marshall, 'Western Arms in Maritime Asia in the Early Phases of Expansion', *Modern Asian Studies*, 1 (1980), pp. 17–19.
33. A.M. Stevens-Arroyo, 'The Inter-Atlantic Paradigm: The Failure of Spanish Medieval Colonization of the Canary and Caribbean Islands', *Journal of Comparative Studies in Society and History*, 35 (1993), pp. 515–43; P. Powell, *Soldiers, Indians and Silver: The Northward Advance of New Spain, 1550–1600* (Berkeley, 1952); P. Gerhard, *The North Frontier of New Spain* (2nd edn, Norman, Oklahoma, 1993), pp. 5–9.
34. R.S. Chamberlain, *The Conquest and Colonization of Yucatán 1517–1550* (Washington, 1948); Gerhard, *The Southeast Frontier of New Spain* (Princeton, 1979); G.D. Jones, 'The Last Maya Frontiers of Colonial Yucatán', in M.J. MacLeod and R. Wassertrom (eds), *Spaniards and Indians in Southeastern Mesoamerica: Essays on the History of Ethnic Relations* (Lincoln, Nebraska, 1983), pp. 64–91.
35. L. de Armond, 'Frontier Warfare in Colonial Chile', *Pacific Historical Review*, 23 (1954), pp. 125–32; R.C. Padden, 'Cultural Change and Military Resistance in Araucanian Chile, 1550–1730', *Southwestern Journal of Anthropology* (1957), pp. 103–21.
36. I.K. Steele, *Warpaths. Invasions of North America* (New York, 1994), pp. 7–13, 33.
37. J. Thornton, *Africa and Africans in the Making of the Atlantic World, 1400–1680* (Cambridge, 1992), pp. 40–1.
38. P. Boucher, *Cannibal Encounters. Europeans and Island Caribs, 1492–1763* (Baltimore, 1993).
39. J. Hemming, *Red Gold: The Conquest of the Brazilian Indians, 1500–1760* (2nd edn, London, 1995), pp. 72–3, 78–9, 90–3.
40. *Ibid.*, pp. 70, 74–6, 89.
41. *Ibid.*, pp. 94–6.
42. L.A. Newson, *Aboriginal and Spanish Colonial Trinidad: A Study in Culture Contact* (London, 1976); F. Moya Pons, 'The Tainos of Hispaniola', *Caribbean Review*, 13 (1984), p. 47; N.D. Cook, *Demographic Collapse: Indian Peru, 1520–1620* (Cambridge, 1981).

43. A. Crosby, *The Columbian Exchange: Bio-logical and Cultural Consequences of 1492* (Westport, Conn., 1969) and *Ecological Imperialism: The Biological Expansion of Europe, 1500–1900* (London, 1986); J.D. Daniels, 'The Indian Population of North America in 1492', *William and Mary Quarterly*, 49 (1992), pp. 298–320.

44. K.S. Mathew, *Portuguese Trade with India in the Sixteenth Century* (New Delhi, 1983).

45. Ayalon, *Gunpowder and Firearms*, p. 113; J.F. Guilmartin, *Gunpowder and Galleys: Changing Technology and Mediterranean Warfare at Sea in the Sixteenth Century* (Cambridge, 1974).

46. Inalcik, 'Socio-Political Effects', pp. 203, 205; Özbaran, 'The Ottoman Turks and the Portuguese in the Persian Gulf, 1534–1581', *Journal of Asian History*, 6 (1972), pp. 45–87.

47. Reid, 'Sixteenth-century Turkish influence in western Indonesia', *Journal of South-East Asian History*, 10 (1969), pp. 395–414; Cipolla, *Guns and Sails in the Early Phase of European Expansion*, pp. 102–3; Pankhurst, *Ethiopia*, pp. 278–9.

48. Reid, *Southeast Asia*, II, 212.

49. T. Abeyasinghe, *Portuguese Rule in Ceylon, 1594–1612* (Colombo, 1966).

50. C. Wessels, *Histoire de la Mission d'Am-boine, 1546–1601* (Louvain, 1934), pp. 85–95; M.A.P. Meilink-Roelofsz, *Asian Trade and European Influence in the Indone-sian Archipelago between 1500 and about 1630* (The Hague, 1962).

51. Stein, *Vijayanagara*, pp. 55, 114–15; Pankhurst, *Ethiopia*, p. 279.

52. J. Vogt, *Portuguese Rule on the Gold Coast, 1469–1682* (Athens, Georgia, 1979).

53. I. Clendinnen, *Aztecs: An Interpretation* (Cambridge, 1991), pp. 111–28, 267–73; H. Thomas, *The Conquest of Mexico* (London, 1993); Hassig, *Aztec Warfare, Mexico and the Spanish Conquest* (Harlow, 1994) and 'War, Politics, and the Conquest of Mexico', in J. Black (ed.), *War and Warfare 1450–1815* (London, 1998). For an Aztec view, M. Leon-Portilla (ed.), *The Broken Spears: The Aztec Account of the Conquest of Mexico* (Boston, 1966). N. Wachtel, *The Vision of the Vanquished. The Spanish Conquest of Peru through Indian Eyes, 1530–1570* (Hassocks, 1977) is more wide-ranging than the title suggests and includes discussion of the Aztecs and Mayas. Aztec warfare is also discussed in Clendinnen, 'The Cost of Courage in Aztec Society', pp. 56–64. On weaponry,

A. Bruhn de Hoffmeyer, 'Las armas de los conquistadores. Las armas de los Aztecas', *Gladius*, 17 (1986), pp. 5–56. For a recent view of the literature that concludes against a technological explanation, G. Raudzens, 'So Why Were the Aztecs Conquered, and What Were the Wider Implications? Testing Military Superiority as a Cause of Europe's Pre-industrial Colonial Con-quests', *War in History*, 2 (1995), pp. 87–104, esp. pp. 102–3.

54. P. Bakewell, *A History of Latin America* (Oxford, 1997), p. 98; C. Hudson et al., 'The Tristán de Luna Expedition, 1559–1561', in J.T. Milanich and S. Milbrath (eds), *First Encounters: Spanish Explorations in the Caribbean and the United States, 1492–1570* (Gainesville, Florida, 1989), pp. 119–34.

55. J.L. Phelan, *The Hispanization of the Philip-pines: Spanish aims and Filipino responses, 1565–1700* (Madison, Wis., 1967).

56. J. Pelenki, *Russia and Kazan: Conquest and Imperial Ideology, 1438–1560s* (The Hague, 1974), pp. 48–9; V.A. Zolotarev (ed.), *Voennaia istoriia otechestva s drevnikh vremen do nashikh dnei. Tom pervyi, glavy 1–13* (Moscow, 1995), pp. 149–52.

57. H. Inalcik, 'The Origin of the Ottoman-Russian Rivalry and the Don-Volga Canal (1569)', *Annales de l'Université d'Ankara*, 1 (1947), pp. 47–110; C. Lemercier-Quelquejay, 'Co-optation of the elites of Kabarda and Daghestan in the sixteenth century', in M.B. Broxup (ed.), *The North Caucasus Barrier. The Russian Advance towards the Muslim World* (London, 1992), pp. 22–3, 39–40.

58. T. Tamrat, *Church and State in Ethiopia 1270–1527* (Oxford, 1972), pp. 297–8.

59. M. Alam, *The Crisis of Empire in Mughal North India. Awadh and the Punjab 1707–1748* (Delhi, 1986), pp. 5–6, 15, 50.

60. Stein, *Vijayanagara*, pp. 71, 110.

61. W.F. Cook, 'The Cannon Conquest of Nāsrid Spain and the End of the Recon-quista', *Journal of Military History*, 57 (1993), pp. 69–70; A.D. McJoynt (ed.), *The Art of War in Spain: The Conquest of Granada* (Mechanicsburg, Penn., 1995).

62. Hess, *The Forgotten Frontier. A History of the Sixteenth-Century Ibero-African Frontier* (Chicago, 1978).

63. Cook, 'Cannon Conquest', pp. 43–70, esp. pp. 50–1, 70.

64. J.F. Powers, *A Society Organized for War* (Berkeley, 1988); Hess, 'The Moriscos: An Ottoman Fifth Column in Sixteenth-

Century Spain', *American Historical Review*, 74 (1968), pp. 1–25.

65. J. Vogt, 'Saint Barbara's Legions: Portuguese Artillery in the Struggle for Morocco', *Military Affairs*, 41 (Dec. 1977), pp. 176–82.

66. S. Soucek, 'The rise of the Barbarossas in North Africa', *Archivium Ottomanicum*, 3 (1971), pp. 238–50; Hess, 'The Battle of Lepanto and its Place in Mediterranean History', *Past and Present*, no. 57 (1972), pp. 53–73. See more generally, J.R. Hale, 'Men and Weapons: the Fighting Potential of Sixteenth-Century Venetian Galleys', in B. Bond and I. Roy (eds), *War and Society* (London, 1975), pp. 1–23.

67. Guilmartin, *Gunpowder and Galleys*, p. 18; Hess, 'Ottoman Seaborne Discoveries', p. 1910.

68. W.E.D. Allen, *Problems of Turkish Power in the Sixteenth Century* (London, 1963); S. Pepper, 'Fifteenth-Century Ottoman Military Architecture: A Reassessment'. I would like to thank Professor Pepper for lending me a copy of this unpublished paper.

69. Cook, 'Warfare and Firearms in Fifteenth Century Morocco, 1400–1492', *War and Society*, 11 (1993), p. 31.

70. E.W. Bovil, *The Battle of Alcazar* (London, 1952); Cook, *The Hundred Years War for Morocco. Gunpowder and the Military Revolution in the Early Modern Muslim World* (Boulder, 1994).

71. M. Newitt, 'Prince Henry and the Origins of Portuguese Expansion', in Newitt (ed.), *The First Portuguese Colonial Empire* (Exeter, 1986), p. 29.

72. A.W. Lawrence, *Trade Castles and Forts of West Africa* (London, 1963).

73. Woods, *The Aqquyunlu*, p. 175; S. Digby, *War Horse and Elephant in the Delhi Sultanate* (Oxford, 1971), pp. 23–82; Phul, *Armies*, pp. 64–6.

74. H.J. Fisher, 'The central Sahara and Sudan', in R. Gray (ed.), *The Cambridge History of Africa IV* (Cambridge, 1975), p. 71. See also G. White, 'Firearms in Africa: An Introduction', and H.J. Fisher and V. Rowland, 'Firearms in the Central Sudan', *Journal of African History*, 12 (1971), pp. 173–84, 215–39; Pankhurst, *Ethiopia*, p. 16.

75. Thornton, 'The Art of War in Angola, 1575–1680', *Comparative Studies in Society and History*, 30 (1988), pp. 360–78.

76. A. Waldron, 'Chinese Strategy from the Fourteenth to the Seventeenth Centuries', in W. Murray, M. Knox and A. Bernstein (eds), *The Making of Strategy. Rulers, States, and War* (Cambridge, 1994), pp. 109, 113.

77. D.M. Brown, 'The Impact of Firearms on Japanese Warfare, 1543–98', *Far Eastern Quarterly*, 7 (1948), pp. 236–53; J.L. Boots, 'Korean weapons and armour', *Transactions of the Korean Branch of the Royal Asiatic Society*, 23, no. 2 (1934), p. 25.

78. J. Needham, *Military Technology: The Gunpowder Epic* (Cambridge, 1987), Needham, 'The Epic of Gunpowder and Firearms, Developing from Alchemy' in his *Science in Traditional China* (Cambridge, Mass., 1981), pp. 27–56, and *Gunpowder as the Fourth Power, East and West* (Hong Kong, 1985); L.C. Goodrich and F. Chia-Sheng, 'The Early Development of Firearms in China', *Isis*, 36 (1946), pp. 114–23.

79. Reid, *Southeast Asia in the Age of Commerce*, II, 219–23.

80. Needham, *Military Technology*, pp. 444, 465.

81. F.W. Mote and D. Twitchett (eds), *The Cambridge History of China. VII. The Ming Dynasty, 1368–1644, Part 1* (Cambridge, 1988), p. 478; Barfield, *The Perilous Frontier: Nomadic Empires and China* (Oxford, 1989), pp. 249–50.

82. A. Chan, *The Glory and Fall of the Ming Dynasty* (Norman, 1982), pp. 51–63.

83. L.Y. Andaya, 'Interactions with the Outside World and Adaptation in Southeast Asian Society, 1500–1800', in N. Tarling (ed.), *The Cambridge History of South-East Asia* (2 vols, Cambridge, 1992), 380–95; Reid, *Southeast Asia*, II, 223–9.

84. Reid, *Europe and Southeast Asia: The Military Balance* (Townsville, Queensland, 1982), and *Southeast Asia*, II, 87–90; M.C. Ricklefs, *A History of Modern Indonesia since c. 1300* (2nd edn, Basingstoke, 1993), p. 24.

85. J.F. Richards, *The Mughal Empire* (Cambridge, 1993), p. 288.

86. Streusand, *Mughal Empire*, pp. 57–63.

87. *Ibid.*, pp. 63–5.

88. Reid, *Southeast Asia*, II, 229–30.

89. J. Lo, 'The Decline of the Early Ming Navy', *Oriens Extremus*, 5 (1958), pp. 151–2.

90. K. So, *Japanese Piracy in Ming China during the Sixteenth Century* (East Lansing, 1975).

91. A.L. Sadler, 'The Naval Campaign in the Korean War of Hideyoshi (1592–8)', *Transactions of the Asiatic Society of Japan*, 2nd ser., 14 (1937), pp. 177–208.

92. Mote and Twitchett (eds), *Cambridge History of China. VII*, p. 573.

93. Hess, 'Ottoman Seaborne Empire', p. 1918.

94. Parker, 'David or Goliath? Philip II and his world in the 1580s', in R.L. Kagan and

Parker (eds), *Spain, Europe and the Atlantic World. Essays in Honour of John H. Elliott* (Cambridge, 1995), pp. 247–8, 254–6; Boxer, 'Portuguese and Spanish Projects for the Conquest of Southeast Asia, 1580–1600', in Boxer, *Portuguese Conquest and Commerce in Southern Asia, 1500–1750* (London, 1985), pp. 118–36.

95. P.Y. Manguin, 'The Vanishing *Jong*: Insular Southeast Asian Fleets in Trade and War', in Reid (ed.), *Southeast Asia in the Early Modern Era* (Ithaca, 1993), pp. 197–213; Reid, *Southeast Asia*, p. 233.

96. C. Tilly, *Coercion, Capital, and European States, AD 990–1990* (Oxford, 1990), p. 65.

97. M.A. Vale, *War and Chivalry: Warfare and Aristocratic Culture in England, France and Burgundy at the End of the Middle Ages* (London, 1981), pp. 129–46; P. Contamine, *War in the Middle Ages* (Oxford, 1984), pp. 249–50; K. DeVries, *Medieval Military Technology* (Peterborough, Ontario, 1992), pp. 143–68, 'The Impact of Gunpowder Weaponry on Siege Warfare in the Hundred Years War', in I.A. Corfis and M. Wolfe (eds), *The Medieval City under Siege* (Woodbridge, 1995), pp. 227–44, and 'The Use of Gunpowder Weaponry by and against Joan of Arc during the Hundred Years War', *War and Society*, 14 (1996), pp. 1–15; M. Mallett, 'Siegecraft in Late Fifteenth-Century Italy', and B.S. Hall, 'The Changing Face of Siege Warfare: Technology and Tactics in Transition', in Corfis and Wolfe (eds), *Medieval City*, pp. 245–55, 256–76; D. Braid, 'Ordnance and Freedom of Thought: the Development of Gunmaking in Bohemia, 1350–1450', *Journal of the Ordnance Society*, 5 (1993), pp. 75–93; B.S. Hall, *Weapons and Warfare in Renaissance Europe* (Baltimore, 1997); M. Mallett, 'The Art of War', in T.A. Brady, H.A. Oberman and J.D. Tracy (eds), *Handbook of European History 1400–1600. Late Middle Ages, Renaissance and Reformation. I. Structures and Assertions* (Leiden, 1994), pp. 535–6.

98. C.J. Rogers (ed.), *The Military Revolution Debate. Readings on the Military Transformation of Early Modern Europe* (Boulder, 1995) should be read, but it does not include contributions from the most severe critics of the thesis. For these, see J. Plowright, 'Revolution or Evolution?', *British Army Review*, 90 (1988), pp. 41–3 and B.S. Hall and K. DeVries, 'The Military Revolution Revisited', *Technology and Culture*, 31 (1990), pp. 500–7. Parker has

robustly replied to the latter, *Military Revolution*, pp. 157, 236–7. More generally, his defence of his thesis (*ibid.*, pp. 155–75, 235–45) is of great importance and reflects his wide-ranging scholarship.

99. Mallett, 'Art of War', p. 544; S. Pepper, 'Castles and cannon in the Naples campaign of 1494–95', in D. Abulafia (ed.), *The French Descent into Renaissance Italy 1494–95. Antecedents and Effects* (Aldershot, 1995), pp. 264, 290; Mallett and Hale, *The Military Organization of a Renaissance State: Venice, c. 1400–1617* (Cambridge, 1984), pp. 81–7.

100. J. Bennett and S. Johnston, *The Geometry of War 1500–1750*, catalogue of exhibition at Museum of the History of Science, Oxford, 1996; A.W. Crosby, *The Measure of Reality. Quantification and Western Society, 1250–1600* (Cambridge, 1997).

101. For the argument that China had already been passed, L. White, *Medieval Religion and Technology. Collected Essays* (Berkeley, 1978), pp. 218–19, and for a recent discussion of European developments and their causes, K. David's 'Technological Change in Early Modern Europe, 1500–1780', *Journal of the Japan-Netherlands Institute*, 3 (1991), pp. 32–44. The issue is of more general interest as it prints the papers of the first conference on the transfer of science and technology between Europe and Asia since Vasco da Gama. This conference, held in Amsterdam and Leiden in 1991, heard some important papers. Ekmeleddin Ihsanoğlu's contribution on Ottoman science and its relation with European science and technology up to 1800 filled a major gap. For the argument that South Asia contained regions with proto-industrialisation comparable to that in Europe, F. Perlin, 'Proto-industrialization and Precolonial South Asia', *Past and Present*, 98 (1983), pp. 30–95, and for persisting strength, Dharampal, *Indian Science and Technology in the Eighteenth Century* (Delhi, 1971).

102. N. Housley, *The Later Crusades, 1274–1580: From Lyons to Alcazar* (Oxford, 1992).

4 The Seventeenth Century

1. D. Sinor, 'The Concept of Inner Asia', in Sinor (ed.), *The Cambridge History of Early Inner Asia* (Cambridge, 1990), p. 3; T.J. Barfield, *The Perilous Frontier: Nomadic Empires and China* (Oxford, 1989); S.

Jagchild and V.J. Symons, *Peace, War, and Trade along the Great Wall: Nomadic-Chinese Interaction through Two Millennia* (Bloomington, Indiana, 1989).

2. B.I. Watson, 'Fortification and the "Idea" of Force in Early English East India Company Relations with India', *Past and Present*, no. 88 (Aug. 1980), pp. 70–87.

3. A. Deshpande, 'Limitations of Military Technology: Naval Warfare on the West Coast, 1650–1800', *Economic and Political Weekly*, 27 (1992), pp. 900–4; C.R. Boxer, *Portuguese Conquest and Commerce in Southern Asia, 1500–1750* (London, 1985), chapter 4; D. Lombard, *Le Sultanat d'Atjéh au temps d'Iskandar Muda, 1607–1636* (Paris, 1967); Ricklefs, *Indonesia*, pp. 43, 45.

4. J.R. Jones, *The Anglo-Dutch Wars of the Seventeenth Century* (Harlow, 1996), pp. 38–42; P. Earle, *Corsairs of Malta and Barbary* (London, 1970), pp. 30, 49–52; J. Glete, *Navies and Nations. Warships, Navies and State Building in Europe and America, 1500–1860* (Stockholm, 1993), p. 122; Parker, 'The *Dreadnought* Revolution of Tudor England' and N.A.M. Rodger, 'The Development of Broadside Gunnery, 1450–1650', *Mariner's Mirror*, 82 (1996), pp. 269–300, 301–24.

5. J.A. Harrison, *Japan's Northern Frontier* (Gainesville, 1953), pp. 7, 10.

6. L. Blussé, 'The Dutch occupation of the Pescadores (1622–1624)', *Transactions of the International Conference of Orientalists in Japan*, 18 (1973), pp. 28–43.

7. E. van Veen, 'How the Dutch Ran a Seventeenth-Century Colony. The Occupation and Loss of Formosa 1624–1662', *Itinerario*, 20 (1996), pp. 59–77.

8. G.D. Winius, *The Fatal History of Portuguese Ceylon: Transition to Dutch Rule* (Cambridge, Mass., 1971).

9. J.I. Israel, *Dutch Primacy in World Trade, 1585–1740* (Oxford, 1989); G.V. Scammell, *The World Encompassed* (London, 1981); K. Glamann, *Dutch-Asiatic Trade, 1620–1740* (2nd edn, The Hague, 1981).

10. R.D. Bathurst, 'Maritime Trade and Imamate Government: two principal themes in the history of Oman to 1728', in D. Hopwood (ed.), *The Arabian Peninsula. Society and Politics* (London, 1972), pp. 99–100, 102–3.

11. C.R. Boxer and C. de Azevedo, *Fort Jesus and the Portuguese in Mombasa 1593–1729* (London, 1960), pp. 59–73, 81–3; J. Kirkman, *Fort Jesus* (Oxford, 1974), pp. 4–5.

12. R. Gray, 'Portuguese musketeers on the Zambezi', *Journal of African History*, 12 (1972), pp. 531–3; M. Newitt, *Portuguese Settlement on the Zambezi* (London, 1973), pp. 1–73.

13. J. Thornton, 'The Art of War in Angola, 1575–1680', *Comparative Studies in Society and History*, 30 (1988), pp. 360–78, and *The Kingdom of Kongo: Civil War and Transition, 1641–1718* (Madison, Wisconsin, 1983).

14. R. Buckley, 'Colonial Military History: A Research Note', *Itinerario*, 5 (1981), pp. 68–77; L.Y. Andaya, *The Heritage of Arung Palakka. A History of South Sulawesi (Celebes) in the Seventeenth Century* (The Hague, 1981), pp. 76–8, 130–3; A. Reid, *Europe and Southeast Asia: The Military Balance*. Occasional Paper, no. 16 (Townsville, Queensland, 1982), p. 8.

15. Ricklefs, *Indonesia*, pp. 62–3; Stein, *Vijayanagara*, p. 125.

16. S. Arasaratnam, *Dutch Power in Ceylon 1658–87* (Amsterdam, 1958); Ricklefs, *Indonesia*, pp. 76–7.

17. E. Winius, 'Portugal's "Shadowy Empire in the Bay of Bengal"', *Camões Center Quarterly*, 3, nos 1 and 2 (1991), pp. 40–1; S. Arasaratnam, *Maritime India in the Seventeenth Century* (New York, 1994); Ricklefs, *Indonesia*, p. 24.

18. G.A. Lantzeff and R.A. Pierce, *Eastward to Empire. Exploration and Conquest on the Russian Open Frontier, to 1750* (Montréal, 1973); T. Armstrong, *Yermak's Campaign in Siberia* (London, 1975); I. Stebelsky, 'The Frontier in Central Asia', in J.A. Bates and R.A. French (eds), *Russian Historical Geography* I (London, 1983), pp. 145–7; Forsyth, *History of the Peoples of Siberia*, pp. 26–83. I am grateful to James Forsyth for his advice on dates.

19. M. Bassin, 'Expansion and colonialism on the eastern frontier: views of Siberia and the Far East in pre-Petrine Russia', *Journal of Historical Geography*, 14 (1988), pp. 3–8.

20. Lantzeff and Pierce, *Eastward to Empire*, p. 175 give an estimate of between 2,000 and 10,000 Manchus against 350 Russians, while N.I. Nikitin, *Sibirskaia Epopeia XVII Weka* (Moscow, 1987), gives 5,000 against 800.

21. M. Mancall, *Russia and China: their diplomatic relations to 1728* (Cambridge, Mass., 1971), pp. 146–62; M.A. Courant, *L'Asie centrale aux XVIIe et XVIIIe siècles: Empire kalmouk ou empire mantchou?* (Lyons, 1912); Barfield, *Perilous Frontier*, pp. 275–87.

22. A. Wood (ed.), *The History of Siberia, From Russian Conquest to Revolution* (London, 1991), pp. 5, 74.

23. R. Law, ' "Here is No Resisting the Country". The Realities of Power in Afro-European Relations on the West African "Slave Coast" ', *Itinerario*, 18 (1994), pp. 51–2; A.H. Schroeder, 'Shifting for Survival in the Spanish Southwest', *New Mexico Historical Review*, 43 (1968), pp. 291–310. On native American divisions, see also L.V. Eid, 'The Ojibwa-Iroquois War: The War the Five Nations Did Not Win', *Ethnohistory*, 26 (1979), pp. 297–324.

24. P.M. Malone, 'Changing military technology among the Indians of southern New England 1600–77', *American Quarterly*, 25 (1973), pp. 48–63, and *The Skulking Way of War. Technology and Tactics among the Indians of New England* (London, 1991); M.L. Brown, *Firearms in Colonial America: The Impact on History and Technology 1492–1792* (Washington, 1980); B. Given, 'The Iroquois and Native Firearms', in B.A. Cox (ed.), *Native Peoples, Native Lands. Canadian Indians, Inuit and Metis* (Ottawa, 1987), pp. 3–13; T.B. Abler, 'European Technology and the Art of War in Iroquoia', in D.C. Tkaczuk and B.C. Vivian (eds), *Cultures in Conflict: Current Archeological Perspectives* (Calgary, 1989), pp. 273–82; D. Delage, *Bitter Feast: Amerindians and Europeans in Northeastern North America, 1600–64* (Vancouver, 1993). On the French in 1682, W.J. Eccles, *Frontenac: The Courtier Governor* (Toronto, 1959), pp. 157–72.

25. G. Raudzens, 'Why Did Amerindian Defences Fail? Parallels in the European Invasions of Hispaniola, Virginia and Beyond', *War in History*, 3 (1996), p. 352; Sinor, 'Concept of Inner Asia', p. 3.

26. W.H. McNeill, *Europe's Steppe Frontier, 1500–1800* (Chicago, 1964), pp. 199–200, 214; M. Raeff, 'The Style of Russia's Imperial Policy and Prince G.A. Potemkin', in G.N. Grob (ed.), *Statesmen and Statecraft of the Modern West* (Barre, Mass., 1967), p. 37.

27. J. Axtell, *Beyond 1492: Encounters in Colonial North America* (New York, 1992), p. 239; F. Jennings, *The Ambiguous Iroquois Empire* (New York, 1984). On the demographic question, more generally, D.K. Richter, *The Ordeal of the Longhouse: The Peoples of the Iroquois League in the Era of European Colonization* (Chapel Hill, N.C., 1992). On the European impact, more generally, see B.G. Trigger and W.E. Washburn (eds), *The Cambridge History of the Native Peoples of the Americas. North America* (Cambridge, 1996).

28. H.E. Selesky, 'Colonial America', in M. Howard, G. Andreopoulos and M.R. Shulman (eds), *The Laws of War: Constraints on Warfare in the Western World* (New Haven, 1994), p. 66.

29. Hemming, *Red Gold*, passim., eg. for 1690s–1700s, pp. 365–79; E. de Vattel, *The Laws of Nations: or the Principles of the Law of Nature, Applied to the Conduct and Affairs of Sovereigns* (English edn, Philadelphia, 1861, of French 1758 original), p. 361. I owe this reference to Armstrong Starkey.

30. L.V. Eid, ' "A Kind of Running Fight": Indian Battlefield Tactics in the Late Eighteenth Century', *Western Pennsylvania Historical Magazine*, 71 (1988), p. 171; A. Hirsch, 'The Collision of Military Cultures in Seventeenth-Century New England', *Journal of American History*, 74 (1987–8), pp. 1187–212.

31. T.V. Mahalingam, *Readings in South Indian History* (Delhi, 1977), p. 154.

32. R. Huang, 'The Lung-ch'ing and Wan-li reigns, 1567–1620', in Mote and Twitchett (eds.), *History of China* VII, pp. 582–3, 602; Barfield, *Perilous Frontier*, pp. 251–7.

33. F. Wakeman, *The Great Enterprise. The Manchu Reconstruction of Imperial Order in Seventeenth-Century China* (2 vols, Berkeley, 1985), I, 178; Barfield, *Perilous Frontier*, pp. 258–65.

34. On Schall, J. Waley-Cohen, 'China and Western Technology in the Late Eighteenth Century', *American Historical Review*, 98 (1993), pp. 1531–2; J.A. Gross, 'Approaches to the Problem of Identity Formation', in Gross (ed.), *Muslims in Central Asia. Expressions of Identity and Change* (Durham, North Carolina, 1992), p. 17.

35. L.A. Struve, *The Southern Ming 1644–1662* (New Haven, 1984).

36. Wakeman, *Great Enterprise*, II, 1047.

37. C.R. Boxer, 'The Siege of Fort Zeelandia and the capture of Formosa from the Dutch, 1661–2', *Transactions and Proceedings of the Japan Society of London*, 24 (1926–7), pp. 16–47.

38. Needham, *Military Technology; The Gunpowder Epic*, pp. 393–8; Waley-Cohen, 'China and Western Technology', p. 1531.

39. L.D. Kessler, *K'ang-hsi and the Consolidation of Ch'ing Rule, 1661–1684* (Chicago, 1976).

40. Needham, *Military Technology*, pp. 392–3.

41. An excellent recent discussion of the trajectory of Safavid military development is offered by R. Matthee, 'Unwalled Cities and Restless Nomads: Firearms and Artillery in Safavid Iran', *Pembroke Papers*, 4(1996), pp. 389–416.

42. J.F. Richards, *The Mughal Empire* (Cambridge, 1993). p. 139. On artillery, W. Irvine, *The Army of the Indian Moghuls: its Organisation and Administration* (Delhi, 1962), pp. 113–59. See also, J. Sarkar, *The Military Despatches of a Seventeenth Century Indian General* (Calcutta, 1969).

43. D.A. Parrott, 'Strategy and Tactics in the Thirty Years' War: The "Military Revolution"', in C.J. Rogers (ed.), *The Military Revolution Debate: Readings on the Military Transformation of Early Modern Europe* (Boulder, 1995), pp. 239, 245–6.

44. P.D. Lockhart, *Denmark in the Thirty Years' War, 1618–1648* (Cranbury, New Jersey, 1996), p. 148.

45. R. Murphey, 'The Ottoman Resurgence in the Seventeenth-Century Mediterranean: the Gamble and its Results', *Mediterranean Historical Review*, 8 (1993), pp. 198–200. See, more generally, K.M. Seton, *Venice, Austria and the Turks in the Seventeenth Century* (Philadelphia, 1991).

46. Lockhart, *Denmark*, pp. 65–6.

47. J. Israel, 'Olivares, the Cardinal-Infante and Spain's Strategy in the Low Countries (1635–1643): the Road to Rocroi', in Kagan and Parker (eds), *Spain, Europe and the Atlantic World*, p. 280.

48. C. Oman, *The Art of War in the Sixteenth Century* (London, 1937), pp. 678–81; J.F. Guilmartin, 'The Military Revolution: Origins and First Tests Abroad', in Rogers (ed.), *Military Revolution Debate*, p. 308.

49. G.E. Rothenberg, 'Christian Insurrections in Turkish Dalmatia 1580–96', *Slavonic and East European Review*, 40 (1961), p. 141.

50. C. Finkel, *The Administration of Warfare: Ottoman Campaigns in Hungary, 1593–1606* (Vienna, 1988), and 'The Costs of Ottoman Warfare and Defence', *Byzantinische Forschungen*, 16 (1990), p. 96.

51. H. Inalcik, 'The Socio-Political Effects of the Diffusion of Firearms in the Middle East', in V.J. Parry and M.E. Yapp (ed.), *War, Technology and Society in the Middle East* (London, 1975), pp. 199–200.

52. A. Arkayin, 'The Second Siege of Vienna (1683) and its consequences', *Revue Internationale d'Histoire Militaire*, 46 (1980), pp. 114–15.

53. J. Stoye, *Marsigli's Europe, 1680–1730. The Life and Times of Luigi Ferdinando Marsigli, Soldier and Virtuoso* (New Haven, 1994), pp. 37–8.

54. R. Hellie, 'The Petrine Army: Continuity, Change, and Impact', *Canadian-American Slavic Studies*, 8 (1974), pp. 239–40.

55. *Ibid.*, p. 242.

56. G. Agoston, 'Ottoman Artillery and European Military Technology in the fifteenth to seventeenth centuries, *Acta Orientalia Academiae Scientiarum Hung.* 47 (1994), pp. 46–78.

57. G.E. Rothenberg, 'Venice and the Uskoks of Senj: 1537–1618', *Journal of Modern History*, 33 (1961), pp. 155–6.

58. R.A. Stradling, *The Spanish Monarchy and Irish Mercenaries: the Wild Geese in Spain 1618–68* (Dublin, 1994); Parker, 'The World beyond Whitehall: British Historiography and European Archives', in R.M. Smuts (ed.), *The Stuart Court and Europe* (Cambridge, 1996), pp. 280–1.

59. Hellie, 'The Petrine Army', pp. 238, 241–3.

60. British Library (hereafter BL.) Stowe Manuscripts, 447 f.1.

61. M.E. Mallett and J.R. Hale, *The Military Organization of a Renaissance State: Venice, c. 1400–1617* (Cambridge, 1984), pp. 71–4; Mallett, 'Venice and the War of Ferrara, 1482–84' in D.S. Chambers, C.H. Clough and Mallett (eds), *War, Culture and Society in Renaissance Venice* (London, 1993), p. 66; A. Santosuosso, 'Anatomy of Defeat in Renaissance Italy: The Battle of Fornovo in 1495', *International History Review*, 16 (1994), pp. 226, 242–3.

62. I have benefited from reading an unpublished paper by Brett Steele, 'Early Modern Science and Military Culture: the European and Ottoman Reactions'. I would like to thank him for providing me with a copy.

63. There is only limited literature on the Uzbeks. I would like to thank David Morgan for providing me with a copy of 'Western Turkestan: The Emergence of the Uzbeks', an unpublished essay by the late Joseph Fletcher that covers the early period of Uzbek history.

64. Mahalingam, *South Indian History*, p. 155.

5 The Pre-Revolutionary Eighteenth Century

1. C.A. Bayly, 'India and West Asia, c. 1700–1830', *Asian Affairs*, 19 (1988), pp. 3–19.

2. A. Deshpande, 'Limited of Military Tech-

nology. Naval Warfare on the West Coast, 1650–1800', *Economic and Political Weekly* (Bombay), 25 Apr. 1992, pp. 902–3; L. Lockhart, 'Nadir Shah's Campaigns in Oman, 1734–1744', *Bulletin of the School of Oriental and African Studies*, 8 (1935–7), pp. 157–73.

3. B.J. Gupta, *Sirajuddaullah and the East India Company, 1756–1757: Background to the Foundation of British Power in India* (Leiden, 1966), pp. 116–26.

4. O. Subtelny, 'Russia and the Ukraine: the Difference that Peter I Made', *Russian Review*, 39 (1980), pp. 10–11.

5. B.H. Sumner, *Peter the Great and the Ottoman Empire* (Oxford, 1949), pp. 39–42; L.R. Lewitter, 'Jean-Nicole Moreau de Brasey's letter on the Moldavian campaign of Peter I', *Jahrbücher Geschichte Osteuropas*, 40 (1992) pp. 517–29; E.V. Anisimov, *The Reforms of Peter the Great: Progress through Coercion in Russia* (Moscow, 1993), pp. 127–34.

6. A contemporary account of the conflict is provided by C.H. von Manstein, *Contemporary Memoirs of Russia from the Year 1727 to 1744*, ed. D. Hume (London, 1856).

7. W.C. Fuller, *Strategy and Power in Russia 1600–1914* (New York, 1992), p. 158.

8. A. Balisch, 'Infantry Battlefield Tactics in the Seventeenth and Eighteenth Centuries on the European and Turkish Theatres of War: the Austrian Response to Different Conditions', *Studies in History and Politics*, 3 (1983–4), p. 51.

9. I. Parver, *Habsburgs and Ottomans between Vienna and Belgrade 1683–1739* (Boulder, Colorado, 1995).

10. R.W. Olson, *The Siege of Mosul and Otoman-Persian Relations 1718–1743. A Study of Rebellion in the Capital and War in the Provinces of the Ottoman Empire* (Bloomington, Indiana 1975). For an important study of the Ottoman failure to adopt scientific military culture, B.D. Steele, 'Early Modern Science and Military Culture: the European and Ottoman Reactions', unpublished paper.

11. J. Keep, 'Feeding the Troops. Russian Army Supply Policies during the Seven Years War', *Canadian Slavonic Papers*, 29 (1987), pp. 24–44.

12. Fuller, *Strategy and Power*, p. 165.

13. For a more critical view, V. Aksan, 'The One-eyed Fighting the Blind: Mobilization, Supply, and Command in the Russo-Turkish War of 1768–1774', *International History Review*, 15 (1993), pp. 221–38.

14. Forsyth, *History of the Peoples of Siberia*, pp. 135–6, 138–40, 144–50.

15. Olson, *Mosul*, p. 45; Anisimov, *Reforms of Peter the Great*, pp. 255–61.

16. A.S. Donnelly, *The Russian Conquest of Bashkiria, 1552–1740* (New Haven, Conn. 1968); M. Khodarkovsky, 'Uneasy Alliance: Peter the Great and Ayuki Khan', *Central Asian Survey*, 7, no. 4 (1988), pp. 25–7, and *Where Two Worlds Met: the Russian State and the Kalmyk Nomads 1600–1771* (Ithaca, New York, 1992); Stebelsky, 'Frontier in Central Asia', pp. 149–51.

17. M.C. Ricklefs, *War, Culture and Economy in Java, 1677–1726* (The Hague, 1990), and *Indonesia*, pp. 85–97.

18. George Monson to Charles Townshend, Secretary at War, 30 Oct. 1762, Public Record Office (hereafter PRO), War Office, 1/319, p. 392.

19. N. Tracy, *Manila Ransomed. The British Assault on Manila in the Seven Years War* (Exeter, 1995).

20. Francis to Jeremy Browne, 26 Oct. 1762, BL. RP. 3284.

21. Call to Colonel Draper, 15 July 1760, BL. India Office Collections (hereafter IO.), H/Misc/96, pp. 28–9, 31.

22. *Bengal and Madras Papers. III, 1757–85* (Calcutta, 1928), 1760 section, p. 29.

23. J. Gommans, *The Rise of the Indo-Afghan Empire c. 1710–1780* (Leiden, 1995), p. 178.

24. For praise of Indian cannon in 1764, private journal of Colonel Alexander Champion, 23 Oct. 1764, IO. H/Misc./198, p. 112, and journal of Captain Harper, IO. Mss. Eur. Orme OV 219, pp. 40–1, 44, and of Mysore cannon fire in 1790, Major Skelly, narrative, BL. Add. 9872 f. 21.

25. J. Gommans, 'Indian Warfare and Afghan Innovation during the Eighteenth Century', *Studies in History*, 11 (1995), pp. 271–3; T.S. Shejwalkar, *Panipat: 1761* (Poona, 1946); H.R. Gupta (ed.), *Marathas and Panipat* (Chandigarh, 1961). For lack of Maratha coordination, pp. 182, 191, 193, 248.

26. G.J. Bryant, 'The Military Imperative in Early British Expansion in India, 1750–1785', *Indo-British Review* 21, 2 (1996), p. 32; J. Gommans, 'The Horse Trade in Eighteenth-Century South Asia', *Journal of the Economic and Social History of the Orient*, 37 (1994), pp. 247, 250.

27. L.Y. Andaya, 'Interactions with the outside world and adaptation in southeast Asian society, 1500–1800', in N. Tarling (ed.), *The Cambridge History of Southeast Asia* (2

28. W.J. Koening, *The Burmese Polity, 1752–1819* (Ann Arbor, Michigan, 1990), pp. 22–5.

29. L. Petech, *China and Tibet in the Early Eighteenth Century. History of the establishment of the Chinese protectorate in Tibet* (Leiden, 1950).

30. T.J. Barfield, *The Perilous Frontier: Nomadic Empires and China* (Oxford, 1989), pp. 290–4.

31. Gommans, *Indo-Afghan Empire*, p. 31.

32. J. Waley-Cohen, 'China and Western Technology in the Later Eighteenth Century', *American Historical Review*, 98 (1993), pp. 1537–9.

33. J.A. Harrison, *Japan's Northern Frontier* (Gainesville, 1953), p. 17.

34. J.R. Perry, *Karim Khand Zand. A History of Iran, 1747–1779* (Chicago, 1979).

35. Gommans, *Rise of the Indo-Afghan Empire, c. 1710–1780.*

36. Gommans, 'Indian Warfare', pp. 274–7.

37. J.F. Searing, *West African Slavery and Atlantic Commerce. The Senegal River Valley, 1700–1860* (Cambridge, 1993), p. 21; R.A. Kea, 'Firearms and Warfare on the Gold and Slave Coasts from the Sixteenth to the Nineteenth Centuries', *Journal of African History*, 12 (1971), pp. 185–213, and *Settlements, Trade, and Politics in the Seventeenth-Century Gold Coast* (Baltimore, 1982), pp. 130–64; R.S. Smith, *Warfare and Diplomacy in Pre-Colonial West Africa* (London, 1976, 2nd edn, London, 1989); J.E. Inikori, 'The Import of Firearms into West Africa', *Journal of African History*, 18 (1977), pp. 339–68; W. Richards, 'The Import of Firearms into West Africa in the Eighteenth Century', *Journal of African History*, 21 (1980), pp. 43–59.

38. Thornton, 'Art of War in Angola', p. 366.

39. R. Law, 'Warfare on the West African Slave Coast, 1650–1850', in R.B. Ferguson and N.L. Whitehead (eds), *War in the Tribal Zone: Expanding States and Indigenous Warfare* (Santa Fé, 1992), pp. 103–26, and ' "Here is No Resisting the Country". The Realities of Power in Afro-European Relations on the West African "Slave Coast" ', *Itinerario*, 18 (1994), pp. 55–6. I have benefited from the advice of Robin Law.

40. Pankhurst, *Ethiopia*, pp. 81, 280–3.

41. H.J. Fisher, 'The Central Sahara and Sudan', in R. Gray (ed.), *The Cambridge History of Africa IV* (Cambridge, 1975), p. 73; J.P. Smaldone, *Warfare in the Sokoto Caliphate* (Cambridge, 1977); Law, *The Oyo Empire c. 1600–c.1836: a West African Imperialism in the Era of Atlantic Slave Trade* (Oxford, 1977), *The Horse in West African History: the role of the horse in the societies of pre-colonial West Africa* (London, 1980), and 'The Horse in Pre-Colonial West Africa', in G. Pezzoli (ed.), *Cavalieri dell' Africa* (Milan, 1995), pp. 175–84; R.L. Roberts, *Warriors, Merchants, and Slaves: the State and the Economy in the Middle Niger Valley, 1700–1914* (Stanford, 1987); S.P. Reyna, *Wars Without End: The Political Economy of a Precolonial African State* (Hanover, New Hampshire, 1990).

42. L. Campbell, 'Recent Research on Andean Peasant Revolts, 1750–1820', *Latin American Research Review*, 14 (1979), pp. 3–50; A. McFarlane, 'Rebellions in Late Colonial Spanish America: a Comparative Perspective', *Bulletin of Latin American Research*, 14 (1995), p. 313.

43. D. Cahill, 'Taxonomy of a colonial "riot": the Arequipa disturbances of 1780', in J.R. Fisher, A.J. Kuethe and A. McFarlane (eds), *Reform and Insurrection in Bourbon New Granada and Peru* (Baton Rouge, 1990), p. 276; S.J. Stern, 'The Age of Andean Insurrection, 1742–1782', in Stern (ed.), *Resistance, Rebellion and Consciousness in the Andean Peasant World. 18th to 20th Centuries* (Madison, Wisconsin), p. 35; O. Cornblit, *Power and Violence in a Colonial City: Oruro from the Mining Renaissance to the Rebellion of Túpac Amaru, 1740–1782* (Cambridge, 1995).

44. Hemming, *Red Gold*, pp. 489–90.

45. A.J. Kuethe, 'The pacification campaign on the Riohacha frontier, 1772–1779', *Hispanic American Historical Review*, 50 (1970), pp. 467–81.

46. D. Sweet, 'Native resistance in eighteenth-century Amazonia: the "Abominable Muras" in War and Peace', *Radical History Review*, 53 (1992), pp. 49–80.

47. P.E. Hoffman, *The Spanish Crown and Defense of the Caribbean, 1535–1585* (Baton Rouge, 1980); P. Pierson, 'The Development of Spanish Naval Strategy and Tactics in the Sixteenth Century', in M.R. Thorp and A.J. Slavin (eds), *Politics, Religion, and Diplomacy in Early Modern Europe* (Kirksville, Missouri, 1994), p. 214.

48. On English garrisons in the Caribbean, S.S. Webb, *The Governors-General: the English Army and the Definition of the Empire, 1569–1681* (Chapel Hill, N.C. 1979).

49. Steele, *Warpaths*, pp. 34–5.

50. C.I. Archer, *The Army in Bourbon Mexico 1760–1810* (Albuquerque, 1977); J.R.

Booker, 'Needed but unwanted: Black militiamen in Veracruz, Mexico, 1760–1810', *Historian*, 55 (1993), p. 259.

51. R.J. Singh, *French Diplomacy in the Caribbean and the American Revolution* (Hicksville, New York, 1977), p. 122.

52. K. Maxwell, *Pombal. Paradox of the Enlightenment* (Cambridge, 1995), p. 120.

53. F. Anderson, *A People's Army. Massachusetts Soldiers and Society in the Seven Years' War* (Chapel Hill, N.C. 1984).

54. R.D. Edmunds and J.L. Peyser, *The Fox Wars. The Mesquakie Challenge to New France* (Norman, Oklahoma, 1993), pp. 142–3, 147.

55. D.W. Marshall, 'The British Military Engineers 1741–1783: a Study of Organization, Social Origin, and Cartography' (PhD, Michigan, 1976), pp. 21–2, 25.

56. W.A. Hunter, *Forts on the Pennsylvania Frontier 1753–1758* (Harrisburg, 1960).

57. D.J. Weber, *The Spanish Frontier in North America* (New Haven, Conn. 1992), pp. 166, 213–14, 220–4, 258, 247; W.A. Beck and Y.D. Haase, *Historical Atlas of the American West* (Norman, Oklahoma, 1989), pp. 17–18; A.B. Thomas, *The Plains Indians and New Mexico, 1751–1778* (Albuquerque, 1940); T.H. Naylor and C.W. Pilzer, *Pedro de Rivera and the Military Regulations for Northern New Spain, 1724–1729* (Tuscon, 1988); W.B. Griffen, *The Apaches at War and Peace: the Janos Presidio, 1750–1858* (Albuquerque, 1988).

58. Edmunds and Peyser, *Fox Wars*; L.P. Kellogg, *The French Régime in Wisconsin and the Northwest* (Madison, 1925); L.H. Gipson, *Zones of International Friction: North America, South of the Great Lakes Region, 1748–1754* (New York, 1939); G.F.G. Stanley, *New France: The Last Phase, 1744–1760* (Toronto, 1968); W.J. Eccles, *The Canadian Frontier, 1534–1760* (2nd edn., Albuquerque, 1983); R. White, *The Middle Ground: Indians, Empires, and Republics in the Great Lakes Region, 1650–1815* (Cambridge, 1991), pp. 199–232; M.N. McConnell, *A Country Between: The Upper Ohio Valley and its Peoples, 1724–1774* (Lincoln, Nebraska 1992), pp. 61–120; C.J. Balesi, *The Time of the French in the Heart of North America, 1673–1818* (Chicago, 1991).

59. H.H. Peckham, *Pontiac and the Indian Uprising* (Princeton, 1947); Eccles, *France in America* (2nd edn, East Lansing, Michigan, 1990), p. 48; McConnell, *Country Between*, pp. 147–81; C. Calloway, *The Western Abenakis of Vermont, 1600–1800*

(Norman, Oklahoma, 1990).

60. H.W. Crosby, *Antigua California. Mission and Colony on the Peninsular Frontier, 1697–1768* (Albuquerque, 1994), pp. 29–33, 39.

61. *Ibid.*, p. 37.

62. A. Wood (ed.), *The History of Siberia* (London, 1991), p. 38.

63. B.B. Misra, *The Central Administration of the East India Company, 1773–1834* (Manchester, 1959), p. 32.

64. Trevor to Onslow Burrish, 5 May 1744, PRO. SP. 110/6.

65. J. Glete, 'The European Navies 1688 to 1713', in 'IVes Journées franco-britanniques d'histoire de la marine', *Guerres maritimes 1688–1713* (Vincennes, 1996), p. 300.

66. G.D. Inglis, 'The Spanish Naval Shipyard at Havana in the Eighteenth Century', in *New Aspects of Naval History. Selected Papers from the 5th Naval History Symposium* (Baltimore, 1985), pp. 48, 56.

67. Mann, 8 Mar. 1779. W. Cobbett, *Parliamentary History of England from . . . 1066 to . . . 1803* (36 vols, London, 1806–20), 20, 224.

6 An Age of Revolution and Imperial Reach, 1775–1815

1. P. Bertaud, *Valmy, la Démocratie en Armes* (Paris, 1970); E. Hublot, *Valmy ou la Défense de la Nation par les Armes* (Paris, 1987); J. Lynn, 'Valmy', *Military History Quarterly*, 51 (1992), pp. 88–97; T.C.W. Blanning, *The French Revolutionary Wars 1787–1802* (London, 1996), pp. 75–80.

2. Cornwallis to Henry Dundas, President of the Board of Control, 15 Oct. 1792, 25 Jan., 24 Mar. 1793, PRO. 30/11/151 fols 138, 148–9, 156; K.C. Chaudhuri, *Anglo-Nepalese Relations from the Earliest Times of the British Rule in India till the Gurkha War* (Calcutta, 1960), pp. 63–9.

3. A. Peyrefitte, *The Collision of Two Civilisations: the British expedition to China, 1792–4* (London, 1993); G. Staunton, *An Authentic Account of an Embassy from the King of Great Britain to the Emperor of China* (3 vols, London, 1797), III, 140–1.

4. Cornwallis to Medows, 28 Dec. 1790, PRO. 30/11/173 f. 38.

5. President and Council at Fort St George to Court of Directors, 31 July 1760, BL. IO. H/Misc/96 p. 61; Josias Du Pré to Robert Orme, 10 June 1769, BL. IO. Mss Eur.

Orme OV 30, pp. 125–8; John Shore to Cornwallis, 4 Oct. 1787, PRO. 30/11/122 f. 33–4.

6. F. Wickwire and M. Wickwire, *Cornwallis. The Imperial Years* (Chapel Hill, N.C. 1980), pp. 117–73.

7. Recent accounts of the struggle are offered by J.M. Black, *War for America. The Fight for American Independence 1775–1783* (Stroud, 1991) and S. Conway, *The War of American Independence 1775–1783* (London, 1995).

8. W.M. Fowler, *Rebels under Sail* (New York, 1976).

9. Skinner to General Lord Amherst, 4 May 1779, PRO. WO. 34/114 f. 104.

10. Burgoyne to Earl of Shelburne, 1 Nov. 1782, Bowood, Shelburne Papers vol. 37. I would like to thank the Earl of Shelburne for permission to consult these papers.

11. N. York, 'Pennsylvania Rifle: a Revolutionary Weapon in a Conventional War?', *Pennsylvania Magazine of History and Biography*, 103 (1979), pp. 302–24.

12. J.M. Hill, 'The Distinctiveness of Gaelic Warfare, 1400–1750', *European History Quarterly*, 22 (1992), pp. 323–45, is valuable, but underrates the continued threat posed by the tactical offensive.

13. See, most recently, D. Showalter, *The Wars of Frederick the Great* (Harlow, 1996).

14. Black, *Culloden and the '45* (Stroud, 1990).

15. F. McLynn, *France and the Jacobite Rising of 1745* (Edinburgh, 1981).

16. J.S. Gibson, *Playing the Scottish Card. The Franco-Jacobite Invasion of 1708* (Edinburgh, 1988).

17. D. Baugh, 'Why did Britain lose command of the sea during the war for America?', in J.M. Black and P. Woodfine (eds), *The British Navy and the Use of Naval Power in the Eighteenth Century* (Leicester, 1988), pp. 161–3.

18. P. Mackesy, *Could the British have won the War of Independence?* (Worcester, Mass., 1976), pp. 23–4.

19. *Ibid.*, p. 28.

20. C.L.R. James, *The Black Jacobins: Toussaint L'Ouverture and the San Domingo Revolution* (London, 1980); D.P. Geggus, 'The Haitian Revolution', in F.W. Knight and C.A. Palmer (eds), *The Modern Caribbean* (Chapel Hill, N.C. 1989), pp. 21–50; L.D. Langley, *The Americas in the Age of Revolution* (New Haven, 1996), pp. 102–35. R.N. Buckley, *Slaves in Red Coats: The British West India Regiments, 1795–1815* (New Haven, Conn. 1979), p. 104.

21. G.A. Smith, 'Storm over the Gulf: America's Destiny Becoming Manifest', in *The Consortium on Revolutionary Europe: Selected Papers, 1994* (Tallahassee, 1994), pp. 510–16; S. Clissold, *Bernardo O'Higgins and the Independence of Chile* (1968); J. Lynch, *The Spanish American Revolutions 1808–1826* (2nd edn, London, 1973); T. Anna, *The Fall of the Royal Government in Mexico City* (Lincoln, Nebraska, 1978).

22. A.C. Bayly, 'The British Military-Fiscal State and Indigenous Resistance. India 1750–1820', in L. Stone (ed.), *An Imperial State at War. Britain from 1689 to 1815* (London, 1994), pp. 324–49.

23. R. Bonney, *Kedah 1771–1821* (Oxford, 1971), p. 100.

24. N. Tarling (ed.), *Cambridge History of Southeast Asia*, p. 580.

25. Fife to William Rose, 7 May 1790, Aberdeen, University Library 2226/131/817; Loughborough to Pitt, 9 Dec. 1792, PRO. 30/8/153 f. 71. B.E. Kennedy, 'Anglo-French Rivalry in India and in the Eastern Seas, 1763–93: A study of Anglo-French tensions and of their impact on the consolidation of British power in the region. (PhD, Australian National University) p. 183.

26. *Archives Parlementaires de 1787 à 1860: Recueil complet des débats législatifs et politiques des chambres françaises* (127 vols, Paris, 1879–1913), XV, 528.

27. R.C. Stuart, *United States Expansionism and British North America, 1775–1871* (Chapel Hill, N.C. 1988), p. 5.

28. W.E. Washburn, 'The Moral and Legal Justifications for Dispossessing the Indians', in J.M. Smith (ed.), *Seventeenth Century America: Essays in Colonial History* (Chapel Hill, N.C. 1959), pp. 24–32; A. Frost, 'New South Wales as *terra nullius*: the British denial of Aboriginal land rights', *Historical Studies*, 19 (1981), pp. 513–23.

29. C. de La Jonquière, *L'Expédition d'Egypte, 1798–1801* I (Paris, 1900); F.-P. Renaut, *La Question de la Louisiane, 1796–1806* (Paris, 1918); G. Blainey, *The Tyranny of Distance* (Melbourne, 1966), pp. 70–98; I. Murat, *Napoléon et le rêve américain* (Paris, 1976); M.E. Yapp, *Strategies of British India: Britain, Iran and Afghanistan 1798–1850* (Oxford, 1980); E. Ingram, *Commitment to Empire: Prophecies of the Great Game in Asia, 1797–1800* (Oxford, 1981); P. Mackesy, *War without Victory. The Downfall of Pitt, 1799–1802* (Oxford, 1984), esp. pp. 144–7; S. Förster, *Die mächtigen Diener der East India Company. Ursachen und Hintergründe der britischen*

Expansions-politik in Südasien, 1793–1819 (Stuttgart, 1992).

30. P.J. Marshall, '"Cornwallis Triumphat": War in India and the British Public in the Late Eighteenth Century', in L. Freedman, P. Hayes and R. O'Neill (eds), *War, Strategy and International Politics* (Oxford, 1990), pp. 60–74.

31. G. Williams, *The Expansion of Europe in the Eighteenth Century: Overseas Rivalry, Discovery and Exploitation* (London, 1966); S. Chapin, 'Scientific Profit from the Profit Motive: the Case of the La Perouse Expedition', *Actes du XII* Congrès International d'Histoire des Sciences* XI (Paris, 1971), pp. 45–9, and 'The Men from across La Manche: French Voyages, 1660–1790', in D. Howse (ed.), *Background to Discovery. Pacific Exploration from Dampier to Cook* (Berkeley, 1990), p. 113; C. Gaziello, *L'Expédition de La Pérouse 1785–1788* (Paris, 1984).

32. J.C. Beaglehole, *The Exploration of the Pacific* (3rd edn, London, 1960), pp. 318–22, and *The Discovery of New Zealand* (2nd edn, Oxford, 1961), pp. 72–3.

33. M.E. Thurman, *The Naval Department of San Blas: New Spain's Bastion for Alta California and Nootka 1767 to 1798* (Glendale, California, 1967); W.L. Cook, *Flood Tide of Empire: Spain and the Pacific Northwest, 1543–1819* (New Haven, Conn., 1973); S. Saavedra et al., *To the Totem Shore: The Spanish Presence on the Northwest Coast* (Madrid, 1986).

34. R.A. Pierce, *Russia's Hawaiian Adventure, 1815–1817* (Berkeley, 1965); J.R. Gibson, *Feeding the Russian Fur Trade: Provisionment of the Okhotsk Seaboard and the Kamchatka Peninsula, 1639–1856* (Madison, Wisc. 1969); G. Barratt, *Russia in Pacific Waters, 1715–1825* (Vancouver, 1981), and *Russia and the South Pacific, 1696–1840* (Vancouver, 1988–90); A.V. Postnikov, *The Mapping of Russian America* (Milwaukee, 1995).

35. C. Totman, *Early Modern Japan* (Berkeley, 1993), pp. 482–93.

36. Forsyth, *A History of the Peoples of Siberia*, pp. 151–2.

37. J. Glete, *Navies and Nations. Warships, Navies and State Building in Europe and America, 1500–1860* (Stockholm, 1993), p. 276.

38. J. Habron, *Trafalgar and the Spanish Navy* (Annapolis, 1988).

39. J.S. Bromley (ed.), *The Manning of the Royal Navy. Selected Public Pamphlets 1693–1873* (London, 1974), p. 71.

40. J.R. Elting, *Amateurs, to Arms! A Military History of the War of 1812* (Chapel Hill, N.C. 1991).

41. R.J.B. Knight, 'The Introduction of Copper Sheathing into the Royal Navy, 1779–1786', *Mariner's Mirror*, 59 (1973), pp. 299–309.

42. P. Webb, 'The Frigate Situation of the Royal Navy 1793–1815', *Mariner's Mirror*, 80 (1996), p. 38.

43. M. Duffy, *Soldiers, Sugar and Seapower. The British Expeditions to the West Indies and the War against Revolutionary France* (Oxford, 1987).

44. J. Hemming, *Amazon Frontier. The Defeat of the Brazilian Indians* (2nd edn, London, 1995).

45. J. Herold, *Napoleon in Egypt* (London, 1961); M. Barthorp, *Napoleon's Egyptian Campaigns, 1798–1799* (London, 1978); R.L. Tignor (ed.), *Napoleon in Egypt. Al-Jabarti's Chronicle of the French Occupation, 1798* (Princeton, 1993).

46. R.B. Barnett, *North India Between Empires. Awadh, the Mughals, and the British 1720–1801* (Berkeley, 1980), p. 229.

47. On value of speedy attack, J. Weller, *Wellington in India* (London, 1972), p. 192. On Fallen Timbers, P.D. Nelson, 'Anthony Wayne's Indian War in the Old Northwest, 1792–1795', *Northwest Ohio Quarterly*, 56 (1984), p. 131, and 'General Charles Scott, the Kentucky Mounted Volunteers, and the Northwest Indian Wars, 1784–1794', *Journal of the Early Republic*, 6 (1986), p. 248. More generally on the war, W. Sword, *President Washington's Indian War: the Struggle for the Old Northwest, 1790–1795* (Norman, Oklahoma, 1985).

48. J. Pemble, 'Resources and Techniques in the Second Maratha War', *Historical Journal*, 19 (1976), pp. 375–404; R.G.S. Cooper, 'Wellington and the Marathas in 1803', *International History Review*, 11 (1989), pp. 36–8.

49. Weller, *Wellington*, pp. 275–6; G.J. Bryant, 'The Cavalry Problem in the Early British Indian Army, 1750–1785', *War in History* 2 (1995), pp. 20–1.

50. Cornwallis to Dundas, 4 Apr. 1790, PRO. 30/11/151 f. 40.

51. P. Carey (ed.), *The British in Java, 1811–1816: a Javanese Account* (Oxford, 1992).

52. G.F. Jewsbury, *The Russian Annexation of Bessarabia: 1774–1828. A Study of Imperial Expansion* (Boulder, 1976), and 'Chaos and Corruption: the Comte de Langeron's Critique of the 1787–1792

Russo-Turkish War', *Studies in History and Politics*, 3 (1983–4), pp. 73–83; A. Balisch, 'Infantry Battlefield Tactics in the Seventeenth and Eighteenth Centuries on the European and Turkish Theatres of War: the Austrian Response to Different Conditions', *Studies in History and Politics*, 3 (1983–4), pp. 53–60.

53. Lang, *Georgian Monarchy*, pp. 182–5, 203–6; Atkin, *Russia and Iran*, pp. 29–30, 37.

54. N.E. Saul, *Russia and the Mediterranean, 1797–1807* (Chicago, 1970).

55. A.W. Fisher, *The Russian Annexation of the Crimea 1772–1783* (Cambridge, 1970), pp. 86–8, 117, 126.

56. S. Shaw, 'The Origins of Ottoman Military Reform: The Nizam-i Cedid Army of Sultan Selim III', *Journal of Modern History* 37 (1965), pp. 291–5.

57. M. Jansen (ed.), *Warrior Rule in Japan* (Cambridge, 1995).

58. B.P. Lenman, 'The Weapons of War in Eighteenth-Century India', *Journal of the Society for Army Historical Research*, 46 (1968), pp. 33–43; S. Bidwell, *Swords for Hire: European Mercenaries in Eighteenth Century India* (London, 1971); Gordon, *Marathas*, p. 168; M. Turlotte, 'La Mission Militaire Française auprès des Nababs du Mysore à La fin de l'ancien régime', *Revue Historiques des Armées*, No. 190 (March 1993), pp. 4–5; G. Bodinier, 'Les officiers français en Inde dc 1750 à 1793', in P. Decraene (ed.), *Trois Siècles de presence française en Inde* (Paris, 1994).

59. J. Pemble, *The Invasion of Nepal. John Company at War* (Oxford, 1971), pp. 26–8; P. Barua, 'Military Developments in India, 1750–1850', *Journal of Military History*, 58 (1994), pp. 610–11.

60. R. Fisher, 'Arms and men on the north-west coast, 1774–1825', *British Columbia Studies* (London, 1976), pp. 3–18; J.B. Townsend, 'Firearms against native arms: a study in comparative efficiencies with an Alaskan example', *Arctic Anthropology*, 20 (1983), pp. 1–33; J.R. Gibson, *Otter Skins, Boston Ships, and China Goods: the Maritime Fur Trade of the Northwest Coast, 1785–1841* (Montréal, 1992), pp. 220–4; T.L. Connelly, 'Indian Warfare on the Tennessee Frontier, 1776–1794: Strategy and Tactics', *East Tennessee Historical Society's Publications*, 36 (1964), pp. 3–22; L.V. Eid, 'The Cardinal Principle of Northeast Woodland Indian War', in W. Cowan (ed.), *Papers of the Thirteenth Algonquian Conference* (Ottawa, 1982), pp. 243–50, and '"A Kind of Running Fight": Indian Battlefield Tactics

in the Late Eighteenth Century', *Western Pennsylvania Historical Magazine*, 71 (1988), pp. 147–71; G.E. Dowd, *A Spirited Resistance: The North American Struggle for Indian Unity 1745–1815* (Baltimore, 1992); C.G. Calloway, *The American Revolution in Indian Country: Crisis and Diversity in Native American Communities* (Cambridge, 1995).

61. A.W. Crosby, *Ecological Imperialism. The Biological Expansion of Europe, 900–1900* (Cambridge, 1986), pp. 236–7.

62. P. Pluchon, *Histoire de la Colonisation Française. I. Le Premier Empire Colonial* (Paris, 1991), pp. 760–4.

63. Smaldone, *Warfare in the Sokoto Caliphate*, pp. 26–37.

64. A. Kahn, *The Plow, the Hammer, and the Knout. An Economic History of Eighteenth-Century Russia* (Chicago, 1985), pp. 7–8.

65. PRO. WO. 34/84 f. 44, 34/126 f. 86–7; R.N. Buckley (ed.), *The Napoleonic War Journal of Captain Thomas Henry Browne 1807–1816* (London, 1987), p. 87.

66. E. Karppinen (ed.), *The War of King Gustavus III and the Naval Battles of Ruotsinsalmi* (Kotka, 1993).

67. S.T. Ross, 'The Development of the Combat Division in Eighteenth-Century French Armies', *French Historical Studies*, 1 (1965), pp. 84–94.

68. R. Quimby, *Background of Napoleonic Warfare: the Theory of Military Tactics in Eighteenth-Century France* (New York, 1957); J. Chagniot, *le Chevalier de Folard* (Paris, 1997).

69. S.F. Scott, *The Response of the Royal Army to the French Revolution. The Role and Development of the Line Army 1787–1794* (Oxford, 1978).

70. Wellington to Lord Stewart, later 3rd Marquis of Londonderry, 8 May 1815, BL. Loan 105 ff. 9–10.

71. F. Winter. *The First Golden Age of Rockets: Congreve and Hale Rockets of the Nineteenth Century* (Washington, 1991).

72. A. Roland, *Underwater Warfare in the Age of Sail* (Bloomington, Indiana 1978).

73. J. Lynn, 'Towards an army of honor: the moral evolution of the French army 1789–1815', *French Historical Studies*, 16 (1989), p. 177; G. Rothenberg, *The Art of Warfare in the Age of Napoleon* (Bloomington, Indiana, 1978), pp. 122–3; J.R. Elting, *Swords around a Throne: Napoleon's Grande Armée* (New York, 1988), p. 263.

74. R.K. Showman (ed.), *The Papers of General Nathanael Greene II* (Chapel Hill, N.C. 1980) 135.

75. Saul, 'The Impact of the Napoleonic War

upon Russian Priorities on Naval Development', in W.B. Cogar (ed.), *New Interpretations in Naval History* (Annapolis, 1989), p. 55.

76. P. Paret, *Yorck and the Era of Prussian Reform* (Princeton, 1966); C. White, *The Enlightened Soldier: Scharnhorst and the Militarische Gesellschaft in Berlin, 1801–1805* (New York, 1989); K. Alder, *Engineering the Revolution: Arms and Enlightenment in France 1763–1815* (Princeton, 1997).

77. W.O. Shanahan, *Prussian Military Reforms 1786–1813* (New York, 1945); R. Glover, *Peninsular Preparation: the Reform of the British Army, 1795–1809* (Cambridge, 1963); D.E. Showalter, 'Hubertusberg to Auerstädt: The Prussian Army in Decline?', *German History*, 12 (1994), pp. 321–33; Rothenberg, *Napoleon's Great Adversaries: the Archduke Charles and the Austrian Army, 1792–1814* (Bloomington, Indiana, 1982); G.J. Evelyn, ' "I learned what one ought not to do": The British Army in Flanders and Holland, 1793–95', and P. Mackesy, 'Abercromby in Egypt: the Regeneration of the Army', in A.J. Guy (ed.), *The Road to Waterloo. The British Army and the Struggle Against Revolutionary France, 1793–1815* (London, 1990), pp. 16–22 and 101–10.

7 The Nineteenth Century

1. J.A. de Moor, 'Warmakers in the Archipelago: Dutch Expeditions in Nineteenth Century Indonesia', in J.A. de Moor and H.L. Wesseling (eds), *Imperialism and War. Essays on Colonial Wars in Asia and Africa* (Leiden, 1989), p. 63; M. Harrison, 'Tropical Medicine in Nineteenth-Century India', *British Journal for the History of Science*, 25 (1992), pp. 299–318.

2. President and Council at Fort St George to Court of Directors, 31 July 1760, IO. H/Misc./96, p. 56; P.D. Curtin, *Death by Migration: Europe's Encounter with the Tropical World in the Nineteenth Century* (Cambridge, 1989); B. Menning, *Bayonets before Bullets: The Imperial Russian Army, 1861–1914* (Bloomington, Indiana, 1992), p. 82.

3. J. Keegan, *A History of Warfare* (London, 1993), p. 305.

4. D. Showalter, *Railroads and Rifles: Soldiers, Technology and the Unification of Germany* (Hamden, Connecticut, 1975), esp., pp. 38–46. On the weakness of Prussia's Aus-

trian opponent, G. Wawro, 'An "Army of Pigs": The Technical, Social, and Political Bases of Austrian Shock Tactics, 1859–1866', *Journal of Military History* 59 (1995), pp. 407–34 and *The Austro-Prussian War: Austria's War with Prussia and Italy in 1866* (Cambridge, 1996).

5. See, more generally, D.R. Headrick, *The Tools of Empire: Technology and European Imperialism in the Nineteenth Century* (Oxford, 1981).

6. Elting, *Swords around a Throne*, pp. 103–6; M. van Creveld, *Technology and War. From 2000 BC* (New York, 1989), pp. 154–6.

7. D.R. Headrick, *The Invisible Weapon. Telecommunications and International Politics 1851–1945* (New York, 1991), esp., pp. 117, 130, 141.

8. C.J. Bartlett, *Great Britain and Sea Power 1815–1853* (Oxford, 1963), pp. 199–200; G.S. Graham, *The China Station. War and Diplomacy 1830–1860* (Oxford, 1978), pp. 140–4; Headrick, *Tools of Empire*, pp. 20–57; A.S. Kanya Forstner, 'The French Marines and the Conquest of the Western Sudan, 1880–1899', in *Imperialism and War*, p. 150.

9. D.K. Brown, *Before the Ironclad: Development of Ship Design, Propulsion and Armament in the Royal Navy, 1815–1860* (London, 1990); A. Lambert, *Battleships in Transition: the Creation of the Steam Battlefleet, 1815–1860* (London, 1984), *The Last Sailing Battlefleet. Maintaining Naval Mastery 1815–1850* (London, 1991), and *Steam, Steel and Shellfire: The Nineteenth Century Naval Technical Revolution* (London, 1992); C.I. Hamilton, *Anglo-French Naval Rivalry, 1849–1870* (Oxford, 1993).

10. R. Luraghi, *A History of the Confederate Navy* (London, 1996), pp. 55–8.

11. E. Hagerman, *The American Civil War and the Origins of Modern Warfare. Ideas, Organization, and Field Command* (Bloomington, Indiana, 1988), pp. xi, xvii.

12. D.B. Ralston, *Importing the European Army. The Introduction of European Military Techniques and Institutions into the Extra-European World, 1600–1914* (Chicago, 1990), pp. 85–93; K. Fahmy, *All the Pasha's Men. Mehmed Ali, his army and the making of modern Egypt* (Cambridge, 1997).

13. J.S. Grewal and I. Banga (eds), *Civil and Military Affairs of Maharaja Ranjit Singh* (Amritsar, 1987); J.-M. Lafont *French Administrators of Maharaja Ranjit Singh* (Delhi, 1988) and *La Presence française dans le royaume sikh du Penjab* (Paris, 1992); P. Barua, 'Military Developments in

India, 1750–1850', *Journal of Military History* 58 (1994), pp. 610–12.

14. P. Avery, G. Mambly and C. Melville, *The Cambridge History of Iran. VII. From Nadir Shah to the Islamic Republic* (Cambridge, 1991), pp. 158–9, 169, 171.

15. D.H.A. Kolff, 'The End of an *Ancien Régime*. Colonial War in India 1798–1818', in de Moor and Wesseling (eds), *Imperialism and War*, pp. 22–49.

16. C.E. Davies, *The Blood-Red Arab Flag. An Investigation into Qasimi Piracy 1797–1820* (Exeter, 1997); B. Gough, *The Falkland Islands/Malvinas. The Contest for Empire in the South Atlantic* (London, 1992), pp. 89–104.

17. N.E. Saul, 'The Impact of the Napoleonic War upon Russian Priorities on Naval Development', in W.B. Cogar (ed.), *New Interpretations in Naval History* (Annapolis, 1989), p. 56.

18. W.E.D. Allen and P. Muratoff, *Caucasian Battlefields: A History of the Wars on the Turco-Caucasian Border, 1828–1921* (Cambridge, 1953), pp. 23–45.

19. Stebelsky, 'Frontier in Central Asia', pp. 154–5.

20. M. Gammer, 'Russian Strategies in the Conquest of Chechnia and Daghestan, 1825–1859', in M.B. Broxup (ed.), *The North Caucasus Barrier. The Russian Advance towards the Muslim World* (London, 1992), p. 58; M. Gammer, *Muslim Resistance to the Tsar. Shamil and the Conquest of Chechnia and Daghestan* (London, 1994).

21. M.C. Ricklefs, *A History of Modern Indonesia since c. 1300* (2nd edn, Basingstoke, 1993), pp. 140, 142, 116–17.

22. C.R. Pennell, 'Dealing with Pirates: British, French and Moroccans, 1834–56', *Journal of Imperial and Commonwealth History,* 22 (1994), p. 63.

23. G.E. Rothenberg, foreword to D.J. Hughes (ed.), *Moltke on the Art of War* (Novato, California, 1993), p. viii; Wawro, *Austro-Prussian War*, pp. 13–25; M. Howard, *The Franco-Prussian War* (London, 1961).

24. L. Sondhaus, *The Habsburg Empire and the Sea: Austrian Naval Policy, 1797–1866* (West Lafayette, Indiana, 1989).

25. W.F. Sater, *Chile and the War of the Pacific* (Lincoln, Nebraska, 1986).

26. G. McWhiney and P.D. Jamieson, *Attack and Die. Civil War Military Tactics and the Southern Heritage* (Tuscaloosa, 1982); R.E. Beringer, et al., *Why the South Lost the Civil War* (Athens, Georgia, 1986); J.M. McPher-son, *Battle Cry of Freedom. The Civil War Era* (Oxford, 1988); E.J. Hess, 'Tactics, Trenches and Men in the Civil War', in S. Förster and J. Nagler (eds), *On the Road to Total War. The American Civil War and the German Wars of Unification, 1861–1871* (Cambridge, 1997), pp. 481–96.

27. S.R. Wise, *Gate of Hell: Campaign for Charleston Harbor 1863* (Columbia, South Carolina, 1994).

28. B.S. Nijjar, *Anglo-Sikh Wars, 1845–1849* (New Delhi, 1976); H. Strachan, *From Waterloo to Balaclava. Tactics, Technology, and the British Army 1815–1854* (Cambridge, 1985), pp. 124–5.

29. J. Pemble, *The Raj, the Indian Mutiny and the Kingdom of Oudh 1801–1858* (Hassocks, 1977); R. Mukherjee, *Awadh in Revolt 1857–1858* (Delhi, 1984).

30. P. Adams, *Fatal Necessity: British Intervention in New Zealand 1830–1847* (Auckland, 1977); J. Belich, *The New Zealand Wars and the Victorian Interpretation of Racial Conflict* (Auckland, 1986).

31. B. Keegan, 'The Ashanti Campaign 1873–4', in B. Bond (ed.), *Victorian Military Campaigns* (London 1967), pp. 163–9; D. Killingray, 'The British and Asante 1870–1914', in de Moor and Wesseling (eds), *Imperialism and War*, pp. 158–67; I. Wilks, *Asante in the Nineteenth Century* (Cambridge, 1975).

32. D. Robinson, *The Holy War of Umar Tel. The Western Sudan in the Mid-Nineteenth Century* (Oxford, 1985), p. 330.

33. J.A. de Moor, 'Warmakers in the Archipelago: Dutch Expeditions in Nineteenth Century Indonesia', in de Moor and Wesseling (eds), *Imperialism and War*, pp. 50–71, esp. 70–1; M. Brossenbroek, 'The Living Tools of Empire: The Recruitment of European Soldiers for the Dutch Colonial Army, 1814–1909', *Journal of Imperial and Commonwealth History,* 23 (1995).

34. W.H. Leckie, *The Military Conquest of the South Plains* (Norman, Oklahoma, 1963); S.L.A. Marshall, *Crimsoned Prairie: the Wars Between the United States and the Plains Indians during the Winning of the West* (New York, 1972).

35. Stebelsky, 'Frontier in Central Asia', pp. 155–63.

36. Ralston, *European Army*, p. 149.

37. R. Hackett, *Yamagata Aritomo in the Rise of Modern Japan, 1838–1922* (Cambridge, Mass., 1971), pp. 81–2; M. and S. Harries, *Soldiers of the Sun. The Rise and Fall of the Imperial Japanese Army* (New York, 1991), pp. 43, 47.

38. G.A. Lensen, *The Russian Push towards Japan: Russo-Japanese Relations, 1697–1875* (Princeton, 1959), pp. 426–7, 442–5.

39. Graham, *China Station*, pp. 373–7.

40. R.J. Smith, *Mandarins and Mercenaries: 'The Ever-Victorious Army' in Nineteenth Century China* (Millwood, New York, 1978).

41. W.J. Hail, *Tsêng Kuo-Fan and the Taiping Rebellion* (New Haven, 1927), p. 125; S.A. Leibo (ed.), *A Journal of the Chinese Civil War 1864* by Prosper Giquel (Honolulu, 1985), pp. xiv, 11, 47–8.

42. Needham, *Military Technology: The Gunpowder Epic*, p. 466.

43. *Cambridge History of Iran*, VII, 177, 191–2, 198, 205; A. Amanat, *The Pivot of the Universe. Nasir al-Din Shah and the Iranian Monarchy, 1831–1896* (London, 1996).

44. B. Langensiepen and A. Guleryuz, *The Ottoman Steam Navy, 1828–1923* (Aldershot, 1995).

45. R.M. Utley, *The Last Days of the Sioux Nation* (New Haven, 1963), and *Frontier Regulars: The United States Army and the Indian, 1866–1891* (New York, 1973); R.K. Andrist, *The Long Death: The Last of the Plains Indians* (New York, 1964).

46. M. Crowder (ed.), *West African Opposition: the Military Response to Colonial Occupation* (London, 1971).

47. J.P.C. Laband and P.S. Thompson, *Field Guide to the War in Zululand and the Defence of Natal 1879* (Pietermaritzburg, 1983), pp. 54–7. For a warning against an exaggeration of the role of firearms, J.J. Guy, 'A Note on Firearms in the Zulu Kingdom with Special Reference to the Anglo-Zulu War, 1879', *Journal of African History* 12 (1971), pp. 557–70.

48. R.H. Rainero, 'The Battle of Adowa: a Reappraisal', in de Moor and Wesseling (eds.), *Imperialism and War*, pp. 188–200.

49. B. Robson (ed.), 'The Kandahar Letters of the Reverend Alfred Cane', *Journal of the Society for Army Historical Research*, 69 (1991), pp. 206, 211–12.

50. R. Hill, *Egypt in the Sudan, 1820–81* (Oxford, 1959); D.L. Lewis, *The Race to Fashoda. European Colonialism and African Resistance in the Scramble for Africa* (London, 1988), pp. 3–4.

51. I. Knight, *The Anatomy of the Zulu Army: from Shaka to Cetshwayo, 1818–1879* (London, 1995).

52. M. Legassick, 'Firearms, Horses and Samorian Army Organisation 1870–1898', *Journal of African History*, 7 (1966), pp. 95–115.

53. P.M. Holt, *The Mahdist State in the Sudan 1881–1898* (2nd edn, Oxford, 1970).

54. Kea, 'Firearms on the Gold and Slave Coasts', p. 201; Law, 'Warfare on the West African Slave Coast', pp. 124–5.

55. Pankhurst, *Ethiopia*, pp. 286–7; D. Crummey, 'Tewodros as reformer and modernizer', *Journal of African History*, 10 (1969), pp. 457–69; R.A. Caulk, 'Firearms and Princely Power in Ethiopia in the Nineteenth Century', *Journal of African History*, 13 (1972).

56. F. Myatt, *The March to Magdala: The Abyssinian War of 1868* (London, 1970); D. G. Chandler, 'The Expedition to Abyssinia, 1867–81, in Bond (ed.), *Victorian Military Campaigns*, pp. 105–59.

57. J. Dunn, '"For God, Emperor, and Country!" The Evolution of Ethiopia's Nineteenth-Century Army', *War in History*, 1 (1994), pp. 278–99; H.G. Marcus, *The Life and Times of Menelik II: Ethiopia, 1844–1914* (Oxford, 1975).

58. R. Law, 'Wheeled Transport in Pre-Colonial West Africa', *Africa*, 50 (1980), pp. 255–7.

59. S. Lone, *Japan's First Modern War: Army and Society in the Conflict with China 1894–1895* (London, 1994).

60. L. Barrows, 'The Impact of Empire', pp. 71, 81, and C. Badesi, 'West African Influence on the French Army of World War One', both in G.W. Johnson (ed.), *Double Impact: France and Africa in the Age of Imperialism* (Westport, Conn., 1985), pp. 96–7; Forstner, 'The French Marines and the Conquest of the Western Sudan, 1880–1899', in de Moor and Wesseling (eds), *Imperialism and War*, pp. 138, 150; Badesi, *From Adversaries to Comrades-in-arms: West Africans and the French Military, 1885–1918* (Waltham, Mass., 1979), p. 20.

61. Lewis, *Road to Fashoda*, pp. 68–70.

62. *Ibid.*, pp. 157, 196, 201–2; I.H. Zueto, *Karari: the Sudanese account of the battle of Omdurman* (London, 1980).

63. B. Robson, *The Road to Kabul – The Second Afghan War, 1878–1881* (London, 1986).

64. D.J.M. Muffett, *Concerning Brave Captains* (London, 1964); O. Ikime, *The Fall of Nigeria. The British Conquest* (London, 1977).

65. C. Fourniau, 'Colonial Wars before 1914: the Case of France in IndoChina', in de Moor and Wesseling (eds), *Imperialism and War*, p. 85.

66. A.S. Kanya-Forstner, *The Conquest of the Western Sudan. A Study in French Military*

Imperialism (Cambridge, 1969); R. Betts, *Tricouleur: The French Overseas Empire* (1978); G.W. Johnson (ed.), *Double Impact: France and Africa in the Age of Imperialism* (Westport, Conn., 1985); W.A. Hoisington, *Lyautey and the French Conquest of Morocco* (Basingstoke, 1995); B. Vandervort, *Wars of Imperial Conquest in Africa, 1830–1914* (London, 1998).

67. J.S. Gallieni, *La Pacification de Madagascar 1896–1899* (Paris, 1900); Y.G. Paillard, 'The French Expedition to Madagascar in 1895', in de Moor and Wesseling (eds), *Imperialism and War*, pp. 168–88.

68. S. Hinde, *The Fall of the Congo Arabs* (New York, 1969).

69. Graham, *China Station*, p. 399.

70. D. Bates, *The Abyssinian Difficulty* (Oxford, 1979).

71. H.D. Napier, *Field Marshal Lord Napier of Magdala* (London, 1927).

72. J.Y. Wong, *Deadly Dreams. Opium, Imperialism and the 'Arrow' War (1856–1860) in China* (Cambridge, 1996).

73. J. Smith, *The Spanish-American War. Conflict in the Caribbean and the Pacific 1895–1902* (Harlow, 1994), p. 176.

74. J.S. Curtiss, *The Russian Army under Nicholas I, 1825–1855* (Durham, North Carolina, 1965) and *Russia's Crimean War* (Durham, N.C., 1979).

75. A. Lambert, *The Crimean War: British Grand Strategy against Russia 1853–1856* (Manchester, 1991).

76. Hamilton, *Anglo-French Naval Rivalry*, p. 94.

77. T.R. Moreman, 'The British and Indian Armies and North-West Frontier Warfare 1848–1914', *Journal of Imperial and Commonwealth History*, 20 (1992), pp. 58–9.

78. T. Pakenham, *The Boer War* (London, 1979); P. Warwick (ed.), *The South African War: The Anglo-Boer War 1899–1902* (London, 1980).

79. A.T. Nolan, 'Confederate Leadership at Fredericksburg', in G. Gallagher (ed.), *The Fredericksburg Campaign* (Chapel Hill, N.C., 1995), pp. 43–4.

80. R. Schwartz, *Lawless Liberators. Political Banditry and Cuban Independence* (Durham, North Carolina, 1989), p. 238.

81. Menning, *Bayonets before Bullets*, p. 104, 107.

82. K. Neilson, 'Russia' in K. Wilson (ed.), *Decisions for War, 1914* (London, 1995), p. 102; D.G. Hermann, *The Arming of Europe and the Coming of World War One* (Princeton, 1996).

83. K.D. Moll, *The Influence of History upon Seapower 1865–1914* (Stanford, 1968), pp. 37–40.

84. N. Ferguson, 'Germany and the Origins of the First World War: New Perspectives', *Historical Journal*, 35 (1992), p. 733.

85. A. Bucholz, *Moltke, Schlieffen, and Prussian War Planning* (1991).

86. A. Gat, *The Development of Military Thought: the Nineteenth Century* (Oxford, 1992), pp. 114–72; D. Porch, *The March to the Marne* (Cambridge, 1981); G. Krumeich, *Armaments and Politics in France on the Eve of the First World War* (Leamington Spa, 1984), p. 22.

87. T. Travers, *The Killing Ground: the British Army, the Western Front and the emergence of modern warfare, 1900–1918* (London, 1987); M. Samuels, *Command or Control? Command, Training and Tactics in the British and German Armies, 1888–1918* (London, 1995).

88. C. Bassford, *Clausewitz in English: the reception of Clausewitz in Britain and America, 1815–1945* (Oxford, 1994).

89. G.E. Rothenberg, 'The Austro-Hungarian Campaign Against Serbia in 1914', *Journal of Military History*, 53 (1989), p. 134.

90. P.M. Kennedy (ed.), *The War Plans of the Great Powers 1880–1914* (London, 1979); J. Snyder, *The Ideology of the Offensive: Military Decision Making and the Disasters of 1914* (Ithaca, N.Y., 1984); Rothenberg, 'Moltke, Schlieffen, and the Doctrine of Strategic Envelopment', in P. Paret (ed.), *Makers of Modern Strategy* (Princeton, 1986), pp. 296–325; G.A. Tunstall, *Planning for War Against Russia and Serbia* (Boulder, 1993).

91. Rothenberg, foreword to Hughes (ed.), *Moltke*, p. ix; A.J. Echevarra, 'A Crisis in War Fighting: German Tactical Discussions in the Late Nineteenth Century', *Militargeschichtliche MiHeilungen*, 55 (1996), pp. 51–68.

92. A.J.P. Taylor, *War by Timetable: How the First World War Began* (London, 1969); M. Trachtenberg, *History and Strategy* (Princeton, 1991), pp. 72, 96, 98.

93. D.M. Schurman, *The Education of a Navy: the Development of British Naval Strategic Thought, 1867–1914* (Malbar, 1984); J.T. Sumida, *In Defence of Naval Supremacy: Finance, Technology, and British Naval Policy 1889–1914* (Boston, 1989); R. Walser, *France's Search for a Battle Fleet: Naval Policy and Naval Power, 1898–1914* (New York, 1992); L. Sondhaus, *The Naval Policy of Austria-Hungary, 1867–1918: Navalism, Industrial Development, and the Politics of Dualism* (West Lafayette, Indiana, 1994); M.N. Vego, *Austro – Hungarian Naval Policy,*

1904–1914 (Portland, Oregon, 1996); S.A. Knight, 'The Evolution and Processes involved in the Manufacture of Armour Plate up to the Great War', *Journal of the Ordnance Society*, 5 (1993), pp. 58–61.

94. Menning, *Bayonets before Bullets*, p. 2.

95. G. Fox, *British Admirals and Chinese Pirates 1832–1869* (Westport, Conn., 1940), pp. 107–8.

96. A. Preston and J. Major, *Send a Gunboat! A Study of the Gunboat and its Role in British Policy, 1854–1904* (London, 1971); M. Rodman and M. Cooper (eds), *The Pacification of Melanesia* (Ann Arbor, 1979).

97. B.M. Gough, *Gunboat Frontier: British Maritime Authority and North-West Coast Indians, 1846–1890* (Vancouver, 1984).

98. M.S. Partridge, *Military Planning for the Defense of the United Kingdom, 1814–1870* (Westport, Conn., 1989); A.T. Patterson, *Palmerston's Folly: the Portsdown and Spithead Forts* (Portsmouth, 1985).

99. N. Stone, *The Eastern Front: 1914–1917* (1975), pp. 148–9.

100. H. Strachan, 'The British Army and "Modern" War: the Experience of the Peninsula and of the Crimea', in J.A. Lynn (ed.), *Tools of War: Instruments, Ideas, and Institutions of Warfare, 1445–1871* (Urbana, 1990), p. 213.

101. Dunn, '"For God, Emperor and Country!"', p. 295.

102. R. Beal and R. Macleod, *Prairie Fire: The North-West Rebellion of 1885* (Edmonton, 1984).

103. I.J. Kerr, *Building the Railways of the Raj 1850–1900* (Oxford, 1995).

104. R. MacLeod and D. Kumar (eds), *Technology and the Raj: Western Technology and Technical Transfers to India 1700–1947* (London, 1995).

105. Headrick, *The Tentacles of Progress: Technology Transfer in the Age of Imperialism* (New York, 1988); I. Inkster, 'Prometheus Bound: Technology and Industrialization in Japan, China and India Prior to 1914 – A Political Economy Approach', *Annals of Science*, 45 (1988), pp. 399–426; T. Morris-Suzuki, *The Technological Transformation of Japan from the Seventeenth to the Twenty-First Century* (Cambridge, 1995).

106. R. Betts, *Tricouleur. The French Overseas Empire* (London, 1978), pp. 28, 134.

107. M.W. Daly, *Empire on the Nile: the Anglo-Egyptian Sudan 1898–1934* (Cambridge, 1987).

108. E.M. Spiers, 'The Use of the Dum Dum Bullet and Colonial Warfare', *Journal of Imperial and Commonwealth History*, 4

(1975), pp. 3–14.

109. D. Featherstone, *Colonial Small Wars, 1837–1901* (Newton Abbot, 1973); L. James, *The Savage Wars. British Campaigns in Africa, 1870–1920* (New York, 1985); H. Whitehouse, *Battle in Africa, 1879–1914* (Fieldhead, 1987); R.H. Dusgate, *The Conquest of Northern Nigeria* (London, 1985).

110. Menning, *Bayonets before Bullets*, p. 108.

111. Kanya-Forstner, 'French Marines', pp. 151–2.

112. C.E. Callwell, *Small Wars: their Principles and Practice* (London, 1896); J. Gottman, 'Bugeaud, Gallieni, Lyautey: the Development of French Colonial Warfare', in E.M. Earle (ed.), *Makers of Modern Strategy* (Princeton, 1944), pp. 234–59; Hoisington, *Lyautey*, pp. 7–8; H.L. Wesseling, 'Colonial Wars and Armed Peace, 1870–1914: a Reconnaissance', *Itinerario*, 5 (1981), pp. 61–3. For the argument that lightly armed mobile units could only achieve so much and that large numbers of regulars supplied with modern weaponry could also be required in some circumstances, D. Porch, *The Conquest of Morocco* (New York, 1983), pp. 184–8.

113. W.H. Schneider, *An Empire for the Masses: the French Popular Image of Africa, 1870–1900* (Westport, Conn., 1982); T.G. August, *The Selling of the Empire: British and French Imperialist Propaganda, 1890–1940* (Westport, Conn., 1985); D. Geyer, *Russian Imperialism: the Interaction of Domestic and Foreign Policy, 1860–1914* (Leamington Spa, 1987); W.R. Katz, *Rider Haggard and the Fiction of Empire: a Critical Study of British Imperial Fiction* (Cambridge, 1989); J. Richards (ed.), *Imperialism and Juvenile Literature* (Manchester, 1989); J. Mackenzie (ed.), *Popular Imperialism and the Military* (Manchester, 1990).

114. R.N. Stromberg, *Redemption by War, the Intellectuals and 1914* (Lawrence, Kansas, 1982).

115. W.M. Pintner, 'The Burden of Defense in Imperial Russia, 1725–1914', *Russian Review*, 43 (1984), pp. 247, 249.

116. Menning, *Bayonets before Bullets*, p. 64.

117. P.D. Jamieson, *Crossing the Deadly Ground: United States Army Tactics, 1865–1899* (Tuscaloosa, 1994); Smith, *Spanish-American War*, p. 215.

118. M.R. Shulman, *Navalism and the Emergence of American Sea Power, 1882–1893* (Annapolis, 1995); W.R. Herrick, *The American Naval Revolution* (Baton Rouge, 1966).

119. S.C. Topik, *Trade and Gunboats. The*

United States and Brazil in the Age of Empire (Stanford, 1996), pp. 145–54.

120. G.N. Sanderson, *England, Europe and the Upper Nile, 1882–1899* (Edinburgh, 1965); D.L. Lewis, *The Race to Fashoda: European Colonialism and African Resistance in the Scramble for Africa* (1987).

121. Headrick, *Invisible Weapon*, p. 85.

8 Warfare and the State, 1450–1900

1. C.C. Bayly, *Mercenaries for the Crimea: the German, Swiss and Italian Legions in British Service, 1854–1856* (Montreal, 1977).

2. N. Tarling, *Britian, the Brookes and Brunei* (Oxford, 1971), and *The Burthen, the Risk and the Glory: a biography of Sir James Brooke* (Oxford, 1982); J.E. Thomson, *Mercenaries, Pirates, and Sovereigns: State-Building and Extraterritorial Violence in Early Modern Europe* (Princeton, 1994).

3. G. Fox, *British Admirals and Chinese Pirates, 1832–1869* (London, 1940); B.M. Gough, 'Pax Britannica: Peace, Force and World Power', *Round Table*, 314 (1990), pp. 173–4.

4. R. Howell, *The Royal Navy and the Slave Trade* (New York, 1987).

5. J. Glete, *Navies and Nations. Warships, Navies and State Building in Europe and America, 1500–1860* (Stockholm, 1993), pp. 477–81; P. Longworth, *The Cossacks* (London, 1969).

6. B.M. Downing, *The Military Revolution and Political Change. Origins of Democracy and Autocracy in Early Modern Europe* (Princeton, 1993); B.D. Porter, *War and the Rise of the State. The Military Foundations of Modern Politics* (New York, 1994); T. Ertman, *Birth of the Leviathan. Building States and Regimes in Medieval and Early Modern Europe* (Cambridge, 1997).

7. A. Reid, *Southeast Asia in the Age of Commerce 1450–1680. II. Expansion and Crisis* (New Haven, 1993), pp. 256–7, 266.

8. For deficiencies, e.g. Mallet, 'Art of War', pp. 551–2; D. Potter, *War and Government in the French Provinces: Picardy, 1470–1560* (Cambridge, 1993), p. 158; J.B. Wood, *The King's Army. Warfare, Soldiers and Society during the Wars of Religion in France, 1562–1576* (Cambridge, 1996), pp. 305–10; R.W. Stewart, 'Arms and Expeditions: the Ordnance Office and the Assaults on Cadiz (1625) and the Isle of Rhé (1627)', in M. Fissel (ed.), *War and Government in Britain, 1598–1650* (Manchester, 1991), p. 126; P.W. Bamford, *Fighting Ships and Prisons: the Mediterranean Galleys of France in*

the Age of Louis XIV (Minneapolis, 1973); D. Parrott, 'French Military Organization in the 1630s: the Failure of Richelieu's Ministry', *Seventeenth Century French Studies*, 9 (1987), pp. 156–67, 'The Constraints on Power: Recent Works on Early Modern European History', *European History Quarterly*, 20 (1990), pp. 101–3, and 'The Military Revolution in Early Modern Europe', *History Today*, vol. 42 (Dec. 1992), p. 25. For a very different impression, M.E. Mallett and J.R. Hale, *The Military Organization of a Renaissance State: Venice, c. 1400–1617* (Cambridge, 1984), pp. 101–52; C.C. Sturgill, 'Money for the Bourbon Army in the Eighteenth Century: the State within the State', *War and Society*, 4 (1986), pp. 17, 23; T. Hayter (ed.), *An Eighteenth-Century Secretary at War. The Papers of William, Viscount Barrington* (London, 1988), pp. 11, 18; J.S. Wheeler, 'The Logistics of the Cromwellian Conquest of Scotland 1650–1651', *War and Society*, 10 (1992), pp. 1–18, and 'English Financial Operations during the First Dutch War', *Journal of European Economic History*, 23 (1994), pp. 329–43; M.J. Braddick, 'An English Military Revolution?', *Historical Journal*, 36 (1993), pp. 965–75; R.W. Unger, 'Admiralties and Warships of Europe and the Mediterranean, 1000–1500', in R.W. Love (ed.), *Changing Interpretations and New Sources in Naval History* (New York, 1980), p. 42.

9. Reid, *Europe and Southeast Asia: The Military Balance* (Townsville, 1982), p. 8; C.R. Phillips, *Six Galleons for the King of Spain. Imperial Defense in the Early Seventeenth Century* (Baltimore, 1992).

10. W.H. McNeill, 'European Expansion, Power and Warfare since 1500', in de Moor and Wesseling (eds), *Imperialism and War*, pp. 17–18; D. Landes, 'The Foundations of European Expansion and Dominion: An Equilibrium Model', *Itinerario*, 5 (1981), pp. 52–3.

11. D.C. Goodman, *Power and Penury. Government, Technology and Science in Philip II's Spain* (Cambridge, 1988).

12. J.R. Bruijn, *The Dutch Navy of the Seventeenth and Eighteenth Centuries* (Columbia, South Carolina, 1993).

13. M. Raeff, *The Well-Ordered Police State. Social and Institutional Change through Law in the Germanies and Russia, 1600–1800* (New Haven, 1983); R. Axtmann, 'The Formation of the Modern State: the Debate in the Social Sciences', in M. Fulbrook (ed.), *National Histories and European History* (London, 1993), pp. 21–45; G. Burgess,

Absolute Monarchy and the Stuart Constitution (New Haven, 1996).

14. R.I. Frost, 'The Polish-Lithuanian Commonwealth and the "Military Revolution"', in M.B. Biskupski and J.S. Pula (eds), *Poland and Europe: Historical Dimensions* (Boulder, 1993), pp. 46–7.

15. R. Hellie, *Enserfment and Military Change in Muscovy* (Chicago, 1971); C.B. Stevens, *Soldiers on the Steppe: Army Reform and Social Change in Early Modern Russia* (De Kalb, Illinois, 1995).

16. W.S. Cormack, *Revolution and Political Conflict in the French Navy 1789–1794* (Cambridge, 1995).

17. R.D. Hurt, *The Ohio Frontier. Crucible of the Old Northwest, 1720–1830* (Bloomington, Indiana, 1996).

18. W. Reinhard, 'Power Elites, State Servants, Ruling Classes, and the Growth of State Power', in Reinhard (ed.), *Power Elites and State Building* (Oxford, 1996), pp. 10–11.

19. P.J. Marshall, 'Western Arms in Maritime Asia in the Early Phases of Expansion', *Modern Asian Studies*, 14 (1980), p. 13.

20. C. Tilly, 'War Making and State Making as Organized Crime', in P.B. Evans et al. (eds), *Bringing the State Back in* (Cambridge, 1985).

21. R.J.W. Evans and T.V. Thomas (eds), *Crown, Church and Estates. Central European Politics in the Sixteenth and Seventeenth Centuries* (London, 1992); N. Henshall, *The Myth of Absolutism: Change and Continuity in Early Modern European Monarchy* (Harlow, 1992) and 'Early Modern Absolutism 1550–1700: Political Reality or Propaganda', in R.G. Asch and H. Duchhardt (eds), *Der Absolutismus – ein Mythos?* (Cologne, 1996), pp. 25–53.

22. Potter, *War and Government in the French Provinces: Picardy, 1470–1560.*

23. F.J. Baumgartner, *Louis XII* (Stroud, 1994).

24. H.G. Koenigsberger, *Mars and Venus: Warfare and International Relations of the Casa de Austria* (Portsmouth, 1994), pp. 19–22.

25. Fissel, *The Bishops' Wars. Charles I's campaigns against Scotland, 1638–1640* (Cambridge, 1994); M.E. Berry, *The Culture of Civil War in Kyoto* (Berkeley, 1994).

26. C. Storrs and H.M. Scott, 'The Military Revolution and the European Nobility, c. 1600–1800', *War in History*, 3 (1996), pp. 1–41. For Denmark, where the monarchy was more powerful after 1660 than was the case in most of Europe, and officership relatively less aristocratic, G. Lind, 'Military

and Absolutism: the Army Officers of Denmark-Norway as a Social Group and Political Factor, 1660–1848', *Scandinavian Journal of History*, 12 (1988), pp. 221–43.

27. Charles Delafaye, Under Secretary of State, to Earl Stanhope, 12 June 1719, PRO. State Papers 43/61.

28. J.F. Richards, *The Mughal Empire* (Cambridge, 1993), pp. 20–4; D.H.A. Kolf, *Naukar, Rajput and Sepoy: the Ethnohistory of the Military Labour Market in Hindustan, 1450–1850* (Cambridge, 1990).

29. J. Goody, *The East in the West* (Cambridge, 1996).

30. V.A. Ryazanovsky, *Fundamental Principles of Mongol Law* (Tientsin, 1937), pp. 46–52.

31. H. Inalcik, 'Military and Fiscal Transformation in the Ottoman Empire 1600–1700', *Archivum Ottomanicum*, 6 (1980), pp. 283–377; Richards, *Mughal Empire*, pp. 142–3.

32. J. Hathaway, *The Politics of Households in Ottoman Egypt. The Rise of the Qazdağlis* (Cambridge, 1997); J.J.L. Gommans, *The Rise of the Indo-Afghan Empire* c. *1710–1780* (Leiden, 1995), p. 3.

33. M. Alam, *The Crisis of Empire in Mughal North India. Awadh and the Punjab 1707–1748* (Delhi, 1986), pp. 50–3.

34. B.D. Steele, 'Muskets and Pendulums: Benjamin Robins, Leonhard Euler, and the Ballistics Revolution', *Technology and Culture*, 35 (1994), pp. 348–82.

35. C.A. Bayly, *Imperial Meridian. The British Empire and the World 1780–1830* (Harlow, 1989), pp. 164–92, esp. 164–5.

36. C.N. Parkinson, *Edward Pellew, Viscount Exmouth, Admiral of the Red* (London, 1934), pp. 419–72.

37. F. Braudel, *The Mediterranean and the Mediterranean World in the Age of Philip II* (2 vols, London, 1966).

38. An important recent attempt to find a long-term pattern in global conflict is offered by K.A. Rasler and W.R. Thompson, *The Great Powers and Global Struggle 1490–1990* (Lexington, Kentucky, 1994) and G. Modelski and Thompson, *Leading Sectors and World Powers. The Coevolution of Global Politics and Economics* (Columbia, South Carolina, 1996). On lack of unity, M. Finley, *The Most Monstrous of Wars. The Napoleonic Guerrilla War in Southern Italy, 1806–11* (Columbia, South Carolina, 1994), p. 133.

39. E. Kedourie, *Nationalism* (London, 1960), p. 1; E.J. Hobsbawm, 'The Nation as Novelty', in Hobsbawm, *Nations and*

Nationalism since 1780: Programme, Myth, Reality (2nd edn, Cambridge, 1992), pp. 14–45; J.C.D. Clark, *The Language of Liberty: Political Discourse and Social Dynamics in the Anglo-American World 1660–1800* (Cambridge, 1993), chapter 1; J. Breuilly, *Nationalism and the State* (2nd edn, Manchester, 1993). Other important works included E. Gellner, *Nations and Nationalism* (Oxford, 1983); A. Smith, *The Ethnic Origins of Nations* (Oxford, 1986).

40. H. Schulze, *States, Nations and Nationalism from the Middle Ages to the Present* (Oxford, 1996), p. 181.

41. D. Laven, 'Machiavelli, *italianità* and the French invasion of 1494', in D. Abulafia (ed.), *The French Descent into Renaissance Italy, 1494–95. Antecedents and effects* (Aldershot, 1995), pp. 363–4.

42. J.W. Geary, *We Need Men: the Union Draft in the Civil War* (De Kalb, Illinois, 1991).

43. P. Paret, 'Conscription and the End of the Old Regime in France and Prussia', in his *Clausewitz and the History of War: Essays* (Princeton, 1993), pp. 53–74; A. Forrest, *Conscripts and Deserters: the Army and French Society during the Revolution and Empire* (Oxford, 1989); J. Lynn, 'War of Annihilation, War of Attrition, and War of Legitimacy: a Neo-Clausewitzian Approach to Twentieth-Century Conflicts', *Marine Corps Gazette*, 80, no. 10 (Oct. 1996), pp. 64–71.

44. D. Moon, 'Peasants into Russian Citizens? A Comparative Perspective', *Revolutionary Russia*, 9 (1996), pp. 65–7; V.R. Berghahn, *Militarism. The History of an International Debate 1861–1979* (Cambridge, 1984), p. 16.

45. J. Gooch, *Army, State and Society in Italy, 1870–1915* (London, 1989), pp. 21–2.

46. G.W. Gallagher, 'Another Look at the Generalship of R.E. Lee', in Gallagher (ed.), *Lee. The Soldier* (Lincoln, Nebraska, 1996), p. 285.

47. M. Howard, *The Franco-Prussian War* (London, 1961), p. 455; M.S. Coetzee, *The German Army League. Popular Nationalism in Wilhelmine Germany* (Oxford, 1990).

48. W.L. Kahrl (ed.), *California Water Atlas* (North Highlands, California, 1978); J. Smith, *The Spanish-American War. Conflict in the Caribbean and the Pacific, 1895–1902* (Harlow, 1994).

49. R.W. Johannsen, *To the Halls of the Montezumas: the Mexican War in the American Imagination* (New York, 1985).

50. W.A. Hoisington, *Lyautey and the French Conquest of Morocco* (Basingstoke, 1995).

51. J.M. Hitsman, *Safeguarding Canada,* *1763–1871* (Toronto, 1968); H. Strachan, 'Lord Grey and Imperial Defence', in I.F.W. Beckett and J. Gooch (eds), *Politicians and Defence: Studies in the Formulation of British Defence Policy* (Manchester, 1981), pp. 8–10.

52. P.K. Taylor, *Indentured to Liberty. Peasant Life and the Hessian Military State, 1688–1815* (Ithaca, N.Y. 1994); F. Redlich, *The German Military Entrepreneur and his Work Force* (Wiesbaden, 1964–5).

53. M.E. Yapp, *The Near East since the First World War* (Harlow, 1991), p. 77; E.M. Spiers, 'Army Organisation and Society in the Nineteenth Century', in T. Bartlett and K. Jeffrey (eds), *A Military History of Ireland* (Cambridge, 1996), pp. 355–7.

54. J.C. Scott, *Weapons of the Weak. Everyday Forms of Peasant Resistance* (New Haven, 1985), pp. xvi–xvii.

55. K. Holsti, *The State, War, and the State of War* (Cambridge, 1996).

56. S. Forster and J. Nagler (eds), *On the Road to Total War. The American Civil War and the German Wars of Unification, 1861–1871* (Cambridge, 1996).

9 Twentieth-Century Reflections

1. H.J. Mackinder, 'The Geographical Pivot of History', and subsequent debate, *Geographical Journal*, 23 (1904), pp. 436, 443, 440. Amery's contribution is discussed in W.R. Louis, *In the Name of God, Go! Leo Amery and the British Empire in the Age of Churchill* (New York, 1992), pp. 54–5.

2. J. Villiers, 'The Estado da India in Southeast Asia', in M. Newitt (ed.), *The First Portuguese Colonial Empire* (Exeter, 1986), p. 61.

3. Hoisington, *Lyautey and the French Conquest of Morocco*, p. 22; R.E. Dunn, *Resistance in the Desert: Moroccan Responses to French Imperialism, 1881–1912* (London, 1977).

4. D. Porch, *The Conquest of the Sahara* (London, 1985), pp. ix, 220.

5. Ricklefs, *Modern Indonesia*, pp. 136–7, 139–40.

6. D.G. Herrmann, 'The paralysis of Italian strategy in the Italian – Turkish War, 1911–1912, *English Historical Review*, 104 (1989), pp. 332–56; J. Ellis, *From the Barrel of a Gun. A History of Guerrilla, Revolutionary and Counter-Insurgency Warfare, from the Romans to the Present* (London, 1995), p. 156.

7. S.F. Wells, 'British Strategic Withdrawal from the Western Hemisphere, 1904–1906', *Canadian Historical Review*,

49 (1968), pp. 335–56; S.R. Rock, 'Risk Theory Reconsidered: American Success and German Failure in the Coercion of Britain, 1890–1914', *Journal of Strategic Studies*, 11 (1988), pp. 342–64.

8. D. Healy, *Gunboat Diplomacy in the Wilson Era: the U.S. Navy in Haiti, 1915–1916* (Madison, Wisc., 1976) and *Drive to Hegemony: the United States in the Caribbean, 1898–1917* (Madison, Wis., 1988).

9. B.A. Linn, *The U.S. Army and Counterinsurgency in the Philippine War, 1899–1902* (Chapel Hill, N.C. 1989) and 'The Long Twilight of the Frontier Army', *Western Historical Quarterly*, 27 (1996), p. 157.

10. B.F. Cooling, *Gray Steel and Blue Water Navy: The Formative Years of America's Military – Industrial Complex, 1881–1917* (Hamden, Conn., 1979); W.R. Braisted, *The United States in the Pacific, 1897–1909* (Austin, Tex., 1958), and . . . *1909–1922* (Austin, Tex., 1971).

11. E.M. Spiers, 'Haldane's Reform of the Regular Army: Scope for Revision', *British Journal of International Studies*, 6 (1980), pp. 79–80; D. Stevenson, *Armaments and the Coming of War. Europe 1904–1914* (Oxford, 1996).

12. This term is deliberately used in a somewhat anachronistic fashion; it is generally applied to the German campaigns of 1939–41. See, more generally, Raudzens, 'Blitzkrieg Ambiguities: Doubtful Usage of a Famous Word', *War and Society*, 7 (1989), pp. 77–94.

13. A. Livesey, *The Viking Atlas of World War I* (London, 1994), pp. 74, 124.

14. T. Lupfer, *The Dynamics of Doctrine: the Changes in German Tactical Doctrine during the First World War* (Leavenworth, Kansas, 1981); B. Gudmunsson, *Stormtrooper Tactics* (New York, 1989); R. Paschall, *The Defeat of Imperial Germany 1917–1918* (New York, 1989), pp. 128–62; M. Samuels, *Command or Control? Command, Training and Tactics in the British and German Armies, 1888–1918* (London, 1996)

15. S. Bidwell and D. Graham, *Firepower. British Army Weapons and Theories of War, 1904–1945* (London, 1982); J. Terraine, *White Heat. The New Warfare 1914–18* (London, 1982); T. Travers, *The Killing Ground: the British Army, the Western Front, and the Emergence of Modern Warfare, 1900–1918* (London, 1987) and *How the War Was Won: Command and Technology in the British Army on the Western Front, 1917–1918* (London, 1992); P. Griffith, *Battle Tactics of the Western Front: the*

British Army's Art of Attack, 1916–18 (New Haven, 1994) and (ed.), *British Fighting Methods in the Great War* (London, 1996).

16. D. Trask, *The AEF and Coalition War-Making* (Lawrence, Kansas, 1993); G. Martin, 'German Strategy and Military Assessments of the American Expeditionary Force, 1917–18', *War in History*, 1 (1994), p. 178.

17. K. Burk, *Britain, America and the Sinews of War* (London, 1985).

18. P.G. Halpern, *A Naval History of World War I* (London, 1994), pp. 334, 442–4.

19. D. Richter, *Chemical Soldiers: British Gas Warfare in World War I* (Lawrence, Kansas, 1992).

20. G.J. De Groot, *Blighty: British Society in the Era of the Great War* (Harlow, 1996); J. Sumida, 'British Naval Administration and Policy in the Age of Fisher', *Journal of Military History*, 54 (1990), p. 22, and 'Forging the Trident: British Naval Industrial Logistics, 1914–1918', in J.A. Lynn (ed.), *Feeding Mars. Logistics in Western Warfare from the Middle Ages to the Present* (Boulder, Col., 1993), pp. 217–49, and 'British Naval Operational Logistics', *Journal of Military History*, 57 (1993), pp. 447–80.

21. J.F. Godfrey, *Capitalism at War: Industrial Policy and Bureaucracy in France 1914–1918* (Leamington Spa, 1987).

22. G. Feldman, *Army, Industry, and Labour in Germany, 1914–1918* (1966).

23. L.H. Siegelbaum, *The Politics of Industrial Mobilization in Russia, 1915–1917: a Study of the War-Industries Committees* (New York, 1984); N. Stone, 'Organizing an Economy for War: The Russian Shell Shortage, 1914–1917', in G. Best and A. Wheatcroft (eds), *War, Economy and the Military Mind* (London, 1976).

24. J.W. Chambers, *To Raise an Army: the Draft Comes to Modern America* (New York, 1987); H. Cecil and P.H. Liddle (eds), *Facing Armageddon* (London, 1996); J. Kocka, *Facing Total War: German Society, 1914–1918* (Cambridge, Mass., 1985).

25. M. Cornwall, *The Last Years of Austria-Hungary* (Exeter, 1996); R. Bessel, 'Mobilization and demobilization in Germany, 1916–1919', in J. Horne (ed.), *State, society and mobilization in Europe during the First World War* (Cambridge, 1997), pp. 220–1.

26. B. Lincoln, *Red Victory. A History of the Russian Civil War* (London, 1990), p. 447; E. Mawdsley, *The Russian Civil War* (Boston, 1987); J.D. Smele, *Civil War in Siberia. The anti-Bolshevik government of Admiral Kolchak, 1918–1920* (Cambridge,

1996), pp. 672–9.

27. K.O. Morgan, *Consensus and Disunity: the Lloyd George Coalition Government 1918–1922* (Oxford, 1979), p. 342; B. Gökay, *Clash of Empires. Turkey between Russian Bolshevism and British Imperialism, 1918–1923* (London, 1996).

28. C. Townshend, *The British Campaign in Ireland 1919–21* (Oxford, 1975).

29. D. Porch, *The Conquest of Morocco* (New York, 1983), p. 204.

30. C.G. Segrè, *Fourth Shore: the Italian Colonization of Libya* (Chicago, 1974).

31. M. Broxup, 'The Last *Ghazawat*. The 1920–1921 Uprising', and A. Avtorkhanov, 'The Chechens and Ingush during the Soviet Period', in M. Broxup (ed.), *The North Caucasus Barrier* (London, 1992), pp. 112–45, 157–61, 183.

32. J.W. Kipp, 'Lenin and Clausewitz: the Militarization of Marxism, 1915–1921', in W. Frank and P. Gilette (eds), *Soviet Military Doctrine from Lenin to Gorbachev, 1915–1991* (Westport, Conn., 1992), pp. 64–78.

33. E.O. Goldman, *Sunken Treaties: Naval Arms Control between the Wars* (College Station, Penn., 1994).

34. E.L. Dreyer, *China at War, 1901–1949* (Harlow, 1995).

35. T.R. Moreman, 'The Arms Trade and the North-West Frontier Pathan Tribes, 1890–1914', *Journal of Imperial and Commonwealth History*, 22 (1994), p. 211; Fazal-ur-Rahim Marwat, Abdul Karim Khan and Sayed Wiqar Ali Shah Krakakhel, 'Faqir of Ipi', in Rahim and Krakakhel (eds), *Afghanistan and the Frontier* (Peshawar, 1993), pp. 235–73. I have greatly benefited from the advice of Alan Warren on this conflict.

36. I.F.W. Beckett (ed.), *The Roots of Counter-Insurgency. Armies and Guerilla Warfare 1900–45* (London, 1988).

37. I. Talbot, *Punjab and the Raj 1849–1947* (Riverdale, Md., 1988); S.L. Menezes, *Fidelity and Honour. The Indian Army from the Seventeenth to the Twenty-first Century* (New Delhi, 1994); D. Omissi, *The Sepoy and the Raj. The Indian Army, 1860–1940* (Basingstoke, 1994); J. Greenhut, 'The Imperial Reserve: the Indian Infantry on the Western Front 1914–15', *Journal of Imperial and Commonwealth History*, 12 (1983). For India's contribution in World War Two, P. Barua, 'Strategies and Doctrines of Imperial Defence: Britain and India, 1919–45', *ibid*, 25 (1997), p. 259–60.

38. C. Badesi, 'West African Influence on the French Army of World War One', in G.W. Johnson (ed.), *Double Impact. France and Africa in the Age of Imperialism* (Westport, Conn., 1985), pp. 93–104.

39. P.S. Khoury, *Syria and the French Mandate: the Politics of Arab Nationalism, 1920–1945* (Princeton, 1987).

40. P. Kennedy, 'Grand Strategies and Less-Than-Grand Strategies: a Twentieth-Century Critique', in L. Freedman, P. Hayes and R. O'Neill (eds), *War, Strategy and International Politics* (Oxford, 1992), p. 230.

41. H. Schmidt, *The United States Occupation of Haiti, 1915–1934* (New Brunswick, 1971); B.J. Calder, *The Impact of Intervention: the Dominican Republic during the US occupation of 1916–1924* (Austin, Tex., 1984).

42. R. Wohl, *A Passion for Wings: Aviation and the Western Imagination* (New Haven, 1994); A. Gollin, *No Longer an Island: Britain and the Wright Brothers, 1902–1909* (London, 1984) and *The Impact of Air Power on the British People and their Government 1909–14* (London, 1989).

43. P.E. Coletta, *Admiral Bradley A. Fiske and the American Navy* (Lawrence, Kansas, 1980).

44. R.R. Muller, 'Zeppelins', in S.C. Tucker (ed.), *The European Powers in the First World War, an Encyclopedia* (New York, 1996), p. 766.

45. L. Kennett, *The First Air War, 1914–1918* (New York, 1991), p. 170. See, more generally, J. Morrow, *The Great War in the Air, Military Aviation from 1909 to 1921* (Washington, DC, 1993).

46. J.S. Murray, 'The Face of Armageddon', *Mercator's World*, 1, no. 2 (1996), pp. 30–7.

47. R. Higham, *Britain's Imperial Air Routes, 1918–1939* (Hamden, Conn., 1960); R.L. McCormack, 'Imperialism, Air Transport and Colonial Development: Kenya 1920–1946', *Journal of Imperial and Commonwealth History*, 17 (1989), pp. 374–95.

48. D.E. Omissi, *Air Power and Colonial Control. The Royal Air Force 1919–1939* (Manchester, 1990).

49. H.G. Marcus, *A History of Ethiopia* (Berkeley, 1994), pp. 128–9.

50. J. Zdanowski, 'Military Organisation of the Wahabi Emirates (1750–1932)', in R.L. Bidwell, G.R. Smith and J.R. Smart (eds), *New Arabian Studies* II (Exeter, 1994), p. 137.

51. A. Waldron, *From War to Nationalism. China's Turning Point, 1924–1925* (Cambridge, 1996).

52. Omissi, *Air Power*, pp. 129–31.

53. F.K. Mason, *Battle over Britain: a History of German Air Assaults on Great Britain, 1917–1918 and July–December 1940, and*

of the Development of Britain's Air Defenses between the World Wars (New York, 1969); U. Bïaler, *The Shadow of the Bomber: the Fear of Air Attack and British Politics, 1932–1939* (London, 1980).

54. G. Douhet, *The Command of the Air* (New York, 1942); A.F. Hurley, *Billy Mitchell* (New York, 1964); M. Smith, *British Air Strategy Between the Wars* (Oxford, 1984).

55. G.W. Baer, *One Hundred Years of Sea Power. The U.S. Navy, 1890–1990* (Stanford, 1993), pp. 139–44; G. Till, 'Adopting the Aircraft Carrier. The British, American, and Japanese Case Studies', in W. Murray and A.R. Millett (eds), *Military Innovation in the Interwar Period* (Cambridge, 1996), pp. 191–226.

56. B.H. Liddell Hart, *The Tanks, 1914–1939* (New York, 1959); B. Bond, *Liddell Hart: a Study of his Military Thought* (London, 1972); J. Erickson, *The Road to Stalingrad* (1st pub. 1975, London, 1993), pp. 3–5, 26–7; A.J. Trythall, *'Boney' Fuller: The Intellectual General, 1878–1966* (London, 1977); J.J. Mearsheimer, *Liddell Hart and the Weight of History* (Ithaca, 1988); A.J. Smithers, *A New Excalibur. The Development of the Tank, 1909–1939* (London, 1988); H.R. Winton, *To Change an Army, General Sir John Burnett-Stuart and British Armoured Doctrine, 1927–1938* (Lawrence, Kansas, 1988); J.P. Harris, *Men, Ideas and Tanks: British Military Thought and Armoured Forces, 1903–1939* (Manchester, 1995); W. Murray, 'Armoured Warfare. The British, French, and German Experiences', in Murray and Millett (eds), *Military Innovation*, pp. 6–49.

57. Harris, *Men, Ideas and Tanks*, pp. 306–7.

58. Murray, 'Armoured Warfare', pp. 29, 45. For a more positive view of British generals, D. French, 'Colonel Blimp and the British Army: British Divisional Commanders in the war against Germany, 1939–1945', *English Historical Review*, 111 (1996), pp. 1996–7.

59. J.M. House, *Towards Combined Arms Warfare: a Survey of Twentieth Century Tactics, Doctrine, and Organization* (Fort Leavenworth, Kansas, 1984).

60. For a case study that emphasises change and adaptability in a sphere not generally noted for either, J.T. Sumida '"The Best Laid Plans": the Development of British Battle-Fleet Tactics, 1919–1942', *International History Review*, 14 (1992), pp. 682–700.

61. A. Mockler, *Haile Selassie's War: the Italian-Ethiopian Campaign, 1935–1941* (New York, 1985).

62. S.G. Payne, *A History of Fascism 1914–45* (London, 1995), p. 235.

63. M. Knox, *Mussolini Unleashed, 1939–1941, Politics and Strategy in Fascist Italy's Last War* (Cambridge, 1982), p. 16.

64. L. Samuelson, 'Mikhail Tukhachevsky and War–Economic Planning: Reconsiderations on the pre-war Soviet Military build-up', *Journal of Slavic Military Studies*, 9 (1996), pp. 804–47; L.A. Humphreys, *The Way of the Heavenly Sword: the Japanese Army in the 1920s* (Stanford, 1995).

65. J.W. Morley (ed.), *The China Quagmire. Japan's Expansion on the Asian Continent 1933–1941* (New York, 1983), pp. 6–7; M.A. Barnhart, *Japan Prepares for Total War: the Search for Economic Security, 1919–1941* (Ithaca, New York, 1987).

66. B. Farcau, *The Chaco War: Bolivia and Paraguay, 1932–1935* (Westport, Conn., 1996)

67. A. Horne, *To Lose a Battle: France 1940* (Harmondsworth, 1969); R.A. Doughty, *The Breaking Point: Sedan and the Fall of France, 1940* (Hamden, Conn., 1990).

68. M.A. Stoler, 'The "Pacific-First" Alternative in American World War II Strategy', *International History Review*, 2 (1980), p. 434.

69. J. Erickson, *The Road to Berlin* (London, 1983).

70. R.J. Overy, *The Air War 1939–1945* (London, 1987); H. Boog (ed.), *The Conduct of the Air War in the Second World War: an International Comparison* (New York, 1992); Sir Arthur Harris, *Despatch on War Operations*, (ed.) S. Cox (London, 1995).

71. W.M. Leary, 'The CIA and the "Secret War" in Laos: the Battle for Skyline Ridge, 1971–1972', *Journal of Military History*, 59 (1995), p. 507.

72. D.E. Fisher, *A Race on the Edge of Time: Radar – the Decisive Weapon of World War II* (New York, 1988).

73. R.H. Jones, *The Road to Russia: United States Lend-Lease to the Soviet Union* (Norman, Oklahoma, 1969).

74. M. Rupert, *Producing Hegemony. The Politics of Mass Production and American Global Power* (Cambridge, 1995).

75. J.K. Ohl, *Supplying the Troops. General Somervell and American Logistics in World War Two* (DeKalb, Illinois, 1994).

76. Harries and Harries, *Soldiers of the Sun*, p. 207.

77. R.J. Overy, *Why the West Won* (London, 1995). I would like to thank Jeremy Noakes for his advice.

78. T.R. Philbin, *The Lure of Neptune. German-Soviet Naval Collaboration and*

Ambitions, 1919–1941 (Columbia, S.C., 1994), p. xiv.

79. M.J. Neufeld, *The Rocket and the Reich. Peenemünde and the Coming of the Ballistic Missile Era* (Washington, D.C., 1995), pp. 274–5, 278.

80. E.J. Drea, *MacArthur's ULTRA: Code-breaking and the War Against Japan, 1942–1945* (Lawrence, Kansas, 1992); R. Bennett, *Behind the Battle. Intelligence in the War with Germany, 1939–45* (London, 1994). See, more generally, Raudzens, 'War-Winning Weapons: the Measurement of Technological Determinism in Military History', *Journal of Military History*, 54 (1990), pp. 403–33, an article that criticises such determinism and concentrates on the two world wars.

81. M. Walker, *German National Socialism and the Quest for Nuclear Power, 1939–1949* (New York, 1989).

82. S. Nicholas, *The Echo of War. Home Front Propaganda and the Wartime BBC, 1939–45* (Manchester, 1996), pp. 269–74; R.D. Herzstein, *The War that Hitler Won: the Most Famous Propaganda Campaign in History* (London, 1979); N.J. Cull, *Selling War: The British Propaganda Campaign against American 'Neutrality' in World War II* (Oxford, 1995).

83. M.E. Porter, *The Competitive Advantage of Nations* (London, 1990), pp. 305–6.

84. A. Clayton, *The Wars of French Decolonization* (Harlow, 1994).

85. J.A. Huston, *Outposts and Allies: US Army Logistics in the Cold War, 1945–1953* (Selinsgrove, Pennsylvania, 1988).

86. D.R. Devereux, *The Formulation of British Defence Policy towards the Middle East, 1948–56* (1990); P. Darby, *British Defence Policy East of Suez 1947–1968* (Oxford, 1973); K. Pieragostini, *Britain, Aden and South Arabia: Abandoning Empire* (1991).

87. C. MacDonald, *Korea: The War Before Vietnam* (New York, 1986); W. Stueck, *The Korean War: An International History* (Princeton, 1995).

88. S.H. Lee, *Outposts of Empire. Korea, Vietnam and the Origins of the Cold War in Asia, 1949–1954* (Liverpool, 1995), p. 85.

89. R.A. Hunt, *Pacification. The American Struggle for Vietnam's Hearts and Minds* (Boulder, Col. 1995); E.M. Bergerud, *The Dynamics of Defeat. The Vietnam War in Hau Nghia Province* (Boulder, Col. 1990). Among the numerous books on the Vietnam War, the military dimension from the American perspective is covered ably in D.R. Palmer, *The Summons of the Trumpet: a History of the Vietnam War from a Military Man's Viewpoint* (New York, 1984). The war is seen as unwinnable in J. Prados' recent *The Hidden History of the Vietnam War* (Chicago, 1995).

90. R.H. Collins, 'The Economic Crisis of 1968 and the Waning of the "American Century"', *American Historical Review*, 101 (1996), pp. 413, 417.

91. W.J. Duiker, *Sacred War: Nationalism and Revolution in a Divided Vietnam* (New York, 1995). For the American failure to understand North Vietnamese military concepts, R.E. Ford, *Tet 1968. Understanding the Surprise* (London, 1995). For Vietnam in the context of the limitations of limited war, R. Brown, 'Limited War', in C. McInnes and G.D. Sheffield (eds), *Warfare in the Twentieth Century: Theory and Practice* (London, 1988), pp. 177–84. See also M. McClintock, *Instruments of Statecraft: U.S. Guerilla Warfare, Counter-insurgency and Counter-Terrorism, 1940–1990* (New York, 1992).

92. E. O'Ballance, *Malaya: the Communist Insurgent War, 1948–60* (London, 1966).

93. J. and D.S. Small, *The Undeclared War. The Story of the Indonesian Confrontation 1962–1966* (London, 1971), pp. 192–3.

94. A.K. Wildman, *The End of the Russian Imperial Army: the Old Army and the Soldiers' Revolt, March–April 1917* (Princeton, 1980).

95. L.V. Scott, *Conscription and the Attlee Governments. The Politics and Policy of National Service, 1945–1951* (Oxford, 1993).

96. G.Q. Flynn, *The Draft, 1940–1973* (Lawrence, Kansas, 1993).

97. M. Howard, *War in European History* (Oxford, 1976), pp. 142–3; B. Bond, 'The British Experience of National Service, 1947–1963', in R.G. Foerster (ed.) *Die Wehrpflicht: Eintstehung, Erscheinungsfomen und politisch-militärische Wirkung* (Munich, 1994), pp. 207–15; A. Horne, *The French Army and Politics 1870–1970* (Basingstoke, 1984), p. 89.

98. Bond, *The Pursuit of Victory. From Napoleon to Saddam Hussein* (Oxford, 1996); Ricklefs, *Modern Indonesia*, pp. 233, 302.

99. J.S. Ikpuk, *Militarisation of Politics and Neo-Colonialism: the Nigerian Experience* (London, 1995).

100. A. Banani, *The Modernization of Iran, 1921–1941* (Stanford, 1961); S. Cronin, *The Army and the Creation of the Pahlavi State in Iran, 1910–1926* (London, 1996).

101. R.M. Levine, *The Vargas Regime: the Critical Years, 1934–1938* (New York, 1970).

102. R. Potash, *The Army and Politics in*

Argentina, 1928–1945 (Stanford, 1969).

103. Omissi, *Air Power and Colonial Control*, p. 131.
104. A.H. Young and D.E. Phillips (eds), *Militarization in the Non-Hispanic Caribbean* (Boulder, Colorado, 1986), p. 129.
105. E. O'Ballance, *Wars in the Caucasus, 1990–1995* (Basingstoke, 1996).
106. H. Feldman, *The End and the Beginning: Pakistan 1969–1971* (London, 1975); H. Zaheer, *The Separation of East Pakistan: the Rise and Realization of Bengali Muslim Nationalism* (New York, 1994).
107. H. Crouch, *The Army and Politics in Indonesia* (2nd edn, Ithaca, 1988), p. 344. For Pakistan see C. Dewey, 'The Rural Roots of Pakistani Militarism', in D.A. Low (ed.), *The Political Inheritance of Pakistan* (Basingstoke, 1991), pp. 255–60.
108. K. Krause, *Arms and the State: Patterns of Military Production and Trade* (Cambridge, 1995).
109. D.G. Muller, *China as a Maritime Power* (Boulder, Colorado, 1983), pp. 18–19, 29, 38.
110. A. Ilan, *The Origin of the Arab-Israeli Arms Race* (Basingstoke, 1996), pp. 153–74.
111. S. Green, *Living by the Sword: America and Israel in the Middle East 1968–1987* (London, 1988); A. Vitan, 'The Soviet Military Presence in Egypt 1967–1972: A New Perspective', *Journal of Slavic Military Studies*, 8 (1995), pp. 547–65.
112. S.P. Cohen, *The Pakistan Army* (Berkeley, 1984), pp. 134–41; A. Varas, *Militarization and the International Arms Race in Latin America* (Boulder, Colorado, 1985), p. 49.
113. P.C. Schmitter (ed.), *Military Rule in Latin America. Function, Consequences and Perspectives* (London, 1973).
114. J. Pay, 'The Battlefield since 1945', in C. McInnes and G.D. Sheffield (eds), *Warfare in the Twentieth Century: Theory and Practice* (London, 1988); G. Hartcup, *The Silent Revolution: Development of Conventional Weapons 1945–85* (Oxford, 1993).
115. J.T. Sumida, *In Defence of Naval Strategy: Finance, Technology and British Naval Policy 1889–1914* (Boston, 1989).
116. R.A. Gabriel and K.S. Metz, *A History of Military Medicine, II: From the Renaissance through modern times* (Westport, Conn., 1992). See, more generally, M. Harrison, 'Medicine and the Management of Modern Warfare', *History of Science*, 34 (1996), pp. 379–410.
117. J.F. Dunnigan and A. Bay, *From Shield to*

Storm: High-Tech Weapons, Military Strategy and Coalition Warfare in the Persian Gulf (1992) exaggerates the effectiveness of American weaponry.
118. M. and S. Harries, *Soldiers of the Sun. The Rise and Fall of the Imperial Japanese Army* (New York, 1991), p. vii.
119. *The Times*, 15 April. 1996, p. 10.
120. M. Galeotti, *Afghanistan. The Soviet Union's Last War* (London, 1995).
121. A. Raevsky, 'Russian Military Performance in Chechnya: An initial evaluation', *Journal of Slavic Military Studies*, 8 (1995), pp. 681–90.
122. D. Holloway, *Stalin and the Bomb: the Soviet Union and Atomic Energy, 1939–1956* (New Haven, 1994); J.W. Lewis and X. Litai, *China's Strategic Seapower. The Politics of Force Modernization in the Nuclear Age* (Stanford, 1995).
123. Neufeld, *Rocket and the Reich*, p. 275.
124. R. Cockett (ed.), *My Dear Max. The letters of Brendan Bracken to Lord Beaverbrook, 1925–1958* (London, 1990), p. 112.
125. M.J. White, *The Cuban Missile Crisis* (Basingstoke, 1995).
126. C. Gray, 'The Changing Nature of Warfare?', *Naval War College Review*, 96, no. 2 (Spring 1996), p. 14; A. Irvin, 'The Buffalo Thorn: The Nature of the Future Battlefield', *Journal of Strategic Studies*, 19 (1996), pp. 238–40, 245–6; L.W. Grau and T.L. Thomas, 'A Russian View of Future War: Theory and Direction', *Journal of Slavic Military Studies*, 9 (1996), pp. 508–12.
127. N. Myers (ed.), *The Gaia Atlas of Planet Management* (London, 1985); M. Kidron and R. Segal, *The State of the World Atlas* (London, 1995).
128. R.H. Johnson, *Improbable Dangers: U.S. Conceptions of Threat in the Cold War and After* (New York, 1994); W.J. Durch (ed.), *UN Peacekeeping, American Policy and the Uncivil Wars of the 1990s* (Basingstoke, 1996).
129. A valuable recent emphasis on such characteristics is provided by J.A. Lynn, 'The Evolution of Army Style in the Modern West, 800–2000', *International History Review*, 18 (1996), p. 507.
130. For an important recent discussion, S.P. Rosen, 'Military Effectiveness. Why Society Matters', *International Security*, 19 (1995), pp. 5–31, especially, pp. 25–30, and his *Societies and Military Power: India and her Armies* (Ithaca, N.Y. 1997).

Index